GREEN

GLOBE

YEARBOOK

1995

# GREEN GLOBE YEARBOOK

of International Co-operation on

Environment and Development

# 1995

an independent publication on environment and development

from the Fridtjof Nansen Institute, Norway

Editors-in-Chief:
*Helge Ole Bergesen and Georg Parmann*

Documents and Production Editor:
*Øystein B. Thommessen*

**Oxford University Press**

*This text paper is made predominantly from genuine waste fibre and
the endpapers are made from 100% recycled waste paper.*

*Oxford University Press, Walton Street, Oxford OX2 6DP*
*Oxford  New York*
*Athens  Auckland  Bangkok  Bombay*
*Calcutta  Cape Town  Dar es Salaam  Delhi*
*Florence  Hong Kong  Istanbul  Karachi*
*Kuala Lumpur  Madras  Madrid  Melbourne*
*Mexico City  Nairobi  Paris  Singapore*
*Taipei  Tokyo  Toronto*
*and associated companies in*
*Berlin  Ibadan*

*Oxford is a trade mark of Oxford University Press*

*Published in the United States by*
*Oxford University Press Inc., New York*

*© The Fridtjof Nansen Institute 1995*

*Maps: GRID-Arendal, Norway*
*Cover design and layout: Ellen Larsen, Norwegian University Press*
*Paste-up: Morten Mathiesen, Norwegian University Press*

*British Library Cataloguing in Publication Data*
*Data available*

*Library of Congress Cataloging in Publication Data*
*Data available*
*ISBN 0–19–823325–6*
*ISSN 0–0803–9011*

*Printed in Great Britain by*
*Bath Press Ltd*
*Bath, Avon*

# Acknowledgements

We gratefully record, once more, our sincere thanks to the staff of the Nansen Institute for invaluable support for this undertaking. We are particularly indebted to Willy Østreng for his never-ending enthusiasm, to Morten Sandnes and Anne-Christine Thestrup for practical assistance, and to G. Kristin Rosendal and Davor Vidas for editorial advice. Professor Raino Malnes of the University of Oslo has also assisted efficiently in the editorial work.

We acknowledge the financial support provided by the Research Council of Norway, NORAD, and the Ministry of the Environment and the respect they maintain for our editorial independence.

We appreciate the smooth and effective co-operation we have established over the years with Oxford University Press and our editor, Andrew Schuller, and assistant editor, Enid Barker.

Morten Mathiesen, Norwegian University Press, and Torstein Olsen, GRID-Arendal, deserve mention for professional technical support and Susan Høivik, International Peace Research Institute, for efficient editorial assistance.

We extend our sincere thanks to the numerous officials and international secretariats for their timely answers to our annual queries.

Finally, we wish to express once more our sincere, annual appreciation of the tireless efforts undertaken by our documents and production editor, Øystein B. Thommessen, who remains essential for every aspect of this yearbook.

The Editors-in-Chief

# Advisory Panel to the Green Globe Yearbook

Homero Aridjis, President,
  Groupo de los Cien Artistas e Intelectuales,
  A.C., Lomas Barrilaco, Mexico

Alicia Bárcena, Executive Director,
  Earth Council,
  San José, Costa Rica

Solita Collas-Monsod, Professor,
  Department of Economics,
  University of the Philippines,
  Manila, The Philippines

Bruce W. Davis, Professor and Deputy Director,
  Institute of Antarctic and
  Southern Ocean Studies,
  University of Tasmania,
  Hobart, Australia

Margarita Marino de Botero, Executive Director,
  El Colegio Verde de Villa de Leyva,
  Bogotà, Colombia

Raimonds Ernšteins, Director,
  Institute for Environmental Education and Information,
  University of Latvia,
  Riga, Latvia

Susan George, Professor,
  Transnational Institute,
  Amsterdam, The Netherlands

Ernst B. Haas, Professor,
  University of California,
  Berkeley, California, USA

Stuart J. Hayward, MP, Correspondent,
  de Fontes Broadcasting,
  Pembroke, Bermuda

Calestous Juma, Executive Director,
  African Centre for Technology Studies (ACTS),
  Nairobi, Kenya

Martin Kohr, Director,
  Third World Network,
  Penang, Malaysia

Geoffrey Lean, Environment Correspondent,
  The Independent on Sunday,
  London, United Kingdom

Jeremy Leggett, International Science Director,
  Greenpeace International,
  London, United Kingdom

Magnar Norderhaug, Director,
  Worldwatch Norden,
  Tønsberg, Norway

David Pearce, Professor and Director,
  Centre for Social and Economic Research on the Global
  Environment (CSERGE),
  University College,
  London, United Kingdom

Amulya K. Reddy, Professor and President,
  International Energy Initiative (IEI),
  Bangalore, India

Bruce M. Rich, Senior Attorney and Director,
  Environmental Defense Fund (EDF),
  Washington, DC, USA

Richard Sandbrook, Executive Director,
  International Institute for Environment and Development
  (IIED),
  London, United Kingdom

Lawrence Susskind, Professor,
  Department of Urban Studies and Planning, Massachu-
  setts Institute of Technology,
  Cambridge, Massachusetts, USA

Anders Wijkman, Director-General,
  Swedish Agency for Research Cooperation with Devel-
  oping Countries (SAREC),
  Stockholm, Sweden

Alexey V. Yablokov, Professor and Chairman,
  Interagency Commission on Ecological Security,
  Russian Federation National Security Council,
  Kremlin, Moscow,
  Russian Federation

Willy Østreng, Director and Chairman of the Panel,
  Fridtjof Nansen Institute,
  Lysaker, Norway

# Contents

## Section II: References
*International Agreements on Environment and Development*

## Non-Governmental Organizations (NGOs)

# Contributors in this Yearbook

*Helge Ole Bergesen* is Senior Research Fellow at the Fridtjof Nansen Institute (FNI). He is a graduate in Political Science from the University of Oslo, specializing in international relations, and was Assistant Professor of Political Science for two years (1978–9) at the University of Odense, Denmark. Since 1980 he has been working for the Fridtjof Nansen Institute, where he established and, until 1988, directed its research programme on international energy policy. He is also Associate Professor with the Norwegian School of Management. He is currently in charge of a multi-disciplinary research project on climate, energy, and the environment, involving participants from the fields of economics, political science, and engineering. Mr Bergesen is editor-in-chief of the *Green Globe Yearbook* and he has published widely on international energy relations, North-South conflicts, and environmental policy.

*Betty Ferber* is the International Co-ordinator of the Group of 100, a Mexico-based environmental coalition of writers, artists, and scientists. She organized the First and Second Morelia Symposia, 'Approaching the Year 2000'.

*Janine Ferretti* is Executive Director of the Pollution Probe Foundation, a Canadian non-profit research-based environmental advocacy group. She has also held positions with the Union for the Conservation of Nature and Natural Resources in Bonn, Germany, and the Environmental Liaison Center International (ELCI) in Nairobi, Kenya. Ms Ferretti is also currently a member of the International Trade Advisory Committee, and the Task Force on Trade and the Environment of Foreign Affairs and International Trade in Canada.

*Lynn Fischer* is a Latin American Policy Specialist with the Natural Resources Defense Council (NRDC), where she is responsible for heading the organization's efforts on implementation of the North American Free Trade Agreement (NAFTA). Ms Fischer has co-authored a variety of documents on NAFTA and US-Mexico relations.

*Harris Gleckman* served as Chief of the Environment Unit at the former United Nations Centre on Transnational Corporations (UNCTC). He has authored or supervised numerous research projects, books, and articles, including key UNCTC publications. Among these are: *Benchmark Survey on Corporate Environmental Management* (1993); *Options to Facilitate Transfer of Environmentally Sound Technologies to Developing Countries Under Favorable Terms* (1993); and *Criteria for Sustainable Development Management* (1989). Currently on leave from the United Nations, Dr Gleckman acts as a consultant to a number of clients, including World Wide Fund For Nature (WWF) International, the UK NGO Trade Network, the Norwegian government, and the University of Southern Maine. His broad area of specialism is environmental research and policy analysis at national and international levels, with a focus on transnational corporate management.

*Michael Grubb* is Head of the Energy and Environmental Programme at the Royal Institute of International Affairs, where he directs a wide range of research on international energy and environmental issues. He is well known for his work on the policy implications of climate change, with publications in this area including a report on the issues and options for negotiating an agreement on limiting carbon dioxide emissions, and a two-volume international study entitled *Energy Policies and the Greenhouse Effect*, together with many journal publications on economic and political aspects of the problem. He has also led an extensive study resulting in the book *Emerging Energy Technologies*, and most recently published a book examining the outcome and implications of the United Nations Conference on Environment and Development (UNCED).

*Vladimir Kotov*, Dr.Habil., is a Professor at the School of Business Management of the Russian Academy of Transport in Moscow, and is an associate at the International Institute for Applied Systems Analysis (IIASA) in Laxenburg, Austria. He has worked at the Institute of World Economy and International Relations and the Institute of Economy at the Russian Academy of Sciences, as an expert of the Russian Union of Entrepreneurs. He has also served as visiting professor at the University of Augsburg in Germany. Professor Kotov is currently focusing on the implementation of environmental policies under transition to a market economy. He is an author of four books published in Russia and in Japan, and of numerous articles published in Russia and in the West.

*John Lanchbery* is Director of Environmental Projects at the Verification Technology Information Centre (VERTIC) in London. He is also working as a research scholar on the project 'Effectiveness of International Environmental Commitments' at the International Institute for Applied Systems Analysis (IIASA) in Laxenburg, Austria, and as Co-ordinator of the European Commission sponsored project 'Greenhouse Gas Inventories: National Reporting Processes and Implementation Review Mechanisms'. He is a tutor in technology for the Open University. On joining VERTIC Mr Lanchbery worked mainly on verification issues relating to the then forthcoming Climate Convention but is now also researching the reporting and review processes in a wide range of environmental agreements. Prior to joining VERTIC he worked for over twenty years on research in applied physics, mainly in technologies related to sensors and microelectronics.

*Marc Levy* is Assistant Professor of Politics and International Affairs at Princeton University. He has published on acid rain, East-West environmental co-operation, UNCED, and the effectiveness of international environmental institutions. Professor Levy is currently engaged in research on the use of financial transfers for international environmental problems, and is working with scholars at the International Institute for Applied Systems Analysis (IIASA) in Laxenburg, Austria, to create a database of international environmental regimes. He is co-editor of *Institutions for the Earth*.

*Elena Nikitina*, Ph.D. is a Senior Researcher at the Institute of World Economy and International Relations, Russian Academy of Sciences, and associate at the International Institute for the Applied Systems Analysis (IIASA) in Laxenburg, Austria. Her research focus is the problems of international environmental regimes. She is the author of a number of articles published in Russia and abroad. Her most recent book is *World Meteorological Organization and the World Ocean*.

*G. Kristin Rosendal* is a doctoral student at the Fridtjof Nansen Institute (FNI). She has worked as a research fellow at FNI since graduating in Political Science from the University of Oslo in 1989. Her main research work has been in the field of international environmental negotiations, focusing on the North–South debate on genetic resources and property rights. Her most recent publication is 'The Biodiversity Convention: Implications of the US "no" in Rio', in Calestous Juma and Vincente Sánchez (eds.) *Biodiplomacy*.

*David Victor* is co-leader of the project 'Effectiveness of International Environmental Commitments' at the International Institute for Applied Systems Analysis (IIASA) in Laxenburg, Austria. Previously he was at the Department of Political Science, Massachusetts Institute of Technology, undertaking research on how international agreements are enforced. Mr Victor has held many scholarships for teaching and research, including work at the Center for International Affairs at Harvard University, and the Carnegie Commission on Science, Technology, and Government. He has served as a consultant to the US Information Agency, the US Environmental Protection Agency, and the United Nations Conference on Trade and Development (UNCTAD). He received his undergraduate degree in History of Science from Harvard University. Mr Victor has contributed articles and book chapters to various publications, including *Nature*, *Climate Change*, and *International Journal of Hydrogen Energy*.

# Introduction

*Helge Ole Bergesen and Georg Parmann*

One of the major achievements of the UN Conference on Environment and Development (UNCED) and the 'Rio process' was the signing of the UN Framework Convention on Climate Change (FCCC). This agreement attracted support from developing and industrialized countries with amazing speed, which led to its entry into force less than two years later, on 21 March 1994. For a global agreement with such wide-ranging implications this is remarkable. This obliged the northern state parties to submit national reports on emissions and future measures to combat or regulate them, thereby initiating the first phase of a broad international review process. The formal intergovernmental machinery established under the Convention forces the political issues related to the greenhouse effect back on the international agenda. In March/April 1995 the first Conference of the Parties is held in Berlin, which makes it necessary for governments to face the basic questions once more:

• How serious is the potential threat of climate change, for the globe as a whole and its different parts?

• Who bears the responsibility for taking the first steps to counteract the assumed risk, and what are the appropriate measures to be taken in the 1990s?

• How can national action by individual governments be co-ordinated in a way that makes sense, confronted with a global problem?

In this edition of the *Green Globe Yearbook* we do not purport to present answers to these complicated and controversial questions, but we intend to focus attention on the major problems of international collaboration in this area.

In one of our papers the authors—Lanchbery and Victor—emphasize the crucial interface between science and politics, in particular the role of the Intergovernmental Panel on Climate Change (IPCC). Another contributor (Grubb) points to the European Union as a small-scale test case for regional solutions of a kind that could, if successful, show the way towards innovative global schemes of a similar type. Finally, in our focus section on climate change, Bergesen demonstrates the sensitive and critical links between international commitments and national reporting and implementation.

Three of the other articles included in this edition of the *Yearbook* (by Rosendal, Gleckman, and Ferber, Ferretti,

and Fischer) are also concerned with the initial phases of establishing international norms or rules for environmental conduct—the NAFTA negotiations, the biodiversity convention, and the discussions on business and sustainable development. The two former ones have reached the legal stage in the form of binding agreements, while the latter remains informal. In all cases the process of implementation of formal and informal commitments will be essential.

The question of national follow-up is in a different manner pursued by Kotov and Nikitina in their study of the problems facing Russia in implementing its obligations under international environmental agreements. Again, we learn how long the way from legal text to real life can be. This yearbook has been established in order to highlight attention on this very problem.

Finally, Levy's article on acid rain shows that over time states can reach agreement on more committing and effective national action if there is sufficient common understanding of the problem at hand and continuing political support on the domestic scene. Even then, implementation is not without difficulties.

The *reference section* follows the design established in the three previous editions, focusing on a careful selection of agreements and organizations, which in our judgement have an impact on real-life developments. This year we have expanded the coverage to include a few new entries, among them the new International Convention on Desertification, the restructured Global Environmental Facility (GEF), and the new World Trade Organization (WTO). The entries covering the UNEP Regional Seas Programme, the International Convention on the Establishment of an International Fund for Compensation for Oil Pollution Damage (Fund Convention), and the Convention on Long-Range Transboundary Air Pollution (LRTAP) have been extensively revised since the previous volume. Most importantly, all the data included have been updated as of late October 1994. All organizations and secretariats listed have had an opportunity to comment on a draft description of their activities, but we take responsibility for both the selection of entries, the organization of information, and the contents. We welcome comments from readers who disagree with our presentation of information (see Questionnaire).

As to maps and tables, we follow official UN procedure,

which means that every country recognized by the UN is included. In addition we have included Taiwan as it *de facto* is a part of the international community. The table covering international organizations and degrees of participation also includes some territories. Newly independent states do not inherit international membership or commitments from their successor. So, if they have not explicitly joined an organization or acceded to an agreement, they are considered non-participants.

Polhøgda, Lysaker, Norway
November 1994

# Russia and International Environmental Co-operation

*Vladimir Kotov and Elena Nikitina*

## Changes in Policy and Institutional Framework of Co-operation

Following the disintegration of the USSR in late 1991 Russia has become its legal successor in various international environmental agreements. Currently it is a member of nearly one hundred international accords on nature and resource protection and conservation. Approximately seventy of these are multilateral and the rest bilateral. Russia participates in the environmental activities of international intergovernmental and non-governmental organizations, in their co-operative research programmes.

Significant changes are under way in the policy and institutional framework of Russia's international environmental co-operation. However, the system of co-operation is still far from its final form, and is of a transitional character. In large measure it reflects the serious political and economic changes initiated in Russia during 'transformation'—a transition from a totalitarian to a democratic state, from a command-based to a market economy. Environmental co-operation today represents a conglo-meration of new and old approaches, of changing tenets, perceptions, and concepts. It involves both the inertia of older days and an impulse towards the new; dis-illusionment with the past and a desire to escape from it. A set of different factors defines the general framework of co-operation and shapes its structure, as well as new potentials for the development of co-operation and its limitations.

*Perestroika* followed by 'transformation' in Russia marked a turning-point in the environmental co-operation system. In particular, national and international environmental policies abandoned the ideological and institutional framework of a totalitarian regime. A new basis for international co-operation with the West was under formation. Progressive environmental policy started taking shape, with restructuring of environmental management, adoption of new legal and economic mechanisms, and an upsurge of the environmental movement and environmental *glasnost*. Environmental policy became decentralized, with wider rights granted to the regional and local levels. New independent environmental institutions have now been created in Russia, destined to represent Russian interests in international environmental co-operation.

However, there are also serious limits to the effectiveness of international environmental co-operation. The development of international environmental co-operation between Russia and the West has been defined largely by an inertia acquired back in Soviet totalitarian times, when the major reasons for active participation in co-operation lay rather far from a true environmental involvement. These goals were mainly of a declarative character, highly politicized in their essence, and tightly integrated into the foreign policy priorities of a communist state. Numerous international environmental commitments were undertaken by the Soviets without any in-depth evaluation of their effects on the national scale, of the possibilities for compliance, and the opportunities they might present—in balance, of real environmental interests. Some former institutional characteristics and perceptions continue to have an impact on the system of international environmental co-operation, which is still, as mentioned, in a transitional phase.

It is not only the legacy of communism that shapes Russia's major problems in the field of international environmental co-operation today, and the implementation of international environmental obligations. The 'transformation' process has, in addition to its positive effects on environmental policy formation, had certain negative implications for ecological stability in the national scale, as well as for international environmental security. It has imposed certain limits on environmental problem-solving in Russia, and on the effectiveness of Russia's participation in international environmental co-operation.[1] Due to the general weakening of state authority during 'transformation', the state has seen a sharp decrease in its potential for effective action in the field of environmental protection, and this in turn negatively affects the prospects of international environmental co-operation. Industrial production has plummeted (by as much as 50 per cent in 1994 compared to the 1990 level), thereby limiting the financial opportunities of the state for implementation of its national and international environmental policies. Investment has come to a standstill, largely as a result of extreme inflation. Subsequently, the processes of structural changes in the economy, the introduction of clean technologies, and the installation of purification facilities have been frozen. Domestically there seems to be a widening gap between Russia's recent progressive intentions in international environmental co-operation in general and in dealing with global environmental changes in particular, and their implementation under the current situation.

During the 1990s Russia has also become involved in the UNCED (United Nations Conference on Environment and Development) process. This has had a considerable influence not only on its national environmental policy, including adoption of the concept of sustainable development among its priority goals, but also on strategies towards participation in international environmental co-operation towards solving the major issues on the global environmental change agenda.

How can we evaluate the recent modifications in the political, ideological, institutional, and economic framework of Russia's international environmental co-operation? It seems that in general environmental issues are beginning to rank higher on the national scale of priorities (despite some short-term fluctuations). Environmental issues have been depoliticized, and are becoming more independent of other goals. We cannot yet say that they are playing the major role in the political and public life of contemporary Russia, that they do in Western societies. However, the clear increase in the significance of environmental issues and of the international environmental agenda indicates that important systemic alterations are under way in this country.

Recently there have been institutional changes in the framework of international co-operation. Under the previous total supremacy of the state under communism, no social function (no matter how important) not performed by a special governmental institution had any chance for realization. Throughout practically the whole Soviet era Russia's natural endowment was not represented institutionally within the structure of power. It was considered that the industrial ministries that exploited natural resources and the environment were to protect them as well. In fact, within this system ministries were over-exploiting natural resources, polluting the environment—and regulating themselves in their own activities. There was no specialized state institution to protect nature, nor any specialized institution dealing with issues of international environmental co-operation.

As a result of *perestroika*, major institutional changes were undertaken in this field. The State Committee on Environmental Protection was formed in 1988, and that meant that control functions over polluters and resource-users were withdrawn from the latter. The Committee became responsible for co-ordinating international environmental co-operation, as other ministries had transferred their functions of regulating the implementation of international environmental agreements. Thus, the environmental management function acquired its independence. Later on, during 'transformation', sectorial industrial ministries were dismantled in Russia, while the State Committee on Environmental Protection saw its status raised, and was turned into the present Ministry of the Environment and Natural Resources. A 1994 statute underlines its special institutional role in the regulation of international environmental co-operation. The ministry is to be in charge of the implementation of the country's environmental obligations as result of Russia's participation in environmental conventions and accords, and in activities of international organizations; moreover, international activities of other governmental bodies in the sphere of the environment and resource use are to be co-ordinated with the ministry. Currently a special inter-agency body is being established within the ministry with participation of other governmental organs. It is to be responsible for the implementation of international environmental projects with participation of the World Bank and other international financial organizations. Following the decentralization of environmental management in Russia, a considerable amount of environmental ministry competence was transferred to regional and local organs. This meant greater opportunities for foreign partners to establish closer environmental co-operation at the local level.

The introduction of a new system of economic mechanisms of environmental management in Russia has also spread to the sphere of international co-operation. Charges and fines for pollution and resource use are being applied to solving not only domestic environmental problems, but global ones as well. Carbon-dioxide emission charges are now being adopted in Russia, together with a system of fees for the production and consumption of ozone-depleting substances. These are meant to induce enterprises to finance industrial restructuring and to switch over to alternatives to ozone-depleting substances.

New actors—independent producers, non-governmental organizations, the mass media—that were previously totally controlled by the state, have appeared on the national arena. It is inevitable that the structure of interests that they represent and implement in the environmental sphere will change. This issue is of high importance, especially for the West trying to create new patterns of co-operation with Russia. Previously environmental interests were suppressed. With democratization, they are being gradually realized and revealed. We may expect them to take shape in the sphere of international environmental policy in the near future, associated with a return to the normal international practice of identifying and protecting national interests.

Such a return to conventional practice would help to enhance the predictability of Russia's international environmental policies, making it dependent on ecological imperatives, not on exogenous pressures. That would have a positive effect on international environmental co-operation with Russian participation. On the other hand, one should take care not to view the future prospects associated with these changes through rose-coloured spectacles. Many obstacles still exist. One of them lies in the deep-rooted habits of Russian bureaucracy, and in its aspirations to control completely the processes within its competence. Without constant assessment and pressures from the democratic public on the bureaucratic apparatus, serious failures are possible.

## Goals and Strategies of International Environmental Co-operation

The early 1990s have been marked in Russia by the formation of new strategies of environmental co-operation, developed within the framework of significant modifications in environmental policies. These strategies have been normatively fixed at the governmental level in a number of official documents. Basic among them is the Law on Environmental Protection (19 December 1991), the first in the history of the country. It envisages that in its environmental policies Russia will proceed from the necessity to provide international environmental security and the development of international environmental co-operation. The following major principles are to guide national approaches in this field:

- every state has the right to use its environment and its natural resources for purposes of economic development and providing for the needs of its people;
- the environmental welfare of one state cannot be provided at the expense of others;
- the economic activities of a state should not damage the environment within and beyond its jurisdiction;
- any activity with unpredictable environmental consequences is inadmissible;
- global, regional, and local control should be provided over the state of the environment and changes in it;
- free international exchange of ecological information and environmentally safe technologies should be maintained;
- states should provide mutual assistance in case of environmental emergencies;
- all environmental disputes are to be settled by peaceful means.[2]

Article 92 of the Law, in which these principles are set out, has a declarative character, announcing the state's obligations towards its public and to the international community to work towards environmental security. The major principles of environmental co-operation stated there were already established at the international level (the 1972 Stockholm Conference, the 1982 World Charter on Nature). Russia's environmental law was adopted in the midst of the most romantic period of reforms; as a result, some of its provisions, including those dealing with the issues of international co-operation, are characterized by a certain detachment from hard reality. For instance, if principles of environmental damage or of exclusion of environmental risk are to be executed in practice, then Russia will have to halt a greater part of its economic activities.

As yet, no final concept for Russia's participation in international environmental co-operation has been shaped. The Ministry of the Environment has indicated in the major federal programme, 'Environmental Security of Russia', that it is necessary 'to work out a concept and prior directions' for Russian participation in international environmental co-operation during a period of transition to a market economy, as well as 'major measures to provide compliance with international obligations in support of international environmental security'. Though these goals were set by the ministry early in 1993,[3] as yet no results of its efforts on the issue have been announced.

Today the UNCED process provides the framework for the elaboration of conceptual designs and strategies of Russia's international environmental co-operation. Participation in UNCED preparations was initiated by the Soviet Union, and Russia as its successor took part in the Rio Conference (in which seven states of the former USSR participated) and in the implementation of its provisions. The UNCED process has had a rather strong impact on Russia's environmental policies and strategies. During UNCED, Russia signed the Convention on Biological Diversity and the Framework Convention on Climate Change, and supported *Agenda 21* as well as principles of rational use, conservation, and utilization of forests. Russia is also a member of the Commission on Sustainable Development. After the Conference, Russia held parliamentary hearings on the implementation of the Rio provisions in 1993. Institutional structures—an inter-agency commission on the realization of UNCED provisions—were established, and mechanisms for control over their adherence are being instituted.

Russia is one of few countries to adopt a national action plan on the issue—'the National Plan of Action for Realization of the UNCED Decisions'. This serves as a basis for Russia's domestic efforts to provide sustainable development, and it incorporates major items of strategies and concrete measures in environmental protection along the lines fixed in *Agenda 21*, with sections on environmental management, international co-operation, environmental education, priority measures to improve the state of the environment, and mechanisms for realization of the plan.

The major impact of the Rio process would seem to be that

the concept of sustainable development is becoming a foundation for Russia's environmental policy. According to a recent presidential decree (No. 236 of 4 February 1994), a national programme is to be elaborated on implementation of a strategy of sustainable development. This strategy is to envisage concrete actions and principles of national policy realization both at the domestic and international levels.

A wide range of provisions on international co-operation are conceived in Russia's national plan of action on UNCED implementation. First, it indicates the major directions for realizing the 1992 intergovernmental environmental agreement of the Commonwealth of Independent States (CIS) and for developing international co-operation between the former Soviet republics. Secondly, it notes that the international obligations of Russia within a framework of environmental accords need close integration with other countries, especially European ones; the special role of European ministerial conferences on the environment is stressed. Thirdly, implementation of the UNCED national action plan requires an expansion of foreign financial and technical assistance at the bilateral level and within the framework of international financial organizations, especially the World Bank and the European Bank for Reconstruction and Development.

In evaluating the impact of the Rio process on Russia, V. Danilov-Danilian, Russia's minister of the environment, indicated that the major priorities of *Agenda 21* aimed at providing environmental policy formation in the developing countries, and expanding their environmental activities. Various actions had already been undertaken in Russia in this field, especially regarding its scientific potential, development of environmental protection mechanisms, and environmental monitoring. The minister stressed that the real problem today lay in defining the mechanisms of international co-operation to provide financing for global environmental problem-solving, as well as the formation of national control mechanisms over the distribution and use of financial resources earmarked for this purpose.[4] At the Rio Conference, Russia, together with other countries of Eastern Europe, was accorded the special status of a state in transition to a market economy, with certain privileges granted in financing of environmental measures, in technology transfers, and in financial allocations to international environmental funds. Provisions for the transitional period were reflected in the Russian national plan of action which envisaged modifications in management mechanisms to adapt to a market economy, including a gradual shift from a centralized and strictly controlled system of management to a decentralized one.

In the course of the post-Rio process Russia took part in the 1993 Lucerne Conference on the environment in Central and Eastern Europe, where a programme of action to solve the most urgent problems in these countries with transitional economies was adopted. Russia has proposed a list of specific sites and territories which need foreign aid in order to improve their environmental situation.

The Rio process has affected and diversified the framework of Russia's environmental activities, especially within the agenda for global environmental change. The process of formulating goals and strategies and undertaking actions is developing—some of these initiated earlier on certain aspects of global change management, and some of them to be shaped in the near future. Together with more traditional issues (ozone-layer protection, climate change, trans-boundary air pollution), new fields of international co-operation for Russia have emerged. These include protection of biodiversity, conservation of forests, development of nature-protection areas and reserves, environmentally benign destruction of chemical and nuclear weapons, and solving transboundary environmental problems between the states of the former Soviet Union. The domestic implementation of international provisions on these issues requires serious restructuring and behaviour adaptation on the part of various actors. For instance, the domestic realization of the Rio principles on conservation of forests requires certain amendments to Russia's national forestry strategies. It is necessary to increase control over timber-cutting and export, to develop legislative norms for forest conservation, and to adopt a national programme for the conservation and reproduction of Russian's forests. Indeed, these forests account for a quarter of the world's total forest resources and are important in providing ecological stability on a planetary scale. Domestic implementation of the provisions of the bio-diversity convention necessitates the elaboration of a national strategy for conservation and sustainable use of elements of biodiversity, including preservation of *in situ* and *ex situ* species, as well as scientific research and specialist training. Particular attention should be paid to establishing mechanisms of access to information on genetic resources and technologies, and national measures to finance the implementation process.

Assessing the first steps which Russia has taken in formulating its national goals and strategies for international environmental co-operation, one might conclude that, despite the abundance of official government documents regulating the country's international environmental co-operation, there is as yet no clear and comprehensive concept on this issue. However, participation in international environmental co-operation is not engaged in for its own sake: it is motivated by the necessity of solving environmental problems at the national and international levels. What major environmental concerns is Russia now facing whose solutions will require such mechanisms as international co-operation? Unfortunately it is still rather difficult to get clear answers to this question. Several official documents published recently in the press and covering goals and strategies on international environmental co-operation share a common serious shortcoming. Basically, they seem to be mere summary lists of ministerial guide-lines, composed with such remarkable bureaucratic skilfullness as to be reminiscent of the old adage 'a tongue is given to conceal one's thoughts'. In Russia, government documents on environmental issues ought to be expressed in the most democratic way, so that the public can catch their essence. Instead, they often follow the old bureaucratic traditions—in the form of a charade created for the purposes of internal bureaucratic games.

## Environmental Interactions of Russia within the Commonwealth of Independent States (CIS)

The disintegration of the Soviet Union had a considerable effect on Russia's environmental co-operation. Fourteen new neighbours emerged, with their specific environmental interests and priorities. Serious problems arose in connection with adherence to the international environmental obligations of the former USSR, accompanied by problems in environmental interaction between former Soviet republics and the settlement of previously latent controversies between them. During the Soviet period these disputes had been mitigated by the central government, which had defined for all Soviet republics their common strategy of participation in international environmental regimes. The approaches of Ukraine and Belarus as UN charter members were co-ordinated with the position of the USSR, so that all of them functioned as a single actor. The central government controlled compliance with international environmental obligations, and determined major directions and implementation patterns for the Soviet republics.

Now new states have acquired sovereign rights over their natural resources and jurisdiction over environmental protection, and are shaping their own independent environmental policy, also in international environmental co-operation. This has resulted in considerable variations in national approaches towards participation in international environmental regimes and adherence to the treaty obligations of the former USSR. Today the implementation of certain environmental commitments is in jeopardy, and the extent of compliance with them is decreasing.

A new set of questions has emerged recently. Russia has declared itself the successor to all international obligations of the former USSR, but what is the actual division of responsibilities between the other new states on this issue? How will the new actors interact, with Russia representing them in international regimes? What is to be the role of the new states in connection with the global environmental change agenda? Will CIS become a member of international

regimes, as is the case of the European Community?

Considerable deviations have become apparent in the approaches taken by the new states towards global environmental changes, especially as regards the issues of global climate change, ozone-layer depletion, and acid rain. Attitudes towards the assessment of global-warming risk are addressed from national perspectives, with consequent variations in response. The distribution of temperature and precipitation patterns as a result of climate change might have differing effects on nature and the economy of the various states. Considerable differences exist in the 'input' of certain states as regards global warming—much greater in the case of the industrially developed regions of Russia, Ukraine, Belarus, and the Baltic states. This means that they would have to bear higher costs to restructure their industries to meet environmental requirements. All these factors affect their attitudes to the emerging international climate-change regime.

The regional prospects of implementing the ozone-layer protection regime within the CIS are rather uncertain as well. After the disintegration of the Soviet Union, the problem of co-ordinating ozone-layer protection activities among the former republics emerged. On the initiative of Russia's Ministry of the Environment, an inter-state co-ordination meeting was convened in late 1992 on ozone layer protection, with the participation of the CIS, the three Baltic states, and Georgia. Issues of compliance with the Montreal Protocol were discussed, as well as those of scientific technological co-operation. Also on the agenda were the problems of other states participating in the international ozone layer regime, and the possibility of joint obligations as a group of states, with mutual obligations, as well as the question of creating a multilateral fund to finance co-operative research. The possibility of establishing a joint co-ordination mechanism within the CIS was indicated. Among the important questions dealt with was adherence to the international obligations of Russia in terms of control over trade in restricted chemicals, including with non-parties. Though the major production and consumption of ozone-depleting substances is concentrated in Russia, various ties exist between the former republics (technologies, raw materials, export–import operations). The amendment to the Montreal Protocol regarding trade restrictions would affect the interests of many of them. However, as yet no solution has been found to the problem of how to modify trade patterns to adhere to international provisions.

A range of interstate environmental problems within the CIS has come into existence. In particular these concern air and water pollution regulations and protection of living resources of the inland seas of the former Soviet Union. New joint approaches are urgently needed to protect the biological resources of the Caspian Sea—including the elaboration of an interstate agreement between Kazahkstan, Turkmenistan, Russia, and Azerbaijan on fisheries conservation and reproduction, especially sturgeon stocks. Another item on the interstate environmental agenda concerns solving the problem of the Aral Sea by mutual efforts, not only of the regional states, but on a broader basis. As yet there is no environmental protection programme for the rivers and seas of the Arctic basin. Russia needs to regulate with Kazahkstan the issues of pollution prevention in the rivers Irtish and Ishim, which bring their highly polluted waters from Kazahkstan, and deliver them to the Arctic Ocean. Co-ordination between Russia and Ukraine is necessary to regulate transboundary water pollution in the rivers of the North Donets, and the Desna, and between Russia and Belarus, on the River Dneper.[5]

Various factors define the potential for environmental interstate disputes. In 1993 the local council of Krasnoyarsk in Russia imposed a ban on deliveries from Ukraine of wastes from nuclear power stations for recycling at the chemical plant Krasnoyarsk-2. However, this ban was not called because of environmental considerations: Ukraine had not been meeting its obligations for foodstuff deliveries to Siberia, and in response to proposals for negotiations just kept silent but continued its nuclear wastes deliveries.[6]

Serious disagreements may arise between Russia, Ukraine, Belarus, Moldavia, and Kazahkstan on transboundary air pollution. Russia, for instance, receives ten times more air pollutants from Ukraine and Belarus than it sends in the opposite direction. The major source within the former Soviet republics is Ukraine, with air pollutants export totalling that of Germany and Poland combined (in 1990 its $SO_2$ and $NO_x$ exports to Russia accounted for 405,000 and 118,000 tons respectively). Russia is sending to Kazahkstan about twice as much air pollutants as it receives (in 1990, 70,000 and 40,000 tons).[7] The question of regulating this problem within the common Soviet territory had not been raised before. Inter-republican fluxes were not controlled within the Long Range Transboundary Air Pollution (LRTAP) regime, since they were considered internal. Recently they have gained international status, but they are still not regulated. New CIS members not previously members of the LRTAP regime might decide to join. The Baltic states have already declared their intention. As to Moldova, however—a considerable source of transboundary air pollution in Europe—the prospects are still uncertain.

At present, priority is being given to the institutionalization of environmental interactions of new independent states with each other, as well as with the West. Various efforts have been undertaken to co-ordinate their environmental activities. A multilateral interstate environmental agreement was signed within the CIS at the beginning of 1992 (by Azerbaijan, Armenia, Belarus, Kazahkstan, Kirghizia, Moldova, Russia, Tajikistan, Turkmenistan, and Uzbekistan), which envisages co-ordination of environmental policies and joint financing of environmental programmes. It has laid a basis not only for international co-operation between CIS members, but also for co-ordination and elaboration of joint approaches towards their participation in international environmental regimes. The major goals of this agreement are harmonization of environmental legislation, norms, and standards; co-ordination in introducing economic mechanisms of environmental management; and implementation of joint projects aimed especially at solving transboundary problems. Also foreseen are promotion of environmental monitoring systems, data exchange, a system of national parks, and mutual assistance in case of environmental emergencies. An interstate environmental council and environmental fund have been established for implementation of this agreement.

Several bilateral environmental agreements have recently been adopted between Russia and other CIS members, with the emphasis on co-operation on specific environmental problem areas. In 1992 Russia signed intergovernmental agreements with Kazahkstan and Ukraine on the joint use and protection of transboundary watercourses. However, a long way lies between their signing and actual implementation within the CIS.

## Russia and the Global Environmental Change Agenda

During the final years of its existence the Soviet Union, and thereafter Russia, became involved in the process of international regime formation dealing with global environmental problems—acid rain, ozone layer depletion, and global climate change. In connection with the management of these three environmental risks we may trace different histories and patterns of domestic implementation, and varying results when it comes to fulfilling international obligations.

### Acid Rain and Transboundary Air Pollution
The elaboration of the 1979 Convention on Long Range Transboundary Air Pollution (LRTAP) coincided with the period of East–West detente in the late 1970s. The national approaches taken by the USSR and its readiness for domestic implementation had their national specificities. The major issue was that, due to westerly air currents, the import of air pollutants to the European part of the country was considerably higher than their export across the Soviet Union's western border. The USSR, and Russia within it, were victims of transboundary air pollution. By the beginning of the 1990s about 1,730,000 tonnes of sulphur dioxide ($SO_2$) was carried annually across the western border of the

USSR from Europe, whereas five times less was going in the opposite direction. Nitrous oxide ($NO_x$) imports accounted for about 930,000 tons, with their export being fifteen times less. The major fluxes originated in Poland, Germany, Czechoslovakia, Hungary, and Finland. The exception was Scandinavia: $SO_2$ export from the USSR was higher than import, but the situation for $NO_x$ flows was quite the opposite. Norway and Sweden were net-importers of $SO_2$.

A provision envisaging regulation either of air pollutant emissions or their transborder flows was introduced into the convention at the request of the Soviet Union. For the USSR this meant that in order to comply with the Sulphur Protocol, major efforts to reduce air pollutant emissions would have to be concentrated mainly at enterprises situated along its western borders. Only the European part of the country was included in the area covered by the convention. Thus, measures to restructure polluting industries were not to be applied to the industrialized regions of non-European Siberia.

Domestic implementation of this international regime coincided with considerable structural changes in Soviet energy policy. At the end of the 1970s and the beginning of the 1980s the energy sector of the European part of the USSR was in the process of shifting from coal to natural gas and to nuclear energy development. These radical changes in the national energy balance that needed considerable governmental capital investments were not attributable to the Soviet entry into the international regime. Rather, these changes were the result of the impact of indigenous factors—the exhaustion of energy resources in the European USSR, the necessity of their transportation from the north and Siberia, and the shift to cheaper fuel—natural gas, and so on. All these factors served to facilitate for the USSR compliance with the Sulphur Protocol. From the beginning of the 1980s an active national policy for air protection was launched—with adoption of the law on air protection, elaboration of norms and standards, installation of air purification facilities at industrial enterprises, and the compiling of a register of air pollution sources.

Various efforts were undertaken to reduce emissions from industrial enterprises engaged in the production of energy, ferrous and non-ferrous metals, chemicals, and fertilizers that contributed to transboundary air pollution. As a result, $SO_2$ transborder flows were reduced, and national obligations were met. Sulphur dioxide emissions from the European USSR dropped by 29 per cent during the years 1980–90. In Russia today we can note a 41 per-cent reduction from the base level of 1980.[8] However, these reductions are also attributable in part to the severe decline in industrial production in Russia as a result of economic crisis. In June 1994 Russia became a party to the Protocol to the LRTAP Convention on Further Reduction of Sulphur Emissions.

Nevertheless, despite numerous attempts to solve the problem of reconstructing the non-ferrous enterprises on the Kola Peninsula—major contributors to transborder pollution of Scandinavia—a satisfactory answer has not been found. In 1992 $SO_2$ emissions from the Severonikel and Pechenganikel smelters on Kola accounted for 300,000 tons according to official figures.[9] In addition to transborder damage, these emissions have an extremely negative impact on the Kola Peninsula and nearby Karelia. Emissions affect about 126 hectares of forests, one-third of the territory of the Lapland biosphere reserve, and residential areas of the natives of the north. At present, consideration is being given to options for solving this problem by the joint efforts of regional states. As a result of a tender invited by the Russian Ministry of the Environment, it seems likely that a Scandinavian consortium of Norwegian and Swedish companies will be involved in this work.

The issue of $NO_x$ air pollution has not been solved in Russia. Discharges from transport have increased considerably during recent years. This problem is receiving considerable attention in Russia, since these emissions constitute about 41 per cent of the total $NO_x$ emissions, and there is a stable upward trend. Envisaged for the near future in Russia are measures to control emissions from cars and to introduce new emission standards similar to those in the West, as well as to shift transport to natural gas and to use catalytic converters. It appears that it is much more difficult to control $NO_x$ emissions than $SO_2$ discharges. But in the absence of innovations and of control and monitoring over car emissions, the situation might deteriorate further in the future.

### Ozone Layer Protection

Over the two past decades the Soviet Union and then Russia have taken an active part in international research activities aimed at ozone layer protection. As a result of monitoring the dynamics of the stratospheric ozone layer, extensive data have been accumulated and analysed. At present a system of twenty-nine monitoring stations is functioning in Russia (forty-three in the USSR), created at the end of the 1950s as a result of the International Geophysical Year. The national system is incorporated into an international one, and there is daily monitoring of the state of the ozone layer over Russian territory. In line with international co-operative arrangements, data from German and Bulgarian stations are used in these evaluations. Operational data exchange on the state of the ozone layer over the Arctic was staged recently between Russia, Finland, and Canada, with Russia responsible for the publication of maps on its dynamics. Regular ozone layer monitoring has been organized on the four stations in Antarctica, and in 1987 this programme was expanded into a co-operative effort with German scientists.

Russia has also participated in several projects within the framework of the World Meteorological Organization and UNEP (the United Nations Environment Programme).

Russia is responsible for about 9–10 per cent of the world's production of ozone-depleting substances. According to official figures in 1990 total production and consumption of ozone-depleting substances including halons accounted for 124,652 tons (with halons alone at 4,242 tons).[10] Russia's Ministry of the Environment has indicated that in 1991 CFC (chlorofluorocarbons) production decreased from the previous year by 16 per cent, and halons by 40 per cent. The main production of ozone-depleting substances in the former Soviet Union is concentrated in Russia (80 per cent), and about 15 per cent in Tajikistan; other producers are located in Ukraine, Belarus, Lithuania, and Latvia.

From the mid-1980s the Soviet Union became involved in work on the formation of an international regime for the ozone layer. After signing the international agreement, a process of domestic implementation was initiated, including institutional formation,[11] organizational measures, and elaboration of responses to the risk of ozone layer depletion. Two national programmes were adopted on this issue: on research into the ozone layer (1990), and on elaboration of technologies of ozone-benign halon production (1992). Attempts to shape national goals and strategies were undertaken at the end of the 1980s. It was decided to approach the task of reducing and preventing the risk of ozone depletion by means of control over production and consumption of ozone-depleting substances, with the goal being first to reduce, and finally to phase them out completely by the year 2000; provision was also made for research and monitoring of the state of the ozone layer.[12] The provision to reduce and then to cease production and consumption of ozone-depleting substances was introduced in Russia's 1991 Law on Environmental Protection.[13]

Nevertheless, practical measures to implement the provisions of environmental law and environmental programmes have been realized rather slowly and ineffectively. Adequate government financing has not been provided, and specific reduction goals have not yet been imposed on target groups. This has resulted in partial adherence to international treaty obligations. According to an official statement issued by the Ministry of the Environment, Russia is currently not complying totally with the Vienna Convention and its Montreal Protocol. In 1992 obligations to reduce production and consumption of ozone-depleting substances were met, as well as the Protocol's provisions on information exchange and scientific research. However, due to the critical economic situation in Russia, the remaining obligations were not fulfilled, it was reported in 1992 at the fourth meeting of the parties to the Montreal Protocol.[14] An additional set of serious obligations has been imposed on Russia after it signed the 1992 amendments to the Montreal Protocol. Starting from 1996 Russia is to halt completely the production and consumption of refrigerants containing CFCs, as well as exclude all trade in them (at present about 50 per cent of the refrigerators produced in Russia are exported). Experts have warned that it may be difficult to restructure the industrial production completely during the remaining period and to meet international obligations.[15]

Russia is currently in the process of elaborating a national programme: 'Production of ozone-benign refrigerants and compliance with international obligations of Russia to protect the ozone layer.'[16] This programme envisages continuing ozone layer research, including the construction of a model of interactions between the ozone layer, man, and the biosphere, to provide regular monitoring of ozone layer dynamics. It presupposes elaboration of concrete actions to convert Russian enterprises to ozone-benign technologies,[17] collecting and recycling existing ozone-layer depleting substances. However, given the prevailing economic crisis in the country, the prospects of programme implementation would seem uncertain, and a gap might emerge between the programme as it has been elaborated and its actual implementation.

## Protection of the Global Climate

Russian scientists have been involved in international scientific co-operation on the global climate (Global Atmosphere Research Programme, World Climate Programme, as well as in world climate conferences, and activities of the International Panel on Climate Change, etc). Since the 1950s M. Buidyko and his school have been engaged in research on global climate change; and their work, especially the scientific results of analogue palaeoclimatic reconstructions, has become famous in the world scientific community. Forecasts of global warming were presented internationally in the early 1970s. The results of analysis of data compiled in Russia for over a century, combined with the results of palaeoclimatic reconstructions, served as a basis for evaluations of global climate change and its impact on a national scale, as well as for the formulation of national responses.[18]

Until recently, the management of global climate-change risk was not a priority item on Russia's national environmental agenda. The specifics of national perceptions of the effects of climate change have defined Russia's approaches towards the problem, as well as towards the formulation of goals and strategies, and participation in the international regime under formation. Russia's attitudes to this issue have been quite similar to those of the USA. According to Russian scientists, there still exists considerable uncertainty in perceptions on the comparative role of anthropogenic and natural factors in global warming. There are as yet no well-defined answers concerning the consequences of global warming for man and nature on a national scale. For instance, according to the work of M. Buidyko and other scientific assessments, most of the former Soviet territory, and especially areas north of 50°N latitude might benefit from global warming. On a national scale, a 5 per-cent increase in grain production is possible due to a predicted increase in the duration of the growing season by ten to fifteen days by the year 2005, and due to the positive agricultural effect of increased carbon dioxide content on crop production. The boundary of agricultural zones might expand northwards because of permafrost zone reductions.[19] On the other hand, there might also be negative impacts of global warming. Due to changes in precipitation patterns droughts might increase, especially in the southern areas, as well as the probability of crop failure. Changes in the permafrost areas might negatively affect engineering constructions.

National approaches to climate-change risk management were formulated by the end of the 1980s, based on the necessity to reduce the negative impacts. The goal was formulated: to stabilize greenhouse gas concentrations in the atmosphere at a level that excludes the negative anthropogenic impact on the global climate, in combination with an adaptation to the risk.[20] After signing the UN Framework Convention on Climate Change in 1992 Russia began to undertake national institutional responses. In 1994 the Interagency commission to co-ordinate national activities on the climate-change issue was established, and Russia has outlined an action plan for domestic implementation of the UN Framework Convention. The plan contains a set of measures, including preparation of national registers of emissions by sources and removals by sinks of greenhouse gases, and making these data available at the international level. Efforts in this direction for nitrous and carbon oxides were undertaken by the former State Committee on Hydrometeorology; similar activities are currently being organized for a broader range of greenhouse gases, including carbon dioxide. Another group of national obligations includes national efforts to limit greenhouse gas emissions and to enhance sinks so that by the year 2000 carbon-dioxide emissions will have been stabilized at the 1990 level of about 650–700 million tons.[21] The national programme foresees elaboration of measures to mitigate the impacts of global warming, as well as measures of industrial and social adaptation. It envisages the development of integrated plans for coastal zone management, agriculture, and water resources, and for protection of regions that might be affected by desertification, droughts, and floods.

A major potential for lowering greenhouse gas emissions appears to lie in the restructuring of national energy production and consumption patterns. The current energy intensity of Russia's GNP (gross national product) is two times higher than in the countries of Western Europe, and about one-third of the energy resources are wasted.[22] Compliance with Russia's international obligations to reduce greenhouse gas emissions requires considerable investments in restructuring the energy balance. Despite the availability of various modern technologies in the energy, transport, and industrial sectors which might enable a downward trend in greenhouse gas emissions, during the past five years no policy of structural changes in Russia has been implemented, nor have new technologies been installed, due to the lack of financial resources for industrial investment. However, Russia has been granted a certain flexibility in terms of time-scales and emission-level reductions, by classifying it as one in a group of states with economies under transition. In recent years, a 7–10 per cent drop in carbon-dioxide emissions in comparison with the 1990 level has been noted in Russia as a result of lower industrial production. Russia would seem to have considerable prospects in international co-operation on the global warming issue connected with enhancing its greenhouse gas sinks, and especially through conservation and reproduction of its vast forest resources. According to figures from the Russian federal forestry service about one third of the national anthropogenic carbon-dioxide emissions are absorbed by the Russian forests.

## Concluding Observations: New Prospects, New Potentials

Although Russia has undertaken a progressive reshaping of its environmental policies, serious difficulties still remain. It will not be easy to solve the problems not only of compliance with international obligations, but also of the national implementation of international environmental agreements. The situation is defined by a wide range of political, socio-economic factors deeply rooted in the specifics of the transitional period in Russia.

The recent weakening of state authority has had extremely negative consequences for Russia's adherence to its international obligations. Due to the lack of adequate administrative control, environmental standards and norms adopted in compliance with international provisions are being violated. Weaker border controls, and higher levels of poaching in the country result, for instance, in increased non-compliance with the obligations undertaken under the Convention on International Trade in Endangered Species of Wild Fauna and Flora (CITES).

A certain shift can be noted towards giving priority to solving urgent environmental problems on the national and local scales, rather than problems of a global character. According to data from the early 1990s, practically none of the 750 non-governmental environmental groups registered in the former Soviet Union indicated global environmental protection among their established goals. Their activities were focused instead on regional and local environmental issues.[23]

A crucial limiting factor is the lack of financial resources for domestic implementation of international obligations. Russia's 1994 federal budget allocates for environmental purposes about 0.6 per cent of its spendings, or about 0.15 per cent of GNP. Moreover, it seems that this downward trend in state financing of environmental activities will continue. Currently about one-tenth of the environmental programmes of the Ministry of the Environment receive funding. Only 37 per cent of the envisaged financial resources were actually allotted in 1993 to the major federal environmental programme 'Ecological Security of Russia'.[24] This deficit of federal resources for environmental purposes is accompanied by a crisis situation concerning capital investments in the environmental sphere. As a result, the installation of purification facilities and modern resource-saving technologies has been reduced considerably during recent years. Financial shortages are a major factor in Russia's non-compliance with some provisions of international environmental commitments. This was illustrated in connection with the violation of the international ozone layer regime, and with restructuring the non-ferrous industries of the Kola Peninsula to reduce $SO_2$ emissions as agreed under the international Long-Range Transboundary Air Pollution regime.

The current domestic financial deficit means that the outlook is serious for environmental problem-solving associated with international environmental co-operation in various forms. Here we could mention the special environmental loans from the international financial institutions, especially from the World Bank and the European Bank for Reconstruction and Development. Recently the World Bank agreed to an environmental loan to Russia for US$65 million. Within the World Bank, much attention is paid to projects at the regional and local levels—about 80 per cent of the financial resources allotted by the World Bank for elaboration of Russia's national environmental strategy is to be provided at the local level. The major aims of this credit are to assist in building environmental policy, to support restructuring of institutional mechanisms, to develop sectorial efforts in environmentally vulnerable areas, and to provide for implementation of the global change agenda—protection of biodiversity, reductions of greenhouse gas emissions, development of alternative technologies for CFC production and consumption, as well as rational use of natural resources, mainly of oil and gas.

The motives for financial aid are broader than mere assistance to solve environmental problems in Russia that endanger environmental stability in the West. They are supplemented by the new economic opportunities for private investments and the development of new markets, opened in the course of the transformation in Russia. New prospects have opened up as a result of decentralization and emergence of new independent producers on the national arena. The possibilities of impact from the West indirectly improving the environmental situation in Russia are increasing. For instance, the West could exert its influence at the local level, especially in the regions of resource production where export interests are concentrated. Environmental arrangements with local authorities in exchange for financial, technical, and economic assistance could play an important role in getting them to shift to more progressive environmental policies. On the other hand, non-tariff instruments of influence to preserve environmental standards are becoming increasingly important—providing access to foreign markets for Russian resource producers might be an important item in exchange for compliance with environmental security provisions.

Democratization and the transition to a market economy in Russia have revealed new chances for developing environmental co-operation on a bilateral basis, especially with the countries of Western Europe. Whereas previously bilateral contacts were limited mainly to joint research projects and exchange of information, today the range of this type of co-operation has expanded to involve environmental management and joint implementation of international commitments. Within the framework of the highly centralized Soviet state, bilateral co-operation was provided via Moscow, which totally controlled the process. Today, however, with the decentralization of environmental management, the various regions of Russia are playing an important role in the co-operation, and this is also more in line with the interests of the West. For example, for the comparatively small Scandinavian countries it is more logical to concentrate their interests and to establish contacts not with distant areas of vast Russia, but with the neighbouring regions of Karelia, Murmansk, and St Petersburg. This provides for more specifically targeted co-operation, for greater flexibility of joint projects, and for solving of common transboundary environmental problems.

Some new trends in co-operation with international financial institutions can be indicated here. Mention should be made of the possibilities of providing certain privileges (lower interest rates on loans, longer credit-return periods) in the terms of loans and technical assistance from the West within the framework of environmental projects aimed at the reconstruction of obsolete plants and rationalization of resource use. New opportunities seem to be emerging in connection with the restructuring of Russia's external debt in some of its environmental activities. For instance, reductions in external debt could be provided in line with the costs of measures aimed at shifting to new technologies to reduce greenhouse gas emissions.

Even though financial assistance from the West is of great significance, Russian experts doubt that it can solve entirely the environmental problems of Russia, as well as the problems concerning adherence to its international obligations. It might definitely help in reducing the time-limits of environmental restructuring and *perestroika*, and contribute to success in this field.

The transitional period in Russia necessarily involves greater instability in the major prerequisites for international environmental co-operation. Effective implementation of international environmental obligations would seem to be closely linked with the success of this transitional period, and whether a solution can be found to Russia's internal political, economic, and social problems. Success in the domestic implementation of international agreements depends on progress in systemic transformation—on the rapid creation of market-based and democratic institutions and culture. Realization of an environmental strategy in Russia is dependent on overcoming the economic recession. Thus, for a relatively long period of time, solving the most urgent environmental problems in Russia, as well as domestic implementation of international environmental commit-ments and compliance with international obligations, will remain intertwined with the prospects of general economic normalization, and with the stabilization of the state.

Solving the environmental problems of Russia and increasing the effectiveness of international environmental co-operation are closely associated with democratization, a necessary prerequisite for exposing and defending environmental interests. This is especially important in the case of Russia, because the environmental consciousness and political will of political leaders on this issue still tend to be rather weak. Political pressures from the green movement and the public are of crucial importance. Indeed, this field might be regarded as one of the important directions for international co-operation. Co-ordination of actions between NGOs in Russia and in the West is inevitable. Pressures from foreign NGOs exerted in Russia can be even more effective than the desperate efforts of local NGOs and the local public to solve environmental problems.

## Notes and References

This article is inspired by the research initiated by the authors within the international project 'Implementation and Effectiveness of International Environmental Commitments' headed by E. Skolnikoff and D. Victor at The International Institute for Applied Systems Analysis, Laxenburg, Austria.

1. V. Kotov and E. Nikitina (1993), 'Russia in Transition: Obstacles to Environmental Protection', *Environment*, 35 (Dec.), 10–20.

2. 'Zakon Rossiiskoy Federacii ob Ohrane Okruizhauishei Prirodnoy Sredy' (Law of the Russian Federation on Environmental Protection) (1992), *Vedomosti Siezda Narodnyh Deputatov Rossiiskoy Federacii i Verhovnogo Soveta Rossiiskoy Federacii*, 10: 629.

3. 'Federalnaya Celevaya Kompleksnaya Nauchno-Tehnicheskaya Programma "Ekologicheskaya Bezopasnost Rossii" (1993–5)' (Federal Complex Science and Technology Programme 'Environmental Security of Russia') (1993), *Zelenyi Mir* (special issue), 9.

4. V. Danilov-Danilian (1993), 'Tochki nad i', *Zelenyi Mir*, 14: 7.

5. *Gosuidarstvennyi Doklad. O Sostoyanii Okruizhauishei Prirodnoy Sredy Rossiiskoy Federacii v 1992 Godu* (State Report. On the State of the Environment in the Russian Federation in 1992) (1993) (Moscow: Evrasia), 67.

6. *Izvestia* (1993), 4 Jan.

7. *Zelenyi Mir* (1992), 39–40: 9.

8. 'Obzor Zagriaznenia Okruizhauishei Prirodnoi Sredy v SSSR' (Overview of the Environmental Pollution in the USSR) (1991), (Moscow: Hydrometeoizdat), 9; *Gosuidarstvennyi Doklad* (n. 5 above), 92.

9. *Gosuidarstvennyi Doklad* (n. 5 above), 60.

10. Data presented to the UN Environmental Programme.

11. After signing the Vienna Convention in 1985 according to a resolution of the Council of Ministers of the USSR, an Inter-departmental Commission was set up to implement the provisions of the regime. The State Committee on Hydrometeorology was nominated at the head of it to co-ordinate activities of other ministries. In 1987 the Ministry of Chemical Industry became responsible for the elaboration of measures aimed at reducing the production and consumption of ozone-depleting substances.

12. *Ekonomicheskaya Gazeta* (1988), (July), 1.

13. 'Zakon Rossiiskoy Federacii ob Ohrane Okruizhauishei Prirodnoy Sredy' (n. 2 above), 616–17.

14. *Gosuidarstvennyi Doklad* (n. 5 above), 92.

15. *Segodnya* (1994), 18 June.

16. *Zelenyi Mir* (1993), 20: 12.

17. Such measures include: introduction of ozone-benign halons for refrigerators, components of foam plastics, aerosol cans using ozone-benign propellants or on a non-propellant basis. Producers of ozone-depleting substances are to be reconstructed and shifted to hydrocarbon propellants, fluorine-containing solvents should be substituted, and the creation of alternatives to CFCs and halons is foreseen.

18. M. Buidyko (1989), 'Introduction', Greenhouse Effect, Climate Change, and Ecosystems (Leningrad: Gidrometeoizdat), 10–16.

19. *Nacionlny Doklad SSSR k Konferencii OON 1992 goda po Okruizhayushei Srede i Razvitiy* (USSR National Report for the 1992 UNCED Conference) (1991) (Moscow: Mineco), 168.

20. Governmental resolution (1989), 'On Prevention of the Negative Consequences of Climate Change for National Economy' (18 May).

21. Major discharges are attributed to the energy sector: natural gas (33.7%); oil and gas condensate (32.1%); coal, shale, and peat (30.1%). 'Obzor Zagriaznenia . . .' (n. 8 above), 13.

22. *Izvestia* (1992), 14 July.

23. *Spravochnik Ekologicheskyh Obshestvennych Ob'dinenyi na Territorii SSSR* (Compendium of the Environmental Public Organizations on the Territory of the USSR) (1991) (Moscow: VNIIC Ekologia), 245.

24. *Rossisky Vesti* (1994), 17 June.

# The Role of Science in the Global Climate Negotiations

*John Lanchbery and David Victor*

## Introduction

Perceptions vary as to how large a role science and scientists played in the negotiations which led to the signature of the Climate Change Convention at the Earth Summit in Rio[1] and, indeed, have continued to play in the negotiations prior to the first Conference of the Parties (CoP) in Berlin, in March 1995.

'Science' certainly put the climate issue on the political agenda, and scientists have retained a visible role in the negotiations on the Convention, but the nature and extent of their influence on the negotiations are unclear and widely misunderstood. One common perception is that the Convention, together with the international ozone agreements,[2] represents a new type of international response to global environmental issues, where the scientific community plays a major part both in identifying problems and in shaping the regimes designed to solve them. Another, opposing, view is that the negotiations on the Convention were dominated by political and economic considerations and that scientific evidence about possible climate change was given scant consideration.

In this article we seek to clarify the role of science in the climate negotiations before and after Rio. We adopt the perspective that, in addition to putting the climate-change issue on the agenda, science has shaped the convention in limited ways. Our view rests between the contrasting views mentioned previously: the Convention is neither all science nor all politics. The types of expert advice that the core natural science research programme can offer are increasingly less relevant to implementing the detailed workings of the international legal machinery on climate change. With the passage of time, the international organizational framework for assessing climate science has become more distant from its connection and relevance to the Climate Convention.

We first address some basic considerations, such as what causes the greenhouse effect and why the climate might change as a result of human activities. We then relate how the debate on climate change arose, first amongst scientists and later in political fora, eventually leading to the negotiations on the Climate Convention. Some major issues under debate during preparations for the first Conference of the Parties (CoP) to the Convention are then discussed, and

we conclude with a discussion of possible future roles of science in the development of the Convention.

## The Nature of the Greenhouse Problem

*Heat Balance in the Natural Atmosphere*

The concept of global warming is the enhancement of the natural phenomenon known (incorrectly)[3] as the 'greenhouse effect', which has been understood for nearly a hundred years. The effect is caused by certain trace gases, particularly water vapour and carbon dioxide, which occur naturally in the atmosphere. These gases absorb energy in the infra-red region[4] of the electromagnetic spectrum but do not absorb much energy in the visible region. Consequently, most of the energy (mainly visible light) radiated by the sun passes through the atmosphere to the Earth's surface where it is absorbed and then re-radiated, primarily as infra-red radiation (heat). This heat is absorbed by the trace gases in the atmosphere and finally re-radiated back into space. The greenhouse gases thus act rather like a blanket, absorbing and re-radiating heat.

The heat absorbed by the atmosphere as a result of the greenhouse effect maintains the average temperature at the Earth's surface about 33 °C higher than it would be if it contained no heat-absorbing (greenhouse) gases.[5] The greenhouse effect is thus essential for the existence of life on Earth, certainly in its present forms.

The concentration of greenhouse gases[6] in the atmosphere is quite low, totalling less than 1 per cent of all gases, and it is maintained by a balance between emission sources[7] and 'sinks'.[8] Concentrations can change if either the sources or the sinks (or both) change and, indeed, the natural sources and sinks of all the greenhouse gases have varied in the past.

*Anthropogenically Induced Climate Change*

Current concerns about climate change arise from the fact that mankind is causing greenhouse gas concentrations to rise significantly and at a comparatively high rate. This trend is forecast to continue and could have effects on the climate. Many human activities give rise to greenhouse gas emissions, particularly those associated with energy use and agriculture. Burning of coal, oil and gas (fossil fuels) generates carbon dioxide ($CO_2$); rice paddies release methane

$(CH_4)$; and nitrogen-based fertilizers used in agriculture tend to release nitrous oxide $(N_2O)$. Increased industrial and agricultural activity over the last 200 years, coupled with the rapid rise in the human population, have led to a significant increase in emissions of greenhouse gases and a consequent rise in their atmospheric concentrations. Human activities have also reduced the size and capacity of some sinks, particularly forests, further increasing the concentrations of some gases. As a result, carbon dioxide concentrations in the atmosphere have increased by more than one-quarter since the Industrial Revolution, methane concentrations have more than doubled over the same period, and nitrous oxide concentrations have increased by more than 15 per cent since 1950.[9] Moreover, mankind has invented and released into the atmosphere some wholly artificial greenhouse gases, notably chlorofluorocarbons (CFCs).

If greenhouse gas concentrations in the atmosphere have been increased by human activities, it should follow from 'greenhouse theory' that the atmosphere will trap more of the sun's heat and become warmer. The nub of the debate about climate change is the magnitude of this warming ('climate sensitivity') and the extent to which it will have adverse consequences in terms of things that society values, such as crop yields and the protection of coastal zones.

There is no dispute amongst scientists about the fact that greenhouse gas concentrations have been, and are,[10] increasing; but there is dispute about the degree to which they are coupled to rising temperatures. The Intergovernmental Panel on Climate Change 'judge that'[11] the average global temperature has risen by between 0.3 and 0.6 °C in the last hundred years (with a concomitant rise in mean sea level of 10–20 cm). Many scientists think that it is more than likely that some of the increased temperature is due to rising greenhouse gas concentrations, but a definitive fingerprint of climate warming due to greenhouse gases does not yet exist. The crucial question is what may happen in the future, if greenhouse gas concentrations rise significantly. IPCC forecasts[12] from current models, that the mean global surface temperature will continue to rise at an average rate of 0.3 °C per decade if no action is taken to control emissions. However, this is only one of many possible predictions because the relevant models are very complex and dependent upon many assumptions. Forecasting the effects and impacts of any such changes is thus fraught with difficulty; research into the impacts of changing climate on society is generally at an early stage.

## Identification of the Climate 'Problem' and Responses To It

### Identification

Although the greenhouse effect was identified and described by the Swedish scientist Svante Arrhenius[13] at the turn of the century, and many scientists realized that anthropogenic emissions of greenhouse gases must be increasing, little systematic research was done on the topic of climate change until the early 1970s. Some small, scattered, research projects were conducted, mainly in Sweden, the UK, and the USA as early as the 1930s and 1940s. These projects included some measurements of atmospheric carbon dioxide concentrations and led to speculation about the sources and consequences of climate change (most thought that warming would be a welcome 'improvement' in the weather).[14]

Systematic measurement of air and sea temperatures began around the turn of the century, much earlier in a few locations, with the creation of meteorological services. However, continuous measurements of atmospheric carbon dioxide only began in the 1950s as part of the International Geophysical Year (IGY), in an effort to understand better the global carbon cycle. The other main greenhouse gases (methane, CFCs, and nitrous oxide) have been measured continuously only since the late 1970s. Indeed, much of the research conducted prior to the last three decades was limited in scope and did not fire the imagination of the public. It was undertaken because of its intrinsic intellectual interest to a few curious scientists, not because of its relevance to policy or society.

The main reasons for lack of systematic attention to anthropogenic climate change were probably threefold. First, until the 1950s most scientists believed in 'gradualism' (that changes in nature occur gradually, usually over very long periods of time), and they were thus predisposed to think that the climate could not change significantly in the course of a generation or two. Secondly, virtually all scientists were sceptical that the actions of humans could change climate on a planetary scale. There was abundant evidence of local changes, including heat island effects near cities, but global consequences were much more difficult to fathom.[15] Scientists consistently underestimated the future volume of carbon dioxide emissions, probably because they did not imagine exponential growth in these sources, and this further reduced the likelihood that they would take the possibility of global climate change seriously. Thirdly, the evidence for climate change was inconclusive and contradictory. Temperatures had risen after the turn of the century but declined in the 1940s and 1950s. There was no clear sign of temperatures rising continuously and significantly.

The predisposition not to study climate change systematically reversed in the 1950s, primarily because of the new role of science in Western society after the Second World War. 'Big science' came to atmospheric, oceanic, and geological research with the International Geophysical Year (1957 to 1958), during which many climate-related measurements were made around the globe, some of which have continued to the present (the first permanent Antarctic stations were, for example, established in the IGY).

Generally, the war changed the relationship between government and science, especially in the USA and in US universities, in part because it demonstrated the practical values of science and engineering research (RADAR and the atomic bomb were both products of basic science). A 'social contract' of government support for basic science, therefore, emerged after the war, particularly in the USA but also in many Western European nations. In the USA the contract has been nurtured by a scientific élite that has simultaneously steered not only science but also government policy concerning it. The disciplines that became climate research, as with most sciences, benefited from this support. The cold war included a race in science which bolstered the contract. Indeed, one of the challenges to emerge since the cold war is how to sustain the contract and its support for basic science. In general, climate science has attracted sustained support after the cold war because of popular concerns about 'the environment' including fears of global warming; scientists in other areas, notably theoretical physics, have found that justification for their work has become more difficult and they now face severe cuts in government funding.

Following the measurement programmes begun in the IGY, the 1960s saw the development of the first theoretical models of the circulation of atmospheric air currents. Begun in the 1940s, the early models were funded by the US Defense Department, initially as part of a numerical weather prediction programme. (This new field of research was made possible by the development of computing machines, also a product of the war and defence funding.) From the mid-1960s onwards it was commonplace to illustrate the sensitivity of such models by showing their response to a doubling of carbon dioxide concentrations in the atmosphere, not because of fears that carbon dioxide would double but rather because this was, and remains, a convenient benchmark. More widely applicable General Circulation Models (GCMs) began in this way at Princeton University: at present, perhaps two dozen exist world-wide, a third of which are 'state of the art'. Virtually all of these are now used for the development of scenarios for possible climate change.

The politically detached nature of greenhouse science changed in the 1960s, largely because of the rise of popular environmentalism, leading eventually to the Stockholm Conference on the Human Environment in 1972, which prompted an increase in research both into possible climate change and allied issue areas. In science it became common to identify the practical environmental consequences of one's research, and global warming was no exception. The science of global warming cuts across many other environmental issues, and thus when scientists worried about the effects of supersonic aircraft on climate (a fear of the late 1960s) or the effects of perturbations in the global atmospheric chemistry (possibly leading to stratospheric ozone depletion, a fear beginning in the mid-1970s), what they learned was also relevant to the understanding and eventual prediction of climate change.

There were many sources of fears about climate change in the mid-1970s, some related to possible global cooling, and these helped to build up climatology as a multidisciplinary field. For example, in the 1980s climate studies focused on the possible consequences on climate of nuclear war or of an asteroid or comet impacting the Earth (such as probably led to extinction of the dinosaurs). Other fields of science experienced a similar development. In particular, energy economics grew markedly in response to the first oil crisis (1973), and a large amount of expertise in forecasting energy use became available 'off the shelf' when fears of global warming prompted efforts to predict future emissions from burning fossil fuels and concomitant policy responses for reducing greenhouse gas emissions. The first full assessment of the climate problem by the US National Academy of Sciences (published in 1983) was originally commissioned to examine the effect on climate of high-carbon synthetic oil ('synfuels'), which the USA was contemplating using as part of a strategy to reduce dependence on imported oil.

*Responses*

By the end of the 1970s scientists had begun to see climate change as a potentially serious problem. Some politicians and international bodies, notably some within the UN, had also become acquainted with the issue and had begun to consider policy-related actions for the mitigation of climate change. By 1979 there was sufficient interest, globally, for the World Meteorological Organization (WMO) to call the first World Climate Conference in Geneva. At the end of the Conference the following statement was issued:

The present understanding of the climate process leads to the recognition of the clear possibility that these (anthropogenic) increases in carbon dioxide may result in significant and possibly major long-term changes of the global-scale climate.

The first Climate Conference, which was attended mainly by scientists, was followed in rapid succession by a series of other meetings sponsored by the WMO, the United Nations Environment Programme (UNEP), and the International Council of Scientific Unions (ICSU) which were held at

Villach, in Austria, in 1980, 1983, and 1985, followed by further independent meetings in 1987.[16] At the domestic level some countries were, and had been, conducting assessments of possible climate change. The US National Academy of Sciences conducted a small-scale assessment in 1979, which reported an estimate of 1.5 to 4.5 °C global warming in response to a doubling of carbon dioxide emissions—a number based on an informal poll of participants, but which is now conventional wisdom because it is repeated so often. The Academy also produced a study in 1983, mentioned earlier. The US Department of Energy published a massive assessment in 1985, and the US Environmental Protection Agency increased its research into climate in the 1980s, publishing an assessment in 1983 and a full assessment later in the decade. Other countries lagged behind, but many had assessments under way or completed by the late 1980s. In this context of domestic and international attention the now famous Toronto Conference was held in 1988.[17]

The Toronto Conference marked the beginning of high-level political debate on the climate-change issue.[18] It concluded with a call for political action, and included suggestions as to what targets might be adopted for greenhouse gas emission reductions, the so-called Toronto Targets.[19] The final statement from the Conference included the following remarks:

The Earth's atmosphere is being changed at an unprecedented rate by pollutants resulting from human activities, inefficient and wasteful fuel use, and the effects of rapid population growth in many regions. These changes represent a major threat to international security and are already having harmful conse-quences over many parts of the globe . . . Far reaching impacts will be caused by global warming and sea level rise which are becoming increasingly evident as a result of atmospheric concentrations of carbon dioxide and other greenhouse gases.

This was probably an overstatement, if not a distortion, of the scientific evidence, but it did serve to prompt a flurry of political activity. This activity was further reinforced by a series of hot summers and natural disasters in the 1980s, notably the hot summer of 1988 in the USA, which led to high-visibility hearings in the USA and created a momentum that did not die to do something about climate change. There was, and is, no credible evidence that the hot summers of the late 1980s were due to anthropogenically induced global warming, but they did create an opportunity that was seized upon by environmentalists and interested climate scientists to push for policy action on global warming. The Toronto Conference became an international focal point for such action.

The Toronto Conference and the public concern about climate issues had two main outcomes in terms of institutional development, one with implications for further research into climate change, and one which led eventually to the development of the Climate Convention.

The political attention to climate change elevated by the Toronto Conference, and furthered by domestic and international environmental pressure to do something about global warming, helped make the activities of the nascent Intergovernmental Panel on Climate Change (IPCC) more salient. Independent of the Toronto Conference, the IPCC was set up by the WMO and UNEP in 1988 and dates to discussion earlier in the decade.[20] The Panel, which is composed mainly of government scientific representatives from all over the world, has since been generally accepted as the main, expert, scientific body on climate change issues. Evidence that governments view the IPCC process as credible and legitimate is the fact that there are many fewer national assessments of the climate problem than might be expected given the salience of the issue; most governments are content to rely upon the international review process of the IPCC.

Additionally, two months after the Toronto Conference the Maltese government proposed to the UN that the global climate be declared a 'common heritage of mankind', reminiscent of the developing countries' claims to the deep seabed floor in the Law of the Sea negotiations. This led the General Assembly, in December 1988, to adopt a resolution on the protection of the climate for present and future generations of mankind which, in turn, led to discussion amongst policy-makers as to what legal and policy options might be adopted by the international community in response to the perceived threat of climate change. The Maltese effort was the most salient of many attempts to get international negotiations under way, but no sustained negotiations began until after the publication of the first IPCC Report in 1990.

The scientific and policy-making processes were not, initially, strongly linked, although it was always assumed that the former would inform the latter. However, the results of the first IPCC scientific report,[21] which were widely known beforehand, stimulated considerable debate amongst policy-makers. By the time of the second World Climate Conference in November 1990 political interest was sufficient for the UN General Assembly to agree to establish an Inter-governmental Negotiating Committee (INC) for a Framework Convention on Climate Change in December 1990. That the General Assembly did this—and not UNEP, WMO, or some other agency—is important because the General Assembly's patrimony has helped make the negotiations broader in character, focusing on development as well as environmental aspects of climate change. The importance of the process has probably increased because the General Assembly is the supreme body of world governance. We trace the General Assembly's role in part as an extension of its earlier activities led by Malta and, in part, to dissatisfaction by developing countries with UNEP's highly visible role in promoting the environmental aspects of earlier international environmental agreements, at the expense of economic development and resource transfers.

The INC was charged with drawing up a Convention for signature by world leaders at the Earth Summit in Rio de Janeiro in June 1992. This the INC did, but in a rather incomplete manner which left large sections of the agreement open to a variety of different interpretations. Consequently, the INC has continued to meet since Rio in order to try to clarify exactly what the Parties should do, and how they should do it, at the first Conference of the Parties (CoP) to the Convention, which will be held in March 1995 in Berlin.[22]

The remainder of this article is devoted to an examination of the relationship between scientists, in particular the IPCC, and the INC. First, however, it is worth recounting in a little more detail how the IPCC has developed.

## The Development of the IPCC

### The Origins and Structure of the IPCC

The IPCC was set up by the WMO and UNEP in 1988 to undertake three main tasks: to assess how much the climate might change as a consequence of human activities; to estimate what the environmental and socio-economic impacts of any climate change might be; and to formulate response strategies for the management and mitigation of any adverse environmental impacts. To carry out these three tasks the IPCC was originally divided into three groups:

- *Working Group One* (WG1), composed mainly of climate scientists whose job was to gather information about, and come to considered judgements on, the likelihood and extent of any change in climate resulting from anthropogenic emissions of greenhouse gases;
- *Working Group Two* (WG2), a multidisciplinary group whose task was to assess the impacts of any climate change;
- *Working Group Three* (WG3), another multidisciplinary group whose job was to formulate response strategies and policy options for coping with climate change.

The IPCC as a whole was headed by Professor Bert Bolin, an eminent Swedish climatologist who is still chairman of the panel, and the chairs of the three working groups were divided between the UK (WG1), Russia and Australia (WG2), and the USA (WG3).
From the outset WG1, chaired by Sir John Houghton of the UK Meteorological Office, was the dominant group. This was partly because of general interest in its scientific findings and partly because natural scientists are better organized and have a long history of conducting focused reviews and comparisons of the literature, which is the main mode of IPCC's operation. At the time that the IPCC was set up there was considerable popular interest in whether or not global warming was occurring, stimulated by a series of natural phenomena at the time (hot summers, droughts, unusually severe storms, and so on) which seemed to indicate that the climate was changing. This interest was enhanced by the importance attached to the group by some political leaders (notably UK prime minister Margaret Thatcher). However, the dominance of WG1 principally stems from the fact that the outcome of its work would necessarily determine the work of the other two groups. (Without evidence of a changing climate, and its extent and magnitude, there was evidently little point in trying to assess impacts or policy options.) Partly because of this, Working Groups 2 and 3 never really got their acts together, even after the publication of the first WG1 report in 1990 which gave some basis for their work.

It is generally accepted that the IPCC WG1 has done a good job in summarizing scientific findings concerning climate change, and the scientific strengths of the group have been widely praised. However, we contend that it also has weaknesses which are especially evident in the way it communicates with the INC and the domestic policy-makers who control it. These weaknesses derive both from the backgrounds and experience of members of the group and from its mode of working. For example, the sheer size of WG1 limits its effectiveness both in making and communicating decisions, and certainly, the fact that most governments can be, and are, represented on the IPCC and its committees means that it is very slow at coming to decisions. The adverse effects of its size are aggravated by the panel's mode of making decisions. Like most international institutions associated with the UN, it operates broadly by consensus.

Apart from taking up a lot of time, the combined effects of size and the consensus mechanism tend to result in the IPCC never making recommendations of a radical nature or reaching conclusions which are at all controversial. By its very nature, a consensus-oriented process finds it difficult to deal with extreme views, in spite of the fact that clearly a credible review of climate science must identify not only the central views of mainstream experts but also those of 'outliers' and 'outsiders'—the science of potential climate change is so uncertain and surprise-ridden that unorthodox views cannot be discounted simply because they are not part of the mainstream. However, although non-controversial conservatism may be quite a good feature in a body designed to reflect the balance of scientific thought, it is not necessarily a good feature in a body called upon to inform a negotiating process.

The IPCC undoubtedly fulfils its role as a provider of balanced scientific judgements but it is much less comfortable, and much less effective, in its role as an informer of the treaty negotiating process. Indeed, this is a role that it has never quite accepted. The IPCC is, therefore, always likely to fail to provide timely information for the treaty negotiating process.

The IPCC's reluctance to act as an advisor to the negotiating process is a problem, in that the INC increasingly looks to the IPCC for scientific advice on specific questions and the IPCC often feels unable to reply sufficiently rapidly or in sufficient detail to satisfy the INC (or rather the nationally based policy-makers who direct the course of the negotiations in the INC). This apparent vagueness derives, in part, from the complexities and uncertainties inherent in trying to assess the extent of climate change, but it is also due to differences between the way in which the scientists are trained to report and the types of report which diplomats and policy-makers are used to receiving. Policy-makers are used to founding their judgements on reports which are based largely on opinions and 'best guesses'. Scientists, on the other hand, tend to be extremely cautious in venturing unsubstantiated opinions. Scientific culture stresses evidence, careful testing, scepticism, and constant doubting.

Conservatism within the IPCC has tended to increase as it has developed and this is probably, to some extent, inevitable.[23] In its role as a provider of balanced scientific advice it is desirable that it be (and be perceived to be) a careful, methodical, and rather conservative group. It is, after all, meant to give advice on matters of global importance. It cannot afford to make many mistakes, and should not, perhaps, be rushed. On the other hand, the negotiating process is sometimes rushed and the negotiators have, generally, only the IPCC to turn to for reliable scientific advice. In the absence of such advice the INC, the Conference of the Parties (CoP), and policy-makers have to get their information from elsewhere, and this is likely to be less sound than that of the IPCC. We will return to the question of what types of information are needed and demanded by the international negotiating process later.

## The Role of Science in the Development of the INC

*The Development of the Negotiating Process: Early Days*[24]
In the early INC meetings the IPCC played a central, if largely tacit, role. The INC had, after all, been established by the UN General Assembly partly as a result of the first IPCC report,[25] which concluded that:

emissions resulting from human activities are substantially increasing the atmospheric concentrations of the greenhouse gases . . . These increases will enhance the greenhouse effect, resulting on average in an additional warming of the Earth's surface.[26]

This carefully worded message did not give much sense of direction to the INC, and at its first few meetings the Committee was unsure of what was required of it. It was particularly uncertain about the level of commitments it should contain concerning limiting greenhouse gas emissions. The UN General Assembly, when establishing the INC, had envisaged a 'framework' convention in which the level of commitments might be changed as necessary, but this did not help to resolve the question of what level of commitments to include in the first place. The first IPCC report had stated that a cut in anthropogenic emissions to less than 50 per cent of 1990 levels would be needed to stabilize greenhouse gas concentrations in the atmosphere, but did not say whether this was necessary in order to limit dangerous climate changes. When speaking on this point to the INC, the IPCC, usually in the person of Professor Bolin, avoided answering this question. Such an answer would have depended on a full assessment of the impacts of climate change, and an estimate of the optimal policy required to balance the costs of impacts with the costs of mitigation and adaptation. The IPCC had only conducted a partial analysis of impacts and, in its first assessment, essentially no analysis of the economics of adaption.

At the time the IPCC was not in a position to forecast the exact extent of any climate change, nor was it in a position to estimate the impacts of any change. However, it was in a far better position than any other group to give a well-informed estimate of the likely extent of any climate change and what might be done about it. It would have helped the negotiations considerably if the IPCC had given the INC an opinion at this early stage.

Here it should be stressed that the INC negotiators are, generally, scientifically literate. It is commonly supposed that delegates to the INC are diplomats and lawyers and that there is consequently a large comprehension gap between the negotiators and scientific advisors such as the IPCC. This is not generally the case. Although many delegations are headed by professional diplomats and lawyers, many of these have specific expertise in environmental agreements. Moreover, many of the more influential delegations include one or more trained scientists from their environment ministries. Also, some smaller nations send as their sole representatives to the INC the same people who attend meetings of the IPCC. Comprehension gaps, therefore, tend to occur not between the IPCC and the INC negotiators but mainly between the negotiators and their domestic political masters.

As a consequence of their backgrounds, the members of most delegations to the INC have always had a very good idea of what the IPCC is doing and what its best guess would be on the level of commitments that should be included in a convention designed to limit climate change. Their actions have, however, been severely curtailed by their national governments. This has led to a characteristic feature of many INC debates, where delegations, particularly from northern countries, have proposed courses of action in which they did not personally believe and the arguments for which they regarded as insupportable. In general, this has only applied to countries whose delegation leaders were senior civil servants and do not change with their governments, but even within delegations led by political appointees, notably the US, clearly visible fights have broken out between delegates and their governments.

In many respects, a broad range of scientific views was better put by observers to the INC process (particularly non-govern-mental environmental organizations) than by delegations or international scientific bodies such as the IPCC and WMO. Indeed, the non-governmental organizations (NGOs) played an important role, not only in informing the INC process but also in raising scientific and technical issues, particularly sensitive issues which delegations were reluctant to raise. For example, some of the environmental NGOs, who considered that significant and damaging climate change was likely, conducted their own research into what the more extreme consequences of climate change might be, at a time when most governments were considering more conservative scenarios. They also often acted as problem-solvers to the process, researching complex issues such as 'Joint Implementation' in far more depth than most negotiators, and acting as legal and scientific advisors to both small and large delegations and to the secretariat.

Like the IPCC, progress in the INC is slow because of consensus decision-making. (The use of the consensus approach is understandable, given that the Convention needs large-scale support, but it does not need universal support.) This slowness was particularly evident in the early days of the negotiations, when there were many diverse ideas on what form the Convention might take. Achieving consensus on matters of importance, such as commitments, invariably proved difficult. Frequently, adopting options agreeable to a substantial majority of delegations would be delayed by one or two; for example, the Saudis and Kuwaitis were not in favour of any limitations on emissions,[27] and they hampered moves to introduce substantial commitments on this topic. This type of occurrence eventually led, just before the Rio Conference, to the consensus mechanism being temporarily and unofficially suspended, but in the meantime it had wasted a considerable amount of time.

## Drafting the Climate Convention

By the end of 1991 most governments were clear that they wanted a Climate Convention to sign at the Earth Summit in Rio in 1992. While most agreed that they had to do something, there was considerable divergence between governments about the level of commitment to emission reductions that should be included in the agreement. There was not even much agreement between traditional regional and economic groupings. Within the OECD, for example, Germany was committed to substantial emission reductions in line with the Toronto targets, whereas the UK and the USA were opposed to any cuts. Similarly, amongst the developing countries' negotiating alliance, the Group of Seventy Seven (G77),[28] many larger nations, such as India and China were opposed to emission reductions except in the north,[29] whereas the Alliance of Small Island States (AOSIS), a new group within the G77 created for the climate talks, who risk inundation if sea-level rise occurs, were in favour of massive cuts in emissions. Both the G77 and AOSIS favoured resource transfers, the former generally and the latter especially to help compensate and adapt to changing climate and rising sea level.

Arguments for or against emission reductions turned on quite fine interpretations of the IPCC findings, in particular, on the rate at which the climate might change as a result of anthropogenic emissions and what changes would be dangerous to mankind. The basic finding that the climate had probably changed was not challenged. Both the USA and the UK, for example, took the possibility of climate change seriously, and yet both were heavily influenced against cutting their emissions by fears of the economic consequences (fanned by fossil-fuel and industrial lobbies), whereas Germany, with if anything a far greater reliance on fossil fuels and heavy industry, was determined to cut emissions drastically.[30] The economic argument promoted by governments such as the USA and the UK was that any emission reductions would necessarily mean cutting energy (fossil fuel) use, and that this would be costly to industry and harm job prospects. The main ramification of that argument was that the Convention should not contain commitments to cut greenhouse gas emissions unless quite large, rapid, and dangerous climate change was more certain. The USA was the most important advocate of this argument[31] and was a key player in the INC debates, not simply because of its general political and economic power but also because it emits more greenhouse gases than any other single country. Participants in the INC process thus appropriately expected the USA to take the lead on any commitments on emission reductions. Europe could have pushed for a more stringent treaty that excluded the USA, hoping that it would be forced by domestic political pressure ultimately to join the agreement, but the Europeans lacked the political will and cohesion for this risky strategy. Probably, many actually preferred a weak Convention and were secretly delighted that the USA was bearing the criticism.

The debate before the Rio Conference thus centred around

the now standard issues of the likelihood, magnitude, and rate of climate change. The IPCC did not contribute to this debate other than via its 1990 Report. The negotiating process might have benefited considerably from its advice in early 1992, and at that time the IPCC was compiling a supplementary report to its first 1990 report. As it happens, this did not contain any substantial new ideas that might have informed the INC debates, but it was perhaps indicative of the IPCC process that the report was published just after the Rio Conference, in what appeared to some as a deliberate attempt to distance the IPCC from 'political' matters in general, and the negotiating process in particular. Fundamentally, the IPCC had little to say about impacts of climate change (the Impacts Report was of very low quality) and nothing to say about the economic costs and benefits. Yet these were the issues that governments now faced as they negotiated what policy measures were warranted. As the INC process had evolved, the kinds of advice it needed gradually drifted away from the broad advice of the IPCC towards more detailed issues of law, organization, and policy areas where the panel had little expertise and little desire to contribute.

By the time of the last INC meeting before the Rio Conference the draft treaty was a mess. There was little agreement on all of the more important issues and, in particular there was no consensus on what commitments states should make in terms of limiting their greenhouse gas emissions. The negotiations might have been expected to founder at this stage. However, the political imperative to have some sort of agreement for signature in Rio was paramount. The Earth Summit was originally to have seen the opening for signature of three major environmental agreements: the Climate Convention, the Biodiversity Convention, and the Forests Convention. Negotiations on the Forests Convention had already failed and those on biodiversity were nearing possible completion but were acrimonious and unsatisfactory to many negotiators. Climate was the treaty flagship of the Rio Conference, and the pressure for some agreement was intense. In the final days the key countries, therefore, agreed on a compromise text.

## The Convention Signed in Rio

The Convention signed in Rio contains no substantial commitments concerning emissions other than, loosely, for some (primarily developed) countries to limit greenhouse gas emissions at 1990 levels by the year 2000. Indeed, the Convention is full of ambiguities reflecting the compromises that needed to be made in order for the INC to reach consensus on the document and thus the exact interpretation of its obligations is contentious. Nevertheless, the treaty does lay down some clear and helpful guide-lines as to how it should evolve with time, and probably it is better to have an

agreement on which to build rather than try to negotiate another (which would probably be impossible for some time into the future without the political imperative of the Earth Summit).

Some of the more attractive features of the agreement which might serve to make it effective in the long term are that it lays the foundations for reviewing not only the implementation of the Convention, but also the adequacy of national policies for mitigating climate change and the overall adequacy of commitments. The commitments can be changed should the Parties be convinced of the need.

The Convention sets up a body for reviewing scientific and technical matters. A strong scientific component is thus firmly embedded in the treaty, although exactly what form this body might take is left unclear and will be decided by the INC, or rather by the first Conference of the Parties (CoP) in March 1995.[32] Indeed, although the Convention is now in force, all of its more important features are still under negotiation.

## The Negotiations since Rio[33]

In the months following the Rio Conference most aspects of international environmental diplomacy experienced depression and exhaustion. The Rio process had been so exhaustive in terms of time and resources that the characteristic mood of the INC in the immediate post-Rio phase was one of relief. However, the Climate negotiations resumed in December 1992, on the principle that, although the Convention was not yet in force, the negotiations could productively work through some issues that had not been fully addressed by the agreement and which needed to be resolved if the Convention was to get off to a prompt start. This principle has proved itself. By the time of the first Conference of the Parties in March 1995 as many Negotiating Committee meetings will have been held since Rio as were held before it. The subsequent meetings have been productive, elaborating terms of the Convention that were left constructively vague in the rush to get an agreement before Rio, for example, although the agreement mentions reporting and review processes, they are not specified in any detail and much work remained to be done on exactly how to implement them.

Fundamental aspects of the negotiations have not changed. There is still deep disagreement about financial and technological resources, expressed in debates over the proper role of the financial mechanism created under the Convention. Some governments want to move quickly to negotiating protocols to limit global warming more stringently, but there is little agreement on exactly what form these protocols might take. There has, for example, been talk amongst some northern nations of a 'fast track' protocol on carbon dioxide, but this probably lacks sufficient support to be a realistic prospect for the first CoP. The arguments about the likelihood of climate change and its consequences remain much as before Rio. The underlying physical sciences and impact assessments are still highly uncertain. The change in government in the USA has led to a more conciliatory US delegation, but its fundamental position against more stringent abatement of greenhouse gas emissions remains as before, as do the basic positions of most other states.

Broadly, science has not been very relevant in the post-Rio negotiations. Most of the issues facing negotiators are either not scientific or are only very narrowly so. The IPCC's 1992 Supplementary Report appeared after the Rio Conference, but it contained little new information, and none of it has been directly relevant to the negotiations on the Convention since Rio.[34] The IPCC is now in the midst of its Second Assessment Report, which will be formally published after the first CoP in 1995. Drafts of some chapters will be circulating for peer review prior to this meeting, so perhaps some of the results, if any are relevant, will be reflected in these discussions. Also, the IPCC is publishing a special report of six critical chapters drawn from the larger Assessment in late 1994, in time for the first CoP, although these will be on science—not impacts. The Assessment will be a reorganized repeat of the first IPCC 1990 Report published by Working Group 1 in 1990. Working Group 1 remains on the scene. Working Groups 2 and 3, which are now officially merged, are still working on impacts, 'cross-cutting issues', and economics, including issues of fairness and assessments of earlier IPCC emissions scenarios.

Working Group 1 of the IPCC has been actively engaged in devising inventory compilation methods for states to use when compiling their formal reports on emissions to the Convention. They have shared this task with the OECD, which has played an important part in ensuring that the compilation system really works and can be based, to a large extent, on data already collected by governments for other purposes (in particular, energy related statistics). The system has been of considerable assistance to the participants in the INC process (later to be the CoP) and it has been delivered in time for the developed countries to use its methodologies in the first reports they submitted beginning in September 1994. Both the IPCC and the OECD deserve credit for this achievement. However, there is some doubt as to whether the OECD will wish to be involved in continued development of the system, and whether the IPCC will continue to regard such work as part of their key role or roles. The system is fairly simple at present—deliberately so—but if it is to continue to be useful in the future it will need to be developed in the light of practical experience and the demands placed on it by the review processes in the Convention.

With the exception of the inventories work, the IPCC and the INC have been drifting apart, as evidenced by the creation by the INC of a separate subsidiary body for scientific and technological advice. The functions of that body are still unclear, but many in the INC hope that it will be a forum for raising and answering technical questions that are directly relevant to the Convention. What these might be is unclear; one area of potential advice is on how to apply Global Warming Potentials for converting different greenhouse gas emissions into common units, and on this issue there are many opinions—the IPCC's is only one.[35] In short, the IPCC and the INC might continue to drift apart, with the former perhaps relevant only in a very broad sense.

The IPCC could ultimately provide more useful advice if it included disciplines that are directly relevant to the evolution of the Convention, notably law and organizational science which have much to offer to the treaty and have a track record of research findings that can be reviewed and applied to the case of climate. Just as the relevant natural sciences have been reviewed by the IPCC, the IPCC could also become more relevant if it were to engage in giving more timely advice. In some cases this need only take the form of a fairly simple adjustment, such as publishing reports before rather than after critical meetings on the Convention. (Finishing and publishing the Second Assessment Report before the 1995 Conference of the Parties is impossible, but if the IPCC publishes a third assessment it should aim to do so before the 1998 review of the adequacy of commitments mandated by the Convention.) However, a regular and timely advisory function by the IPCC could require large changes in the mandate and culture of the panel, away from detached reviews of the science and into a more pro-active mode.

Some governments have conducted their own reviews of possible climate change and its likely consequences for their countries. Also, of course, most industrialized countries have begun the process of preparing national reports to the Climate Convention and a few have considered how they might implement greenhouse abatement strategies. In general, governments are finding that devising and implementing realistic policies to slow down global warming is much more difficult than they assumed before Rio. This is a matter for some concern, because widespread non-implementation of the Convention could prove a very serious impediment to serious negotiations about further commitments.

## Conclusion

Science put the greenhouse issue on the political agenda as a matter meriting serious attention at an international level. The fear of global warming became an issue of prime public policy attention when public concern about the issue was raised by the unusual climatic events of the 1980s, a concern which was further stimulated by environmental groups and some scientists. Science was not irrelevant in the international policy-making process on climate change but, beyond its broad importance, science is only one of many factors that has shaped the debate.

Since the late 1980s a number of international processes have led to the development of international policy concerning climate change. The IPCC was created to assess the findings of climate science, which it did admirably, at least for the physical sciences. The IPCC has helped in achieving an understanding of the climate problem, and it continues as an international assessor of scientific research. The negotiations that led to the Framework Convention on Climate Change were largely initiated by the first IPCC Report, but as time has passed the IPCC has become more distant from the negotiations in the INC. Maintaining some distance between the two bodies is probably wise, if only to avoid the appearance of conflict between the negotiating process and the IPCC scientific assessments, which are supposed to be detached and objective. However, the existence of a large gulf between the two reflects the decreasing relevance of formal science to the INC process. The IPCC might help reconnect physical science to the negotiating process by producing reports which are more timely and which involve disciplines that are more directly relevant to the problems now facing the Convention: such as those which address how to design policies, legal instruments, and organizations. But, even with those changes, science will remain only one of many factors that shape greenhouse policy.

The IPCC will always face two major tensions that will necessarily keep it from being the central or sole international source of advice. First, it is an inherently conservative enterprise which was designed to review and assess the state of the science and then subject those reviews to a massive peer review process. In this mode the IPCC finds it difficult to address extreme views. Extreme views will, therefore, primarily affect the Convention outside the normal scientific process, such as through media reports. Presentation of the full range of scientific opinion, including extreme views,

will remain a noisy process. Secondly, science and diplomacy operate in very different ways: scientists enjoy the time to conduct thorough reviews and analysis, but diplomats have erratic and unpredictable demands for information. A body of scientists, especially one conceived around the task of conducting large-scale reviews over long periods of time, with extensive peer review, will always find it difficult to influence diplomatic processes. We do not lament most of these attributes, but merely note that they further limit the direct relevance of the international scientific review processes to the international negotiations.

The power of the IPCC in large measure stems from its being 'scientific', and thus for it to sustain its power it must maintain its scientific culture, despite the fact that the culture leads to time-consuming peer review and some distance between the scientific and diplomatic processes. The culture of science confers a power on its élite spokesmen akin to the oracle power of clergy in centuries past. None the less, a distance remains between science and the production of useful advice.[36]

Ultimately, what matters most is what happens at the domestic level, where the pressure to negotiate agreements originates and where international agreements are implemented. Here we have focused on the use of science within the international negotiation and policy-making process, and especially the role of the IPCC. We have suggested that at the domestic level the broad advice of the IPCC is being used, but we urge analysts of the policy-making process to be to be aware of other sources of domestic expert advice. Within countries that have well-developed scientific infrastructures, domestic advice will be more important. Indeed, although there has been a lull in domestic assessments of the causes and effects of climate change (we have suggested that this stems from the adequate job of the IPCC at the international level and because the IPCC has followed, confirmed, and extended earlier domestic assessments) now that governments must implement the Climate Convention and decide whether it is in their interest to strengthen the treaty, domestic assessments may become more numerous.

## Notes and References

The authors thank Jill Jäger for reviewing this paper. Remaining errors are those of the authors. The authors also thank the W. Alton Jones Foundation, the Commission of the European Communities and IIASA for funding work on which this paper was based.

1. The United Nations Framework Convention on Climate Change was opened for signature on 5 June 1992 at the United Nations Conference on Environment and Development (UNCED) in Rio de Janeiro. By the end of the Conference representatives of more than 150 nations had signed the Convention, which came into force in March 1994 after being ratified by fifty states. For negotiating histories see n. 24 and 33.
2. The Vienna Convention for the Protection of the Ozone Layer (1985), the Montreal Protocol on Substances that Deplete the Ozone Layer (1987), and the Amendments to the Protocol (London, 1990 and Copenhagen, 1992).
3. Greenhouses (or 'hothouses') work primarily by blocking convection. The clear glass in a greenhouse allows visible light to enter and warm the plants inside. In the open atmosphere that warm air would then rise and carry the heat elsewhere in the atmosphere, but the glass enclosure contains the air inside the structure. The error in interpretation dates to the mid-19th century, with Fourier's experiments where he described the heating of the atmosphere as a 'hothouse'. For more on the prehistory of the

climate issue see generally the annotated bibliography of Handel and Risbey, special issue of *Climatic Change*.

4. Infra-red radiation is heat radiation, i.e. having fairly long wavelength. (The infrared waveband spreads from about 1 micrometre—near infrared—to about 1 mm—far infrared/microwave but the more energetic radiation is in the near infrared, 1 to about 20 micrometres.

5. J. T. Houghton, G. J. Jenkins, and J. J. Ephraums, (eds.) (1990), *Climate Change: The IPCC Scientific Assessment* (Cambridge: Cambridge University Press).

6. The main naturally occurring greenhouse gases are water vapour, carbon dioxide, methane, and nitrous oxide. For details of all of these gases see the IPCC reports mentioned in reference n. 5 above.

7. Natural greenhouse gas sources include all animal life, which 'burns' its carbon-based food in oxygen to give carbon dioxide; all ruminants, which emit methane; and volcanoes, which emit a variety of greenhouse gases.

8. Sinks take up and retain (sequester) greenhouse gases and come in many different forms. For example, carbon dioxide is absorbed by the oceans in which it dissolves and can then be incorporated into the skeletons of marine animals as carbonates. Carbon dioxide is also taken up by all green plants which combine it with water to form carbohydrates and more complex organic compounds.

9. See n. 5 above.

10. There is evidence that growth in all of the major greenhouse gases stalled in the late 1980s and early 1990s—some may even decrease in the mid-1990s—but there is no consensus on why.

11. See n. 5 above.

12. The forecast is based on a set of complex assumptions about population growth, fossil fuel-burning, agricultural activities, and human life-styles.

13. S. Arrhenius (1896), 'On the Influence of Carbonic Acid upon Temperature at the Ground', *Phil. Mag.* 41, 237.

14. The history given here is very brief. For more extensive coverage see primarily David G. Victor and William C. Clark, (1991), 'The Greenhouse Effect in the US: A History of the Science up to 1985' (Jan.). Contribution I-2 on the project on Social Learning in the Management of Global Environmental Risks and references therein. See also W. W. Kellogg, (1987), 'Man's Impact on Climate: The Evolution of an Awareness', *Climatic Change*, 10, 113–36, and M. D. Handel and J. S. Risbey (eds.) (1992) 'An Annotated Bibliography on the Greenhouse Effect and Climate Change', special issue of *Climatic Change*, 21: 2 (June), 97–255. A helpful analysis and history of the co-evolution of climate politics, climate research, and international scientific advice on climate is: Sonja Boehmer-Christiansen (1994), 'Global Climate Protection Policy: The Limits of Scientific Advice, Part 1', *Global Environmental Change*, 4: 2, 140–59; and Sonja Boehmer-Christiansen, 'Global Climate Protection Policy: The Limits of Scientific Advice, Part 2', *Global Environmental Change*, 4: 3, 185–200. (Notably, Boehmer-Christiansen offers a sceptical conclusion about the role of scientific advice, arguing that scientists have used the IPCC and fears of global warming to the advantage of their own scientific institutions).

15. For scientists studying the atmosphere, the regional and global effects of fallout from atmospheric nuclear testing in the 1950s helped reverse the perception that climatic effects of human activities could not occur on a planetary scale.

16. Continued in Bellagio, Italy, 1987.

17. The World Conference on the Changing Atmosphere: Implications for Global Security.

18. Some observers mark the 1985 Villach conference as the beginning of high level debate (e.g see Sonja Boehmer-Christiansen's essays, notably part 1, cited in n. 14). Our opinion is that Villach marks the beginning of sustained high level attention among scientists and, crucially, is a starting point for the development of an international group of scientific advisors (and, ultimately, the IPCC). However, the Toronto conference marks the beginning of sustained high level political attention.

19. Essentially the 'targets' were a return to 1988 levels of greenhouse gas emissions by the year 2000 and a 20% cut by the year 2005. Some countries have unilaterally adopted these targets, notably Germany, one of the larger emitters of greenhouse gas.

20. For a review of the different international scientific events and their connection to the IPCC, see Sonja Boehmer-Christiansen, n. 14 above.

21. See n. 5 above. The report said that anthropogenic greenhouse gas emissions will enhance the greenhouse effect resulting in additional warming of the Earth's surface. It also, with less certainty, gave estimates of the rates of temperature and sea-level rise.

22. For more on the development of the Convention and subsequent negotiations, see below and n. 24 and 33.

23. e.g. a sense of ownership of, and a tendency to defend, its own reports is bound to occur in any organization, and this occurred in the IPCC after the publication of the first and second WG1 reports.

24. For an extensive review of the development of the Convention, especially its legal aspects, see D. Bodansky (1993), 'The United Nations Framework Convention on Climate Change: A Commentary', *The Yale Journal of International Law*, 18: 2 (summer).

25. See n. 5 above.

26. The IPCC also predicted, with provisos, that during the next century the mean global temperature would rise by about 0.3 °C per decade.

27. Because they did not want any lessening of their oil revenues.

28. The G77 consists of most of the developing countries. It does not have, and never had, seventy-seven members. The name was derived as a sort of pun on the G7 group of industrialized countries.

29. Partly on the grounds that they would impede their development and partly because climate change was perceived to be a mess created by the 'North', whose job it was to clean it up.

30. The German government unilaterally committed its country to, essentially, the Toronto targets. Denmark, Luxembourg, and a few local governments have made similar statements.

31. The US administration's economic argument was, of course, based largely on domestic considerations. The year that the Convention was to be ready for signature, 1992, was a presidential election year and the US economy was in recession. The Bush administration (the EPA had no say in this) was not going to risk upsetting his electorate by telling them that they had to cut back on energy use.

32. One option is that the IPCC WG1 may be asked to fulfil this role.

33. An overview of negotiations for the period since the Convention was signed is: David Victor and Julian Salt, (1994), 'Climate since Rio', *Environment* (forthcoming, Nov.).

34. The one exception is the use of Global Warming Potentials (GWP) to convert emissions (and sinks) of different greenhouse gases into common greenhouse units. On this topic, the 1992 Supplementary Report dampened the 1990 IPCC report's claims that GWPs could be quantified. Notably, the indirect effects of different greenhouse gases—which must be quantified in order to quantify an overall GWP—are quite uncertain. The original IPCC report over-stated the extent to which indirect effects could be quantified, and the 1992 report simply reported the sign (but not the magnitude) of indirect effects. GWPs remain unquantifiable in detail.

35. See n. 34 above.

36. A stronger version of this argument is that the IPCC has become purposely more distant because it has served the interests of the IPCC élite and the institutions of science to be seen as apolitical advisors. See Sonja Boehmer-Christiansen, especially part 2, n. 14 above.

# European Climate Change Policy in a Global Context

*Michael Grubb*

## Introduction

The purpose of this paper is to analyse the evolution and state of policy towards climate change in the European Union (EU), to assess prospects for the EU meeting its carbon dioxide $CO_2$ emission target, and to consider future options for EU climate policy and their international implications. Because detailed accounts of the science are available elsewhere, for this paper it is sufficient to say that, although there have been significant advances in aspects of our scientific understanding, for policy purposes we remain uncertain but concerned:

- uncertain because, although the science is beyond dispute at the most fundamental level (i.e. that greenhouse gases such as $CO_2$ act to warm the earth's surface and that human emissions are increasing their concentration), we do not understand adequately the various positive and negative feedbacks associated with the water cycle, and longer-term responses associated with natural carbon and methane cycles; nor do we understand the critically important issue of ocean-current behaviour;
- concerned because we know that $CO_2$ and (to a lesser extent) other greenhouse gas emissions are making a large perturbation to the natural balance of flows of greenhouse gases and that this must ultimately affect climatic patterns and possibly the ocean-current flows that we believe have been implicated in past climatic instabilities.

Since concerns about human-induced climatic change first emerged as a major political issue in the mid- to late 1980s, governments in the European Union and Scandinavia have been in the forefront of efforts to start addressing the problem. Some EU countries, and later the EU itself, adopted unilateral emission goals and sought to follow these through with policies to limit particularly $CO_2$ emissions. Building upon this, the EU sought to lead the international process established by the UN General Assembly towards a strong Framework Convention on Climate Change.

The Convention which emerged from this process, signed by 153 countries at the UN Conference on Environment and Development at Rio in June 1992 (and by several more since), now forms the legal basis for the international development of responses to the climate problem.

## International Importance of EU Climate Strategy

*EU Emissions in the International Context*

Figure 1 shows the contribution of different regions to fossil-fuel $CO_2$ emissions in 1993, in terms of emissions per capita compared against population (the product—the area of the blocks—is thus proportional to total emissions). The USA was the biggest emitter, accounting for 25 per cent of the global total; the countries of Central/East Europe, including Russia, in total accounted for another 17 per cent, but following the breakup and economic contraction of this region, the EC is left as the second-biggest cohesive economic group, emitting 14.5 per cent of global $CO_2$ emissions (the accession of Austria and Scandinavian countries will add another per cent or so). Emissions from developing countries are rising rapidly, and now account for over a quarter of the global total.

On a per-capita basis, the USA is again the most profligate emitter and forms a distinct group along with Canada and Australia; European per-capita emissions are in a range similar to Japan and (now) to the former USSR, at about half this level. On this measure there is a big gulf compared with most developing countries, where emissions per capita are typically several times lower than in developed countries.

Because of this and differences in wealth, and the fact that the developed countries have dominated emissions historically, developing countries have taken the attitude that stabilization of emissions from industrialized countries is a precondition for them to consider any substantive abatement action. The economic collapse of the former Soviet Union means that emissions are contracting there anyway, and precludes them from taking a more active position. The focus is thus upon OECD countries.

The US Clinton Administration published its national strategy for 1990–2000 stabilization[1] of greenhouse gases relatively early, as did the United Kingdom. Japan has committed to a target of per-capita 1990–2000 $CO_2$ stabilization, published an Action Plan to Arrest Global Warming, and is working on more detailed measures. Japan has also emphasized the long-term nature of the problem, and technological strategies towards this long term. Action in all three of the OECD's major economic groupings is important, but there is a particularly strong spotlight upon Europe, which led the declarations of emissions stabilization

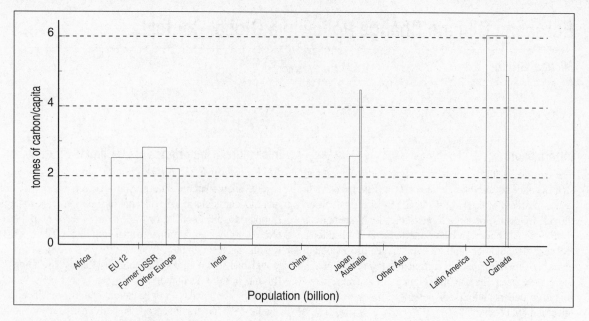

**Fig. 1 Carbon emissions per capita and population, 1993**
(*Source*: Derived by the author from *BP Statistical Review of World Energy (1994)* and *World Population Prospects*, UN.)

but which has yet to agree on any coherent strategy for achieving it.

### Internal Differences: The EU as a 'Test Case' and Nucleus

Another reason why the EU position is important is because in several ways the EU represents a microcosm of the global problem. EU member countries vary with respect to economic and institutional factors, and some of the problems faced by the EU reflect those that could arise, on a larger scale, at the global level in the negotiation of a co-ordinated climate change strategy. There is a 'North–South' dimension, with four countries in a markedly less advanced development stage; Spain, Portugal, Ireland, and Greece. Their relatively homogeneous economic situation is the basis for their common position on some aspects of climate change policy: these 'cohesion countries' do not want to bear the responsibility for past emissions of other EU countries, and they fear any constraint on energy consumption as an obstacle to the main aim of economic growth. Moreover, the economic costs of limiting emissions to 1990 levels would be higher for the currently less-developed countries as their economies are likely to grow faster, and start from a lower basis. Climate policy declarations in the EU have recognized the disparity, and that emissions from these countries are likely to grow in the context of overall stabilization, requiring reductions from some other member states.

Beside the decision on the extent of action, economic

factors also affect the choice of policy instruments. The same strategy will have different costs for different countries depending on the economic structure, existing taxation (average fossil-fuel prices in EU countries vary mainly because of differing taxes), and resource availability. For example, in the discussion on the carbon tax, the size of the nuclear contribution in France has motivated support for a tax entirely based on the carbon content of fuels rather than on a mix of carbon and energy; the opposite is true for Germany. Also, similar instruments would not be equally easy or efficient in all countries, given their differing political, cultural, and economic situations.

Political and institutional variations include the general national approach to policy-making; specific elements that influence the position on the particular climate change issue; and the state of the debate on sovereignty, subsidiarity, and the strength of EU decision-making powers. Wynne[2] draws a distinction between a 'top-down' approach centred on formal policy institutions (e.g. the Netherlands, Germany), and a 'bottom-up' approach (e.g. the United Kingdom) in which diverse actors other than the formal institutions play an important role in policy development and implementation, rather than simply adapting to it. Acceptance of policies can also be influenced by other developments; for example, the United Kingdom population is most unlikely to accept additional energy taxation just after the government has fought to introduce VAT on domestic energy consumption.

All these differences complicate the process of achieving agreement among EU countries, but they are small compared with the differences that exist at the global level. Compared with the differences between the USA, Russia, and China, for example, the EU is quite a homogeneous group, with strong co-ordinating institutions already in place. If concrete international action to counteract global warming has any chance of being taken in the near future, it will be easier for a small group of relatively homogeneous countries such as EU member states to take the lead. Such action may also demonstrate possible avenues for implementing agreements between states with different economic conditions, cultures, and sensitivities. The demonstration effect of EU policy may thus strongly influence the approach taken at the global level. Furthermore, there exist various ways in which an initial coalition—such as the EU—may itself form a nucleus for an expanding regime, over and above the fact and impact of political leadership.[3] Hence the importance of EU climate policy for the world.

## The Development of EU Climate Policy[4]

*The EU CO$_2$ Stabilization Declaration*
The European Community has taken a forward stance on the issue of climate change, and CO$_2$ emissions in particular. EC member countries were amongst the first to adopt targets for limiting CO$_2$ emissions, and to urge the international community to negotiate a binding Convention including emission constraints. The decision with the single greatest impact on the development of the issue, both within the EC and on the broader international discussions, was the declaration by the joint Council of EC Energy and Environment Ministers of Member States, on 29 October 1990, that: 'The European Community and Member States assume that other leading countries undertake commitments along [similar] lines and, acknowledging the targets identified by a number of Member States . . . are willing to take actions aiming at reaching stabilization of the total CO$_2$ emissions by 2000 at 1990 level in the Community as a whole.'

This falls into the pattern of 'constructively ambiguous' declarations that mark many stages of the development of climate policy, most notably the Convention itself; it expresses 'willingness to take action aiming at . . .', and 'assumes' that other countries will take similar measures, but does not make the goal explicitly conditional upon such action. The UN Climate Convention, which the European Union signed some twenty months later at Rio, reiterates this 'aim' for all industrialized country signatories.

The EU's CO$_2$ stabilization goal has been repeatedly reaffirmed, most importantly with the EU Council's Monitoring Decision—a legal instrument in terms of EU law—that contains a preamble highlighting repeated reaffirmations of the goal (see below). Also, both the process

and outcome of developing the Convention have added greatly to the status and importance of the EU's commitment. To renege upon it now would undermine the UN Convention in the very area in which the EU fought hardest for stronger wording, and would be used by developing countries as a prima facie reason why they should not take significant action. Given that the target has already been reaffirmed by the Union's Council of Ministers, it would also make the EU look foolish, if not actually devious. Accordingly, there are now strong pressures to ensure that the EU stabilization goal is not abandoned, and to find ways of achieving it.

Stabilization by the EU is not the same thing as stabilization by all individual states, since the former allows emissions by some countries to increase *if* others reduce accordingly. The less-developed Cohesion countries—notably Spain, Portugal, Greece, and Ireland, which start from a base of per-capita emissions far below the EU average—made it plain that they would *not* stabilize their own emissions. They signed the Convention on the same basis, drawing on the provision for joint implementation of the stabilization goal—namely, their participation in the EU goal—as their commitment. The Council Declarations, and the Monitoring Decision, clearly recognize that these countries are likely to increase emissions—and by implication that others in the EU must reduce correspondingly to achieve the collective goal.

To meet the legal requirements of the Convention, a full EU report, detailing strategy in place to achieve stabilization, should be lodged with the Secretariat by 21 September 1994. The difficulties in preparing this—which at the time of writing seem unlikely to be resolved in time to meet the deadline—reflect the fundamental dilemmas and unresolved tensions in EU climate policy.

*EU CO$_2$ Emissions Stabilization: National Composition*
The EU's stabilization goal was not a random choice. Nor did it reflect simply a recognition that such 1990–2000 stabilization was fast becoming a standard symbolic and psychological demonstration to the developing world that developed countries could, and intended to, start addressing the problem by at least ensuring that their CO$_2$ emissions did not continue to rise. It was also a reflection that the targets already declared by member countries, if achieved, would be almost sufficient to achieve 1990–2000 stabilization across the EU. This is indicated in Table 1, which shows various measures of 1990 emissions by member countries, and the declared national emission targets. Set against these are the emissions projected in the absence of any abatement measures for the Reference Scenario calculated by the European Commission's Energy Directorate.[5]

The table illustrates several points about the EU situation.

Total emissions are dominated by Germany and the United Kingdom, and then Italy and France. There are wide differences in the starting per-capita emissions, with those from Germany and the United Kingdom being about twice the level in Spain, with Portugal even lower. This reflects different patterns of economic development, but also other factors like climate and energy-supply mix, as indicated by the relatively low per-capita level of France and Italy.

The reference projections indicated that $CO_2$ emissions, excluding the former East German territory ('old-EC'), were expected to rise about 13 per cent above 1990 levels by 2000

in the absence of abatement measures. The Commission acknowledged considerable uncertainty in such projections—and outlined also a 'higher growth' scenario in which emissions by the year 2000 from the big four (Germany, the United Kingdom, Italy, and France) are 3–5 per cent higher than in the reference case.[6]

*The Five-Part Strategy*

The year 1990, with the completion of the Maastricht Treaty and confident movement towards the '1992' Single European Market, was the year of peak optimism about European integration. In the climate discussions, the European Council decided very early on that an arrangement of explicit burden-sharing through national emission targets was not appropriate for a converging Community, and the European Commission was, in 1990, asked by member governments to prepare an EC-wide strategy for turning the projections of 12–14 percent emissions increase into a collective stabilization. Extended discussions, and to some extent commandeering of existing EC programmes for addressing Europe's energy needs, led to a five-part strategy being advanced by the Commission, backed up by a series of analyses and discussion documents:[7]

- direct measures to improve energy efficiency through implementation of the existing SAVE proposals (Specific Actions for Vigorous Energy Efficiency) for a series of Directives on energy efficiency standards. It was estimated that these would reduce EC $CO_2$ emissions in 2000 by 3 per cent below the reference projection;
- strengthening of existing measures for promoting the dissemination of better energy conversion and use technologies, primarily through new phases in the EC's THERMIE programme. These were estimated to save another 1.5 per cent of projected $CO_2$ emissions. The JOULE programme for energy RD&D would also encourage development of better technologies primarily for longer-term reductions;
- a programme of support for renewable energy technologies, which emerged as the ALTENER Directive which set goals for the contribution of renewable energy. This would have most impact after the year 2000, but was projected to reduce emissions by another 1 per cent by that year;
- a combined energy/carbon tax, to be introduced at a level of three dollars per barrel of oil equivalent (US$3/boe) in 1993, rising by US$1/boe annually to a level of US$10/boe in 2000.[8] The reduction in year 2000 emissions would be 'between slightly more than 3% and some 5.5% of the 1990 level according to the policy stance on industry exemptions and the way of taxing electricity'; and
- additional measures taken by Member States, which would

**Table 1. EU CO$_2$ emissions: 1990 levels and projections for 2000**

| Country | CO$_2$ reduction target (%) | 1990 emissions (Million tonnes of CO$_2$) | | | Projected emissions to the year 2000 (Million tonnes of CO$_2$) | |
|---|---|---|---|---|---|---|
| | | % EU | Per capita | Total | CEC reference* | National targets |
| Belgium | -5 (2000,1990) | 4.0 | 11.2 | 112 * | 121.7 | 106 |
| Denmark | -20 (2005,1988) | 1.8 | 9.9 | 51 * | 65.5 | 48 ** |
| France | stabilization at 2tC/cap | 13.2 | 6.5 | 366 * | 431.4 | 425 |
| Germany (West) | -25 (2005,1987) | 25.5 | 11.3 | 709 | 800.6 | 674 ** |
| Greece | +25 (2000,1990) | 2.7 | 7.4 | 74 * | 96.6 | 92 |
| Italy | 0 (2000,1990) | 14.4 | 6.9 | 400 | 464.0 | 400 |
| Ireland | +20 (2000,1990) | 1.1 | 8.8 | 31 | 36.0 | 37 |
| Luxembourg | 0 (2000,1990) | 0.5 | 35.1 | 13 * | 13.7 | 13 |
| Netherlands | -3 to -5 (2000,1989) | 6.6 | 12.2 | 182 | 178.1 | 177 |
| Portugal | +29 to 39 (2000,1990) | 1.4 | 4.1 | 40 | 57.0 | 55 |
| Spain | +25 (2000,1990) | 7.6 | 5.4 | 211 * | 259.8 | 263 |
| United Kingdom | 0 (2000,1990) | 21.1 | 10.2 | 587 | 614.1 | 587 |
| EU12 | 0 (2000,1990) | | | 2,776 | 3,138.5 | 2,877 |
| % increase relative to 1990 | | | | | 13.1 | 3.6 |
| Germany (East) | | 10.7 | 18.3 | 298 | 236.8 | n.a. |

*Notes:*\*Data from Commission of the European Communities, 'A View to the Future', *Energy in Europe*, special issue (Sept. 1992), CEC-DGXVII, Brussels. Otherwise data are taken from national plans or statements.

\*\*In figures for countries which have a year-2005 target, 20% reductions are estimated as a 5% reduction achieved by the year 2000, because many measures can contribute substantially only after 2000.

report their national strategies to the Commission, which would then be empowered to monitor and review them, and if progress towards the target were inadequate, propose new measures.

Full implementation of the Community-wide measures would thus reduce projected emissions by 8.5–11 per cent, leaving a rather small gap to be filled by additional Member-State initiatives under the 'monitoring' proposals.

It was originally intended by the Commission (and indeed governments) that this package of measures would be agreed by the European Council of Ministers before the Rio 'Earth Summit' Conference. However, agreement of a draft directive on the carbon/energy tax by the Commission proved to be very difficult. Concerns about the impact of the tax on industrial competitiveness led to substantial exemptions for energy-intensive industries, and it was decided (due partly to electricity trade complications) that the tax should apply to electricity output rather than input fuels; both weaken the impact on emissions, limiting the likely emission reductions to little more than 3 per cent of the reference projection by 2000. In a further crucial change, the tax proposals were also made[9] 'conditional on the introduction by other member countries of the OECD of a similar tax or of measures having an financial impact equivalent to the measures provided for in this Directive'.

The failure of other OECD countries to implement such fiscal measures has been part of the justification for those opposed to the EU tax proposals, but the opposition lies deeper. In presenting its March 1993 budget the UK government signalled fundamental opposition, in declaring that it would not accept taxes 'imposed by Brussels' and announcing a very different package involving VAT on domestic energy, and steadily rising vehicle-fuel excise duties. Indeed, by the time the Commission presented its five-part package, the winds of Unification had turned 180 degrees to re-emphasize the role of national-level policy-making (subsidiarity), and there was a general decline in the priority accorded to environmental concerns as Europe sank into recession. Climate policy was one of the earliest victims of these changes. Of the Commission's five-part strategy:[10]

- the tax proposal is essentially dead for the present. Neither the Cohesion countries nor the United Kingdom show any willingness to accept a harmonized energy/carbon tax, and it now seems clear that Denmark is the only EU country prepared to push ahead with one on its own;
- the SAVE programme of energy efficiency standards has been largely sacrificed on the altar of subsidiarity, with an understanding that member states are free to pick and choose measures, subject to EU competition law;
- the THERMIE programme for promoting energy-efficient technologies through demonstration and enhanced diffusion schemes can only make a marginal contribution;

- the ALTENER programme for promoting renewable energy technologies likewise can have little impact by 2000, because of inherent timing constraints and lack of funding;
- the result is to place nearly all the weight upon the fifth component of the strategy, namely the 'monitoring mechanism' by which Member Countries develop and submit to the Commission their own national strategies for abatement—which presumably have to subsume the original SAVE proposals and considerably more.[11]

The central place now given to national strategies is reflected in the fact that the Monitoring Decision is the only substantive piece of Union legislation yet to have passed through Council. As indicated in the box, it establishes a legal and institutional basis for working towards $CO_2$ stabilization in the Union. The problem is that the national programmes submitted under this do not convincingly add up to EU stabilization.

*EU Emissions Outlook*
With the exception of the United Kingdom moving its target date for returning emissions to 1990 levels forward from 2005 to 2000, little has changed in the emission commitments by Member States since 1990. The national targets set would keep old-EC emissions growth to 3.6 per cent above 1990 levels, with nearly all the difference (compared with the CEC reference scenario) coming from abatement in Germany, Italy, the United Kingdom, Belgium, and Denmark;[12] Spanish emissions would increase to nearly 10 per cent of the total.[13] However, if the collapse in $CO_2$ emissions from the former East Germany projected by the Commission does materialize and is incorporated, *and* the rest of Germany were to achieve the separate reductions illustrated in Table 1, this brings the total to within a per cent or two of stabilization. Therefore, there are hopes that the problem of projecting 1990–2000 stabilization will solve itself.

But there are three problems with this neat solution. First, the ambiguity of the centrally important German position, arising both from the fact of Unification during the 1990 base year, and the fact that a German goal or projection for 2000 has never been presented—at the time of writing, Germany thus remains in breach of its legal obligation under the Monitoring Decision. Secondly, even if one took the plans at face value, a per cent or two more reduction across Europe needs either most countries to agree to a bit more than current goals (which are mostly simple national stabilization), or one or two countries to do much more—and neither is politically simple.

Thirdly—and most importantly—some of the national plans and the associated emission goals frankly look implausible. The first round of national plans are of very variable quality and some are little more than a combination of 'business as usual' projections with a list of technical options for emissions limitation. This is essentially the experience that the Commission had already gone through by 1990. As experience shows, the central issues are to do with policy and implementation. Also, projections tend to swing with the economic mood: the recession induced hopes that the goal would achieve itself, but the gradual emergence from recession during 1994 is lowering the perceived credibility of such projections.

## Ways Forward
*The EU Report to the Conference of Parties*
The most immediate dilemma facing the Commission at the time of writing is what to report to the Conference of Parties. The discussion above indicates the fragility of emission projections. Given the gift of East German reductions, Europe is within striking distance of 1990–2000 stabilization, and the blunt fact is that it could choose the projection that best suits its interests.

But it is unclear where those interests lie. For the Commission to question, in an official report to a UN body, the veracity or reliability of reports and projections submitted by Member States, is at best politically tricky; and to state that Europe will not meet the target that it has so often berated others for not formally adopting is scarcely feasible. Blind acceptance of the national projections, coupled with judicious choice of emissions base-line definitions (for example, in the treatment of emissions from East Germany and accession countries), and/or slight modification of some national targets, could allow Europe to present a picture of being on track. For the Member Countries this would be most appealing.

But for the Commission, the resulting implication that nothing needs to be done at Community level would not be so attractive. Perhaps the most likely outcome, therefore, is to admit uncertainty: if all Member States deliver their promised projections, Europe might reach its goal, but this still depends upon policies yet to be delivered and uncertain projections. Consequently there is likely to be a need to revisit, and fundamentally reconsider, Community-wide policies to limit $CO_2$ emissions—a conclusion which is somewhat embarrassing to admit globally, but which would suit the Commission perfectly well and is probably the most honest assessment.

*The Policy Dilemma*
This outcome would bring the Community almost full circle to the situation in November 1990, and serve to emphasize that whilst the EU's commitment to stabilization is an important step, the real difficulties, as so often in

environmental policy, lie in the implementation. There needs to be a fresh look at the problems, and recognition of the special difficulties involved in addressing a pervasive and crucial sector like energy, in the complex and evolving political make-up of the EU.

What are the fundamental dilemmas? Brute politics aside, they lie in the fact that the policies required to implement emission constraints logically involve action at a variety of levels, combined with a lack of real incentives on the part of member states to contribute to the collective goal. For some of the relevant measures, such as efficiency standards on tradeable goods, there clearly is a strong case for harmonizing action across the EU. There are sound reasons also for seeking to harmonize fiscal measures, though variations in existing tax structures and political attitudes create genuine difficulties and these, combined with the fact that tax issues require unanimity, have so far proved powerful obstacles. Yet, having other measures established at the Union level makes little sense: building-insulation standards are very relevant, for example, but no one trades buildings, and even if they did they would hardly want the same standards in Portugal as in Denmark. Indeed, all kinds of issues—the form of utility regulation, VAT distortions, transport policy, and so on—affect $CO_2$ emissions, and it is clearly not realistic to suppose that all of these can or should be co-ordinated across the EU as part of the stabilization policy.

This, combined with the broader political and cultural differences between Member States, makes it clear that the key energy-policy decisions required to stabilize emissions cannot and should not all be taken centrally. Yet the goal remains inherently a collective one.

*National Emission Targets*
An opposite approach to that of centralized development of energy policies for limiting $CO_2$ is simply to negotiate $CO_2$ emission targets for each Member State, such that the total adds up to the stabilization goal. In form, this would be just like the Large Combustion Plant Directive for limiting sulphur dioxide emissions. This has the political advantage of being a very simple and well-understood approach, which leaves the specific energy-policy decisions required to meet the emission targets to the Member States.

In one sense, the existence of national targets already declared means that Europe is already some way down this road. But there are several problems with relying on these national targets, backed up by the Monitoring Directive. Most importantly, it is far from clear how seriously some governments will ensure that their targets are met, because there is no direct incentive—other than political face-saving—for ensuring this. The Commission, through the Monitoring Directive, can sound the alert when national policies are not adequate to meet the declared emission

goals—and it has done so. But what steps are then open?

Attempting to convert existing national targets into legal commitments, through a directive analogous to the Large Combustion Plant Directive for $SO_2$, faces a number of problems. These arise principally because $CO_2$ is a much more fundamental issue with potentially higher costs and much less scope for closely targeted reductions in emissions by installation of clean-up equipment.

Thus in the context of $CO_2$, the approach of setting fixed national targets is not flexible, because the process of setting such targets is so fraught and difficult politically that the prospects for revising the distribution of emissions between countries, if this proves justified in the light of national trends and experience, is negligible. This same factor creates a very powerful incentive on all the negotiating parties to ensure that they get the highest-possible emission target, with maximum headroom for uncertainty in emissions.

Nor is such a system efficient, because the targets might require more difficult or high-cost measures in one country whilst simpler abatement opportunities elsewhere remain unexploited; an argument that has already been used to oppose such a system. Also, an agreement on fixed and binding emission targets would give no incentive upon countries to do better than their negotiated target. If some breached their target, then—quite apart from the question of what sanctions might be invoked—it is most unlikely that other countries would seek to exceed theirs sufficiently to enable the EU goal to be met. On the contrary, it now seems likely that certain EU countries could readily 'over-achieve' their target, and at present they have an incentive to defer abatement policies so as to leave themselves with a high base for subsequent negotiations. On such a system, the EU would lose most of the potential benefits of being a union. In the aftermath of the October 1990 declaration, the approach was cursorily examined and politically rejected.

*Tradable Emission Quotas: Principles*
A way out of this dilemma could be to negotiate initial national emission 'quotas', but with the critical distinction that the Member States, or their industries, would be free to 'trade' them with others. In other words, the Union could create 'emission quotas' for carbon totalling the already agreed level (i.e. stabilization in 2000 at the 1990 level) and negotiate an initial division, but these would not form fixed targets. Participants would undertake to ensure that their emissions in the target year (2000) do not exceed the quotas they hold in that year. If their initially agreed quota allocation proves insufficient, they would have to obtain, from other Member States, additional quotas. Thus, some countries could let their emissions exceed their initial allocation if they obtain quotas from others whose abatement efforts leave them with spare—and who would thus be rewarded

accordingly.

In essence this would create an internal EU 'market' in entitlements to emit $CO_2$, and harness market incentives for the purpose of achieving the stabilization goal. There would be a direct incentive on all countries to minimize emissions (either to minimize the payment for quotas or to maximize the revenue from selling them) irrespective of whether they were meeting some pre-defined national target. National bureaucracies—and in particular finance ministries—would be faced directly with the fact that $CO_2$ emissions involve a tangible cost, and could thus balance internally the benefits of constraint against more-traditional energy policy goals. Ultimately, the 'price' of such quotas should settle at a point which reflects the least costly way of meeting the stabilization target anywhere in the Union. The efficiency benefits could be considerable; one study suggests that the costs of an approach which allows such inter-country flexibility could be just one-fiftieth of the costs involved if each country were bound to stabilizing $CO_2$ emissions individually.[14]

Such a system ensures that the collective goal of stabilizing total emissions is attained, because this is established by the total number of quotas issued. But it is much more flexible than the allocation of fixed targets. It is also fully consistent with the 'polluter pays' principle by ensuring that increases in emissions above the agreed initial quotas are paid for, and additional constraint is rewarded.

Governments would retain control over the policies used to limit emissions, but components could be adjusted for mutual benefit under the broad thrust of overall EU harmonization. The Commission could still promote Europe-wide components to energy and climate policy; indeed, governments might be more receptive to them because the benefit of limiting emissions would be more tangible. Energy pricing is important, and reform of tax systems to place greater weight on energy/carbon taxation over time is an important strategic component of climate policy; such measures could and should continue to be promoted in concert with a tradable quota system. But many other measures would be relevant, and a harmonized tax agreement across the EU would not be the focus of success or failure to achieve the stabilization goal.

The approach would thus provide an efficient and feasible way of meeting the declared goal, whilst being consistent with two major policy principles enunciated by the EU and agreed by the Member States: the subsidiarity principle, by devolving the detailed energy policy decision-making as far as is consistent with Union objectives; and the polluter-pays principle.

## Tradable Emission Quotas: Practicalities
Obviously, setting up such a system would be complex and would require both analysis and negotiations to address a range of complex questions concerning allocation, management, and practical operation of such a system, as compared with the alternatives. Many of these are considered elsewhere, in a more detailed study conducted between a number of European institutes.[15]

Negotiating the initial allocation of quotas would inevitably be a politically fraught and difficult process, though as experience to date reveals it is not unique in facing the problem of negotiating 'burden sharing', which ultimately has to be faced in any substantive EU effort. As compared with fixed targets, the difficulties might be eased by the added flexibility: countries would no longer have to err on the side of extreme caution because of uncertainties about being able to meet particular emission targets. It could also offer a politically feasible way out from existing declarations about the unacceptability of particular targets.

Although this is introduced in the context of the 1990–2000 stabilization goal, in practice it makes most sense if developed as an instrument for emissions control over a longer period. This recognition could also ease the initial development of the system. Countries would negotiate in the knowledge that the goal of 1990–2000 stabilization is likely to be but the first step, and that if a tradable quota system is established as an effective and efficient mechanism, there are likely to be further rounds of allocation. A country which ends up with a large surplus of quotas in the year 2000 would be pressured to a lower allocation in subsequent rounds; and if the situation arises because it held out for an unreasonably high allocation, based on implausibly high projections of $CO_2$ emissions, the credibility of its negotiation position for subsequent rounds would be seriously weakened.

Furthermore, this opens the possibility of 'banking' quotas for future use. In other words, if, under the incentive of the system, it proves possible to do better than the stabilization goal, and the price of quotas drops correspondingly to low levels, parties with spare quotas could elect to 'bank' them for later use—or for selling in the future—based on their expectation of how much emission constraints may tighten after 2000. This both improves the stability of the system and improves the prospects for exceeding and strengthening the environmental goal. The importance of allowing such banking has been clearly demonstrated in US experience with tradable permits.

The benefits of designing a system which can, if necessary, be extended over time raises a number of other possible design issues. Grubb and Sebenius[16] develop a proposal for a system of permits with extended lifetimes, of which a fraction are retired every few years and reissued according to the need to tighten the emissions control and/or expand the range of participants.

It is this possibility which points to the real importance of finding a workable and flexible solution to the EU's climate dilemmas. It must, anyway, be an approach that can cope with expansion of the Union. Implicitly, it could also form the practical basis for an expanding regime of climate control, that could enlarge to include non-member states: OECD countries like Japan that may only be able to meet their commitments as part of a larger group; and perhaps beyond that, developing countries who see it as an effective and practical means of developing a global regime with mutual benefits. This possibility brings us back to the starting-point of this article: if the EU system can find a way of implementing its emissions commitment in an effective and efficient manner, its greatest value may be as a demonstration and nucleus for a global solution.

As indicated, there are many practical and political issues that would need to be resolved. But what is needed at present is political recognition that such an approach could offer an effective way forward for implementing the European Union's $CO_2$ commitment, and a commitment to open high-level discussions on the possible design of such a system as part of the EU strategy.

## Conclusions and Prospects

Climate change remains as a real concern. The institutional regimes established globally and within the EU during the past three years partially insulate government policy from the ebb and flow of popular concern, and generate internal pressures which force governments to keep addressing the issue and reviewing whether progress is adequate. These developments have strongly reinforced the original EU undertaking to stabilize $CO_2$ emissions at 1990 levels by the year 2000, and the Monitoring Decision forms the legal and institutional basis for achieving this. But the national programmes are not all convincing; nor do they fully achieve the declared goal, which is but the beginning of likely longer-term needs. With the effective collapse of the carbon/energy tax and drastic weakening of the SAVE programme, Europe does not have a strategy to achieve its $CO_2$ undertaking.

The first meeting of the UN Conference of Parties will be held in Germany, and the submission of the European strategy has to be made during the course of the German presidency. At present, unless there are very rapid developments, Germany and the EU face a politically and environmentally damaging failure. The roots of this failure would lie in the same elements that underlie the global endeavour: how to implement collective commitments among diverse and jealously sovereign states in an area as fundamental as energy policy.

Yet there are substantial pressures to find some convincing strategy. If there is substantive political will, perhaps during the period of the sequential German–French–Spanish presidencies, then political realities may force Member States to launch negotiations on binding targets or, more promisingly, tradable national-emission quotas—to ensure the 1990–2000 goal, and/or for implementing longer-term emission constraints. At present the omens are not promising; but if Europe can successfully develop an effective system for collective control of its emissions, it may yet fulfil its claim to lead the world in combating the threat of climate change.

## Notes and References

1. I use this term to describe the aim that emissions in the year 2000 should not exceed 1990 levels. Stabilization in full implies a commitment that emissions should not rise again thereafter.
2. B. Wynne (1993), 'Implementation of Greenhouse Gas Reductions in the European Community: Institutional and Cultural Factors', *Global Environmental Change*, 3/ 1, 101–28.
3. C. Carraro and D. Siniscalco (1993), 'Policy Coordination for Sustainability: Commitment, Transfers and Bandwagon Effects', in I. Goldin and L. A. Winders (eds.), *Sustainable Development* (CEPR and Cambridge University Press); C. Carraro, A. Lanza, and A. Tudini (1993), 'Technological Change, Technology Transfer and the Negotiation of International Environmental Agreements', *International Environmental Affairs* (forthcoming).
4. An earlier but more extensive account of the development of EU climate policy and the implications of the UN Climate Convention is given in Pier Vellinga and Michael Grubb (eds.) (1993), *Climate Change Policy in the European Community* (London: Royal Institute of International Affairs).
5. Commission of the European Communities (1992), 'A View to the Future', *Energy in Europe*, special issue (Sept.) (Brussels: CEC-DGXVII).
6. Ibid.
7. CEC (1991), 'A Community Strategy to Limit Carbon Dioxide Emissions and to Improve Energy Efficiency', SEC(91) 1744 final, Brussels (14 Oct.); CEC (1992), 'Draft Communication on Community $CO_2$ Stabilisation by the Year 2000—Energy Evaluation', COM(92) 158/2, Brussels (23 Apr.); CEC (1992), 'A Community Strategy to Limit Carbon Dioxide Emissions and to Improve Energy Efficiency', COM(92) 246 final, Brussels (1 June); CEC (1992), 'Proposal for a Council Directive Introducing a Tax on Carbon Dioxide Emissions and Energy', COM(92) 226 final (30 June).
8. This was later clarified as a tax, split 50 : 50 on the energy and carbon components, starting in 1993 at 0.21 ECU/GJ (European Currency Units per gigajoule) plus 2.81 ECU/t$CO_2$, and rising by a third of this starting amount annually to a level of 0.7 ECU/GJ plus 9.4 ECU/t$CO_2$ in the year 2000. 1ECU = US$1.2 in late 1992. The final tax level equates to a total of around US$80 per tonne of carbon. Small hydro and new renewable energy sources were exempted.
9. CEC (1992), COM(92) 226 final, Brussels (30 June).
10. CEC, 'A Community Strategy to Limit Carbon Dioxide Emissions and to Improve Energy Efficiency', COM(92) 246 final, Brussels, 1 June 1992.
11. CEC (1992), 'Proposal for a Council Decision for a Monitoring Mechanism of Community $CO_2$ and other Greenhouse Gas Emissions,' SEC(92) 854 final, Brussels (May).
12. There is little additional saving from the Netherlands shown in the table because the Dutch government has already adopted a substantive National Environmental Policy Plan to limit emissions, so that abatement measures are already reflected in the Commission's reference scenario.

13. The Commission's estimates in Table 1 may be compared with the figures presented by the Spanish government, which show much higher reference emissions and slightly higher 1990 and 2000 target emissions (Luis C. M. Garcia, 'Strategies and Perspectives towards Climate Change in Spain', in Pier Velling and Michael Grubb (eds.) (n. 4 above). It remains one of the quaint and troubling facts of the European situation that the Commission's projections frequently vary from those of the Member States, and there are no institutional mechanisms for exploring the reasons for differences and achieving consistency. The Spanish official national target is a substantial reduction compared with their own 'business as usual' projections, but a fractional increase on the Commission's projection.

14. Scott Barret (1992), 'Reaching a $CO_2$ Emission Limitation Agreement for the Community: Implications for Equity and Cost-effectiveness', (Brussels: CEC-DG-II).

15. M. Grubb, J. Jäger, A. Tudini, H. O. Bergesen, and J. C. Hourcade (1994), *Implementing the European $CO_2$ Commitment: A Policy Proposal* (London: Royal Institute of International Affairs).

16. M. Grubb and J. Sebenius (1994), 'Participation, Allocation and Adaptability', with J. Sebenius, in OECD (1992), *Climate Change: Designing a Tradeable Permit System* (Paris: OECD), 185–225.

# A Global Climate Regime—Mission Impossible?

*Helge Ole Bergesen*

The year 1994 brought an addition to the already large collection of international environmental agreements when the UN Framework Convention on Climate Change (FCCC) came into force on 21 March. Similarly, 1995 adds a new institution to the ranks of intergovernmental bodies—the Conference of the Parties to this Convention—which meets for the first time in Berlin in March–April 1995. This ends a long period of international negotiation aimed at establishing a framework for dealing with climate change at the global level. Time is ripe, then, for an assessment of experience so far and future options.

Such an evaluation should build upon a proper understanding not only of the subject-matter at hand—the complexities of climate change issues—but also of the relations between policy and behaviour at the national and international levels. I begin with a brief account of the volatile nature of this issue-area and the consequent barriers to political interference. Secondly, I will present a simplified model of environmental policy-making and behaviour, with a focus on the interface between national and international processes. On this basis, I seek to answer the questions: what is a realistic level of ambition for a global climate regime, and how can it be achieved within a reasonable time-frame? What are the most promising avenues for the turn of the century, and what are the probable dead ends for international collaboration in this field?

## The Nature of the Problem

Several empirical studies have demonstrated that the development of international environmental diplomacy is largely conditioned, not by the goodwill of governments or concerned citizens, but by the structure of the matter at hand.[1] Effective political intervention, whether at the global or the national level, requires (1) a well-founded scientific identification of the problem in ecological terms and a reliable assessment of the basic cause-and-effect relations; (2) a credible understanding of the relationship between the issue at hand, as defined by natural science, and human behaviour; and (3) a reasonable set of assumptions about how societal measures can influence the latter in the desired direction. In addition, matters are made easier if those who are affected by the problem have a corresponding interest in its solution.

For decades now, climate scientists have been struggling with their part of the problem; since 1988 within the framework of the Intergovernmental Panel on Climate Change (IPCC) established by UNEP and the World Meteorological Organization.[2] Despite considerable progress in identifying the mechanisms and sources behind the accumulation of greenhouse gases,[3] large gaps remain in the understanding of impacts on natural systems in different parts of the world. So, precondition 1 above is met only partly, and the rest of the story is even less encouraging: While we do know in general terms what kind of human behaviour is linked to climate change—especially emissions of carbon dioxide—we have little but guesswork as to how it can be affected by political action. What we know for sure is that climate change—if it is real—will be the result of millions of large and small actions taken across the world over a long period, and the impacts, whatever they might be, will become apparent only years later—decades, if not centuries. The critical question is whether the underlying decisions by millions of people possibly leading to climate change can be brought under social control: do the basic political and economic problems simply escape intervention by governments or other public agents? I do not purport to have a definite answer to this. Indeed, the question is primarily meant to indicate the approach to the politics of climate change which I have chosen to pursue in this article.

## Dealing with Climate Change at the National Level

Innumerable analyses, reports, and seminars have in recent years been devoted to *how* governments can best exert influence on large and small decision-makers so as to avoid a continuation of the trends that might lead to uncontrollable man-made climate change. Despite the remaining gaps in scientific knowledge, we know fairly well which direction we should aim for if the IPCC consensus is not completely off the mark. We—that is, well-informed governments and citizens—know quite well what kind of action to *avoid* at both the macro and micro level. The problem is *how* to avoid it.

In principle, public agencies can choose from a menu consisting of four clusters of policy measures:

- information, encouragement, and persuasion;
- regulation;
- economic incentives;
- research and development.

In debates over climate policy, the discussion seems to have come full circle. It started in many countries with the well-established instruments of environmental policy as developed in the 1970s and 1980s, with a focus on command and control, to varying degrees supported by information campaigns and public research funding. At the insistence of the entire profession of economists, the focus was soon redirected from such dated, ineffective measures and towards economic instruments instead. But as governments have recently experienced the practical barriers to such policies, whatever their academic merits, we now see a return to voluntary agreements, often combined with the veiled threat of old-fashioned regulation. It takes little imagination to foresee that within a few years the emphasis on voluntarism and persuasion, backed by command measures, will have exhausted its potential, and economic incentives will again take front stage. As in other walks of life, fashions come and go, but always with some new twist. Each new trend is different, but clearly recognizable to the observer with a memory longer than the fashion-makers.

This continuous search for viable policies, as witnessed throughout the OECD area in the 1990s, underscores the intrinsic difficulties of the climate issue: it is hard to find proper motivation for the necessary measures, as the benefits to be reaped are long-term and diffuse. It is even harder to identify a constituency promoting a 'climate policy'— normally a prerequisite for government action in democratic societies. It is not, however, difficult to identify the opponents to climate measures, who range from fossil-fuel producers and energy-intensive industries to ordinary motorists. In addition, anything resembling a coherent 'climate policy' would have to cut across well-established boundaries of authority among public agencies, which is bound to meet fierce resistance from the vested interests involved.[4]

If political intervention is difficult, apparently intractable, at the domestic level, what can we expect beyond that? The facile conclusion would be that meaningful action at the international level is inconceivable, given this state of affairs. That would be self-defeating, since national measures, even for the largest countries, can be meaningful only if other governments also take appropriate action. Hence the dual difficulty: fragile, dithering measures at the domestic level must somehow be co-ordinated inter-nationally if they are to make any sense in relation to the assumed collective problem.

**Table 1. International collaboration in environmental issue areas**

|  | Acid rain | Ozone depletion | Climate change |
|---|---|---|---|
| Early warning | late 1960s/ early 1980s | 1974– | early 1970s– |
| Scientific assessment | EMEP 1978– | CCOL 1977– | IPCC 1988– |
| Intergovernmental negotiations | ECE 1978– | UNEP 1981– | INC 1990– |
| Framework convention | LRTAP | Vienna | FCCC |
|   Signed | 1979 | 1985 | 1992 |
|   Into force | 1983 | 1988 | 1994 |
| Protocol | SO$_2$   NO$_x$ | Montreal | |
|   Signed | 1985  1988 | 1987 | |
|   Into force | 1987  1991 | 1989 | |
| Amendment/revision | | | |
|   Signed | 1994 | 1990 | |
|   Into force | | 1992 | |
| Amendment/revision | | | |
|   Signed | | 1992 | |
|   Into force | | | |

*Source*: Compiled from (1994) *Green Globe Yearbook* (Oxford: Oxford University Press), and other sources.

## An Emerging Climate Regime?

International environmental relations within a given issue-area seem to pass through certain stages. In the first phase, early-warning signals appear in the form of alarming reports from individual scientists, which will often be neglected or refuted by others, equally reputable. For the general public and politicians alike the situation is confusing. If the scientific debate continues to produce evidence or serious indications of environmental risk, arousing media attention, at least some governments will feel obliged to act, which in turn brings the process to the second stage: the organized scientific assessment initiated by an intergovernmental organization (IGO) or a group of states. If this leads to the conclusion that international action is required to deal with the problem, the governments concerned can hardly avoid the next step—the tortuous process of negotiating a suitable international agreement. In recent years this has normally begun with a framework convention, establishing the organizational and procedural basis for consequent protocols with targets and commitments.

Table 1 shows how international collaboration in the issue-areas of acid rain (largely in Europe), ozone depletion, and climate change has developed through these stages. In the first two cases, scientific discussion started in the late 1960s or early 1970s, but serious political bargaining did not get off the ground until a decade later. It was not until the mid-1980s that intergovernmental negotiations began to produce tangible results in the form of protocols with verifiable commitments. Since 1985, when the sulphur dioxide protocol and the Vienna Framework Convention on Protection of the Ozone Layer were signed, progress has been remarkably swift compared with the previous ten years. This wave of international environmentalism reached its peak by the early 1990s, at the same time as IPCC published its first landmark assessment of climate change.[5] In my judgement, this timing goes a long way to explain how the UN Framework Convention on Climate Change could be negotiated within a year-and-a-half and enter into force less than two years thereafter. For a global agreement with such wide-ranging implications, such an astounding pace can hardly be accounted for by governmental interest in this issue as such.[6] The rapid progress is more likely a by-product of the green beauty contest among political leaders that developed around the Rio Conference in 1992. No government has wanted to be branded an environmental laggard in the run-up to this mega-media event.

The question now facing the governments that have signed the Convention is whether this interest is declining so fast as to erode the basis for meaningful international collaboration. The year 1995 is a critical juncture for the infant world-climate regime: It has a legal basis with impressive adherence among states (one hundred rati-fications by the end of October 1994). It has a long-term objective, to prevent dangerous man-made interference with the global climate, as well as a short-term commitment by the OECD countries to stabilize emissions by the year 2000. However, it is widely recognized that these commitments are insufficient and that the regime must make considerable progress in both substantive and procedural terms, if it is not to be relegated to the ranks of the paper tigers of environmental diplomacy. This brings us to the questions, how can international collaboration in a complex field like this influence behaviour at the national and sub-national level?[7]

## A Model of Environmental Policy-Making

In order to answer this, we need to know how decisions on environmental matters are normally formulated and executed in open societies.[8]

I would identify three main driving forces. First, *popular concern*: if voters don't care about the environment, governments certainly won't. Secondly, experience since the mid-1980s has shown that particular *events* have been decisive in shaping both public opinion and political response. Suffice it to mention accidents like Chernobyl and Exxon *Valdez*—without them, current environmentalism would probably have been much less of a political force. And thirdly, *science* has been crucial in focusing attention on specific environmental issues. Indeed, in all the three issue-areas mentioned above—acid rain, ozone depletion, and climate change—the political process at both the national and the international level has been driven primarily by science, often by scientific assumptions and forecasts of a problem to come.

Concern, events, and science are the motors that drive the environmental policy process—the continuous bargaining over objectives, measures, and concrete decisions among public agencies, political parties, interest groups, and NGOs. This takes place within and outside governments and parliaments, always aimed at influencing public policy either in the environmental field itself or in other areas with ecological consequences, such as energy. This 'machinery' produces domestic policies intended to solve or at least affect specific real-life problems, like emissions of greenhouse gases, as well as national positions in the intergovernmental arena. If the bargaining among governments is successful, common understanding or an international regime will gradually develop. This may be formalized in a convention and an IGO, or may be less structured; the purpose is in any case to influence behaviour of relevance to the given problem *at the national level*. This critical relationship can work through various connections—whether the long way through science or concern or directly via the domestic policy process. Either way, objectives or targets agreed to at the international

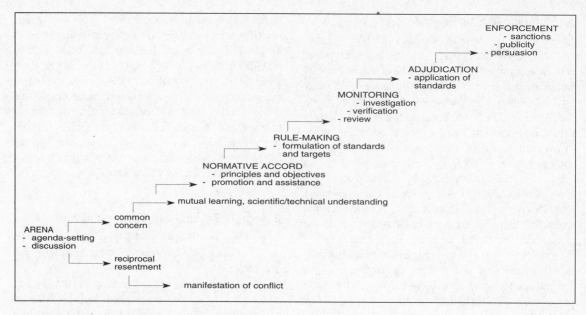

**Fig. 1. IGO functions in the field of the environment**
(*Source*: adapted form Helge Ole Bergesen, *Norms Count, But Power Decides,* Lysaker: The Fridtjof Nansen Institute, 1985.)

level must somehow be translated into national policies and action, which will normally give ample room for discretion, manœuvre, and bargaining. This outcome will in turn feed back into the IGO process, as compliance or non-compliance with the regime. If verification is possible, it will in due time affect the national policy process. This continuous interaction between the national and international level is the core of greenhouse politics, as in many other fields of international collaboration. At best it is constructive and dynamic, at worst a mere paper exercise, highly dependent on the tasks performed within the IGO arena.

## IGO Functions

An intergovernmental organization can have a variety of functions vis-à-vis the participating states.[9] In its simplest form an IGO is merely a forum for discussion among state representatives. But even this apparently technical task can have the effect of setting an environmental issue on the agenda for governments, forcing them to consider the subject-matter.[10] If the issue is sensitive or controversial, this *arena function* may well develop into a forum for regular manifestation of conflict. UN discussions of population issues comes to mind. The large and small gatherings since the first World Population Conference in 1974 do not seem to have fostered mutual understanding, but have rather reinforced reciprocal resentment over the matters involved.

In the environmental field, however, we have several cases where discussions have led to common concern among most, if not all, participating states.[11] This is normally the starting

point for climbing the ladder of ever-more ambitious IGO functions, as illustrated in Figure 1. The first step on the way upwards includes mutual learning and developing a joint scientific and technical understanding of the issues. The importance of these functions can be clearly seen from the development of European bargaining over acid rain in the 1970s and 1980s. As long as scientists openly disagreed on the major issues, there was little governments could do. By contrast, in the ozone negotiations a tight network of experts gradually developed a joint understanding of the nature and magnitude of the problem, which formed the basis for subsequent political deals.

A common scientific basis is a necessary but not sufficient condition for further progress. Once the underlying issues are reasonably well understood, politics takes over, as governments face the question of distribution of costs and benefits. They also have to figure out the best combination of measures to combat the problem identified by scientists. If they agree, the IGO is used for creating norms of behaviour, in the form of general objectives like 'stabilization of greenhouse gas concentrations in the atmosphere at a level that would prevent dangerous anthropogenic interference with the climate system'.[12] Such normative accord will often be supported by promotion activities, like training of national experts, and assistance to reluctant parties to strengthen their capacity to deal with the issue.

The process goes a vital step further when (or if) the principles are translated into standards or targets against which national performance can be measured and verified. This is the key distinction from objectives, which are usually too vague for anybody to tell the difference between compliance and non-compliance. The change from the Vienna Framework Convention on Protection of the Ozone Layer to the Montreal Protocol with amendments illustrates the point: the latter contains commitments to which the participating states can be held accountable, the former does not.

But formulating verifiable targets or standards for national action does not in itself touch on the delicate issue of monitoring, which is the next step on the ladder. It is possible, indeed not uncommon, in international affairs simply to leave implementation to individual governments, relying on their goodwill. In the environmental field, with its persistent free-rider problems, states will hesitate to take costly action on their own unless they can be reassured that others will follow up on their part of the deal.[13] Thus, targets will often have scant importance unless a reliable monitoring function is performed within the same IGO. The least controversial option here is also the most common— intergovernmental review of national reports: governments describe what measures they have taken to fulfil their obligations, and submit their self-assessment to the others. This can have a certain deterrent effect in the sense that the responsible national agencies will have in mind the duty to report when formulating national policies. But self-reporting will not necessarily lead to a clear-cut distinction between compliance and non-compliance. Governments as represented by diplomats tend to be too polite to draw such unambiguous and uncomfortable conclusions.

The next monitoring option is, however, explicitly designed to verify the contents of national reports: through the relevant IGO, governments authorize an expert body to scrutinize the material submitted by the participating states and publish its findings, according to a specific set of procedures.

Investigation is even more drastic. An independent body can in this case, on its own initiative, or following a complaint, ask a participating government for information on a particular case falling within the scope of the agreement.

Adjudication implies a litigation-like procedure, where a body under the IGO makes a ruling on a particular case involving alleged violations of rules or standards. This function resembles that of national courts and is therefore a rare commodity in international relations, but the International Labour Organization (ILO) has made very interesting experience in this direction.

Once such a ruling has been made, the question of enforcement comes to the fore: how to deal with violators once their non-compliance has been demonstrated? Even if trade sanctions have been incorporated in a few recent environmental agreements, notably the Montreal Protocol, the primary method of enforcement in the international system remains a combination of persuasion and publicity. How effective this will be depends on the domestic context within the country in question, which brings us back to the link between the national and the international level.

## Feedback to National Policy-Making

As an international regime develops up the ladder of IGO functions, the potential for feedback to the domestic level changes dramatically. As noted above, the fundamental driving forces behind environmental policy are located primarily within national boundaries. This is the case today and will, in my judgement, remain so for the foreseeable future. In the absence of a domestic constituency, negative feedback in the form of critical remarks on dubious compliance or negative publicity will have no significant effect, unless the outside world is willing to resort to strong coercive measures, like trade sanctions. And experience has shown that even this may not work if the other party is intransigent enough.

Hence the importance of the links to domestic politics: the first of them concerns the 'science' element in the national context. As many scientific efforts concerning the environment are international, the relation to the outside world will often be visible from the first discussions of an issue. However, an international assessment process, like IPCC, will strengthen the scientific capability in the participating countries and thereby probably enhance the standing and independence of scientists in the domestic arena.

Secondly, formulating objectives, standards, or targets at the international level will, in a similar way, improve the credibility and position of those domestic actors who have argued for such purposes, like environmental NGOs. It will also strengthen the hand of the political parties most sympathetic to green issues. This tendency will be further reinforced if the monitoring function of the IGO acquires more teeth than standard self-reporting. The more likely that a government will be exposed to a critical scrutiny, the more likely that it will pay close attention to its performance.[14] If NGOs are entitled to file complaints against governments, the risk of exposure increases manifold.

## Implications for the Climate Convention

It then follows that if the nascent global climate regime is to have an impact not only on the itinerary of diplomats and government experts, but also on substance—the ever-increasing emissions of greenhouse gases—the critical question is: how can the regime be designed and developed to give maximum constructive feedback to the domestic policy process, in Western, ex-communist, and developing countries? On the basis of the analysis of the transnational links, I will offer five suggestions.

## 1. Targets Are Essential, Not Protocols

If the climate convention is to develop beyond an organizational framework, it must be extended from general objectives to normative standards against which future behaviour can be evaluated. The current commitments contained in its Article 4.2(a) suffer from serious flaws.[15] They are open to diverging interpretations; most importantly, they do not go beyond the year 2000, where most of the real challenges lie. The present decade is an inappropriate time-frame for any meaningful climate policy.

As this is widely recognized, considerable attention since the Convention was signed in Rio in 1992 has focused on the form and content of future commitments.[16] Many OECD governments have adopted national objectives or targets, more or less specific, more or less conditional, but most of them hesitate to announce verifiable targets and supporting policies because they are sceptical of domestic political and economic costs, and because they are uncertain whether others will follow suit.[17] Here we see a classic free-rider problem, to which the standard reaction in environmental diplomacy is to call for a legally binding protocol. Whether such negotiations are confined to separate gases or sinks or are more comprehensive in character, they will be extremely time-consuming, with the final outcome highly uncertain.

In my view, the question is not how to design negotiations on a follow-up protocol to the framework convention, but whether this is the best approach to formulating more tangible commitments. The alternative way is for governments to record in political statements their national targets and on this basis encourage an open-minded discussion of adequacy. If backed by national NGOs, this might over time develop into a core of commitments by, hopefully, most OECD governments, consisting of targets and standards with substantive contents. These could include reduction targets for particular emissions, or a national aggregate, quantified objectives for expanding renewable energy supplies, or energy-efficiency goals, defined in a meaningful, measurable way. Initially, commitments would probably vary considerably from one government to the next, as they do today, but if the domestic process works properly the laggards might feel the pressure over time to keep up with the front-runners. This presumes that environmental concern does not decline significantly, but if it does, there is little to be done on the international arena anyway.

The advantage with this approach, often referred to as 'pledge and review' among negotiators, is that it manages to circumvent all the legal technicalities of ratification and entry into force. More importantly, it deprives the vocal anti-environmental minority, primarily the OPEC governments, of their veto power and most of their formal influence. If formal negotiations on a protocol are opened, however designed, these procrastinators will have all the opportunities they need to tie down the political energy of other governments in endless bargaining sessions with a highly uncertain outcome. Why give them that chance?

## 2. Voluntary Monitoring For a Start

Targets and standards must be followed by monitoring, if the feedback to the domestic arena is to work properly. If a government can just state an objective, subsequently announce its own impeccable performance, and get away with it, nothing is gained. However, developing formal procedures with legally binding force will be highly controversial and extremely cumbersome. Any review procedure that goes beyond national self-reporting is bound to meet vehement opposition from governments preoccupied with preserving their national sovereignty. Again, an informal, voluntary approach is the best way to get around such hard political sentiments. There is nothing to prevent OECD governments from suggesting and funding, on an interim basis to gain experience, a monitoring procedure that includes independent scrutiny. If they are really concerned about free-rider problems, this would be in their own best interest. The more transparent the monitoring, the easier to uncover cheating on national commitments. An open, rational process with adequate independent expertise, NGO participation, and even public hearings would act as a powerful deterrent against possible free-riders. Once a government has recorded its commitment, it does not want to be embarrassed in the subsequent monitoring phase, for fear of its own reputation and a political backlash at home. Western governments have experience with performance review within the OECD, but this suggestion goes further in two ways: monitoring activities are explicitly linked to a national target or commitment, and they will be far more transparent. Governments would have to answer to difficult questions in public, not behind closed doors, and independent assessments would be published without prior consent from the government in question.

If OECD governments initiate a monitoring process of this kind, which could very well begin in 1995, the sensibilities of their developing-country counterparts can be put aside for some time. Under the terms of the Convention, they do not have to submit reports until 1997 and can therefore, from the outset, participate as observers in the review procedures. Hopefully they will learn that this is not necessarily an adversarial exercise, but that it can contribute to mutual learning. Let us likewise hope that Southern NGOs will see the value of such open procedures and, over time, work to persuade their governments that this is the only way to avoid cheating, given the structure of the international society.

## 3. Joint Implementation on Experimental Basis

Another controversial issue within the Convention is whether states can fulfil their commitments through joint action. Some Western governments see this as a promising option, to cut costs and (though it is never publicly admitted) avert domestic barriers. Third World representatives are sceptical, arguing that joint implementation could relieve the pressures for structural change in the West, and fearing that Western governments or companies could hoard the cheapest reduction options in the South at little expense. While the theoretical attractions are indisputable and have been documented in numerous studies,[18] the practical and institutional obstacles to such a system remain formidable.[19] In my view, the institutional setting is not yet ripe for joint implementation, *including emission credits*, apart from within the European Union. Opening negotiations in 1995 on a regime of this kind could very well prove premature. It will require much more confidence among the participating states and more institutional experience in joint problem-solving before a sophisticated system of this kind can play a constructive role. This does not exclude experimental projects as part of the mutual learning process, which is the crux of the monitoring procedures sketched above, but the funders of such experiments in a pilot phase should take care not to preclude the outcome by calculating the credits before they have been authorized. It may take a decade or two before governments in North and South muster enough joint ambition and joint political will to permit joint implementation, without undermining the objectives of the Convention. The trouble with such schemes is not the transfer of resources or technology, but keeping track of the credits and making sure that quotas are respected. So far, governments have been very reluctant to grant IGOs such powers of supervision. Economists around the world may continue to lament the waste of resources that follows in the absence of joint implementation or emission trading; others may recognize that in the world we live in, it is often necessary to put up with third- or fourth-best solution for a long time.

## 4. Expanding Scientific Co-operation

One of the most promising aspects of international climate collaboration so far has been the expansion of joint scientific efforts stimulated by the IPCC. Despite its shortcomings in a bargaining context, as pointed out by Lanchbery and Victor in their contribution to this volume, the panel has played an essential role in building credibility and legitimacy for climate science around the world. A major difficulty in political terms has been the concentration of participants from Western countries, which reflects the general unequal distribution of scientific resources. In the future it will be essential to expand and improve the technical capability of developing-country institutions, if forthcoming assessments are to gain widespread support among governments. Equally important, Southern institutions must be able to analyse the impact of climate change on their own societies, and thereby become a force to be reckoned with in the domestic policy process—on a par with the critical role often played by science in environmental discussions in the West.

## 5. Pragmatic Approach to North–South Tensions

The negotiations that led to the Climate Convention were marred by North–South conflicts which continue to haunt negotiators and governments alike. The Convention itself is a veritable minefield of time-bombs that can be activated at any time. Third World representatives have made it clear that the West must pay the price for climate-related measures to be taken in developing countries. Governments in the latter have not taken on any substantive obligations under the Convention, but have agreed to submit national communications of a fairly general character. The expenses involved in such an exercise are to be borne by industrialized-country governments by providing 'new and additional financial resources to meet the agreed full costs'.[20] This could set a precedent for future burden-sharing, highlighting the most emotional and intractable issues on the entire North–South agenda: how to define 'additionality' in resource transfers?[21] What is a reasonable level of development assistance from the North to the South? Such discussions could easily stall the forthcoming international climate bargaining for the rest of the 1990s—which some governments and some observers would be only to happy to see. Avoiding this will not be easy, as the preference of many Third World governments in international climate discussions has been to press the West for increased resource transfers. They perceive the vulnerability as lying on the other side, as Western opinion is concerned about environmental dangers, and do their best to take advantage of it. In reality, developing countries, in particular the poorest ones, may prove far more vulnerable to the impact of climate change—but apart from the small island countries, this has not yet had much effect on their positions.

The problem in relation to the international regime is, again, how to connect activities at the global level with the societies of the South. As long as the focus is limited to funding, governments are the sole external agents, as they will be the recipients of increasing transfers. If, however, more attention is paid to substantive action that can be taken in the Third World to constrain emissions of greenhouse gases and enhance forest cover, interesting feedbacks at the domestic level may begin to appear. If, for example, the international community made an obligation as part of a global climate regime to support energy efficiency, renewable energy, and sustainable forestry in developing countries, then a number of actors in the Third World would become 'parties' in a real, if not legal, sense to the world-wide bargain. Funding from the West could be made increasingly available for such purposes, without touching on 'additionality'. Some LDC (least-developed country) governments would most likely raise the issue, but they would hardly veto increased funding within such a context in the absence of evidence of additionality. In exchange for such transfers, Western governments could encourage—not dictate—their Southern counterparts to draw up and submit plans for sustainable energy development and forestry, as a basis for international discussions of how external funding could yield maximum benefit at both the local and the global level. The futile effort to distinguish between the two, which has taken up so much attention in the World Bank and the Global Environment Facility, has led nowhere and is better left aside.

If this works—if some governments of developing countries can be sufficiently tempted to produce and submit such plans—the first steps towards a global monitoring system will have been taken from the South, almost inadvertently. If others follow suit, this could gradually develop into a comprehensive review based on a logical *quid pro quo*: Western governments report on their commitments, targets, and policies to reduce greenhouse emissions, while Southern states contribute plans, hopefully including targets and policies, for their energy and forestry sectors. And on both sides, NGOs and other domestic interests can use the information provided and the assessments made to influence their governments at home.

If such a regime can be established, in practice though not in legal terms, by the end of the 1990s, both governments and negotiators will have reason to be satisfied.

## Notes and References

1. For a review of these issues, see Steinar Andresen and Jørgen Wettested (1992), 'International Resource Management and the Greenhouse Problem', *Global Environmental Change*, 2: 4, 277–91.
2. For an account of this history see Leiv Lunde (1991), *Science and Politics in the Global Greenhouse*, EED:008 (Lysaker: Fridtjof Nansen Institute), and the contribution by John Lanchbery and David Victor to this volume.
3. Intergovernmental Panel on Climate Change, 1992 IPCC Supplement, WMO and UNEP.
4. This particular aspect of institutional adaptation to a new environmental challenge is elaborated by Tim O'Riordan in his introduction to Jill Jäger and Tim O'Riordan, (eds.) (1995 forthcoming), *The Politics of Climate Change in Europe* (London: Routledge).
5. J. T. Houghton, G. J. Jenkins, and J. J. Ephraums (1990), *Climate Change: The IPCC Scientific Assessment* (Cambridge: Cambridge University Press).
6. For a review of the interests behind negotiating positions and barriers to further progress, see Helge Ole Bergesen and Anne Kristin Sydnes (1992), 'Protection of the Global Climate: Ecological Utopia or Just a Long Way to Go?', in H. O. Bergesen, M. Norderhaug, and G. Parmann (eds.), *Green Globe Yearbook* (Oxford: Oxford University Press), 35–48.
7. For a broad review of current and future options, see Jill Jäger and Reinhard Loske (1994), *Options for the Further Development of the Commitments within the Framework Convention on Climate Change* (Wuppertal: Institute for Climate, Environment and Energy).
8. The following is based on empirical studies of climate policies in different OECD countries carried out by the Fridtjof Nansen Institute.
9. The following is adapted from Helge Ole Bergesen (1985), *Norms Count, But Power Decides. International Regimes—Wishful Thinking or Realities?* R:002-1985 (Lysaker: Fridtjof Nansen Institute), which in turn builds on Harold Jacobson (1979), *Networks of Interdependence* (New York: Alfred A. Knopf).
10. For the importance of agenda-setting, see Peter M. Haas, Robert O. Keohane, and Marc A. Levy (1993), *Institutions for the Earth* (Cambridge, Mass.: MIT Press), ch. 1.
11. Haas, Keohane, and Levy, *Institutions for the Earth* comprises several case-studies where development of common concern is a critical variable.
12. Art. 2 of the FCCC.
13. They need a proper contractual environment, in the terminology used by Haas, Keohane, and Levy.
14. The OECD performance reviews are intended to have this function. For elaboration of this and other corresponding arrangements, see Olav Schram Stokke (1993), 'Environmental Performance Review: What? Why? How?', *International Challenges*, 13: 4 (Lysaker: Fridtjof Nansen Institute), 17–27.
15. 'Each of these Parties [OECD and countries in transition to a market economy] shall adopt national policies and take corresponding measures on the mitigation of climate change, by limiting its anthropogenic emissions of greenhouse gases and protecting and enhancing its greenhouse gas sinks and reservoirs. These policies and measures will demonstrate that developed countries are taking the lead in modifying longer-term trends in anthropogenic emissions consistent with the objective of the Convention, recognizing that the return by the end of the present decade to earlier levels of anthropogenic emissions of carbon dioxide and other greenhouse gases not controlled by the Montreal Protocol would contribute to such modification . . .'.
16. David G. Victor and Julian B. Salt (1994), 'Climate since Rio', *Environment* (Nov.), summarizes these discussions in the Intergovernmental Negotiating Committee, INC.
17. For an extensive review of such policies, see International Energy Agency (1994), *Climate Change Policy Initiatives, 1994 Update*, vol. I *OECD Countries* (Paris: OECD).
18. UN Conference on Trade and Development (1992), *Study on a Global System of Tradeable Carbon Emission Entitlements* (New York: United Nations).
19. For a recent review of critical factors, see Reinhard Loske and Sebastian Oberthür (1994), 'Joint Implementation under the Climate Change Convention—Opportunities and Pitfalls', *International Environmental Affairs*, 1.
20. Art. 3 of the Convention.
21. Olav Kjørven and Anne Kristin Sydnes (1992) have shown the difficulties and contradictions inherent in the concept in *Funding for the Global Environment: The Issue of Additionality*, EED:004 (Lysaker: Fridtjof Nansen Institute).

# International Co-operation to Combat Acid Rain

*Marc A. Levy*

## The Nature of the Problem

The combustion of some fossil fuels releases compounds into the atmosphere that are capable of travelling hundreds of miles. When they eventually land they can cause damage to crops, ecosystems, buildings, and human health. This phenomenon has been given the name 'acid rain', because often deposition occurs through mixing with precipitation, and because often the mechanism that does the damage is acidification. But 'acid rain' has come to mean more than acid rain. The label is now used to cover the long-range transport of pollutants (whether or not deposition occurs through precipitation) that cause harm through mechanisms of either acidification or oxidization. The most important pollutants are sulphur dioxide ($SO_2$), nitrogen oxides ($NO_x$), and volatile organic compounds (VOCs).

Both acid precipitation and long-range transport of air pollution were known long before acid rain became the subject of international controversy. The Scottish chemist Robert Angus Smith described acid rain as a consequence of high levels of coal burning in nineteenth-century England, publishing his accounts in an 1872 book (that coined the term).[1] And Ibsen wrote of the foul air that travelled across the sea from Britain. But the contemporary understanding of acid rain is of more recent origin. It began in 1967, when Swedish chemist Svante Odén hypothesized that the increasing acidity in Swedish rivers and lakes was attributable to air pollution travelling from continental Europe and Britain.[2] Odén called this 'an insidious chemical war', and warned that it would reduce fish populations, harm forests, increase plant diseases, and damage materials.[3] With scientific acumen and activist zeal, Odén launched the modern acid rain controversy.

Since then the acid rain problem in Europe has gone through three distinct phases—a long period of stalemate, lasting until 1982; a period that witnessed dramatic change in domestic policies, roughly from 1982 to 1988; and finally the current period in which international policies are undergoing significant change.

### 1968–1982: Stalemate

Between the time of Odén's discovery and 1982 the primary lines of conflict were fixed. On the one side were Sweden and Norway, which recognized serious domestic acid rain damage in lakes and streams, much of it caused by imported sulphur dioxide. On the other side was the entire rest of Europe, which was being blamed for exporting sulphur dioxide. During this period Sweden and Norway attempted,

without success, to persuade their neighbours to reduce emissions of $SO_2$. The rest of Europe had little incentive to comply with these requests. Other countries were free of acid rain damage, as far as they knew, and reducing emissions was bound to be expensive. The persuasive effort continued, however. Sweden highlighted the issue at the 1972 Stockholm Conference on the Human Environment. Sweden and Norway persuaded the Organization of Economic Co-operation and Development (OECD) to carry out studies of the phenomenon, and to issue principles on transboundary air pollution. An important triumph for Scandinavian diplomacy occurred in the mid-1970s, when the unlikely ally of the Soviet Union joined forces to push for a regional convention on acid rain. The Soviets were not concerned about acid rain as an environmental problem, but saw in it a potentially useful vehicle for furthering the *détente* process. In 1979 the Convention on Long Range Transboundary Air Pollution (LRTAP) was signed by thirty-three states, including Canada and the United States.

LRTAP was an important victory for the Scandinavians, but it did not reap immediate benefits. The convention committed parties to broad principles and joint research activities, but not to any concrete measures to reduce acid rain. For the first few years of LRTAP's existence there was little indication that the rest of Europe was going to behave any differently just because a convention had been signed.

### 1982–1988: Least-Common-Denominator Agreements

But all this changed in 1982, and this year therefore marks the beginning of the second phase of the conflict, lasting approximately up to 1988. In 1982 the German biologist Bernhard Ulrich discovered a new kind of forest sickness, *Waldsterben*, and hypothesized that it was caused by acid rain. Ulrich announced his findings at the 1982 Stockholm Conference on Acidification of the Environment, where German government officials announced they had joined Norway and Sweden in seeking reductions in $SO_2$ emissions. This was a key turning-point for many reasons. German support guaranteed not only serious $SO_2$ reductions in a large polluter, it also added a powerful political ally to the Scandinavian cause. Moreover, the discovery that terrestrial ecosystems might be threatened by acid rain drastically altered the geopolitical map. Acid rain was no longer a Scandinavian problem; it was potentially a continent-wide problem.

International co-operation during the second phase entailed two related activities—collaborative science and adversarial diplomacy. The combination of the two resulted in a pair of protocols to the LRTAP convention—a 1985 protocol signed in Helsinki to reduce sulphur emissions, and a 1988 protocol signed in Sofia to freeze emissions of $NO_x$.

The collaborative science, organized through LRTAP working groups, was important for advancing the state of consensual knowledge about the extent of acid rain damage and about the nature of transboundary flows. The politically most important science was probably that conducted under the auspices of the Working Group on Effects and the European Monitoring and Evaluation Programme (EMEP). The Working Group on Effects oversaw collaborative research on forests, materials, freshwater ecosystems, crops, and integrated monitoring. This research helped solidify a consensus about the importance of the acid rain problem, and in some cases led countries to discover domestic acid rain damage that they had not expected to find. The United Kingdom probably represents the starkest example of this latter phenomenon.

EMEP engaged in highly sophisticated monitoring of pollution flows and modelling of transborder flows. It grew out of early OECD work in the 1970s, when a priority was to determine whether acidifying compounds really did travel long distances. As EMEP grew in sophistication it acquired the capacity to pinpoint with increasing precision the origin and eventual deposition of sulphur dioxide and nitrogen oxides. This furthered the scientific goal of understanding the acid rain problem on a continental scale. It also contributed two key political benefits. First, it established quite clearly who the 'good guys' and 'bad guys' were. And secondly, it created a verification capability that made it almost impossible to cheat on a promise to reduce emissions without getting caught.

The adversarial diplomacy built on the foundation of this collaborative science. Growing knowledge of the severity of the acid rain problem, and of who was responsible for it, helped put pressure on states to reduce emissions. The focal points for this diplomacy were the Sulphur and $NO_x$ Protocols. The Sulphur Protocol asked states to reduce their emissions by 30 per cent by the year 1994, using 1980 as a baseline. Between 1983 and 1985 the number of supporters of the protocol grew from six to twenty-one. High-level meetings in Ottawa and Munich in 1984 helped keep the conversion process going. In the end, the United Kingdom and Poland refused to sign the protocol, as did the United States; but all other significant contributors to the acid rain problem agreed to reduce emissions.

They signed for a variety of reasons. One group, including the Scandinavians, Netherlands, Germany, Switzerland, and Austria did so because of an awareness that acid rain was a serious domestic problem that required multilateral action. Another group calculated that reductions were going to

happen anyway, thanks to changing energy policies; this group included France, Belgium, and Italy. Finally, many eastern bloc governments signed for opportunistic reasons, aiming both to keep alive the fruits of their co-operation with Scandinavia and to embarrass the United States and Britain, while never intending to undertake serious reduction measures at home.

The result was a protocol in which not a single signatory planned to use the instrument as a guide to sulphur reductions. The first two groups were able to ignore it because their domestic measures exceeded the required 30 per cent; and the final group intended to cheat from the beginning. The only exception is the Soviet Union, which probably did take the protocol seriously, owing to its high diplomatic stakes in the convention. This is an exception without a difference, however. The Soviet Union engineered an exception into the protocol permitting it to reduce 'transborder fluxes' instead of total emissions. As a large country it could, therefore, easily comply by shifting some sources to the east (among other ways, by building more nuclear facilities in the west). In most places the prevailing winds push Soviet emissions away from Western Europe, so they were not considered a central part of the political conflict. Again, the exception proves the rule: in the Kola peninsula, where nickel smelters emit enormous quantities of sulphur dioxide that blow across to Norway, emissions have never been reduced.[4]

Following the 1985 Sulphur Protocol, work began almost immediately on a protocol governing $NO_x$. As with the Sulphur Protocol, a combination of collaborative science and adversarial diplomacy bore fruit in a protocol that was signed in 1988 by twenty-seven states. This protocol required states to freeze $NO_x$ emissions at 1987 levels by 1995. A group of NGOs pressured a group of twelve states to sign a separate, declaratory pledge to go beyond the freeze and reduce by 30 per cent. This pledge was entered into by more states than actually intended to aim seriously for a 30 per cent reduction. In fact, by the time of the signing of the protocol even some states who signed the protocol itself were in some doubt as to their ability to achieve a freeze.[5] None the less, the $NO_x$ Protocol had in common with the Sulphur Protocol the fact that when initial negotiating positions were formulated prior domestic plans set fixed baselines beyond which governments did not budge.

Both the 1985 Sulphur Protocol and the 1988 $NO_x$ Protocol were therefore variants of 'least-common-denominator' protocols. In neither case did any party sign intending to use the protocol as a guide to revisions in its domestic emission-reduction policies. In fact, there is no evidence that any state (with the possible exception of the Soviet Union) signed any protocol without first determining that already-planned policies would bring it into compliance more or less automatically. (By contrast, the 1987 Montreal Protocol *was* used by most signatories as a guide to alterations in domestic policies.) Analyses of LRTAP that overlook this fact come to the mistaken view that these protocols somehow brought about the reductions in emissions that took place afterwards.[6] On the contrary, it was the change in emission policies that made the protocols possible. It would be misleading, however, to dismiss these protocols as ineffectual. Often least-common-denominator agreements are criticized because they do no more than codify the *status quo*.[7] But under the right conditions they can help advance the *status quo*, and this is what happened in the case of these two protocols. Their power lay not in binding states to undertake measures they otherwise would not (as the Montreal Protocol does), but in helping shift states' perceptions of their self interest.[8]

### 1989–Present: Creative Problem-Solving

After the 1988 $NO_X$ Protocol LRTAP entered a new phase. Instead of using protocols as instruments of normative persuasion that influence parties during the negotiations but not after signature, negotiators are now seeking to use them as genuine regulatory instruments that impose serious constraints on domestic policies after they are signed.

This shift in the negotiating style reflects an underlying shift in the nature of the acid rain problem in Europe. The most important change has been the conversion of all the important opponents to acid rain controls, with Great Britain's shift in late 1988 being the most dramatic. Once Britain reversed its opposition to acid rain controls, the need for normative persuasion lessened considerably; it became possible for the first time to engage in collective problem-solving around mutual perceptions of the problem.

The exercise in collective problem solving has had two concrete manifestations: the 1991 protocol on volatile organic compounds, and the 1994 revised Sulphur Protocol.

The 1991 VOC Protocol is qualitatively different from the earlier protocols because it commits states to emission-reduction policies that in most cases go beyond what these states had earlier committed themselves to domestically. In fact, most states had no VOC regulations in place prior to the protocol. During the negotiations on sulphur and nitrogen, battle-lines were drawn based on calculations governments had made on the costs of abatement measures and the perceived benefits from reducing acidic deposition; not surprisingly, low cost and high benefit countries favoured steep reductions, and high cost and low benefit countries opposed them.[9] When VOCs were considered, however, the changed atmosphere lent itself to a different mode of interaction. Acrimonious exchanges were largely absent; in fact, disputes over abatement costs and damage estimates were relegated to the sidelines because no government had

any reliable estimates of what these were anyway. Instead, debate focused on what sorts of instruments would be most likely to bring about the desired environmental results, and on how variations in national situations could be accommodated most productively. Neither of these debates had a chance during the sulphur or nitrogen negotiations.

This is not to say the tug and pull of politics disappeared. There was a fair degree of suspicion voiced about the Norwegian, Russian, and Canadian proposal to restrict VOC emissions only within designated 'Tropospheric Ozone Management Areas', for example; the idea had technical merit but evoked suspicions that its proponents were trying to escape their fair share of the burden. But such conflicts took a back seat to the mutual search for effective solutions, in stark contrast to the earlier negotiations.

The most dramatic way in which the acid rain problem in Europe has changed is the use of critical loads as a management tool. Critical loads are defined as 'the highest load that will not cause chemical changes leading to long-term harmful effects on the most sensitive ecological ecosystems' in a designated area.[10] They are similar to toxicity thresholds. They were seen as overcoming a number of limitations of the use of flat-rate reductions. Flat-rate reductions were inevitably arbitrary from a scientific point of view—there was no ecological basis for settling on a 30 per cent reduction in sulphur emissions or a freeze on nitrogen emissions. Flat-rate reductions also ignored the fact that some countries had undertaken reductions prior to the negotiation of a protocol, while others had not. Perhaps most important, flat-rate reductions overlooked the reality that both sensitivity to pollution and the cost of reducing emissions varied markedly across Europe.

Swedish scientists and government officials were the first actively to promote the use of critical loads as the guiding principle in regulating European acid rain controls.[11] Jan Nilsson was the chief proponent, first arguing in the early 1980s that thresholds should be determined for acidifying compounds and that these thresholds ought to guide policy. A series of LRTAP sponsored workshops formalized a definition of critical loads and began specifying methodologies for measurement and mapping. These workshops enjoyed broad support among government scientists across Europe. Presenting a practically united front, these scientists succeeded in thoroughly transforming the political agenda. The 1988 $NO_X$ Protocol and the 1991 VOC Protocol both contain language specifying that they are only 'first steps' towards later regulations based on critical loads. And the 1994 Sulphur Protocol, which replaces the 1985 instrument, is explicitly based on critical loads.

The use of critical loads was intended to proceed in a series of technical and political activities aimed at deepening the collective regulations in a way that was politically fair and scientifically sound. The most fundamental building-block in this exercise was to be the creation of critical-load maps for Europe. These maps are created by identifying the most sensitive receptor within a given grid, determining the critical load of that receptor using dose–response data, and then aggregating the data onto maps for all of Europe. Methodologies were harmonized and dose–response data were agreed on consensually so that national maps would be readily comparable and integrated.[12]

Vital to this exercise was the RAINS Model, a computerized assessment tool that integrated data on critical loads, transport and emissions data, and reduction cost data to permit negotiators to seek out optimum reduction scenarios and to assess the environmental and economic consequences of alternative regulatory options.[13]

Although the 1994 Sulphur Protocol represents in a way the most complete realization of the critical-loads approach to date, the full effect of critical loads as an organizing principle cannot be grasped by looking only at the protocol. In fact, it is not difficult to evaluate the protocol, narrowly construed, as a return to politics as usual and a failure to realize the promise of critical loads as a means for elevating the science of environmental protection above the politics of expediency.

Such a narrow assessment acquires plausibility (though ultimately falls short) because of the numerous compromises that were required to cement the coalition supporting the protocol. The first concession to political constraints was to focus on 5-percentile critical-load maps, which specify levels of deposition that will protect all but the most sensitive 5 per cent of a grid. This was seen as a necessary concession to political and economic reality, since protecting the most vulnerable 5 per cent of ecosystems would add prohibitively to the cost.[14] However, when the negotiations over the Sulphur Protocol turned to the concept of 'gap closure', politics was appearing to get a double concession. Beginning in late 1993 negotiators started working with a formula by which states would commit themselves to emission targets that would reduce by 60 per cent the gap between 1980 emissions and emission levels needed to achieve critical loads. Because the gap closure was measured against the critical loads baseline, and critical loads were already calculated on a 5-percentile basis (that is, they already had a gap built in), to some observers the shift in the debate to gap closure was giving away the same concession a second time, this time on an even bigger scale. When, in early 1994, the focus shifted from 60 per-cent gap closure to 50 per-cent gap closure, the concession looked bigger still.
As other deviations from the original model became necessary for political reasons, the accumulated effect was to cast the exercise into some disrepute. Some governments sought permission to use alternatives to RAINS in calculating

## Table 1. Obligations under the 1994 Sulphur Protocol (as % reduction in 1980 emissions)

| | Target Year | | |
| --- | --- | --- | --- |
| | 2000 | 2005 | 2010 |
| Austria | 80 | | |
| Belarus | 38 | 46 | 50 |
| Belgium | 70 | 72 | 74 |
| Bulgaria | 33 | 40 | 45 |
| Canada (national) | 30 | | |
| Canada (SOMA)* | 46 | | |
| Croatia | 11 | 17 | 22 |
| Czech Republic | 50 | 60 | 72 |
| Denmark | 80 | | |
| Finland | 80 | | |
| France | 74 | 77 | 78 |
| Germany | 83 | 87 | |
| Greece ** | 0 | 3 | 4 |
| Hungary | 45 | 50 | 60 |
| Ireland | 30 | | |
| Italy | 65 | 73 | |
| Liechtenstein | 75 | | |
| Luxembourg | 58 | | |
| Netherlands | 77 | | |
| Norway | 76 | | |
| Poland | 37 | 47 | 66 |
| Portugal ** | 0 | 3 | |
| Russian Federation | 38 | 40 | 40 |
| Slovakia | 60 | 65 | 72 |
| Slovenia | 45 | 60 | 70 |
| Spain | 35 | | |
| Sweden | 80 | | |
| Switzerland | 52 | | |
| Ukraine | 40 | | |
| United Kingdom | 50 | 70 | 80 |
| European Community | 62 | | |

*Note*: * SOMA = Sulphur Oxide Management Area, an area designated for different levels of reductions.
** Greece and Portugal are actually permitted to increase emissions against their 1980 baselines, by 48% and 14% respectively. The text of the protocol avoids singling them out in this way by using their emission ceilings for the year 2000 as the basis for reduction targets. Formally, each country's commitments are specified in terms of emission ceilings, not percentage reductions.

*Source: Protocol to the 1979 Convention on Long-Range Transboundary Air Pollution on Further Reduction of Sulphur Emissions.*

the emission reductions needed to achieve a particular level of gap closure. Some governments sought to use a different base year for use in calculating percentage reductions, and some sought to set later target years than others. As these deviations from the initial idea behind critical loads accumulated it soon became evident that what was happening was that states were finding ways to couch their commitments in such a way that they required no further action beyond what they had already planned domestically. The new sulphur protocol, so radically new in its original design, was ending up having a lot in common with the old.

Between mid-1993 and early 1994, for example, one witnessed almost the mirror image of the ground-swell of support that culminated in the signing of the first Sulphur Protocol. Instead of states rushing to jump on the 30 per-cent club bandwagon, this time they were rushing to jump off the critical-loads bandwagon, at least as it was originally designed. Even under the less ambitious 50 per-cent gap-closure target, the United Kingdom, Belgium, Denmark, France, Ireland, and Spain all sought weaker reduction targets, pitting themselves against a coalition of Sweden, Norway, Finland, Germany, the Netherlands, Austria, and Switzerland.[15] As this conflict emerged, the politics came to resemble, on the surface at least, those of a decade ago. Swedish and Norwegian officials branded the United Kingdom an irresponsible renegade guilty of damaging Scandinavian resources. In one heated moment Norwegian environment minister Thorbjørn Berntsen publicly called his British counterpart, John Gummer, a shitbag.[16]

As the political conflict heightened, this protocol that was supposed to rationalize the management of acid rain seemed to be having an altogether different effect. For the editorial board at the *Energy Economist*, it had become 'self-consciously pointless', and 'a humiliating blow to the scientific effort that has underpinned the running of the protocol. The reply delivered to the scientists has been: "No, you are wrong, there is no role for science in international negotiations, we are going to ignore you, you might as well not have bothered to carry out this work".'[17]

This pessimistic view is just as wrong as the rosy assessments of the 1985 Sulphur Protocol that give that instrument credit for all the sulphur reductions that took place over the 1980s. It is true that the protocol commits states no further than they had already planned to go domestically. And it is true that during the final months of negotiating there was only a very weak role for science in the political deliberations. But although intense political negotiations are the stuff of great drama (anything that can prompt a Norwegian minister to lose his temper in public qualifies as drama), in the overall course of things they are far from the most important phenomena. An accurate evaluation of the use of critical loads in the LRTAP process requires an assessment of the difference that critical loads made in the course of preparatory work leading up to the 1994 Sulphur Protocol as well as in the protocol itself.

On these grounds the effort looks more effective. The most fundamental effect that critical loads had was to shift the nature of the public debate, both internationally and in many domestic settings, away from determining who the bad guys were, and towards determining how vulnerable each party was to acid rain. The case of Britain is the best illustration of this phenomenon. Before the critical-loads approach Britain spent most of its time within LRTAP trying to defend its refusal to go along with the activist states' demands to reduce sulphur and nitrogen emissions.[18] After the critical-loads approach was adopted Britain threw itself heartily into the exercise and quickly emerged as an intellectual and entrepreneurial leader in the effort, along with the Dutch, Swedes, and Norwegians. The effect of the switch was so profound that a British government scientist, Robert Wilson, was appointed chairman of the Working Group on Effects, which oversees the critical-loads mapping efforts.

Within Britain as well critical loads thoroughly trans-formed the debate. Instead of a bruising stalemate between hard-line Thatcherite conservatives and Labour, Liberal Democrats, and a few wet Tories, which dominated the early 1980s, Britain went about the technical and uncontroversial work of mapping critical loads. As this work progressed it became evident that one of the unquestioned assumptions of British acid rain policy—that while the United Kingdom might or might not be responsible for acidification abroad, at least it had no domestic acid rain problem to worry about—was simply false. The British critical-load maps revealed a sizable swathe of highly vulnerable ecosystems in Scotland and Wales, as well as other sensitive areas. The constituency supporting acid rain controls expanded from environmental activists and élites concerned about the standing of Britain abroad to include those worried about the fate of the British countryside—a much larger group.

Whereas Britain had fought very hard against a European Community directive on sulphur and nitrogen emissions from large combustion plants, eventually signed in 1988, in 1990 it committed itself in principle to adopting even stricter emission-reduction standards based on critical loads.[19] By 1993, when the new protocol was negotiated, Britain was voluntarily pursuing policies aimed at reductions on the order of 70 per cent.

A 11 March 1994 headline in the *Financial Times* reflects how deeply the British debate had shifted. Whereas a decade earlier the focus had been on whether or not Britain was wrongfully polluting its neighbours, now the focus was on a report showing that 'Half of Country "is Damaged by Acid Rain" '.[20]

Other factors were pushing Britain in a more green direction, so critical loads and LRTAP cannot claim all the credit for the change in British acid rain policies. Beginning in 1988 the British government underwent a transformation away from obstructionism on international environmental issues towards a more activist bent; this transformation was realized in a number of issues beyond acid rain, including ozone depletion, climate change, and biodiversity. In addition, much of the power sector was privatized, which had the twin beneficial effects of dispersing the political power which had formally rested in the Central Electricity Generating Board, and especially, of freeing the power generators to switch fuels away from coal, which was politically popular, and towards gas, which was economically sensible. Because gas produces radically less sulphur than coal, privatization deserves a sizable amount of the credit for British sulphur reductions.

The impact of critical loads on Britain, the above exogenous factors notwithstanding, are highly important because of Britain's contribution to European air pollution. It has the third highest emission levels, and contributes a significant percentage of the deposition in Sweden and Norway, two of Europe's most vulnerable countries. Any solution to the European acid rain problem will require active British co-operation, yet until the last few years this appeared an elusive goal.

The critical-loads concept has influenced other countries as well. Among the governments that incorporate critical loads into their domestic acid rain policies are Austria, Denmark, Finland, France, the Netherlands, Norway, Sweden, Switzerland, the United Kingdom, and Russia.[21] The Netherlands, for example, was one of the first govern-ments to embrace critical loads as a guiding tool for domestic policy. This caused a shift in emphasis away from specific pollutants and towards vulnerable ecosystems, which were found to be seriously endangered. This in turn led to a steady ratcheting downwards of the target deposition loads, and a search for broader sources of acidifying compounds that could be reduced. This last task resulted in a series of measures aimed at reducing ammonia emissions from livestock—this innovation would likely not have occurred without the impetus of critical loads.[22]

### LRTAP as a Qualified Success

A number of characteristics of the evolution described above warrant the characterization of LRTAP as a success.

One clear success was the ability to shift from rigid, positional disputes to collective problem-solving. The early years of the acid rain problem were dominated by efforts to assign and deflect blame. Since the late 1980s blaming has declined in salience (perhaps not disappearing entirely), giving way to a broad-based collective search for mutually beneficial solutions to shared problems. Whether in personal life or international politics this is not an easy transformation to bring about, and it is a sign of great success that it happened in this case.

A related aspect of LRTAP's success was that this shift to collective problem-solving occurred in a political envir-onment characterized by a deep ideological divide. The East–West conflict in which LRTAP operated (indeed, to which LRTAP owes its existence) never seriously undermined the effectiveness of the convention. In fact, LRTAP had a

significant effect in helping to build up scientific and technical capacity for assessing acidification problems in Eastern Europe and the Soviet Union.[23]

Another clear success is the way LRTAP has helped broaden the scope of action as understanding of the acid rain problem has expanded. Instead of getting stuck in initial ideas about how best to respond to the acid rain problem, LRTAP has proved quite flexible at adding $NO_x$ and VOCs to its agenda, and now has even started investigating such far afield issues as heavy metals and complex organic compounds.

Finally, LRTAP has had a significant effect in the emergence of a number of transnational networks that play important roles in the management of the acid rain issue. It serves as the focal point for a dense scientific network that links acid rain researchers across North America, Scan-dinavia, Eastern Europe, Russia, and EC members. It has helped form looser networks among environmental activists.

What accounts for these successes? Managing international environmental problems is a complex task, with numerous factors interacting to produce results that are difficult to evaluate. Some success is really just luck, some apparent failures are really successes at keeping things from getting worse. With those cautions in mind, it is possible to identify some factors where more than luck was involved.

First, LRTAP defined its task consistently in terms of environmental impacts rather than particular causes of the problem. In practical terms this meant organizing scientific working groups around identifying and understanding phenomena such as lake acidity, forest health, materials damage, and so on, rather than strictly around various methods for responding to these problems. LRTAP does organize working groups around specific pollutants in connection with the negotiation of protocols, but these are transient and given specific, pragmatic tasks. It is the effects-oriented groups that endure.[24]

Secondly, the LRTAP process integrated knowledge-building exercises artfully with the task of negotiating international regulations. In the initial years it used regulatory protocols as vehicles for focusing public attention, for embarrassing laggards, and for building transnational alliances. These uses of the protocol made use of the underlying scientific exercises, and at the same time added to the momentum that kept these scientific efforts thriving.

## Obstacles to Effective International Solutions

The effort to cope with acid rain is far from an unqualified success, and we may learn from the shortcomings of international efforts as much as from their victories. In contrast to the successes, which centre around the way people see the problem, the failings all centre around the actions people take.

## Weak Transnational Action-oriented Networks

One clear failure is that, in contrast to the tight integration and transnational links that LRTAP has helped promote around awareness and understanding of the problem, it has contributed very little to such links around the issue of implementing strategies for managing the acid rain problem. There is scarcely any collaborative research and development on technological options for reducing emissions. In fact, on technological issues conflict remains much more openly combative than it is on questions of impacts. Unlike the Montreal Protocol, LRTAP has consistently failed to spark any reassessments of technical or economic constraints within domestic constituencies. Although LRTAP has helped tremendously to solidify a thriving network of scientists and activists seeking action, it leaves them to their own devices to convince domestic opponents who argue that reduction measures are too costly.

LRTAP faces considerable difficulty correcting this failure. Many of the most important industrial sectors are under government control and have weak transnational connections. This is the case for the two biggest polluting sectors, power generation and transportation. In other environmental problems, where the economic sectors are private and have extensive transnational links, technical knowledge diffuses more readily. Multinational corporations competing with each other for a share of the global market, for example, are more inclined to experiment with new technology in case it presents competitive advantages than are firms that do not face competition. The power industry in Europe (as in the world at large) is dominated by quasi-monopolistic, state-protected firms. The auto industry has similar constraints on a somewhat smaller scale. Many firms are protected or partially owned by their home governments, limiting their incentives to assess pollution control technology realistically.

A long-term, effective solution to the acid rain problem will require replicating the dense transnational network that exists with regard to awareness and understanding in the realm of action. The so-far elusive goal of a single European energy market would be a great help in this regard.

## Little Attention Paid to Coping with Impacts

Another failing is the lack of creative attention to coping with the impacts of acidification as opposed to taking only the preventive measure of reducing emissions. At the domestic level the Scandinavians engage in a significant amount of liming of lakes and soils to help cope with the effects of increasing acidic deposition. Where drinking water supplies are highly acidic, water authorities often add buffering agents to prevent harmful effects to human health. LRTAP has done practically nothing to share expertise and knowledge on how these adaptive measures work and where they might currently be under-supplied. In a prospective vein, it is now clear that emissions of ground-level ozone precursors are going to increase in Europe into the near future. This means that stresses on human health and agricultural crops will increase. An effective international response to this problem calls for sharing of information and strategies, and perhaps for joint exploration of new strategies, around the issue of coping with these impacts.

There is strong resistance, however, to addressing the need to cope with impacts at the international level. As one Swedish official put it: 'We considered doing that, but decided it would reduce the pressure to cut emissions.'[25] But in the absence of reliable assurances that current adaptive measures are adequate, especially in the former eastern bloc countries with poor historical records on these matters, this argument is irresponsible.

## No Mechanism for Financial Transfers

One of the biggest failures of LRTAP has been its inability to contribute to any significant transfer of financial resources from west to east. Although it has been realized since the early 1980s that some of the most severely affected countries (such as Sweden) could achieve reduced deposition at far lower cost if they could find a way to finance emission reductions in poor, highly polluting countries (such as Poland), very little practical progress was made towards putting this idea into practice. To be sure, there were some good reasons for treading lightly in these waters before the changes of 1989. Some carefully conducted experiments at linking financial assistance and emission reductions might have generated significant benefits, however, and they ought to have been tried. Such experiments might have helped avoid some of the floundering and squandering that occurred with East–West environmental assistance in the immediate years after the changes of 1989.[26] They might have helped integrate Eastern Europe, Russia, and the former Soviet Republics more directly into the negotiation of the 1994 Sulphur Protocol, instead of shunting them once again on to the margins, forced to hope for either a continued recession or a technological miracle to bring them into compliance with their commitments. For so much of the LRTAP agenda to be taken up over 1993 and 1994 with debates over whether the United Kingdom should reduce 76 per cent or 80 per cent (and similar matters), while so little was devoted to discussing such matters as how to help Poland and the Czech Republic finance the measures needed to implement their targets, is almost farcical.

In any event, there is now a widespread consensus that, regardless of whether early action was possible, now is the time to pursue the matter vigorously. The Working Group on Strategies within LRTAP has been directing attention to this issue since 1992, mainly by way of commissioning studies evaluating the prospects for competing cost-sharing mechanisms. One possibility is to create an 'acidification fund' within LRTAP, which would be used to finance emission-abatement projects.[27] Wealthy countries would pay into the fund and poor countries take from it. Another option is to permit joint implementation, in which a wealthy country would meet its own reduction commitment, in part, by financing reductions elsewhere.[28] Finally, a third option that has been examined is a tradable permits scheme.[29] Countries could meet their reduction targets through a combination of reduction measures and purchase of permits from abroad.

The discussion within the Working Group on Strategies, at least as reflected in the papers it has commissioned, has some way to go before workable ideas will emerge. Some of the ideas are politically naïve. Why, for example, would all the wealthy LRTAP signatories contribute to an acid abatement fund when many (such as the United Kingdom and France) stand to gain almost nothing in return? All the ideas are weak on the institutional infrastructure required to support the transfer schemes. There is almost no discussion of how compliance with the terms of financial transfer will be guaranteed, for example, nor of how the value of tradeable permits will be safeguarded (what happens if A buys a permit from B, but B emits anyway?). The Protocol makes oblique reference to joint implementation in Article 2, section 6, but leaves it to future decisions by the Executive Body to determine under which conditions it will be permitted.

These are not insurmountable problems; indeed, they are faced to one degree or another in every environmental financial transfer. But they require politically feasible solutions arrived at through joint deliberation. LRTAP signatories have not yet begun those deliberations.

Should LRTAP fail to develop a financial transfer scheme, the fall-back option is to rely on the current mix of financing measures under way: a combination of loans and grants from multilateral banks and bilateral aid agencies. These programmes suffer the disadvantage of having no formal link to LRTAP, and therefore being unable to exploit either joint implementation possibilities or to make direct use of compliance incentives. They have the advantage, however, of being part of a broader effort to co-ordinate the economic restructuring of the region; that might give them a greater long-term chance of success.

### Fragile Compliance Procedures

Finally, LRTAP is poised to cross a threshold in how it treats questions of compliance. If it crosses that threshold successfully, a range of new opportunities will be available; if it fails, many promising ideas will be threatened. The threshold presents itself by virtue of the heightened attention given to compliance questions during the negotiation of the 1994 Sulphur Protocol. With earlier protocols, which simply codified the *status quo*, compliance issues were never highly salient; the only states that cheated were states that everyone thought would cheat from the beginning. But because the 1994 Protocol was intended to be different, to go beyond the *status quo*, compliance was given much more serious attention.

Article 7 of the Protocol represents the result of that increased attention. It establishes an 'Implementation Committee' to review implementation and compliance by parties. It is to report to the Executive Body with recommendations, which may then 'call for action to bring about full compliance with the present Protocol, including measures to assist a Party's compliance with the Protocol, and to further the objectives of the Protocol'.

This may sound timid, but it signals a break with the past, when instances of non-compliance and lack of implementation were treated very lightly. The unwritten rule in the past was not to embarrass states by bringing their failures out into the open. In practice, even such a simple procedure as taking note of implementation and compliance failures and developing corrective courses of action might make a big difference.

The way the article is written, there is nothing to guarantee that it will make a difference; it might prove just as timid in practice as prior protocols were. Success will require energetic and creative procedures that will be a departure for LRTAP. Useful models are to be found in the OECD, IMF, and GATT performance reviews.[30]

## Future Prospects

### A New NO_x Protocol?

Sulphur is the easiest compound LRTAP has to worry about. Its effects are well understood and most of its emissions can be controlled by regulating a single activity (power generation). Nitrogen is tougher, both because its effects are more complicated and therefore less well understood, and because its sources include power generation plus transportation. That is one reason the activist countries were forced to abandon their initial hopes for a 30 per-cent reduction protocol for $NO_x$, and why some of those activist countries are having a difficult time meeting their commitments.[31] A new $NO_x$ protocol, to replace the current one which lapses in 1996, will be much tougher to negotiate than the second sulphur protocol.

Some analysts are arguing that instead of a second $NO_x$ protocol, LRTAP ought to combine $NO_x$ and VOCs and negotiate new regulations for both classes of compounds in a single protocol. The argument is that, because $NO_x$ and

VOCs are both precursors of ground-level ozone, there is no way to negotiate a protocol based on critical loads that does not incorporate both classes of compounds. The problem this presents is that VOCs are easily an order of magnitude more complicated, on both chemical and political grounds, than $NO_X$.[32] To regulate both at once may significantly slow down progress on a revised $NO_X$ regulation.

## Substantive Links to North America

The United States and Canada are signatories to LRTAP because they were caught with Western Europe in the same diplomatic net thrown by the Scandinavian–Soviet initiative in the 1970s. No one in Europe ever really considered North American emissions to be a European problem, however, nor vice versa. Now, though, as European emissions fall and transport modelling becomes more sophisticated, there is emerging a real, substantive reason for integrating North American and European acid rain policies.

The advantages of such integration lie in the long run. Although current depositions in Europe of North American emissions are quite small, these will increase in importance if Europe continues to reduce; if the goal of meeting critical loads is taken seriously, then every last percentile of deposition makes a difference. In addition, LRTAP is beginning to cast an eye toward regulating emissions of complex organic compounds, toxic chemicals that travel very long distances. Regulation of complex organic compounds, on scientific grounds, ought to involve both North America and Europe, because their emissions travel into each-others' territories.

However, the principal difficulty is that the United States bases its air pollution regulations on technical standards, not environmental quality standards. It will, therefore, be reluctant to commit itself to international instruments cast in terms that are incompatible with its domestic regulatory apparatus.

## Acid Rain Outside Europe and North America

In 1980 Europe and North America accounted for approximately 62 per cent of the global sulphur emissions. It is precisely because emissions were concentrated in this relatively small geographic area that the acid rain problem emerged there first. But like most environmental problems associated with industrialization, acid rain is destined to spread. Growing population and per-capita fossil fuel use mean that acid rain problems are likely to emerge in Latin America, Africa, and especially Asia, where sulphur emissions are projected to exceed total European and North American emissions by 2010.[33]

General awareness of potential acid rain problems outside Europe and North America is mainly low, however. The clearest exception is in Japan, where concern over the possibility that Chinese emissions may pose an environmental threat is growing. But relatively low geological sensitivities in Japan make it unlikely that it will be the next country to experience serious damage. An explicit effort to transfer some of the European experience to Asia more broadly, in anticipation of acid rain problems there, is now under way, with funding from the World Bank and the Asian Development Bank. One intended product of this effort is a RAINS-ASIA model, similar to the RAINS model that has played an important role in Europe.

For those who are serious about reducing the scale of acidification-induced damage in Asia and elsewhere in the developing world, equal attention ought to be paid to the challenge of transferring financial and technological resources where they can most effectively be used. Even if the RAINS model is exported completely successfully, effective responses will not be forthcoming in the absence of creative solutions to the problems that continue to plague East–West relations in Europe. Particular attention will need to be paid to efforts to organize the mobilization, transfer, and control of financial resources; to efforts to transfer proven technologies in the power-generation and transport sectors; and to efforts to uncover novel strategies suited to local circumstances. Each of these problems is currently stalling efforts to reduce emissions of acidifying compounds in Eastern Europe, some twenty-six years after they were identified as a problem. Any forward-looking strategy aimed beyond Europe ought to place these problems, however difficult they may be, front and centre.

## Notes and References

1. Ellis Cowling (1982), 'Acid Precipitation in Historical Perspective', *Environmental Science and Technology*, 16 (Feb.), 111A.
2. Svante Odén (1968), 'The Acidification of Air and Precipitation and its Consequences in the Natural Environment', *Ecology Committee Bulletin Number 1*, Swedish National Science Research Council (Stockholm). This is the first scientific publication with Odén's results, though Odén had made his results known in the press in 1967. I am grateful to Ellis Cowling for conversations on Odén and his work.
3. Cowling, 'Acid Precipitation' (n. 1 above), 114A–115A.
4. Rune Castberg (1993), 'Common Problem—Different Priorities: Nordic–Russian Environmental Cooperation and the Nickel Works of the Kola Peninsula', *International Challenges*, 13: 3, 23–33.
5. I am grateful to Jørgen Wettestad for clarifying this to me.
6. Amy A. Fraenkel (1989), 'The Convention on Long-Range Transboundary Air Pollution: Meeting the Challenge of International Cooperation', *Harvard International Law Journal*, 30: 2 (Spring), 471.
7. Lawrence Susskind (1994), *Environmental Diplomacy: Negotiating More Effective Global Agreements* (Oxford University Press, New York).
8. Marc A. Levy (1993), 'European Acid Rain: The Power of Tote-Board Diplomacy', in Robert O. Keohane, Peter M. Haas, and Marc A. Levy (eds.), *Institutions for the Earth: Sources of*

*Effective International Environmental Protection* (Cambridge, Mass.: MIT Press).

9. Detlef Sprinz and Tapani Vaahtoranta (1994), 'The Interest-based Explanation of International Environmental Policy', *International Organization*, 48: 1 (Winter), 77–105.

10. Jan Nilsson, (ed.) (1986), *Critical Loads for Sulphur and Nitrogen: Report from a Nordic Working Group*, National Swedish Environment Protection Board, Solna.

11. I am grateful to William F. Dietrich for discussion on the spread of critical loads.

12. Juha Kämäri, *et al.* (1992), 'The Use of Critical Loads for the Assessment of Future Alternatives to Acidification', *Ambio*, 21: 5 (Aug.), 377–86.

13. Leen Hordijk (1991), 'Use of the RAINS Model in Acid Rain Negotiations in Europe', *Environmental Science and Technology*, 25: 4, 596–602; Joseph Alcamo, Roderick Shaw, and Leen Hordijk (eds.) (1990), *The Rains Model of Acidification: Science and Strategies in Europe* (Kluwer, Dordrecht).

14. According to the RAINS model, the cost of protecting the 96th through 98th percentiles costs the same as the entire first 95, while the last 2 per cent cannot be protected at any cost. *Energy Economist* (Nov. 1993).

15. *Financial Times*, 5 Nov. 1993, 'Power Europe' section.

16. *Independent*, 18 Sept. 1993, p. 9. Berntsen used the Norwegian term *drittsekk*, which is slightly (but only slightly) less offensive than its English equivalent. The two ministers later were reconciled at an EC Council of Ministers meeting.

17. *Energy Economist*, Nov. 1993.

18. Typical in this regard is 'UN ECE Convention on Long-Range Transboundary Air Pollution, Review of Strategies and Policies of the Contracting Parties to the Convention, United Kingdom Response', n.d. (1986), typescript, 13 pp.

19. 'This Common Inheritance: Britain's Environmental Strategy', Cm 1200 (London: HMSO, Sept. 1990), 149.

20. *Financial Times*, 11 Mar. 1994, p. 10; citing 'Critical Loads of Acidity in the United Kingdom', Department of the Environment, 1994.

21. EB.AIR/WG.5/R.24/Rev.1 (1991).

22. I am grateful to Gerda Dinkelman for sharing information on Dutch acid rain policy with me.

23. For such an argument, see Marc A. Levy, 'East–West Environmental Politics After 1989', in Stanley Hoffmann, Robert Keohane, and Joseph Nye (eds.) (1993), *After the Cold War: International Institutions and State Strategies in Europe, 1989–1991* (Cambridge, Mass,: Harvard University Press).

24. By contrast, the International Maritime Organization organizes its work around such specific response options as tanker regulations, safety standards, and oil reception facilities; as a result the IMO has contributed quite little to understanding of the marine oil pollution problem.

25. Confidential interview with Swedish acid rain official, Uppsala, 19 Aug. 1994.

26. For more details on the problems with the initial rush of environmental assistance, see Levy, 'East–West Environmental Politics After 1989' (n. 23 above).

27. Options for organizing such a fund are analysed in Johan Sliggers and Ger Klaasen, 'Cost Sharing for the Abatement of Acidification in Europe: The Missing Link in the Sulphur Protocol', paper prepared for Working Group on Strategies, Executive Body for the Convention on Long Range Transboundary Air Pollution, 1993.

28. This option is reviewed in Paul Ruyssenaars, Johan Sliggers, and Henk Merkus, 'Joint Implementation in the Context of Acidification Abatement', paper prepared for Working Group on Strategies, Executive Body for the Convention on Long Range Transboundary Air Pollution, 1993.

29. Ger Klaasen, 'Trade Offs in Exchange Rate Trading for Sulfur Emissions in Europe', paper prepared for Working Group on Strategies, Executive Body for the Convention on Long Range Transboundary Air Pollution, 1993.

30. See Abram Chayes and Antonia Handler Chayes (1995), 'The New Sovereignty: Compliance with Treaties in International Regulatory Regimes' (Cambridge, Mass.: Harvard University Press).

31. See e.g. Per Elvingson, (1994), 'Nitrogen Oxides: Norway Gives Up', *Acid News*, 2 (Apr.), 3.

32. Hundreds of compounds qualify as VOCs, and they are emitted in a wide range of industrial activity. Their life-span in the atmosphere, the distances they travel, and the amount of ozone they are responsible for are all the subject of ongoing scientific controversy.

33. D. M. Whelpdale (1992), 'An Overview of the Atmospheric Sulphur Cycle', in R. W. Howarth, J. W. B. Stewart, and M. V. Ivanov (eds.), *Sulphur Cycling on the Continents*, SCOPE (London: John Wiley & Sons), 5–26.

# The Convention on Biological Diversity: A Viable Instrument for Conservation and Sustainable Use?

*G. Kristin Rosendal*

## Introduction

The International Convention on Biological Diversity entered into force on 29 December 1993, having achieved the required thirty ratifications three months earlier. This article traces the main challenges in the process leading to the BioConvention, and examines whether some of the same stumbling-blocks may reappear further along the road. An essential controversy revolves around wildlife and habitat *preservation* versus *utilization* of biological diversity. This is inherently linked to the dispute over property rights to genetic resources. I will examine this conflict, and then follow the debate on property rights through those international forums in which it has been most prominent: briefly reviewing the debate in the United Nations Food and Agricultural Organization (FAO) and the General Agreement on Tariffs and Trade (GATT), and more extensively covering the negotiation process and the signing of the Convention on Biological Diversity in Rio de Janeiro. Finally, I will consider the remaining challenges and future prospects for the BioConvention, focusing on three topics: (1) the articles in the Convention concerning biotechnology and intellectual property rights; (2) how the developing countries might use the framework of the BioConvention to improve their bargaining position with a view to biodiversity prospecting deals; and (3) the prospects concerning the financial mechanism (GEF). First, however, a brief introduction to the nature of the problem as well as its historical background is in order.

Biological diversity is a broad concept, embodying as it does the variability among all living organisms, including diversity within species, among species, and among ecosystems. Genetic resources are the hereditary material (genes) in all animals, plants, and micro-organisms; the concept refers to genetic material with actual or potential use or value for humanity. Genetic diversity or variability is a necessary condition to sustain vitality in both wild and domesticated plants and animals, and also for the development of new and improved products.[1]

The conservation of biological diversity constitutes one of today's greatest challenges, as environmental degradation world-wide has led to species extinction at a hitherto unprecedented rate. Estimates of the number of existing species in the world vary from about 5 to 100 million,[2] of which only some 1.4 million have been described scientifically.[3] As the new biotechnologies make it possible to utilize the full potential of the world's genetic resources (it is now possible to transfer any gene into any organism), the economic incentive to conserve biological diversity increases.[4] Hence, the interest in genetic material is arising from environmental concerns, as well as being based on technological developments. By the year 2000 farm-level sales of products of agricultural biotechnology are expected to have reached some US$100 billion; the value of global trade in plant-based pharmaceuticals was estimated at US$20 billion for the year 1986.[5] Apart from the ethical and aesthetic value of species diversity, we should note that mankind depends on genetic resources for food, medicines, and for raw materials in the chemical industries.

The international debate on genetic resources is concerned not only with conservation, but just as much with the distribution of benefits derived from using this material. The main bulk of the global genetic resources is found in the Third World, but it is the developed countries that possess the (bio)technology to exploit these resources. This potential conflict was realized by the World Commission on Environment and Development which urged: 'Industrialized nations seeking to reap some of the economic benefits of genetic resources should support the efforts of the Third World nations to conserve species' and 'developing countries must be ensured an equitable share of the economic profit from the use of genes for commercial purposes'.[6]

The BioConvention is not the first international treaty to address species or habitat conservation, but it is the first to address conservation of all biological diversity and the first to include sustainable utilization of these resources. There exist a great many agreements pertaining to international co-operation on the conservation of various species of plants and animals and their habitats. The Ramsar Convention on Wetlands is one of the most important global measures concerned with habitat protection (Ramsar, 1971). For the Arctic area, there is the Convention on the Conservation of Antarctic Marine Living Resources (CCAMLR, Canberra, 1980). Whales (ICRW, Washington, 1946) and tuna (ICCAT, Rio de Janeiro, 1966) have their own Conventions. Another example is the Convention on International Trade in Endangered Species of Wild Fauna and Flora (CITES, Washington, DC, 1973).

Until the early 1980s the focus for both national and international conservation work was still on wild species of plants and animals. An important shift came when the question of access to and control over plant genetic resources was raised by governments of the developing world. The forum for this heated debate was the UN Food and Agricultural Organization (FAO); the result was the FAO International Undertaking on plant genetic resources, then representing the most comprehensive agreement in terms of linking genetic resources conservation to social and economic concerns.[7] In 1989 the UN Environment Programme (UNEP) was given the formal mandate of negotiating what was to become the all-encompassing Convention on biological diversity, which was adopted in Nairobi in May and signed in June at the 1992 UN Conference on Environment and Development in Rio de Janeiro.[8] A first crucial question was whether to include both wild and domesticated species. In the background lurked the question of property rights to genetic resources.

## Genetic Resources: Properties and Property Rights

Genetic resources are generally defined as genetic material of actual or potential value.[9] The world's genetic resources are raw materials for biotechnology. With the advent of the new biotechnologies has come an increased realization of the value of genetic resources. In the 1970s the transnational seed and chemical corporations started applying these new technologies in plant breeding and agrochemicals, and in the course of the 1980s the biotechnology industry grew big. This realization has had a profound impact on the understanding of property rights to genetic resources. The story begins with the principle of a common heritage of mankind and ends with patents and state sovereignty.

Common property resources are usually defined by their character of non-rivalry and non-exclusiveness. Non-rivalry implies that it is possible for more than one person to use or consume the good without diminishing the amount available to others. Non-exclusiveness indicates that it is hard to exclude others from using or consuming the good. The air we breathe is generally regarded as an example of a non-rival and non-exclusive good. This used to be the case with clean water as well, but its character of non-rivalry is rapidly declining in many parts of the world. The combined case of non-exclusiveness and rivalry may give rise to problems of collective action, unless some kind of management regime can be established to control access to the resource in question.[10]

Basic to the idea of common heritage is always an element of non-exclusiveness or open access: the absence of well-defined property rights. This was the case with ocean fisheries in the past century, in the Grotian doctrine of the freedom of the high seas.[11] Common heritage, however, is not necessarily identical with the idea of open access as practised under the high seas doctrine.[12] Open access merely implies that no one can be excluded from using the resources, save by lack of economic and technological capacity. Conversely, the common heritage principle may imply that everyone (all mankind) has a right to benefit from exploitation of the resources.

In international negotiations the common heritage principle was first introduced at the UN Conference on the Law of the Sea (UNCLOS) in 1967 by the Maltese ambassador to the UN, Arvid Pardo, as a guiding principle in governing the exploitation of minerals on the deep sea-bed. Both in the UNCLOS negotiations and later in the Antarctic Treaty negotiations, the idea was to secure greater equity between developed and developing countries in the exploitation of a 'common' resource. The majority of industrialized states objected to the principle as being legally diffuse and practically impossible.

All along, however, the principle of common heritage did constitute the international regime for exchange of and access to plant genetic resources, in other words, seeds. International gene-banks were stocked with seeds from the most commonly used food plants, these seeds were primarily collected from the extensive variation found in the Third World, and the gene-banks were based on the principle of open access. 'Technically', the collection of seed samples was considered by all as a non-rival and non-exclusive activity. Moreover, no one questioned this practice on moral grounds, as the seeds of our most utilized food plants were seen to be of basic significance to all mankind.

While most gene-banks still operate on the basis of open access to genetic resources, the common heritage regime for genetic resources is rapidly becoming a thing of the past. This change may be traced back to the 1930s, with the introduction of hybridization, tailored to secure exclusive rights to superior plant varieties. More recently, the regime change has come about swiftly, primarily as a reaction to the introduction of intellectual property rights for organic material, which allow private ownership to genetic resources through patents or plant breeders' rights. Prior to this development it became necessary to change, or rather reinterpret, national patent laws.

The moral notion that food and medicinals should be excluded from patentability because of their fundamental importance to basic human needs is rapidly losing ground. On the other hand, there have also been technical barriers to patentability. National and international patent legislation draws no a priori distinction between various sectors of technology. Traditionally, it is true, the patent system was limited to technologies dealing with non-organic material.

Biological material was regarded as natural products rather than industrial products—discoveries rather than inventions.[13] Biological products or processes were originally excluded from patentability on the grounds that such inventions could not meet all the requisite patent criteria. For an invention to be patented, it must meet four fundamental criteria. First, the invention must be novel, meaning basically that it has not been published anywhere before. Secondly, there is the criterion of non-obviousness—the invention must display an inventive step. The third criterion states that the invention must have an industrial application—a practical utility. One function of this utility requirement is to distinguish between basic research, considered to belong to the public domain, and applied technology, which is eligible for patenting. Finally, the patent application must fulfil the criterion of reproducibility, in the sense that it must describe the invention in such detail that other experts may repeat the experiment and arrive at the same results. In addition to these criteria, patent legislation commonly excludes from patentability inventions whose utilization would run counter to 'public order or morality'.

The barriers represented by these patent criteria have now been largely overcome by developments in the new biotechnologies. These developments have not only made patenting a practical possibility: they have also created a need for it, from the perspective of the US, Japanese, and West-European biotechnology industries. Research in biotechnology often involves high costs, as compared to traditional breeding methods. Competition is fierce, and research is increasingly being carried out by the private sector. The biotechnology sector has been arguing strongly for compensation in terms of royalties, along the lines of other fields of technology.

The principal ruling on the patentability of biological material appeared in the German Federal Supreme Court in 1969 (the Red Dove Case), which determined that a breeding process for animals was indeed patentable.[14] In the Chakrabaty Case of 1980 the US Supreme Court of Justice decided, by five against four, to allow industrial patents for naturally occurring living matter, including both asexually and sexually reproduced plants.[15] A judge from this case was later employed by the EC Commission in drawing up its formulation of a directive on industrial patents in biotechnology.

Plant varieties can be protected by 'plant breeders' rights', as under the US Plant Variety Protection Act of 1970. Intellectual property rights may also be granted through the 'plant breeders' rights' of the 1961 UPOV Convention (the Union for the Protection of New Varieties of Plants). In order to be subject to UPOV protection, a plant variety must be 'uniform, stable and distinct from existing varieties'. In order to attain protection by breeders' rights or patents,

some kind of systematic breeding is required. This is seldom the case with Third World breeders' lines, however.

This controversy is not confined to the agricultural sector. There is a growing awareness that the largely unexplored components of biodiversity may conceal treasures, for example, of great medicinal value. A much-cited case from medicine is the Rosy Periwinkle, a native plant of Jamaica and Madagascar. Two components from the plant have been turned into a medicine for treatment of Hodgkin's Disease and certain types of leukaemia by the US pharmaceutical firm Eli Lilly. The company's annual return on the invention is about £60 million, none of which is returned to the country of origin.[16]

As patenting was catching on rapidly in the industrialized world, the governments of developing countries started to question whether the common heritage principle would eventually apply solely to resources from the South. They reasoned that the elaborated material of the industrialized countries was based largely on material from the South, and should thus also be seen as part of the common heritage. This view met with strong resistance from the industrialized countries, who argued that such an arrangement would not be compatible with Northern 'breeders' rights' and patent legislation.

Third World governments abandoned the claim for an all-embracing common heritage regime and turned the argument around. Their new line of argumentation was to claim *national sovereignty* over their genetic heritage, regarding it as a national asset along the lines of other natural resources, like oil and minerals. Genetic resources differ, however, from oil and minerals in being non-rival and largely non-exclusive goods. Nor is species distribution necessarily confined to national borders. These characteristics will obviously hamper state control over genetic resources. Nevertheless, national sovereignty ended up as the only passageway for reaching consensus about property rights between the North and the South.

The next section traces this international debate through the international forums in which it took place during the 1980s and early 1990s.

## International Cacophony

*FAO and the Undertaking for Plant Genetic Resources*
The issue of control and access to genetic material was first put on the FAO agenda by Mexico in 1981. Third World governments and NGOs started questioning the one-way, free-of-charge flow of genetic resources from the South to the North.[17] This resulted in, among other things, a non-binding International Undertaking and a Fund for Plant Genetic Resources.

It was seen as a great victory for the developing world

when the Undertaking of 1983 laid down the principle that *all* categories of plant genetic resources should be subject to free exchange for exploration, preservation, evaluation, plant breeding, and scientific research. Article 1 of the Undertaking declared that genetic resources were the 'heritage of mankind and consequently should be available without restrictions'. Responding to the emerging regime of intellectual property rights, however, an *Agreed Interpretation* of the Undertaking was signed in 1989. With regard to elaborated material subject to legal protection under national legislation, this material was to be made available 'on mutually agreed terms', according to the reinterpreted Undertaking. Basically, such 'mutually agreed terms' signify an acceptance of payment for legally protected varieties. Since the Agreed Interpretation regarded intellectual property rights as compatible with the Undertaking, the developing countries abandoned the 'common heritage of mankind' strategy.

The main idea of the FAO Fund for Plant Genetic Resources is crystallized in the concept of 'farmers' rights', meant to represent a counterpart to 'plant breeders' rights'. The Fund aims to provide compensation for 'the enormous contributions generations of farmers have made to the conservation, selection, domestication and development of plant genetic resources. If breeders, who provide the finishing touches to this process, can secure a title and handsome profits for their efforts, then the farmers too should receive compensation . . .'.[18] The promotion of this idea can be credited largely to the International Coalition for Development Action (ICDA), an NGO which played a central role in informing developing countries about their common interests and thus facilitated the maintenance of a strong Third World alliance.[19]

The fact that 'farmers' rights' was put on the agenda and achieved consensus is still regarded as a Third World victory. To date, however, the concept has had little practical effect. This may primarily be put down to the inability of the FAO Fund to attract funding, basically due to widespread scepticism about FAO among donor countries. Another explanation may be found in the difficulties inherent in applying the concept to practical policy. First, there is the problem of tracing the 'contributor' to whom compensation should be made. These plant genetic resources have not been subject to systematic breeding, and rarely fulfil, for example, the UPOV criteria of stability and uniformity—on the contrary, their greatest value lies in their evolving diversity. Over the years seeds have crossed so many borders and been developed in such diverse parts of the world that such a system would be hard to design, let alone administer. As the FAO Global System on Plant Genetic Resources was not cast in a legally binding mould, the parties are presently discussing whether to include relevant parts of it in protocols under the BioConvention.

## Trade-Related Aspects of Intellectual Property Rights (TRIPs) in GATT

While the developing world seemed to find approval for some of its argumentation in FAO, the issue was dealt with in a somewhat different manner elsewhere. Although Third World governments may have achieved some kind of stronghold in international development assistance agencies, industrialized countries generally dominate the forums on economy and trade. Most significantly, questions concerning the widening scope of industrial patents were brought up in the Uruguay Round of TRIPs in GATT.

This discussion soon became one of the fiercest arenas for the North–South patent controversy. The USA, Japan, and the EC advocated the principle that all countries should provide and respect intellectual property protection in all technical fields—including biotechnology. Disregarding this principle would constitute a contravention of GATT regulations, making the offending country liable to economic sanctions.

Third World governments have been strongly opposed to these proposals, maintaining that patents benefit those states that are already technologically and economically strong.[20] This is a point hard to refute, as Third World countries hold no more than 1 to 3 per cent of all patents world-wide.[21] In the initial rounds, India argued against patenting of plant and animal varieties as well as food and pharmaceutical products, citing concern for basic human needs.[22] For a great many developing countries this is not merely a matter of contesting theoretical principles. With the introduction of industrial patents, access to improved breeding material may be hampered, as prices for seed increase.[23] Some fear that patents will place constraints on technology transfers in general. As the Uruguay Round drew to a close in December 1993 most Third World delegations had resigned, but grass-roots organizations were still mobilized in large numbers: Indian farmers, Latin American pharmaceuticals manufacturers, and Guyami Indians demonstrated in Geneva against the patent regime proposed in GATT.

The opposition has had some success in GATT. The final agreement on Trade-Related Aspects of Intellectual Property Rights (TRIPs), grants the parties the right to exclude from patentability (a) diagnostic, therapeutic, and surgical methods for the treatment of humans and animals, and (b) plants and animals other than micro-organisms.[24] The parties are bound to introduce some kind of intellectual property rights for plants, however, as TRIPs require members to provide for the protection of plant varieties, either by patents, or by an effective *sui generis* system.

The latter part of the TRIPs agreement has prompted the farmers' movement in India, among others, to propose that such a *sui generis* system should focus on the rights of farmers in protecting and improving plant genetic resources:

'Common Intellectual Property Rights.'[25] As to whether the new GATT regulations on patenting will have harmful effects for Third World farmers, the answer is probably no, in the short-term. The inherent threat in the expanding patent legislation—that farmers must pay royalties for reusing seeds—is still a long way from being enforceable. A far more harmful effect of the GATT patent regulations is that they bolster a North–South conflict line in an issue-area where common solutions and co-operation are of paramount importance.

## The BioConvention: Negotiation Process

The BioConvention was negotiated by a UNEP *ad hoc* Working Group of legal and technical experts, which later changed its name to the Intergovernmental Negotiating Committee (INC). The first meeting in the *ad hoc* group drew experts from twenty-five countries, as well as some NGO observers (including the World Conservation Union (IUCN) and World Wide Fund for Nature (WWF) and IGOs (such as FAO). The number of delegates expanded rapidly. Negotiations started in November 1989, and the Bio-Convention was signed by 153 countries and the European Community at UNCED in Rio de Janeiro on 5 June 1992.

When the issue of biodiversity was first moved to UNEP several parties suspected that this was in fact an attempt to un-link the politicized plant genetic resources debate in FAO from the more traditional values of wildlife conservation in protected areas. That is exactly what it was: an attempt, led by the USA and the IUCN, to retain a focus on *in situ* conservation, rather than tackle the controversial issue of 'sustainable use of biological resources'. Their fears were legitimate enough, as linking these packages would clearly cause hotter negotiations. The USA hoped that the move to UNEP would quench the fire, and refused to include any mention of biotechnology or to talk about the value of genetic resources. Obviously, the controversy concerning conser-vation and sustainable utilization of biological resources was further fired by the consequences this would eventually have for financing: first, because putting a price-tag on biodiversity might disclose how profits in the agricultural and pharmaceutical sectors in the North are extracted from genetic resources from the South. Secondly, because the new perspectives draw attention to biodiversity in a much wider sense and could lead to stricter regulations on agricultural and forestry practices in all parts of the world.

Environmental and wildlife management NGOs like IUCN and WWF feared that no conservation agreement would in the end be reached, either for wild or domesticated species, if the latter was to be included in the negotiations.[26] Hence, the first IUCN draft convention presented to the participants reflected the Western traditions of nature conservation in full. The role of IUCN was also symptomatic of the NGOs

represented as observers in the UNEP negotiations. These were mainly concerned with habitat and species protection, rather than what had been the case in FAO, where the International Coalition for Development Action (ICDA) helped to advocate the interests of Third World farmers.

The UNEP agenda was characterized by a high degree of flexibility, and participants kept adding on new elements. Nevertheless, for a long time the agenda was dominated by a focus on protecting biological 'hot-spots' like tropical rainforests and other places of high biological diversity. It was primarily the Nordic delegations which emphasized the development aspects and an improved utilization of resources as a means to provide incentives for better conservation of natural species or habitats. They also stressed that bio-diversity conservation is essential in all countries, regardless of the number of species—thus trying to counter the bias towards tropical forests. Eventually the developed countries realized that putting off these issues would mean that the developing countries, especially countries like Brazil and Malaysia, would not join the BioConvention. And, as the main bulk of biodiversity is located in the tropics, negotiations simply could not proceed without them.

## The BioConvention: Negotiation Output

As of 3 October 1994 the Biodiversity Convention has been signed by 167 states and the European Community, and has been ratified by ninety-two Parties, including the Europan Community. The objective of the Convention is twofold:

- to ensure conservation and sustainable use of biological diversity; and
- to promote a fair and equitable sharing of the benefits arising from the utilization of genetic resources.

The Convention sets out obligations and objectives for nations to combat the destruction of plant and animal species and ecosystems. Among other things, the Contracting Parties shall integrate conservation and sustainable use of biological diversity into relevant sectoral plans and policies and develop systems of protected areas. The international community is given the responsibility for conserving biodiversity in developing countries, including the most environmentally vulnerable, such as those with arid and semi-arid zones, and coastal or mountainous areas. Each Contracting Party is to present reports on the measures it has taken towards implementing the provisions of the Convention and how effective these have been in meeting the objectives. It is left to each Party to decide on which measures are most effective to conserve biodiversity. Furthermore, the Contracting Parties agree to respect, preserve, and maintain knowledge and practices of indigenous and local communities, and encourage the equitable sharing of the benefits arising from the utilization of such knowledge and practices.

The BioConvention states that each country has the sovereign authority to determine access to its genetic resources, that access to genetic resources requires prior informed consent and must be on mutually agreed terms, and that a country providing genetic resources is entitled to benefit from the commercial use of its resources. The Convention envisages three basic mechanisms by which a country may benefit from the use of its genetic resources: participation in the research using the resources, receiving technology which embodies or utilizes the resources, and sharing the financial benefits realized from commercial exploitation of the genetic material or resource. This sovereignty does not include genetic material in international gene-banks which was collected prior to the Convention entering into force.

In Article 39 the Global Environment Facility (GEF) of the United Nations Environment Programme, the United Nations Development Programme, and the World Bank is accepted as the interim financial mechanism of the Convention. It is up to the Conference of the Parties to decide on policy, programme priorities, and eligibility criteria relating to access to the financial mechanism.

As far as patenting is concerned, the Convention stipulates that technology transfers 'shall be provided on terms which recognize, and are consistent with, the adequate and effective protection of intellectual property rights'. Seeking to reconcile the conflicting interests in the patent issue, the BioConvention states that the Contracting Parties shall co-operate to ensure that intellectual property rights '*do not run counter to its objectives*' (emphasis added). This sentence was one of the main reasons why US president George Bush refused to sign the BioConvention in Rio. Moreover, this is still a major concern with the current Clinton administration, as the decision to sign the Convention was followed by an interpretative statement addressing intellectual property rights as well as the provisions for financial mechanisms.

As regards links to biotechnology, the final version of the Convention also sought to smoke out another controversial issue. As the USA was fervently opposed to international regulations on 'living modified organisms resulting from biotechnology', it was left to the Parties to consider the 'need for, and modalities of' a protocol on biosafety in the future.

### The BioConvention: An Assessment
Before considering the remaining challenges and future prospects of the BioConvention, a brief assessment of the negotiation output is in order: how was it possible to reach agreement on this Convention in spite of the high conflict level?

Negotiations at the international level are inherently riddled by the lack of authority to implement mechanisms for control and sanctions. Consequently, unless the parties involved feel comfortable about the solutions, there is always the chance that they may opt for free-rider strategies (according to which the optimal situation is that in which everybody contributes, except themselves). According to current theories in political science some of these shortcomings of the international system may be mitigated by designing well-functioning forums for negotiations, geared towards achieving agreement from relevant parties.[27] Lacking this, formal decisions will be of little effect in the implementation phase. If the parties do not regard rules and regulations as legitimate, they cannot be counted on to comply with them.

Concerning the negotiations leading up to the Bio-Convention, a striking question is how could the parties manage to achieve consensus in the face of what were apparently insurmountable differences. One external complicating factor here was clearly the ongoing and contrary process in GATT. Three factors seem to have encouraged consensus. First, the negotiation forum itself may be credited for some of the success. As the negotiations proceeded, the UNEP secretariat was able to integrate controversial items, one after another, into the agenda. Thus, the conflict level was raised, but in order to secure the agreement of all relevant parties (especially the multi-diversity tropical countries) this was accepted as a necessary move. Secondly, as June 1992 and UNCED were approaching, the chairman of the Intergovernmental Negotiating Committee and the executive director of UNEP set up small working groups focused on reaching consensus on the issues still remaining.[28] This may also have boosted the overall contractual environment. Thirdly, the Nordic countries maintained the confidence of the developing countries, and helped to present several compromise formulations which seem to have played an important role in conciliating the parties.

The final Convention does represent a delicately balanced package deal with many relatively vague formulations. The real test of its success will obviously come in the implementation phase. Only then will it be possible to determine with greater certainty whether the new bio-regime may be successful in appeasing the underlying conflicts, or whether the Convention will become a useless international instrument for affecting state behaviour. This is not to say that evaluating the implementation phase will be a straightforward matter: The objectives of the Convention do not include any tangible standards for measuring activity. Hence, any conclusions regarding improvement of conservation efforts and improved equality in sharing will have to be approached in a qualitative manner. The next section will look at some of the major leads which may affect future developments.

## Remaining Challenges and Future Prospects

*The BioConvention and the Biotechnology Industry*

One crucial test for the future implementation and development of the BioConvention is probably linked to whether industrialized states regard the treaty primarily as a threat or as a possible advantage for their growing biotechnology industries. The USA has signed but not yet ratified the Convention, although it is expected to do so shortly in order to attend the first meeting of the Conference of the Parties in November/December 1994.

Let us look at the US behaviour as a test case. The US government is still fighting the BioConvention on several important points. First, its ratification will be accompanied by a statement of interpretation, seeking to tone down any articles that may seem to put restrictions on biotechnology industry. Such statements are not uncommon in international treaties, but in this case it may have the serious effect of upsetting the delicate equilibrium of the BioConvention. Secondly, the US government is still arguing against a protocol on biosafety. While the USA was alone in this argumentation initially,[29] it now seems that others may follow. The Convention parties are split as to whether to aim for non-binding guide-lines on biosafety or a legally binding protocol.[30] The need for a biosafety protocol stems from the realization that environmental consequences of releases of genetically modified organisms are non-reversible and unpredictable. It is feared that strict regulations at 'home' may lead transnational corporations to use developing countries, where legislation and the administrative capacity are weaker, as testing grounds.[31]

Despite these controversies, the US government seems willing to ratify the BioConvention. Why? First, explanations may be sought by applying a power-based, cost–benefit analysis of US policy, looking at how it deals with the possible threats and advantages in the Convention: the reinterpretative statement may thus be seen as a way to circumvent the perceived threats in the BioConvention; that is, refuting the costs which the USA fears might be put on its biotechnology industries, while retaining the benefits associated with the Convention. In this perspective the USA is powerful enough to get away with this policy, as no other state can pressure it to ratify the Convention as it is.

This approach does not, however, explain why the USA should bother to ratify. If the power-based explanation were taken to its logical extreme, the USA might as well do without an international convention on biological diversity. The crucial point is what indeed are the benefits of the BioConvention to the USA, as well as other powerful industrialized countries. The major benefit seems clear enough: 'access to genetic resources.' At face value, this could mean that our structural power perspective might still

hold: the gene-rich developing countries have greatly increased their power, to the extent that they are able to pressure the USA into the fold (see, for example, the case of Venezuela in the next section). In a short-term perspective, however, with free access to genetic material in most of the world's gene-banks, this is hardly an adequate picture of the power relations between gene-exporting and gene-importing countries. Rather, a major benefit of the BioConvention seems to lie in gene-importing countries being accepted as legitimate partners in international transactions with genetic resources. Thus, the Convention may come to have some influence as an international instrument for affecting state behaviour. If the US government chooses to ratify, this implies that it does not appreciate the idea of being (solely) left out of the international agreement. It would hurt its 'green image' as well as leaving it with no possibility of making an impact on further developments of the Convention.

This would seem to go some way towards explaining why the US government may choose to ratify—but not fully why it was so reluctant to sign in the first place. While the 'real' benefits of the Convention may not be explicitly realized, there may also be reason to believe that the threats have been exaggerated.[32] At the May 1992 meeting where the Bio-Convention was adopted, the US negotiating delegation hoped and believed that the Convention would prove acceptable to the US government. One week later, however, the Bush Administration backed out in Rio. This may partly be explained by a 'contextual interpretation': the combined effect of the formulations in the BioConvention became too much for the Bush Administration, even though it might have been willing to swallow each article separately (UNCLOS is an example of this same phenomenon).

Part of that explanation may also be found at the domestic level.[33] First, there is the US bureaucratic style in dealing with international agreements. Typically, the US government is very cautious in committing itself to international agreements, but once it has done so it has a relatively high score on compliance. Secondly, the domestic decision-making process was characterized by internal bargaining and a high conflict level between different agencies. Illustrative of the internal strife within the US administration was the US biotechnology industry and its main political supporters (then US vice-president Dan Quayle and his Council on Competitiveness) whose influence won through in the final round. Their fears, however, appear to have been loosely founded. The US government refused to sign the Biodiversity Convention, mainly because of its formulations on intellectual property rights. There are several reasons why the Biodiversity Convention is unlikely to impose severe limitations on biotechnology companies. Patenting in biotechnology is becoming increasingly widespread, and there are thus no indications that the Convention has had any prior diminishing effects on this practice. This is linked to the increasing privatization in the agricultural sector,[34] and may be observed in several developing countries, even some of the most zealous in opposing the international patent quest in the GATT Uruguay Round. Today most of those developing countries that can manage to sustain a patent system, like India, Brazil, and Mexico, are well on the way to accepting parts of it.[35]

For various reasons, however, the patent question may in fact not constitute such a serious constraint to implementation of the Convention. As the patent-system reaches world-wide acceptance, it will be increasingly hard to side with the US biotechnology industry in arguing that they alone will be harmed by the Convention's regulations on biotechnology. The crucial question is whether the delicate balance in the BioConvention can be kept up—whether the combined regime of patents and national sovereignty over genetic resources will become viable. It seems a safe bet that if only one part of the deal is honoured, exchange of and access to genetic material will come to involve considerable future conflict.

## The BioConvention as a Framework for Bio-prospecting Deals

A significant loss of biodiversity would affect all sectors of human activity. As with the case of climate change, it is clear that a single nation cannot deal with the issue adequately by itself. However, while global environmental issues like these have gained significant awareness in industrialized countries, Third World governments maintain that alleviation of poverty continues to be their overriding concern. In the least developed countries (LDCs) the costs of conservation activities may prove to be too high, as these may undermine basic human needs today.[36] This pertains both to wildlife conservation and to conservation of domesticated biological resources. It is thus pertinent to ask whether governments as well as local populations in developing countries may be able to benefit from the formulations in the BioConvention, in order to strengthen conservation and use of biodiversity.

Donor governments tend to prefer bilateral arrangements—especially when these can be arranged without the impediment of international regulations. This position was also noticeable in the biodiversity negotiations. There are already a number of bilateral deals in effect in the biodiversity field. Most popularly quoted is the contract between the US multinational corporation, Merck & Co. Pharmaceuticals, and the Costa Rican National Institute of Biodiversity. The latter provides plant and animal species for drug research which Merck gets exclusive rights to develop; in return Merck pays US$1 million as well as royalties for any drug developed. Training of local 'parataxonomists' and institutional capacity-building are also part of the deal. In the environmental and developmental NGO community there is still dispute concerning the quality of the contract. All the same, this raises the question of whether the developing countries need a framework convention for concluding such deals, since this deal already existed prior to the Bio-Convention.

That the BioConvention is seen as an important instrument in this respect was clear from the reaction of Venezuela when US president Bush refused to sign the Convention in Rio. As a direct response Venezuela proclaimed that it would stop signing new agreements with US scientific institutions, collecting and screening biodiversity in the country.[37] There are also examples of this concept gaining ground among collecting agencies. The UK Royal Botanic Gardens at Kew now states that any net profits derived from collaboration will be shared equally between itself and the supplier. There is also the case of Biotics, a private British for-profit company that acts as a broker between companies and in-country collectors, granting the latter 50 per cent of Biotics' royalties.[38]

From the legalistic perspective one of the most relevant formulations in the BioConvention is linked to the principle of *prior informed consent*. It indicates that the country providing genetic resources must provide national legislation regulating the appropriation of genetic material.[39] A weak point in this regulation is that in order to turn down a request for genetic material, the providing country, depending on its national legal system, may have to refer to such legal provisions. In the absence of such provisions, there is still a substantial risk that the gene-flow must continue free of charge.[40] Obviously, this may represent an impediment to governments, especially in LDCs, which lack the administrative capacity both to enact and to enforce a legal framework. There will be a need for specially designated bodies to conduct the deals, and to establish information databases on the genetic material. Moreover, the providing country will have to set priorities with regard to compensation mechanisms for its genetic material, as well as making clear the relationship to genetic resources held by local communities and gene-banks.

In view of the problems facing Third World governments in connection with enforcing catch quotas for foreign fisheries under UNCLOS, the problems regarding regulation of genes are striking. In addition to the general administrative burdens, the non-exclusive character of genetic resources further complicates control of their movements. This is partly negated, however, by the need for a user to obtain information about the genetic material in question. Without this, it may be difficult to screen genetic material for potentially valuable and interesting traits in secrecy.

This brings to light another aspect in which gene exchange

differs from deals on catch quotas: the rights and knowledge of local communities. The 200-mile exclusive zones, which include the fish stocks within them, are generally regarded as state property, so rights to control access and levels of exploitation of fish are usually vested exclusively in government. Genetic resources, on the other hand, may have been developed through the work of local communities of farmers; or their valuable medicinal traits may be known only to indigenous or local communities. Government authority over their utilization may thus be more seriously questioned. Throughout history local people have often been victimized as global and national interest has been spurred in these resources: the western ideology of traditional wildlife management views man as an alien element in preservation areas, and central governments may increase their control over natural resources and groups within the population by employing the ideology, legitimacy, and technology of Western preservation ideology.[41]

The BioConvention mentions explicitly that the Contracting Parties shall respect, preserve, and maintain knowledge and practices of indigenous and local communities, and encourage the equitable sharing of the benefits arising from the utilization of such knowledge and practices. A probable interpretation of the BioConvention is that governments may regulate the activities of their citizens regarding export of genetic material. Enforcement is less clear, as this brings up the tricky question of interference in domestic affairs, as well as how to identify who should be rewarded. One approach to ensuring the interests of local and indigenous people may be to include and elaborate the FAO principle of 'farmers' rights' in a protocol under the BioConvention. This principle applies to collectives and not individuals, but it would have to be expanded outside the area of plant genetic resources and agriculture to include, among others, the forestry sector. A more general approach could be to link the concept of compensation to capacity building at the local level.

User countries may also improve the effectiveness of the *prior informed consent* principle by enacting national legislation on the import side: along the lines of the rules governing international trade in endangered species of flora and fauna (CITES), national legislation could be tailored to prohibit illegal import of genetic resources, that is, collections conflicting with prior informed consent export rules in the providing country. Likewise, companies and other importers could be obliged to keep records of imported genetic material, in order to facilitate monitoring by government authorities. Another interesting suggestion is to require patent applications to give information about how genetic material was obtained.[42] Efforts to fight the expanding scope of patent legislation has so far hardly been rewarded. A more promising avenue may be to direct attention to what can be done with the legislation itself.

Finally, the parties to the BioConvention will have to consider the legal vacuum surrounding genetic resources in international gene-banks. Biological materials collected prior to the Convention's coming into force are not covered by the Convention, and are thus still subject to the principle of free access for all. These resources, obtained largely from farmers in developing countries, represent important breeding material for improvement of world food production. Third World governments and environmental and developmental NGOs argue that this genetic material should be included in the FAO Global System on Plant Genetic Resources with the intention of developing a protocol to the BioConvention on 'farmers' rights' to place such material under democratic intergovernmental governance. A similar proposal was included in the Nairobi Final Act, adopted by the parties negotiating the BioConvention.[43] An agreement between FAO and the Consultative Group on International Agricultural Research is anticipated on this issue, aimed at making the germ-plasm in international agricultural research centres part of the FAO international network of gene-banks. Gene-banks within this network are based on the principles of making genetic material available for breeding and research while respecting the rights of the providers of germ-plasm.[44] Environmental and developmental NGOs have warned against the World Bank taking over leadership of international germ-plasm collections, fearing a loss of intergovernmental control over this valuable material.[45]

National legislation is an important vehicle for enhancing implementation of the objectives in the BioConvention. Institution and capacity building in developing countries must be strengthened in order to increase their ability to reap benefits from their own valuable resources. Ideally, contracts on biodiversity prospecting should include components of technology transfers, institution building, and environmental concerns as compensation for access to genetic resources. The Merck–Costa Rica deal does integrate these different components, though some still object that there should be more of each component. Payment mechanisms such as these will hardly suffice to secure full conservation and sustainable use of genetic resources (whatever this may mean). Moreover, there is a renewed danger that the developing countries may become increasingly segregated in the scramble for biodiversity prospecting deals. It would seem, however, that if the BioConvention could succeed in strengthening equity in international gene transactions, this would legitimize its other objectives with the developing world.

*Prospects Concerning the Financial Mechanism*
The possibilities for Third World governments to achieve compensation from external use of genetic resources may,

at least for the time being, still be limited. The major source of income for conservation will obviously come from direct funding from bi- and multilateral sources.

The North–South controversy over funding was barely resolved by the compromise that the Global Environment Facility (GEF) of the World Bank, UNDP, and UNEP should be used for an interim period, and on condition that it become more democratic. The latter condition was a concession to Third World governments who would have preferred a new funding mechanism over which they could have more control. This reflects the fundamental conflict regarding the South's concern about national sovereignty over its own natural resources, and the North's claim for some degree of conditionality tied to its spending on global environmental projects.

One main reason why GEF was accepted for an interim period despite certain shortcomings in its democratic structure was its assumed ability to attract major funding. In its pilot stage, GEF has already been active in financing several global environmental projects: besides biodiversity, it covers climate change, international waterways, and ozone depletion. The important question is whether GEF will prove to be a suitable tool for the conservation of biodiversity. This concerns criteria for funding of projects in the GEF portfolio and whether GEF can be adjusted to reach small-scale farmers who are so central in growing and maintaining a diversity of food crops in the fields.

GEF has already been active in funding global environmental projects for four years. Reporting on their review of the GEF biodiversity portfolio, however, a group of experts agreed there were various shortcomings:[46] among others, that projects take too little consideration of the expertise and interests of local people, and that GEF has been biased towards biodiversity protection through the establishment of protected areas. This bias is related to the traditional approach of the agencies operating GEF: the World Bank deals mainly with large-scale programmes, whereas what is believed to be needed for biodiversity conservation is small-scale, community-based projects. A crucial factor in the further development of the GEF mechanism would seem to be its 'Small Grants Programme' for NGOs, which so far constitute only 2–3 per cent of the total GEF portfolio.

A major concern at the first intergovernmental follow-up meeting on the BioConvention held in October 1993, was to provide input to the GEF meeting the following December.[47] The parties did not succeed in this objective. There was some agreement that biodiversity conservation can scarcely be understood in terms of 'global benefits' versus 'national benefits', but as yet no solution has been reached for dealing with the concept of 'incremental costs' in GEF. These incremental costs are intended as an incentive for developing countries to include in projects a global conservation benefit which may not be in their immediate national interest. This division seems to work fairly well in projects concerned with ozone depletion and climate change, but in the biodiversity area, the separation of national and global benefits rarely make sense.

Some examples may illustrate how it may seem that 'some benefits are more global than others':

• By establishing a wildlife reserve to conserve threatened or endemic species of trees or animals, a country may lose revenue from timber extraction, as well as contracting extra costs in terms of resettlement of local populations originally living in the area. On the positive side, the country may gain revenue through increased tourism. The deficit in this budget (the difference between lost revenue from timber and gained revenue from tourism) constitutes the incremental costs, and will most likely be accepted as a global benefit component.
• By continued use of a diversity of local varieties of rice plants, instead of the widespread introduction of uniform, high-yielding rice varieties, a country might experience an economic loss in terms of reduced yields. In this budget one must first subtract the lower costs of input factors in the first place (less costly seeds, less need for pesticides). The conservation component of the activity is the benefits derived from conserving a large variety of food plants in the field, securing breeding material for the future: how much of this benefit can be counted as a national benefit, and what part of it is truly global?

As the debate has worn on, some of the G77 governments have begun to complain that 'global benefits' in fact equal 'Northern benefits'. Rather, they claim, global benefits in biodiversity projects should be defined as national benefits. This would erase any semblance of conditionality—and is thus obviously out of the question for Northern governments. The central dilemma remains: how to define global benefits in biodiversity conservation in line with the precautionary principle, that is, without risking a bias towards biological 'hot-spots', at the expense of biodiversity of less immediate economic value. The BioConvention itself does not prescribe global benefits as a criterion; rather, funding is tied to fulfilment of the objectives of the BioConvention. What it does is provide a basis for setting priorities in biodiversity conservation: including high diversity and high numbers of endemic and threatened species, as well as species or habitats of social, economic, cultural, or scientific importance. This comes closer than the notion of 'global benefits' with regard to guaranteeing a diversity of projects in the GEF portfolio.

Currently, the bottom line in GEF is to maintain the division between development aid and biodiversity conservation. This issue was much debated during a recent intergovernmental meeting on scientific aspects of the BioConvention.[48] India, Brazil, and Malaysia argued against scientific input providing a basis for setting priorities about conservation projects (primarily in terms of GEF financing). As the most resourceful among the developing countries, they insist on having political control over GEF money in terms of development, rather than accepting what they claim to be Western scientific priorities. In the end, the parties of the Convention are expected to have the final say regarding programme priorities and eligibility criteria for GEF funding. This question will be further debated in November/December at the first Conference of the Parties.

## Concluding Remarks

Biotechnology regulations, equitable sharing through compensation for use of genetic resources, and criteria for financial transfers for conservation projects—these remain linked and controversial issues. With regard to biotechnology regulations, a crucial question is whether the US government will succeed in blocking the development of a biosafety protocol under the BioConvention. There is also the question of whether Northern governments will comply with the new regime regulating access to and exchange of genetic resources and technology. As far as compensation mechanisms for access to genetic resources are concerned, it is now up to national governments to enact appropriate legislation. The North–South conflict on funding of biodiversity projects basically concerns the perennial question of sovereignty versus conditionality.

Whether compensation for use of genetic resources will become a viable concept depends on whether the new dual property rights regime of the BioConvention will take hold. New policies on equitable sharing adopted by Britain's Royal Botanic Gardens at Kew and by Biotics are indications that these ideas are catching on. Such a system will also depend on the capacity of Third World governments to enact and enforce appropriate legislation. As long as the developed countries have free access to germ-plasm through international gene-banks, they have an incentive to remain free-riders in reaping the benefits from genetic resources. Tracing germ-plasm back to its origin is scarcely feasible in all cases, so what is needed is a general system of recording how the material was obtained. This could be developed in a protocol to the Convention. An important incentive for Northern governments to enact legislation in line with the principle of prior informed consent, however, would be for them to be considered legitimate purchasers of genetic resources. This is basically a question of the strength of the new bio-regime in establishing common norms which the actors in gene transactions can find acceptable and fair. In terms of the larger related picture regarding prospects for a new economic world order, this idea might seem far-fetched, but it could have a viable chance within a limited issue-area.

The funding for conservation and compensation for use of genetic resources may lead to discord among developing countries, as they differ in terms of gene and species richness and also with regard to technological capacity. In the aftermath of UNCED many fear that the least developed, gene-poor countries will be left increasingly at the losing end—in two respects: limited funding for biodiversity conservation, and reduced access to improved breeding material. As the GEF evaluation has demonstrated, there is a tendency to disregard the potential importance of genetic resources in arid and semi-arid areas, and to focus on tropical rainforests instead. The explanation is most likely found in the old paradigm of wildlife conservation, which still links 'global benefits' to biodiversity 'hot-spots'. For biodiversity conservation in a long-term perspective, this does not bode well for the implementation of the Biodiversity Convention. Unlike the FAO debate, there are few rallying factors available for the G77, for example, in the form of NGOs. As NGO representation gained legitimacy and increased during and following UNCED, so has the plurality of their voices, and thus their difficulties in rallying around common goals. The schism between wildlife conservation and agricultural biodiversity (like on-farm conservation and the use of traditional food plants) still constitute a hurdle in this respect. If environmental and developmental NGOs are to have a positive impact on biodiversity conservation in a long-term perspective, the old dispute between wildlife conservation and agricultural biodiversity will have to be laid to rest.

Discontent with the financial aspects of the BioConvention is not restricted to gene-poor countries. Biologically rich countries like Brazil and Malaysia are expected to become the greatest beneficiaries from the North's focus on global environmental issues, but they have no desire to be told what to do with this money. The sovereignty issue looms large in this part of the follow-up of the BioConvention, as the North is unlikely to accept financial obligations without conditionality. Donor governments cannot be expected to abandon their demand for scientific criteria as a basis for setting priorities in biodiversity conservation. A pertinent lesson from the forestry sector is that the temperate countries of the North must commit themselves to the same standards of conservation and sustainable utilization as they request from the tropical countries, in order to gain legitimacy and credibility for their argumentation. In this way the conditionality/sovereignty trap may be evaded.

Applying a long-term perspective to biodiversity conservation, compensation for use of genetic resources is probably more important than direct funding of piecemeal wildlife conservation measures. It is also more important to integrate biodiversity perspectives into the large social sectors of agriculture, forestry, and fisheries, than to establish small islands of preservation areas. If biodiversity conservation is necessary for future use, this may certainly be most effectively reflected by how we use it today. Biodiversity conservation is essentially about the ability to engage in a diversity of activities at the same time. Considerable scientific uncertainty remains regarding the relationship between species and ecosystems, and about what happens when small or larger parts of diversity disappear. Some priorities will certainly have to be made; but with the present scientific uncertainty, it may prove just as dangerous to neglect plant genetic resources in Mali as animal species of the Amazon jungle. Additional resources resulting from UNCED, as well as conventional development aid, need to be strengthened to integrate sustainable use of genetic resources. This may include the use of traditional plants in agriculture, as well as the development of incentives for integrated methods for agri-forestry and aqua-culture.

In this perspective, GEF funding is indeed necessary, but far from sufficient. Even though resources for overall conservation are strained, GEF should still be made available also for projects outside the traditional preservation portfolio. The GEF concepts of incremental costs and cost efficiency must be treated with utmost care in relation to biodiversity projects. Moreover, the very nature of the biodiversity complex makes it more natural to concentrate on small-scale projects rather than big, top-down ones. Likewise, GEF should also be used for capacity building. The overall benefits from helping developing countries to secure revenue from the utilization of genetic resources may prove to be the best investment for ensuring their future.

## Notes and References

I would like to thank Veit Koester, Head of the Ecological Division with the Danish Ministry of Environment, and Erik Steineger, special advisor to the Norwegian Ministry of Environment, for their valuable comments at various stages in my work with this article. The full responsibility for any shortcomings reside of course with the author.

1. As defined in the Convention on Biological Diversity, Rio de Janeiro, 5 June 1992.
2. Edward O. Wilson (1992), *The Diversity of Life* (Cambridge, Mass.: Harvard University Press).
3. Edward O. Wilson (ed.) (1988), *Biodiversity* (Washington, DC: National Academy Press).
4. While the 'old' biotechnology includes traditional activities like brewing beer and baking bread, the concept of 'new biotechnologies' refers to activities like tissue culture and recombinant-DNA (r-DNA) techniques.
5. Report of Panel II, UNEP/Bio.Div/Panels/Inf.2, Nairobi, 28 Apr. 1993.
6. WCED, World Commission for Environment and Development (1987), *Our Common Future* (Oxford: Oxford University Press).
7. For an extended exposé of the historical background for the seeds issue as a North–South conflict area, as well as a thorough examination of the FAO debate, see Cary Fowler (1993),

8. 'Biological Diversity in a North–South Context', in *Green Globe Yearbook 1993* (Oxford: Oxford University Press), 35–44.
9. For more information on the treaties and agreements see reference section in *Green Globe Yearbook* (Oxford: Oxford University Press). For an extended analysis of the debate leading up to the arrangements in FAO, see G. Kristin Rosendal (1989), *A Sustainable Development for Plant Genetic Resources: The Output of the Debate in FAO; a Sisyphean Victory for an Environmental Organisation?* (Lysaker: Fridtjof Nansen Institute, R:010-1989). For a similar analysis of the UNEP debate, see id. (1991), *International Conservation of Biological Diversity: The Quest for Effective Solutions* (Lysaker: Fridtjof Nansen Institute, R:012-1991).
9. As defined in the Convention on Biological Diversity, Rio de Janeiro, 5 June 1992.
10. See e.g. Gareth Hardin's now-classic article: (1968), 'The Tragedy of the Commons', *Science*, 162, 1243–8.
11. Hugo Grotius (1609), *Mare Liberum sive de iure quod Batavis competit ad Indicana commercia dissertatio*, (Leiden: Elsevier). See also Hedley Bull, Benedict Kingsbury, and Adam Roberts (eds.) (1992), *Hugo Grotius and International Relations* (Oxford: Clarendon Press).
12. R. B. Bilder (1980), 'International Law and Natural Resources Policies', *Natural Resources Journal*, 20 (July), 451–86.
13. R. S. Crespi (1988), *Patents: A Basic Guide to Patenting in Biotechnology* (Cambridge: Cambridge University Press).
14. Pat Mooney, Cary Fowler, Eva Lachkovics, and Hope Shand (1988), 'The Laws of Life: Another Development and the New Biotechnologies', *Development Dialogue* (Dag Hammarskjöld Foundation, Uppsala), 1–2.
15. S. A. Bent, R. L. Schwaab, D. G. Conlin, and D. D. Jeffery (1987), *Intellectual Property Rights in Biotechnology Worldwide* (New York: Stockton Press).
16. F. Pierce (1992), 'Brazil, Where the Ice Cream Comes From', *New Scientist* (17 July), 47.
17. G. Kristin Rosendal (1989) (n. 8 above).
18. FAO, Working Group of the Commission for PGR, CPGR/89/9, 1989.
19. G. Kristin Rosendal (1989) (n. 8 above). ICDA has recently changed its name to GRAIN (Genetic Resources Action International), and is still active lobbying in the international biodiversity debates.
20. GATT (1989), *Communication from India: Standards and Principles Concerning the Availability, Scope and Use of Trade-Related Intellectual Property Rights* (GATT Secretariat, MTN GNG/NG11/W/37) (July).
21. WCED, World Commission for Environment and Development (1987) (n. 6 above).
22. GATT (1989) (n. 20 above)
23. Keystone International Dialogue on Plant Genetic Resources (1990), *Final Consensus Report* (Madras Plenary Session, Keystone, Colo.) (14 Feb.).
24. Multilateral Trade Negotiations, the Uruguay Round, the Negotiations Committee, MTN.TNC/W/124, 13 Dec. 1993, MNT/FA II-Annex 1C. Sec. 5, Art. 27 in the agreement on Trade-Related Aspects of Intellectual Property rights.
25. Vandana Shiva (1994), 'The Need for Sui Generis Rights', *Seedling* (Mar.), 11–15.
26. G. Kristin Rosendal (1989) (n. 8 above).
27. See e.g. Arild Underdal (1980), *The Politics of International Fisheries Management: The Case of the Northeast Atlantic* (Oslo: Norwegian University Press).
28. Ulf Svensson (1993), 'The Convention on Biodiversity—A New Approach', in Sjøstedt, Svedin, and Hägerhäll Aniansson (eds.), *International Environmental Negotiations; Process, Issues and Context* (Stockholm: FRN Utrikespolitiska Institutet).

29. Expert Panel IV concluded that there is a need for a protocol on biosafety, against the sole vote of the USA. Expert Panel to follow up on the Convention on Biological Diversity, Report of Panel IV (1993): *Consideration of the Need for and Modalities of a Protocol Setting Out Appropriate Procedures Including, in Particular, Advance Informed Agreement in the Field of the Safe Transfer, Handling and Use of any Living Modified Organism Resulting from Biotechnology that May Have Adverse Effect on the Conservation and Sustainable use of Biological Diversity* (UNEP/Bio.Div./Panels/Inf.4, Nairobi, 28 Apr.).

30. Second session of the Intergovernmental Committee for the Convention on Biological Diversity, Nairobi (20 June–1 July 1994).

31. K. Hindar, G. K. Rosendal, and H. N. Trønnes (1990), *Bioteknologi og norsk tilpasning til EFs indre marked* (Trondheim: Norsk Institutt for Naturforskning NINA).

32. G. Kristin Rosendal (1992), 'The Biodiversity Convention: Analysing the Footwork of Bush in Rio', *International Challenges* (Lysaker: Fridtjof Nansen Institute), 12: 3, 15–23.

33. G. Porter (1993), 'The United States and the Biodiversity Convention', *International Conference on the Convention on Biological Diversity*, African Centre for Technology Studies, Nairobi, Kenya, (26–9 Jan.); and G. Kristin Rosendal (1994), 'The Biodiversity Convention: Implications of the US "No" in Rio', in Vincente Sánches and Calestous Juma (eds.), *Biodiplomacy* (Nairobi: ACTS Press).

34. J. H. Barton and W. E. Siebeck (1992), 'Intellectual Property Issues for the International Agricultural Research Centres: What are the Options?', *Issues in Agriculture*, 4 (Washington, DC: Consultative Group on International Agricultural Research).

35. J. van Wijk (1991), 'Diminishing National Sovereignty in Intellectual Property Protection: Enforced Global Recognition of Patents in Biotechnology', paper presented at the International Symposium and Experts Workshop: *Property Rights, Biotechnology and Genetic Resources* (African Centre for Technology Studies and World Resources Institute, Nairobi, 10–14 June).

36. Raino Malnes, (1990) *The Environment and Duties to Future Generations, An Elaboration of 'Sustainable Development'* (Lysaker: Fridtjof Nansen Institute, EED:002-1990).

37. Walter Reid (1992), 'Bush Biodiversity Policy Risks Dangerous Side Effects', *Wall Street Journal*, 8 Oct.

38. Sarah A. Laird (1993), 'Contracts for Biodiversity Prospecting', in *Biodiversity Prospecting* (Baltimore: World Resources Institute Publications), 99–130.

39. This article has been studied in detail by Frederic Hendrickx, Veit Koester, and Christian Prip (1993): 'Convention on Biological Diversity. Access to Genetic Resources: A Legal Analysis', *Environmental Policy and Law* 23: 6. Veit Koester played a central role throughout the biodiversity negotiation process, acting both as chairman and vice-chairman during various parts of negotiations, among others, leading Working Group II.

40. Hendrickx, *et al.* (1993) (n. 39 above).

41. In a recent World Bank technical paper, the issue is described as follows: 'The establishment of national parks and reserves, which may attract tourists and foreign exchange for the government, exclude and have often directly displaced rural communities from land they have traditionally considered to be their own. Anti-poaching laws turn the centuries' old practice of subsistence hunting into a crime, and people are often even prevented from eliminating "problem" animals to protect their crops, their livestock and themselves. In the simplest terms, rural people bear the significant costs of living with wildlife but have progressively been excluded from obtaining any benefit from them' (World Bank (1990), Agnes Kiss (ed.), *Living with Wildlife. Wildlife Resource Management with Local Participation in Africa*, Technical Paper No. 130, Washington, DC.)

42. Hendrickx, *et al.*, 1993 (n. 39 above).

43. Nairobi Final Act, Resolution 3, Nairobi, 22 May 1992.

44. FAO report to the Second Session of the Intergovernmental Committee on the Convention on Biological Diversity, Nairobi, 20 June–1 July 1994; 'Progress Report on Resolution 3 of the Nairobi Final Act: Ex Situ Collections and Farmers' Rights'.

45. Second Session of the Intergovernmental Committee of the Convention on Biological Diversity (see previous note).

46. GEF (1992), *Summary Report on the Review of the GEF Biodiversity Portfolio* (Nov.) (Washington, DC).

47. Intergovernmental Committee on the Convention on Biological Diversity (ICCBD) in Geneva, Oct. 1993.

48. The open-ended Intergovernmental meeting of Scientific Experts on Biological Diversity (ISE) in Mexico in April.

# Building an Environmental Protection Framework for North America: The Role of the Non-Governmental Community

*Betty Ferber, Janine Ferretti, and Lynn M. Fischer*

## Introduction

On 1 January 1994 the North American Free Trade Agreement (NAFTA) officially entered into force, creating the world's largest trading bloc, and the first ever reciprocal free-trade agreement between developing and industrialized countries. The treaty, along with its side agreements, represents the first time environment has been given serious consideration in a trade agreement. The fact that environment was given such high-profile treatment was largely due to organized pressure and participation by environmental groups in Mexico, Canada, and the USA. The accords reflect the new importance of the North American environmental community as a tri-national non-governmental movement.

The debate in North America over NAFTA was a complex one, involving many sectors of society. In all three countries, elements of the labour community, human-rights activists, and environmental advocates, in addition to traditional trade interests from the business community, sought to influence the outcome of the negotiations. The environmental community in particular was highly successful in organizing across borders and in articulating its agenda.

In September 1990, the Mexican president Carlos Salinas de Gortari officially sought the opening of negotiations for a free-trade agreement between the USA and Mexico. Shortly afterwards President Bush notified Congress that the negotiations would go forward. Non-governmental environmental organizations in all three countries were quick to express their concern regarding the potentially adverse impact which a trade agreement of this scope would have on the conservation of natural resources and on the health of the 360 million inhabitants of North America. From the beginning, they argued for an inclusion of environmental issues within the negotiations, to ensure that a North American Free Trade Agreement would promote environmentally sustainable development, rather than further environmental degradation.

The urgency and high visibility of three issues in particular created a climate in which the governments felt compelled to deal with a series of serious environmental concerns:

- the rapid industrialization and population growth along the US–Mexico border provided particularly vivid images of potential environmental problems arising from increased economic growth. The problems in the region are many, including insufficient infrastructure to deal with water-treatment and waste-disposal needs, rising levels of air pollution, and abysmal housing conditions around factories;
- the 1991 GATT decision in the Tuna–Dolphin case, which deemed that efforts by the USA to protect resources (dolphins in this case) beyond its borders were inconsistent with international trade rules, raised a red flag for environmental and consumer protection advocates. The highly publicized case raised fears that trade agreements could weaken human health- and natural-resource protection measures;
- the weakness of environmental law enforcement in Mexico created widespread concern about the possible repercussions of expanded trade. On the one hand, industry, labour, and environmentalists in Canada and the USA feared the possible creation of so-called 'pollution havens' that would produce unfair advantages for industry operating in Mexico. This was compounded by the more generalized and realistic fear that bad enforcement practices combined with growth in the industrial sector would lead to further degradation of the Mexican environment.

The response of the environmental groups to the above concerns, and others detailed further in this article, was organized and swift. The groups quickly joined forces across borders, identifying anticipated environmental and public-health problems associated with increased trade. Later, after gaining a better understanding of trade rules, some environmentalists began offering solutions to trade and environment conflicts. The concrete solutions offered by many environmental groups eventually laid the groundwork for NAFTA and its environmental side agreements.

## Anticipated Impacts of NAFTA

From an economic point of view, NAFTA is predicted to promote additional economic growth in all three North American economies, through the specialization and economies of scale resulting from freer trade and investment flows. A US International Trade Commission synthesis of economic models concluded that NAFTA would result in additional economic growth of less than 0.5 per cent of the gross national product (GNP) for Canada and the USA. Growth of up to 11 per cent of the GNP was predicted for Mexico.[1] Greater investment is also predicted, especially in Mexico. Analysis shows growth in exports for the USA and Mexico, increased wages in all sectors except agriculture, and improved returns on investment in both countries.[2]

Despite overall growth, certain sectors such as corn production in Mexico are expected to experience large reductions in output due to increased competition from imports.[3] The most widely recognized negative outcomes are in small-scale agriculture and small business in Mexico. Increased competition from cheaper US and Canadian grain production is expected to cause significant dislocation for Mexican peasant farmers. This dislocation was already under way, as a result of recent reforms in Mexican land-tenure laws. Small and medium-sized manufacturing industries in Mexico are also expected to suffer in the short term as they are forced to compete with large and more efficient US and Canadian firms.

From an environmental perspective, economic growth can have potentially negative impacts on natural resources and human health; it is likely to be accompanied by increased production of hazardous waste, greater energy and natural-resource consumption and extraction, and rising agricultural output using more water and agricultural chemicals. Without proper infrastructure and enforcement of environmental laws, all of these will exacerbate existing environmental problems in Canada, Mexico, and the USA.

Furthermore, the predicted dislocation in the rural regions of Mexico could result in serious degradation of the environment. Environmental damage as a result of rural poverty, including accelerated deforestation and over-cropping of marginal lands, is well documented. Migration from rural to urban areas places additional stresses on already overtaxed urban infrastructures, creating human health and environmental problems. Many of these problems would occur without NAFTA, as a result of the elimination of the collective farming system in Mexico and the shortage of credit for small farmers.

In addition to these general problems, environmentalists raised a number of specific concerns in the NAFTA debate which are detailed below. Environmental NGO participation in the process was largely aimed at preventing or mitigating these anticipated and existing problems.

### Weakening of Environmental Laws and Standards

Environmental advocates feared that NAFTA would limit each nation's ability to manage and conserve its own resources and enact high standards for public health and environmental protection. Fears revolved around harmonization or attempts to create uniform standards throughout the free-trade region. Many feared that harmonization efforts would force high national standards down to a lowest common denominator or to international standards that are frequently lower than the strong environmental and consumer protection laws in the USA and Canada. Another key concern was that the agreement would open to challenge as trade barriers federal, state, and local laws designed to conserve natural resources and protect human health. There were further fears that competition from firms operating in countries with lower standards would gain an unfair advantage over firms operating in the country with higher standards, thus causing a movement of industry and jobs to the nation with the weakest laws, or creating political pressures to lower standards in the country with stricter laws. This last issue became less of a concern once environmentalists discovered that Mexico's environmental laws were relatively strong, if badly enforced.

### Insufficient Funding for Environmental Protection and Infrastructure

Budgetary constraints hamper the implementation of Mexico's environmental laws and programmes. Although Mexico nearly tripled its federal pollution-control budget between 1990 and 1992, as part of a significant increase in overall environmental spending, resources continue to fall short of actual needs. State and local governments in Mexico are particularly ill-equipped to enforce environmental laws and protect public health. To make matters worse, a recent restructuring of Mexico's environmental authority has placed more responsibility with those same entities, further exacerbating enforcement problems.

A key concern during the NAFTA negotiations was ensuring that Mexico have access to sufficient funds to consider the environment in its development plans and to comply with domestic laws and international protocols and conventions. There was a general consensus that Mexico needed money to train more personnel, to develop the technical capacity to deal with complex environmental problems, and to create a sufficient infrastructure to absorb new development. There is currently a shortage of funds and qualified personnel for monitoring the existing industrial plants and implementing extant Mexican laws and international agreements.

## Degradation of the Border Environment

Related to the above were particular concerns about degradation of the US–Mexico border environment due to a lack of infrastructure accompanied by rapid industrial growth. Many saw the border as a predictor of future problems throughout Mexico. Much focus in the media and by environmental organizations was placed on the inadequate housing situation on both sides of the border, lack of water-treatment and waste-disposal capabilities, clandestine hazardous-waste sites, and worsening air quality in many of the cities in the region.

## Lack of Enforcement of Environmental Laws

Over the last few years, Mexico has made important strides in the development of strong environmental laws and regulations. Nevertheless, environmentalists feared that serious enforcement problems in Mexico would be exacerbated by increased trade and investment, possibly attracting polluting industry to Mexico.

For example, a 1992 US General Accounting Office (GAO) sample found that none of six US majority-owned 'maquiladora' factories surveyed had prepared an environmental impact assessment for new plants established in Mexico, as required under Mexico's 1988 General Ecology Law.[4] The GAO findings are consistent with the observations of Mexican environmentalists, who have described chronic and widespread violations of Mexico's environmental impact requirements. The implementation of those requirements has routinely neglected a timely disclosure of assessment documents, as well as full notice and comment procedures that are essential to informed public participation.[5]

Enforcement problems are due in large part to a lack of money and technical resources, exacerbated in some cases by inefficiency, corruption, and a lack of political will. Another factor resulting in weak enforcement is that citizens and environmental groups, who play an important part in the enforcement of environmental law in other countries, are not given the opportunity to participate fully, thus limiting the already under-funded enforcement efforts. Although an 'Attorney-General' for the environment was created in Mexico in 1992, providing a citizen-complaint procedure, many environmental groups in Mexico expressed dissatisfaction with the process.

## Insufficient Public Participation In Decision-making Processes

NGOs were concerned about getting a seat at the table in both the NAFTA process, and more generally in guaranteeing a greater role for citizens in the enforcement and decision-making process in all three countries, especially Mexico. In particular, Mexican environmentalists were concerned about the general lack of democratic processes in Mexico,

particularly in the arena of environmental decision-making.

Under the GATT dispute-resolution procedures, used during the Tuna–Dolphin case and others, for example, the entire process was closed to the public and no NGO input was allowed. The same rules prevailed under the US–Canada free-trade agreement. Environmentalists and others had a strong interest in opening up these processes and ensuring that environmental disputes included input from experts.

At the national level, particularly in Mexico, citizens are not given important information or allowed to participate in decision-making processes. For example, Mexican citizens have no access to information about toxic emissions or potentially harmful industrial activities, as Mexican law does not require reporting or public release of this data. Mexican NGOs have repeatedly called for the creation in Mexico of a toxic-release inventory and the passage of right-to-know legislation. Such requirements were seen as even more important in light of the trade agreement, as more foreign companies set up operations in Mexico.

## Changes in the Mexican Constitution and Environmental Law During the NAFTA Process

Many Mexican environmentalists expressed particular concern about the changes that were made in the Mexican constitution in order to conform with NAFTA.

The most striking example is the reform of Article 27, eliminating the collective farming system know as the *ejido*. While agricultural policy in Mexico has long had negative social and environmental effects in rural areas, the abrupt removal of all support for the small-scale farmer is expected to create widespread problems in Mexico. Removal of the law which has hitherto forbidden sale of communal *ejido* property, especially in coastal and heavily forested areas, presents a serious threat of additional deforestation, destruction of wetlands, and environmentally unsound tourism development. In addition, many experts predict that foreign competition under the trade agreement will exacerbate the problems of dislocation and under-employment.

## The NGO Role in the NAFTA Process

When the USA entered into trade negotiations with Canada in 1986, the major US environmental and consumer-protection organizations showed little interest. During 1990, as the Uruguay round of GATT appeared to be drawing to a close, some of the environmental–consumer concerns mentioned in the previous section were raised for the first time. The NAFTA negotiations, however, created great concern that regional integrations would directly threaten natural resources and public health in Mexico as well as the viability of US and Canadian environmental and health standards.

For much of the environmental community the early 1991 GATT dispute over the US ban on tuna imports from Mexico set off alarm bells. GATT ruled in favour of Mexico in August of that year, stating that the USA could not fairly ban the importation of Mexican tuna to protect dolphins. Concerns triggered by the GATT ruling, coupled with growing dissatisfaction with the US–Canada free-trade agreement, as well as the enforcement, participation, and infrastructure concerns mentioned in the previous section, set the stage for a cross-border coalition of environmentalists interested in improving or preventing NAFTA.

Environmental organizations from Mexico and the USA worked closely together during the free-trade discussions. Products of this collaboration have included conferences and seminars to develop recommendations for NAFTA and joint submissions to each country's trade negotiators.[6]

### Building Tri-National Coalitions

The problems described above prompted concerns from groups thoughout the region, and became the platform for the environmental community. Soon after the intention to negotiate an agreement was announced, environmentalists in the USA, Mexico, and Canada began collaborating. In March 1991 the Grupo de los Cien—a Mexican advocacy group— initiated contacts with American and Canadian groups. On 5 April a *Common Declaration by Environmental Groups in Mexico, the United States and Canada Regarding the North American Free Trade Agreement*[7] was released to the press in all three countries. The communities quickly developed a mutually beneficial relationship which afforded groups in Mexico support and leverage in their attempts to influence the negotiations and allowed American and Canadian groups to demonstrate that concern for Mexico's environment was not exclusive to environmentalists in the USA.

Later, at a meeting held in Mexico City in January 1992, representatives of environmental groups in Mexico, Canada, and the USA developed recommendations for specific actions their governments could take to evaluate and mitigate environmental risks posed by NAFTA.[8]

A number of joint and individual declarations were made over the following months; however, the response from the negotiators was less than satisfactory.

### Inadequate Government Response

As an initial response to concerns voiced by the environmentalists, the US and Mexican environmental authorities (EPA and SEDUE) produced the *Integrated Plan for the Mexican–US Border Area* (Border Plan).[9] The US Trade Representative also released the *Review of US–Mexico Environmental Issues*[10] (Environmental Review), in place of a more formal environmental impact assessment.

A draft of the Border Plan was released in August 1991 for public comment. Hundreds of Mexican and US citizens testified at the seventeen public hearings organized along the border by the Mexican Secretaria de Desarrollo Urbano y Ecologia (SEDUE) and the US Environmental Protection Agency (EPA). Major criticisms of the draft focused on lack of financing, recommendations for future study rather than plans for immediate action, failure to address health-related pollution problems, insufficient attention to hazardous waste, superficial treatment of water supply and pollution, lack of provisions for bi-national enforcement of pollution regulations, inadequate public access to information, and omission of wetlands and wildlife protection from the plan.

The final plan was released in February 1992, to further criticism from Mexican and US groups. They condemned it as an 'inadequate response to existing environmental problems and increased pressures under [the] free trade agreement',[11] emphasizing that the Border Plan does not prescribe any significant changes to existing environmental laws and institutions.

A draft of the Environmental Review was released for comment in October of 1991. It too was widely criticized by US and Mexican environment groups for its nearly exclusive focus on the border region and its biased analysis of many issues.[12] The final Environmental Review was released in February 1992, without taking into account most of the comments from environmentalists.

### Detailed and Specific Proposals from the Environmentalists

Unhappy with the response from the negotiators, a number of environmental groups joined together to formulate concrete and detailed recommendations to the negotiators. The documents focused on environmental safeguards to be included in NAFTA. In early 1992, working in parallel on both sides of the border, a number of US and Mexican organizations resolved to transform their concerns into specific proposals. The Mexican groups prepared a package of 'Environmental Safeguard Clauses' for inclusion in the agreement.[13] Following the Mexican groups' example, environmentalists in the USA and Canada drew up similar proposals.[14] The respective documents were delivered to trade negotiators in all three governments in May and June of 1992.

The groups strongly urged the creation of a permanent, independent, trilateral panel or commission, in addition to public participation in dispute-resolution processes, better enforcement procedures, and additional funding for environmental infrastructure. In July of that year, fifty-one Mexican, US, and Canadian groups signed an open letter to negotiators from the three countries, again urging the inclusion of environmental safeguards within NAFTA, whose final text was then nearing completion. Emphasizing their common aims, they again argued for language in NAFTA which would ensure public participation and oversight, guarantee improved enforcement of environmental legislation, increase funding for environmental programmes, and protect local, state, and national standards for public health and the environment.[15]

### Improved NAFTA Text

The NAFTA negotiators incorporated some recommendations offered by environmental organizations into the final text of the treaty. In disputes involving health and environmental measures, for example, the agreement places the burden on challenging countries to prove inconsistency with NAFTA's trade rules.[16] The Preamble of the agreement promises to '[u]ndertake . . . [the agreement] in a manner consistent with environmental protection and conservation' and '[p]romote sustainable development'.[17] Article 1114 in the investment chapter warns the parties against a weakening of domestic law to attract investment.[18]

Most environmental groups in all three countries were quick to reject the final NAFTA text as insufficient because it did not address the key concerns of improving enforcement and funding environmental infrastructure. In addition, many expressed concerns that, despite improvements, the new NAFTA standards language did not fully address risks of possible trade challenges to environmental and public-health laws.

### Creating a North American Environment Commission

On 17 September 1992, in a partial response to joint NGO proposals, the environmental ministers of Canada, Mexico, and the USA announced their intention to create a North American Commission for the Environment.[19]

Several weeks later, twenty-three Mexican environmental organizations made public a detailed proposal for the establishment of a 'North American Commission on Trade and the Environment', drawn up jointly with their counterparts in the USA and Canada.[20] A number of proposals from various organizations were circulated; most requested the basic principles of independence, public participation, a procedure for citizen complaints or submissions, and the ability to focus a 'spotlight' on environmental problems in the region.

### Additional Funding for the Environment

The issue of additional funding was also not addressed in the original agreements, leading to many proposals for cross-border taxes and other mechanisms to pay for the needed clean-up and infrastructure. The most detailed and promising of these proposals came from a broad coalition of environmental and social groups in the USA, led by three national Latino organizations. The coalition proposed the creation of a North American Development Bank (NADBank) to provide funding for environmental infrastructure and community development projects in the USA, Canada, and Mexico.

Originally presented by the National Council of La Raza, Southwest Voter Research Institute, and the Mexican American Legal Defense and Education Fund, the NADBank proposal gained support from a number of environmental organizations and elected officials. NADBank supporters envisioned a new type of multilateral development bank that would loan directly to communities experiencing negative economic impacts from NAFTA, in addition to providing loans for environmental projects throughout the region.[21]

## The Governments' Final Response to Environmental Concerns

In response to the concerns voiced by environmentalists in the three countries, the governments finally negotiated one trilateral and one bilateral agreement to deal with environmental concerns raised during the trade debate. In addition, the USA allocated US\$20 million for biodiversity and natural-resource protection in Mexico, and provided additional clarification of the NAFTA language ensuring that the environmental laws would not be weakened by the agreement. The following section briefly describes and assesses the agreements and the new institutions created.

### The North American Agreement on Environmental Co-operation

The cornerstone of the governments' response to the environmental communities is the environmental side agreement signed by Canada, Mexico, and the USA. The North American Agreement on Environmental Co-operation (Side Agreement or NAAEC), obligates the countries to enforce their environmental laws, creates an independent commission to facilitate enforcement and co-operation, and ultimately permits the parties to impose trade sanctions in cases of persistent non-enforcement of environmental laws.

The North American Commission for Environmental Co-operation (NACEC or Commission), created by the Side Agreement, has a three-part structure. It is governed by a three-member council made up of the environment ministers of each country. The NACEC will be staffed by an independent secretariat headed by an executive director, who will serve a renewable three-year term. The first executive director, the Mexican economist Victor Lichtinger, enjoys support from environmentalists in all three countries.

**North American
Free Trade Agreement
(Canada — Mexico — USA)**

North American Commission
for Environmental Co-operation
(Canada — Mexico — USA)

North American Commission
for Labor Co-operation
(Canada — Mexico — USA)

Border Environment
Co-operation Commission

North American
Development Bank
(Mexico — USA)

*Note:* Two tri-national institutions and one bi-national institution were created by the NAFTA side agreements, to address environment and employment concerns related to the agreement. Though part of the NAFTA package, the new instiutions are not limitid to addressing trade-related problems.

**Fig. 1. NAFTA and side agreements**

The secretariat, which will be housed in Montreal, Quebec, will employ approximately eighteen people, to be expanded to thirty or forty in 1995. It is loosely organized into two divisions, headed by directors from Canada and the USA. One division will focus on policy and co-operative programmes, with 'committees' dealing with the specialty areas of enforcement, pollution prevention, conservation and biodiversity, transboundary and border issues, and production process-related issues. The other division will handle administrative and legal concerns, including disputes over failure to enforce environmental laws. The Council and Secretariat will be advised by a fifteen-member Joint Public Advisory Committee (J-PAC), with five members from each county. In addition, each party may create National Advisory Committees (NACs), with broad non-governmental representation.[22]

The role of NACEC (pronounced NAY-sec) will fall into three broad categories: (1) facilitating co-operation among the NAFTA parties on a range of environmental concerns; (2) preparation of reports and recommendations to improve natural-resource and human-health protection throughout the continent; and (3) investigation of citizen complaints related to non-enforcement of environmental laws.

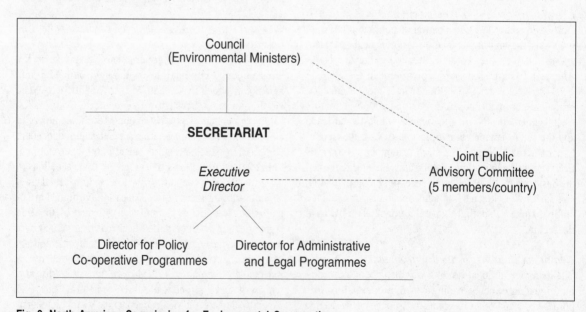

**Fig. 2. North American Commission for Environmental Co-operation**

## Assessment of NACEC

While NACEC does provide an important step forwards in improving environmental protection in North America, it falls short in some areas. On the one hand, the agreement largely met the demands of the mainstream environmental community by (1) providing an international institution with an independent secretariat; (2) establishing a mechanism for citizen complaints; and (3) obligating countries to enforce domestic environmental laws.

On the other hand, there are flaws in the procedures for openness and public access to the institution. Many of the documents produced by the secretariat, such as investigations of complaints and reports on environmental issues, will require a two-thirds vote of the parties to be released to the public.[23] Failure by the parties to release such information will seriously limit the ability of NACEC to spotlight environmental problems and will diminish the credibility of the institution. In addition, the side agreement is vague in defining the role of the public advisory committees. It is silent on the organization and size of the secretariat. Very few guide-lines are given in the agreement for preparation of reports, while nineteen open-ended potential topics are listed for consideration.

Overall, the institution has a lot of potential. Environmental groups across the continent, including opponents of NAFTA, have begun to participate in the process of naming advisors to the Commission and making recommendations for rules of procedure and priorities for the work-plan.[24]

If appropriate rules of procedure are adopted, and the national governments refrain from using the institution for political ends, the Commission could play an important role

in spotlighting environmental problems and recommending co-operative actions that the countries could take. The executive director, Victor Lichtinger, was widely endorsed by environmental groups,[25] and is seen as a highly independent proponent of environmental protection, with excellent managerial experience. His appointment further guarantees the independent nature of the Commission.

## The Border Environment Co-operation Commission and the North American Development Bank

In a bilateral agreement, the USA and Mexico created the Border Environment Co-operation Commission (Border Commission or BECC) and the North American Development Bank (NADBank).[26] The two institutions are designed to co-ordinate, prioritize, and fund environmental infrastructure projects in the US–Mexico border region.[27]

BECC's mandate is to assist border communities in addressing waste-water treatment, drinking-water supply, and municipal waste-management needs. It will provide technical assistance, packaging, and certification of projects. BECC will be located in Ciudad Juarez in Chihuahua, Mexico.

The NADBank is capitalized by US$112 million in paid-in capital, in equal shares from Mexico and the USA. The bank is expected to be able to use leverage to acquire between US$2 and US$3 billion in loans and guarantees for border projects. It will be the lead bank in funding projects certified by the Border Commission. It is expected to play an important role in putting together financing packages of private capital, NADBank loans and guarantees, and grants from federal and state governments. The environmental window of the bank is located in San Antonio, Texas.

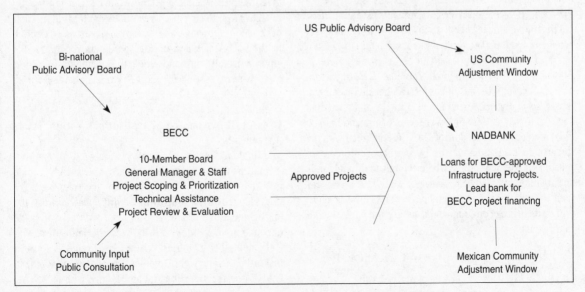

**Fig. 3. Border Environment Co-operation Commission. North American Development Bank**

## Assessment

Both the NADBank and BECC have been met with widespread optimism on the part of both the financial and environmental communities. The bottom-up project design system presents an important alternative to the traditional development-bank approach. If successful, the NADBank could well offer a starting-point for future reforms of the World Bank and the other multilaterals.

On the negative side, there are some concerns about the potential for economic success of NADBank loans. The payment stream for projects is expected to come from user fees imposed on the communities benefiting from the projects. Given the level of poverty found in many US and Mexican border communities, there is some question about the ability of these communities to pay sufficient user fees. In addition, half of the capital of the bank which can be called upon is from Mexico. The investment markets may not be willing to accept this Mexican callable capital as a guarantee for bonds issued by the bank, with the result that the bank will be limited in its lending capacity to the paid-in capital plus the capital which can be called upon from the USA.

## Looking to the Future

### A Focus on the North American Environment

It is difficult to predict specific effects of the trade agreement and the new institutions on environmental protection in the hemisphere. Much will depend on the successful implementation of the institutions and on the continued commitment from the three governments. Recent political upheavals in Mexico make predictions even more difficult—environmentalists in that country will be struggling to keep their concerns at the top of the government's list of priorities.

The increased attention focused on environmental problems and the likelihood of increased international co-operation will probably result in better management of transboundary environmental problems. Scrutiny from NACEC may provide incentives for stronger environmental laws, especially in Mexico but also in US and Canadian states and provinces with lower levels of protection. The citizen-complaint procedure of NACEC combined with the threat of trade sanctions may well lead to better enforcement practices in Mexico and elsewhere, though additional funds and training will also be necessary. Finally, there is every indication that the increased funding for border infrastructure will result in better environmental quality and public health in that region.

### Improving Relations Among NGOs

Clearly, the stronger ties between the non-governmental communities of all three countries have already had a positive effect. All indications are that some of the ties created during the NAFTA process will continue during and beyond the implementation phase of the new institutions. For example, many organizations are already planning joint submissions to NACEC.

The success of the environmental movement in achieving better environmental protection as part of NAFTA was largely due to the high level of co-operation among NGOs. This presents an important lesson for other social movements, such as labour and human-rights groups in North America. It also provides a useful model for future trade negotiations with Chile and other countries in Latin America.

### Creating Models for Future Trade Agreements

NAFTA sets an important precedent for treatment of the environment in future trade talks. The agreement recognizes for the first time the legitimacy of environmental concerns in international trade. NAFTA and its side agreements will provide a useful starting-point for future negotiations.

### Process-Related Standards

In the contentious debate over process-related standards,[28] the language in NAFTA and the side agreement represents a first step towards including process-related concerns within future trade agreements. The provisions relating to enforcement of environmental laws in the environmental side agreement[29] and the reference to international environmental agreements in Article 104 of NAFTA suggest that the environmental practices of a nation are of legitimate concern to its trading partners, even if those practices are not directly related to a product or its characteristics. While falling short of explicitly allowing trade restrictions based on production methods, NAFTA and it side agreement recognize that environmentally unsound production methods can distort trade patterns, as well as negatively affect natural resources and public health.

### Creating Environmental Institutions within Trade Agreements

The final NAFTA package reflects the need for environmental institutions as an independent counterweight to trade institutions. NACEC clearly provides the framework for that balance in its ability to identify and address the environmental effects of trade. Particularly if trade negotiations move forward in the Western Hemisphere with Chile and other countries, NACEC will provide a model institutional framework, whether those countries accede to NAFTA or negotiate bilateral agreements with the USA.

## Creating a Climate of Openness and Public Participation

The openness and participatory elements of the environmental Commission created by the side agreement is likely to pervade not just NAFTA itself, but future trade agreements. The NAFTA agreement requires that environmental experts be called upon in the case of trade disputes involving the environment. The Commission goes even further in allowing some participation by the non-governmental sector in disputes over enforcement of environmental laws. Once this door is opened it will be difficult to shut in future negotiations, especially those planned for the Western Hemisphere.

## Conclusions

Whether or not one believes that the NAFTA package provides sufficient safeguards for natural resources and public health (the authors are split on this point) the environmental community of North America deserves substantial credit for significantly advancing the linkage of trade and the environment. In all arenas, NAFTA represents an important step forwards.

In the area of environmental protection, the language of NAFTA itself presents a significant improvement over previous trade agreements. The preamble cites sustainable development and resource conservation as goals of the treaty.[30] Specific provisions in the agreement discourage countries from weakening environmental laws to attract investment.[31] Explicit protection is provided for certain International Environmental Agreements, in cases where the trade provisions of those treaties are in conflict with NAFTA.[32] Language in the standards portion of the treaty significantly improves upon previous trade agreements in its protection of strong domestic laws and standards.[33]

In addition to progressive language in the agreement itself, NAFTA generated path-breaking environmental side agreements. The tri- and bi-national institutions created by the side agreements are unique in laying the groundwork for improved enforcement and co-operation among countries. The institutions provide mechanisms allowing for citizen participation and complaints, as well as creating an independent secretariat with reporting and investigative capabilities, as requested by environmental organizations.

Perhaps most significantly, the process of negotiation of NAFTA and its side agreements set new precedents for participation by non-governmental organizations and the public in general in trade policy decisions. While uneven and far from satisfactory in Mexico, consultation with environmental groups in all three countries during the process was a first in the trade negotiation process. Unfortunately, in Mexico trade negotiators did not officially meet with a broad segment of the environmental community until after the text of the Agreement had been completed. In the USA and Canada, however, trade negotiators met numerous times with representatives of environmental groups and acted on many of the suggestions made by those groups. For example, as described in this article, the concept of a North American environment commission originated with environmentalists;[34] detailed recommendations for the structure and role of the institution were elaborated on a tri-national coalition of NGOs.[35] The environment commission structure finally negotiated by the governments retains many of the features first proposed by the NGO community.

In what is likely to have significant long-term benefits in North America, NAFTA generated unprecedented co-operation among the environmental communities of Canada, Mexico, and the USA, creating important leverage for environmental advocates and ensuring future co-operation and joint efforts to protect the environment of North America. In fact, the high level of co-ordination among the NGO communities in the three countries allowed Mexican environmentalists to play an important role in the process despite the lack of opportunities for participation provided by the Mexican government.

Lastly, NAFTA will provide a useful starting-point for future multilateral and bilateral trade agreements. It is widely predicted that Chile will soon join the agreement or at a minimum negotiate a bilateral agreement with the USA. In addition, there has been much discussion recently of a Western Hemisphere trading bloc including all of the countries of Latin America, the USA, and Canada. Recent attention has been focused on the formation of the World Trade Organization (WTO), created during the last round of the General Agreement on Trade and Tariffs, as well as preliminary discussions of a 'Green Round' of world trade negotiations. The new mechanisms for environmental protection created by NAFTA present an important model for these and other future trade talks.

The implementation of NAFTA and its side agreement will be the key to the success of environmental protection in North America. If environmentalists in all three countries continue to work together to ensure effective implementation of NAFTA and its side accords, the agreements can become an important tool for protecting public health and natural resources on the North American continent. The environmental communities deserve much credit for the achievements of NAFTA, and will play a key role in determining the continued success of the institutions they helped to create.

# Notes and References

1.  US General Accounting Office (1993), *North American Free Trade Agreement: Assessment of Major Issues*, vol. 2 (GAO/GGD-93-137 NAFTA), 132.
2.  Raul A. Hinojosa, Jeffrey D. Lewis, and Sherman Robinson (1994), 'Regional Integration in Greater North America: NAFTA, Central America and the Caribbean' (Mar.), draft.
3.  Ibid.
4.  US General Accounting Office (1992), *US–Mexico Trade: Assessment of Mexico's Environmental Controls for New Companies* (GAO/GGD-92-113) (Aug.), 13.
5.  Human Rights Watch and NRDC (1992), *Defending the Earth: Abuses of Human Rights and the Environment* (June), 69–70.
6.  See e.g. Natural Resources Defense Council, Instituto Autónomo de Investigaciones Ecológicas, and Grupo de los Cien (1991), *Comments on the US Trade Representative's 'Draft Review of US–Mexico Environmental Issues'*, (Dec.).
7.  *Common Declaration by Environmental Groups in Mexico, the United States and Canada Regarding the North American Free Trade Agreement* (5 Apr. 1991). Endorsing organizations in Mexico: Grupo de los Cien, Colectivo Ecologista Jalisco, Comunidad Ecologista de Occidente, Enlace Ecológico, Grupo Ecologista del Mayab, Instituto Autónomo de Investigaciones Ecológicas, Movimiente Ecologista Mexicano, Pacto de Grupos Ecologistas, Partido Verde Ecologista de Mexico, Proyecto Fronterizo de Educación Ambiental; in the USA: National Wildlife Federation, Arizona Toxics Information, Border Ecology Project, Community Nutrition Institute, Environmental Defense Fund, Friends of the Earth, Natural Resources Defense Council, National Toxics Campaign, Public Citizen, Texas Center for Policy Studies; in Canada: Pollution Probe, Canadian Arctic Resources Committee, Canadian Environmental Law Association, Rawson Academy of Aquatic Science.
8.  Instituto Autónomo de Investigaciones Ecológicas, Natural Resources Defense Council, National Wildlife Federation, (1992) Conference: 'El Medio Ambiente y el Tratado de Libre Comercio', Mexico City, (30–1 Jan.).
9.  US Environmental Protection Agency and Secretaria de Desarrollo Urbano y Ecología (1992), *Integrated Environmental Plan for the Mexican–US Border Area* (First Stage, 1992–4)(Feb.).
10.  US Environmental Protection Agency and Secretaria de Desarrollo Urbano (1991), 'Review of US–Mexico Environmental Issues' (Oct.), draft.
11.  Natural Resources Defense Council, Instituto Autónomo de Investigaciones Ecológicas and Grupo de los Cien, (1002) Press Release, *US and Mexican Groups Hit Plan for Border Environment* (25 Feb.).
12.  See e.g. Justin Ward and Lynn Fischer (1991), *Comments on the 'Draft Review of US–Mexico Environmental Issues'*; Prepared for the Natural Resources Defense Council, Grupo de los Cien, and the Instituto Autónomo de Investigaciones Ecológicas; (Dec.).
13.  Grupo de los Cien, Instituto Autónomo de Investigaciones Ecológicas, Asociación Ecológica de Coyoacan, *et al.* (1992), *Proyecto de cláusulas de salvaguardia ambiental para un Tratado Norteamericano de Libre Comercio* (May).
14.  Natural Resources Defense Council (1992), *Environmental Safeguards for the North American Free Trade Agreement* (June); National Wildlife Federation and Pollution Probe (1992), *Minimal Environmental Safeguards to be Included in the North American Free Trade Agreement* (May).
15.  Natural Resources Defense Council, National Wildlife Fund, Grupo de los Cien, Instituto Autónomo de Investigaciones Ecológicas, Asociación Ecológica de Coyoacan, Pollution Probe, *et al.* (1992), *Open Letter to North American Trade Negotiators*, (20 July).
16.  NAFTA (1992), Art. 765(6).
17.  Ibid., Preamble.
18.  Ibid., Art. 1117.
19.  US Environmental Protection Agency and Secretaria de Desarrollo Social (1992), Press release (17 Sept.).
20.  Unión de Grupos Ambientalistas, Grupo de los Cien, Consejo para la Defensa de la Costa del Pacifico Mexicano, Instituto Autónomo de Investigaciones Ecológicas, Asociación Ecológica Coyoacan, *et al.* (1992), *Acuerdo que Establece la Comisión Norteamericana para Comercio y Medio Ambiente* (Oct.).
21.  Albert Fishlow, Sherman Robinson, and Raul Hinojosa-Ojeda (1991), 'Proposal for North American Regional Development Bank and Adjustment Fund' (University of California, Berkeley) (May).
22.  The USA has appointed a NAC with broad participation from the environmental community. As of October 1994 Mexico was in the process of creating a NAC, Canada had not yet decided whether to create additional advisory committees.
23.  See e.g. North American Agreement on Environmental Co-operation, (1993) Art. 15(7) and 16(7), related to release of complaint investigations to the public and to the Joint Public Advisory Committee.
24.  See e.g. *NGO Recommendations for Implementation of the North American Commission for Environmental Cooperation* endorsed by thirty-one organizations from Canada, Mexico, and the USA (22 Feb. 1994).
25.  See e.g. NRDC letter of 15 June 1994 to Robert Sussman, deputy administrator of the US Environmental Protection Agency, (On behalf of the Environmental Defense Fund and National Audubon Society); and Center for Mexican Environmental Law letter of 21 June 1994 to Mexican president Carlos Salinas.
26.  *Agreement between the Government of the United States of America and the United Mexican States concerning the Establishment of a Border Environment Commission and a North American Development Bank* (1993).
27.  The border region is specifically defined as 100 km. on either side of the border.
28.  Process-related standards or Product Production Methods (PPMs) are laws or standards that regulate the method or process used to manufacture or produce a good or service, as opposed to the quality of the good or service.
29.  *North American Agreement on Environmental Co-operation* (1993), Art. 3, 5, 6, 7.
30.  NAFTA (1992), Preamble.
31.  Ibid., Art. 1114.
32.  Ibid., Art. 104.
33.  Kenneth Berlin (undated) *The NAFTA Environmental Agreements*; for the law firm Winthrop, Stimpson, Putnam & Roberts (undated), Washington, DC, 19–21.
34.  The first reported suggestion for a 'tri-national environmental commission' was by John Adams, executive director of the Natural Resources Defense Council, in a meeting with US president George Bush in early 1991; the concept was further elaborated in Pollution Probe-Canada (1991), *The Environmental Dimensions of Free Trade* (June).
35.  Unión de Grupos Ambientalistas, Grupo de los Cien, *et al. Acuerdo que Establece la Comisión Norteamericana para Comercio y Medio Ambiente*; and Natural Resources Defense Council, Environmental Defense Fund, *et al.* (1993), *Recommendations for a North American Commission on the Environment* (Mar.).

# Transnational Corporations' Strategic Responses to 'Sustainable Development'

*Harris Gleckman*

'There were two issues we missed out on: transnationals and the military.'

(Comment from a Brazilian delegate on the closing day of UNCED.)

Transnational Corporations (TNCs) can play a critical role in a sustainably managed world or serve as major impediments in this transition. The relationship between TNCs and environmental performance came under scrutiny in the buildup to the 1992 Rio United Nations Conference on Environment and Development (UNCED). By way of background, this paper provides a critical review of the buildup in the corporate world to the UNCED. It then argues that there were strategic reasons why UNCED avoided an overall analysis of international investment and sustainable development. UNCED did raise a number of major intellectual and political issues about the relationship between TNC activity and sound environmental practice, and the management of this relationship within the corporate world and between the corporate and non-corporate worlds. These questions raise several others, and this paper will review three of them:

- Who defines sustainable behaviour?
- Who regulates transnational corporate environmental activity?
- How does society pay for environmental resource extraction and depletion?

TNCs clearly have a global environmental impact. Some TNCs have become leaders in the field of global environmental management. They recognize a growing global 'green' market in goods and services. Their international trade associations have made major recommendations for corporate environmental performance improvements. On balance, however, changes have occurred among a very small minority of TNCs. Most firms are unconcerned about the environmental impacts of their business processes. Those that are actively improving environmental performance tend to pick away at aspects of the problem—recycling, emissions, and the like—rather than take a systemic approach.

TNC environmental performance has come under the microscope as the global environmental crisis has loomed before us. But because TNCs operate outside national political boundaries, they are not treated as a group or subjected to public scrutiny or accountability. The UNCED put TNC environmental activity on the table for the first time, asking the question: what should be the relationship between TNCs and sustainable development? The question raised much heat among corporate leaders, government, trade associations, citizens groups, and workers. It also generated a flurry of activity within the TNC community because, unlike the other groups in this discussion, TNCs have never before had to act as a group on environment and development issues: they have no institutional history, no established leadership, or method to reach consensual positions. But here was an occasion where their very terms of business were potentially being challenged.

In some ways, this is a re-run in the international arena of a 200-year old debate within national democratic systems, of what the relationship should be between the state and its economic actors. Historically, northern democracies created a variety of checks and balances on the free play of economic forces. National industry generally has not welcomed national regulation, but acknowledges the need for regulation to maintain competition and the legitimacy of the market. Consequently there is a permanent love–hate relationship between national government and industry in all democratic societies.

In the international arena there are now highly complex TNCs operating in a literally unregulated international environment. In this international arena, international corporations and national political actors have resisted the concept of international regulation, and have been unenthusiastic about extending the authority of multilateral institutions. The response of TNC leaders illuminates what the issues are for TNCs, and what trends we can expect in the coming years.

## What is the Relationship Between TNCs and the Global Environmental Crisis?

In the public mind the issue is clear: there is a level of unacceptable environmental behaviour for multinational enterprises operating abroad. The Gallup *Health of the Planet* survey, conducted in the developed and developing world, showed that 'there is widespread concern for the environment among citizens of *all* types of countries'. In most countries, citizens believe that business and industry are *the* major cause of environmental problems.[1] In contrast, TNCs do not accept that they are the cause of the global economic crisis, but they are beginning to accept that environmental issues need to be managed in some fashion. What are the facts?

The impact of TNC activity on the environment is extensive. TNC importance stems from their vast corporate networks and technological resources and the international consequences of their decision-making. More than 50 per cent of global greenhouse gas emissions are in the province of TNCs.[2] TNCs invest more than US$225 billion each year outside their home countries, and 95 per cent of these investments come from firms based in industrialized countries. Seventy per cent of world trade involves TNCs, who also hold 90 per cent of all technology and product patents. Every major natural resource extraction and processing industry involves TNCs. The environmental impacts of TNCs extend to the service sector (product advertising) and the financial services sector (investment loans).

To put it another way: if all transnational corporations were to adopt sound environmental policies, then the following would occur:

- at least one quarter of the world's assets would be better managed environmentally;
- 70 per cent of the products in international trade would be better labelled;
- 80 per cent of the world's land cultivated for export-oriented crops would use fewer toxic pesticides and more sustainable agricultural policies;
- a large share of the world's new technological innovations would be better evaluated for their health-and-safety effects.

There is every reason to believe that the political–economic–environmental role of TNCs will increase in the coming years. This will continue as the international market adapts to the new World Trade Organization (WTO) and its arrangements on trade and investment, the trade-related investment measures agreement, and the WTO standards code.

In recognition that there is some relationship between TNCs and global environmental issues, some TNCs have adopted new attitudes to environmental issues (see Box 1). Corporate-wide policy statements have been transmitted from headquarters to affiliates; new markets for pollution control equipment and environmental services have been created; global environmental management has turned into a profession; executives are more receptive to work with international organizations on corporate environmental

The International Chamber of Commerce has stated that industry needs '*to integrate (environmentally sound) policies, programmes, and practices (for conducting operations) fully into each business as an essential element of management in all its functions.*'

A grouping of international banks has declared: '*We . . . recognize that ecological protection and sustainable development are collective responsibilities and must rank among the highest priorities of all business activities, including banking. We will endeavour to ensure that our policies and business actions promote sustainable development; meeting the needs of the present without compromising those of the future.*'

The Keidanren, the largest Japanese industrial trade association, asserted: '*[the] formulation of a complete policy for the protection of the environment of the host country is a responsibility of good corporate citizenship on the part of the expanding corporation and it is hoped that each corporation will establish specific policies with this in mind.*'

**Box 1. Some recent comments on environmental responsibility from major international trade associations**

issues; environmental impact assessments and hazardous waste disposal appraisals have become common tools for a good number of transnational corporations; and long-term targets and goals have been set for the control of emissions and the use of natural resources. Without doubt, the preparatory process for Rio generated a good deal of constructive attention in the corporate world. The paths set during the preparatory phase will have a lot to do with the future momentum on these issues.

These pioneering efforts show that environmental and economic excellence can be compatible. Resource recovery and recycling can produce both an environmentally desirable and an economically beneficial outcome. Durable and energy-efficient products make good economic sense and are requisites for good environmental management. Global environmental issues like climate change can be met by innovative environmental and economic solutions. Macroeconomic data also show that environmental leadership and competitive advantage are closely linked. Market leaders in new technologies are firms from home countries that have strong regulatory standards. Within countries, firms operating in sectors with high environmental costs have strengthened their international trade performance.

## TNCs and Environmental Responsibility: How UNCED Put the Issue on the Table and How Business Responded

Although the question of transnational corporate environmental responsibility has been the subject of some activist campaigns, it has received scant attention in intergovernmental discussions, because it falls outside the sphere of national political influence. The first international conference on the environment was in Stockholm in 1972, and the International Chamber of Commerce (ICC) gave a fifteen-minute presentation. In the fall–winter of 1989 the General Assembly agreed to hold a second international conference on the environment in 1992 and to broaden the scope of the conference to integrate environment and development as common themes.

Several groups were interested in reformulating the concept of the traditional corporation so that environmental concerns were embedded into traditional business concerns. Recommendations and strategies were needed at the intergovernmental, non-governmental, and corporate levels to change existing transnational corporations into sustainably managed firms. As a first step, the UN Economic and Social Council (ECOSOC) asked the United Nations Centre on Transnational Corporations (UNCTC)[3] to prepare a set of recommendations on 'large industrial enterprises, including transnational corporations' and their role in sustainable development that governments might use in the drafting of *Agenda 21*.[4] UNCTC had a good track record in this area. The Centre had prepared the first set of standards for sustainable development management, the *Criteria for Sustainable Development Management*,[5] had undertaken research on the environmental policies and programmes of the world's largest firms,[6] had drafted innovative proposals to increase the flow of environmentally sound technologies to developing countries on favourable terms,[7] and had reviewed the state of international and domestic environment law affecting transnational corporations.[8]

It was bound to be difficult to convert a new conceptual definition of sustainable enterprise into operational terms, so care was taken in drafting the document *Transnational Corporations and Sustainable Development: Recommendations of the Executive Director* to ensure that each central recommendation was currently *in use* by a major transnational corporation. As a twenty-year work plan, the *Recommendations* worked backwards from a twenty-year goal and identified key events that would need to take place within fifteen, ten, and five years. These components of the *Recommendations* involved changes in global corporate environmental management, the minimization of risk and hazard in all operations, the encouragement of environmentally sound consumption patterns, the use of full-cost

environmental accounting, and compliance with environmental conventions, standards, and guide-lines.[9]

In parallel, the UNCED secretariat prepared a draft of a chapter entitled 'Business and Industry' in a section dealing with the role of major groups, and omitted direct reference to TNC responsibility. In early 1992 the United Nations Industrial Development Organization (UNIDO) hosted a conference on Sound Ecological Development which concluded with some environmental policy proposals affecting TNCs.

For the corporate community the challenge was this: how can business respond to the global environmental crisis and play its part in global regeneration? This was a completely new terrain for TNCs, and one in which the UN and some TNC firms moved rapidly. Efforts to involve TNCs in the 1992 conference began in 1989, a year before the UNCED conference was authorized by the General Assembly. In this period a handful of major firms and some trade associations took leadership of this issue within the TNC community. They began to incorporate environment *and* economic development concerns into business language. They achieved some notable and important shifts in business principle and practice. At the same time, they claimed the right to define a sustainable enterprise and measure its performance.

Many international organizations now claim to speak on behalf of international business, but in truth there is no organization that is the legitimate representative of TNCs on any subject. None of the existing organizations can claim a democratic decision-making system involving all major enterprises. None of the business–environmental organizations can make agreements on behalf of TNCs. In general, all lack the authority to negotiate on behalf of large industrial enterprises, transnational corporations, or industry. The question to the industry, then, of how TNCs would respond to the issue of sustainable development, also called for an industry leader or spokesperson.[10]

The International Chamber of Commerce in Paris, the oldest organization in this area, released its first environmental statement entitled *Environmental Guidelines* in 1965. It incorporated its first reference to environmental standards in its revision to the *Guidelines on Multinational Enterprises* only in 1992. The ICC is an international network of national chambers of commerce. In most cases, the national chambers of commerce in their own countries are not leaders in the field of environmental protection.

The ICC historically assigned its policy-work in this area to its Commission on the Environment in Paris. After its first World Industry Conference on Environmental Management (co-sponsored with the United Nations Environment Programme), it supplemented the Commission with a programme delivery office in an International Environment

Bureau. The ICC Commission functions at the level of vice-presidents of corporations and makes its major decisions by consensus. The ICC Commission has for years argued that environmental standards hamper the market-place and should be accepted only if they apply to all industry. They have also argued that the UN should reduce its attention to environmental matters affecting the international market. At the same time, the membership of the ICC Commission has been almost wholly drawn from individual TNCs.

In response to UNCED and the *Valdez* Principles[11]—a set of corporate environmental principles drafted by US social investors in the wake of the Exxon/*Valdez* oil-spill—the ICC Commission on the Environment decided to prepare a voluntary statement on sustainable development. While portraying itself as a tool for sustainable management, the term 'sustainable development' appears only in the title and in one sub-paragraph. The remainder of the *Business Charter of Sustainable Development* is a series of partial statements on environmental protection.[12]

During the drafting process a number of individual corporations resisted any texts that might require major departures from their existing practices. After discarding a number of drafts, the final version of the *ICC Business Charter on Sustainable Development* utilized the first ten steps of the *UNCTC Criteria on Sustainable Development Management* extensively—without citation or acknowledgment. Currently endorsed by over 1,000 TNCs and trade associations, the Business Charter has been translated and reprinted in over ten languages. The Centre, while pleased that its original ideas were being widely used but aware of the implications for the battle on intellectual property rights, chose not to clarify the origin of the key passages of the Business Charter. On the other hand, the ICC continued to criticize heavily United Nations work on TNCs and the environment. After the second World Industry Conference on Environmental Management (WICEM) in Rotterdam—also co-sponsored with UNEP—the ICC published *From Ideas to Action*, of environmentally good case studies from various industrial sectors;[13] it did not mention problem cases or lessons to be learnt from corporate mistakes.

After Rio, the ICC re-configured the International Environmental Bureau into an expanded World Industry Council of the Environment (WICE). This body will take a more active role than its ICC predecessors in carrying the environmental message to business and national chambers of commerce and in carrying the business message to international organizations and government delegations. Yet the membership of WICE is by invitation and by private corporate dues, so its claim to 'represent' world industry is even more diluted than that of the ICC itself.

Independent of the ICC is a series of specialized trade associations that address environmental issues from a sectoral perspective. The associations, like the oil industry CONCAWA and the International Federation on Metals and the Environment, seek to develop internally acceptable positions on the environment. In the past five years there has been a proliferation of environmental statements from these trade associations covering topics as diverse as contract terms for the transfer of potentially hazardous chemical technologies to the conditions for sustainable tourism. Besides getting in on a currently fashionable topic, these policy statements and new industrial sector associations can be seen as attempts to soften potentially difficult topics for individual sectors and to reassure a sceptical international community that there are environmentally responsible firms within the industry. Yet this trend among trade associations to develop environmental policy statements does not necessarily have a practical result. Most of these guide-lines do not ask signatories to commit themselves to the principles or activities they recommend.

In addition there are various national or regional business organizations that have formalized policy statements on global environment and development issues. The Keidanren (Federation of Economic Organizations) in Japan, for example, has a specific guidance document for its member firms operating abroad.[14] The Chemical Manufacturers Association (US) is probably the only trade association that has even established minimum environmental standards for its member firms covering their operations in their home country.

In part because of the minimal positions taken by the ICC and because of a driving interest by Maurice Strong, secretary-general of UNCED, to actively involve TNC chief executive officers in the preparations for Rio, the post of corporate advisor to UNCED was created. The corporate advisor to UNCED established the Business Council on Sustainable Development (BCSD).

The Business Council was immediately seen as being in competition with the old-guard ICC.[15] The BCSD is an association of fifty chief executive officers who speak in their personal capacities, not on behalf of their enterprises. It functioned at a more senior level than the ICC. While the BCSD and the corporate advisor privately provided advice on UNCED's manuscripts and draft conference proposals, their public involvement was focused on influencing ministers of state and heads of government. With few exceptions, the BCSD did not participate actively in the public sessions of the preparatory committees for UNCED.

The BCSD focused a good part of its attention on an issue which was called by the UNCED resolution the 'transfer of environmentally sound technologies to developing countries on favourable terms'. The BCSD held a series of meetings with industry and government representatives in order to convince them that it would be more appropriate to use

Alliance Internationale de Tourisme
American Hardware Institute
American Plastics Council
American Textile Manufacturers Institute
American Petroleum Institute
Association of International Banks
Association of Petrochemicals Producers in Europe (APPE)
Business Council for Sustainable Development
Bundesverband der Deutschen Industrie e.V
Canadian Chemical Manufacturers Association (CCMA)
Canadian Manufacturers of Chemical Specialities Association (CMCS)
Chemical Industries Association (UK)
Chemical Manufacturers Association (CMA)
The Coalition for Environmentally Responsible Economies (CERES)
Confederation of British Industry (CBI)
Environmental Marketing and Advertising Council (EMAC)
European Auto Manufacturers (ACEA)
European Chemical Manufacturers Association (CEFIC)
European Confederation of Pulp, Paper and Board Industries (CEPAC)
Federchimica
Institute of Petroleum
International Chamber of Commerce
International Council on Metals and the Environment
International Federation of Consulting Engineers (FIDIC)
International Fertilizer Industry Association (IFA)
International Iron and Steel Institute
International Road Transport Union (IRU)
Keidanren
Keizai Doyukai
Schweizerische Gesellschaft für Chemische Industrie (SGCI)
Verband der Chemischen industrie (VCI)
World Tourism Organization

**Box 2. Selected list of international business organizations that have formulated positions statements on environmental performance or sustainable development**

'technology co-operation' as the umbrella term for this issue. As self-selected corporate leaders on sustainable development, one of the primary tasks of council members is to convince other senior corporate executives to take sustainable development seriously. Their report, *Changing Course*,[16] is an enlightened long-term strategy document that contrasts sharply with the ICC and other trade associations' recommendations for UNCED. However, it also avoids addressing TNCs directly.

As actors on the world stage, TNCs play two conflicting parts. On the one hand, they publicize their global power and global reach. On the other, they deny that their activities, as a group, could have negative consequences, and they deny that, as a group, they have the power to influence events.[17] Both roles were played out during UNCED. For two-and-a-half years before the Conference there was a series of specialized meetings and intergovernmental preparatory conferences to agree on a multi-year plan of action for sustainable development and on a broad declaration of commitment to an integrated approach to environment and development. Concurrently the international community negotiated on environmental conventions on climate change and on the preservation of biodiversity. Within the Rio Conference proceedings there was silence on the role of TNCs; across from the Conference Centre and in São Paulo major meetings of corporate executives from around the world were held to plan further expansions of transnational investment and trade in environmental technologies.[18] The multi-year plan of action, called at the end *Agenda 21*, contains forty-two chapters on a wide range of economic, social, and environmental issues.

After all the fuss, what does *Agenda 21* say about TNCs? When the General Assembly accepted the report of UNCED in December 1992 the international community adopted more substantial references to the responsibilities of transnational corporations developed under the sustainable development umbrella than in any other area considered by the General Assembly. These standards are expressed in eight different technical sections of *Agenda 21*. They have been rearranged in policy categories in the Annex section at the end of this paper.

The key passages of *Agenda 21* adopted by the General Assembly dealing with TNCs are clearly stronger than any other equivalent texts adopted by prior general assemblies, ECOSOC, OECD, or the World Bank. Certain of these passages are likely to foretell new areas of international law. The General Assembly agreed, for example, that TNCs and other large industrial enterprises should introduce policies and commitments to adopt equivalent or not-less stringent standards of operation as in the country of origin and they should undertake research into the phase-out of those processes that pose the greatest environmental risk based on the hazardous waste generated. *Agenda 21* also calls for an annual report on routine emissions of toxic chemicals to the environment, even in the absence of the host country. Without Rio, this text would not even have been considered by the General Assembly. The efficacy of these new statements in altering behaviour will depend in large part on the follow-up by the Commission on Sustainable Development, the Earth Council, the various specialized international business associations, and the NGO community.

The Rio conference could have started a serious consideration of what 'sustainable enterprise' means and how international economic activity could be brought in line with global environmental requirements. As will be explained later, the international business community and the governments of the industrialized countries looked at this possibility for substantive change and flinched. They opted for a narrow definition and lobbied hard to prevent the public scrutiny that lay at the foundation of the question. The key question was what definition would be used of sustainable TNC activity. It is crucial, as perceptions of what the relationship should be between TNCs and sustainable activities will guide public expectation, litigation, and the thinking that occurs around national or international regulation—all of which have implications for the business profitability.

## Who Defines Sustainable TNC Behaviour?

The definition of acceptable environmental performance has obvious public-relations implications. For the corporate world, it is crucial that the public believes that there will be no more 'Bhopal-type incidents'. The events involving Occidental Petroleum at Love Canal, Sandoz, with the pollution of the Rhine, Hoffman-LaRoche in Seveso, Italy, Occidental Petroleum again in the North Sea, and Exxon with its *Valdez* tanker must not be seen as evidence that transnational corporations are regularly causing 'difficulties' for the environment.

The definition of acceptable environmental behaviour also has legal and financial consequences. Recent years have seen a proliferation of court cases involving TNCs. Some cases were initiated in the North and then taken to Southern courts (for example, Bhopal); others were undertaken in developing-country court systems with public campaigns of support from the developed countries (for example, the de-registration of pharmaceutical products in Bangladesh); some have started as Northern activist exposés and continued as developing-country legal proceedings (for example, Italian waste dumping in Nigeria); and some 'accidents' in Southern countries have found a court-room in the North (for example, Central American DBCP pesticide victims

are before a Texas court).

The general public's view is that there is some inherent concept of minimum international environmental standards below which firms and countries can no longer operate, and that it is the job of governments to enforce these. Firms cannot, even in states with lax regulations and enforcement, discharge mercury, lead, or other heavy metals into the air and water without public indignation and/or legal action. TNCs, irrespective of explicit laws, cannot maintain vastly different health and safety standards for their workers without serious adverse labour criticism and/or civil liability suits. And TNCs cannot be involved in industrial accidents in developing countries and expect to walk away without costs through skilful manipulation of the corporate veil and relocation of assets.

In legal terms, this may herald the evolution of international environmental standards roughly equivalent to the now recognized human rights standards. Even if countries authorize torture, the international community can react with economic and/or diplomatic sanctions. When firms ignore minimum international environmental standards, the world media will find a sympathetic audience when reporting disparate practices. Many firms may behave outside highly regulated markets with a cavalier attitude to environment and development. They are increasingly likely to discover constraining state legal actions and unexpected public-relations costs. But below this threshold of unacceptable behaviour is a vast grey area where TNCs operate outside public scrutiny or government regulation. In this area, TNCs claim that they should be responsible for corporate environmental improvements, and point to successes already achieved.

Published reports of TNC environmental successes celebrate single case studies. The celebratory genre of corporate environmental reporting seen in the ICC book *From Ideas Into Action* has been duplicated in corporate reports and in several reports of 'trends' produced by industry and consulting houses. These reports tend to be popular among business readers. They are defended on the grounds that they lead by example and show what is possible if industry is allowed to be innovative and not over-regulated. At the same time, the limits of their definition of sustainable environmental management must be recognized. They are self-referring, concentrating on 'improvements' in selected areas—often emissions or recycling—over previous performance. They concentrate on discretionary changes that can be profitable.

Leading environmental TNCs announce with pride that they have improved their environmental practices, reduced emissions, cut the generation of hazardous waste, and minimized the likelihood of industrial accidents. In annual report after annual report these firms make impressive public claims and display attractive statistical charts. But these claims are difficult to document unless there is a recognized disclosure standard and an accepted method of measurement. Clearly something has happened for a good number of TNCs, but the overall significance for the firm and the environment is difficult to assess. Even sophisticated users of annual reports are at a loss to compare meaningfully the relative environmental impact of two large firms. For instance, one firm reports that it cut $SO_2$ emissions over the past three years but fails to relate this reduction to a corporate reorganization that closed down a particular affiliate. Another firm states that it has a corporate goal to reduce hazardous waste by 10 per cent per year over five years without providing the definition of hazardous waste used or the starting amount. Such claims have excellent short-run advantages in the media, but they damage long-term credibility with environmentalists, social investors, and government officials.

## Who Regulates Transnational Corporate Environmental Activity?

The issue of what the relationship should be between the nation-state and its business community has generated a sound body of literature. In contrast, there is very little work done on the relationship between international economic actors and international institutions of governance, and the assumptions of corporate governance are not transferred from the national to the international arena. Currently, conventions are drafted and signed by governments on behalf of nation-states. TNCs are not formally part of this process, nor are they directly addressed in the conventions. On the global economic stage, the lead players are in the wings: they neither participate in the process of preparing a convention nor are they obligated by its conclusions. This is a contradiction that is beginning to get some attention, particularly in a post-Uruguay GATT world.

Consequently, environmental conventions that do have industrial consequences are written in a roundabout fashion. The Basel Convention on hazardous waste is designed to restrict the shipment of hazardous waste. Governments sign conventions but firms ship waste. So the Basel Convention says governments will take measures to prevent firms from exporting hazardous waste. The USA, for example, does not have an export review system, except for military-related products. So it really does not have the capacity to control waste exports directly. Another example of this indirect method to control industrial pollution that has global effects is the approach in the Montreal Protocol on Ozone Depletion. While governments negotiated and adopted the Protocol, industry manufactures and uses ozone-depleting compounds. The Montreal Protocol states that member governments should take actions to reduce and eliminate certain classes of ozone-depleting compounds within their national boundaries, but there is no effective corporate verification procedure. One effect of this approach is that some non-signatory countries may choose not to become members of the Montreal Protocol as a device to encourage foreign investment in their countries.

What prompts TNCs to establish corporate-wide environmental management systems? The *Benchmark Corporate Environmental Survey* asked TNCs this question. Respondents were offered nine choices including:

• consumer protests;
• negative media publicity;
• potential legal costs;
• home country environmental regulations;
• host country environmental regulations; and
• accidents at their firm and accidents at other firms.

The results showed that the largest single factor motivating the establishment of a global environmental policy is the development of environmental laws and regulations *in the home country*. It appears that for large firms it may make more technological and managerial sense to have firm-wide environmental policies and procedures rather than to attempt effective management of internal, often contradictory, practices and technological standards. It is interesting that this reality is recognized by citizens around the world. In the Gallup Survey, over 55 per cent of the respondents 'strongly favour' that home countries formulate model environmental laws to put appropriate restrictions on business and industry.[19]

More surprisingly, and in marked contrast to the hype around 'self-regulation' created by leading trade associations and individual corporations, international business strongly believes that there *is* a major role to be played by the United Nations (and, presumably, other multilateral organizations) in regulating international corporate environmental performance. In the only statistical sampling done to date on TNCs and environmental performance, two-thirds of TNCs thought that the UN should work towards standardizing national environmental rules and regulations. A majority also felt that the UN should be active in setting international policy guide-lines.[20] Both positions are directly opposed to the views expressed by the ICC, and are not widely publicized. There is a major question here, of who represents international industry and who represents the views of international industry on sustainable business practice.

At the same time as TNCs recognize that better environmental practices will only happen through legislation, most firms take strong public exception to international environmental regulations. This is to be expected: few firms have ever called for environmental regulations in their home markets. One might assume, therefore, that TNCs would not take the lead in international environmental regulations. However, it may be more important to conduct the debate about regulations in the international arena than the national one, where some constraints already exist.

The campaign in favour of international self-regulation by individual firms and industry trade associations has been energetic and has been supported by almost all the international business trade associations. While not generally recognized as such, 'self-regulation' is really an oxymoron. Potential polluters cannot make 'laws' (that is, regulate) and order 'sanctions' (that is, authorize penalties and fines) that are against their self-interest. Further, state regulation presumes that there is a political process that defines a level of pollution, and regulations are issued to disperse this standard equitably over the generators of the pollution. No individual 'self-regulator' can determine the publicly approved level of pollution or allocate to itself the correct amount of pollution.

Although not explicitly made, the self-regulation argument at its most extreme is tantamount to advocating for the international arena only municipal/provincial/state laws and the cancellation of all national health and safety institutions and laws. While not advocating that untenable public position in home country markets, TNCs do not factor the 'common good' into their international economic activity. The demand for 'self-regulation' is couched in the language of trade and competitiveness and is remarkably value-free. It also reflects a double standard. It would be unimaginable to advocate cancelling the laws and institutions in a TNC home country that protect worker safety, water quality, product safety, pharmaceutical standards, or the environment.

National history holds a lesson here. Business cannot be expected to author its own regulation. Moreover, its requirements of government are inherently contradictory—wanting freedom and protection at the same time. Regulations in some form will be needed to maintain mature and stable democratic international economic relations. History shows that the proper debate should be on what kind of regulations are appropriate, not whether they should exist at all. It may have suited short-term TNC needs to try to eliminate references to transnational corporations in *Agenda 21*. But it may not suit them so well in the longer term. And it does not diminish their impact on the environment or their potential contribution to economic development.

In general, citizens' groups and non-governmental organizations call for some level of international standards. For example, the NGO text from Rio calls for 'democratic control of transnational corporations'.[21] There are other supporters of a clearer statement on TNC environmental responsibilities. Governments acknowledge that they cannot create and maintain a regulatory system in their own country that is technologically and scientifically dynamic. Scholars have argued that a 'level playing field' requires a globally consistent set of environmental norms and standards.

## Consequences of TNC Self-Regulation

An illustration of how important the definition of sustainable development is to TNCs can be seen in industry's rejection of UN proposals on corporate environmental management. The UN has no environmental enforcement powers against individual enterprises. But when UNCTC's *Criteria for Sustainable Development* was published, it was heavily criticized by industry proponents of 'self-regulation'. There were several reasons. First, while some criteria were already in operation, others would require some corporate-wide changes that they were disinclined to make. Secondly, the 'self-regulation' momentum could not be advanced if the UN or any other intergovernmental body could be seen *in the public eye* to be setting expectations for international business activities. These principles might lead some national governments to adopt laws and regulations based on these recommendations. Thirdly, 'self-regulation' would be weakened if it was understood that corporations could not define for themselves what constituted a sustainably managed firm. Were firms to be seen as unable to formulate sustainable management criteria and using something produced by intergovernmental bodies (or by governments), it would strongly suggest that they lacked even rudimentary 'self-regulatory' capabilities.

Another example is provided by the history of the passage of the UNCTC *Recommendations . . . on Transnational Corporations and Sustainable Development*. When it reached the Fourth Preparatory Committee for UNCED in March 1992, major developed countries, the ICC, and the Business Council for Sustainable Development launched a frontal effort to avoid any reference to TNCs and their potential contribution to sustainable development.[22] Some developing countries and NGOs continued to raise issues regarding TNCs and environmental responsibility during the Fourth Preparatory Committee meeting, to little avail.[23]

TNC leaders resisted all attempts made by multilateral organizations to table meaningful definitions of sustainable development, and ignored offerings from citizens groups. One could understand their criticism of the burdensome nature of international regulations if these really existed or were being proposed. But there is not a body of international conventions and agreements nor a set of agencies monitoring the implementation of corporate health, safety, environmental, and workers' standards. The world does not have agencies with administrators who collect standardized data on emissions. There are no administrative judges who rule and fine for violations of international standards. Inspectors

The Recommendations of the Executive Director of UNCTC to the Preparatory Committee for UNCED articulated a series of interrelated principles regarding acceptable international corporate environmental behaviour. Amongst the principles were:

Transnational corporations should apply the highest practicable principles and standards for environmental protection equivalently throughout each firm's global operations; conform to the provisions of international and regional environmental standards, guide-lines, and conventions to the extent that they are applicable to corporate activities, even though not mandatory under national/local law; and observe all national and local laws and regulations, subject to the overriding responsibility to conform with regional and international standards.

Transnational corporations should include environmental considerations in corporate accounting and reporting in order to relate an enterprise's environmental activities to its financial position and performance. Subsequently firms should incorporate the full environmental costs into the production of goods and services in order to send the right signals to producers and consumers.

**Box 3. Selections from the recommendations of the executive director of the UNCTC to the preparatory process for UNCED**

are not appointed internationally to visit operating plants in developing countries. In the absence of any regulation, the battle is nevertheless focused on preventing any—even a minimal system—from gaining public acceptance.

There are some positive aspects of the self-regulation approach. Most importantly, it is important to the leaders that they are not embarrassed by more Bhopal or *Valdez*-type public disasters. Corporate 'free-riders'—those firms who benefit from the lack of international environmental standards regulations but have not made any structural changes themselves—present a difficult case. They cannot be ordered by other firms to take environmental protection seriously but they can prevent the public from developing a 'green' image for TNCs in general.

'Self-regulation' leaders also have to make a convincing case to industry for environmental protection. They do this in a three-part argument. The first is built around traditional rationales for business activities; the second set is couched in defensive external terms,[24] and the third is a joint appeal

to governments to make environmental protection profitable.

The traditional argument is that 'environmental protection' is really good business. This line of approach is no different than, say, business consultants recommending streamlined management systems as a good business practice. The environmental version generally has these claims. Good environmental practices will lead to:

- new markets and increased profitability;
- diminished costs of production through reduced purchases of raw materials and inputs;
- increased efficiency of production through internal recycling; and
- reduced operating and maintenance costs through standardization of technological standards.

The defensive approach stresses the likelihood of external 'attack' on TNCs that could be deflected or delayed if firms understand the relative importance in the public mind of environmental issues. This line of approach is similar to strategies adopted by domestic trade associations selling their public affairs services to their corporate clientele. The sustainable development version tends to claim that a good programme can

- avoid or postpone domestic and international regulations;
- minimize costs from civil liability suits;
- counter public criticism; and
- protect consumer markets from media exposés which can discourage consumer purchases and brand loyalty.

The joint appeal to governments is related to the campaign for 'self-regulation.' Rather than maintain an enforceable set of rules, it is argued that governments should use the market to reward financially good environmental behaviour. On the domestic level, incentives *above and beyond* legal requirements can be a powerful lever towards greater levels of environmental protection and regional economic growth. The core concept is that, with a base set of enforceable standards and regulations in place for all enterprises, the state could give incentives to environmentally sound business practices. It could finance supplemental environmental activities by business enterprises. It could induce special regional investment programmes through a variety of incentive programmes.[25] This appeals to firms not currently committed to sustainable development. The benefits of an incentive system on the international level might even be more lucrative as there are no base international environmental standards. It is a potentially large expenditure of resources by governments without a guarantee from firms to raise overall environmental performance. The approach financially rewards firms for doing 'good', but does not constrain them (or others) when they don't.

Despite its publicity through trade associations and leading firms, self-regulation has not spurred a trend towards improved TNC environmental performance. Most TNCs maintain a 'do-nothing' approach: comply with local and national environmental regulations, advertise environmental concerns when appropriate, but keep politically quiet on sustainable development.

Constructive corporate environmental initiatives involve a handful of firms. The former UNCTC estimated that there are now some 35,000 TNCs. At the same time that over 1,000 firms signed the ICC Charter, only 650 attended the major industrial pre-conference to Rio and some 200 TNCs co-operated with the UNCTC in its *Benchmark Corporate Environmental Survey*. Many of these firms were involved in only one major activity in the global public corporate policy arena from 1990 to 1992. One area of improvement, or a handful of case studies, are usually all that are cited in corporate claims to be 'sustainable'.

In practice, the best 'environmentally sound firms' are uni-dimensional or limited in the scope of their environmental efforts. Progressive environmental strategies mean that a TNC has safe worker protection rules *or* good products *or* good waste recycling *or* good environmental audits, but not a broad range of environmental and health and safety standards. The *Benchmark Corporate Environment Survey* identified twenty-two areas which could require corporate policies for environmental protection. The average respondent had publicly available statements in only five areas.[26]

Firms that do recognize environmental issues often treat sustainable development as just another social issue that requires periodic expressions of concern while avoiding any negative messages on the subject. A component of this strategy is to establish a specialized unit on environmental management in a relatively marginal position in the global structure of the firm. A third strategy is to carve out a segment of the growing green market, say green saving in industrial recycling, and extensively publicize the firm's environmental concerns. Only a very small minority re-examine the structures, markets, product mixes, and engineering practices to take on board environmental concerns. This could entail designing a management system that incorporates environmental change into the future growth of the main lines of business. Even then, most corporations are reluctant to have these changes audited by external observers or by external criteria.

When CERES released their *Valdez* Principles (since renamed the CERES Principles), they made it clear that information disclosure was going to be at the heart of the public debate. CERES distributed a detailed data collection form to major firms which were interested in becoming signatories to their principles. The data collection form asked for information over a five-year period on such items as energy efficiency of production lines, waste production per unit of output, and plans for future compliance with the Montreal Protocol on ozone-depleting chemicals. In response to the *Valdez* data collection plans and challenges to the veracity of corporate environmental claims, a number of trade associations have proposed that quantifiable and comparative environmental standards be drafted by industry.

The task is immensely complicated. Does one only measure 'emissions' from a plant but not the rate of use of 'inputs' from nature (for example natural resources)? Does one measure only 'popular' emissions like $CO_2$, $NO_X$, and $SO_2$, but not specialist chemical by-products? Does one only measure the environmental impact of manufacturing industries and not consider the agricultural and growing service industries? How does one assign values to the non-manufacturing or mining use of natural resources like scenic beauty and biological diversity that are generally outside the frame of contemporary accounting? With such diverse measurement questions, the task will take a good deal of technical study and political effort.

Yet even the effort to define measurable environmental standards has caused difficulties for a significant number of TNCs who 'committed' themselves to a green world without making real changes throughout the firm. It also causes difficulties for environmental corporate leaders seeking to attract non-committed firms who now reasonably wonder what will be asked of them to document if they 'sign on' to corporate sustainable development campaigns.

In spite of these cautions, the debate today comes down to who should author disclosure standards—trade associations, individual firms, professional associations, governments, activists, or a combination of the above; and who should carry out the audits—the firm itself, external examiners, or the government. The precedent from the corporate accounting world is that the state sets the basic ground rules and allows specialized professional bodies, like the Financial Advisory Standards Board (FASB) in the USA, to draft detailed rules of accounting and reporting. In the environmental field, there is not yet a recognized body with the capacity to take on this task and command respect from the industry, government, and the general public. With regard to verification of data, the 'self-regulation' advocates generally oppose 'external' audits, which generally mean audits by independent corporate service firms. The tension, then, is between the need for publicly reliable data and the anxiety that a professional body might undertake verification of environmentally oriented data.[27]

Preoccupation with self-measurement of environmental impacts and provable assertions to be a good 'green' enterprise leaves little attention on the measurement of the other side of sustainable development, the development component. To date no trade association has recommended formulating comparative standards to assess the social and economic development impacts and benefits of commercial activity.

## Who Pays For Environmental Resource Extraction and Depletion?

In addition to the arguments regarding the disclosure of information, the most complex argument affecting the debate on TNCs and sustainable development is the inclusion of environmental costs in overall production costs or, more generally, the internalization of environmental costs.

There is general agreement that environmental costs need to be internalized. In non-technical language, the economic impacts of business on the environment has historically been left out of the firm's costs of production. The costs of cleaning up waste, for example, were previously passed on to the community. Now it is expected that these and other environmental costs are made internal to the firm's production accounting. This view appears in—or is assumed by—every major policy statement on the economy and the environment by industry associations, developed-country governments, and UN agencies. But there is no agreement on how that should happen while maintaining the current competitive structures of the market system. Proponents of the free market vociferously assert that the market can take care of the problem, without acknowledging that the market has not done so in the past. What is missing is an agreement on the methods needed to 'alter' the market without undermining the independence of the market-place.

Objectively there is a series of major avenues using market mechanisms that can internalize costs. These are:

- an effective, enforced regulatory system that sets costs for previously free goods (land damaged by waste disposal is given a clean-up cost);
- a civil liability system that 'punishes' firms/executives for not taking care of health, safety, and the environment (for example, health damages are paid by the polluter);
- a corporate accounting system that reflects 'real' environmental costs during the internal decision-making process (for example, recycling costs are included in budget forecasts);
- an eco-labelling system that encourages consumers to make purchases on the basis of the product's environmental impact (so that consumer purchasing choices could penalize unacceptable environmental business decisions);
- a national tax system based on the use of natural resources rather than on income flows (taxes could be charged on the consumption of non-renewable resources rather than

on income flows);
- a mandated requirement that manufacturers have a responsibility for their products' full life-cycle uses (for example, costs for a public recycling plan are paid for by the manufacturer); and
- an end to government programmes that underprice natural resources and therefore encourage their over-use or misuse (costs for soil depletion are not subsidized by agricultural programmes).

With the exception of the last item, these proposals are frequently criticized even by the corporate environmental leadership as unacceptable on other economic and political grounds. It is often difficult to have a good assessment of these mechanisms because they clearly have significant short-term costs, and generally can result in unpredictable consequences for individual firms and sectors. The business community wants to incorporate a share of environmental costs—so as to equalize the corporate burden on a sound environmental pricing system—but wishes to avoid the associated ideological costs that could be used to incorporate environmental costs into the price of goods.

The current deadlock, then, is that using market signals to convey environment and development costs is well accepted, but the specific available mechanisms are generally scorned as unworkable or impractical. This dilemma needs to be faced. Either the market is self-correcting with self-regulation and self-reporting, or some significant external intervention by the state, by consumers, or by workers needs to take place to prompt the internalization of environmental and natural resources prices into the cost of production.

## Conclusion

The confrontation of issues around the theme of corporate responsibility raised in the preparation for the UNCED will continue for a good number of years. The battle for a definition of an acceptable international corporate behaviour and the precision of standards for environmental disclosure will continue largely in the media, in legislative bodies, and in court systems. The battleground on a minimum set of international environmental regulations after Rio will shift primarily to fora drafting the protocols to the climate, biodiversity, and waste conventions, and to campaigns by sustainable development NGOs based on their Rio agreements. Efforts to increase voluntary corporate international environmental management practices and systems will be reflected in increased management seminars, training of environmental auditors, and specialized trade media, and in the further exposés by journalists and NGOs in developing countries. Intra-corporate leadership battles will be reshaped in light of the post-Rio institutional discussions at the UN and the individual assessments within the industrial associations of the durability of public interest in sustainable development.

Following the structure of issues raised in UNCTC's *Recommendations . . . on Transnational Corporations and Sustainable Development*, one can also expect further developments in the methods for global corporate management of large industrial enterprises and in the effort to minimize risk and hazard from products, processes, and services from the manufacturing, mining, and consumer sectors. One can also expect that environmentally sounder consumption patterns will be supported by a broader range of corporate products and services. What is not so clear is the time-scale for these changes or the extent of their implementation by all international investors and technology suppliers. It does seem, however, that efforts for greater use of full-cost environmental pricing and accounting, and for greater acceptance of international standards are less likely in the near future.

With such a significant share of world investment and technology resource involving TNCs, there remains a compelling need to address a range of issues related to the environmental activities of these firms. From a UN perspective it is, of course, best if this were done through negotiation and consensus-building involving all the major stakeholders in the process. Over the coming years public reaction to future 'Bhopal-events' may create opportunities for enhanced attention to the general practices of international investment and technology acquisition. Individual governmental bodies, particularly the EU, may undertake efforts that encourage TNCs to become stronger advocates of a more even international environmental playing-field. It is reasonable to expect that some of the contradictions in the current debate, for example, the now recognized need for internationally recognized, quantifiable measurements of environmental impact, could open avenues for a broader reconsideration of a variety of environmental and development practices of TNCs.

Furthermore, as the post-Rio process starts to gain momentum, some of the principles and tasks articulated in *Agenda 21* could raise the overall level of environmental commitment and discussion in the corporate world. While the high-visibility opportunity of the Rio conference for a major new breakthrough was lost, other international forums may allow more incremental developments on these themes.

## Annex. Review of *Agenda 21* on TNC-related issues

This Review was produced by the UN Centre on Transnational Corporations in a document, *Followup to the United Nations Conference on Environment and Development as Related to Transnational Corporations: Report of the Secretary General to the Commission on Transnational Corporations*, April 1993 (E/C. 10/1993/14). It organizes the relevant elements of *Agenda 21* under thematic categories established in the UNCTC document: *Transnational Corporations and Sustainable Development: Recommendations of the Executive Director* (E/C.10/1992/2).

A. *Agenda 21* states that *transnational corporations* along with other industrial actors should:

*in the area of global corporate environmental management*:
1. introduce policies and commitments to adopt equivalent or not less stringent standards of operation as in the country of origin;
2. recognize environmental management as among the highest corporate priorities and as a key determinant to sustainable development;
3. be encouraged to establish world-wide corporate policies on sustainable development;
4. ensure responsible and ethical management of processes from the point of view of health, safety, and environmental aspects;
5. establish environmental management systems, including environmental auditing of production or distribution sites;
6. strengthen partnerships to implement the principles and criteria for sustainable development;[28]
7. have a special role and interest in promoting co-operation in technology transfer and in building a trained human resource pool and infrastructure in host countries;
8. share their environmental management experiences with the local authorities, national governments, and international organizations;
9. report annually on their environmental record as well as on their use of energy and natural resources;

*in the area of environmentally sound production and consumption patterns:*
10. play a major role in reducing impacts on resource use and the environment through more efficient produc-tion processes, preventive strategies, cleaner production technologies, and procedures throughout the product life-cycle;
11. integrate cleaner production approaches into the design of products and management practices;
12. arrange for environmentally sound technologies to be available to affiliates in developing countries;
13. increase research and development of environ-mentally sound technologies and environmental management systems in collaboration with academia, scientific/engineering establishments, and indigenous peoples;
14. establish clean production demonstration projects/networks by sector and by country;
15. integrate cleaner production principles and case studies into training programmes and organize environmental training programmes for the private sector and other groups in developing countries;
16. consider establishing environmental partnership schemes with small- and medium-sized enterprises;

*in the area of risk and hazard minimization:*
17. undertake research into the phase-out of those processes that pose the greatest environmental risk based on the hazardous wastes generated;
18. encourage affiliates to modify procedures in order to reflect local ecological conditions;

19. provide data for substances produced that are needed specifically for the assessment of potential risks to human health and the environment;
20. develop emergency response procedures and on-site and off-site emergency response plans;
21. apply a 'responsible care' approach to chemical products, taking into account the total life-cycle of such products;
22. be transparent in their operations and provide relevant information to the community that might be affected by the generation and management of hazardous waste;
23. adopt, on a voluntary basis, community right-to-know programmes based on international guide-lines, including sharing information on the causes of accidental releases or potential releases and the means to prevent them;
24. make available to governments the information necessary to maintain inventories of hazardous wastes, treatment/disposal sites, contaminated sites that require rehabilitation, and information on exposure and risks;
25. report annually on routine emissions of toxic chemicals to the environment even in the absence of host country requirements;
26. phase out, where appropriate, and dispose of any banned chemicals that are still in stock or in use, in an environmentally sound manner;

*in the area of full-cost environmental accounting:*
27. be invited to participate at the international level in assessing the practical implementation of moving towards greater reliance on pricing systems that internalize environmental costs;
28. co-operate in developing methodologies for the valuation of non-marketed natural resources and the standardization of data collection;
29. work towards the development and implementation of concepts and methodologies for the internalization of environmental costs into accounting and pricing mechanisms;
30. work with governments to identify and implement an appropriate mix of economic instruments and normative measures such as laws, legislation, and standards;

*in the area of environmental conventions, standards and guide-lines:*
31. develop an internationally agreed-upon code of principles for the management of trade in chemicals;

*in the area of post-UNCED follow-up:*
32. be full participants in the implementation and evaluation of activities related to *Agenda 21.*

B. Further, *Agenda 21* states that *transnational corporations* and other corporate actors should co-operate with Governments and international organizations which are asked to

*in the area of environmental conventions, standards, and guide-lines:*
1. consider adopting policies based on accepted pro-ducers' liability principles as well as precautionary, anticipatory, and life-cycle approaches to chemical management, covering manufacturing, trade, transport, use, and disposal;
2. adopt regulatory and non-regulatory measures to identify and minimize exposure to toxic chemicals by replacing them with less-toxic substitutes;
3. phase out those chemicals that pose unreasonable and otherwise unmanageable risks and those that are toxic, persistent, and bio-accumulative, the use of which cannot be adequately controlled;
4. develop guide-lines and policies for manufacturers, importers, and others to disclose toxicity information declaring risks and emergency response arrange-ments;
5. co-operate in developing guide-lines on public communications on chemical risks;

6. co-operate in developing common criteria to determine which chemicals are suitable candidates for concerted risk-reduction activities;

*in the area of risk and hazard minimization:*
7. undertake concerted activities to reduce risks from toxic chemicals, taking into account the entire life-cycle of the chemicals;
8. minimize or eliminate as far as feasible risks from the storage of outdated chemicals;
9. develop procedures for monitoring the application of the 'cradle-to-grave' approach, including environ-mental audits;
10. generate the data necessary for hazard assessment of toxic chemicals;
11. promote mechanisms to increase collaboration in risk assessment of chemicals and related processes;
12. give high priority to hazard assessment of chemicals, that is, of their intrinsic properties as the appropriate basis for risk assessment;
13. launch a project on the harmonization of classi-fication of chemicals and compatible labelling systems for chemicals using all official UN languages and pictograms;
14. prepare an inventory of hazardous-waste production sites;

*in the area of global corporate environmental management:*
15. conduct environmental audits of existing industries to improve in-plant regimes for the management of hazardous wastes;
16. improve databases and information systems on toxic chemicals, such as emission inventory programmes;
17. establish a technical exchange programme to produce a core of trained personnel with each participating country; and
18. establish technical co-operation with, and provide information to developing countries, especially those with a shortage of technical expertise.

## Notes and References

This paper was written with Dr Riva Krut, co-director in Benchmark Environmental Consulting.

1. Respondents chose, as causes of environmental problems, between overpopulation, home government, individual waste, lack of education, business and industry, and technology. Technology was ranked second. George H. Gallup Memorial Survey (1992), *The Health of the Planet Survey: A Preliminary Report on Attitudes Toward the Environment and Economic Growth Measured by Surveys of Citizens in 22 Nations to Date* (Princeton, NJ: George H. Gallup International Institute), ii. 16–17.
2. UNCTC (1990), *Transnational Corporations and Climate Change* (New York: United Nations).
3. In Feb. 1992 UNCTC was reorganized into a Division on Transnational Corporations and Management in the Department of Economic and Social Development (DESD), New York. In Jan. 1993 the section was reorganized again into a Programme on Transnational Corporations in United Nations Conference on Trade and Development (UNCTAD), Geneva.
4. Before starting with this analysis, I should make clear that I served as the chief of the environment unit of the UNCTC, a body that was generally regarded with scepticism by the international business community.
5. United Nations Centre on Transnational Corporations (1990), *Criteria for Sustainable Development Management* (New York: United Nations).
6. United Nations Commission on Trade and Development (1993), *Environmental Management in Transnational Corporations: Report of the Benchmark Corporate Environmental Survey* (Geneva: United Nations).

7. United Nations Commission on Transnational Corporations (1994), *Options to Increase the Flow of Environmentally Sound Technologies to Developing Countries on Favourable Terms* (Geneva: United Nations).

8. United Nations Centre on Transnational Corporations (1990), *Transnational Corporations and the Disclosure of Information on Hazards and Risks* (New York: United Nations); United Nations Department of Economic and Social Development (1992), *Emerging Trends in the Development of International Environmental Law at the Regional and Global Level: Implications for Transnational Corporations* (New York: United Nations).

9. United Nations Centre on Transnational Corporations (1991), *Transnational Corporations and Sustainable Development: Recommendations of the Executive Director. Report of the Secretary-General E/C.10/1992/2* (New York: United Nations), subsequently referred to as 'Recommendations'.

10. These factions take temporary allies from academic institutions, mainstream environmental organizations, and UN system agencies. For example, the International Chamber of Commerce has links with the United Nations Environment Programme's Industry and Environment Office in Paris; the Business Council for Sustainable Development worked with the Corporate Conservation Council and the Stern School of Business, New York University, in preparing for a joint US–Japanese chief executive officers' meeting on the environment and with the new Canadian think-tank, the International Institute for Sustainable Development, in preparing a report on corporate disclosure practices (*Business Strategy for Sustainable Development: Leadership and Accountability for the '90s*, offset, no date ).

11. The *Valdez* Principles were formulated in the USA by the Coalition for Environmentally Responsible Economics (CERES), a group of social investors and environmental leaders, following the grounding of the Exxon tanker *Valdez* in Alaskan waters. The principles have been renamed the Ceres Principles.

12. The imperative of the ICC Charter is not clear from its drafting. The Charter contains a series of infinitive clauses (to cause . . . , to design . . .) without a subject (executives, industry, TNCs, manufacturing firms) and without a main verb (shall announce, will require, may consider, might recommend). This grammatical vagueness can allow a large number of firms and trade associations to assert accurately that they are in conformity to the Charter.

13. International Chamber of Commerce (1992), *From Ideas to Action* (Paris: ICC).

14. Keidanren (1991), *Keidanren Global Environmental Charter* (Tokyo).

15. The new executive director of Business Council on Sustainable Development, Hugh Faulkner, had recently been replaced as the executive director of the International Chamber of Commerce.

16. Steven Schmidheiny (1992), *Changing Course* (Cambridge, Mass: MIT Press).

17. e.g. Stephen Schmidheiny, chairman of the Business Council for Sustainable Development: 'the multinational companies are among the few private organizations powerful enough to influence international environmental and development problems. They often take a longer term and more international view than governments themselves.' 'Our Common Enterprise', *Development*, 1992: 2 (Journal of the Society for International Development, Rome).

18. For example, the ICC three-day conference in Rio omitted any direct discussion of the future tasks expected from national industries or TNCs in *Agenda 21*. The meeting provided TNCs with an opportunity to declare their commitment to 'sustainable development' without clarifying the ways in which they could use their considerable resources to implement a sustainable future.

19. Gallup, *Health of the Planet Survey* (n. 1 above), table 11.

20. In the questionnaire, the largest transnational firms were asked to rank the potential role for the UN system in terms of what would benefit the firm most. Choices included reducing the differences in national regulations, setting international policy guide-lines, recognizing the good leadership of individual firms, advising developing countries on inspection systems, serving as a potential neutral partner to resolve environmental conflicts involving foreign investors, and distributing publicity on industry standards.

21. During the Global Forum, NGOs negotiated various 'treaties' reflecting their interest in key topics of the UNCED agenda. Amongst the general principles in the NGO treaty on transnationals are that these enterprises 'should be held to the highest environmental, health, safety, and labour standards in all countries of operation', and that 'the precautionary approach, which places the burden of proof of no harm on the potential polluter rather than on the environment or potential victims, should govern TNC practices'. (Rio de Janeiro, no date), mimeo.

22. The EC declined to participate in one of the pre-session weekend reviews of the Recommendations; Japan opposed concepts that even the Japanese industrial trade association, Keidanren, had adopted; the US mis-characterized the Recommendations in an intentionally pejorative fashion, calling them a 'regulatory system'; Sweden and Norway introduced text based on the Recommendations then withdrew it two days later; and Canada hosted a series of meetings to co-ordinate the impact of industry representatives on the negotiations.

23. The two NGO newspapers, *Crosscurrents* and *Earth Summit Times*, carried accounts of the NGO and government interaction during the Fourth Preparatory Committee meeting.

24. Both of these lines of arguments were recently used in the background paper for a high-level meeting between US and Japanese chief executive officers on sustainable development sponsored by Business Council for Sustainable Development, International Chamber of Commerce, and the Corporate Conservation Council. Thomas Gladwin (1992), *Building the Sustainable Corporation: Creating Environmental Sustainability and Corporate Advantage*, commissioned for the Synergy 92 Conference of the National Wildlife Federation-Corporate Conservation Council (offset, Washington, DC).

25. Such environmental subsidies may no longer be allowed under GATT.

26. This is dealt with at length in the UNCTAD *Benchmark Survey*.

27. Norsk Hydro does produce an annual environment and development report through the use of internal and external examiners. Norsk Hydro's report is available in Norwegian and English.

28. UNCTC, Criteria for Sustainable Development Management, 1989.

# Section II: References

**International Agreements on Environment and Development**

# Convention on Environmental Impact Assessment in a Transboundary Context (Espoo Convention)

## Objectives
- to enhance international co-operation in assessing environmental impacts, in particular in a transboundary context;
- to promote environmentally sound and sustainable development;
- to support the development of anticipatory policies and of measures preventing, mitigating, and monitoring significant adverse environmental impacts in general and more specifically in a transboundary context;
- to promote measures taken at an early planning stage of proposed activities aimed at preventing potentially harmful environmental impacts, in particular those with a transboundary dimension, and to strive towards convergence of relevant national policies and practices;
- to provide for notification and consultation among states concerned on all major projects under consideration that are likely to cause significant adverse environmental impact across boundaries;
- to promote public information and public participation in relevant decision-making processes.

## Scope
*Legal scope*
Open to member countries of the United Nations Economic Commission for Europe (UN/ECE), the European Union (EU), and other European States having consultative status with the UN/ECE.

*Geographic scope*
Regional. UN/ECE region (Europe and North America).

## Time and place of adoption
25 February 1991, Espoo.

## Entry into force
Not yet in force. Enters into force ninety days after the deposit of 16 instruments of ratification, acceptance, approval, or accession.

## Status of participation
6 Parties, by 15 September 1994. 25 Signatories, including the European Union, without ratification, acceptance, or approval.

## Affiliated protocols, annexes, and organizations
The Convention also contains seven *Appendices* (see rules and standards below) which form an integral part of the Convention.

The *Secretary-General of the United Nations* acts as depositary.

The *Executive Secretary of the UN/ECE* carries out the Secretariat functions.

## Secretariat
UN/ECE, Environment and Human Settlements Division (ENHS), Palais des Nations, CH-1211 Geneva 10, Switzerland
*Telephone*:  +41-22-9171234
*Telefax*:  +41-22-9070107

## Finance
Not applicable.

## Rules and standards
The Convention stipulates measures and procedures to prevent, control, or reduce any significant adverse effect on the environment, particularly any transboundary effect on human health and safety, flora, fauna, soil, water, climate, landscape, and historical monuments, which is likely to be caused by a proposed economic activity or any major change to an existing economic activity listed in *Appendix 1*.

Appendix 1 covers 17 groups of activities, such as nuclear and thermal power stations, road and railway construction, chemical installations, waste-disposal facilities, oil refineries, oil and gas pipelines, mining, steel production, pulp and paper manufacturing, and the construction of dams and reservoirs.

Concerned Parties may apply the provisions of the Convention also to other activities (general guidance is included in *Appendix III* for this purpose), and enter into bilateral or multilateral agreements.

Parties will have to establish an environmental impact assessment (EIA) procedure involving public participation and the preparation of EIA documentation described in *Appendix II*. An EIA has to be carried out before the decision is taken to authorize or undertake a proposed activity listed in *Appendix I*.

Parties will also endeavour to ensure that the EIA principles are applied to policies, plans, and programmes. A country under the jurisdiction of which a proposed activity is envisaged will have to notify accordingly any country likely to be affected by it as early as possible and no later than when informing its own public about the proposed activity. The country of origin has to transmit to the affected country or countries the relevant EIA documentation on the proposed activity and its possible transboundary effects, for comments.

Arrangements will have to be made in order to ensure that the public, including the public of the affected country or countries, is given the opportunity to submit comments on or objections to the proposed activity.

Consultations may be held between the countries concerned in respect of possible alternatives to the proposed activity, including the no-action alternative and possible measures to mitigate adverse effects. Affected countries will be informed about the final decision on the proposed activity and the reasons and considerations on which it is based. Post-project analysis may be undertaken in order to monitor compliance with the conditions set out in the authorization of the activity and the effectiveness of mitigation measures.

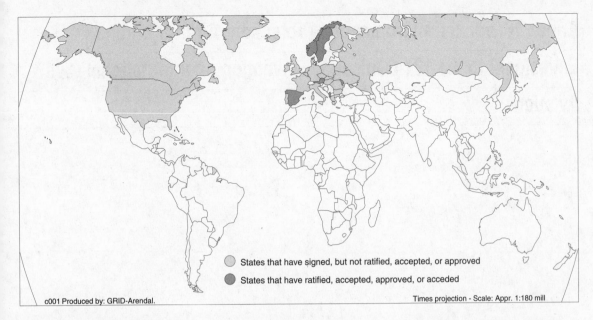

States that have signed, but not ratified, accepted, or approved

States that have ratified, accepted, approved, or acceded

c001 Produced by: GRID-Arendal.                    Times projection - Scale: Appr. 1:180 mill

## Monitoring/implementation

*Review procedure*
The Parties to the Convention shall keep under continuous review the implementation of the Convention and with this purpose in mind:
• review the policies and methodological approaches to EIA by the Parties with a view to further improving EIA procedures in a transboundary context;
• exchange information regarding experience gained in concluding and implementing bilateral and multilateral agreements;
• seek, where appropriate, the services of competent international bodies and scientific committees in methodological and technical aspects.

When a country considers that it may be affected by a significant adverse trans-boundary impact of a proposed activity, and when no notification has taken place, the concerned countries shall, at the request of the affected country, exchange sufficient information to enable discussions to take place on whether there is likely to be a significant adverse trans-boundary impact.

If those countries agree that there is likely to be a significant adverse trans-boundary impact, the provisions of the Convention will apply accordingly. If those countries cannot agree whether there is likely to be a significant adverse trans-boundary impact, any such country may submit that question to an inquiry

commission in accordance with *Annex IV* to the Convention to advice on the likelihood of significant adverse trans-boundary impact, unless they agree on another method of settling this question.

*Dispute-settlement mechanisms*
If a dispute arises between two or more Parties about the interpretation or application of the Convention, they shall seek a solution by negotiation or by any other method of dispute settlement acceptable to the parties to the dispute.

The Parties may submit the dispute to the International Court of Justice or to an arbitration procedure set out in Appendix VII.

## Decision-making

*Political bodies*
In their Resolution on Environmental Impact Assessment in a Transboundary Context, adopted by the Senior Advisers to UN/ECE Governments on Environmental and Water Problems at their fourth session in Espoo on 25 February 1991, the Signatories to the Convention decided to strive for its entry into force as soon as possible and to seek to implement it to the maximum extent possible pending its entry into force.

Three meetings of the Signatories to the Convention, open to all UN/ECE member countries, were held in 1991, 1992, and 1994. These meetings reviewed actions taken by Signatories to

implement the Convention pending its entry into force, considered legal, administrative, and methodological aspects of its practical application, discussed ways and means of strengthening the capability of future Parties, particularly countries with economies in transition, to comply with the obligations under the Convention, and establish a work programme.

Once the Convention has entered into force, the *Conference of the Parties* will meet annually in order to review national policies and strategies promoting EIA, consider relevant methodological and technical aspects, and exchange information regarding experience gained in concluding ad implementing relevant bilateral and multilateral agreements.

Where appropriate, the meeting will consider and, where necessary, adopt proposals for amendments to the Convention. Agreement on the proposed amendment should be reached by consensus. If no agreement is reached, the amendment shall, as a last resort, be adopted by a three-quarter majority vote of the Parties present and voting at the meeting.

## Publications
• ECE Environmental Series;
• *Environmental Conventions Elaborated under the Auspices of the UN/ECE*, 1992.

# Annex 16, vol. II (Environmental Protection: Aircraft Engine Emissions) to the 1944 Chicago Convention on International Civil Aviation

## Objectives
- to provide international standardization, through certification procedures, of limitations on aircraft and engine emissions in the vicinity of airports;
- to ensure that replacements with newly designed engines employ the best available emissions-reduction technology.

## Scope
*Legal scope*
Membership restricted to International Civil Aviation Organization (ICAO) members. A Convention providing for the establishment of ICAO was signed at Chicago, 7 December 1944. The organization came into existence on 4 April 1947, after 26 states had ratified the Convention.

*Geographic scope*
Global.

## Time and place of adoption
30 June 1981, Montreal.

## Entry into force
18 February 1982. Entry into force of ICAO Annexes is facilitated by a 'tacit consent' procedure, enabling dissenting countries to notify their differences within a specified time-limit, after which the Annexes become generally applicable.

## Status of participation
183 member States, by 7 October 1994. All ICAO member States are potentially involved, although in practice only those ICAO member States manufacturing aircraft and engines are directly involved.

## Affiliated protocols, annexes, and organizations
Annex 16 was originally drafted by a Committee of Experts nominated by member States plus observers from international organizations. Annexes to the Chicago Convention on Civil Aviation are adopted and revised by the ICAO Council upon recommendation by the expert committee (see below).

The most recent amendment entered into force on 11 November 1993. This amendment is a significant change in that it was an increase of 20 per cent in the stringency of the nitrogen oxides emissions standards for future production engines.

All States have the opportunity to comment on the provisions before adoption or to disapprove them and file differences. (Article 38 of the Convention).

Related instrument is the Annex 16, vol. I (Environmental Protection: Aircraft Noise).

Administrative functions under the Chicago Convention are performed by the ICAO secretariat in Montreal.

*Co-ordination with related instruments*
There is currently no co-ordination with drafting work regarding other international agreements or instruments.

## Secretariat
International Civil Aviation Organization (ICAO),
1000 Sherbrooke Street West,
Montreal,
Quebec H3A 2R2,
Canada
*Telephone*: +1-514-2858221
*Telefax*: +1-514-2884772
*E-mail*: yulcaya (sitatex)

*Secretary-General (ICAO)*
Dr Philippe Rochat.

*Chief, Public Information*
Mr Hutton G. Archer.

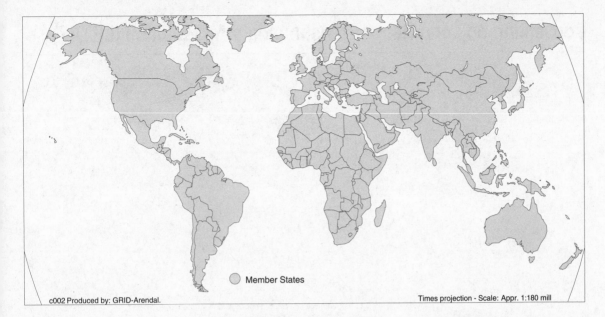

Member States

c002 Produced by: GRID-Arendal.

Times projection - Scale: Appr. 1:180 mill

## Finance

*Budget*
The Annex does not provide for regular meetings and programme activities. Costs of meetings, documentation, and secretariat services are covered by the regular ICAO budget.

*Special funds*
None.

## Rules and standards

Member States are not required to report compliance, only non-compliance.

## Monitoring/implementation

*Review procedure*
The objectives are considered to have been met in that all newly designed aircraft engines meet the requirements of Annex 16, although a number of countries have filed notifications under Article 38 of the Convention regarding different national standards.

Notifications of national differences in standards are recorded and regularly communicated to all members, by way of supplements to Annexes. With regard to Annex 16, vol. II, 11 member States had notified national differences, 23 had reported conformity. The remaining members are presumed to be tacitly conforming. The following States have notified ICAO of differences, by October 1991: Australia, Canada, Germany, Italy, Japan, Malawi, Netherlands, Saudi Arabia, Singapore, the United Kingdom, and the USA. These notifications are made public.

Potential factors affecting compliance include technical difficulties in meeting the requirements, disagreement with the need for specific aspects of the requirement, and the cost of compliance testing. A problem of major concern to developing countries is the potential for unilateral or regional operating restrictions on older aircraft not conforming to Annex 16.

Continuous review of Annex 16 by the expert committee and the ICAO Council takes into account inputs from manufacturers, operators, airport management, etc. The flexible ICAO procedure for amendment of technical annexes allows timely adjustment.

*Monitoring*
No observations or inspections by the Convention as such.

*Trade sanctions*
None.

*Dispute-settlement mechanisms*
Disputes are normally considered by the ICAO Council, with possible recourse to international arbitration or adjudication.

## Decision-making

*Political bodies*
The *Assembly*, composed of delegates from all the Contracting States, meets every three years. The *Council*, the executive organ, is composed of 33 representatives of Contracting States elected by the Assembly. It is in session almost continuously. The Council elects its own president.

*Scientific/technical bodies*
Four *ad hoc* meetings of expert committees on Annex 16 have been held since 1978. The expert committee reviews, refines, and updates the provisions as necessary.

## Publications

The ICAO secretariat publishes current activities in *ICAO Journal* and, in addition, a wide range of information materials for government and public distribution.

# Convention on Long-Range Transboundary Air Pollution (LRTAP)

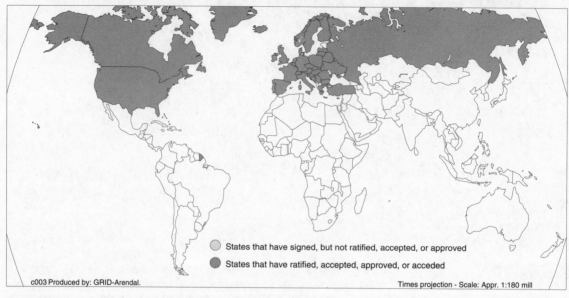

States that have signed, but not ratified, accepted, or approved

States that have ratified, accepted, approved, or acceded

c003 Produced by: GRID-Arendal.    Times projection - Scale: Appr. 1:180 mill

## Convention on Long-Range Transboundary Air Pollution (LRTAP)

### Objectives
• to protect man and his environment against air pollution;
• to limit and, as far as possible, gradually reduce and prevent air pollution, including long-range transboundary air pollution.

### Scope
*Legal scope*
Open to member States of the United Nations Economic Commission for Europe (UN/ECE), the European Community, and other European States having consultative status with the UN/ECE.

*Geographic scope*
Regional. Europe and North America.

### Time and place of adoption
13 November 1979, Geneva.

### Entry into force
16 March 1983.

### Status of participation
39 Parties, including the European Community, by 15 September 1994. 2

Signatories without ratification, accession, acceptance, or approval.

### Affiliated protocols, annexes, and organizations
• *Protocol to the Convention on Long-Range Transboundary Air Pollution on Long-term Financing of the Co-operative Programme for Monitoring and Evaluation of the Long-Range Transmission of Air Pollutants in Europe (EMEP), Geneva, 28 September 1984.* Entered into force on 28 January 1988. 35 Parties, including the European Community, by 15 September 1994. No Signatories without ratification, approval, or acceptance. The basic objective of the Protocol is:
• to share the costs of a monitoring programme which forms the backbone for review and assessment of relevant air pollution in Europe in the light of agreements on emission reduction. EMEP has three main components: collection of emission data for $SO_2$, $NO_x$, VOCs, and other air pollutants; measurement of air and precipitation quality; and modelling of atmospheric dispersion.
• *Protocol to the Convention on Long-Range Transboundary Air Pollution on Further Reduction of Sulphur Emissions*

*(1994 Sulphur Protocol), Oslo, 14 June 1994.* [Not yet in force.] No Parties, by 15 September 1994. 26 Signatories, including the European Community, without ratification, accession, acceptance, or approval. Enters into force on the ninetieth day after the deposit of the sixteenth instrument of ratification, approval, or accession. The Protocol follows the former Sulphur Protocol, adopted in Helsinki on 8 July 1985 which entered into force on 2 September 1987. The basic objective of the first Protocol was to reduce the annual sulphur emissions or the transboundary fluxes by at least 30 per cent as soon as possible and at the latest by 1993, using 1980 levels as the basis for calculation of reductions. The basic objective of the new 1994 Sulphur Protocol is:
• to set individual targets for each country in accordance with the contribution their sulphur emissions make to exceedances of 'critical loads'; the rates of sulphur deposition which ecosystems and other receptors can tolerate in the long term without suffering damage.
• to achieve a '60 per cent gap closure' between current sulphur deposition and critical loads in all but the most acid-sensitive regions of Europe.
• *Protocol to the Convention on Long-*

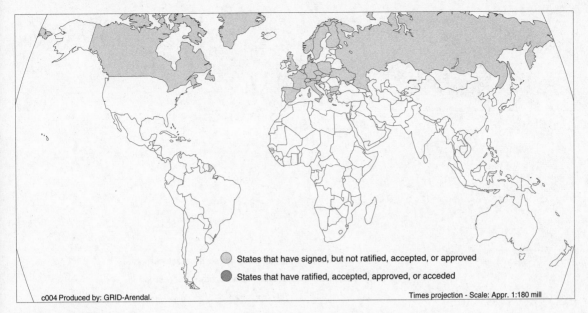

States that have signed, but not ratified, accepted, or approved

States that have ratified, accepted, approved, or acceded

c004 Produced by: GRID-Arendal.                                                Times projection - Scale: Appr. 1:180 mill

## Sulphur Protocol

*Range Transboundary Air Pollution concerning the Control of Emissions of Nitrogen Oxides or their Transboundary Fluxes (NO$_x$ Protocol), Sofia, 31 October 1988.* Entered into force on 14 February 1991. 24 Parties, including the European Community, by 15 September 1994. 4 Signatories, without ratification, accession, acceptance, or approval. The basic objective of the Protocol is:
• to take effective measures to control and/or reduce the Parties' national annual emissions of nitrogen oxides or their transboundary fluxes so that these, at the latest by 31 December 1994, do not exceed their national annual emissions of such substances for 1987 or any previous year to be specified upon signature.
• *Protocol to the Convention on Long-Range Transboundary Air Pollution concerning the Control of Emissions of Volatile Organic Compounds or their Transboundary Fluxes (VOC Protocol), Geneva, 18 November 1991.* [Not yet in force.] 9 Parties, by 15 September 1994. 14 Signatories, including the European Community, without ratification, accession, acceptance, or approval. Enters into force on the ninetieth day after the deposit of the sixteenth instrument of ratification, acceptance, approval, or accession. The basic objective of the Protocol is:

• to control and reduce the emissions of Volatile Organic Compounds (VOCs) in order to reduce the transboundary fluxes and the fluxes of the resulting secondary photochemical oxidant products so as to protect human health and the environment from adverse effects.
    This Protocol offers flexibility to the Parties, which is a completely new feature of this type of international agreement. There are not only options to selection of base year, but also for designation of particular areas within a country in which the reduction obligation apply, as well as for freeze instead of reduction in countries with very low total emissions.
    The *Secretary-General of the United Nations* acts as depositary.
    *United Nations Economic Commission for Europe (UN/ECE)*, through the Air Pollution Section of the UN/ECE Environment and Human Settlements Division plays a central role for the elaboration of the Convention and its protocols and for follow-up action to implement them.

*Co-ordination with related instruments*
Drafting work on revised or new protocols are co-ordinated through the ECE secretariat, with other competent bodies, especially as regards airborne pollution of adjacent regional sea areas,

e.g. the Baltic Sea, through the Helsinki Commission (see this section) and the North Sea, through the Oslo and Paris Commission (see this section).

## Secretariat

UN/ECE Environment and Human Settlements Division (ENHS), Palais des Nations, CH-1211 Geneva 10, Switzerland
*Telephone*:         +41-22-9171234
*Telefax*:              +41-22-9070107

*Deputy Director (ENHS Division)*
G. de Bellis.

*Number of staff*
6 professionals and 2 support staff (Oct. 1994).

## Finance

Costs of meetings, documentation, and secretariat services are covered by the regular budget of UN/ECE. International co-ordination costs for the EMEP programme are financed by mandatory contributions from the Parties to a UN-administered trust fund and were approximately $US1 million for 1990. Costs of other co-operative programmes are covered by voluntary contributions of participating Parties.

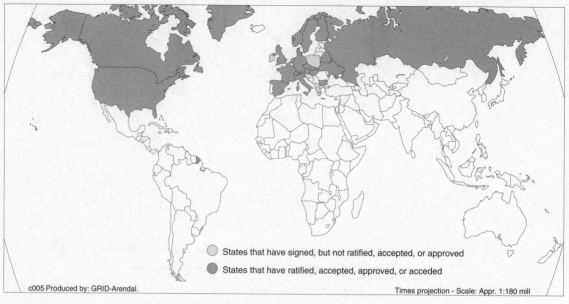

States that have signed, but not ratified, accepted, or approved

States that have ratified, accepted, approved, or acceded

c005 Produced by: GRID-Arendal.                    Times projection - Scale: Appr. 1:180 mill

## NO$_x$ Protocol

*Budget*
The actual budget for the EMEP programme was $US1,797,600 for 1993,
$US1,882,915 for 1994, and is
$US1,900,915 for 1995.

## Rules and standards

Parties are committed to:
• by means of exchanges of information,
consultation, research, and monitoring,
develop without undue delay policies
and strategies which shall serve as a
means of combating the discharge of air
pollutants;
• exchange information on and review
their policies, scientific activities, and
technical measures aimed at combating,
as far as possible, the discharge of air
pollutants which may have adverse
effects, thereby contributing to the
reduction of air pollution, including
long-range transboundary air pollution;
• develop the best policies and strategies, including air-quality management
systems, and as part of them, control
measures compatible with balanced
development, in particular by using the
'best available technology' (BAT) that is
economically feasible and low- or non-
waste technology.

The sulphur emission reductions in the
following schedule give the obligations
referred to in the new *1994 Sulphur
Protocol* (% sulphur emissions reductions taking 1980 as the base year):

| Year | 2000 | 2005 | 2010 |
|---|---|---|---|
| Austria | 80 | | |
| Belarus | 38 | 46 | 50 |
| Begium | 70 | 72 | 74 |
| Bulgaria | 33 | 40 | 45 |
| Canada | 30 | | |
| Croatia | 11 | 17 | 22 |
| Czech | | | |
| Republic | 50 | 60 | 72 |
| Denmark | 80 | | |
| Finland | 80 | | |
| France | 74 | 77 | 78 |
| Germany | 83 | 87 | |
| Greece | 0 | 3 | 4 |
| Hungary | 45 | 50 | 60 |
| Ireland | 30 | | |
| Italy | 65 | 73 | |
| Liechtenstein | 75 | | |
| Luxembourg | 58 | | |
| Netherlands | 77 | | |
| Norway | 76 | | |
| Poland | 37 | 47 | 66 |
| Portugal | 0 | 3 | |
| Russian | | | |
| Federation | 38 | 40 | 40 |
| Slovakia | 60 | 65 | 72 |
| Slovenia | 45 | 60 | 70 |
| Spain | 35 | | |
| Sweden | 80 | | |
| Switzerland | 52 | | |
| Ukraine | 40 | | |
| United | | | |
| Kingdom | 50 | 70 | 80 |
| European | | | |
| Community | 62 | | |

## Monitoring/implementation

*Review procedure*
Compliance with the commitments of the
Convention, including the obligation to
submit annual reports and other information, is reviewed by the Executive Body
at its meeting and in special four-year
reviews based on detailed questionnaires.
At the same time, monitoring data on
actual depositions of air pollution are
collected and analysed under the EMEP
programme and submitted to the Executive Body.

For the 1990 major review, 24 of the
32 Parties submitted their national
reports. 25 Parties (71 per cent of the
Parties) submitted national reports as
requested under the Convention in 1991,
23 Parties (66 per cent of the Parties) in
1992, and 28 Parties (76 per cent of the
Parties) in 1993. A major review for
1994 is in preparation (Oct. 94).

The national emission data and other
information required from Parties of the
*1985 Sulphur Protocol* and the *NO$_x$
Protocol* are further specified in work
plans for implementation of the Convention, adopted annually by the Executive
Body. Annual data reporting to the
EMEP international centres is generally
satisfactory.

18 Parties (90 per cent of the Parties)
submitted national reports required under
the *1985 Sulphur Protocol* in 1991, 15
Parties (75 per cent of the Parties) in

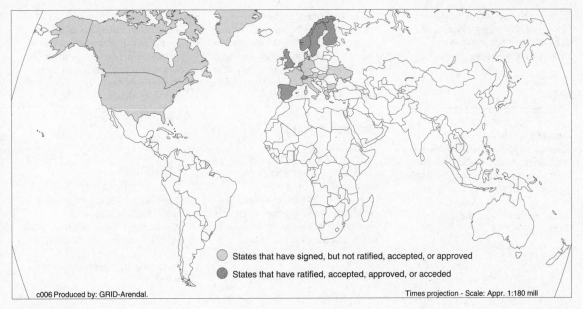

| | |
|---|---|
| ○ | States that have signed, but not ratified, accepted, or approved |
| ● | States that have ratified, accepted, approved, or acceded |

c006 Produced by: GRID-Arendal.                                                                    Times projection - Scale: Appr. 1:180 mill

## VOC Protocol

1992, and 18 Parties (86 per cent of the Parties) in 1993.

15 Parties (79 per cent of the Parties) submitted national reports required under the $NO_x$ *Protocol* in 1991, 17 Parties (85 per cent of the Parties) in 1992, and 20 Parties (87 per cent of the Parties in 1993.

Periodic public reviews of national reports and the data collected through EMEP and other co-operative programmes under the Convention have served as an effective mechanism to induce compliance. The reviews are published after derestriction by the Executive Body for the Convention. The publicity caused by NGO participation in the annual review meetings may be considered a contributing factor.

The *1994 Sulphur Protocol* establishes an Implementation Committee to review the implementation of the Protocol and compliance by the Parties with their obligations. It shall report to the Parties at sessions of the Executive Body and make such recommendations to them as it considers appropriate. The Protocol will be subject to review by the Parties at these sessions, with the first being due for completion in 1997.

Taken as a whole, the 21 Parties to the *1985 Helsinki Protocol* reduced 1980 sulphur emissions by 46 per cent by 1993 (using the latest available figure, where no data were available for 1993).

In the whole of Europe, including non-parties to the Protocol, that sum of emissions is just below 30,000 kt which corresponds to a reduction of 43 per-cent compared to 1980. Individually, based on the latest available data, all but one Party to the Sulphur Protocol have reached the reduction target. Also four non-parties to the Protocol have achieved sulphur emission reductions of 30 per cent or more. Eleven Parties have achieved reductions of at least 50 per cent; two of these have actually reduced their emissions by 80 per cent or more.

Concerning the emissions of nitrogen oxides, the general reference year is 1987 with the exception of the USA that chose to relate its emission target to 1978. For all Parties to the Convention overall emissions of $NO_x$ had been stabilized by 1990 at the 1987 level and by 1993 (or an earlier year, where no figures are available for 1993) they had been reduced by 3 per cent. Taking the sum of emissions of Parties to the $NO_x$ *Protocol* in 1993, or a previous year, where no recent data are available, also a slight reduction of 3 per cent compared to 1987 can be noted. 17 of the 24 Parties to the 1988 Sofia Protocol have reached the target and stabilized emissions at 1987, or in the case of the USA 1978, levels, or reduced emissions below that level according to the latest emission data reported. Among the other cases

four cannot be evaluated because of a lack of data for the base year and the three remaining Parties to the Protocol have increased emissions by 4 to 36 per cent above 1987 levels. Four Parties to the Convention (including one non-party to the Sofia Protocol) have reduced $NO_x$ emissions by more than 25 per cent. They are all countries with economies in transition. It can also be noted that, in general in southern Europe $NO_x$ emissions have increased, in some cases significantly, above the 1987 levels.

*Observations or inspections*
None by the Convention as such.

*Environmental monitoring programmes*
Monitoring data on actual depositions and concentrations of air pollution are collected and analysed under the EMEP programme (see above). The programme was originally established in 1977 by UN/ECE, WMO, and UNEP. EMEP collects precipitation gas and aerosol chemistry data from some 100 ground-level monitoring stations in 33 UN/ECE countries. The data are collected daily and are analysed to establish the transportation patterns of essential pollutants. These data are analysed and results published by EMEP's Chemical Co-ordinating Centre (CCC) in Norway. Two Meteorological Synthesizing Centres (MSCs) are established by

EMEP in Norway and in the Russian Federation, to develop model calculations of long-range transport and deposition of acidifying compounds.

*Data and information system programmes*
The scheme for emission reductions of the 1994 Sulphur Protocol is based on a computer simulation model known as the Regional Acidification Information and Simulation Model (RAINS), developed by the International Institute for Applied Systems Analysis (IIASA) in Austria.

*Trade sanctions*
None.

*Dispute-settlement mechanisms*
If a dispute arises between two or more Parties as to the interpretation or application of the Convention, they shall seek a solution by negotiation or by any other method of dispute settlement acceptable to the parties to the dispute.

## Decision-making
*Political bodies*
The *Executive Body*, formed of the Contracting Parties, meets at least annually. The Body reviews the implementation of the Convention and has established working-groups to prepare appropriate studies, documentation, and recommendations to this end.

*Scientific/technical bodies*
The Executive Body has established several standing subsidiary bodies to provide the necessary scientific expert advice for policy-making decisions. They are at present:
• *Working Group on Effects*;
• *Working Group on Strategies*;
• *EMEP Steering Body*;
• *Working Group on Technology*.

## Publications
Up-to-date information on the operation of the Convention and its protocols is disseminated through documents for UN/ECE meetings, the UN/ECE *Air Pollution Studies* series, the unofficial *MonitAir Newsletter* of the EMEP programme, public-information brochures, etc.

# Framework Convention on Climate Change (FCCC)

## Objectives
• to stabilize greenhouse gas concentration in the atmosphere at a level that would prevent dangerous anthropogenic interference with the climate system, within a time frame sufficient to allow ecosystems to adapt naturally to climate change;
• to ensure that food production is not threatened;
• to enable economic development to proceed in a sustainable manner.

## Scope
*Legal scope*
Open to states members of the United Nations, or of its specialized agencies, or that are Parties to the Statute of the International Court of Justice, and to regional economic integration organizations.

*Geographic scope*
Global.

## Time and place of adoption
9 May 1992, New York.

## Entry into force
21 March 1994.

## Status of participation
95 Parties, including the European Economic Community, by 3 October 1995. 74 Signatories without ratification, acceptance, or approval.

## Affiliated protocols, annexes, and organizations
The Conference of the Parties (CoP) at its first session will review the adequacy of the commitments of the developed-country Parties. The inputs to this review will include recent information from the IPCC. If the CoP would conclude that present commitments are inadequate in the light of the objective of the Convention they may decide on additional commitments.

Since proposals for a protocol have been received in time (that is, six months before the session), the CoP could already at its first session adopt a protocol or set the mandate and timetable for a new round of negotiations, possibly aiming at a protocol at a later stage.

The *Secretary-General of the United Nations* acts as depositary.

## Secretariat
*Mailing address*
Climate Change Secretariat (UNFCCC), Palais des Nations, CH-1211 Geneva 10, Switzerland

*Office location*
Geneva Executive Centre, 11/13 Chemin des Anémones, 1219 Châtelaine, Geneva, 
*Telephone*:       +41-22-9799111
*Telefax*:       +41-22-9799034
*E-mail*:  secretariat.unfccc@unep.ch

(Information is also available through the UNEP/WMO Information Unit on Climate Change (IUCC), Geneva Executive Center, CP 356, CH-1219 Châtelaine, Geneva, Switzerland. Telephone: +41-22-9799242. Fax: +41-22-7973464. Contact person: Mr Michael Williams.)

Establishment of a permanent secretariat will be approved at the first Conference of the Parties, scheduled for 28 March to 7 April 1995 in Berlin.

*Executive Secretary*
Mr Michael Zammit Cutajar.

*Information officer*
Mr Horacio Peluffo.

*Number of staff*
18 professionals and 14 support staff (Oct. 1994).

## Finance
The Global Environment Facility (GEF) (see IGOs) of the United Nations Development Programme (UNDP), the United Nations Environment Programme (UNEP) (see IGOs), and the International

Bank for Reconstruction and Development (IBRD) (see IGOs, World Bank) has been entrusted with the operation of the financial mechanism of the Convention on an interim basis. On 16 March 1994 the participants in the GEF accepted the 'Instrument for the establishment of the restructured Global Environment Facility' and the resources of the Facility were replenished with some \$US2 billion for the period from 1 July 1994 to 30 June 1997 for its four programme areas. This interim arrangements is to be reviewed by the Conference of the Parties at its first session in March–April 1995.

*Budget*
The cost of the interim secretariat is presently covered by the UN regular budget under the Department for Policy Co-ordination and Sustainable Development with additional contributions from UNEP, WMO, and bilateral donors. The budget of the permanent secretariat will be discussed at the first session of the CoP and shall enter into effect as of 1996.

## Rules and standards
The Parties undertake:
• to develop, periodically update, publish, and make available to the Conference of Parties national inventories of emissions from sources and removals by sinks of all greenhouse gases not controlled by the Montreal Protocol (see this section), using comparable methodologies;
• to formulate, implement, publish, and regularly update national and, where appropriate, regional programmes containing measures to mitigate climate change by addressing emissions, sinks, and reservoirs of greenhouse gases and to facilitate adequate adaption to climate change;
• to promote and co-operate in the development, application, and diffusion of technologies, practices, and processes that control, reduce, or prevent greenhouse gas emissions;
• to promote sustainable management, and promote and co-operate in the conservation and enhancement, as

appropriate, of all sinks and reservoirs of greenhouse gases;
• to promote and co-operate in scientific, technical, socio-economic, and other research, systematic observation, and development of data archives related to the climate system.

The developed-country Parties (including countries that are undergoing the process of transition to a market economy) shall adopt national policies and take corresponding measures on the mitigation of climate change, by limiting their anthro-pogenic emissions of greenhouse gases and protecting and enhancing their greenhouse gas sinks and reservoirs. These policies and measures will demonstrate that developed countries are taking the lead in modifying longer-term trends in anthropogenic emissions consistent with the objective of the Convention, recognizing that the return by the end of the present decade to earlier levels of anthropogenic emissions of greenhouse gases not controlled by the Montreal Protocol would contribute to such modification.

These Parties may implement such policies and measures jointly with other Parties and each of these Parties should communicate, within six months of the entry into force of the Convention, and periodically thereafter, detailed information on its policies and measures, as well as on its resulting projected anthropogenic emissions by sources and removals by sinks of greenhouse gases, with the aim of returning these emissions individually or jointly to their 1990 levels.

In accordance with Article 4.2.b and 12 of the Convention the interim secretariat had received national communications as of 5 October 1994, from the following Parties listed in Annex I: Australia, Austria, Canada, Denmark, Germany, Japan, the Netherlands, New Zealand, Norway, Spain, Sweden, Switzerland, United Kingdom, and USA.

The developed-country Parties (*not* including countries that are undergoing the process of transition to a market economy) shall provide new and additional financial resources to meet full agreed costs incurred by developing country Parties in complying with their obligations concerning communication of information.

The developed-country Parties shall also provide such resources, including those for transfer of technology, needed by the developing-country Parties to meet the agreed full incremental costs of implementing their commitments.

Each developing-country Party shall make its initial communication within three years of the entry into force of the Convention for that Party or of the availability of financial resources.

The extent to which developing-country Parties will effectively be able to implement their commitments under the Convention will depend on the effective implementation by developed-country Parties of their commitments under the Convention relating to financial resources and their willingness to transfer of technology and take fully into account that economic and social development and poverty eradication are the first and overriding priorities of the developing-country Parties.

Parties that are least-developed countries may make their initial communication at their discretion.

## Monitoring/implementation

*Review procedure*
The Conference of the Parties shall keep under regular review the implementation of the Convention and any related instruments that the Conference may adopt and shall make the decisions necessary to promote the effective implementation of the Convention. To this end it shall:
• periodically examine the obligations of the Parties;
• promote and facilitate the exchange of information on, and the co-ordination, as appropriate, of, policies, strategies, and measures adopted by the Parties to address climate change and its effects;
• promote and guide the development and periodic refinements of comparable methodologies;
• assess the implementation of the Convention by the Parties, the overall effects of the measures taken pursuant to the Convention, in particular environmental, economic, and social effects, and the extent to which progress towards the objective of the Convention is being achieved;

• consider and adopt regular reports on the implementation of the Convention and ensure their publication;
• seek to mobilize financial resources.

*Environmental monitoring programmes*
The Intergovernmental Panel on Climate Change (IPCC) was established in 1988 by UNEP and WMO (see IGOs). The IPCC assesses scientific information related to the various components of the climate change issue, such as emission of major greenhouse gases, and evaluates the environmental and socio-economic impacts of climate change.

The Parties shall support international and intergovernmental efforts to develop and strengthen the capacities and capabilities of the developing countries in these activities, and promote access to, and exchange of, data and analysis thereof obtained from areas beyond national jurisdiction.

*Data and information system programmes*
As part of its activities on technical co-operation, the Interim Secretariat has continued its work jointly with UNEP on the *Climate Convention Information Exchange Programme (CC:INFO)*, (previously CLIMEX). The main objective is to assist countries in finding resources to undertake country activities on climate change. The information collected is being continuously processed and updated in a computerized database, and made available via printed and electronic means.

*Trade sanctions*
None.

*Dispute-settlement mechanisms*
In the event of a dispute between Parties concerning the interpretation or application of the Convention, the Parties concerned shall seek a settlement through negotiation or any other peaceful means of their own choice.

## Decision-making

*Political bodies*
The Conference of the Parties, the supreme body of the Convention, consists of representatives of Parties to the Convention.

Any Party may propose amendments to the Convention. The Conference of

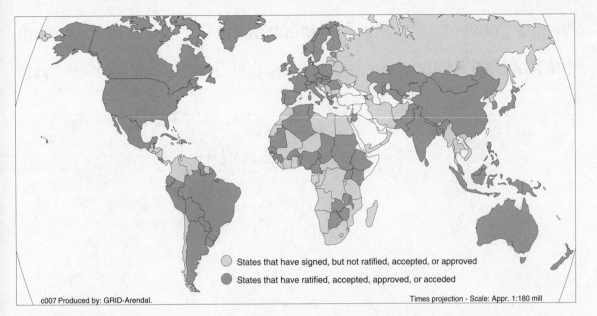

○ States that have signed, but not ratified, accepted, or approved

● States that have ratified, accepted, approved, or acceded

c007 Produced by: GRID-Arendal.    Times projection - Scale: Appr. 1:180 mill

the Parties may adopt amendments, annexes, and protocols to the Convention in accordance with the procedure set forth in the Convention. The Parties shall make every effort to reach agreement on any proposed amendment or annex to the Convention by consensus. If all efforts at consensus have been exhausted, the amendment shall, as a last resort, be adopted by a three-quarters majority vote of the Parties present and voting at the meeting.

Any body or agency, whether national or international, governmental or non-governmental, which is qualified in matters covered by the Convention, and which has informed the Secretariat of its wish to be represented at a session of the Conference of the Parties as an observer, may be so admitted unless at least one-third of the Parties present object.

A subsidiary body for scientific and technological advice and a subsidiary body for implementation have been established to provide the Conference of the Parties with timely information and advice on scientific and technological matters and to assist the Conference in the assessment and review of the effective implementation of the Convention, respectively.

## Publications

Up-to-date information on the Convention is available through the Interim Secretariat, or through the UNEP/WMO Information Unit on Climate Change (see above).

# Vienna Convention for the Protection of the Ozone Layer, including the Montreal Protocol on Substances that Deplete the Ozone Layer

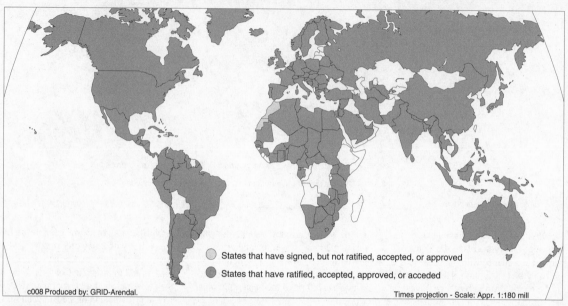

States that have signed, but not ratified, accepted, or approved

States that have ratified, accepted, approved, or acceded

c008 Produced by: GRID-Arendal.
Times projection - Scale: Appr. 1:180 mill

**Vienna Convention for the Protection of the Ozone Layer**

## Objectives
• to protect human health and the environment against adverse effects resulting or likely to result from human activities which modify or are likely to modify the ozone layer;
• to adopt agreed measures to control human activities found to have adverse effects on the ozone layer;
• to co-operate in scientific research and systematic observations;
• to exchange information in the legal, scientific, and technical fields.

## Scope
*Legal scope*
Open to all States and regional economic integration organizations.

*Geographic scope*
Global.

## Time and place of adoption
22 March 1985, Vienna.

## Entry into force
22 September 1988.

## Status of participation
141 Parties, including the European Economic Community, by 12 September 1994. 1 Signatory without ratification, acceptance, or approval.

## Affiliated protocols, annexes, and organizations
*Montreal Protocol on Substances that Deplete the Ozone Layer, Montreal, 16 September 1987.* Entered into force on 1 January 1989. 139 Parties, including the European Economic Community, by 12 September 1994. 2 Signatories without ratification. The basic objective of the Protocol is:
• to protect the ozone layer by taking measures leading to total elimination of global emissions of substances that deplete it on the basis of developments in scientific knowledge, taking into account technical and economic considerations and the needs of developing countries.

*Amendment to the Montreal Protocol on Substances that Deplete the Ozone Layer (London Amendment), London, 29 June 1990.* Entered into force on 10 August 1992. 92 Parties, including the European Economic Community, by 12 September 1994. The London Amendment added 12 new chemicals to the list of controlled substances and 34 new chemicals to the list of transitional substances with reporting requirements. It added provisions relating to technology transfer and established a financial mechanism which included the establishment of an Interim Multilateral Fund to assist eligible Parties to comply with the control measures. The Fund, which became operational on 1 January 1991, is administered by an Executive Committee of the Parties. Contributions are made by the developed countries. Developing countries with an annual consumption of more than 0.3 kg per capita of CFCs and more than 0.2 kg per capita of halons also make contributions to the Multilateral Fund.

Adjustments strengthening the reduction schedules for the original controlled substances came into force automatically in March 1991. The third meeting of the Parties added Annex D, a list of products containing substances from Annex A to

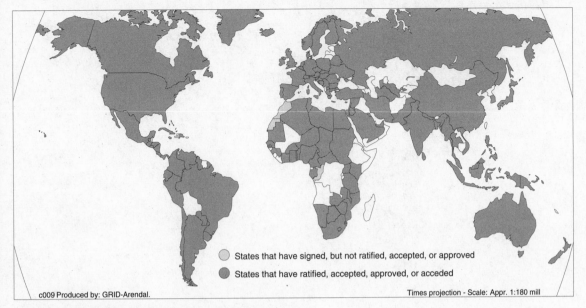

States that have signed, but not ratified, accepted, or approved

States that have ratified, accepted, approved, or acceded

c009 Produced by: GRID-Arendal.                    Times projection - Scale: Appr. 1:180 mill

**Montreal Protocol on Substances that Deplete the Ozone Layer**

the Protocol. From 27 May 1993, Parties cannot import these products from non-Parties.

*Amendment to the Montreal Protocol on Substances that Deplete the Ozone Layer (Copenhagen Amendment), Copenhagen, 25 November 1992.* Entered into force on 14 June 1994. 32 Parties, by 12 September 1994. The Copenhagen Amendment speeded up the phase-out dates for many ozone-depleting substances, included hydrochlorofluorocarbons (HCFCs) and methyl bromide on the list of controlled substances (see below), and firmed up financial arrangements for funding the Multilateral Fund (see below).

*Annex I* of the Convention sets forth important issues for scientific research on and systematic observation of the ozone layer. *Annex II* of the Convention describes the kinds of information to be collected and shared under its terms.

The *Secretary-General of the United Nations* acts as depositary.

*World Meterological Organization (WMO)* (see IGOs) together with *United Nations Environment Programme (UNEP)* (see IGOs) plays a central role in harmonizing the policies and strategies on research.

## Secretariats

UNEP, Ozone Secretariat,
PO Box 30552,
Nairobi,
Kenya
*Telephone*:        +254-2-621234
*Telefax*:          +254-2-521930/
                    226890/226886
*Telex*:            22068 UNEPKE
*Cable address*:  UNITERRA, NAIROBI

*Co-ordinator*
Mr K. M. Sarma.

*Number of staff*
4 professionals and 5 support staff
(Oct. 1994).

Secretariat of the Multilateral Fund for the Implementation of the Montreal Protocol,
Montreal Trust Bldg.,
1800 McGill College Ave.,
Montreal H3A 3J6,
Canada
*Telephone*:        +1-514-2821122
*Telefax*:          +1-514-2820068

*Chief Officer*
Dr Omar E. El-Arini.

*Number of staff*
8 professionals and 7 support staff
(Oct. 1994).

## Finance
*Budget*
The 1990/91 biennial administrative budget for the *Convention* amounted to $US800,000. For 1991, the budget was $US813,000; for 1992, $US351,000; and for 1993, $US877,000. Budgets are financed through a Trust Fund, administered by UNEP (see IGOs) to which Parties contribute according to an agreed assessment schedule.

The administrative budget of the Secretariat of the Multilateral Fund for the Implementation of the Montreal Protocol was $US9 million for the period from 1991 to 1994, of which approximately $US2 million was contributed by the government of Canada for hosting the Secretariat in Montreal.

*Main contributors*
Main contributors to the to the Multilateral Fund in the 1991–94 period were the USA, Japan, Germany, United Kingdom, Spain, and Canada, by 31 August 1994.

*Special funds*
The Vienna Convention Trust Fund and Montreal Protocol Trust Fund are intended to ensure adequate finance for the Ozone Secretariat, to service the meeting and participation of developing countries. The original *Protocol*, signed in 1987, established a ten-year grace period before developing countries were

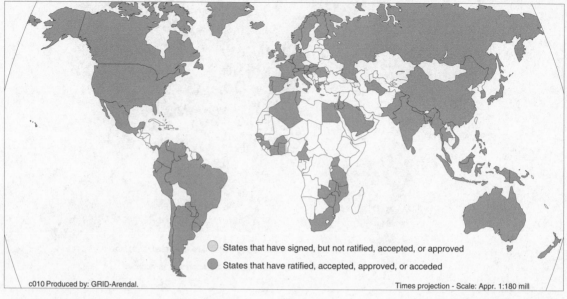

States that have signed, but not ratified, accepted, or approved

States that have ratified, accepted, approved, or acceded

c010 Produced by: GRID-Arendal.                                    Times projection - Scale: Appr. 1:180 mill

## London Amendment

obligated to follow the agreed reduction schedule for controlled substances. The Interim Multilateral Fund was established in 1990, with an initial three-year budget of up to $US240 million, to meet agreed incremental costs to developing countries of implementing the control measures. The UNDP, the World Bank, and UNEP (see IGOs) serve as implementing agencies of the Fund. After the entry into force of the London Amendment, in 1992, the 'interim' Fund has formally become the Multilateral Fund from 1 January 1993.

At the fifth Meeting of Parties in November 1993, a three-year budget of $US510 million for the period from 1994 to 1996 was approved.

The United Nations Industrial Development Organization (UNIDO) (see IGOs) became the fourth implementing agency after signing an agreement with the Executive Committee in October 1992.

## Rules and standards

Parties of the *Montreal Protocol* are committed to:
(*a*) control measures to reduce production and consumption of specific substances;
(*b*) control of trade with non-parties;
(*c*) regularly scheduled assessment and review of control measures;
(*d*) reporting of data;

(*e*) co-operation in research, development, public awareness, and exchange of information;
(*f*) establishment of a financial mechanism and transfer of technology to assist developing countries.

If a developing country considers itself unable to comply with control measures because of inadequate financial or technological assistance provided under the Protocol, it may notify the Ozone Secretariat and the Parties can consider not invoking non-compliance procedures against the notifying Party. Decisions by the Meeting of Parties are to be governed by a balanced voting procedure: a two-thirds majority of Parties, comprising separate simple majorities among the developing and industrialized nations.

As amended by the 1990 second Meeting of Parties in London, commitments on measures relating to substances that deplete the ozone layer (paragraph (a) above), involve the phase-out of a specified list of chlorofluorocarbons (CFCs) and halons, and of carbon tetrachloride, by the year 2000; also the phase-out of methyl chloroform by 2005; with scheduled interim reductions for each of the above classes of chemicals.

The *London Amendment* stipulates the reduction of consumption and production of CFCs by 50 per cent in 1995, a 85 per cent reduction in 1997, and a 100 per cent reduction in 2000.

The 1992 fourth Meeting of Parties adopted the *Copenhagen Amendment* to bring forward the phase-out of chlorofluorocarbons (CFCs) and carbontetrachloride and methyl chloroform by four or more years. For the first time the Parties agreed to bring methyl bromide, a substance used for preserving fruit and grain, under the Protocol. The new agreement also stipulates industrialized countries should phase out:
• halons by January 1994 instead of January 2000;
• hydrochlorofluorocarbons (HCFCs), a less damaging substitute for CFCs, by 2030.

Beginning in 1990, and at least every four years thereafter, the Parties will assess the control measures provided for in the Protocol on the basis of available scientific, environmental, technical, and economic information. Such assessments have so far been completed in 1990 and 1992. The next assessment will be done in 1995.

## Monitoring/implementation

*Review procedure*
Parties to the *Vienna Convention* report to the Secretariat a summary of measures undertaken in the various categories of scientific research and co-operation. These are reviewed and discussed at the Conference of Parties every two years.

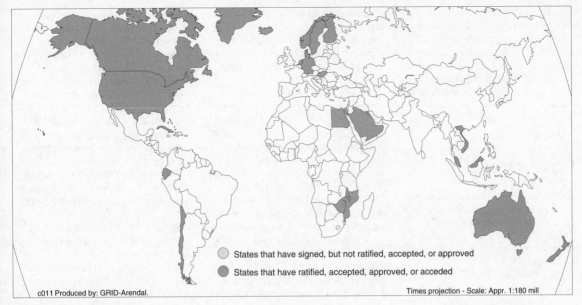

States that have signed, but not ratified, accepted, or approved

States that have ratified, accepted, approved, or acceded

c011 Produced by: GRID-Arendal.

Times projection - Scale: Appr. 1:180 mill

## Copenhagen Amendment

The reports are public. 50 per cent of the Parties are submitting reports as required under the Convention. These reports are due only once in two years by each Party.

Compliance with obligations under the *Montreal Protocol* is measured through specific reporting requirements. Compliance in general is monitored through consultations among the Parties and with the Secretariat, and through deliberations of the annual Meeting of Parties.

Parties to the Protocol provide the Secretariat with annual statistical data on production, imports and exports of controlled substances, including imports and exports to Parties and non-Parties. The Secretariat prepares a report to the annual meeting of the Parties by aggregating data in such a way that data declared by Parties at the time of their reporting remains confidential. These reports are public.

At the third Meeting of Parties to the Montreal Protocol in June 1991 the Implementation Committee noted that reporting was not satisfactory: of 71 Parties (at that time), only 31 had reported complete data for 1986, which is the base year used to calculate required phase-down of the original list of controlled substances. Of the remainder, 19 Parties had submitted incomplete data, 6 had reported no data available and/or requested assistance, 2 had

reported that their data were included in those of another party, and 13 Parties, including 4 European Community members, had submitted no data at all. Of 48 Parties required to report data for 1989, the base year for substances added to the controlled list at the 1990 Meeting of Parties, only 23 Parties had complied by May 1991, of which 20 had submitted complete data.

Up to 30 September 1993, of 74 Parties due to report for 1991, 46 (60 per cent) have reported completely. The due date for reporting for each year is the 30 September of the succeeding year. Of the 99 Parties due to report for 1992, 23 (23 per cent) have reported by 30 September 1993.

The reports are prepared in such a way that the information declared as confidential by the Parties at the time of their reporting is not revealed. The reports contain enough information for any reader to verify the compliance of the Parties with the Protocol.

*Observations or inspections*
None by the Convention as such.

*Environmental monitoring programmes*
None by the Convention as such. The Global Ozone Observing System, established by WMO (see IGOs), is the only provider of ozone related information to UNEP's Global Environmental Monitoring Systems (GEMS) (see IGOs).

It has approximately 140 monitoring stations world-wide which are complemented by remote sensing techniques. It is capable of providing data on both the horizontal and vertical distribution of ozone and also the total atmospheric concentration.

*Trade sanctions*
Trade sanctions are embodied in the Montreal Protocol. The objective of such restrictions is to stimulate as many nations as possible to participate in the Protocol by preventing non-participating countries from gaining competitive advantages and by discouraging the movement of CFC production facilities to such countries.

Each Party shall ban the import of controlled substances from any State not party to the Protocol. As of 1 January 1993 no Party may export any controlled substance to any State not party to the Protocol. As of 27 May 1993, no Party may import products, specified in Annex D of the Protocol, containing substances of Annex A to the Protocol from any non-Party.

*Dispute-settlement mechanisms*
When approving the Convention, a Party may declare in writing that, for a dispute not resolved by negotiation, or through the good offices or mediation of a third party, it will accept one or both of the following means of dispute settlement as

compulsory: arbitration in accordance with procedures adopted by the Conference of the Parties, or submission to the International Court of Justice. If Parties have not accepted either procedures, the dispute shall be submitted to a conciliation commission created by the Parties to the dispute, the recommendations of which 'the Parties shall consider in good faith'.

## Decision-making

*Political bodies*

The basic administrative mechanism for the *Vienna Convention* is the *Conference of Parties* held every two years. The *Bureau of the Conference of the Parties* to the Vienna Convention meets intersessionally.

The Conference of Parties is open to all governments, whether or not they are Parties to the Protocol, as well as observers from international agencies, industry, and non-governmental organizations. States that are not Parties and observers have no voting rights.

The basic administrative mechanism for the *Montreal Protocol* is the annual *Meeting of the Parties*. An *Implementation Committee* has been created, consisting of 10 Parties, equally split between developing and industrialized nations. The Committee is charged with considering and reporting to the Meeting of Parties any cases of non-compliance coming to its attention. The Meeting is ultimately responsible for deciding upon and calling for steps to bring about full compliance with the protocol, including measures to assist a Party's compliance.

The *Open-Ended Working Group of the Parties* and the *Bureau of the Montreal Protocol* meet intersessionally to develop and negotiate recommendations for the Meeting of the Parties on protocol revisions and implementation issues.

The *Executive Committee of the Multilateral Fund* (see above) consists of 14 Parties made up of seven developing countries and seven industrialized countries. The Committee is responsible for developing and monitoring the implementation of specific operational policies, guide-lines, and administrative arrangements, including the disbursement of resources for the purpose of achieving the objectives of the Fund. It is assisted by a Secretariat located in Montreal.

The operations of the Executive Committee and the Fund Secretariat are financed by the Multilateral Fund. By October 1994, the Executive Committee had held fourteen meetings and taken decisions on policy issues and made disbursements amounting to over $US217 million. This money will be used by the implementing agencies to implement specific actions for the phase out of about 42,000 tonnes of ozone-depleting substances. In a matter of less than four years since the inception of the Multilateral Fund, this Committee has approved 42 country programmes and has expanded the coverage of the Fund activities to over 77 countries. These country programmes account for more than 95 per cent of the ODS consumption in article 5 countries, including all the major consuming countries. In 1994, nine projects have been completed with about 1,000 tonnes of CFCs eliminated annually.

The Meetings of the Parties and the Open-Ended Working Group of the Parties are open to all governments, whether or not they are Parties to the Protocol, as well as to observers from international agencies, industry, and non-governmental organizations.

*Scientific/technical bodies*

The *Conference of Parties to the Vienna Convention* has established a *Meeting of Ozone Research Managers* which meets every two years, composed of government experts on atmospheric research and on research related to health and environmental effects of ozone layer modification. This group, working closely with WMO (see IGOs), reviews ongoing national and international research and monitoring programmes to ensure proper co-ordination of these programmes and to identify gaps that need to be addressed. The group pro-duces a report to the Conference of Parties with recommendations for future research and expanded co-operation between researchers in industrialized and developing countries.

At the 1989 Meeting of Parties to the *Montreal Protocol*, an *ad hoc Working Group of Legal Experts on Non-Compliance Procedure* was established. The Working Group is charged with elaborating further procedures on non-compliance.

The Montreal Protocol has established three Panels of Experts, to be convened at least one year before each assessment: (*a*) the *Scientific Assessment Panel*, charged with undertaking the review of scientific knowledge in a timely manner as dictated by the needs of the Parties; (*b*) the *Technology and Economics Assessment Panel*, which includes many industrial and non-governmental representatives. It analyses and evaluates technical options for limiting the use of ozone depleting substances, estimates the quantity of controlled substances required by developing countries for their basic domestic needs and the likely availability of such supplies, and assesses the costs of technical solutions, the benefits of reduced use of controlled substances, and issues of technology transfer; (*c*) the *Environmental Effects Assessment Panel*, surveys the state of knowledge of impacts on health and environment of altered ozone levels and the resultant increased ultraviolet radiation reaching the Earth's surface.

The assessment panels include experts from the non-governmental sector.

Other bodies:
• *ad hoc Group of Experts on Data Reporting*;
• *ad hoc Technical Advisory Committee on Destruction Technologies*.

## Publications

• *Montreal Protocol Handbook*;
• *OzonAction*, newsletter published quarterly;
• *Assessment Reports*.

# Convention on the Ban of the Import into Africa and the Control of Transboundary Movements and Management of Hazardous Wastes within Africa (Bamako Convention)

## Objectives

To protect human health and the environment from dangers posed by hazardous wastes by reducing their generation to a minimum in terms of quantity and/or hazard potential.

## Scope

*Legal scope*
Limited to member states of the Organization of African Unity (OAU).

*Geographic scope*
Regional.

## Time and place of adoption

30 January 1991, Bamako.

## Entry into force

Not yet in force. To enter into force on the ninetieth day after the date of deposit of the tenth instrument of ratification.

## Status of participation

7 Parties. 18 Signatories without ratification, acceptance, or approval, by 18 September 1994.

## Affiliated protocols, annexes, and organizations

*Annex I* contains forty-seven categories of wastes which are subject to control under the Convention. The wastes are classified as either entirely hazardous, such as radionuclides, or as wastes having hazardous substances as part of their constituents, such as metal carbonyls or arsenic.

*Annex II* specifies the characteristics which identify waste as hazardous. There is, however, a catch-all provision which makes substances subject to regulation under the Convention if they have been declared hazardous and banned or if registration has been refused or cancelled by the country of manufacture. An additional list of regulated substances may arise from the provisions, which requires the Parties to inform the Secretariat of any substances not in Annex I which, under their national laws, are defined as hazardous. Similarly, radioactive wastes which are subject to international controls systems because of their characteristics are covered by the Convention.

*Co-ordination with related instruments*
Wastes from the operation of ships, the discharge of which is covered by other instruments, are specifically excluded from the applications of the Convention.

## Secretariat

Information on the Convention is available from:
Organization of African Unity (OAU),
ESCAS Department,
PO Box 3243,
Addis Ababa,
Ethiopia
*Telephone*:      +251-1-517700
*Telefax*:      +251-1-512622
*Telex*:      21046

*Director (ESCAS Department)*
Amb Shaban F. Gashut.

*Head, Press and Information Division*
Dr Ibrahim Dagash.

*Number of staff*
16 professionals and 12 support staff (Sept. 1994).

## Finance

The scale of contribution by the Parties to cover administrative expenses is to be decided at the first Conference of the Parties (see below).

## Rules and standards

All Parties shall take appropriate legal, administrative, and other measures to prohibit the import of all hazardous wastes, when imported by third parties, from entering the territories of the Contracting Parties.

The Parties agree to ban the dumping of such wastes in the territorial sea, continental shelf, and the exclusive economic zone.

On wastes generated within Africa, the Parties undertake to submit the details thereof to the Secretariat established by the Convention. Moreover, the Party within whose territory the wastes are generated is urged to ensure availability of disposal facilities; to minimize the output, and to impose strict liability on those generating the wastes. Such Parties are also required to ensure the adoption of precautionary measures to prevent release of such wastes and to enhance clean production methods. Every case of transfer of polluting technologies to Africa is to be kept under systematic review by the Secretariat, which is to make periodic reports to the Conference of the Parties.

Parties shall:
• prevent the export of hazardous wastes to the states, which they know have prohibited the same;
• prevent the export of such wastes to a state which does not have the requisite disposal facilities.

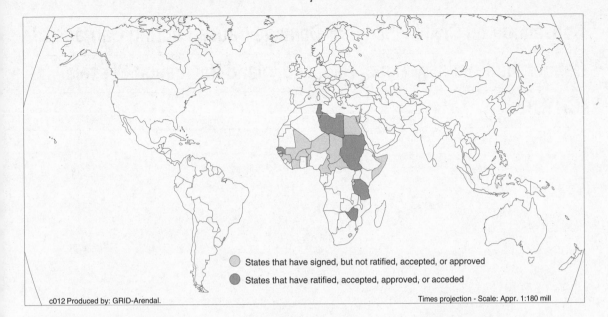

○ States that have signed, but not ratified, accepted, or approved

● States that have ratified, accepted, approved, or acceded

c012 Produced by: GRID-Arendal.                    Times projection - Scale: Appr. 1:180 mill

In every case, the exported wastes must be handled in an environmentally sound manner.

To protect Antarctica, the Parties agree to prohibit any disposal within any area south of 60°S.

Each Party informs the Secretariat of the wastes banned under the Convention. The Secretariat, in turns, informs all other Parties. It is thereafter the duty of every Party to prohibit the export of such wastes (see above), except for any Party which consents to the importation in writing. In every case, the Parties shall prohibit the export of such wastes to non-Parties which are developing countries.

## Monitoring/implementation

*Review procedure*
Each Party undertakes to adopt national legislation to implement the Convention for the protection of human and environmental health. To that effect, they agree to adopt standards which are more stringent than those under the Convention or any other provision of international law.

The Conference may adopt amendments and protocols to the Convention in accordance with the procedure set forth in the Convention.

When a Party has reason to believe that another Party is violating the provisions of the Convention, it shall inform the Secretariat and, concomitantly, convey the information to the Party against which the allegation is made. The Secretariat is required to take measures to verify the claim and to report to other Parties on its findings.

*Observations or inspections*
None by the Convention as such.

*Trade sanctions*
None.

*Dispute-settlement mechanisms*
In the event of a dispute between Contracting Parties concerning interpretation or application of, or compliance with the provision of the Convention, the Parties involved shall seek solution by negotiations or any other peaceful means of their own choice. Should this fail, the dispute shall be submitted either to an *ad hoc* organ set up by the Conference for this purpose, or to the International Court of Justice.

## Decision-making

*Political bodies*
The *Conference of the Parties*, the supreme body of the Convention, consists of representatives of all the Contracting Parties. The first meeting of the Conference shall be convened by the Executive Director of OAU not later than one year after the entry into force of the Convention. The Conference determines the frequency of meetings.

Any body or agency, whether national or international, governmental or non-governmental, which is qualified in matters relating to hazardous wastes, and which has informed the Secretariat of its wish to be represented at a session of the Conference of the Parties as an observer, may be so admitted according to the rules of procedure of the Convention.

*Scientific/technical bodies*
The Conference of the Parties establishes such subsidiary bodies as are deemed necessary for the implementation of the Convention.

## Publications

Up-to-date information on the Convention is made available through OAU.

# Convention on Civil Liability for Damage Caused during Carriage of Dangerous Goods by Road, Rail, and Inland Navigation Vessels (CRTD)

## Objectives

To establish uniform rules ensuring adequate and speedy compensation for damage during inland carriage of dangerous goods by road, rail, and inland navigation vessels.

## Scope

*Legal scope*
Open to all States. Regional integration organizations are not specified in the Convention.

*Geographic scope*
Global.

## Time and place of adoption

10 October 1989, Geneva.

## Entry into force

Not yet in force. The Convention requires 5 ratifications, acceptances, approvals, or accessions to enter into force.

## Status of participation

2 Signatories, no instrument of ratification, acceptance, or approval, by 16 September 1994.

## Affiliated protocols, annexes, and organizations

The *Secretary-General of the United Nations* acts as depositary.

The *Inland Transport Committee of the United Nations Economic Commission for Europe (UN/ECE)* fulfils the function of a standing forum for deliberations in matters concerning the Convention.

*Co-ordination with related instruments*
An instrument addressing liability for dangerous activities is under consideration within the Council of Europe. The corollary instrument addressing liability for damage from maritime transport of dangerous substances is currently being prepared within IMO (see IGOs).

## Secretariat

UN/ECE,
Transport Division,
Palais des Nations,
CH-1211 Geneva 10,
Switzerland
*Telephone*:      +41-22-9172401
*Telefax*:        +41-22-9170039

*Director of Transport Division*
Mr J. Capel Ferrer.

*Responsible officer for the transport of dangerous goods, Transport Division*
Mr O. Kervella.

## Finance

*Budget*
The Convention does not provide for regular meetings and programme activities, or a secretariat. Therefore, under the Convention, regular administrative costs do not arise.

*Special funds*
None.

## Rules and standards

The carrier, e.g. the registered owner or other person controlling a road vehicle, or an inland navigation vessel, or the operator of a railway line, is liable for damage caused during transport of dangerous goods.

Damage extends to loss of life or personal injury, loss or damage of property, loss or damage by contamination to the environment, including reasonable measures for the reinstatement of the environment, and the costs of preventive measures.

The carrier's liability shall be covered by insurance or financial security, except that States or their constituent parts when acting as carriers, do not require insurance cover.

The carrier may limit his liability per incident, in case of a road or rail carrier, to Special Drawing Rights: SDR 18 million for claims concerning loss of life or personal injury, and to SDR 12 million with respect to other claims; and

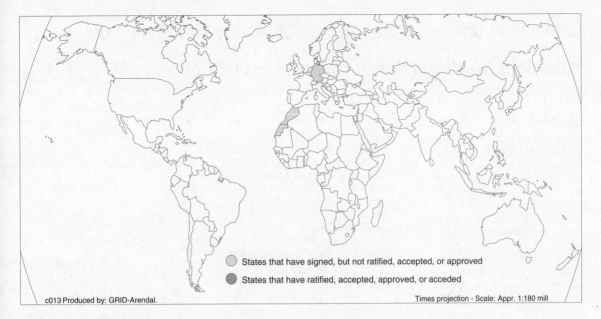

States that have signed, but not ratified, accepted, or approved

States that have ratified, accepted, approved, or acceded

Times projection - Scale: Appr. 1:180 mill

in the case of inland navigation vessels to SDR 8 million and SDR 7 million respectively.

No claim may be made beyond the regime jurisdiction against the carrier or any person engaged in the transport operation or in related salvage activities.

Action may be brought in the courts of Contracting Parties in which the incident occurred, or damage was sustained, or preventive measures were undertaken, or the carrier has his habitual residence. The carrier may establish a limitation fund in one of the courts where action has been brought. The court where the fund has been established will be responsible for deciding distribution of compensation.

## Monitoring/implementation
*Review procedure*
The Convention does not require Parties to report implementation or supply data regularly and there are no mechanisms for a regular or periodic review of the regime. However, Parties having made reservations to the Convention shall notify to the depositary the contents of their national law.

The Convention also provides for simplified procedures for amendment of compensation figures. Requests for such amendments shall be supported by one-quarter, but at least three, of the Parties. Requests are considered by a Committee of the Parties which adopts amendments

of limitation figures by a two-thirds majority. An amendment shall have been accepted if, within a period of 18 months, at least one-quarter of the Parties have communicated their non-acceptance. Accepted amendments are binding on all Parties. In deciding, the Committee shall take into account past experience with incidents, changes in monetary value, and the anticipated impact of an amendment on insurance costs.

There are no procedures or mechanisms for the regular taking into account of scientific and technical information, except that dangerous goods are defined as those substances or articles which are either listed in the classes, or covered by a collective heading of the classes of the European Agreement concerning the International Carriage of Dangerous Goods by Road (ADR), or subject to the provisions of that Agreement. The regional ADR is regularly updated in the light of scientific and technical information.

*Observations or inspections*
None by the Convention as such.

*Trade sanctions*
None.

*Dispute-settlement mechanisms*
No mention is made in the Convention of the settlement of disputes.

## Decision-making
*Political bodies*
The Convention does not provide for the establishment of a separate institutional mechanism. The Inland Transport Committee of the ECE fulfils the function of a standing forum for deliberations in matters concerning the Convention. Upon request of one-third, but at least three, of the Parties, the Inland Transport Committee shall convene a Conference of Parties for revising or amending the Convention. Moreover, the Inland Transport Committee shall convene, upon request of one-quarter, but at least three, of the Parties, a Committee constituted of one representative from each Contracting Party for amending compensation amounts according to simplified amendment procedures.

There has been no meeting of the Committee of Contracting Parties or any Conference of Parties up till now.

*Scientific/technical bodies*
None.

## Publications
• *Annual Report of the ECE*;
• *Explanatory Report* (ECE/TRANS/84);
• *Transport Information*, published annually by the ECE.

# Convention on the Control of Transboundary Movements of Hazardous Wastes and their Disposal (Basel Convention)

## Objectives
- to control and reduce transboundary movements of wastes subject to the Convention;
- to minimize the hazardous wastes generated, ensuring their environmentally sound management, including disposal and recovery operations, as close as possible to the source of generation;
- to assist developing countries in environmentally sound management of the hazardous and other wastes they generate.

## Scope
*Legal scope*
Open to all States and political and/or economic regional organizations.

*Geographic scope*
Global.

## Time and place of adoption
22 March 1989, Basel.

## Entry into force
5 May 1992.

## Status of participation
74 Parties, including the European Economic Community, by 21 October 1994. 13 Signatories, without ratification, acceptance, or approval.

## Affiliated protocols, annexes, and organizations
At the first meeting of the Conference of the Parties (CoP) to the Convention, an Ad Hoc Working Group of Legal and Technical Experts was set up to consider and develop a 'Draft Protocol on Liability and Compensation for Damage Resulting from the Transboundary Movements of Hazardous Wastes and Their Disposal'.

The second meeting of the CoP to the Basel Convention, in March 1994, confirmed the adoption of the Framework Document on the Preparation of Technical Guidelines for the Environmentally Sound Management of Wastes subject to the Basel Convention and four sets of Technical Guidelines, namely on hazardous wastes from the production and use of organic solvents (Y6), on waste oils from petroleum origins and sources (Y8), on wastes comprising or containing PCBs, PCTs, and PBBs (Y10), and on waste collected from household (Y46) (it was issued as SBC publication no 94/005).

It also adopted provisionally three draft technical guide-lines on: specially engineering landfill (D5), incineration on land (D10), and used oil re-refining or other reuses of previously used oil (R9).

*Co-ordination with related instruments*
Co-ordinated activities are taking place with:
- IAEA (see IGOs), regarding *Code of Practice on the International Transboundary Movement of Radioactive Waste*;
- IMO (see IGOs), regarding the *London Convention 1972* (see this section);
- IMO and IAEA, regarding a draft code for the safe carriage of irradiated nuclear fuel, plutonium, and high-level radioactive wastes on board ships;
- Co-ordinating Unit for the Mediterranean Action Plan (see Conventions within the UNEP Regional Seas Programme, this section) in the preparation of a protocol on the prevention of pollution of the Mediterranean Sea resulting from the transboundary movements of hazardous wastes and their disposal;
- UNEP (see IGOs) and UN Economic and Social Commission for Asia and the Pacific (ESCAP), regarding a joint project on illegal traffic in hazardous wastes;
- draft regional treaty on hazardous wastes for the South Pacific region.

## Secretariat
UNEP Secretariat for the Basel Convention (SBC),
Geneva Executive Center,
Building D,
Chemin des Anémones 15,
CH-1219 Châtelaine,
Switzerland
*Telephone*:     +41-22-9799111
*Telefax*:     +41-22-7973454

*Co-ordinator*
Dr Iwona Rummel-Bulska.

*Number of staff*
5 professionals and 4 support staff (Oct. 1994).

## Finance
The Secretariat of the Convention's budget is funded by the Parties as well as by voluntary contributions from non-parties.

*Budget*
The approved budget of the Secretariat (Trust Fund for the Implementation of Basel Convention Secretariat) was $US1,474,650 in 1993, $US1,760,540 in 1994, and is $US2,587,248 in 1995.

The approved budget to assist developing Parties in the implementation of the Convention (Technical Co-operation Trust Fund) was $US788,740 in 1993, $US937,990 in 1994, and is $US1,297,240 in 1995. The Fund is entirely financed by voluntary contributions.

*Special funds*
An Emergency Trust Fund to assist developing countries in the event of a waste emergency is being considered, as well as a Compensation Fund to be linked to the proposed protocol on liability and compensation (see above).

## Rules and standards
Parties shall:
- not allow the export of hazardous wastes or other wastes for disposal within the area south of 60°S, whether or not such wastes are subject to transboundary movement.
- prohibit the export of hazardous wastes and other wastes if the State of

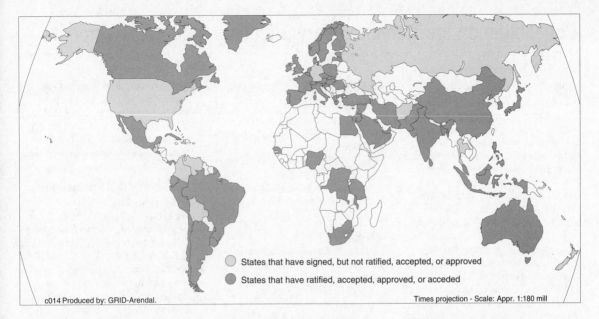

States that have signed, but not ratified, accepted, or approved

States that have ratified, accepted, approved, or acceded

c014 Produced by: GRID-Arendal.    Times projection - Scale: Appr. 1:180 mill

import does not consent in writing to the specific import, if the State of import has not prohibited the import of such wastes;

• prohibit all persons under their national jurisdiction from transporting or disposing of hazardous wastes or other type of wastes unless such persons are authorized or allowed to perform such types of operations;

• designate or establish one or more competent authorities and one focal point.

State Parties of export shall not allow the generator of hazardous wastes or other wastes to commence the transboundary movement until they have received written confirmation that the notifier has received the written consent of the State of import.

In case of an accident occurring during transboundary movement of hazardous or other wastes or their disposal likely to present risks to human health and the environment in other States, those States must be immediately informed.

Parties shall adopt technical guide-lines for the environmentally sound management of wastes subject to the Convention.

Waste exports are allowed only if the country of export does 'not have the technical capacity' or 'suitable disposal sites', and provided that the country of import has this capacity and facilities, in order to ensure environmentally sound disposal of the waste.

Technical and scientific co-operation

between Parties and co-operation between Parties and the competent international organizations are encouraged, for the purposes of exchange of information, planning, education, etc.

## Monitoring/implementation

*Review procedure*
The Conference of the Parties (CoP) shall keep under continuous review and evaluation the effective implementation of the Convention and shall undertake an evaluation of its effectiveness three years after the entry into force of the Convention, and at least every six years thereafter.

Before the end of each calendar year, the Parties shall transmit, through the Secretariat, to the CoP, a report on the previous calendar year which, *inter alia,* will contain information on the measures adopted by them in implementation of the Convention.

Verification for a breach should be undertaken through the Secretariat, to which the Party which acted in breach of its obligations has the obligation upon the request of any Party to submit all relevant information pertaining to the breach.

Compliance, monitoring, and enforcement of the Convention has begun with the submission of reports to an Open-ended Ad Hoc Committee which is the only mechanism established by the first meeting of the CoP to monitor the

implementation and make its recommendations to the CoP. 30 national reports (58 per cent of the Parties) were submitted in 1992 and 45 national reports (63 per cent of the Parties) were submitted in 1993.

*Trade sanctions*
None.

*Dispute-settlement mechanisms*
Becoming a member of the Convention, Parties may, by a written declaration, recognize as compulsory, in relation to any Party accepting the same obligation:

• submission of disputes to the International Court of Justice; and/or

• arbitration in accordance with procedures set out in Annex 6.

## Decision-making

*Political bodies*
The *Conference of the Parties* shall keep under review and evaluate implementation of the Convention, harmonize policies, establish subsidiary bodies, and undertake additional actions.

*Scientific/technical bodies*
A *Technical Working Group* is responsible for the preparation of technical guide-lines.

## Publications

• Annual Reports;
• *Technical Guidelines*;
• *SBC Newsletter*.

# Convention on the Transboundary Effects of Industrial Accidents

## Objectives

• to promote prevention of, preparedness for, and response to industrial accidents capable of causing transboundary effects, and international co-operation in these fields by mutual assistance, research, and development as well as exchange of information and technology regarding industrial accidents in general, and to this end to strive towards convergence of relevant national policies and practices;
• to provide for notification among States concerned (*a*) on any proposed or existing hazardous activity capable of causing transboundary effects in the event of an industrial accident, and (*b*) on an industrial accident, or imminent threat thereof, which causes or is capable of causing transboundary effects;
• to promote public information and participation in relevant decision-making processes.

## Scope

*Legal scope*
Open to member countries of the United Nations Economic Commission for Europe (UN/ECE), the European Union (EU), and other European States having consultative status with the UN/ECE.

*Geographic scope*
Regional. UN/ECE region.

## Time and place of adoption

17 March 1992, Helsinki.

## Entry into force

Not yet in force. Enters into force ninety days after the deposit of 16 instruments of ratification, acceptance, approval, or accession.

## Status of participation

6 Parties, by 15 September 1994. 22 Signatories, including the European Union, without ratification, acceptance, or approval.

## Affiliated protocols, annexes, and organizations

The Convention contains also 13 *Annexes* which form an integral part of the Convention.

The *Secretary-General of the United Nations* acts as depositary.

The *Executive Secretary of the UN/ECE* carries out the secretariat functions.

## Secretariat

UN/ECE, Environment and Human Settlements Division (ENHS), Palais des Nations, CH-1211 Geneva 10, Switzerland
*Telephone*:      +41-22-9171234
*Telefax*:      +41-22-9070107

## Finance

Not applicable.

## Rules and standards

The Convention stipulates measures and procedures:
• to reduce the risk of industrial accidents and improve preventive, preparedness, and response measures, including restoration measures;
• to obtain and transmit identification of hazardous activities that are reasonably causing a transboundary effect;
• to co-operate with other countries to develop off-site and on-site contingency plans, including joint contingency plans regarding industrial accidents in order to respond properly and mitigate effects including transboundary effects;
• to ensure that adequate information is given to the public;
• to receive notification in the event of an industrial accident or imminent threat thereof;
• to request assistance from other countries in the event of an industrial accident in order to minimize its consequences including its transboundary effect;
• to facilitate the exchange of safety technology and the provision of technical assistance;
• to benefit from international co-operation concerning prevention of, preparedness for, and response to industrial accidents, including exchange of information and experience gained from past industrial accidents and research and development in this field.

## Monitoring/implementation

*Review procedure*
The Parties shall report periodically on the implementation of this Convention.

The Conference of the Parties shall, at its first meeting, decide on the method of work, including the use of national centres, co-operation with relevant international organizations, and the establishment of a system with a view to facilitating the implementation of the Convention, in particular for mutual assistance in the event of an industrial accident, and building upon pertinent existing activities within relevant international organizations.

If there is a doubt whether an activity is likely to have a significant adverse transboundary impact and the Parties concerned do not agree on whether the activity is hazardous, in accordance with *Annex I*, the state which could be affected may submit the question to an inquiry commission in accordance with *Annex II*. The requesting Party or Parties shall notify the Secretariat that it or they is (are) submitting questions to an inquiry commission. The notification shall state the subject-matter of the inquiry, in accordance with *Annex III*, and all Parties will immediately be informed of it by the Secretariat. The inquiry commission will consist of three members. Both the requesting party and the other party to the inquiry procedure shall appoint a scientific or technical expert and the two experts so appointed shall designate by common agreement a third expert, who shall be the president of the commission. The parties to the inquiry procedure must facilitate the work of that commission by providing it with all relevant documents, facilities, and information and by enabling it to call witnesses or experts and receive their evidence. If one of the parties to the inquiry procedure does not appear before

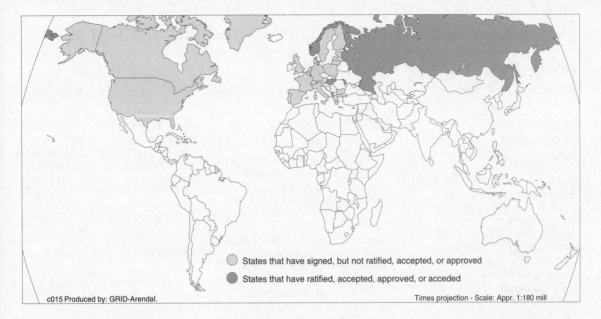

States that have signed, but not ratified, accepted, or approved

States that have ratified, accepted, approved, or acceded

c015 Produced by: GRID-Arendal.                                    Times projection - Scale: Appr. 1:180 mill

the commission or fails to present its case, the other party may request the commission to continue the proceedings and complete its work. The final opinion of the inquiry commission shall reflect the view of the majority of its members and shall include any dissenting view.

*Observations or inspections*
None by the Convention as such.

*Trade sanctions*
None.

*Dispute-settlement mechanisms*
If a dispute arises between two or more Parties as to the interpretation or application of the Convention, they shall seek a solution by negotiation or by any other method of dispute settlement acceptable to the parties to the dispute.

The Parties may submit the dispute to the International Court of Justice or to an arbitration procedure set out in Appendix XIII.

## Decision-making

*Political bodies*
In the decision on the Convention on the Transboundary Effects of Industrial Accidents adopted at their resumed fifth session in Helsinki on 17 March 1992, the Senior Advisers to UN/ECE Governments on Environmental and Water

Problems called on the Signatories to strive for the entry into force of the Convention as soon as possible and to seek to implement it to the maximum extent possible pending its entry into force.

In the light of this decision, three meetings of the Signatories to the Convention, open to all UN/ECE member countries, were held from 1992 to 1994, which have developed a work plan for its implementation. These meetings reviewed actions taken by Signatories to implement the Convention pending its entry into force, *inter alia*, development policies and strategies to reduce the risks of industrial accidents; development and implementation of training programmes for the staff involved in preparedness for, and response to industrial accidents, in particular in countries in transition through the Regional Co-ordinating Centre for Industrial Training and Exercises in Warsaw (Poland); development and implementation of preventive measures in the ECE countries, especially these in transition through the Regional Co-ordinating Centre for the Prevention of Industrial Accidents in Budapest (Hungary); and improving of communications and development of UN/ECE Accident Notification Systems in the event of an industrial accident.

Once the Convention has entered into

force, the *Conference of the Parties* will meet at least annually in order to review the implementation of the Convention and fulfil such other function as may be appropriate under the provisions of the Convention.

Where appropriate, the Conference of the Parties will consider and, where necessary, adopt proposals for amendments to the Convention. Agreement on the proposed amendment should be reached by consensus with the exception of Annex I. When all efforts at consensus have been exhausted and no agreement reached, the amendment to Annex I shall, as a last resort, be adopted by a nine-tenths majority vote of the Parties present and voting at the meeting.

*Scientific/technical bodies*
The Conference of the Parties will establish, as appropriate, working groups and other mechanisms to consider matters related to the implementation and development of the Convention and, to this end, to prepare appropriate studies and other documentation and submit recommendations for consideration by the Conference of the Parties.

## Publications

*Environmental Conventions Elaborated under the Auspices of the UN/ECE,* 1992.

# European Agreement Concerning the International Carriage of Dangerous Goods by Road (ADR)

## Objectives

- to increase the safety of international transport by road;
- to lay down provision concerning classification, packaging, labelling, and testing of dangerous goods, including wastes, in harmony with other requirements for other modes of transport, on the basis of the UN Recommendations on the Transport of Dangerous Goods;
- to lay down conditions as to the construction, equipment, and operation of vehicles carrying dangerous goods by road.

## Scope

*Legal scope*
Open to all States members of the United Nations, United Nations Economic Commission for Europe (UN/ECE), other European States and other States members of the UN which may be invited to participate in the work of the UN/ECE for questions of specific interest to them, such as the transport of international dangerous goods. Not open to regional integration organizations.

*Geographic scope*
Regional (Europe, USA, and Canada) but, due to its legal scope and the international nature of transport, may extend globally.

## Time and place of adoption

30 September 1957, Geneva.

## Entry into force

29 January 1968.

## Status of participation

27 Parties, by 16 September 1994. No Signatories without ratification, acceptance, or approval.

## Affiliated protocols, annexes, and organizations

Two *annexes* attached to the Agreement, concerning conditions of transport, transport equipment, and transport operations. One Protocol of signature and one Protocol on amendment is also attached.

The only amendment to the Agreement itself deals with the procedure for amendment of the annexes. A new Protocol amending the Agreement itself (dealing with the definition of vehicle and again with the procedure for amendment of the annexes) was adopted on 28 October 1993, but is not yet in force. The annexes are regularly amended (usually every two years) in parallel with other agreements dealing with the transport of dangerous goods by other modes such as the Regulations concerning the International Carriage of Dangerous Goods by Rail (RID), International Maritime Dangerous Goods Code (IMDG Code), International Civil Aviation Organization (ICAO)'s Technical Instructions for the Safe Transport of Dangerous Goods by Air, on the basis of the regular updating of the UN Recommendations on the Transport of Dangerous Goods.

The *Secretary-General of the United Nations* acts as depositary and ensures the administration of the Agreement through the *United Nations Economic Commission for Europe (UN/ECE)*. The *Inland Transport Committee* of UN/ECE fulfils the function of a standing forum for deliberations in matters concerning the Agreement.

*Co-ordination with related instruments*
The UN Economic and Social Committee (ECOSOC)'s Committee of Experts on Transport of Dangerous Goods issues recommendations every two years. All international instruments dealing with the transport of dangerous goods, including this Agreement, RID, IMDG Code, ICAO Technical Instructions, as well as national regulations, are regularly revised and amended on the basis of

these recommendations. Annex III of the Basel Convention (see this section) is also based on the UN Recommendation of the Transport of Dangerous Goods. This mechanism ensures co-ordination and harmonization of provisions relating to classification, labelling, marking, packing, documentation, etc.

## Secretariat

UN/ECE,
Transport Division,
Palais de Nations,
CH-1211 Geneva 10,
Switzerland
*Telephone*:     +41-22-9172456
*Telefax*:      +41-22-9170039

*Director of Transport Division*
Mr J. Capel Ferrer.

*Responsible officer for the transport of dangerous goods, Transport Division*
Mr O. Kervella.

*Number of staff*
3 professionals and 2 support staff (Oct. 1994).

## Finance

Budget allocated by the United Nations.

*Budget*
No information available.

*Special funds*
None.

## Rules and standards

The Parties have agreed to ensure that certain dangerous goods are not accepted for international transport and that other goods be transported under conditions laid down in the annexes. However, transport operations to which the Agreement applies shall remain subject to national or international regulations applicable in general to road traffic, international road transport, and international trade.

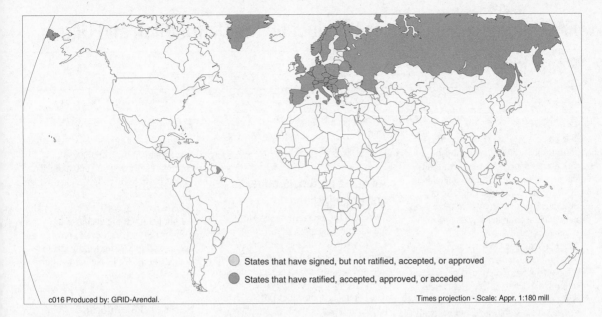

States that have signed, but not ratified, accepted, or approved

States that have ratified, accepted, approved, or acceded

c016 Produced by: GRID-Arendal.                                    Times projection - Scale: Appr. 1:180 mill

*Annex A* contains: general provisions; list of dangerous goods; special provisions for each class (conditions of packing, marking and danger labels, documentation); and classification tests and criteria (packaging standards, and testing and specifications of labels).

*Annex B* contains: provisions concerning transport equipment and transport operations (mode of carriage, special requirements to be fulfilled by the means of transport and its equipments general service requirements, special provisions concerning loading and unloading, operation of vehicles); provisions concerning tank-vehicles and tank-containers; electrical equipment; certificates (approval of vehicles, driver training); list of substances which may be carried in tanks; and danger identification numbers.

## Monitoring/implementation

*Review procedure*
Distribution of documents of the Inland Transport Committee and its subsidiary bodies is limited to governments, specialized agencies, and to intergovernmental and non-governmental organizations, which take part in the Committee and its subsidiary bodies.

There is no reporting requirements under the Agreement. Problems relating to the international transport of dangerous goods are regularly discussed by the UN/ECE Working Party on the Transport

of Dangerous Goods (see below). Compliance with the ADR is controlled by the police/control authorities of each Contracting Party. Penalties for non-compliance are imposed in accordance with the national legislation of each Contracting Party.

The Agreement is regularly updated in the light of scientific and technical information.

*Observations or inspections*
None by the Agreement as such. Inspections are the responsibility of the competent authority of each Contracting Party.

*Trade sanctions*
None.

*Dispute-settlement mechanisms*
The Parties shall as far as possible settle disputes between them by negotiation. Any dispute which is not settled by negotiation shall be submitted to arbitration and the arbitration shall be binding on the parties to the dispute.

## Decision-making

*Political bodies*
The Agreement does not provide for the establishment of a separate institutional mechanism. The *Inland Transport Committee* of the UN/ECE fulfils the function of a standing forum for deliberations in matters concerning the

Agreement. Upon request of any Party, the Secretary-General of the United Nations shall convene a *Conference of Parties* for revising or amending the Agreement.

*Scientific/technical bodies*
*UN/ECE Working Party on the Transport of Dangerous Goods*, meets twice a year, and has 54 members of the UN/ECE, other interested international organizations and non-governmental organizations. It discusses problems relating to the international transport of dangerous goods. There are joint meetings of the Working Party and of the RID Safety Committee.

## Publications

The ADR and its annexes are published every two years. Diskettes are available. Other regular publications from UN/ECE are:
• *Annual Report of the ECE*;
• *Transport Information*, published annually by the ECE;
• *UN Recommendations on the Transport of Dangerous Goods*.

# FAO International Code of Conduct on the Distribution and Use of Pesticides

## Objectives

The objectives of this Code are to set forth responsibilities and establish voluntary standards of conduct for all public and private entities engaged in or affecting the distribution and use of pesticides, particularly where there is no national law or an inadequate one to regulate pesticides.

Specifically the Code seeks:
• to promote practices which ensure efficient and safe use of pesticides while minimizing health and environmental concern;
• to establish responsible and generally accepted trade practices;
• to assist countries which have not established controls designed to regulate the quality and suitability of pesticide products needed in that country;
• to ensure that pesticides are used effectively for the improvement of agricultural production and of human, animal, and plant health.

## Scope

*Legal scope*
The Code was adopted unanimously by the FAO Conference at its 1985 session. Membership of FAO is confined to nations; Associate Membership to territories or groups of territories. The European Union is given membership as a regional integration organization and can vote on behalf of its member countries in certain matters.

*Geographic scope*
Global.

## Time and place of adoption

19 November 1985, Rome.

## Entry into force

Non-mandatory.

## Status of participation

Not applicable. FAO, which has adopted the Code, has 170 members, including the European Union, by 9 November 1993. Puerto Rico (territory of the USA) is an associate member.

## Affiliated protocols, annexes, and organizations

The code was amended in 1989 to include the principle of *Prior Informed Consent (PIC)*, which is particularly related to the control of pesticide imports into and exports to developing countries. By July 1994 125 countries had designated national author-ities (DNA) for the implementation of the PIC procedure. The Code is supported by guide-lines on all aspects of pesticide management and control.

The Code is directed at many segments of society including governments, industry, trade, and interested public-sector organi-zations and international organizations. FAO, in close collabora-tion with other UN agencies such as UNEP and ILO (see IGOs), assists governments to implement the Code.

*Co-ordination with related instruments*
The FAO Conference authorized the Director-General to establish a pro-gramme jointly with UNEP for the implementation of PIC procedures.

## Secretariat

Food and Agricultural Organization (FAO),
Viale delle Terme di Caracalla,
I-00100 Rome,
Italy
*Telephone*:    +39-6-52251
*Telefax*:      +39-6-52253152
*E-mail*:       telex-room@fao.org

*Director-General (FAO)*
Dr Jacques Diouf.

*Director, Information Division (FAO)*
Mr Richard Lydiker.

*Chief, Plant Protection Service*
Dr N. A. Van Der Graaff.

## Finance

*Budget*
The administrative core budget is approxi-mately $US500,000 annually. This is covered by FAO's regular budget.

*Special funds*
Additional funds are available for technical assistance. Several projects are operational to assist governments to implement the Code. No precise infor-mation can be given.

## Rules and standards

Although the Code itself is voluntary in nature, it promotes the promulgation and enforcement of legislation governing the import, manufacture, sale, and use of pesticides. The Code takes into account the special circumstances of developing countries.

The supply of data for the registration and approval of pesticides for use in a country is based on harmonized pesticide registration requirements formulated by FAO. Such data, including toxicological information on the pesticide and its environmental effects, are provided by the pesticide industry for officials in the country to decide whether to approve or disapprove the use of the pesticide based on benefit#risk evaluation under condi-tions of use in the country.

The principle of PIC (see above) concerns the export and import of pesticides that are banned or severely restricted for health or environmental reasons. Designated National Authorities (DNAs) in participating countries have been invited to communicate their decisions on 12 pesticides and 5 indus-trial chemicals. A control action taken for health or environmental reasons by any single country which is communi-cated to UNEP or FAO is sufficient to make a pesticide subject to the PIC procedure.

The Code describes the shared responsi-bility of many segments of society, including governments, indi-vidually or in regional groupings;

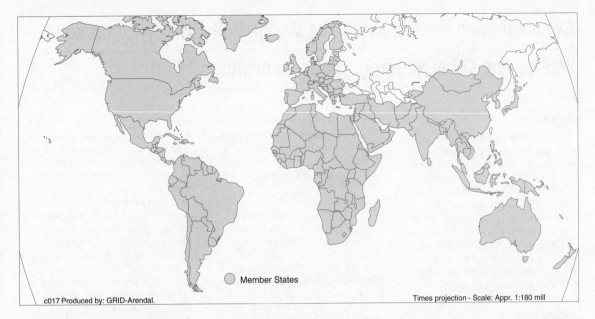

c017 Produced by: GRID-Arendal.

Member States

Times projection - Scale: Appr. 1:180 mill

industry, including manufacturers, trade associations, formula-tors, and distributors; users; and public-sector organizations such as environ-mental groups, consumer groups, and trade unions.

The possibility of converting the FAO Code of Conduct into a binding legal instrument instead of the present voluntary Code is under consideration.

## Monitoring/implementation

*Review procedure*
The current information on the operation and implementation of the code is made through reports to the FAO Conference and reports of meetings and workshops which are published and sent to governments. The reports are public.

The provisions of the Code and progress in its implementation are reviewed regularly by panels of experts appointed to deal with specific topics on pesticides. These also include the joint FAO/UNEP panel which specifically deals with PIC (see below).

In the implementation of PIC, FAO, jointly with UNEP, has published the *Guidance for Governments* document. In addition, FAO has published a Decision Guidance Document (DGD) for each pesticide in the PIC procedure, while UNEP has published similar documents on the industrial and consumer chemicals.

There is no actual compliance monitoring or enforcement. Implementa-

tion required a preparatory phase, which included the appointment of designated national authorities by their respective governments and development of a joint database on banned and severely restricted pesticides and other chemicals. The database now includes notifications of control actions, information sent to Designated National Authorities, responses from importing countries, notifications from exporting countries, addresses of DNAs, and text of DGDs.

Several countries have, consequent to the introduction of the Code, introduced laws in their countries for the effective control of pesticides. Certain countries have, on their own accord, incorporated the code into their national pesticide legislation. Implementation is also carried out through regional and bilateral projects in individual countries. FAO holds regional workshops on the implementation of the PIC procedure.

*Trade sanctions*
None.

*Dispute settlement mechanisms*
None, except discussions and persuasion of member governments and the industry.

## Decision-making

*Political bodies*
The *FAO Conference*, which meets every two years, reviews the Code and makes

recommendations to promote the implementation of the Code. The Conference is the major policy-making organ of FAO (see IGOs).

*Scientific/technical bodies*
FAO and UNEP (see IGOs) have established a *Joint Expert Group on Prior Informed Consent*. The function of the group is to provide advice and guidance for the implementation of PIC, to prepare and review Decision Guidance Documents (DGDs) and other technical matters. The first meeting of the group was held in December 1989. Up to September 1994, the group has met seven times.

## Publications

The Code has been published as a booklet. Current information on the operation and implementation of the Code is made through reports to the FAO Conference and reports of meetings and workshops are available from FAO. Additional guide-lines on the Code are available from FAO.

FAO distributes a circular to DNAs twice a year that summarizes the import status in participating countries of pesticides and industrial chemicals subject to the PIC procedure and outlines follow-up actions expected in those countries.

# Convention on the Prevention of Marine Pollution by Dumping of Wastes and Other Matter (London Convention 1972)

## Objectives

To prevent indiscriminate disposal at sea of wastes liable to create hazards to human health, to harm living resources and marine life, to damage amenities, or to interfere with other legitimate uses of the sea. The fundamental principle of the Convention is the prohibition of dumping of certain wastes, the requirement of a specific permit prior to dumping of others, and the demand for a general permit for the rest. The two first categories are determined by Annexes.

## Scope

*Legal scope*
Open for accession by 'any State'. Not open to regional integration organizations. Inter- and non-governmental organizations participate with observer status at the Consultative Meetings of the Convention.

*Geographic scope*
In addition to the global seas it includes the territorial waters of the coastal States.

## Time and place of adoption

13 November 1972, London.

## Entry into force

30 August 1975.

## Status of participation

73 Parties, by 1 September 1994. 5 Signatories without ratification, acceptance, or approval.

## Affiliated protocols, annexes, and organizations

• *Annex I* ('black list') includes radioactive wastes, organohalogenic compounds, mercury and its compounds, and persistent plastics;
• *Annex II* ('grey list') includes products containing significant amounts of, among other things, lead, arsenic, copper, zinc, cyanides, fluorides, pesticides, and their by-products;
• *Annex III* concerns the criteria governing the issuing of permits and specifies the nature of the waste material, the characteristics of the dumping site, and method of disposal.

*International Maritime Organization (IMO)* (see IGOs) is responsible for secretariat duties. Its duties include convening consultative meetings, preparing and assisting in the development of procedures for determining exceptional and emergency procedures, and communicating information and notifications received from contracting parties.

*Co-ordination with related instruments*
The requirements of the permitting system for low-level radioactive wastes incorporate the standards of the International Atomic Energy Agency (IAEA) (see IGOs).

## Secretariat

c/o International Maritime Organization (IMO) (see IGOs).

## Finance

*Budget*
Costs are covered by the regular IMO budget. No core budget related to the Convention is available.

*Special funds*
None.

## Rules and standards

The Parties are committed:
• Individually and collectively to promote effective control of all sources of pollution of the marine environment and to take all practicable steps to prevent pollution of the sea caused by dumping of waste and other matter;
• to take effective measures individually and collectively to prevent marine pollution caused by dumping and to harmonize their policies;
• to prohibit dumping of waste or other matter except as specified;
• to designate an appropriate authority to issue permits, keep records of dumping, monitor the condition of the seas, and report on these matters to IMO;
• to apply measures required to implement the Convention for all vessels and aircraft registered in its territory or flying its flag; loading in its territory or territorial sea any matter to be dumped; or believed to be engaged in dumping under its jurisdiction;
• to take measures to prevent and punish contravention of the Convention; develop procedures for effective application on the high seas.

The Convention prohibits the dumping of wastes or other matter including high-level radioactive wastes under Annex I (the 'black list') of the Convention. Grey-listed wastes such as low-level radioactive wastes are categorized under Annex II and may be released only under a special permit based on conditions set by the Convention and its technical advisers. Dumping of matter listed in Annex III is allowable only by general permit.

A moratorium on low-level radioactive wastes was approved in 1983 and extended in 1985, and again in 1988 for five years. In 1993 the ban was made permanent by means of an amendment to the Convention which entered into force on 21 February 1994. On the same date the incineration of wastes at sea was prohibited and it was agreed that dumping of industrial wastes at sea will be phased out by 31 December 1995. The International Atomic Energy Agency (IAEA) (see IGOs) is the adviser to the Convention on radiological matters.

## Monitoring/implementation

*Review procedure*
Each Contracting Party shall take appropriate measures in its territory to prevent and punish conduct in contravention of the Convention. The Parties also undertake to issue instructions, assist one another, and work together in

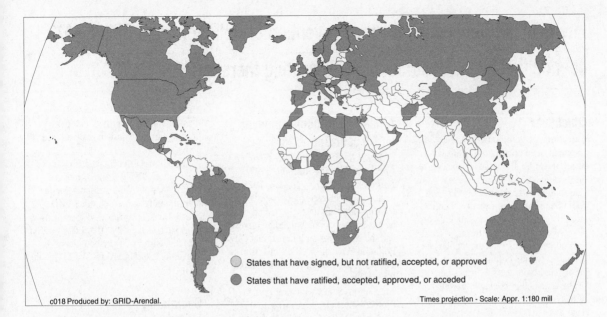

States that have signed, but not ratified, accepted, or approved

States that have ratified, accepted, approved, or acceded

c018 Produced by: GRID-Arendal.                                    Times projection - Scale: Appr. 1:180 mill

the development of co-operative proce-dures for the application of the Conven-tion.

The Parties are required to notify IMO directly or through regional secretariats of the nature, quantity, location, time, and method of dumping of all permitted matter, and of their monitoring of the condition of the sea, and of criteria, measures, and requirements adopted in issuing permits. 25 national reports (36 per cent of the Parties) were submitted in 1991 and 24 national reports (34 per cent of the Parties) were submitted in 1992. These reports are public.

Compliance is monitored and meas-ured by the Consultative Meeting of the Contracting Parties. The Consultative Meeting is able to exercise some control over compliance through notification of dumping activities and monitoring reports, but no formal non-compliance procedures, prior notification procedures, or multilateral consultation procedures have been established.

Notification procedures adopted by the Consultative Meeting also call for the Parties to report compliance monitoring and environmental impact assessments. Only 60 per cent of contracting parties have fulfilled their obligations under the Convention in this respect, and the Consultative Meeting has sought more effective implementation.

Review of data or information in national reports is made by the Secre-tariat. These reviews are public and the Secretariat distribute publication lists of such reviews. There is no independent verification of data or information.

*Observations or inspections*
None by the Convention as such.

*Trade sanctions*
None.

*Dispute-settlement mechanisms*
Disputes concerning interpretation or application are to be settled by negotia-tion, or by other agreed means.

If this is not possible, the dispute shall be submitted, by agreement of the Parties to the dispute, to the International Court of Justice, or at the request of one of them to arbitration. (There is no known use of the procedure.)

## Decision-making bodies
*Political bodies*
The *Consultative Meeting of the Con-tracting Parties* to the London Conven-tion is the governing body and meets annually. *Special Meetings* to be con-vened at the request of two-thirds of the Parties.

*Scientific/technical bodies*
The *Consultative Meeting* requests advice on issues needing multi-discipli-nary expertise from the *Group of Experts on Scientific Aspects of Marine Pollution (GESAMP)*. It has also established *ad hoc* groups to provide advice on specific issues such as incineration at sea. An Inter-Governmental Panel of Experts on Radioactive Waste Disposal at Sea was established in 1986.

The *Scientific Group on Dumping* responds to scientific requests, reviews the provisions of the Annexes, prepares lists of hazardous substances, develops guide-lines on monitoring programmes, and generally maintains awareness of the impacts on the marine environments of inputs from all waste sources. It is the task of this group to draw the attention of the Consultative Meeting to any emerg-ing or worsening problems.

## Publications
Up-to-date information on the operation of the Convention is available through *IMO News* (quarterly), and other reports from IMO.

# International Convention for the Prevention of Pollution from Ships, 1973, as modified by the Protocol of 1978 relating thereto (MARPOL73/78)

## Objectives

• to eliminate pollution of the sea by oil, chemicals, and other harmful substances which might be discharged in the course of operations;
• to minimize the amount of oil which could be released accidentally in collisions or strandings by ships, including also fixed or floating platforms.
• to improve further the prevention and control of marine pollution from ships, particularly oil tankers.

The Convention contains special provision for the control of pollution from more than 400 liquid noxious substances, as well as for sewage, and garbage disposal.

## Scope

*Legal scope*
Open to all States. Not open to regional integration organizations. NGOs participate with observer status at IMO meetings.

*Geographic scope*
The global seas.

The Convention designates the Antarctic, Mediterranean, Baltic, Red, and Black Seas, and the Persian Gulf area as special areas in which oil discharge is virtually prohibited and the Wider Caribbean and the North Sea as special areas subject to more-stringent requirements governing the disposal of ship-generated garbage into the sea.

## Time and place of adoption

2 November 1973 and 17 February 1978 (Protocol), London.

## Entry into force

2 October 1983.

## Status of participation

87 Parties, by 1 September 1994. 34 States have made exceptions for annexes III (24), IV (34), or V (19). No Signatories without ratification.

## Affiliated protocols, annexes, and organizations

*Protocol Relating to the International Convention for the Prevention of Pollution from Ships, London, 1978.* The Protocol introduced stricter regulations for ships and stipulates that a ship may be cleared to operate only after surveys and the issuing of an International Oil Pollution Prevention (IOPP) Certificate. The procedure in effect meant that the Protocol had absorbed the parent convention. States which ratify the Protocol must also give effect to the provisions of the Convention; there is no need for a separate instrument of ratification for the latter. The Protocol and the Convention should therefore be read as one instrument.

The governing scheme of the technical *Annexes I–V* is regulation according to type of pollutant: oil, noxious liquid, harmful substances, sewage, and garbage. The only MARPOL annex not yet in force is Annex IV.

Several *amendments* have been adopted since 1984 and have come into force. The 1992 amendments, which came into force on 6 July 1992, are generally regarded as the most important changes to be made to the Convention since the adoption of the 1978 Protocol. In the past MARPOL, the 1978 Protocol, and many amendments have been concerned mainly with minimizing operational pollution and they have been concentrated mainly on new ships. The 1992 amendments also introduced new regulations which are designed to reduce drastically pollution from accidents; and they apply to existing as well as new tankers.

*International Maritime Organization (IMO)* (see IGOs) receives reports, acts as depositary, carries out secretariat functions, and considers amendments to the Convention and its Annexes.

*Co-ordination with related instruments*
The Convention is a combination of two treaties adopted in 1973 and 1978 respectively. Although it is now one instrument it is described under two headings to show how it evolved (see above).

The Marine Environment Protection Committee (MEPC), one of four main committees of IMO, is responsible for co-ordinating work with other IMO conventions, and with UNEP conventions such as the 1989 Basel Convention for the Control of Transboundary Movements of Hazardous Waste (see this section).

## Secretariat

MARPOL
c/o International Maritime Organization (see IGOs).

## Finance

*Budget*
Costs are covered by the regular IMO budget. No core budget available.

*Special funds*
None.

## Rules and standards

The principal obligations of State Parties are:
• to give effect to the provisions of the Convention and Annexes in order to prevent pollution of the marine environment;
• to prohibit violations, establish sanctions thereto under the law of the administration of the ship concerned, and instigate proceedings if informed of a violation and satisfied that sufficient evidence is available.
• to prohibit violations, and establish sanctions for violations, within the jurisdiction of any Party, and either to cause proceedings to take place or furnish information to the administration of the ship;
• to apply the provisions of the Convention as may be necessary to ensure that more-favourable treatment is not given to ships of non-Parties;
• to co-operate in the detection of

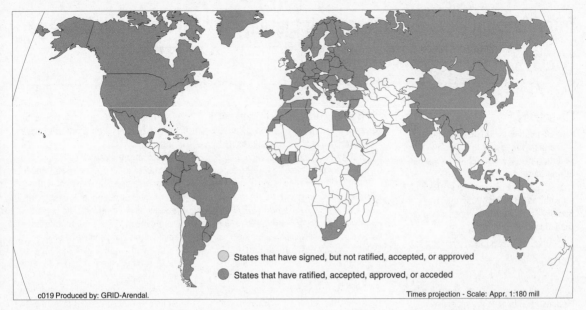

States that have signed, but not ratified, accepted, or approved

States that have ratified, accepted, approved, or acceded

c019 Produced by: GRID-Arendal.                                     Times projection - Scale: Appr. 1:180 mill

violations and in the enforcement of the Convention.

## Monitoring/implementation

*Review procedure*
Compliance with these commitments is primarily monitored and measured by circulating reports made to IMO to the Parties. Reports made by port States following inspections also enable some monitoring of compliance with their obligations by flag States.

Under the mandatory reporting system of MARPOL, Annex I, annual reports have to be submitted to the Convention Secretariat, for consideration by the MEPC at its annual session. The following matters must be reported:
(*a*) *Annual enforcement reports* by port and flag States.
(*b*) *Annual summary report* by the Party State's administration of incidents involving spillages of oil of more than 100 tons.
(*c*) *Annual assessment report*, including
• a statistical report by the port State on the effectiveness of port State control (number of inspections and compliance rate);
• reports by the port State on MARPOL violations by ships resulting in detention or denial of entry into port;
• report on penalties imposed by the port State for violations of MARPOL.

A survey of all types of reports for the period 1985–89 discloses the following

record of compliance with reporting requirements:
    1990: 15 States
    1988: 15 States
    1987: 18 States
    1986: 22 States
Only 16 of 83 Parties provided the Secretariat with the mandatory annual reports required by the Convention for 1991 and 1992. 19 per cent submitted reports under the Convention in 1993. The reports are public, but the quality of information supplied, however, is often inadequate and insufficient to enable useful conclusions to be drawn. There is no independent verification of data or information.

There are no formal provisions for a meeting of the Parties or for a non-compliance procedure.

The MSC and MEPC have reported a variety of causes which might contribute to the lack of effective implementation by flag States. These include the lack of trained and experienced technical personnel within the flag State administration; the inability to retain skilled personnel; inappropriate delegation of inspection authority, or the use of insufficiently qualified and experienced surveyors. In addition, the record of port States in supplying reception facilities has been poor in some areas because of financial constraints. Provision of finance and technical assistance is an important factor in enabling some developing States to implement the

Convention. The reports of the MSC and MEPC are public (see below).

*Observations or inspections*
None by the Convention as such, but it reaffirms the police powers of the port State where a ship is found.

*Trade sanctions*
None.

*Dispute-settlement mechanisms*
There is no provision for dispute settlement. Resort to IMO is a possibility.

Any dispute between two or more Parties shall, if settlement by negotiation has not been possible and if the Parties do not otherwise agree, be submitted, upon the request of any of them, to arbitration as set out in Protocol 2 to the Convention.

## Decision-making

*The Marine Environment Protection Committee (MEPC)* of IMO is established as a main forum for activities relating to the Convention. The MEPC approximately meets every 8 months. 59 member States participated in these meetings in 1994.

## Publications

*IMO News*, and reports of the Marine Environment Protection Committee (MEPC) and Maritime Safety Committee (MSC) of IMO.

# International Convention on Civil Liability for Oil Pollution Damage (CLC)

## Objectives

• to ensure that adequate compensation is available to persons affected by pollution damage through oil escaping during maritime transport by ship;
• to standardize international rules and procedures for determining questions of liability and adequate compensation in such areas.

## Scope

*Legal scope*
Open to all member States of the United Nations, members of the specialized agencies, the IAEA (see IGOs), or Parties to the Statute of the International Court of Justice. Not open to regional integration organizations.

*Geographic scope*
The global seas. The 1984 Protocol (see below) extended the scope into the territorial sea and the exclusive economic zones of the Contracting States.

## Time and place of adoption

29 November 1969, Brussels.

## Entry into force

19 June 1975.

## Status of participation

87 Parties, by 1 September 1994. 3 Signatories without ratification, approval, or acceptance.

## Affiliated protocols, annexes, and organizations

• *Protocol to the International Convention on Civil Liability for Oil Pollution Damage, London 1976.* Entered into force on 8 April 1981. 49 Parties, by 1 September 1994. No Signatories without ratification, acceptance, or approval.
• *Protocol to amend the International Convention on Civil Liability for Oil Pollution Damage, London 1984.* [Not yet in force.] 9 Parties, by 3 October

1994. 10 Signatories without ratification, acceptance, or approval. 10 ratifications, accessions, acceptances, or approvals required to enter into force, including 6 by States having at least a million units of gross tanker tonnage.
• *Protocol to amend the International Convention on Civil Liability for Oil Pollution Damage, London 1992.* [Not yet in force.] 6 Parties, by 3 October 1994. 8 Signatories without ratification, acceptance, or approval. Enters into force 12 months after the deposit of 8 ratifications, accessions, acceptances, or approvals, including 4 by States having at least a million units of gross tanker tonnage. It is expected that this will make entry into force easier than the 1984 Protocol because it will not necessitate acceptance by all the major oil-importing countries.

The *Secretary-General of the International Maritime Organization (IMO)* performs depositary functions.

*Co-ordination with related instruments*
The International Maritime Organization (IMO) (see IGOs) is responsible for co-ordinating work with the International Convention on the Establishment of an International Fund for Compensation for Oil Pollution Damage (Fund Convention) (see this section).

## Secretariat

c/o International Maritime Organization (IMO) (see IGOs).

## Finance

*Budget*
Because IMO provides the deliberation forum and necessary servicing functions, secretariat and administrative costs do not arise under the CLC.

## Rules and standards

The Convention establishes a regime on civil liability for oil pollution damage. The main commitment imposed on Contracting States is to incorporate the

regime into domestic law, whereas actual liability will arise exclusively for owners of oil tankers.
  Other commitments:
• The owner of an oil tanker is liable for pollution damage caused by oil without proof of fault or negligence, except for some special exemptions. The regime therefore clearly identifies an addressee against whom claims must be addressed—without, however, denying the owner's right of recourse under domestic law;
• The owner has to cover his liability by insurance or other financial instruments. Bankruptcy or dissolution of the company, therefore, will not preclude compensation;
• The owner may limit his liability depending upon the tonnage of the ship, but not exceeding the amount of 210 million gold-based francs. In practice, the limits have been set with reference to the structure of the insurance market. No claim which is not based on the conventional regime may be made against any person engaged in the operation or salvage of a ship;
• The right to limit liability is based upon the formation of a fund with a competent court or authority in one of the Contracting Parties in which a claim has been brought or where damage has occurred.
  The fund is exclusively established for disbursing claims in compensation for pollution damage occurring in the territory zone of a Contracting Party and for measures to prevent such damages. The oil pollution liability regime therefore exists alongside traditional maritime liability regimes which cover other claims.
  The Convention does not apply to warships and other state-owned ships not engaged in commercial activities.
  The objective of the 1976 Protocol is to replace the gold-based unit of accounts by Special Drawing Rights (SDR) of the International Monetary Fund (IMF) (see IGOs). Figures were adjusted accordingly to SDR13 million (CLC),

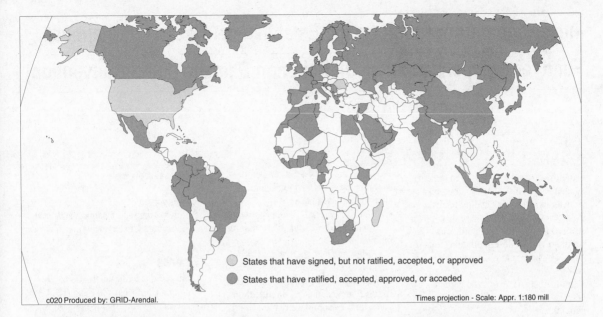

States that have signed, but not ratified, accepted, or approved

States that have ratified, accepted, approved, or acceded

c020 Produced by: GRID-Arendal.      Times projection - Scale: Appr. 1:180 mill

SDR30 million (Fund Convention) (see this section), and SDR60 million (limit for action by the Assembly).

The objectives of the 1984 Protocol are:
(*a*) to draw conclusions in the context of past legal and Fund Practice; and
(*b*) to adapt ceilings with reference to inflation and increased economic risks involved in maritime transport of oil. Ceilings have been raised to SDR59.7 million for owner liability under the revised CLC (applicable to large tankers) and to SDR135 million for compensation with respect to the revised Fund Convention (including amount paid under CLC); this amount is to be increased to SDR200 million in case certain major contributors join the Fund Convention as revised by the Protocol.

Contracting States have certain auxiliary duties to perform. They shall:
• ensure that competent authorities attest and certify that shipowners cover risks of oil pollution by appropriate insurance;
• mutually accept certificates issued by Contracting States;
• ensure that oil tankers, wherever registered (also in non-contracting states), do not enter or leave ports or offshore installations situated in their territory or territorial sea without such a certificate;

• ensure that courts have necessary competences;
• recognize judgments of courts competent under the Convention;
• waive immunity concerning ships which are state-owned but involved in commercial trading.

The objective of the 1992 Protocol is to increase the compensation available to victims of oil spills from approximately £54 million for each accident under the previous system to a limit of approximately £122 million.

## Monitoring/implementation

*Review procedure*
Institutionalized monitoring of the implementation of these duties or reporting obligations does not exist. However, the cost-effective part of the CLC liability regime, the coverage of economic risk by insurance, is subject to decentralized control by port States.

*Observations or inspections*
None by the Convention as such.

*Trade sanctions*
None.

*Dispute-settlement mechanisms*
None.

## Decision-making

*Political bodies*
The CLC does not have its own institutional apparatus, such as a regular conference of Parties. Commitments are not regularly reviewed. However, IMO, as depositary organization, shall convene a conference of Contracting Parties if so desired by at least one-third of the Parties. Such a conference has been called three times: for the adoption of Protocols in 1976, in 1984, and in 1992.

The IMO Legal Committee (see IGOs), is responsible for the general supervision and review of the CLC.

*Scientific bodies*
The CLC regime has no system or rules by which scientific and technical knowledge is incorporated into the decision-making process. As the regime is primarily concerned with allocation of economic risks involved in maritime transportation of oil, the input of scientific and technical knowledge plays a minor role in the decision-making process.

## Publications

Up-to-date developments are reported in *IMO News*, published quarterly.

# International Convention on the Establishment of an International Fund for Compensation for Oil Pollution Damage (Fund Convention)

## Objectives

• to provide for a compensation system, supplementing that of the International Convention on Civil Liability for Oil Pollution Damage (CLC) (see this section) in order to ensure full compensation to victims of oil pollution damage caused by persistent oil spills from laden tankers;

• to distribute the economic burden between the shipping industry and oil cargo interests.

## Scope

*Legal scope*
Open to States Parties to the International Convention on Civil Liability for Oil Pollution Damage (CLC) (see this section).

*Geographic scope*
Pollution damage caused on the territory, including the territorial sea, of Contracting States. The 1992 Protocol (see below) extended the scope into the exclusive economic zone of Contracting States.

## Time and place of adoption

18 December 1971, Brussels.

## Entry into force

16 October 1978.

## Status of participation

60 Parties, by 1 September 1994. 4 Signatories without ratification, approval, or acceptance.

## Affiliated protocols, annexes, and organizations

• *Protocol to the International Convention on the Establishment of an International Fund for Compensation for Oil Pollution Damage, London 1976.*

Entered into force on 22 November 1994. 27 Parties, by 1 September 1994. No Signatories without ratification, approval, or acceptance.

• *Protocol to amend the International Convention on the Establishment of an International Fund for Compensation for Oil Pollution Damage, London 1984.*
[Not in force.] 5 Parties, by 1 September 1994. 9 Signatories without ratification, approval, or acceptance. 8 ratifications, accessions, or approvals required, and a minimum representation of 600 million tonnes of contributing oil. The Protocol shall not enter into force prior to the entry into force of the CLC Protocol of 1984. Governments are called to ratify only the 1992 protocol to avoid a situation in which two conflicting treaty regimes are operational. It is practically certain that this Protocol will never enter into force.

• *Protocol to amend the International Convention on the Establishment of an International Fund for Compensation for Oil Pollution Damage, London 1992.*
[Not yet in force.] 3 Parties, by 1 September 1994. 8 Signatories without ratification, approval, or acceptance. 8 ratifications, accessions, or approvals required, and a minimum representation of 450 million tonnes of contributing oil. It is expected that the 1992 Protocol will enter into force during the first half of 1996.

The *Secretary-General of the International Maritime Organization* performs depositary functions.

## Secretariat

International Oil Pollution Compensation Fund (IOPC Fund),
4 Albert Embankment,
London SE1 7SR,
United Kingdom
*Telephone*:     +44-71-5822606
*Telefax*:        +44-71-7350326

*Director*
Mr Måns Jacobsson.

*Number of staff*
5 professionals and 5 support staff at the Fund Secretariat (Oct. 1994).

## Finance

Contributions to the International Oil Pollution Compensation Fund (IOPC Fund) are assessed on the basis of the quantity of oil received in a Contracting State after sea transport. The Japanese oil industry has been the major contributor to the IOPC Fund to date.

*Budget*
Annual Secretariat costs account for approximately £1.2 million. Expenses are paid by receivers of crude or heavy fuel oil, and not by Contracting States.

## Rules and standards

*Compensation system*
• The IOPC Fund provides compensation up to a flat-rate ceiling if:
  • the shipowner is exonerated from liability;
  • the shipowner is financially incapable of paying; or
  • the victims are not fully compensated by the shipowner under the CLC (see this section).
• The IOPC Fund also indemnifies the shipowner for a part of the liability imposed upon him.
• IOPC Fund compensation for a single incident is limited to 900 (gold) francs.
• The IOPC Fund is financed by contributions of persons who receive more than 150,000 tonnes of crude or heavy fuel oil after sea transport in a Contracting State during a calendar year. Contributions are determined in proportion to the quantity of oil received.
• The Fund Convention imposes on Contracting Parties primarily the

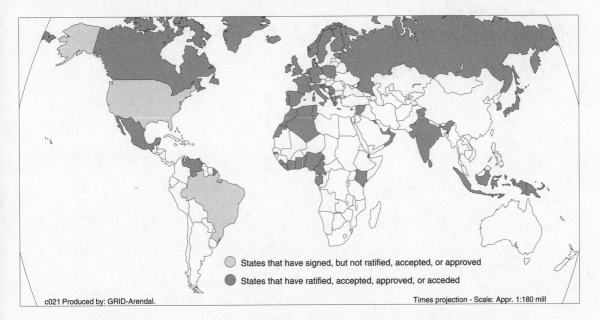

States that have signed, but not ratified, accepted, or approved

States that have ratified, accepted, approved, or acceded

c021 Produced by: GRID-Arendal.

Times projection - Scale: Appr. 1:180 mill

obligation to incorporate its provisions into domestic law.

• The objective of the 1976 Protocol is to replace the gold-based unit of account by Special Drawing Rights (SDR) of the International Monetary Fund (see IGOs). Figures were adjusted accordingly to SDR13 million (CLC) (see this section), SDR60 million (present Fund Convention limit).

• The objectives of the 1992 Protocol are to provide enhanced scope and high limits of compensation. Ceilings of compensations have been raised to SDR59.7 million for owner liability under the revised CLC (applicable to large tankers) and to SDR135 million for compensation with respect to the revised Fund Convention (including amount paid under CLC); this latter amount is to be increased to SDR200 million if, as a result of certain States ratifying the Protocol, the total quantity of contributing oil reaches a certain level.

## Monitoring/implementation

*Review procedure*
Parties shall communicate annually a list of oil-receiving persons under their jurisdiction and the quantity of oil received by each person. These reports are private.

The Convention does not provide for organized monitoring of implementation. The annual submission of lists of contributing persons is closely monitored by the IOPC Fund Secretariat.

The IOPC Fund Secretariat is well-informed about relevant national law and maintains close informal relations with the administrative units of Contracting Parties responsible for implementation of the regime. The implementation process is promoted by informal consultations. IOPC
Fund activities are reported to the Assembly of Contracting States and to the Executive Committee (see Decision-making, below).

*Observations or inspections*
None by the Convention as such.

*Trade sanctions*
None.

*Dispute-settlement mechanisms*
None.

## Decision-making

A Secretariat, led by the IOPC Fund Director, is responsible for the conduct of business, including collection of contributions and settlements of claims.

*Political bodies*
The Fund Convention has established two decision-making organs, the *Assembly* of Contracting States which meets annually, and the *Executive Committee* comprising 15 Contracting States, which meets several times a year.

*Scientific bodies/technical bodies*
None.

## Publications

Current developments are reported in the IOPC Fund's Annual Report. Also published periodically are a General Information Booklet and a *Claims Manual*.

# International Convention on Oil Pollution Preparedness, Response, and Co-operation (OPRC)

## Objectives

- to prevent marine pollution by oil, in accordance with the precautionary principle;
- to advance the adoption of adequate response measures in the event that oil pollution does occur;
- to provide for mutual assistance and co-operation between States for these aims.

## Scope

*Legal scope*
Open to all States. Not open to regional integration organizations. An international conference comprised of 90 States drafted the final text and adopted the Convention.

*Geographic scope*
The global seas.

## Time and place of adoption

29 November 1990, London.

## Entry into force

13 May 1995.

## Status of participation

16 Parties, by 3 October 1994. 19 Signatories without ratification, approval, acceptance, or accession.

## Affiliated protocols, annexes, and organizations

The *Annex* to the Convention provides general principles concerning reimbursements for the costs incurred by nations that assist in responding to spills. In the absence of an existing bilateral or multilateral arrangement, the requesting nation shall reimburse the assisting nation for the costs incurred. However, if an assisting nation acts on its own initiative, it will bear the costs. The costs are to be calculated according to the law and custom of the assisting nation.

10 affiliated *Resolutions* were adopted by the Conference dealing with e.g. institutional matters, expansion of scope to hazardous substances, and technical co-operation and transfer of technology.

*International Maritime Organization (IMO)* (see IGOs) shall act as clearing-house for information submitted to it by the Parties, and to facilitate co-operation among the Parties in technical and educational matters. These functions will be carried out after entry into force of the Convention. Provision for an interim arrangement has been made through implementation of Article 12 dealing with Secretariat responsibilities. The *Secretary-General of the International Maritime Organization* performs depositary functions.

*Co-ordination with related instruments*
As a follow-up to the Convention and, in particular, to the provision requiring all ships to carry oil-pollution emergency plans, the Marine Environment Protection Committee (MEPC), one of four main committees of IMO, adopted amendments to Annex 1 of MARPOL 73/78 (see this section). Co-ordination with regional organizations or arrangements are recognized.

## Secretariat

c/o International Maritime Organization (IMO) (see IGOs).

## Finance

*Budget*
The Convention does not provide for regular meetings and programme activities, nor a Secretariat. Therefore, under the Convention regular administrative costs do not arise.

*Special funds*
None.

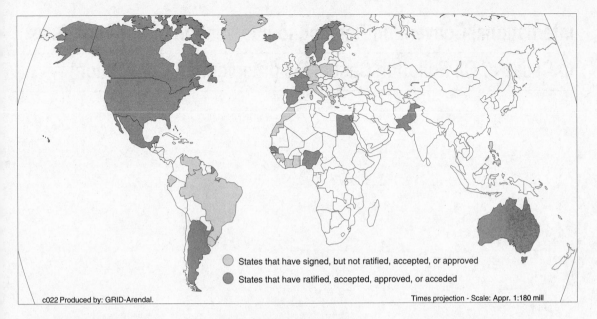

States that have signed, but not ratified, accepted, or approved

States that have ratified, accepted, approved, or acceded

c022 Produced by: GRID-Arendal.

Times projection - Scale: Appr. 1:180 mill

## Rules and standards

Parties must require ships, offshore units, and sea ports under their jurisdiction to have oil-pollution emergency plans. These are required for:
• oil tankers of 150 gross tons and above, and other ships of 400 gross tons and above;
• any fixed or floating offshore installation or structure engaged in gas or oil exploration, exploitation, production activities, or loading or unloading oil;
• any seaport and oil handling facility that presents a risk of an oil pollution incident.

The Convention has established a reporting procedure on oil pollution incidents. Under this procedure, all persons having charge shall be required to report such incidents to the competent national authority, which must assess the incident and inform other states and/or IMO. Parties shall establish national and, as far as possible, regional systems for preparedness and response. They shall co-operate in pollution response, research, and technical matters.

## Monitoring/implementation

*Review procedure*
Beyond the general obligations to co-operate in research and technical assistance, no provision for disclosure of data is made. Parties are required to ensure that current information is provided to IMO response and preparedness systems. Parties shall evaluate the effectiveness of the Convention together with IMO. No evaluation criteria or time-scales are given.

The MEPC has established an OPRC Working Group that is open to representatives from all IMO members, UN organizations, and intergovernmental organizations in consultative status with IMO. The Working Group reports to the MEPC and meets in conjunction with MEPC meetings. According to the current work plan, the Working Group shall recommend ways and means to improve the involvement of industry (oil, shipping, oil spill clean-up) in the implementation of the Convention.

*Observations or inspections*
None by the Convention as such.

*Trade sanctions*
None.

*Dispute-settlement mechanisms*
None.

## Decision-making

The Convention does not establish a meeting of the Parties or similar institution. The *Marine Environment Protection Committee (MEPC)* of IMO is responsible for co-ordinating and administering the activities.

## Publications

*IMO News* and reports of the Marine Environment Protection Committee (MEPC).

# International Convention Relating to Intervention on the High Seas in Cases of Oil Pollution Casualties (Intervention Convention)

## Objectives
• to protect the interest of peoples against the grave consequences of maritime casualties resulting in danger of oil pollution of the sea and coastline;
• to recognize that measures of an exceptional character to protect such interests might be necessary on the high seas, provided these do not affect the principle of freedom of the high seas.

## Scope
*Legal scope*
Membership is open to member States of the United Nations, or any specialized agency, or the IAEA (see IGOs), or Parties to the Statute of the International Court of Justice.

*Geographic scope*
The global seas.

## Time and place of adoption
29 November 1969, Brussels.

## Entry into force
6 May 1975.

## Status of participation
62 Parties, by 1 September 1994. 6 Signatories without ratification, approval, or acceptance.

## Affiliated protocols, annexes, and organizations
*Protocol Relating to Intervention on the High Seas in Cases of Marine Pollution by Substances Other Than Oil, London, November 1973.* 31 Parties, by 1 September 1994. The basic objective of the Protocol is to extend the 1969 Convention to apply also to substances other than oil, such as noxious substances, liquefied gases, and radioactive substances.

*International Maritime Organization (IMO)* (see IGOs) receives reports, acts as depositary, and considers amendments to the Conventions and its Annexes.

*Co-ordination with related instruments*
IMO is responsible for co-ordinating work with other IMO conventions.

## Secretariat
c/o International Maritime Organization (IMO) (see IGOs).

## Finance
*Budget*
Costs are covered by the regular IMO budget. No core budget available.

## Rules and standards
The following commitments are imposed on Parties:
• to consult with other States affected before taking measures;
• to notify proposed measures to any person or company known to have interests which can reasonably be expected to be affected by those measures;
• to use best endeavours to avoid risk to human life and to afford assistance to persons in need;
• to notify without delay States and persons or companies concerned and the secretary-general of IMO;
• to set up and maintain a list of independent experts;
• to ensure that measures taken are proportionate to the damage, actual or threatened, and necessary to protect the interest of the coastal State;
• to pay compensation for measures taken in excess of those reasonably necessary.

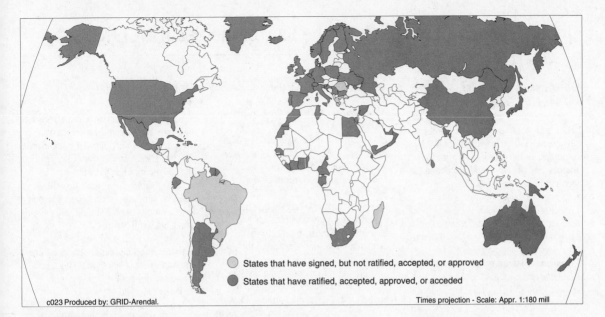

States that have signed, but not ratified, accepted, or approved

States that have ratified, accepted, approved, or acceded

c023 Produced by: GRID-Arendal.                    Times projection - Scale: Appr. 1:180 mill

## Monitoring/implementation

*Review procedure*
The Parties are required to report on
measures taken under the Convention to
IMO and to other States affected. No
reports have been received by IMO.

*Monitoring*
No observations or inspections by the
Convention as such.

*Trade sanctions*
None.

*Dispute-settlement mechanisms*
No dispute is known to have arisen
among any of the Parties concerning
measures taken to deal with pollution
casualties, nor is any Party known to
have been obliged to pay compensation.
The dispute-settlement mechanism has
not been invoked. The Convention
provides for unilateral resort to conciliation or, if unsuccessful, to arbitration.

## Decision-making

IMO acts as reporting facility, and
depositary, and maintains a list of
independent experts.

## Publications

Up-to-date information on the operation
of the Convention is made available
through *IMO News* (quarterly).

# United Nations Convention on the Law of the Sea (UNCLOS)

## Objectives
• to establish a comprehensive legal order to facilitate international communication and promote peaceful uses of the oceans, rational utilization of their resources, conservation of living resources, and the study and protection of the marine environment.
• to establish basic environmental protection principles and rules on global and regional co-operation, technical assistance, monitoring, and environmental assessment, and adoption and enforcement of international rules and standards and national legislation with respect to all sources of marine pollution.

## Scope
*Legal scope*
Open to all States, certain self-governing associated States and territories, and international organizations, to which their member States have transferred competence over matters governed by the Convention.

*Geographic scope*
Global. All seas and oceans, both within and beyond the limits of national jurisdiction.

## Time and place of adoption
10 December 1982, Montego Bay, Jamaica.

## Entry into force
16 November 1994.

## Status of participation
67 Parties, by 15 October 1994. [96 Signatories, including 1 territory (the Northern Mariana Islands) and the European Community, without ratification or formal confirmation.]

## Affiliated protocols, annexes, and organizations
Nine *annexes* are attached to the Convention, forming an integral part thereof. The Convention was adopted together with four resolutions, forming an integral whole.

*Agreement relating to the Implementation of Part XI of the United Nation Convention on the Law of the Sea of 10 December 1982.* Adopted by the 48th session of the General Assembly of the United Nations. Provisions of the Agreement and of Part XI of the Convention shall be interpreted and applied together as a single instrument. Any instrument of ratification or formal confirmation of or accession to the Convention represents also consent to be bound by this Agreement and no State or entity may establish its consent to be bound by the Agreement unless it has to be bound by the Convention. Agreement is applied provisionally from the date of entry into force of the Convention, i.e., 16 November 1994.

Following entry into force, the Convention's institutions will be established: the International Seabed Authority, the International Tribunal for the Law of the Sea, and the Commission on the Limits of the Continental Shelf.

## Secretariat
Division for Ocean Affairs and Law of the Sea,
Office of Legal Affairs, United Nations
2 United Nations Plaza,
New York, NY 10017,
USA
*Telephone*:     +1-212-963-3990/3997
*Telefax*:       +1-212-9635847
*E-mail*:        doalos@undp.org

*Director*
Mr Jean-Pierre Levy.

*Legal Officer*
Mr Moritaka Hayashi.

*Number of staff*
23 professionals and 14 support staff (Oct. 1994).

## Finance
*Budget*
Annual costs are approximately $US4,000,000, paid from the regular UN budget.

## Rules and standards
The States must:
• keep under surveillance the effects of any activities which they permit or in which they engage, in order to determine whether these activities are likely to pollute the marine environment. The results obtained from such surveillance must be communicated to international organizations, which should make them available to all States.
• follow-up their commitment by actively enforcing national and applicable international standards with regard to all sources of pollution under their jurisdiction.
• settle disputes concerning the interpretation and application of the relevant Convention provisions by peaceful means and ensure that recourse is available in their court systems for claims arising from damage to the marine environment caused by persons under their jurisdiction;
• adopt measures for the conservation of living resources and co-operate in taking such measures for high-seas fisheries.

The Convention covers all sources of marine pollution, giving particular attention to the regime for *vessel-source pollution* without interfering with vital commerce. The Convention allocates enforcement responsibilities, as also for the regulation of ocean dumping, among the *Flag State* (state of vessel registry), *Coastal State* (state whose coastal waters the vessel transits), and *Port State* (state whose ports, including offshore terminals, the vessel visits).

The environmental provisions of the Convention do not apply to a warship, naval auxiliary, or other vessels or aircraft being used by the government in non-commercial service, although flag States are urged to apply them so far as is reasonable and practicable.

## Monitoring/implementation
*Review procedure*
The basic objectives of the Convention in the areas of environment and development have been incorporated into most global and regional instruments. National laws have been extensively

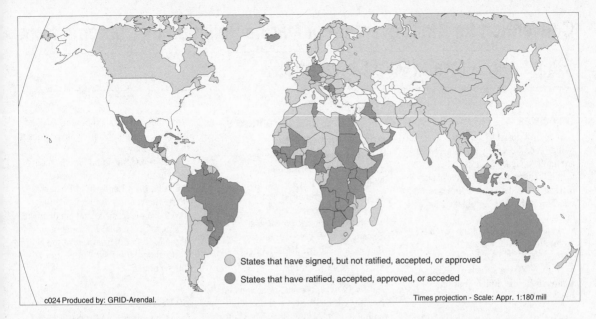

States that have signed, but not ratified, accepted, or approved

States that have ratified, accepted, approved, or acceded

c024 Produced by: GRID-Arendal.

Times projection - Scale: Appr. 1:180 mill

amended and further developed, and new laws adopted, mostly in conformity with the Convention. Several international and regional organizations have also taken measures to adjust their mandate and activities to the provisions of the Convention.

It is left to the Parties to devise the ways and means of individually or jointly pursuing systematic and *ad hoc* monitoring programmes, taking into account similar programmes already established by other treaties and organizations.

States are regularly informed of national, bilateral, regional, and global legislative and policy developments by means of the *Annual Report of the Secretary-General on the Law of the Sea* to the UN General Assembly, the *Annual Review* of main documentary materials, and the *Law of the Sea Bulletin*.

The annual UN General Assembly plenary debate and its regularly annual resolution on the Law of the Sea provide the opportunity for promoting compliance and follow-up on non-compliance in general terms. There is also the practice among States of sending formal protest notes against measures taken by other States which they consider contrary to, or not in conformity with, the Convention. Such protests are published, *inter alia*, in the *Law of the Sea Bulletin* and/or circulated by note verbale to member States at the request of the States concerned. Once in force, the

Convention's dispute-settlement mechanisms will enhance the ability to deal with non-compliance.

*Dispute-settlement mechanisms*
Compulsory procedures entailing binding decisions: the International Tribunal for the Law of the Sea, Arbitration, Special Arbitration. The International Tribunal will be located in Hamburg, Germany.

## Decision-making

The *Secretary-General of the United Nations* is designated as the depositary of the Convention and is required to report on 'issues of a general nature' that have arisen with respect to the Convention. Presently, this is accomplished through the Annual Report to the UN General Assembly. The good offices of the Secretary-General were used to resolve the outstanding problems with provisions on the International Seabed Area which impeded universal acceptance of the Convention as a whole. The Division for Ocean Affairs and the Law of the Sea is responsible for administration of the Convention, including the servicing of the first session of the Assembly of the *International Seabed Authority* as well as the servicing of the meetings of the *Commission on the Limits of the Continental Shelf*.

In the field of the conservation of living resources and the protection and preservation of the marine environment,

the Convention provides for the involvement of 'competent international organizations' in various degrees in the decision-making process. Scientific and technical groups are organized on an *ad hoc* basis to advise on specific issues. The UN Conference on Straddling Fish Stocks and Highly Migratory Fish Stocks is mandated to resolve problems impeding the effective implementation of the relevant Convention provisions on the management and conservation of these resources.

## Publications

• *Report of the Secretary-General*, submitted annually to the General Assembly under the item 'The Law of the Sea'.
• *Annual Review of Ocean Affairs: Law and Policy,* contains texts and selected extracts of documents emanating from global and regional organizations.
• *The Law of the Sea Bulletin,* contains the texts of relevant national legislation and treaties as well as other information on the law of the sea.
• Other Law of the Sea publications include collections of national legislation, legislative histories of Convention provisions, bibliographies, and expert advice on special issues such as baselines, maritime delimitation, exclusive economic zones, high-seas fisheries, continental shelf, and marine scientific research.

# Convention for the Prevention of Marine Pollution by Dumping from Ships and Aircraft (Oslo Convention)

## Objectives
• to take all possible steps to prevent the pollution of the sea by substances that are liable to create hazards to human health, to harm living resources and marine life, to damage amenities, or to interfere with other legitimate users of the sea.
• to prevent pollution of the sea, by prohibiting the dumping of harmful substances from ships and aircraft, and by providing for a system of permits or approvals for the dumping of other substances.

## Scope
*Legal scope*
Membership is based on the States specified in the Convention; others may accede following a unanimous invitation to do so from the Contracting Parties.

*Geographic scope*
Regional, related to the north-east Atlantic including the North Sea. It covers the high seas, the territorial seas, and the internal waters of the Parties.

The Convention sets down a number of ground rules which did not exist before, e.g. 'black' and 'grey' lists which are now to be found in practically all international treaties on marine pollution.

## Time and place of adoption
15 February 1972, Oslo.

## Entry into force
6 April 1974.

## Status of participation
13 Parties, by 25 October 1994. No Signatories without ratification, acceptance, or approval.

## Affiliated protocols, annexes, and organizations
• *Protocol to the Oslo Convention Concerning Incineration at Sea*, Oslo, 2 March 1983. Ratified by all Parties to the Convention, as required. Entered into force on 1 September 1989.
• *Internal Waters Protocol*, Oslo, 5 December 1989. [Not yet in force.] 9 Parties, by October 1994. Although not yet in force the Protocol is being observed on a voluntary basis. Ratifications, approvals, or acceptances by all Parties to the Convention are required to enter into force. The Protocol will extend the geographical scope of the Convention.

*Annex I* ('black list') includes mercury, cadmium, and organohalogen compounds;

*Annex II* ('grey list') includes arsenic, chromium, copper, lead, nickel, and their compounds;

*Annex III* contains provisions governing the issue of permits and approvals for the dumping of wastes at sea, both as to the characteristics of the waste and as to those of the dumping site and method of dumping.

*Annex IV* provides rules on incineration at sea.

The *Oslo Commission (OSCOM)* adopts measures for the prevention of the pollution of the sea, receives reports on the implementation of such measures, on dumping activities, and on the state of the environment, and considers amendments to the Convention and its Annexes.

*Co-ordination with related instruments*
The Oslo Commission and the Paris Commission (PARCOM) (see this section) work together and have a common Secretariat. OSCOM also co-operates with the International Maritime Organization (IMO) (see IGOs) and with ICES (see IGOs).

The Declarations of the ministerial-level North Sea Conferences have laid down principles and targets for the reduction of marine pollution in the North Sea, including dumping. These have been implemented by the Parties to the Oslo Convention.

The Oslo Convention and the Convention for the Prevention of Marine Pollution from Land-based Sources (Paris Convention) (see this section) have been modernized and amalgamated in a new Convention for the Protection of the Marine Environment of the North-East Atlantic (OSPAR Convention) (see this section).

## Secretariat
Oslo Commission (OSCOM),
New Court, 48 Carey Street,
London WC2A 2JQ,
United Kingdom
*Telephone*: +44-71-2429927
*Telefax*: +44-71-8317427

*Executive Secretary*
Ms Claire Nihoul.

*Number of staff*
5 executive staff members and 6 assistants shared with the Paris Commission (Oct. 1994).

## Finance
The annual budget of the Oslo and Paris Commissions is met by funds supplied by the Contracting Parties.

*Budget*
The total budget was £557,070 in 1993, £740,504 in 1994, and is £750,000 in 1995. The actual administrative core budget at the Secretariat was £142,200 in 1993, £143,000 in 1994, and is £150,000 in 1995.

## Rules and standards
Dumping of substances listed in Annex I is prohibited (certain exceptions apply: trace contaminant, *force majeure*). Dumping of any materials requires a permit or approval from the appropriate national authority or authorities.

Each Contracting Party undertakes:

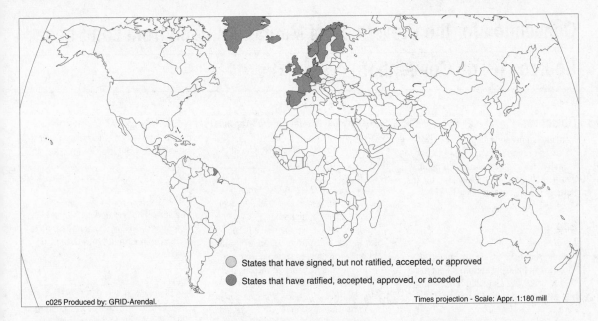

States that have signed, but not ratified, accepted, or approved

States that have ratified, accepted, approved, or acceded

c025 Produced by: GRID-Arendal.                    Times projection - Scale: Appr. 1:180 mill

- to ensure compliance with the provisions of the Convention by ships and aircraft registered in its territory; loading in its territory materials to be dumped, or believed to be engaged in dumping within its internal waters or territorial sea;
- to issue instructions, assist one another, and work together in the development of co-operative procedures for the application of the Convention, particularly on the high seas;
- to take in its territory appropriate measures to prevent and punish conduct in contravention of the Convention;
- to establish complementary or joint programmes of scientific and technical research and to transmit to each other the information obtained.

## Monitoring/implementation

*Review procedure*
Contracting Parties are required to submit records, once a year, of dumping permits and approvals issued, and of dumping which has taken place, to the Commission for its consideration.

Reports were received from all Contracting Parties which issue permits or approvals for dumping or incineration at sea in 1992. The reports of the Contracting Parties are public.

A Prior Consultation Procedure (PCP) has been established whereby Parties proposing to issue a permit for the dumping of wastes containing Annex I

substances, must first inform the other members of the Commission. It also requires Parties to give documented information as to alternative disposal methods to dumping that have been considered.

The Commission exercises overall supervision over the implementation of the Convention; receives and considers the records of permits and approvals issued; reviews generally the condition of the sea and the efficacy of the control measures; keeps under review the contents of the annexes and recommends amendments, additions, or deletions which may be adopted by unanimous vote in the Commissions.

Information in the national reports is reviewed by the relevant specialist subsidiary body of the Commission and subsequently by the Oslo Commission itself (which includes NGO observers). These reviews are public and publication lists are distributed by the Commission.

The following decisions have been made by the Commission:
- incineration at sea was terminated in 1991;
- the dumping of industrial waste in the North Sea was terminated in 1989 and will be phased out in other parts of Convention waters by 1995;
- the dumping at sea of sewage sludge is to be phased out by 1998.

*Observations or inspections*
None by the Convention as such. This is

the responsibility of Contracting Parties, in accordance with the relevant measures adopted by the Commission.

*Dispute-settlement mechanisms*
None.

## Decision-making

*Political bodies*
The *Oslo Commission*, with representatives from the governments of each of the Contracting Parties, is the governing body and meets annually.

*Scientific/technical bodies*
In anticipation of the entry into force of the OSPAR Convention (see this section) and the consequent establishment of an OSPAR Commission, OSCOM and PARCOM have integrated their organizations to a high degree. Within this new structure, the scientific/subsidiary bodies whose tasks include responsibilities derived from the Oslo Convention are:
- *Assessment and Monitoring Committee (ASMO)*;
- *Working Group on Inputs to the Marine Environment (INPUT)*;
- *Working Group on Impacts on the Marine Environment (IMPACT)*;
- *Working Group on Concentrations, Trends, and Effects of Substances in the Marine Environment (SIME)*.

## Publications

Annual Reports.

# Convention for the Prevention of Marine Pollution from Land-based Sources (Paris Convention)

## Objectives
• to take all possible steps to prevent pollution of the sea by adopting individually and jointly measures to combat marine pollution and by harmonizing the Parties' policies in this regard.

## Scope
*Legal scope*
Membership is based on the States specified in the Convention, others may accede following an unanimous invitation to do so from the Contracting Parties.

*Geographic scope*
Regional, related to the north-east Atlantic including the North Sea. It covers the high seas, and the territorial waters and the saline internal waters of the Contracting Parties.

The Convention, being one of the first international agreements aimed at the prevention of pollution from land-based sources, has much potential bearing on global environment protection. The approach it adopted has been used as a model in other regional agreements.

## Time and place of adoption
4 June 1974, Paris.

## Entry into force
6 May 1978.

## Status of participation
13 Parties, including the European Economic Community, by 25 October 1994. 1 Signatory, without ratification, acceptance, or approval.

## Affiliated protocols, annexes, and organizations
*Amending Protocol, Paris, 1986.* Entered into force on September 1989. The objective of the Protocol is to extend the Convention to include the prevention of pollution through the atmosphere by emissions into the atmosphere from land or from man-made structures.

*Annex A, part 1* ('black list') includes mercury, cadmium, organohalogen compounds.

*Annex A, part 2* ('grey list') includes arsenic, chromium, copper, lead, nickel, zinc, and their compounds.

*Annex B* lays down the procedural rules for the constitution of an arbitration tribunal whose award shall be final and binding upon the Parties to the dispute.

*Co-ordination with related instruments*
The Paris Commission (PARCOM) and the Oslo Commission (OSCOM) work together and have a common Secretariat (see this section). PARCOM also co-operates with the International Maritime Organization (IMO) (see IGOs) and with ICES (see IGOs).

The ministerial-level North Sea Conferences have made a significant contribution to the implementation of the Convention, especially with respect to the setting of specific reduction targets for emissions and inputs.

The Paris Convention and the Convention for the Prevention of Marine Pollution by Dumping from Ships and Aircraft (Oslo Convention) (see this section) have been modernized and amalgamated into a new Convention for the Protection of the Marine Environment of the North-East Atlantic (OSPAR Convention) (see this section) which was established at a ministerial conference in Paris, 22 September 1992.

## Secretariat
Paris Commission (PARCOM),
New Court,
48 Carey Street,
London WC2A 2JQ,
United Kingdom
*Telephone*: +44-71-2429927
*Telefax*: +44-71-8317427

*Executive Secretary*
Ms Claire Nihoul.

*Number of staff*
5 executive staff members and 6 assistants shared with Oslo Commission (Oct. 1994).

## Finance
The annual budget of the Oslo and Paris Commissions is met by funds supplied by the Contracting Parties to the Conventions.

*Budget*
The total budget was £557,070 in 1993, £740,504 in 1994, and is £750,000 in 1995. The actual administrative core budget at the Secretariat was £142,200 in 1993, £143,000 in 1994, and is £150,000 in 1995.

## Rules and standards
The Parties are required to implement measures for the elimination of pollution by substances listed in Part 1 of Annex A and for the reduction or elimination of pollution by substances listed in Part 2 of Annex A.

This Convention requires the elimination of 'pollution' by the blacklisted substances (in Part 1 of Annex A), unlike the Oslo Convention which prohibits the dumping of blacklisted substances.

Each Contracting Party undertakes:
• to ensure compliance with the provisions of this Convention;
• to take in its territory appropriate measures to prevent and punish conduct in contravention of the provisions of the Convention;
• to set up and operate a permanent monitoring system.

Parties are required:
• to exchange information in order to assist one another to prevent accidents which may result in pollution from land-based sources;
• to establish complementary or joint programmes of scientific and technical research and to transmit to each other the information obtained.

In case of serious pollution from land-based sources by a substance not listed in

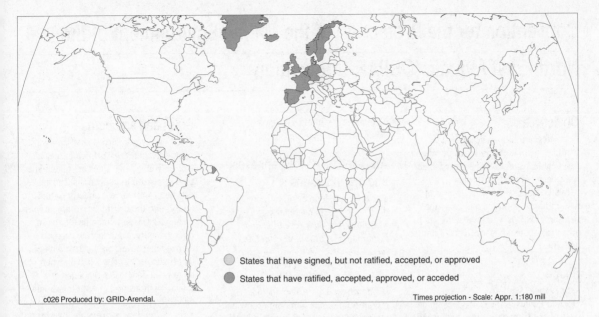

States that have signed, but not ratified, accepted, or approved

States that have ratified, accepted, approved, or acceded

c026 Produced by: GRID-Arendal.

Times projection - Scale: Appr. 1:180 mill

Annex A, Part 1, the Parties shall consult and negotiate a co-operation agreement.

In 1989 the Commission adopted the PARCOM Recommendation 89/2 on the Use of 'Best Available Technology' (BAT). The Parties agreed that BAT should be applied in the programmes and measures adopted under the Convention.

The PARCOM Recommendation 91/1 on the Definition of 'Best Environmental Practice' was adopted by the Commission in 1991. By using the best environmental practice (BET), Parties are required to minimize or eliminate inputs from diffuse sources.

The Commission may adopt recommendations for amendments to Annex A by a three-quarters majority vote of its members.

## Monitoring/implementation

*Review procedure*
Contracting Parties are required to inform the Commission of the legislative and administrative measures they have taken to ensure compliance with the provisions of the Convention.

They are also required to transmit to the Commission:
• the results of monitoring
• the most detailed information available on the substances listed in the Annexes to the present Convention.

National reports are submitted on a wide range of topics by all Contracting Parties (though not all Parties submit reports on all topics) according to agreed timetables. The reports are public.

The Commission exercises overall supervision over the implementation of the Convention. It is the duty of the Commission to promote compliance by reviewing the general condition of the seas, the effectiveness of the control measures adopted, and the need for any additional or different measures. The Commission can also make recommendations when following up on non-compliance.

The relevant specialist subsidiary body of the Commission and subsequently by the Paris Commission itself (which includes NGO observers) reviews data or information in the national reports. These reviews are public and the Secretariat of the Commission distributes lists of such reviews.

*Observations or inspections*
None by the Convention as such. This is the responsibility of Contracting Parties, in accordance with the relevant measures adopted by the Commission.

*Dispute-settlement mechanisms*
Any dispute between Parties relating to the interpretation or application of the Convention, which cannot be settled otherwise by the Parties concerned shall, at the request of any of those Parties, be submitted to arbitration under the conditions laid down in Annex B to the Convention (see above).

## Decision-making

*Political bodies*
The *Paris Commission*, with representatives from each of the Parties, is the governing body and meets annually.

*Scientific/technical bodies*
In anticipation of the entry into force of the OSPAR Convention (see this section) and the consequent establishment of an OSPAR Commission, OSCOM and PARCOM have integrated their organizations to a high degree. Within this new structure, the scientific/subsidiary bodies whose tasks include responsibilities derived from the Oslo Convention are:
• Programmes and Meausures Commitee (PRAM);
• *Working Group on Point Sources (POINT)*;
• *Working Group on Diffuse Sources (DIFF)*;
• *Working Group on Nutrients (NUT)*;
• *Working Group on Radioactive Substances (RAD)*;
• *Working Group on Sea-Based Activities (SEBA)*.

## Publications

Annual Reports. Lists of Oslo and Paris Commissions' publications are available on demand from the Secretariat.

# Convention for the Protection of the Marine Environment of the North-East Atlantic (OSPAR Convention)

## Objectives

• to safeguard human health and to conserve marine ecosystems and, when practicable, restore marine areas which have been adversely affected;
• to take all possible steps to prevent and eliminate pollution and enact the measures necessary to protect the sea area against the adverse effects of human activities.

## Scope

*Legal scope*
Open to Parties to the Oslo Convention or the Paris Convention (see below and this section); any other coastal state bordering the maritime area (see below), any state located upstream on water-courses reaching the maritime area, or any regional economic integration organization having a member state to which the above paragraphs refer.

*Geographic scope*
Regional. The maritime area covers the north-east Atlantic including the North Sea and comprises the internal waters and the territorial sea of the Contracting Parties, the sea beyond and adjacent to the territorial sea under the jurisdiction of the coastal state to the extent recognized by international law, and the high seas, including the bed and subsoil thereof.

## Time and place of adoption

22 September 1992, Paris.

## Entry into force

Not yet in force. Enters into force on the thirtieth day after the deposit of the instruments of ratification, acceptance, approval, or accession by all the Contracting Parties to the Oslo Convention and all the Contracting Parties to the Paris Convention. Upon its entry into force, the Convention shall replace the Oslo and Paris Conventions.

## Status of participation

4 Parties, by June 1994. 12 Signatories, including the European Economic Community, without ratification, acceptance, or approval.

## Affiliated protocols, annexes, and organizations

The different sources of pollution are dealt with in separate annexes:
• *Annex I, On the Prevention and Elimination of Pollution from Land-based Sources*;
• *Annex II, On the Prevention and Elimination of Pollution by Dumping or Incineration*. This Annex includes a moratorium on the dumping of low and intermediate level radioactive substances, including wastes, in the north-east Atlantic which will be imposed for 15 years from 1 January 1993. Once the moratorium expires, nations wishing to dump such waste may be allowed to do so only if they prove that a less dangerous disposal method cannot be found. If no request for dumping is made, the moratorium will be extended for a further ten years;
• *Annex III, On the Prevention and Elimination of Pollution from Offshore Sources*;
• *Annex IV, On the Assessment of the Quality of the Marine Environment*.

The Convention replaces the Convention for the Protection of Marine Pollution by Dumping from Ships and Aircraft (Oslo Convention) (see this section) and the Convention for the Prevention of Marine Pollution from Land-based Sources (Paris Convention) (see this section).

## Secretariat

Information on the Convention is available from the Oslo and Paris Commissions (see this section).

## Finance

*Budget*
Not yet applicable. The Commission to be established under the Convention will draw up its Financial Regulations.

## Rules and standards

The Contracting Parties shall apply:
• the *precautionary principle*: that is that preventive measures are taken when there is reason to believe that substances or energy introduced, directly or indirectly, into the marine environment may create hazards to human health, harm living resources and marine ecosystems, damage amenities, or interfere with other legitimate uses of the sea even when there is no conclusive evidence of a causal relationship between inputs and their effects;
• the *polluter pays principle*, by virtue of which costs of pollution prevention, control, and reduction measures shall be borne by the polluter.

In implementing the Convention, Parties shall adopt programmes and measures containing, where appropriate, time-limits for their completion, which take full account of the use of the *best available technology (BAT)* and *best environmental practices (BET)* designed to prevent and eliminate pollution to the fullest extent.

The Contracting Parties agree to apply the measures they adopt in such a way as to prevent an increase in pollution of the sea outside the maritime area or in other parts of the environment.

No provision of the Convention shall be interpreted as preventing the Parties from taking, individually or jointly, more stringent measures with respect to the prevention and elimination of pollution of the maritime area or with respect to the protection of the maritime area against the adverse effects of human activities.

Contracting Parties shall take, individually and jointly, all possible steps to prevent and eliminate pollution:
• from land-based sources, in particular as provided for in *Annex I*;
• by dumping or incineration of wastes or other matter, in particular as provided for in *Annex II*;
• from offshore sources, in particular as provided for in *Annex III*.

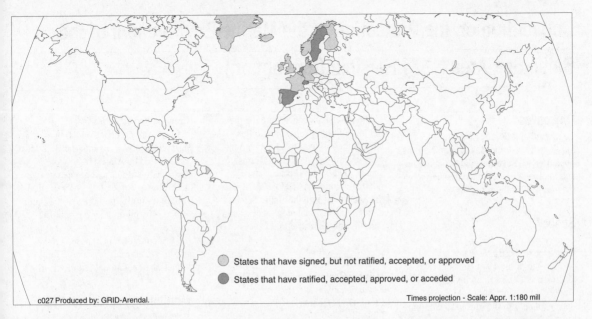

States that have signed, but not ratified, accepted, or approved

States that have ratified, accepted, approved, or acceded

c027 Produced by: GRID-Arendal.     Times projection - Scale: Appr. 1:180 mill

The Parties shall, in particular, as provided for in *Annex IV*:
• undertake and publish at regular intervals joint assessments of the quality status of the marine environment and of its development, for the marine area, or for regions or subregions thereof;
• include in such assessments both an evaluation of the effectiveness of the measures taken and planned for the protection of the marine environment and the identification of priorities for action.

## Monitoring/implementation
### Review procedure
The Parties shall report to the Commission at regular intervals on:
• the legal, regulatory, or other measures taken by them for the implementation of the provisions of the Convention and of decisions and recommendations adopted thereunder, including in particular measures taken to prevent and punish conduct in contravention of those provisions;
• the effectiveness of the measures referred to above;
• problems encountered in the implementation of the provisions referred to above.
    The Commission shall:
• on the basis of the reports submitted by the Parties, assess their compliance with the Convention and the decisions and recommendations adopted thereafter;

• when appropriate, decide upon and call for steps to bring about full compliance with the Convention, and decisions adopted thereunder, and promote the implementation of recommendations, including measures to assist a Party to carry out its obligations.
    The Commission shall supervise the implementation of the Convention and generally review the condition of the maritime area, the effectiveness of the measures being adopted, the priorities, and the need for any additional or different measures.

### Observations or inspections
None by the Convention as such.

### Environmental monitoring programmes
See Oslo and Paris Conventions.

### Dispute-settlement mechanisms
Any dispute between Parties relating to the interpretation or application of the Convention, which cannot be settled otherwise by the Parties concerned shall, at the request of any of those Parties, be submitted to arbitration under the conditions laid down in Article 32 of the Convention.

## Decision-making
### Political bodies
A *Commission*, with representatives of each of the Parties will be established as the governing body and shall meet at

regular intervals. It may establish other subsidiary bodies which it considers necessary and define their terms of reference.
    The Commission may adopt amendments, annexes, and protocols to the Convention by unanimous vote of the Parties. Some Annexes and amendments to Annexes may be adopted by a three-quarters majority vote of the Parties.
    Decisions and recommendations shall be adopted by unanimous vote of the Parties. Should unanimity not be attainable, the Commission may none the less adopt decisions or recommendations by a three-quarters majority vote of the Parties.
    Any body or agency, whether national or international, governmental or non-governmental, which is qualified in matters relating to the Convention, may be admitted as an observer by unanimous vote of the Parties. Such observers may present to the Commission any information or reports relevant to the objectives of the Convention.

### Scientific/technical bodies
To be established.

## Publications
Up-to-date information on the Convention is made available through the Secretariat of the Oslo and Paris Commissions.

# Convention on the Protection of the Marine Environment of the Baltic Sea Area (1974 Helsinki Convention)

## Objectives

To take all appropriate measures, individually or by means of regional co-operation, to prevent and abate pollution and to protect and enhance the marine environment of the Baltic Sea area.

## Scope

*Legal scope*
Restricted to the Baltic States which participated in the 1974 Helsinki Conference. Others upon invitation by all the Contracting Parties. Membership open explicitly to the European Community (EC).

*Geographic scope*
Regional. The Convention covers the Baltic Sea proper with the Gulf of Bothnia, the Gulf of Finland, and the entrance to the Baltic Sea. Internal waters are not included.

## Time and place of adoption

22 March 1974, Helsinki.

## Entry into force

3 May 1980.

## Status of participation

10 Parties, including the European Community, by 20 September 1994. No Signatories without ratification, acceptance, or approval.

## Affiliated protocols, annexes, and organizations

*Annexes* contain detailed operational obligations on substances to be controlled and form an integral part of the Convention.
  *Co-ordination with related instruments*
Upon entry into force of the *1992 Convention on the Protection of the Marine Environment of the Baltic Sea Area (1992 Helsinki Convention)* (see this section) this 1974 Helsinki Convention shall cease to apply.

The provisions concerning the prevention of pollution from ships follow closely the International Convention for the Prevention of Pollution from ships, as modified by the Protocol of 1978 relating thereto (MARPOL 73/78) (see this section) where the Baltic Sea is defined as a 'special area' necessitating strict discharge restrictions.

## Secretariat

Helsinki Commission (HELCOM),
Katajanokanlaituri 6 B,
FIN-00160 Helsinki,
Finland
*Telephone*:        +358-0-6220220
*Telefax*:        +358-0-62202239

*Chairman*
Mr Harald Velner, Estonia.

*Executive Secretary*
Mr Ulf Ehlin.

*Number of staff*
6 professionals and 8 support staff (Sept. 1994).

## Finance

The income to the budget originates in principle from equal contributions from the Contracting Parties as well as an extra contribution by Finland as the host country. In 1993 a special decision for a transition period of maximum three years was taken concerning the system of sharing the contributions.

*Budget*
The administrative core budget was approximately FIM9.1 million for 1992/93, FIM9.1 million for 1993/94, and is FIM8.5 million for 1994/95.

## Rules and standards

The Parties are committed;
• to prevent and control pollution from various sources including pollution from land-based sources, disposal of wastes at sea by ships, or through dumping, and

from sea-bed activities;
• to counteract the introduction of hazardous substances into the Baltic Sea as specified by Annex 1;
• to take measures and co-operate according to Annex 6 in order to eliminate or minimize pollution of the Baltic Sea area by oil or other harmful substances.
  The commitments imposed on the Parties are normally discharge limit values and operational requirements.

## Monitoring/implementation

*Review procedure*
Compliance is controlled by means of obligatory reporting according to a unified procedure, as well as by regular pollution load compilation projects and emission inventories.
  Parties also report on their progress and measures in their respective countries regarding implementing HELCOM Recommendations (see below) according to unified reporting formats. The reports are private. No information is available on number of national reports submitted.
  The appropriate national authorities are obliged to inform the Commission of the quantity, quality, and method of discharge of substances listed in Annex 2, in respect of land-based pollution.
  Only dumping of dredged spoils is permitted, and such dumping activities, as well as emergency dumping, are also reported to the Commission.
  The Parties are required to develop and apply a system for receiving, channelling, and dispatching reports on significant spillages of oil or other harmful substances.
  The Parties must also provide information to the other Parties about their national organizations and regulations on combating pollution at sea by oil.
  The work of the Commission and its subsidiary bodies is focused on implementing the relevant provisions of the Convention, as well as on promoting the compliance with their obligations of the Parties under the Convention's regime.
  Among the intergovernmental organi-

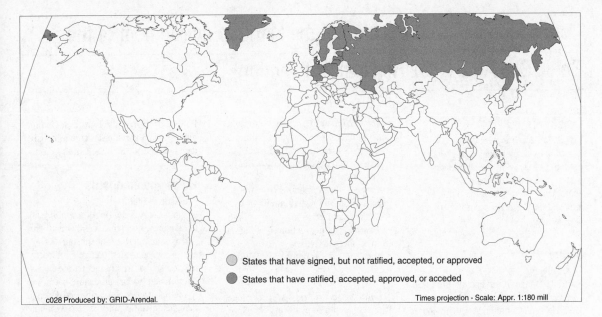

States that have signed, but not ratified, accepted, or approved

States that have ratified, accepted, approved, or acceded

c028 Produced by: GRID-Arendal.    Times projection - Scale: Appr. 1:180 mill

zations participating in the work of the Commission as observers are UNEP, UN/ECE, IMO, WHO, ICES, IAEA, WMO (see IGOs), International Baltic Sea Fishery Commission (IBSFC), and OSCOM/PARCOM (see this section).

Coalition Clean Baltic (CCB), Standing Conference of Rectors, Presidents, and Vice-Chancellors of the European Universities (CRE), European Union for Coastal Conservation (EUCC), European Chlor-Alkali industry (EURO CHLOR), Green-peace, International Council for Local Environmental Governments (ICLEI), Union of the Baltic Cities (UBC), and World Wide Fund For Nature (WWF) have also been granted observer status with the Commission.

Public information on the operation and implementation of the decisions by the Commission is made available to governments through the annual activities reports as well as the private reports from the annual Helsinki Commission meetings. The Secretariat does not distribute publication lists of such reviews.

*Environmental monitoring programmes*
The Parties have agreed upon several monitoring programmes by which data on airborne pollution, radioactive substances, and several determinands of the marine environment are collected.

*Data and information system programmes*
The *Baltic Marine Environment Bibliography* has been produced by the Commission since the 1970s. An on-line version of this database, *BALTIC,* was established in 1987. It contains all aspects of the Baltic Sea area, for example, ecology, fauna, and flora, fisheries, hydrography, pollution, environmental impact, research planning, and administrative measures. It is available on-line through the Swedish Environmental Protection Agency and is updated once or twice per year.

*Dispute-settlement mechanisms*
If a dispute arises between Parties about the interpretation or application of the Convention, they shall seek a solution by negotiation or request mediation by a third Party. If an agreement cannot be achieved the Parties concerned can submit the case to a permanent arbitration tribunal, or to the International Court of Justice.

## Decision-making
*Political bodies*
The *Helsinki Commission (HELCOM)* is established according to the Convention. The offices of chairman and vice-chairman of the Commission rotate between the Parties in alphabetical order every two years.

The decisions by the Commission are taken unanimously and decisions on

measures are most often given in the form of Recommendations to be implemented through appropriate national legislation. The implementation of these Recommendations is under permanent review by the Commission (see above).

*Scientific/technical bodies*
The Commission has established five permanent Committees and several permanent and *ad hoc* working groups as subsidiary bodies to the Commission itself or to the Committees. The permanent committees are:
• Environment Committee (EC);
• Technological Committee (TC);
• Maritime Committee (MC);
• Combating Committee (CC);
• HELCOM Programme Implementation Task Force (HELCOM PITF), which is composed of HELCOM countries, Belarus, Czech Republic, Norway, Slovak Republic, Ukraine, the European Bank for Reconstruction and Development (EBRD), the European Investment Bank, the Nordic Investment Bank/the Nordic Environment Finance Corporation, the World Bank, and the International Baltic Sea Fishery Commission.

## Publications
• *Baltic Sea Environmental Proceedings*, distributed to libraries, laboratories, and institutions inside as well as outside the region;
• *Helcom News.*

# Convention on the Protection of the Marine Environment of the Baltic Sea Area (1992 Helsinki Convention)

## Objectives

To take all appropriate measures, individually or by means of regional co-operation, to prevent and eliminate pollution in order to promote the ecological restoration of the Baltic Sea area and the preservation of its ecological balance.

## Scope

*Legal scope*
Restricted to the States and the European Community which participated in the 1992 Helsinki Conference. Others upon invitation by all the Contracting Parties.

*Geographic scope*
Regional. The Convention covers the Baltic Sea and the entrance to the Baltic Sea bounded by the parallel of the Skaw in the Skagerrak at 57° 44.43'N. Internal waters are included.

## Time and place of adoption

9 April 1992, Helsinki.

## Entry into force

Not yet in force. Enters into force two months after the deposit of the last instrument of ratification or approval by all Signatory States bordering the Baltic and by the European Community.

## Status of participation

3 Parties, including the European Community, by 29 September 1994. 7 Signatories without ratification, acceptance, or approval.

## Affiliated protocols, annexes, and organizations

The following attached *Annexes* form an integral part of the Convention:
• *Annex I*, on harmful substances to be controlled;
• *Annex II*, on criteria for the use of *best environmental practice (BEP)* and *best available technology (BAT)*;

• *Annex III*, on criteria and measures concerning the prevention of pollution from land-based sources;
• *Annex IV*, on prevention of pollution from ships;
• *Annex V*, on exemptions from the general prohibition of dumping of waste and other matter;
• *Annex VI*, on prevention of pollution from offshore activities;
• *Annex VII*, on response to pollution incidents.

*Co-ordination with related instruments*
Upon entry into force of this Convention, the *1974 Convention on the Protection of the Marine Environment of the Baltic Sea Area* (1974 Helsinki Convention) (see this section), shall cease to apply.

The provisions concerning the prevention of pollution from ships follow closely the International Convention for the Prevention of Pollution from Ships, 1973, as modified by the Protocol of 1978 relating thereto (MARPOL 73/78) (see this section) where the Baltic Sea is defined as a 'special area' necessitating strict discharge restrictions.

## Secretariat

In accordance with the Resolution by the Diplomatic Conference the present Secretariat of the 1974 Convention will continue with its duties under the 1992 Convention.

Helsinki Commission (HELCOM),
Katajanokanlaituri 6 B,
FIN-00160 Helsinki,
Finland
*Telephone*: +358-0-6220220
*Telefax*: +358-0-62202239

## Finance

*Budget*
The Commission shall adopt an annual or biennial budget when the Convention enters into force. The total amount of the annual or biennial budget, including any supplementary budget adopted by the Commission, shall be contributed by the

Parties, other than the European Community, in equal parts, unless unanimously decided otherwise by the Commission.

## Rules and standards

The Parties shall:
· apply the *precautionary principle*, i.e. to take preventive measures when there is reason to assume that substances or energy introduced, directly or indirectly, may create hazards in the marine environment to human health, harm living resources and marine ecosystems, damage amenities, or interfere with other legitimate uses of the sea even when there is no conclusive evidence of a causal relationship between inputs and their alleged effects;
• promote the use of *best environmental practice (BEP)* and *best available technology (BAT)*. If the reduction of inputs, resulting from the use of BEP and BAT, as described in Annex II, does not lead to environmentally acceptable results, additional measures shall be applied.
• apply the *polluter-pays principle*;
• ensure that measurements and calculations of emissions from point sources to water and air, and of inputs from diffuse sources to water and air are carried out in a scientifically appropriate manner in order to assess the state of the marine environment of the Baltic Sea area and ascertain the implementation of the Convention;
• use their best endeavours to ensure that the implementation of the Convention does not cause transboundary pollution in areas outside the Baltic Sea area. Furthermore, the relevant measures shall not lead either to unacceptable environmental strains on air quality and the atmosphere or on waters, soil, and ground water. Nor shall they lead to unacceptably harmful or increasing waste disposal, or to increased risks to human health.

| | |
|---|---|
| ◯ | States that have signed, but not ratified, accepted, or approved |
| ⬤ | States that have ratified, accepted, approved, or acceded |

c029 Produced by: GRID-Arendal.                               Times projection - Scale: Appr. 1:180 mill

## Monitoring/implementation

*Review procedure*
Each Party shall implement the provisions of the Convention within its territories, sea, and its internal waters through its national authorities.

Parties shall report to the Commission at regular intervals on:
(*a*) the legal, regulatory, or other measures taken for the implementation of the provisions of the Convention, of its Annexes, and of recommendations adopted thereunder;
(*b*) the effectiveness of the measures taken to implement the provisions referred to in paragraph (*a*) above;
(*c*) problems encountered in the implementation of the provisions referred to in paragraph (*a*) above.

On the request of a Party or of the Commission, the Parties shall provide information on discharge permits, emission data, or data on environmental quality, as far as available.

The Commission shall:
• keep the implementation of the Convention under continuous observation;
• make recommendations on measures relating to the purposes of the Convention;
• keep under review the contents of the Convention, including its Annexes, and recommend amendments as may be required including the lists of substances and materials as well as the adoption of new Annexes;

• define pollution control criteria, objectives for the reduction of pollution, and objectives concerning measures, particularly those described in Annex III;
• receive, process, summarize, and disseminate relevant scientific, technological, and statistical information from available sources;
• seek the services of competent regional and other international organizations to collaborate in scientific and technological research as well as other relevant activities pertinent to the objectives of the Convention.

*Observations or inspections*
None by the Convention as such.

*Data and information system programmes*
The *Baltic Marine Environment Bibliography* has been produced by the Helsinki Commission since the 1970s. An on-line version of this database, *BALTIC,* was established in 1987. It contains all aspects of the Baltic Sea area, for example, ecology, fauna, and flora, fisheries, hydrography, pollution, environmental impact, research planning, and administrative measures. It is available on-line through the Swedish Environmental Protection Agency and is updated once or twice per year.

*Dispute-settlement mechanisms*
If a dispute arises between Parties as to the interpretation or application of the Convention, they shall seek a solution by negotiation or request mediation by a third Party, a qualified international organization, or a qualified person. If an agreement cannot be achieved the Parties concerned can submit the case to an *ad hoc* arbitration tribunal, to a permanent arbitration tribunal, or to the International Court of Justice.

## Decision-making

*Political bodies*
The *Baltic Marine Environment Protection Commission/Helsinki Commission (HELCOM)* is established for the purposes of the Convention. The offices of chairman and vice-chairman of the Commission rotate between the Parties every two years. Meetings of the Commission shall be held at least once a year upon convocation by the chairman. Extraordinary meetings shall, upon the request of any Party endorsed by another Party, be held by the chairman as soon as possible.

Unless otherwise provided under this Convention, the Commission shall take its decisions unanimously. Each Party shall have one vote in the Commission.

*Scientific/technical bodies*
To be established.

## Publications

Up-to-date information on the Convention is made available through the Helsinki Commission.

# Conventions within the UNEP Regional Seas Programme

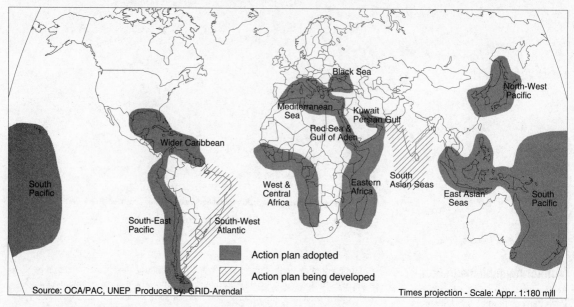

**Areas covered by the UNEP Regional Seas Programme**

## Objectives

The Regional Seas Programme of the United Nations Environment Programme (UNEP) was established in 1974 to tie coastal nations together in a common commitment to mitigate and prevent degradation of the world's coastal areas, inshore waters, and open oceans.

Each programme is tailored to the specific needs of its shoreline participants, but is made of similar components:

• an Action Plan for co-operation on management, protection, rehabilitation, development, monitoring, and research of coastal and marine resources;
• an intergovernmental agreement of a framework convention embodying general principles and obligations;
• detailed protocols dealing with particular environmental problems, such as oil spills, dumping, emergency co-operation, and protected areas.

Funds for these activities come initially from UNEP and then from trust funds set up by the governments involved.

## Scope

*Legal scope*
Open to coastal states in the respective region. In some cases, upon invitation, open to other states and intergovernmental integration organizations.

*Geographic scope*
Regional. The conventions address the needs of particular regions as perceived by the governments concerned. Together with the regional conventions covering the North-East Atlantic (see the Oslo and Paris Conventions and the North-East Atlantic Convention, this section) and the Baltic Sea area (see the 1974 and 1992 Helsinki Conventions, this section), these con-ventions have a global scope.

There are nine regional conventions within the Regional Seas Programme so far, covering:
• the Black Sea;
• the wider Caribbean;
• the East African seaboard;
• the Persian Gulf;
• the Mediterranean;
• the Red Sea and the Gulf of Aden;
• the South Pacific;
• the South-East Pacific;
• the Atlantic coast of West and Central Africa.

Action Plans have been established for the East Asian Seas and the North-West Pacific (September 1994). Action Plans are being formulated for the South Asian Seas and the South-West Atlantic.

## Programme co-ordination

The programme is under the overall co-ordination of the (UNEP) Oceans and Coastal Areas Programme Activity Centre (OCA/PAC) but it depends on the work of specialized agencies and co-operating intergovernmental organizations and centres dealing either with specific regions covered by the programme or with specific subjects common to most or all of the regions.

(UNEP) Oceans and Coastal Areas/
Programme Activity Centre (OCA/PAC),
PO Box 30552,
Nairobi, Kenya
*Telephone*: +254-2-621234
*Telefax*: +254-2-622788
*E-mail*: verlaan.unep@un.org
(internet)

*Director*
Mr Peter Schröder.

*Information Officer*
Ms Ruth Batten.

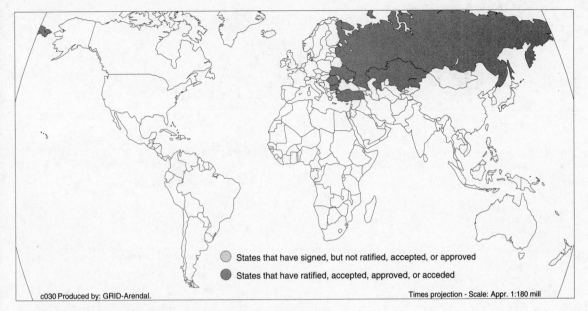

States that have signed, but not ratified, accepted, or approved

States that have ratified, accepted, approved, or acceded

c030 Produced by: GRID-Arendal.                    Times projection - Scale: Appr. 1:180 mill

**Convention on the Protection of the Black Sea against Pollution**

## Convention on the Protection of the Black Sea against Pollution

*Objectives*
• to achieve progress in the protection of the marine environment of the Black Sea and in the conservation of its living resources.

*Time and place of adoption*
21 April 1992, Bucharest.

*Entry into force*
15 January 1994.

*Status of participation*
6 Parties, by 30 September 1994. No Signatories without ratification, acceptance, or approval.

*Affiliated protocols, annexes, and organizations*
The following related protocols are signed, but not ratified, accepted, or approved by the Signatories to the Convention:
• *Protocol on Protection of the Black Sea Marine Environment against Pollution from Land-based Sources*;
• *Protocol on Co-operation in Combating Pollution of the Black Sea Marine Environment by Oil and Other Harmful*

*Substances in Emergency Situations*;
• *Protocol on the Protection of the Black Sea Marine Environment against Pollution by Dumping.*

*Secretariat*
Established in Istanbul for an initial period of three years.

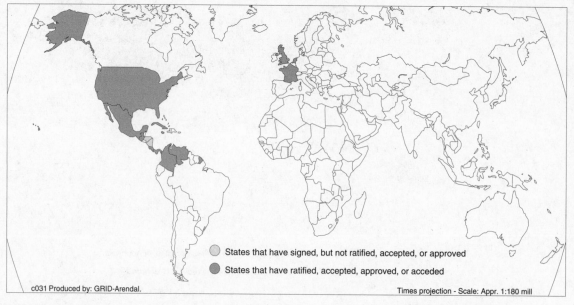

States that have signed, but not ratified, accepted, or approved

States that have ratified, accepted, approved, or acceded

c031 Produced by: GRID-Arendal.                    Times projection - Scale: Appr. 1:180 mill

**Convention for the Protection and Development of the Marine Environment of the Wider Caribbean Region**

## Convention for the Protection and Development of the Marine Environment of the Wider Caribbean Region

### Objectives
• to achieve sustainable development of marine and coastal resources in the Wider Caribbean region through effective integrated management that allows for increased economic growth.

### Time and place of adoption
24 March 1983, Cartagena de Indias.

### Entry into force
11 October 1986.

### Status of participation
19 Parties, by 31 July 1994. 3 Signatories, including the European Community, without ratification, acceptance, or approval.

### Affiliated protocols, annexes, and organizations
• *Protocol Concerning Co-operation in Combating Oil Spills in the Wider Caribbean Region, Cartagena de Indias, 1983*. Entered into force on 11 October 1986. 18 Parties, by 31 July 1994. 2 Signatories, without ratification, acceptance, or approval;
• *Protocol Concerning Specially Protected Areas and Wildlife to the Convention for the Protection and Development of the Marine Environment of the Wider Caribbean Region, Kingston, 1990*. [Not yet in force.] 2 Parties, by 31 July 1994. 13 Signatories, without ratification, accep-tance, or approval. 9 ratifications or accessions required to enter into force.

### Secretariat
UNEP Caribbean Environment Programme,
Regional Co-ordinating Unit (CAR/RCU),
14-20 Port Royal Street,
Kingston,
Jamaica
*Telephone*:          +809-922926-7/8/9
*Telefax*:             +809-922-9292/0195
*E-mail*:              unienet:unx040;
                       econet:uneprcu.ja;
                       environet:une091

### Officer in Charge
Mr Beverly A. Miller

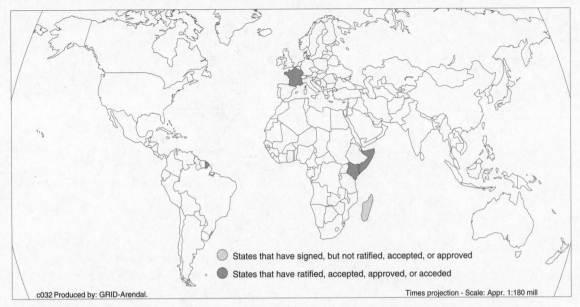

States that have signed, but not ratified, accepted, or approved
States that have ratified, accepted, approved, or acceded

c032 Produced by: GRID-Arendal.                                    Times projection - Scale: Appr. 1:180 mill

**Convention for the Protection, Management, and Development of the Marine and Coastal Environment of the Eastern African Region**

## Convention for the Protection, Management, and Development of the Marine and Coastal Environment of the Eastern African Region

### Objectives
• to protect and manage the marine environment and coastal areas of the Eastern African region.

### Time and place of adoption
21 June 1985, Nairobi.

### Entry into force
Not yet in force. 6 ratifications or accessions required to enter into force.

### Status of participation
5 Parties, by 30 September 1994. 2 Signatories, including the European Community, without ratification, acceptance, or approval.

### Affiliated protocols, annexes, and organizations
• *Protocol Concerning Protected Areas and Wild Fauna and Flora in the Eastern African Region, Nairobi, 1985.* [Not yet in force.] 5 Parties, by 30 September 1994. 2 Signatories, including the European Community, without ratification, acceptance, or approval. 6 ratifications or accessions required to enter into force;

• *Protocol Concerning Co-operation in Combating Marine Pollution in Cases of Emergency in the Eastern African Region, Nairobi, 1985.* [Not yet in force.] 5 Parties, by 30 September 1994. 2 Signatories, including the European Community, without ratification, acceptance, or approval. 6 ratifications or accessions required to enter into force.

### Secretariat
(UNEP) Oceans and Coastal Areas/ Programme Activity Centre (OCA/PAC), PO Box 30552, Nairobi, Kenya
*Telephone*:      +254-2-622029
*Telefax*:          +254-2-622788

### Director
Mr Peter Schröder.

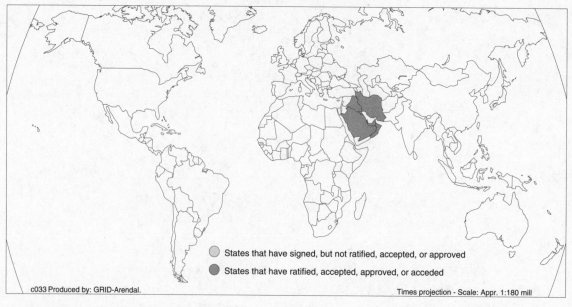

States that have signed, but not ratified, accepted, or approved

States that have ratified, accepted, approved, or acceded

c033 Produced by: GRID-Arendal.                                        Times projection - Scale: Appr. 1:180 mill

**Kuwait Regional Convention for Co-operation on the Protection of the Marine Environment from Pollution**

## Kuwait Regional Convention for Co-operation on the Protection of the Marine Environment from Pollution

### Objectives
• to prevent, abate, and combat pollution of the marine environment in the region.

### Time and place of adoption
24 April 1978, Kuwait.

### Entry into force
1 July 1979.

### Status of participation
8 Parties, by 30 September 1994. No Signatories without ratification, acceptance, or approval.

### Affiliated protocols, annexes, and organizations
• *Protocol Concerning Regional Co-operation in Combating Pollution by Oil and Other Harmful Substances in Cases of Emergency, Kuwait, 1978.* Entered into force on 1 July 1979. Same status of participation as the Convention;
• *Protocol Concerning Marine Pollution Resulting from Exploration and Exploitation of the Continental Shelf, Kuwait 1989.* Entered into force on 17 February 1990. Same status of participation as the Convention;
• *Protocol for the Protection of the Marine Environment against Pollution from Land-based Sources, Kuwait 1990.* Entered into force on 2 January 1993. 6 Parties. 1 Signatory without ratification, accep-tance, or approval.

### Secretariat
Regional Organization for the Protection of the Marine Environment (ROPME), PO Box 26388, 13124 Safat, Kuwait
*Telephone*:          +965-531214-0/3
*Telefax*:             +965-5324172

*Executive Secretary*
H. E. Dr Abdul Rahman Al-Awadi.

*Co-ordinator (Techn. and Admin.)*
Dr Mahmood Y. Abdulraheem.

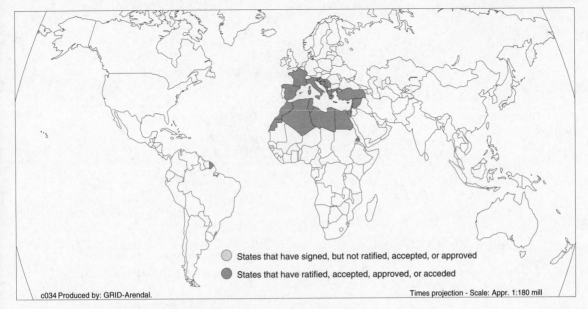

States that have signed, but not ratified, accepted, or approved

States that have ratified, accepted, approved, or acceded

c034 Produced by: GRID-Arendal.                                                                    Times projection - Scale: Appr. 1:180 mill

**Convention for the Protection of the Mediterranean Sea against Pollution**

# Convention for the Protection of the Mediterranean Sea against Pollution

## Objectives
• to achieve international co-operation for a co-ordinated and comprehensive appro-ach to the protection and enhancement of the marine environment in the Mediter-ranean area.

## Time and place of adoption
16 February 1976, Barcelona.

## Entry into force
12 February 1978.

## Status of participation
22 Parties, including the European Community, by 30 September 1994. No Signatories without ratification, acceptance, or approval.

## Affiliated protocols, annexes, and organizations
• *Protocol for the Prevention of Pollution of the Mediterranean Sea by Dumping from Ships and Aircraft, Barcelona, 1976.* Entered into force on 12 February 1978. Same status of participation as the Convention;
• *Protocol Concerning Co-operation in Combating Pollution of the Mediterranean Sea by Oil and Other Harmful Substances in Cases of Emergency, Barcelona, 1976.* Entered into force on 12 February 1978. Same status of participation as the Convention;
• *Protocol for the Protection of the Mediterranean Sea against Pollution from Land-based Sources, Athens, 1980.* Entered into force on 17 June 1983. 19 Parties, including the European Community, by 30 September 1994. No Signatories without ratification, acceptance, or approval;
• *Protocol Concerning Mediterranean Specially Protected Areas, Geneva, 1982.* Entered into force on 23 March 1986. 20 Parties, including the European Community, by 30 September 1994. No Signatories without ratification, acceptance, or approval.

## Secretariat
UNEP/Co-ordinating Unit for the Mediter-ranean Action Plan,
PO Box 18019,
GR-116 10 Athens,
Greece
*Telephone*:        +30-1-7253190-5
*Telefax*:        +30-1-7253196-7
*E-mail*:    unicef network (itt/dialcom)
            unet; unep/athens user id: une058

## Director
Mr Lucien Chabason.

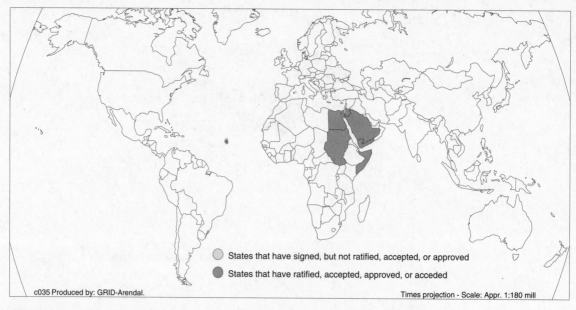

States that have signed, but not ratified, accepted, or approved

States that have ratified, accepted, approved, or acceded

c035 Produced by: GRID-Arendal.                    Times projection - Scale: Appr. 1:180 mill

**Regional Convention for the Conservation of the Red Sea and Gulf of Aden Environment**

## Regional Convention for the Conservation of the Red Sea and Gulf of Aden Environment

### Objectives
• to ensure conservation of the environment of the Red Sea and Gulf of Aden by the promotion, on a regional basis, of environmental protection and natural resources management in the marine and coastal areas of the region.

### Time and place of adoption
14 February 1982, Jeddah.

### Entry into force
20 August 1985.

### Status of participation
6 Parties (+ Palestine, represented by PLO), by 30 September 1994. No Signatories without ratification, acceptance, or approval.

### Affiliated protocols, annexes, and organizations
• *Protocol Concerning Regional Co-operation in Combating Pollution by Oil and Other Harmful Substances in Cases of Emergency, Jeddah, 1982.* Entered into force on 20 August 1985. Same status of participation as the Convention.

### Secretariat
Red Sea and Gulf of Aden Environment Programme (PERSGA),
PO Box 1358,
Jeddah 21431,
Saudi Arabia
*Telephone*:          +966-2-651-4472/9868
*Telefax*:          +966-2-6511424

### Secretary-General
Dr Nizar I. Tawfiq.

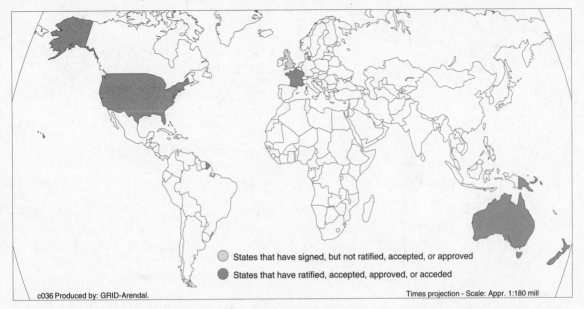

States that have signed, but not ratified, accepted, or approved

States that have ratified, accepted, approved, or acceded

c036 Produced by: GRID-Arendal.                    Times projection - Scale: Appr. 1:180 mill

**Convention for the Protection of the Natural Resources and Environment of the South Pacific Region**

## Convention for the Protection of the Natural Resources and Environment of the South Pacific Region

### Objectives
• to protect and manage the natural resources and environment of the South Pacific Region.

### Time and place of adoption
24 November 1986, Noumea, New Caledonia.

### Entry into force
22 August 1990.

### Status of participation
11 Parties, by 30 September 1994. 4 Signatories without ratification, acceptance, or approval.

### Affiliated protocols, annexes, and organizations
• *Protocol Concerning Co-operation in Combating Pollution Emergencies in the South Pacific Region, Noumea, 1986.* Entered into force on 22 August 1990. Same status of participation as the Convention;
• *Protocol for the Prevention of Pollution of the South Pacific Region by Dumping, Noumea, 1986.* Entered into force on 22 August 1990. 10 Parties, by 30 September 1994. 5 Signatories without ratification, acceptance, or approval.

### Secretariat
South Pacific Regional Environment Programme (SPREP),
PO Box 240,
Apia,
Western Samoa
*Telephone*:        +685-21929
*Telefax*:        +685-20231
*E-mail*: sprep@pactok.peg.apc.org

### Director
Dr Vili Fuavao.

### Information Officer
Ms Wesley Ward.

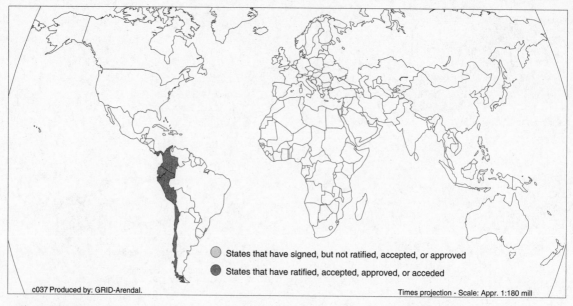

States that have signed, but not ratified, accepted, or approved

States that have ratified, accepted, approved, or acceded

c037 Produced by: GRID-Arendal.　　Times projection - Scale: Appr. 1:180 mill

**Convention for the Protection of the Marine Environment and Coastal Area of the South-East Pacific**

## Convention for the Protection of the Marine Environment and Coastal Area of the South-East Pacific

*Objectives*
• to protect the marine environment and coastal zones of the South-East Pacific.

*Time and place of adoption*
12 November 1981, Lima.

*Entry into force*
19 May 1986.

*Status of participation*
5 Parties, by 30 September 1994. No Signatories without ratification, acceptance, or approval.

*Affiliated protocols, annexes, and organizations*
• *Agreement on Regional Co-operation in Combating Pollution of the South-East Pacific by Hydrocarbons or Other Harmful Substances in Cases of Emergency, Lima, 1981*. Entered into force on 14 July 1986. Same status of participation as the Convention;
• *Supplementary Protocol to the Agreement on Regional Co-operation in Combating Pollution of the South-East Pacific by Hydrocarbons or Other Harmful Substances in Cases of Emergency, Quito, 1983*. Entered into force on 20 May 1987. Same status of participation as the Convention;
• *Protocol for the Protection of the South-East Pacific against Pollution from Land-based Sources, Quito, 1983*. Entered into force on 21 September 1986. Same status of participation as the Convention;

• *Protocol for the Conservation and Management of the Protected Marine and Coastal Areas of the South-East Pacific, Paipa, 1989*. [Not yet in force.] 2 Parties, by 30 September 1994. 3 Signatories without ratification, acceptance, or approval. 3 ratifications or accessions required to enter into force;
• *Protocol for the Protection of the South-East Pacific against Radioactive Contam-ination, Paipa, 1989*. [Not yet in force.] 2 Parties, by 30 September 1994. 3 Signa-tories without ratification, accep-tance, or approval. 3 ratifications or accessions required to enter into force.

*Secretariat*
Comision Permanente del Pacifico Sur (CPPS),
Apartado Postal 2397,
Lima
Peru
*Telephone*:　　+51-14-423640
*Telefax*:　　+51-14-427190

*Secretary-General*
Dr Nicolas Roncagllolo Higueras.

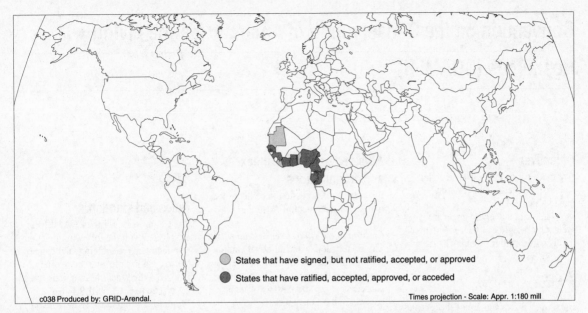

States that have signed, but not ratified, accepted, or approved

States that have ratified, accepted, approved, or acceded

c038 Produced by: GRID-Arendal.                                   Times projection - Scale: Appr. 1:180 mill

**Convention for Co-operation in the Protection and Development of the Marine and Coastal Environment of the West and Central African Region**

## Convention for Co-operation in the Protection and Development of the Marine and Coastal Environment of the West and Central African Region

### Objectives
• to protect the marine environment, coastal zones, and related internal waters falling within the jurisdiction of the States of the West and Central African Region.

### Time and place of adoption
23 March 1981, Abidjan.

### Entry into force
5 August 1984.

### Status of participation
10 Parties, by 30 September 1994. 3 Signa-tories without ratification, accept-ance, or approval.

### Affiliated protocols, annexes, and organizations
• *Protocol Concerning Co-operation in Combating Pollution in Cases of Emergency, Abidjan, 1981.* Entered into force on 5 August 1984. Same status of participation as the Convention.

### Secretariat
(UNEP) Oceans and Coastal Areas/ Programme Activity Centre (OCA/PAC), PO Box 30552, Nairobi, Kenya
*Telephone*:      +254-2-622027
*Telefax*:           +254-2-622788

### Director
Mr Peter Schröder.

# Convention on the Conservation of Antarctic Marine Living Resources (CCAMLR)

## Objectives
• to conserve Antarctic marine living resources (the term 'conservation ' includes rational use);
• to safeguard the environment and protect the integrity of the ecosystem of the seas surrounding Antarctica;

## Scope
*Legal scope*
Open to all States and regional economic integration organizations.

*Geographic scope*
Antarctica, the area south of 60°S, and the area between that latitude and the Antarctic Convergence which encompasses the Antarctic marine ecosystem.

## Time and place of adoption
20 May 1980, Canberra.

## Entry into force
7 April 1982.

## Number of States Parties
29 Parties, including the European Economic Community, by 14 September 1994, of which 21 form part of the Commission. No Signatories without ratification, acceptance, or approval.

## Affiliated protocols, annexes, and organizations
Instruments of accession to be deposited with the Government of Australia.

*Co-ordination with related instruments*
The Convention is an additional component instrument of the Antarctic Treaty System (see this section). The scientific concerns covered by the Treaty are also covered in the Convention.

## Secretariat
CCAMLR,
25 Old Wharf,
Hobart,
Tasmania,
Australia 7000
*Telephone*:      +61-02-310366
*Telefax*:        +61-02-232714
*E-mail*:         ccamlr@antdiv.gov.au

*Executive Secretary*
Mr Estaban de Salas.

*Number of staff*
4 professionals and 6 support staff (Sept. 1994).

## Finance
The Commission adopts its budget and that of the Scientific Committee at each annual meeting. Each member contributes to the budget. Two criteria form the basis for allocating the budget, the amount harvested and equal sharing. The financial activities are conducted in accordance with financial regulations adopted by the Commission and subject to annual external audit.

*Budget*
The administrative core budget was $A1.3 in 1993, $A1.5 million in 1994, and is $A1.6 million in 1995.

*Special funds*
Not applicable.

## Rules and standards
The Commission for the CCAMLR is established with the following functions:
• to facilitate research into and comprehensive studies of Antarctic marine living resources and the Antarctic marine ecosystem (e.g. CCAMLR Ecosystem Monitoring Programme (CEMP) (see below));
• to compile data on the status of and changes in populations of Antarctic marine living resources;
• to ensure the acquisition of catch-and-effort statistics on harvested populations;
• to analyse, disseminate, and publish the information referred to above, and the reports of the Scientific Committee;
• to identify conservation needs and analyse the effectiveness of conservation measures;
• to formulate, adopt, and revise conservation measures on the basis of the best scientific evidence available;
• to implement a system of observation and inspection;
• to carry out such other activities as are necessary to fulfil the objective of the Convention;
• to publish and maintain a record of all conservation measures in force and notify them to all members.

Conservation measures shall become binding upon all members of the Commission 180 days after such notification. If a member, within 90 days, notifies the Commission that it cannot accept the conservation measure, in whole or in part, the measure shall not be binding upon that member.

Parties are required to take any steps necessary for the implementation of the decisions taken.

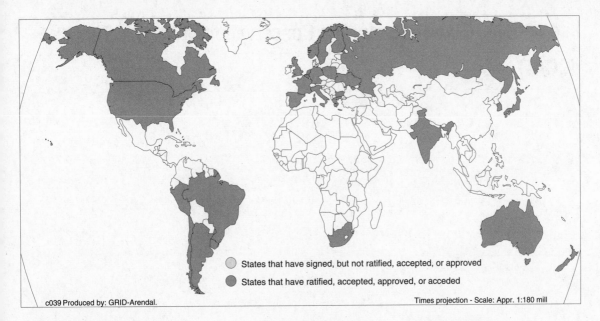

States that have signed, but not ratified, accepted, or approved

States that have ratified, accepted, approved, or acceded

c039 Produced by: GRID-Arendal.                                    Times projection - Scale: Appr. 1:180 mill

## Monitoring/implementation

*Review procedure*
Each Party is required to inform the
Commission of any activities in violation
of the Convention that come to its
knowledge. The Commission then calls
the attention of any State which is not a
party to the Convention to activities of
its nationals or ships which are felt to be
in contravention of the objectives of the
Convention.

National reports are submitted in
yearly, monthly, five-day periods,
depending on the nature of the report.
Some reports are private, others public.
There is no independent verification of
data or information.

*Observations or inspections*
A system of observation and inspection
to verify compliance with measures
adopted by the Commission was established in 1990. Observation implies the
presence of scientific observers on board
fishing vessels throughout the voyage.
Inspection implies the monitoring for
compliance with measures in force. Each
Party is nominating inspectors that are
authorized to conduct inspections during
the seasons.

*Environmental monitoring programmes*
The CCAMLR Ecosystem Monitoring
Programme (CEMP) is intended to detect
changes in the condition, abundance, and
distribution of species which are not
commercially harvested, but which
provide some indication of the dynamics
and well-being of particular ecosystems.
Information obtained from monitoring
'indicator species' can be taken into
account in the regulation of human
activity to ensure conservation principles
of the Convention are met.

*Trade sanctions*
None.

*Dispute-settlement mechanisms*
The Convention provides for disputes
among Parties to be resolved by peaceful
means, including referral of such
disputes by mutual agreement to third-
party procedures for settlement.

## Decision-making

*Political bodies*
Parties to the Convention give effect to
its objectives and principles through the
annual *Meetings of the Commission*.
Adoption of measures, by consensus, is
the exclusive function of the Commission.

*Scientific/technical bodies*
The *Scientific Committee* shall: provide a
forum for consultation and co-operation
concerning the collection, study, and
exchange of information; establish
criteria and methods; analyse data; and
formulate proposals. It provides the
essential input into the Commission's
deliberations. Decisions in the Committee are taken by consensus.

A Standing Committee on Finance and
Administration and a Standing Committee on Observations and Inspection meet
each year.

## Publications

The Secretariat publishes in addition to
different manuals and scientific papers:
• *CCAMLR Newsletter*;
• *Report of the Annual Meeting of the
Commission*;
• *Conservation Measures in Force*;
• *Statistical Bulletin*.

# International Convention for the Conservation of Atlantic Tunas (ICCAT)

## Objectives

To co-operate in maintaining the population of tunas and tuna-like species found in the Atlantic Ocean and the adjacent seas at levels that will permit the maximum sustainable catch for food and other purposes.

## Scope

*Legal scope*
Open to member States of the United Nations or any of its specialized agencies. Not yet open to regional integration organizations (see below).

*Geographic scope*
Regional. Applies to all waters of the Atlantic Ocean and adjacent seas, including the Mediterranean Sea. The longitude of $20^0$ E is used, for scientific purposes, as the border between the Atlantic and the Indian Ocean.

## Time and place of adoption

14 May 1966, Rio de Janeiro.

## Entry into force

21 March 1969.

## Status of participation

22 Parties, by 1 October 1994. 2 Signatories without ratification, acceptance, or approval.

## Affiliated protocols, annexes, and organizations

A protocol enabling regional integration organizations to become Parties to the Convention was adopted in Paris, 10 July 1984. [Not yet in force.] 3 Parties, by 1 October 1994. Enters into force 30 days after the deposit of all instruments of ratification or accession.

A second Protocol was adopted in Madrid in June 1992 to amend Paragraph 2 of Article X of the Convention. [Not yet in force.] 5 Parties, by 1 October 1994. Enters into force after the deposit of instruments of ratification, acceptance, or approval of 75 per cent (currently 17) of the Contracting Parties, including all those classified as developed market economy countries (Group A: Canada, France, Japan, Portugal, South Africa, Spain, and USA). A special procedure was adopted for the entry into force of this Protocol, which takes into account that the contributions of the countries with a developed market economy would increase, while those corresponding to developing countries would decrease.

The *Director General of the Food and Agriculture Organization (FAO)* (see IGOs) acts as depositary.

Based on the Convention, the International Commission for the Conservation of Atlantic Tunas (ICCAT) was established and started its activities in 1969.

## Secretariat

International Commission for the Conservation of Atlantic Tunas (ICCAT),
Principe de Vergara, 17-7°,
E-28001 Madrid,
Spain
*Telephone*: +34-1-4310329
*Telefax*: +34-1-5761968
*Telex*: 46330 ICCAT E
*E-mail*: peter.miyake@iccat.es or papa.kebe@iccat.es

*Executive Secretary*
Dr Antonio Fernández.

*Assistant Executive Secretary*
Dr P. M. Miyake.

*Number of staff*
3 professionals and 11 support staff (Oct. 1994).

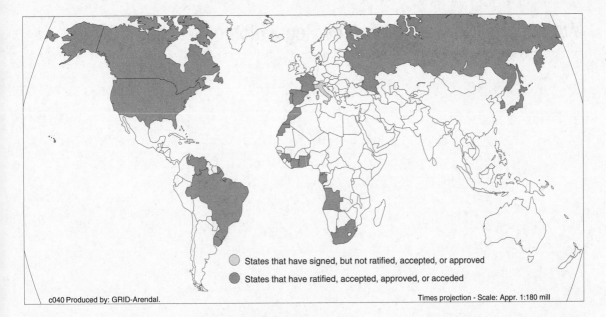

States that have signed, but not ratified, accepted, or approved

States that have ratified, accepted, approved, or acceded

c040 Produced by: GRID-Arendal.

Times projection - Scale: Appr. 1:180 mill

## Finance

*Budget*
The administrative core budget was
Pts133,172,000 in 1993 and
Pts140,268,000 in 1994 contributed by
the Parties.

## Rules and standards

The Commission (see below) shall be
responsible for the study of populations
of tuna and tuna-like fishes and such
other species exploited in tuna fishing in
the Convention area as are not under
investigation by another international
fishery organization.
  Studies include:
• research on the abundance, biometry,
and ecology of the fishes;
• the oceanography of their environment;
• the effects of natural and human
factors upon their abundance.
  If, based on scientific findings, the
Commission considers it necessary, it
recommends to the Parties regulatory
measures to ensure maximum utilization
of the populations of fish. Such regulatory measures may include a minimum
and/or maximum size of fish which may
be caught, restrictions on the amount of
catch and/or effort, etc.

## Monitoring/implementation

*Review procedure*
The Commission implements the
Convention by co-ordinating research,
collecting and disseminating statistics
and other information on the biology and
ecology of tunas, and oceanographic
conditions, and by analysing all this
information regarding the stock status of
fish.
  National reports on the implementation of commitments are submitted once
a year. 15 reports were submitted in
1991, 13 in 1992, and 13 in 1994. The
reports are reviewed by the Commission.
Such reviews are public and publication
lists are distributed by the Secretariat.

*Observations or inspections*
None by the Convention as such.

*Trade sanctions*
None.

*Dispute-settlement mechanisms*
None.

## Decision-making

*Political bodies*
The *International Commission for the
Conservation of Atlantic Tunas (ICCAT)*
is established as a governing body and
meets annually, usually in November.
The Commission, on the basis of

scientific evidence, makes recommendations for the maintenance of the
populations of tuna and tuna-like fish.

*Scientific/technical bodies*
The Commission works through three
standing committees, comprised of
experts representing governments and
others:
• *Research and Statistics Committee
(SCRS)*;
• *Finances and Administration Commit-
tee (STACFAD)*;
• *Infractions Committee*.
  Four panels have also been established
to consider and, if necessary, initiate
regulatory measures on species covered
by the Convention:
• *Panel 1: Tropical tunas*;
• *Panel 2: Temperate tunas (North)*;
• *Panel 3: Temperate tunas (South)*;
• *Panel 4: Other species*.
  A *Permanent Working Group for the
Improvement of ICCAT Statistics and
Conservation Measures* was established
in 1992.

## Publications

The Commission publishes reports of
findings and up-to-date information is
available through a newsletter (periodically).

# International Convention for the Regulation of Whaling (ICRW)

## Objectives

To establish regulations for purposes of conservation and utilization of whale resources, and to serve as an agency for the collection, analysis, and publication of scientific information related to whaling.

## Scope

*Legal scope*
Open to all States. Not open to regional integration organizations.

*Geographic scope*
Global.

## Time and place of adoption

2 December 1946, Washington.

## Entry into force

10 November 1948.

## Status of participation

40 Parties, by September 1994. No Signatories without ratification, approval, or acceptance.

## Affiliated protocols, annexes, and organizations

The *Schedule to the Convention*, adopted annually since 1949 at meetings of the International Whaling Commission (IWC) (see below), is an integral part of the Convention. Its purpose is to set the specific conservation regulations applicable.

Instruments of accession and withdrawal to be deposited with the government of the United States of America.

*Co-ordination with related instruments*
Although there are no formal mechanisms, Parties will be aware of related treaties and conventions, particularly the United Nations Convention on the Law of the Sea (UNCLOS) (see this section).

The Commission contributed to the elaboration of the 1984 UNEP/FAO Global Plan of Action for the Conservation, Management, and Utilization of Marine Mammals and has part of the responsibility for its implementation.

## Secretariat

International Whaling Commission (IWC),
135 Station Road,
Histon,
Cambridge CB4 4NP,
United Kingdom
*Telephone*:        +44-1223-233971
*Telefax*:        +44-1223-232876

*Secretary*
Dr Ray Gambell.

*Number of staff*
3 professionals and 12 support staff (Sept. 1994).

## Finance

The budget is financed mainly by contributions from Parties. There are no special provisions relating to the economic standing of governments, the formula for contributions being based largely on the degree of involvement, and includes shares for membership, whaling activity, and size of delegation.

*Budget*
The annual actual budget was approximately £UK927,300 in 1993, £UK1,000,000 in 1994, and is £UK1,046,570 in 1995. The administrative core budget was £UK714,000 in 1993, £UK754,000 in 1994, and is £UK782,900 in 1995.

*Special funds*
The Commission allots part of its budget towards a research fund for projects related to whales. The most important project has been the Comprehensive Assessment of Whale Stocks.

## Rules and standards

The main duty of the Commission is to keep under review and revise as necessary the measures laid down in the *Schedule to the Convention* governing the conduct of whaling. These include measures:

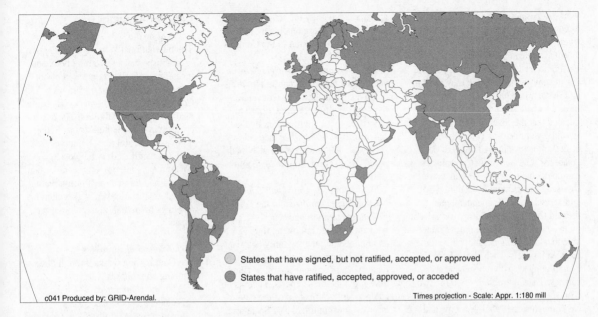

States that have signed, but not ratified, accepted, or approved

States that have ratified, accepted, approved, or acceded

c041 Produced by: GRID-Arendal.                                                    Times projection - Scale: Appr. 1:180 mill

- to provide for the complete protection of certain species of whales;
- to designate specified ocean areas as whale sanctuaries;
- to set the maximum catches of whales which may be taken in one season;
- to prescribe open and closed seasons and areas for whaling;
- to fix size limits above and below which certain species of whales may not be killed;
- to prohibit the capture of suckling calves and female whales accompanied by calves;
- to require the compilation of catch reports and other statistical and biological records.

The Convention requires that amendments to the provisions of the Schedule with respect to the conservation and utilization of whale resources be based on scientific findings.

While the Commission generally acts by simple majority, amendment of the Schedule requires a three-quarter majority vote of those casting an affirmative or a negative vote.

The Convention also establishes certain criteria for amendments to the Schedule and provides for a system of notification which allows Parties 90 days after notification of amendments to register an objection. Under an objection, the relevant passages are not enforceable against the country in question.

The Commission agreed in 1982 to set a zero quota on all commercially exploited stocks for the 1986 coastal and 1985–86 pelagic seasons, and thereafter a so-called moratorium which is still in force, and initiated a comprehensive assessment of whale stocks and the development of a new management procedure that should have been finished by 1990. Five possible management procedures were developed by individuals or pairs of scientists within the Scientific Committee, one of which was recommended as a 'core' procedure and accepted by the Commission in 1991.

At the 1992 Annual Meeting the Commission adopted the specification developed by the Scientific Committee for the calculation of catch limits in a Revised Management Procedure for baleen whales. In 1994 the Commission accepted and endorsed the Revised Management Procedure for commercial whaling and associated Guidelines for surveys and collection of data. However, it noted that work on a number of issues, including specification of an inspection and observer system, remained to be completed before the Commission would consider establishing catch limits other than zero.

In 1979 the Commission established the Indian Ocean north of $55^0$ S as a *whale sanctuary* where commercial whaling is prohibited. This provision has been supported by the coastal states bordering the Ocean, both members and non-members of the IWC, and will be reviewed by the Commission at its Annual Meeting in 2002.

At its 1992 Meeting the Commission received a proposal from France for the establishment of a whale sanctuary in the Southern Hemisphere south of $40^0$ S. The purpose of the proposal was stated to be to contribute to the rehabilitation of the Antarctic marine ecosystem and the protection of all Southern Hemisphere species and populations of baleen whales and the sperm whale on their feeding grounds. This would also link up with the Indian Ocean Sanctuary to provide a large area within which whales would be free from commercial catching.

Working Groups examined the matter at the 1993 Annual Meeting, and intersessionally on Norfolk Island in February 1994. After detailed consideration of the legal, political, ecological, management, financial, and environmental issues, the Commission adopted the Southern Ocean sanctuary at the 1994 Annual Meeting.

A major new development is the Commission's consideration of *whalewatching* as a sustainable use of cetacean resources. In 1993 the Commission invited Contracting Governments to undertake a preliminary assessment of the extent, and economic and scientific value, of whalewatching activities for consideration by a Working Group at the 1994 meeting. As a result the Commission has reaffirmed its interest in the subject, encouraged some scientific work, and established a Working Group to consider the development of guidelines.

With increasing awareness that whales should not be considered apart from the marine environment which they inhabit, and that detrimental changes may threaten whale stocks, the Commission decided that the Scientific Committee should give priority to research on the effects of environmental changes on cetaceans. The Scientific Committee examined this issues in the context of the Revised Management Procedure (RMP) and agreed the RMP adequately addressed such concerns. However, it went on to state that the species most vulnerable to such threats might well be those reduced to levels at which the RMP, even if applied, would result in zero catches. The Committee is holding two workshops, one on the effects of chemical pollutants in 1995 in Norway, and one on the effects of climate change and ozone depletion in 1996 in the USA.

*Aboriginal whaling for subsistence purposes* is carried out by native peoples of Greenland, Bequia, Siberia, and Alaska, and catches for *scientific purposes* by Japan and Norway. Norway has also resumed commercial whaling under the objection procedure provided by the Convention and is setting its own catch limits.

## Monitoring/implementation

*Review procedure*
Parties are required to implement the regulations through internal legislation (copies of which are forwarded to the Secretariat) and submit reports, as appropriate, on any infraction to the Commission. These reports are made public after submission to the Commission.

The *International Observer Scheme* encourages full and accurate reporting of commercial catches. The Convention requires penalties for infractions and reports on these are reviewed by the *Infractions Subcommittee* (see below) each year. These reports are also made public after submission to the Commission.

In addition, the *Aboriginal Subsistence Whaling Subcommittee* and the *Scientific Committee* monitor and report on relevant matters. Following the 1986 ban on commercial whaling, only 'subsistence' and 'scientific' whaling data are required from 6 members, all of which have provided their reports. There is no independent verification of the data or information submitted. The Secretariat does not distribute publication lists of such reviews.

*Observations or inspections*
Compliance with the commercial whaling regulations is monitored by national inspectors and international observers, and their reports and the data submitted are reviewed by the Infractions and Scientific Committee as appropriate (see above).

*Trade sanctions*
None.

*Dispute-settlement mechanisms*
None.

## Decision-making

*Political bodies*
The International Whaling Commission is established as a governing body and meets annually. It is composed of one member (commissioner) from each Contracting Party, who may be accompanied by experts or advisers. The delegates may include industry and other non-governmental representatives as well as scientific advisers. Non-member governments, intergovernmental organizations, and international non-governmental organizations may also attend meetings by invitation in an observer capacity.

*Scientific/technical bodies*
The Commission works through three standing committees:
• *Scientific Committee*;
• *Technical Committee*;
• *Finance and Administration Committee*.

The Scientific Committee reviews scientific information related to whales and whaling, the scientific programmes of the Parties, the scientific permits, and the scientific programmes for which the Parties plan to issue such permits.

In addition, several subcommittees are established such as the *Infractions Subcommittee* and *Aboriginal Subsistence Whaling Subcommittee*.

## Publications

The Commission publishes annual reports and special issues on whale science. It also holds and publishes catch and related data on whaling operations.

# The Antarctic Treaty

## Objectives

- to ensure that Antarctica is used for peaceful purposes only;
- to ensure the continuance of freedom of scientific investigation and international co-operation in scientific investigation in Antarctica;
- to set aside disputes over territorial sovereignty.

## Scope

*Legal scope*

The Antarctic Treaty was ratified by 12 Signatory States. In addition it is open for accession by any State which is a member of the United Nations, or by any other State which may be invited to accede to the Treaty with the consent of all the Contracting Parties whose representatives are entitled to participate in the meetings provided for under Article IX of the Antarctic Treaty (hereinafter: Consultative Meetings).

The Consultative Parties are currently made up of the 12 original Signatories (which retain the consultative status unconditionally) and of the 14 acceding States, which have been acknowledged to the consultative status conditionally, during such times as they demonstrate their interest in Antarctica by conducting substantial research activity there, such as the establishment of a scientific station or the despatch of a scientific expedition. There are also 16 non-Consultative Parties, i.e. states which acceded to the Treaty without acquiring consultative status.

*Geographic scope*

The Antarctic Treaty applies to the area south of 60°S.

## Time and place of adoption

1 December 1959, Washington, DC.

## Entry into force

23 June 1961.

## Status of participation

42 Contracting Parties, by 1 October 1994 (including 26 Consultative Parties and 16 non-Consultative Parties).

## Affiliated international instruments

The Antarctic Treaty system (hereinafter: ATS) provides the umbrella for a complex system of international instruments of importance for the environment. These include:

- the *Antarctic Treaty* itself (text in: United Nations Treaty Series, vol. 402, 71);
- other treaties adopted on the basis of the Antarctic Treaty:

(*a*) *Convention for the Protection of Antarctic Seals*, adopted at London on 1 June 1972, entered into force on 11 March 1978. 16 Parties, by 5 October 1994. 1 Signatory without ratification or acceptance. (Text reprinted in: *International Legal Materials*, 11 (1972), 251);

(*b*) *Convention on the Conservation of Antarctic Marine Living Resources (CCAMLR)*, adopted at Canberra on 20 May 1980, entered into force on 7 April 1982. 29 Parties, by 14 September 1994. (Text reprinted in: *International Legal Materials*, 19 (1980), 837) (see this section);

(*c*) *Convention on the Regulation of Antarctic Mineral Resource Activities (CRAMRA)*, adopted at Wellington on 2 June 1988. [Not in force.] Enters into force on the thirtieth day after the deposit of instruments of ratification, acceptance, approval, or accession by 16 Antarctic Treaty Consultative Parties which participated as such in the final session of

the Fourth Special Antarctic Treaty Consultative meeting, provided that number includes all the States necessary in order to establish all the institutions of the Convention in respect of every area of Antarctica, including 5 developing countries and 11 developed countries. (Text reprinted in: *International Legal Materials*, 27 (1988), 868);

(*d*) *Protocol on Environmental Protection to the Antarctic Treaty (Madrid Protocol)*, with four Annexes (Annex I, *Environmental Impact Assessment*; Annex II, *Conservation of Antarctic Flora and Fauna*; Annex III, *Waste Disposal and Waste Management*; and Annex IV, *Prevention of Marine Pollution*), adopted at Madrid on 4 October 1991. (Text reprinted in: *International Legal Materials*, 30 (1991), 1461). [Not yet in force.] Enters into force on the thirtieth day after the deposit of instruments of ratification, acceptance, approval, or accession by all 26 States which were Antarctic Treaty Consultative Parties at the date of the adoption of the Protocol. 10 Consultative Parties had ratified or accepted, by 1 October 1994. The annexes form an integral part of the Madrid Protocol. Annexes, additional to Annexes I–IV, may be adopted; thus, Annex V, *Area Protection and Management*, was adopted as an annex to Recommendation XVI–10, at the XVI Consultative Meeting, held in Bonn 7–18 October 1991; and

- other international instruments were adopted on the basis of the Antarctic Treaty, and the measures under separate treaties associated with the Antarctic Treaty:

(*a*) *Agreed Measures for the Conservation of Antarctic Fauna and Flora (Agreed Measures)*, approved as Recommendation III–8, at the III Consultative Meeting, held in Brussels 2–13 June 1964;

(*b*) 'measures in furtherance of the principles and objectives of the Antarctic Treaty', so-called *recommendations* of the Antarctic Treaty Consultative Meetings; approximately 200 recommendations have been adopted to date;

(*c*) various *other measures*, such as the results of Meetings of Experts, the decisions of Special Consultative Meetings, etc.;

(*d*) measures adopted and in effect under separate treaties associated with the Antarctic Treaty (e.g. decisions of the CCAMLR Commission).

*Co-ordination with related instruments*
ATS has developed through the negotiation of additional component instruments (see above) rather than by fundamental revision of the Antarctic Treaty itself. Part of this process has reference to regulations embodied in other international treaties such as the International Convention for the Prevention of Pollution from Ships, 1973, as modified by the Protocol of 1978 relating thereto (MARPOL 73/78) (see this section) relating to control of marine pollution in the Antarctic Treaty area.

## Secretariat
For the time being ATS has no permanent secretariat. It operates primarily through annual Consultative Meetings hosted in rotation by Consultative Parties. CCAMLR (see this section) has a permanent Secretariat.

Information on ATS is available nationally from the relevant government department of the Contracting Parties. A recent list of national contact points for all Treaty Parties is published in US Department of State (1994), *Handbook of the Antarctic Treaty System* (April), 8th edn., (Washington), 291–5. Information is also available from the depositary Government to the Antarctic Treaty:

Division of Polar Affairs OES/OA, Room 5801,
Bureau of Oceans and International Environmental and Scientific Affairs, United States Department of State,
Washington, DC 20520,
USA
*Telephone*:    +1-202-6473262
*Telefax*:    +1-202-6471106

Up-to-date *scientific* information and bibliographical references are also available from:

Scientific Committee on Antarctic Research (SCAR),
c/o Scott Polar Research Institute, University of Cambridge,
Lensfield Road,
Cambridge CB2 1ER,
United Kingdom
*Telephone*:    +44-223-336567
*Telefax*:    +44-223-336549

*Executive Secretary*
Dr Peter D. Clarkson.

*Librarian and Information Officer*
Mr William Mills.

## Rules and standards
The Treaty imposes a wide range of obligations on Parties. These include prohibition of all military activities, nuclear explosions, and disposal of radioactive waste in Antarctica, as well as requirements to exchange and make freely available data and observations resulting from scientific research activities (see Monitoring, below).

There is an extensive set of binding conservation measures relating to marine living resources, including obligations to collect catch-and-effort statistics. All human activities are subject to detailed rules relating to: environmental impact assessment; conservation of native fauna and flora, including prohibitions on introduction of alien species; waste disposal and waste management; and prevention of marine pollution. In addition, an extensive system of protected areas has been established.

Related provisions call for environmental monitoring (see below).

The *Madrid Protocol* commits the Parties to a comprehensive protection of the Antarctic environment and its dependent and associated ecosystems and defines the continent as a natural reserve, devoted to peace and science. Building on the existing body of ATS instruments, the Protocol elaborates
detailed, mandatory rules to ensure that activities in Antarctica do not result in adverse environmental effects.

Annex II to the Protocol calls for waste reduction and (where possible) disposal in the country from whose activities the waste has arisen. Waste which is not so removed should be incinerated. Other wastes should not be disposed of in ice-free areas or on to sea-ice, ice-sheets, or ice-shelves. Certain products (such as PCBs, polystyrene packaging materials, etc.) are prohibited.

## Monitoring and implementation
*Review procedure*
The various elements of the ATS make provision for the reporting of the activity of Parties in the Antarctic Treaty area.

The Protocol calls for annual reporting by each Party on what steps have been taken to implement the Protocol. There are also specific requirements under the individual components of the ATS, such as catch data and exploitation effort (see CCAMLR, this section).

*Observations or inspections*
The Antarctic Treaty accords to Consultative Parties rights of inspection of each other's stations, installations, and equipment in the area, to promote compliance. Observers are appointed by each Consultative Party. Both the CCAMLR and the Madrid Protocol build on and extend these provisions.

*Trade sanctions*
None.

*Dispute-settlement mechanisms*
Both the Antarctic Treaty and the CCAMLR provide for a variety of peaceful means of dispute settlement, including a referral of disputes to the International Court of Justice.

The Madrid Protocol introduces compulsory procedures (at the request of any party to a dispute) for its dispute settlement, based on a choice of forum approach (either the International Court of Justice or the special arbitration tribunal, to be instituted in accordance with a schedule to the Protocol).

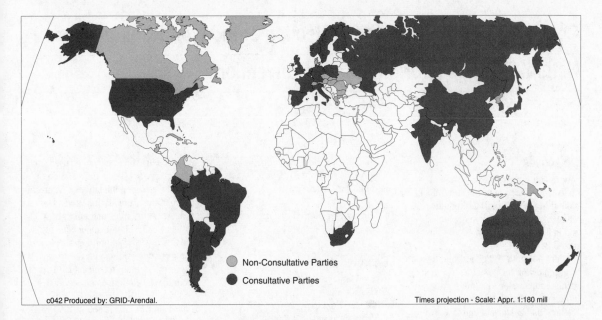

Non-Consultative Parties

Consultative Parties

c042 Produced by: GRID-Arendal.                                    Times projection - Scale: Appr. 1:180 mill

## Decision-making

### Political bodies

The *Consultative Meeting* is the principal decision-making forum of the Antarctic Treaty. Meetings are held annually (every two years up to 1991), hosted in rotation by Consultative Parties. The Consultative Meeting adopts recommendations or formulates other measures to guide the activity in the area.

The Madrid Protocol provides for the establishment of a Committee for Environmental Protection, composed of representatives of Consultative Parties, as an advisory body to the Consultative Meeting. Pending entry into force of the Protocol , the main questions to be dealt with by this Comittee will be, from the XIX Consultative meeting to be held in Seoul, Republic of Korea, in May 1995, considered by a Transitional Environmental Working Group, operating within the Consultative Meeting.

National governmental authorities of Parties have access to the Consultative Meetings, whether as Consultative Parties entitled to decision-making, or as non-Consultative Parties (with quasi-observer status since 1983). Meetings are also attended regularly by the representatives of the Commission for the Conservation of Antarctic Marine Resources, the Scientific Committee on Antarctic Research (SCAR), and the Council of

Managers of National Antarctic Programs (COMNAP), as observers. In addition, by invitation of the Consultative Parties, other inter- and non-governmental organizations, currently including the Antarctic and Southern Ocean Coalition (ASOC), the Intergovernmental Oceanographic Commission (IOC), the International Association of Antarctic Tour Operators (IAATO), the International Hydrographic Organization (IHO), the International Maritime Organization (IMO) (see IGOs), the Pacific Asia Travel Association (PATA), the United Nations Environment Programme (UNEP) (see IGOs), the World Meteorological Organization (WMO) (see IGOs), IUCN (see NGOs), and the World Tourism Organization (WTO), may designate experts to attend the Consultative Meetings.

According to Article XII, the Antarctic Treaty opens the possibility for a special conference to review the operation of the Antarctic Treaty. Such a conference may be convened at the request of any Consultative Party once the Treaty has been in force for 30 years (that is, after 23 June 1991). All Parties, not just Consultative Parties, have the right to participate in this conference.

### Scientific/technical bodies

The Treaty and its various component instruments contain requirements that

activities in the region be scientifically sound. The work of SCAR, a committee of the non-governmental International Council of Scientific Unions (ICSU), forms an integral part of the input to decisions taken by the Consultative Meetings. The Madrid Protocol also requires that environmental policies drawn up and adopted by the Consultative Meeting shall draw upon 'the best scientific and technical advice available'. The role of SCAR and COMNAP is crucial in this respect.

## Publications

Treaty publications are available nationally from the relevant government department of the Contracting Parties. Extensive documentation is published by CCAMLR (see this section). In addition, SCAR produces scientific reports related to Antarctic research.

The eighth edition of the *Handbook of the Antarctic Treaty System* was published by the US Department of State in April 1994. *SCAR Bulletin*, a quarterly publication of SCAR within *Polar Record*, the journal of Polar Publications at the Scott Polar Research Institute (see above), publishes material from Consultative Meetings.

# Convention Concerning the Protection of the World Cultural and Natural Heritage (World Heritage Convention)

## Objectives
• to establish an effective system of collective protection of the cultural and natural heritage of outstanding universal value, organized on a permanent basis and in accordance with modern scientific methods;
• to provide both emergency and long-term protection for monuments, monumental sculpture and painting, groups of buildings, archaeological sites, natural features, and habitats of animals and plants of 'outstanding universal value'.

## Scope
*Legal scope*
Open to all States and members of UNESCO (see IGOs), and to other States upon invitation of the UNESCO General Conference. Not open to regional integration organizations.

*Geographic scope*
Global.

## Time and place of adoption
23 November 1972, Paris.

## Entry into force
17 December 1975.

## Status of participation
139 Parties, by 1 November 1994. No Signatories without ratification, acceptance, or accession.

## Affiliated protocols, annexes, and organizations
*World Heritage List* where 411 sites have been inscribed (305 cultural, 90 natural, and 16 with both cultural and natural attributes) in 95 countries which are Parties to the Convention, by October 1994.
The *Director-General of the United*

Nations Educational, Scientific, and Cultural Organization (UNESCO) acts as depositary.

*Co-ordination with related instruments*
None.

## Secretariat
World Heritage Centre,
UNESCO,
7 Place de Fontenoy,
F-75700 Paris,
France
*Telephone*:      +33-1-45681571
*Telefax*:      +33-1-40569570

*Director of the World Heritage Centre*
Dr Bernd von Droste.

*Number of staff*
10 professionals and 10 general service staff under its Regular Programme and Budget (Oct. 1994).

## Finance
Costs are covered partly by UNESCO's Regular Programme budget and partly by the World Heritage Fund and other extrabudgetary sources.

*Budget*
The administrative core budget was $US327,400 for the biennium 1992–93 and is $US2.7 million for the biennium 1994–95. The figure for the 1994–95 biennium consists of $US2.0 million provided by UNESCO's Regular Programme budget for staff, office space, etc. and $US700,000 from the same source for programme activities.

*Special funds*
Through the *World Heritage Fund*, established in 1978, any individual, nation, or institution may voluntarily contribute (in accordance with their GNP) to the protection of the heritage in countries where national resources are

insufficient. The Fund can be used for preparatory assistance (preparation on World Heritage nominations), technical co-operation (directly for World Heritage properties), training, and emergency assistance. The Fund amounts to approximately $US2.8 million a year with contributions from the Parties to the Convention. Main recipients are Parties from the developing countries. In addition there is a *World Heritage Emergency Fund*, created in 1994, with a total of $US1.0 million for the biennium 1994–95.

*Main contributors*
Main contributing Parties to the World Heritage Fund are the USA, Germany, France, Japan, Russian Federation, and the United Kingdom.

## Rules and standards
Each Party shall:
• recognize that the duty of identification, protection, conservation, and transmission to future generations of the cultural and natural heritage belongs primarily to that State;
• integrate the protection of their heritage into comprehensive planning programmes, set up services for the protection of their heritage, develop scientific and technical studies, and take necessary legal, scientific, administrative, and financial steps to protect their heritage;
• assist each other in the protection of the cultural and natural heritage.
Parties are called upon to draw up an inventory of property belonging to their cultural and natural heritage. A 'World Heritage List' of sites of outstanding universal value has been established by the World Heritage Committee, to be updated every year. A second inventory, 'List of World Heritage in Danger', includes those monuments, buildings, and sites for which major conservation operations are urgently needed.

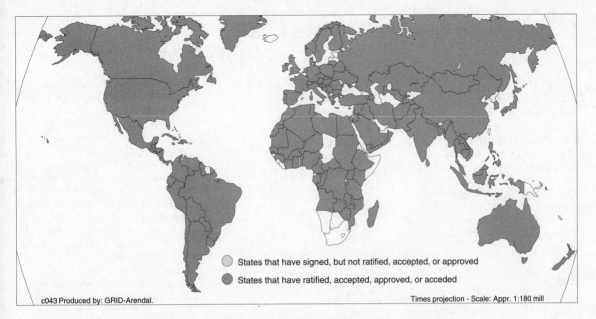

States that have signed, but not ratified, accepted, or approved

States that have ratified, accepted, approved, or acceded

c043 Produced by: GRID-Arendal.

Times projection - Scale: Appr. 1:180 mill

Any Party may request assistance for property forming part of its listed heritage, and such assistance may be granted by the World Heritage Fund in the form of studies, provision of experts, training of staff, supply of equipment, loans, or subsidies.

## Monitoring/implementation
*Review procedure*
Parties report to the UNESCO General Conference in their general reports. Most countries mention World Heritage activities in their reports but this is not systematic, nor does it provide much detail. No national reports on World Heritage activities have been submitted. A complete report from the World Heritage Committee is submitted to the UNESCO General Conference every two years.

The only specific requirements for data disclosure are laid out in forms for nominating properties on the World Heritage List and for requesting international co-operation under the Fund.

Measurement of the compliance of Parties to commitments are undertaken through the procedures for monitoring of the condition and conservation status of World Heritage properties. This task is undertaken for natural properties by the World Conservation Union (IUCN) (see NGOs), which prepares regular reports for the World Heritage Committee, and for cultural sites by the UNESCO

Secretariat, in consultation with the International Council for Monuments and Sites (ICOMOS), the International Centre for the Study of the Preservation and Restoration of Cultural Property (ICCROM), and the countries concerned.

An evaluation of the implementation of the Convention was adopted in 1992. National reports, linked to particular problems of conservation, have been submitted occasionally, but the number of reports requested and submitted is increasing. The reports, which are public, are reviewed by the World Heritage Centre, the advisory bodies to the Convention, the World Heritage Bureau, and the World Heritage Committee. Such reviews are also public. Publication lists of such reviews are not distributed by the Centre.

*Observations or inspections*
None by the Convention as yet, but the World Heritage Center is presently preparing, in co-operation with the advisory bodies, a comprehensive monitoring methodology which should be available by 1995.

*Trade sanctions*
None.

*Dispute-settlement mechanisms*
No provision is made for the settlement of disputes.

## Decision-making
*Political bodies*
The *General Assembly of States Parties* meets during the UNESCO General Conference every two years to elect the *World Heritage Committee*. The Committee makes the decisions relating to the implementation of the Convention, including the allocation of funds. It has established a *World Heritage Bureau*, which performs a number of functions on behalf of the Committee. It meets twice a year.

*Scientific/technical bodies*
Technical and scientific advice is provided by NGOs like IUCN (see NGOs) for the natural heritage and by ICOMOS and ICCROM for the cultural heritage (see above).

## Publications
The World Heritage Centre publishes *World Heritage Newsletter* (three times a year).

UNESCO publishes regularly an up-to-date *World Heritage List* and *List of States Parties*. The UNESCO *Courier* regularly includes information on World Heritage sites. A map of sites is available from the Secretariat.

# Convention on Biological Diversity (CBD)

## Objectives

• to ensure the conservation of biological diversity and the sustainable use of its components;

• to promote a fair and equitable sharing of the benefits arising out of the utilization of genetic resources, including by appropriate access to genetic resources and by appropriate transfer of relevant technologies (taking into account all rights over those resources and to technologies), and by appropriate funding.

## Scope

*Legal scope*
Open to all States and regional economic integration organizations.

*Geographic scope*
Global.

## Time and place of adoption

5 June 1992, Rio de Janeiro.

## Entry into force

29 December 1993.

## Status of participation

92 Parties, including the European Economic Community, by 3 October 1994. 82 Signatories without ratification, acceptance, or approval.

## Affiliated protocols, annexes, and organizations

The Convention has two Annexes which cover:

• identification and monitoring;

• arbitration and conciliation.

   The Convention has no protocols, so far.

*Co-ordination with related instruments*
In keeping with its responsibility to review the implementation of the Convention under Article 23(4), the Conference of the Parties is to contact, through the Secretariat, the executive bodies of conventions dealing with matters covered by the Convention on Biological Diversity. The goal is to establish appropriate forms of co-operation with them.

## Secretariat

UNEP/Interim Secretariat for the Convention on Biological Diversity, CP 356,
15, chemin des Anémones,
CH-1219 Châtelaine,
Geneva, Switzerland
*Telephone*:      +41-22-9799111
*Telefax*:      +41-22-7972512
*E-mail*:      name@unep.ch

*Executive Secretary*
Ms Angela Cropper.

*Number of staff*
7 professionals and 6 support staff (Oct. 1994).

## Finance

The Global Environment Facility (GEF) of the World Bank, UNDP, and UNEP (see IGOs) has been entrusted with the operation of the financial mechanism on an interim basis. The Conference of the Parties will make the decision on the institutional structure to operate the financial mechanism.

*Budget*
The administrative core budget is $US620,000 in 1993 and $US1,302,000 in 1994. The budget for 1995 was decided by the CoP at its first meeting from 28 November to 9 December 1994 in Nassau, the Bahamas.

## Rules and standards

Each Contracting Party shall:

• develop national strategies, plans, or programmes for the conservation and sustainable use of biological diversity or adapt for this purpose existing strategies, plans, and programmes which shall reflect, *inter alia*, the measures set out in the Convention relevant to the Party concerned; and

• integrate, as far as possible and as appropriate, the conservation and sustainable use of biological diversity into the relevant sectoral and cross-sectoral plans, programmes, and policies.

   Access to and transfer of technology to developing countries shall be provided and/or facilitated under fair and favourable terms, including on concessional and preferential terms where mutually agreed, and, where necessary, in accordance with the financial mechanism established by the Convention. In the case of technology subject to patents or other intellectual property rights, such access and transfer shall be provided on terms which recognize and are consistent with the adequate and effective protection of intellectual property rights. The Contracting Parties, recognizing that patents and other intellectual property rights may have an influence on the implementation of this Convention shall co-operate in this regard subject to national legislation and international law in order to ensure that such rights are supportive of and do not run counter to its objectives.

   Each Contracting Party shall:

• take legislative, administrative, or policy measures, as appropriate, to provide for the effective participation in biotechnological research activities by those Parties, especially developing countries, which provide the genetic resources for such research, and where feasible in such Parties;

• take all practical measures to promote and advance priority access on a fair and equitable basis by Parties, especially developing countries, to the results and benefits arising from biotechnologies based upon genetic resources provided by those Contracting Parties. Such access shall be on mutually agreed terms.

   The developed-country Parties shall provide new and additional financial resources to enable developing-country Parties to meet the agreed full incremental costs to them of implementing measures which fulfil the obligations of the Convention.

   The extent to which developing-country Parties will be able effectively to implement their obligations under this Convention will depend on the effective implementation by the developed-country Parties of their commitments

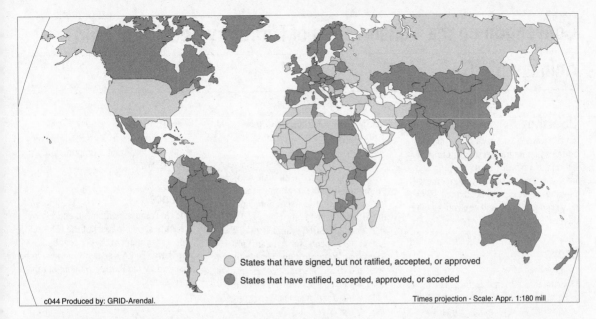

States that have signed, but not ratified, accepted, or approved

States that have ratified, accepted, approved, or acceded

c044 Produced by: GRID-Arendal.

Times projection - Scale: Appr. 1:180 mill

under the Convention related to financial resources and transfer of technology and, their willingness to take fully into account the fact that economic and social development and eradication of poverty are the first and overriding priorities of the developing countries.

There shall be a mechanism for the provision of financial resources to developing-country Parties on a grant or concessional basis. For the purposes of the Convention, the mechanism shall function under the authority and guidance of, and be accountable to, the Conference of the Parties.

## Monitoring/implementation

*Review procedure*
The Conference of the Parties (see below) shall keep under review the implementation of the Convention and establish the form and the intervals for transmitting the information to be submitted in accordance with the Convention and consider such information as well as reports submitted by any subsidiary body.

The Parties shall present reports of measures which they have taken for the implementation of the provisions of the Convention and their effectiveness in meeting the objectives of the Convention.

*Dispute-settlement mechanisms*
In the event of a dispute between

Contracting Parties concerning the interpretation and application of the provisions of the Convention, the Parties involved shall seek solution by negotiation. Should this fail, they may seek the good offices of, or request mediation by, a third party. Upon becoming a member of the Convention, Parties may, by a written declaration to the Depositary, recognize as compulsory, in relation to any Party accepting the same obligation:
• arbitration in accordance with the procedure set out in Part 1 of Annex II; and/or
• submission of the dispute to the International Court of Justice.

If Parties do not accept this procedure, the dispute shall be submitted to a conciliation commission created by the Parties to the dispute, the recommendations of which 'the Parties shall consider in good faith'.

## Decision-making

*Political bodies*
The *Conference of the Parties* (CoP), the governing body of the Convention, consists of representatives of governments. The first meeting of the CoP shall be convened by the Executive Director of UNEP not later than one year after the entry into force of the Convention. Thereafter, ordinary meetings shall be held at regular intervals to be determined by the CoP at its first meeting.

The CoP is the decision-making organ and may adopt amendments, annexes, and protocols to the Convention in accordance with the procedure set forth in the Convention. The Parties shall make every effort to reach agreement on any proposed amendment or annex to the Convention by consensus. If all efforts at consensus have been exhausted, the amendment, shall as a last resort, be adopted by a three-quarters majority vote of the Parties present and voting at the meeting.

Any body or agency, whether national or international, governmental or non-governmental, which is qualified in matters relating to conservation or sustainable use of biological diversity, and which has informed the Secretariat of its wish to be represented at a meeting of the CoP as an observer, may be so admitted unless at least one-third of the Parties present object.

*Scientific/technical bodies*
A subsidiary body for scientific and technological advice has been established. This body shall comprise government representatives competent in the relevant field of expertise.

## Publications
Up-to-date information is made available through the Interim Secretariat.

---

# Convention on the Conservation of Migratory Species of Wild Animals (CMS)

## Objectives

To conserve those species of wild animals that migrate across or outside national boundaries by developing and implementing co-operative agreements, prohibiting taking of endangered species, conserving habitat, and controlling other adverse factors.

## Scope

*Legal scope*
Open to all States and regional economic integration organizations. Membership of subsidiary 'Agreements' under the Convention is open to all Range States (and the relevant regional integration organizations) for the species covered, including States that are not Parties to the parent Convention.

*Geographic scope*
Global.

## Time and place of adoption

23 June 1979, Bonn.

## Entry into force

1 November 1983.

## Status of participation

44 Parties, including the European Union, by October 1994. 9 Signatories without ratification, acceptance, or approval.

## Affiliated protocols, annexes, and organizations

Subsidiary Agreements have been concluded for the conservation of:
• *seals in the Wadden Sea*. Entered into force on 1 October 1991. 3 Parties, by October 1994;
• *bats in Europe*. Entered into force on 16 January 1994. 9 Parties, by October 1994. 4 Signatories without ratification, acceptance, or accession;
• *small cetaceans in the Baltic and North Seas*. Entered into force on 29

March 1994. 6 Parties, by October 1994. 1 Signatory without ratification, acceptance, or accession.

Memoranda of understanding have also been concluded with a view to promoting the conservation of the western and central Asian populations of the Siberian crane (July 1993) and the slender-billed curlew (Sept. 1994). Two further agreements, for African-Eurasian Migratory Waterbirds and for Mediterranean and Black Sea small cetaceans, are at an advanced stage of development.

*Appendix I* covers endangered migratory species.

*Appendix II* covers migratory species which have an unfavourable conservation status and which require international agreements for their conservation and management.

Instruments of accession to be deposited with the Government of Germany.

The *United Nations Environment Programme (UNEP)* (see IGOs) provides the Secretariat and administers the trust fund for the Convention. Institutional arrangements for Agreements vary, being undertaken by various international organizations or governments.

*Co-ordination with related instruments*
Agreements between Range States should take account of related instruments such as the Ramsar Convention (see this section).

## Secretariat

UNEP/CMS Secretariat,
Mallwitzstraße 1–3,
D-53177 Bonn,
Germany
*Telephone:*    +49-228-954350-1/2/3/4
*Telefax:*    +49-228-9543500
*Telex:*    885 556 bfn d

*Co-ordinator*
Mr Arnulf Müller-Helmbrecht.

*Programme Officer*
Mr Douglas Hykle.

*Number of staff*
2 professionals plus 1 professional on temporary basis and 2 support staff (Oct. 1994).

## Finance

The Convention is financed entirely by the Parties, on the basis of the UN scale, with a maximum of 25 per cent by any one Party. The Agreements are also to be financed by the Parties to them, but the basis varies.

*Budget*
The 1994 budget for the Convention adopted by the Conference of the Parties was $US774,841. By October 1994 approximately $US460,000 had been received in contributions from Parties towards the 1994 budget.

The Conference of the Parties, at its fourth meeting in June 1994, adopted a core budget of $US910,780 for 1995, $US920,385 for 1996, and $US1,268,990 for 1997. It also agreed to withdraw an additional $US500,000 from the trust fund in order to finance consultancies during the triennium.

*Special funds*
The core budget includes funds to assist developing- country participants to attend meetings of experts and of the Standing Committee (see below). Further, some funding support for representatives of developing-country Parties for attendance at meetings of the Conference of the Parties and of the Scientific Council has been made available by a few European governments.

The size of the Trust Fund is variable (depends on contributions from member states).

## Rules and standards

With respect to endangered migratory species listed in Appendix I, Parties that are Range States are to prohibit the taking of animals belonging to such species, with a few exceptions. Range

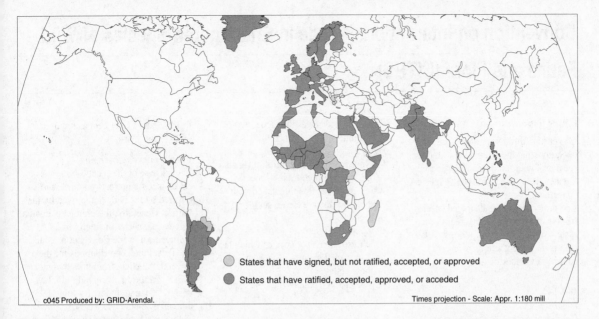

| | States that have signed, but not ratified, accepted, or approved |
| | States that have ratified, accepted, approved, or acceded |

c045 Produced by: GRID-Arendal.

Times projection - Scale: Appr. 1:180 mill

States are to endeavour to conserve and, where possible, restore the habitats of these species; eliminate, prevent, or minimize impediments to their migration; and prevent, reduce, or control factors endangering them.

'Agreements' to benefit species listed in Appendix II are generally regional, sometimes on a north–south gradient, but taken together should have a global effect. These Agreements, within the framework of the 'umbrella' Convention, can stipulate precise conservation measures and implementation mechanisms.

The Convention provides for reservations on joining and with regard to species listed in the Appendices when they are amended. The Agreement on the Conservation of Seals in the Wadden Sea allows no reservations, whereas the Agreements on Bats in Europe and Small Cetaceans in the Baltic and North Seas allow for reservations on species covered.

## Monitoring/implementation

### Review procedure
Parties to the Convention should inform the Conference of the Parties every three years of measures they are taking to implement the Convention for species listed in the Appendices. Initially, provision of information was very poor, but has improved gradually. Nearly half the Parties submitted reports of variable comprehensiveness to the 1994 meeting.

The reports, which are made public, are reviewed by the Secretariat and by the Conference of the Parties. No reviews are made by independent bodies.

Parties also must inform the Secretariat of exceptions made to the prohibition on taking of Appendix I species, but, although the Secretariat is aware informally of some cases of such taking, it has never been informed by Parties officially.

Parties are required to inform the Secretariat of those species in the Appendices of which they consider themselves to be Range States. The Secretariat circulates Range State lists to Parties and experts for comments.

### Dispute-settlement mechanisms
The Convention provides dispute-settlement procedures, that is, bilateral negotiation, followed by referral to the permanent Court of Arbitration. So far such disputes are not known to have arisen.

## Decision-making

### Political bodies
The *Conference of the Parties* is the decision-making organ and can amend the instruments under the Convention and adopt resolutions to improve its implementation. It meets every three years. The *Standing Committee*, consisting of regional representatives and the Depositary Government, provides general policy direction and carries out

activities on behalf of the Conference between the triennial meetings.

Amendments to the Convention may be adopted by the Conference of Parties by a two-thirds majority of members present and voting. They enter into force in regard to all Parties ninety days after the meeting, except for those Parties which filed a written reservation within the ninety-day period.

### Scientific/technical bodies
A *Scientific Council* is established to provide advice on scientific matters to the Conference of the Parties, to the Secretariat, and, when instructed, to any Party. It can recommend research, provide advice on migratory species listed in Appendices I and II, and recommend specific conservation and management measures to be included in agreements. The Council consists of experts appointed by individual Parties and by the Conference, and may include experts from non-governmental organizations in its working groups.

Agreements may provide for advisory bodies or advice from the Convention's Scientific Council.

## Publications
The Secretariat publishes a list of Range States of all migratory species included in the two Appendices, a regular *CMS Bulletin*, and a booklet explaining the aims and operation of the Convention.

# Convention on International Trade in Endangered Species of Wild Fauna and Flora (CITES)

## Objectives

• to ensure, through international co-operation, that the international trade in species of wild fauna and flora does not threaten the conservation of the species concerned;
• to protect certain endangered species from over-exploitation by means of a system of import/export permits issued by a management authority under the control of a scientific authority.

## Scope

*Legal scope*
Open to all States. Not yet open to regional integration organizations.

*Geographic scope*
Global.

## Time and place of adoption

3 March 1973, Washington, DC.

## Entry into force

1 July 1975.

## Status of participation

124 Parties, by 17 November 1994. 4 Signatories without ratification, acceptance, or approval.

## Affiliated instruments

• *Amendment protocol, Bonn 1979.* Entered into force on 13 April 1987. Related to financial provisions;
• *Amendment protocol, Gaborone 1983.* [Not yet in force.] 32 of the States that were Parties on April 1983 have accepted this amendment, by 27 September 1994. 54 instruments of ratification, acceptance, approval, or accession required to enter into force. Related to accession to the Convention by regional economic integration organizations. Same status of participation as the Convention.
• *Appendix I* offers the highest protection and prohibits (with limited exemptions) the commercial international trade in wild-caught specimens of species threatened with extinction;
• *Appendix II* assigns the responsibility to exporting states to control, through a permit system, such trade in species which could become threatened with extinction if there were no such restriction;
• *Appendix III* requires Parties to control trade in specimens of species which have been protected in certain states and listed by those states;
• *Appendix IV* contains a model export permit.

## Secretariat

UNEP/CITES Secretariat,
15, chemin des Anémones, CP 456,
CH-1219 Châtelaine, Geneva,
Switzerland
*Telephone*:        +41-22-979-9139/9140
*Telefax*:        +41-22-7973417

*Secretary-General*
Mr Izgrev Topkov.

*Information officer*
Mr Jean Patrick Le Duc.

*Number of staff*
14 professionals and 11 support staff.

## Finance

*Budget*
The administrative core budget was SFr4,630,751 in 1993, SFr5,955,970 in 1994, and is SFr5,149,313 in 1994.

*Special funds*
The budget is entirely covered by contributions of the Parties to a *Trust Fund* (established in 1984) of UNEP. Contribution from Parties are assessed in accordance with the UN scale of contributions. Contributions received by the CITES Trust Fund in 1992 amounted to approximately $US3.0 million.

Total expenditure relating to the Trust Fund in 1992 was approximately $US2.8 million. Contributors were all Parties to the Convention of which 98.4 per cent fulfilled their financial obligations as required in 1991, 97 per cent as required in 1992, and 91 per cent as required in 1993 (Sept. 1994).

*Counterpart contributions*
The purpose of these contributions is to cover specific projects not necessarily covered by the budget approved by the Parties. Generally, these projects involve surveys of species or improving enforcement of the Convention. Unlike the Trust Fund, contributions for the projects can come from private industry, NGOs, Parties, and any individual who wishes to donate funds. By July 1993 the amount available was $US4.9 million. Main contributors were USA, UK, Japan, France, the European Community (EC), and the World Wide Fund For Nature (WWF).

## Rules and standards

Permits are required for species listed in Appendices I and II stating that export/import will not be detrimental to the survival of the species. Trade in Appendix III listed species is regulated through the issuing of export permits where trade is from the state that listed the species, or otherwise through the issuance of certificates of origin (see below).

If a country does not accept the placing of a species in a certain Appendix, it may enter a reservation.

Each Party is required to maintain records of trade in species covering:
• names and addresses of exporters and importers;
• number and type of permits and certificates granted;
• states with which trade has occurred;
• numbers or quantities and types of specimens and names of species traded.

## Monitoring/implementation

*Review procedure*
The Parties have an obligation to provide an annual report on all trade in species of flora and fauna listed in the appendices to the Convention and to provide a biennial report on legislative, regulatory, and administrative measures taken.

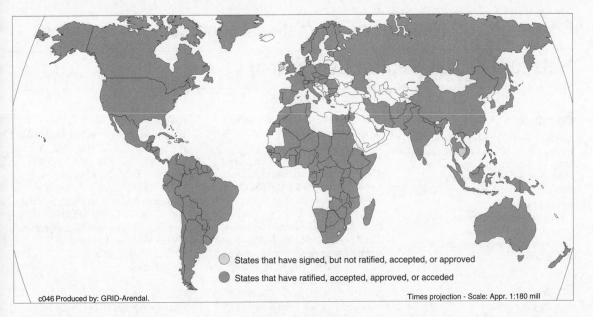

States that have signed, but not ratified, accepted, or approved

States that have ratified, accepted, approved, or acceded

c046 Produced by: GRID-Arendal.                                    Times projection - Scale: Appr. 1:180 mill

Not all Parties meet the reporting requirements; and even those which do submit annual reports often submit them long after the agreed deadlines. Moreover, many of the reports submitted are incomplete. 63 of 109 Parties have submitted national reports for 1990. By 20 October 1993, 69 of 113 Parties have submitted such reports for 1991. A new review on the status of reporting was distributed to the Parties at the end of November 1994 and is public after that date.

The annual statistical reports are a vital tool for monitoring the levels of trade in the listed species and for monitoring the implementation of the Convention. A comparison of the reports of each Party with those of the other Parties often reveals information on trade of which it was unaware, and can help to identify violations. The reports are public. By 20 October 1993, 32 national reports (27 per cent of the Parties) had been submitted, with the deadline on 31 October.

Review of data or information in national reports are reviewed by the Secretariat and the Conference of the Parties, as well as by independent NGOs such as WWF and IUCN (see NGOs).

Each Party is required to establish one or more *Management Authorities* to certify that the species has been obtained within the State's protection laws and that shipment will not be harmful to the living specimen being shipped. In

addition each Party is required to designate one or more *Scientific Authorities* to advise its Management Authority on matters related to the issuance of export permits and Appendix I import permits.

If the Secretariat considers that the provisions of the Convention are not being correctly implemented, it is obliged to inform the Management Authority of the Party concerned, which should reply with the necessary information within one month.

*Observations or inspections*
All enforcement is done at the national level, including inspection of shipments. The Secretariat provides an advisory and co-ordinating role.

*Data and information system programmes*
Wildlife Trade Monitoring Unit holds data on some 2 million trade transactions carried out under CITES.

*Trade sanctions*
Although the Convention does not include any provisions to penalize Parties for non-compliance, the Parties have preferred to avoid being cited in the alleged infractions report. Moreover, in the most serious cases of non-compliance, the Conference of the Parties and/or the Standing Committee (see below), advised by the Secretariat, have gone so far as to recommend a cessation of trade with a particular

country, pending the correction of the implementation problems that have been identified. Such measures were taken against Thailand between April 1991 and April 1992 and against Italy between July 1992 and February 1993.

## Decision-making

The *Conference of the Parties to CITES* meets about every two years to examine progress in the restoration and conservation of protected species, and to revise the Appendices as appropriate. Amendments to Appendices enter into force automatically in accordance with a procedure not requiring ratification.

The *Standing Committee* of the Conference of the Parties may recommend that Parties take certain measures against any Party (e.g. a ban on trade) which seriously and repeatedly infringes the rules of the Convention.

## Publications

*Notifications to the Parties* are also available to NGOs or the public. In addition the Secretariat publishes an *Identification Manual* of animals species included in the appendices (an Identification Manual for plants is under preparation); *The Evolution of CITES*, a reference book; and supports the publication of the quarterly magazine *Conservation and Management/CITES*.

# Convention on Wetlands of International Importance especially as Waterfowl Habitat (Ramsar Convention)

## Objectives

- to stem the progressive encroachment on and loss of wetlands now and in the future, recognizing the fundamental ecological functions of wetlands and their economic, cultural, scientific, and recreational value;
- to encourage the 'wise use' of the world's wetland resources;
- to co-ordinate international efforts for this purpose.

## Scope

*Legal scope*
Membership open to all member States of the United Nations or members of the specialized agencies and the IAEA. Not open to regional integration organizations.

*Geographic scope*
Global.

## Time and place of adoption

2 February 1971, Ramsar, Iran.

## Entry into force

21 December 1975.

## Status of participation

83 Parties, by 10 October 1994. 5 Signatories without ratification, acceptance, or approval.

## Affiliated protocols, annexes, and organizations

- *Protocol to Amend the Convention on Wetlands of International Importance especially as Waterfowl Habitat, Paris, 1982.* Entered into force on 1 October 1986. 83 Parties, by 10 October 1994;
- *Amendments to Arts. 6 and 7 of the Convention, Regina, 1987.* Entered into force on 1 May 1994.
- *List of Wetlands of International Importance.*
The Ramsar Bureau collaborates closely with the *World Conservation Union*

*(IUCN)* (see NGOs) and the *International Waterfowl and Wetlands Research Bureau (IWRB)*.

The *Director-General of the United Nations Educational, Scientific, and Cultural Organization (UNESCO)* (see IGOs) acts as depositary.

*Co-ordination with related instruments*
The Ramsar Convention Bureau meets regularly with the secretariats of other international conventions on nature conservation, such as the Convention on Biological Diversity, the Convention on International Trade in Endangered Species of Wild Fauna and Flora (CITES), the World Heritage Convention, and the Convention the Conservation of Migratory Species of Wild Animals (see this section) to exchange information and to co-ordinate action.

## Secretariat

Ramsar Convention Bureau,
Rue Mauverney 28,
CH-1196 Gland,
Switzerland
*Telephone*:   +41-22-9990170
*Telefax*:      +41-22-9990169
*E-mail*:       ramsar@hq.iucn.ch

*Secretary General*
Mr Daniel B. Navid.

*Information officer*
Ms Mireille Katz.

*Number of staff*
8 professionals and 9 support staff (Oct. 1994).

## Finance

Income comes from the Contracting Parties according to the UN scale of assessments for the core funding. Specific projects of at least a similar magnitude are also undertaken outside the core budget.

*Budget*
Total actual budget was SFr1,944,000 in 1991 and SFr2,313,000 in 1992. The total budget for 1994 is SFr2,148,000; for 1995, SFr2,215,000; and for 1996, SFr2,312,000.

The actual administrative budget was SFr1,678,000 for 1991 and SFr1,995,000 for 1992. The administrative budget for 1994 is SFr2,048,000; for 1995, SFr2,115,000; and for 1996, SFr2,212,000.

*Main contributors*
Main contributors in 1993 were France, the Netherlands, Switzerland, USA, and Japan.

*Special funds*
The *Wetland Conservation Fund* was launched by the Convention in 1990 to assist developing countries by offering financial benefits as well as expert services in the implementation of the Convention. During its first year of existence (1991), contributions amounting to SFr271,246 were received and by October 1994 the contributions totalled SFr473,178. Disbursements in 1992 were SFr292,000 and accumulated disbursements were SFr480,591. Disbursements in 1993 were SFr469,880 and accumulated disbursements were SFr950,472. Contributors in 1991 were Austria, Denmark, the Netherlands, Norway, Sweden, the UK, and USA. 7 projects were approved in 1991, 12 projects were approved in 1992, and 13 projects were approved in 1993. Others were partially funded or referred to other agencies for further study or funding.

## Rules and standards

Parties shall:
- designate at least one national wetland for inclusion in a *List of Wetlands of International Importance*;
- formulate and implement their planning so as to promote the conservation of the wetlands included in the List, and as

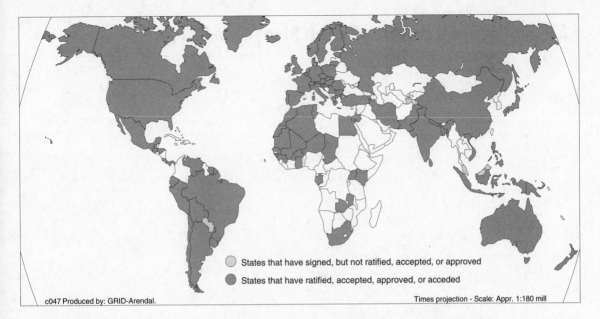

States that have signed, but not ratified, accepted, or approved

States that have ratified, accepted, approved, or acceded

c047 Produced by: GRID-Arendal.

Times projection - Scale: Appr. 1:180 mill

far as possible the wise use of wetlands in their territory;
• establish wetland nature reserves, co-operate in the exchange of information, and train personnel for wetlands management;
• co-operate in the management of shared wetlands and shared wetland species.

## Monitoring/implementation

*Review procedure*
Parties report to each Conference of the Contracting Parties according to an agreed format. Reports are also required when the ecological character of a listed site is changing or is likely to change so that international consultations may be held on the problem. In 1992, 51 national reports (67 per cent of the Parties) on implementation were submitted by the Parties as required under the Convention. The same number was received in 1993. The reports are published. There are no reporting requirements on the implementation of the Protocol. Reviews of data or information in national reports by the Secretariat and the Conference are not public.

A Monitoring Procedure was instituted in 1988 to assist countries in addressing management problems in Ramsar sites. This has been used selectively due to funding restrictions.

In 1990, at Montreux, the Conference

of the Parties called for the maintenance of a Record of Ramsar Sites where changes in ecological character have occurred, are occurring, or are likely to occur.

During 1992 the Monitoring Procedure was applied to 4 Ramsar Sites in Iran, Bulgaria, South Africa, and Iceland; during 1993 to 2 Ramsar Sites in the UK and Uruguay, and during 1994 to 3 Ramsar Sites in Uganda, Trinidad and Tobago, and the UK.

*Observations or inspections*
None by the Convention as such.

*Environmental monitoring programmes*
A Ramsar Database has been elaborated with an agreed classification and data system for all wetland sites.

*Trade sanctions*
None.

*Dispute-settlement mechanisms*
No provisions on dispute settlement. Disputes are resolved by discussions at the Conference of the Contracting Parties, followed by Conference recommendations.

## Decision-making

*Political bodies*
The *Conference of the Contracting Parties* is the governing body and meets every three years. The implementation of the Convention is reviewed at these meetings. Secretariat functions are performed by the *Ramsar Convention Bureau*, responsible to a *Standing Committee of the Contracting Parties*.

*Scientific/technical bodies*
An expert group, the *Scientific and Technical Review Panel* has been established to guide policy decisions by the Conference of the Contracting Parties. It meets twice a year.

Participation by non-governmental observers is encouraged both in meetings of the Contracting Parties and in the Panel.

## Publications

In addition to annual reports, conference proceedings, the Ramsar Bureau publishes:
• *Ramsar Newsletter* (three times a year);
• *Directory of Wetlands of International Importance*;
• *Ramsar Manual*;
• *Towards the Wise Use of Wetlands*, a collection of guide-lines and case studies.

# FAO International Undertaking on Plant Genetic Resources

## Objectives
- to ensure that plant genetic resources (PGR) are conserved and are made as widely available as possible for the purposes of plant breeding, for the benefit of present and future generations;
- to conserve and use plant genetic resources of economic and/or social interest, particularly for agriculture;
- to focus on cultivated varieties of plants, plants or varieties which have been in cultivation in the past, primitive versions of cultivated plants, wild relatives of such plants, and certain special genetic stocks.

## Scope
*Legal scope*
Open to all member States of the United Nations Food and Agriculture Organization (FAO) (see IGOs), non-member States which are members of the United Nations and regional integration organizations.

*Geographic scope*
Global.

## Time and place of adoption
23 November 1983, Rome.

## Entry into force
1 January 1984.

## Status of participation
110 countries have adhered to the Undertaking, by August 1994.

## Affiliated protocols, annexes, and organizations
The principles and articles contained in the Undertaking, and its annexes, are being developed through a number of negotiated elements which form the *FAO Global System of PGR*. This includes:
- *Commission on Plant Genetic Resources (CPGR)* (see below);
- *International Code of Conduct for Plant Germplasm Collecting and Transfer*, which forms an important tool in regulating the collection and transfer of PGR, with the aim of facilitating equitable access to these resources, and promoting their utilization and development. It was adopted by the FAO Conference in November 1993 and became operative in January 1994;
- *Code of Conduct for Biotechnology*, as it affects the conservation and use of PGR;
- *International Network of* ex situ *base collections*, under the auspices and/or jurisdiction of FAO and with the technical assistance of the International Board for Plant Genetic Resources (IBPGR). FAO is currently negotiating 'basic agreements' with more than 30 countries and the International Agricultural Research Centres of the Consultative Group for International Agricultural Research (CGIAR) that have offered to put their gene banks in this network;
- *Network of* in situ *Conservation Areas*, with special emphasis on wild relatives of cultivated plants, as well as on the promotion of 'on-farm' conservation and utilization of land races;
- *World Information and Early Warning System on PGR (WIEWS)*, which collects and disseminates data and facilitates the exchange of information on PGR and related technologies and draws rapid attention to hazards threatening the operation of gene banks and the loss of genetic diversity throughout the world;
- *State of the World's PGR*, periodical reports, which will cover aspects of the conservation and utilization of PGR;
- *Global Plan of Action on PGR*, a rolling plan aimed at rationalizing and co-ordinating efforts in this area. It consists of major national and international institutions which are expected to be involved in the preparation, implementation, and financing of the Plan.

The FAO Conference has suggested a step-by-step process for a negotiated revision of the Undertaking. The negotiation process started in November 1994 initiated by the Commission on Plant Genetic Resources (CPGR). Stage I includes the integration of the Annexes into the main text of the Undertaking and Stage II includes consideration of other

○ States that have adhered to the Undertaking

c048 Produced by: GRID-Arendal.

Times projection - Scale: Appr. 1:180 mill

issues to be incorporated into the revised Undertaking at later stages in the process.

*Co-ordination with related instruments*
FAO is responsible for co-ordinating work with other conventions. Following the approval of the UN Convention on Biological Diversity (see this section), it has been suggested that the Undertaking, duly modified, should become a protocol of the Convention.

## Secretariat

The Secretariat of the FAO Intergovernmental Commission on PGR acts as Secretariat of the Undertaking.

c/o FAO (see IGOs)
*Telephone:* +39-6-52254986
*Telefax:* +39-6-5225-3152/5155
*E-mail:* j.esquinas-fao@cgnet.com

*Secretary*
Dr Jose T. Esquinas-Alcazar.

*Number of staff*
2 professionals supported by a number of professional staff from the FAO Divisions concerned (Oct. 1994).

## Finance

International administration costs are covered by the regular budget of FAO.

*Budget*
Administrative core budget was $US500,000 in 1993, $US600,000 in 1994, and is $US700,000 in 1995.

*Special funds*
In November 1991 the FAO Conference approved a new annex to the Undertaking which established that Farmers' Rights should be implemented through an international fund on PGR to support plant genetic conservation and utilization programmes, particularly in the developing countries. It also established that the priorities of the fund will be overseen by the Commission on PGR (see below).

This fund does not refer to the 'international fund for plant genetic resources' established by FAO in 1988, on an interim basis, to provide a channel for countries, intergovernmental and non-governmental organizations, private industry, and individuals to support activities for the conservation and utilization of PGR. The contributions channelled through this fund have been of the order of $US500,000.

## Rules and standards

The Undertaking covers both *ex situ* and *in situ* conservation as well as sustainable utilization of PGR.

The Parties shall:
• provide access to the materials which have been collected or conserved in pursuance of its terms, and the export of

such material for scientific or plant-breeding purposes is to take place unrestrictedly on the basis of mutual exchange or on the most favourable terms having regard to the characteristics of the person or entity making the request for transfer;
• provide urgent funding in cases where there is reason to apprehend that the effective conservation of material held in a collection centre might be prejudiced;
• mount exploration missions to identify PGR which are endangered by deforestation or development activities. They agree to put in place legislation to protect plants and their habitats and to take steps to collect genetic material;
• pledge themselves to build up institutional and technical capabilities in developing countries, intensifying plant-breeding and germplasm maintenance activities on the international level, establishing an international gene-bank, building up an internationally co-ordinated network of collections, putting in place an international data system, and providing an early-warning system to alert the international community of threats to the continued security of any centre at which plant genetic material is collected.

The Undertaking is regarded by the Parties and by FAO as not imposing legally binding obligations on the Parties.

## Monitoring/implementation

*Review procedure*
States are required to provide the Director-General of FAO with annual reports of the steps which have been taken by them in pursuance of the terms of the Undertaking.

The reports have been received in a heterogeneous and irregular manner. A questionnaire has recently been sent by the Secretariat to the member Countries in order to standardize the information and to collect it on a regular basis. The replies that have been received will serve a double purpose: to develop a country database for the WIEWS (see above), and to provide basic information for the periodical publications on the State of the World's PGR.

The submitting of national reports required under the Undertaking started systematically in 1993. Since February 1993 up to 3 November 1993, 80 national reports (75 per cent of the Parties) have been received.

The reports are reviewed by the Secretariat and the technical consultants and then verified by the States. At this stage the information in the reports becomes public.

The Secretariat revises, processes, analyses, and incorporates the information contained in the national reports into the WIEWS and utilizes it in the preparation of the reports on State of the World's PGR and other publications.

Consolidated information goes to the Commission. Then the State of the World PGR report is presented to the Commission.

The operation of the Undertaking is reviewed at regular meetings of the Commission and its Working Group on PGR (see below).

*Observations or inspections*
None by the Agreement as such.

*Data and information system programmes*
See WIEWS under 'Affiliated protocols, annexes, and organizations' above.

*Trade sanctions*
None.

*Dispute-settlement mechanisms*
The Undertaking makes no reference to dispute settlement. Matters of controversy between the Parties are usually resolved by negotiation and the agreed result endorsed, in appropriate cases, by the Commission or the FAO Conference.

## Decision-making

*Political bodies*
The *Commission on Plant Genetic Resources (CPGR)*, with 122 member Countries, which are donors and users of germplasm, funds, and technologies, monitors the implementation of the Undertaking and discusses, on equal footing, other matters related to the PGR. The Commission has established an intergovernmental *Working Group* with regional representation.

*Scientific/technical bodies*
None, but draws on the resources of the IBPGR (see above), c/o FAO, run by the UNDP (see IGOs)- and FAO-sponsored Consultative Group for International Agricultural Research (CGIAR).

## Publications
• *Plant Genetic Resources Newsletter*, by FAO/IBPGR (three times a year);
• Annual Reports from FAO and IBPGR;
• *State of the World's PGR.*

# International Convention to Combat Desertification (INCD)

## Objectives

To combat desertification and mitigate the effects of drought in countries experiencing serious drought and/or desertification, particularly in Africa, through effective actions at all levels, supported by international co-operation and partnership arrangements, in the framework of an integrated approach which is consistent with *Agenda 21*, with a view to contributing to the achievements of sustainable development in affected areas.

## Scope

*Legal scope*
Open to all member states of the United Nations or any of its specialized agencies, Parties to the Statute of the International Court of Justice, and by regional economic integration organizations.

*Geographic scope*
Global.

## Time and place of adoption

17 June 1994, Paris.

## Entry into force

Not yet in force. The Convention enters into force 90 days after the deposit of 50 instruments of ratification, acceptance, approval, or accession.

## Status of participation

The Convention was signed by 85 States and the European Union at a signing ceremony in Paris on 14–15 October 1994. Open for signature until 13 October 1995 at United Nations Headquarters.

No Parties, by 7 November 1994. 88 Signatories, including the European Union, without ratification, acceptance, or approval.

## Affiliated protocols, annexes, and organizations

The full title of the Convention is the *International Negotiating Committee for the Elaboration of an International Convention to Combat Desertification in Those Countries Experiencing Serious Drought and/or Desertification, Particularly in Africa (INCD)*.

The Convention contains four regional implementation *Annexes* for Africa, Asia, Latin America and the Caribbean, and the northern Mediterranean. The *African Annex* is the most elaborate, both in form and content, of all the annexes. It comprises 19 articles and addresses a broad range of issues including commitments and obligations of both African and developed-country Parties. Explicit reference is made with regard to technical assistance and co-operation to ensure that preference is given to the utilization of less-costly local experts. Emphasis is placed on the need for increased co-ordination among the key players involved in desertification activities, including donors, national governments, NGOs, and local populations. The Annex also contains provisions for financial mechanisms and resources; and co-ordination, partnership, and follow-up arrangements.

The other Annexes are shorter, and reflect the different priorities of the regions. The *Asian Annex* is relatively general in scope, particularly concerning finances. The *Latin American Annex* mentions the important links between desertification and biological-diversity loss, as well as debt issues, unfavourable international economic trade practices, and other socio-economic factors. It also emphasizes traditional knowledge, know-how, and practices. The *Northern Mediterranean Annex* is more scientifically oriented. It stresses urbanization and agricultural practices as economic causes of desertification, and provides for collaboration with other regions in the preparation and implementation of action programmes. It is also unique in that it clearly disqualifies the region from eligibility for funds raised through the main Convention.

The *Secretary-General of the United Nations*, act as depositary.

*Co-ordination with related instruments*
Co-ordinated activities will take place with other relevant international agreements, particularly the Framework Convention on Climate Change (FCCC) and the Convention on Biological Diversity (see Agreements), in order to derive maximum benefit from activities under each agreement while avoiding duplication of effort.

## Secretariat

A permanent secretariat will be set up at the first session of the Conference of the Parties. Until that time (probably over the next two to three years), an interim secretariat will be based in Geneva.

Intergovernmental Negotiating Committee on Desertification (INCD),
Interim Secretariat,
CP 76,
CH-1219 Châtelaine, Geneva,
Switzerland
*Telephone*:     +41-22-979-1234/
                         9410/9404
*Telefax*:         +41-22-9799031
*E-mail*:          secretariat.incd@unep.ch

*INCD Executive Secretary*
Mr Hama Arba Diallo.

*Information officer*
Ms Nada Osseiran.

*Number of staff*
11 professionals and 6 support staff (Nov. 1994).

## Finance

Parties, taking into account their capabilities, shall make every effort to ensure that adequate financial resources are available for programmes to combat desertification and mitigate the effects of drought (see Rules and Standards below).

The Interim Secretariat is funded by the regular budget and voluntary fund contributions.

### Budget

Total core budget for the biennium 1994–95 is $US3,274,100, not including extra-budgetary resources.

## Rules and standards

*Affected Country Parties* undertake:
• to give due priority to combating desertification and mitigating the effects of drought, and allocating adequate resources in accordance with their conditions and capabilities;
• to establish strategies and priorities, within the framework of sustainable development plans and/or policies, to combat desertification and mitigate the effects of drought;
• to address the underlying causes of desertification;
• to promote awareness and facilitate participation of local populations;
• to provide an enabling environment by strengthening relevant existing legislation or by enacting new laws and establishing long-term policies.

*Developed Country Parties* undertake:
• to actively support, as agreed, individually or jointly, the efforts of affected developing-country Parties, particularly those in Africa, and the least developed countries, to combat desertification and mitigate the effects of drought;
• to provide substantial financial resources and other forms of support to assist developing-country Parties, particularly those in Africa, effectively to develop and implement their own long-term plans and strategies to combat desertification and mitigate the effects of drought;
• to promote the mobilization of new and additional funding through the Global Environment Facility (GEF) (see IGOs);

• to encourage the mobilization of funding from the private sector and other non-governmental sources;
• to promote and facilitate access by affected country Parties, particularly affected developing-country Parties, to appropriate technology, knowledge, and know-how.

*National Action Programmes* shall:
• incorporate long-term strategies to combat desertification and mitigate the effects of drought;
• give particular attention to the implementation of preventive measures;
• enhance national climatological and hydrological capabilities;
• promote policies and strengthen institutional frameworks;
• provide for effective popular participation;
• require regular review of implementation.

Elements of the National Action Programmes may include:
• improvements of national economic environments with a view to strengthening programmes aimed at the eradication of poverty and at ensuring food security;
• sustainable management of natural resources;
• sustainable agriculture practices;
• development and efficient use of various energy sources;
• strengthening of capabilities for assessment and monitoring;
• capacity building, education, ad public awareness.

Subject to their respective national legislation/policies, Parties shall exchange information on local and traditional knowledge, ensuring adequate protection for it and providing appropriate return from the benefits derived from it, on an equitable basis and on mutually agreed terms, to the local populations concerned.

## Monitoring/implementation

### Review procedure

Each Party shall communicate to the Conference of the Parties for consideration at its ordinary sessions, reports on the measures which it has taken for the implementation of the convention. The Conference of the Parties shall determine the timetable for submission and the format of such reports.

### Observations or inspections

None by the Convention as such.

### Trade sanctions

No provisions on trade sanctions to penalize Parties for non-compliance.

### Dispute-settlement mechanisms

Parties shall settle any dispute between them concerning the interpretation or application of the Convention through negotiation or other peaceful means of their own choice.

Becoming a member of the Convention, Parties may, by a written declaration, recognize as compulsory, in relation to any Party accepting the same obligation:
• arbitration in accordance with procedures adopted by the Conference of the Parties in an annex as soon as possible;
• submission of disputes to the International Court of Justice.

## Decision-making

### Political bodies

The *Conference of the Parties* shall keep under review and evaluate implementation of the Convention, harmonize policies, establish subsidiary bodies, and undertake additional actions.

### Scientific/technical bodies

A *Committee on Science and Technology* appointed by the Parties is established under the Convention. The Committee shall identify areas related to desertification where additional reflection and research could usefully be undertaken. The Conference of the Parties may, as necessary, appoint *ad hoc* panels to provide information and advice through the Committee on specific issues regarding science and technology.

## Publications

Up-to-date information on the operation of the Convention is made available through the Interim Secretariat.

# International Tropical Timber Agreement (ITTA)

## Objectives

• to provide an effective framework for co-operation and consultation between countries producing and consuming tropical timber;
• to promote the expansion and diversification of international trade in tropical timber and the improvement of structural conditions in the tropical timber market, improving market access and prices which are remunerative to producers and equitable to consumers;
• to promote and support research and development with a view to improving sustainable forest management and wood utilization;
• to improve market intelligence with a view to ensuring greater transparency in the international tropical timber market;
• to encourage the development of national policies aimed at sustainable utilization and conservation of tropical forests and their genetic resources, and maintaining the ecological balance in the regions concerned;
• to facilitate the achievement of the Year 2000 Objective, through which ITTO member Countries are seeking to ensure that all tropical timber entering international trade will be produced from forests under sustainable management by the year 2000, through international assistance and co-operation.

## Scope

*Legal scope*
Open to any State that produces or consumes tropical timber, and to regional integration organizations.

*Geographic scope*
Global.

## Time and place of adoption
18 November 1983, Geneva.

## Entry into force
1 April 1985.

## Status of participation
52 members, comprising 25 producing and 27 consuming members, including the European Economic Community, by October 1994.

## Affiliated protocols, annexes, and organizations
The *International Tropical Timber Organization (ITTO)* is established by the Convention and receives reports from the members.

*Co-ordination with related instruments*
With the ITTA, 1983, close to expiry, negotiations were commenced in 1993 under the auspices of the UN Conference on Trade and Development (UNCTAD)

to formulate a successor agreement. Negotiations were successfully concluded on 26 January 1994, when a successor agreement, the International Tropical Timber Agreement, 1994, was adopted in Geneva thereby enabling the current agreement to be extended pending the entry into force of the successor agreement. Though essentially focused on tropical timber and tropical forests, the successor agreement provides for sharing of information among members on the global timber trade and the sustainable management of all forest types. The successor agreement also provides for a review of its scope four years after its entry into force. A new fund, the Bali Partnership Fund, was also established to assist producer members progress towards ITTO's Year 2000 Objective. The new agreement thus provides a stronger and more realistic basis for international co-operation to promote the conservation, management, and sustainable development of tropical forests.

## Secretariat
International Tropical Timber Organization (ITTO),
International Organizations Center, 5th Floor,
Pacifico-Yokohama,
1-1-1, Minato-Mirai,
Nishi-ku,
Yokohama,

220 Japan
*Telephone*:   +81-45-2231110
*Telefax*:      +81-45-2231111
*E-mail*:  100-201, 3035 (compuserve
           address)

*Executive Director*
Dr B. C. Y. Freezailah.

*Number of staff*
14 professionals and 16 support staff
(Oct. 1994).

## Finance
The administrative budget is financed by
annually assessed contributions from all
Member Countries in proportion to their
votes in the International Tropical
Timber Council (ITTC) (see below). In
hosting ITTO, the government of Japan
and the city of Yokohama provide office
accommodation, pay for costs of transla-
tion and interpretation, and provide three
support staff.

*Budget*
The annual administrative budget was
$US3.5 million in 1992, $US3.6 million
in 1993, and $US3.8 million in 1994.
The proposed budget for 1995 is $US4.3
million. The administrative budget is
shared equally between the producing
and consuming members of the organization.

*Main contributors*
Main contributors in 1994 were all
member Countries, except the European
Economic Community *per se*.

*Special funds*
Funding of project activities is from the
*Common Fund for Commodities*;
relevant regional and international
financial institutions; and voluntary
contributions from members and interested organizations. Generally, target
contributions from donor members are
made at the sessions of the Council held
twice a year. Projects are prepared by the
States and technically appraised by a
Panel of Experts with the assistance of
the Secretariat before being examined by
the relevant Permanent Committees.
Project funding is dependent upon
donors. $US90 million have been
donated for implementation of projects
and pre-projects by October 1994.

Accumulated disbursements are
$US54,890,000.

Main contributors are Japan, Switzerland, the USA, the United Kingdom,
Denmark, the Netherlands, Finland,
Sweden, Norway, Germany, France, as
well as the Common Fund for Commodities and other donors including NGOs
and the private sector. 69 per cent of the
members fulfilled their financial obligations as required by the Convention in
1991 (85 per cent of expected financial
contributions), 71 per cent fulfilled their
obligations in 1992 (85 per cent of
expected financial contributions), and 64
per cent fulfilled their obligations in
1993 (77 per cent of expected financial
contributions).

Recipients are producer member
Countries and some executing agencies
in consumer member Countries.

The idea is to encourage consumer
States and their importing industries to
contribute towards achieving sustainable
use and conservation of tropical forests.
The private sector and conservation
organizations also make financial
contributions to ITTO's project activities.

## Rules and standards
Member Countries are required:
• to pay their assessed contributions to
the Administrative Account;
• to provide data to create transparency
of the tropical timber economy and
enable the Secretariat to prepare an
Annual Review and Assessment of the
World Tropical Timber Situation.

Members are committed to the Year
2000 Objective. It is ITTO's goal that,
by the year 2000, all tropical timber
entering international trade will be
produced from tropical forests under
sustainable management. Members are
invited to submit reports to the Council
annually on their progress towards
achieving Year 2000 Objective, initiated
in 1990.

Members have adopted 'Guidelines for
the Sustainable Management of Natural
Tropical Forests', 'Guidelines for the
Establishment and Sustainable Manage-
ment of Planted Tropical Forests', and
'Guidelines for the Conservation of
Biological Diversity in Tropical Produc-
tion Forests', as well as 'Criteria for the
Measurement of Sustainable Tropical

Forest Management'. The Organization
is also currently preparing 'Guidelines
for the Sustainable Development of
Forest Industries' and 'Guidelines for the
Protection of Tropical Forests Against
Fire'. The ITTO Manual for Project
Formulation also contains guide-lines for
ensuring local community participation
in the project cycle and guide-lines to
take account of the environmental
impacts of projects.

All these commitments and guide-lines
have been adopted by the ITTC (see
below), after due consultation in the
ITTO forum, where, apart from members, non-governmental conservation
organizations and timber trade associations also take part. Legal implementation and enforcement of practical
measures are left to member Countries
themselves.

The operational activities of the
Council and the Permanent Committees
are:
• formulation and implementation of
projects in research and development,
market intelligence, further processing in
producing countries, and reforestation;
• monitoring commercial activity in
tropical timber; reviewing the future
needs of the trade and assistance provided for production; and encouraging
transfer of knowledge and technology.

## Monitoring/implementation
*Review procedure*
Members are expected to submit data
annually on their production and trade of
tropical timbers for the Annual Review
and Assessment of the World Tropical
Timber Situation. Members are also
required to report on progress towards
ITTO's Year 2000 Objective annually.
10 members submitted such reports
during 1993–94. 40 statistical reports (85
per cent of members) were submitted in
1991, 42 reports (85.7 per cent of
members) were submitted in 1992, and
33 reports (63 per cent of members) were
submitted in 1993–94. These reports are
public.

The assessment of compliance by
Members to ITTA principles is the
responsibility of the Council and the
Permanent Committees. Emphasis is
placed on monitoring and review of
ITTO projects and the programme set up
by the Action Plan. An Expert Panel has
been established for the technical

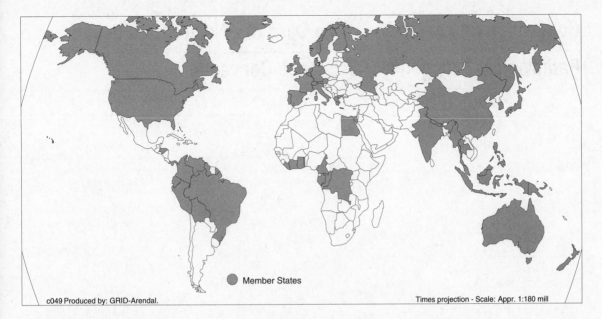

Member States

c049 Produced by: GRID-Arendal.

Times projection - Scale: Appr. 1:180 mill

assessment of project proposals. There is no independent verification of data or information, but non-governmental organizations (NGOs) may address report issues in the Council (see below). They are accorded observer status and are given the chance to speak. These reviews are public and the Secretariat distributes publications list and Council Reports.

*Observations or inspections*
None by the Agreement as such.

*Environmental monitoring programmes*
ITTO supports several projects, pre-projects, and activities that include various environmental monitoring components.

*Trade sanctions*
None.

*Dispute-settlement mechanisms*
Any complaint that a member has failed to fulfil its obligations under the Agreement and any dispute concerning the interpretation or application of the Agreement shall be referred to the Council for decision. Decisions of the Council shall be final and binding.

## Decision-making

*Political bodies*
The ITTA, 1983, has established the *International Tropical Timber Organization (ITTO)*, which functions through its supreme governing body, the *International Tropical Timber Council (ITTC)*. The Council meets twice a year and consists of the members of the Organization. Its work consists in formulating overall policies, approving the programme of work for the Organization, allocating funds for its implementation, and undertaking an annual review and assessment of the tropical timber market

and economy. Non-member governments and organizations may attend upon invitation from the Council as observers of the meetings of the Council.

*Scientific/technical bodies*
The Permanent Committees are:
• *Committee on Economic Information and Market Intelligence*;
• *Committee on Reforestation and Forest Management*;
• *Committee on Forest Industry*;
• *Committee on Finance and Administration*, established by Council decision.

## Publications

Annual Reports, Annual Review of the World Tropical Timber Situation, Council Reports, Technical Series, Policy Development Series, Information Papers, pre-project and project reports, and reports of seminars and workshops are published regularly. ITTO has also two serial publications: *Forest Management Update* and *Market News Service* (Newsletter).

# Convention on Assistance in the Case of a Nuclear Accident or Radiological Emergency (Assistance Convention)

## Objectives
• to set out an international framework aimed at facilitating the prompt provision of assistance in the event of a nuclear accident or radiological emergency, directly between States Parties, through or from the International Atomic Energy Agency (IAEA) (see IGOs), and from other international organizations;
• to minimize consequences and to protect life, property, and the environment from effects of radioactive releases.

## Scope
*Legal scope*
Open to all states, international organizations, and regional integration organizations.

*Geographic scope*
Global.

## Time and place of adoption
26 September 1986, Vienna.

## Entry into force
26 February 1987.

## Status of participation
67 states and 3 intergovernmental organizations (FAO, WHO, and WMO) (see IGOs) were Parties, by October 1994. 24 Signatories without ratification, acceptance, or approval.

## Affiliated protocols, annexes, and organizations
No amendments have been proposed.

The *International Atomic Energy Agency (IAEA)* (see IGOs) acts as depositary and the Secretariat is in charge of administering the Convention.

*Co-ordination with related instruments*
The IAEA Board of Governors has established an Expert Working Group to consider additional measures to improve co-operation in the field of nuclear safety.

## Secretariat
IAEA (see IGOs).

## Finance
*Budget*
Costs are covered by the regular IAEA budget.

*Special funds*
Not applicable.

## Rules and standards
Parties shall co-operate between themselves and with the International Atomic Energy Agency (IAEA) to facilitate prompt assistance in the event of a nuclear accident or radiological emergency.

Parties shall request the Agency to use its best endeavours in accordance with the provisions of this Convention to promote, facilitate, and support the co-operation between the Parties provided for in this Convention.

If a Party needs assistance in the event of a nuclear accident or radiological emergency, whether or not such an accident or emergency originates within its territory, jurisdiction, or control, it may call for such assistance from any other Party, from the Agency, or from other intergovernmental organizations.

A Party to which a request for such assistance is directed shall promptly decide and notify the requesting Party, directly or through the Agency, whether it is in a position to render the assistance requested, and the scope and terms of the assistance.

A Party may request assistance relating to medical or temporary relocation into the territory of another Party of people involved in a nuclear accident or radiological emergency.

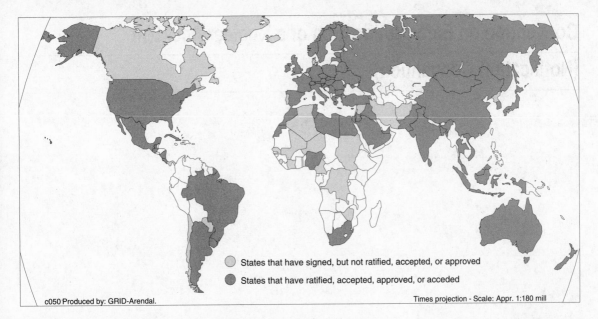

States that have signed, but not ratified, accepted, or approved

States that have ratified, accepted, approved, or acceded

c050 Produced by: GRID-Arendal.

Times projection - Scale: Appr. 1:180 mill

A Party requesting assistance shall provide the assisting State with such information as may be necessary for that Party to determine the extent to which it is able to meet the request.

Parties shall notify the IAEA of experts, equipment, and materials which could be made available in case of a nuclear accident or radiological emergency.

## Monitoring/implementation

*Review procedure*
There are no reporting obligations under the Convention unless a nuclear accident or radiological emergency occurs, which has not been the case since 1986. The IAEA was, however, asked for assistance four times in the framework of this Convention: in the case of the radiological accidents at Goiânia, Brazil in September 1987, in El Salvador in February 1989, in Vietnam in January 1993, and in Costa Rica in May 1993.

No compliance controls are provided.

All information on implementation of the Convention is made available directly to Governments and the competent authorities designated. In addition, IAEA issues a wide range of public information materials relating to the Convention. There is no independent verification of data or information.

At national level, designated national authorities are responsible for issuing and receiving notifications and information.

*Observations or inspections*
None by the Convention as such.

*Trade sanctions*
None.

*Dispute-settlement mechanisms*
In the event of a dispute between the Parties, or between a Party and the IAEA, concerning the interpretation and application of the Convention, the Parties shall consult with a view to settling the dispute by negotiation or by any other peaceful means.

However, if the dispute cannot be settled within one year from the request for consultation, the dispute shall be submitted to arbitration or referred to the International Court of Justice for decision.

A Party may declare that it does not consider itself bound by either or both of these dispute settlement procedures when signing, ratifying, approving, or acceding to the Convention.

## Decision-making

*Political bodies*
The only organ referred to in the Convention is the IAEA. No meeting of Parties has taken place so far.

*Scientific/technical bodies*
Technical assistance is provided by the IAEA. No long-term scientific advisory functions or participation from NGOs and industry are foreseen.

## Publications

Up-to-date information is available through *IAEA Bulletin* (quarterly) and the IAEA's Annual Report.

# Convention on Early Notification of a Nuclear Accident (Notification Convention)

## Objectives

To provide relevant information about nuclear accidents with possible international transboundary consequences as early as possible in order to minimize environmental, health, and economic consequences.

## Scope

*Legal scope*
Open to all States, international organizations, and regional integration organizations.

*Geographic scope*
Global.

## Time and place of adoption

26 September 1986, Vienna.

## Entry into force

27 October 1986.

## Status of participation

70 states and 3 intergovernmental organizations (FAO, WHO, and WMO (see IGOs) are Parties), by October 1994. 21 Signatories without ratification, acceptance, or approval.

## Affiliated protocols, annexes, and organizations

No amendments have been proposed.

The *International Atomic Energy Agency (IAEA)* (see IGOs) acts as depositary and the Secretariat is in charge of administering the Convention.

*Co-ordination with related instruments*
The IAEA Board of Governors has established an Expert Working Group to consider additional measures to improve co-operation in the field of nuclear safety.

## Secretariat

IAEA (see IGOs).

## Finance

*Budget*
Costs are covered by the regular IAEA budget.

*Special funds*
Not applicable.

## Rules and standards

In the event of any nuclear accident with actual or potential transboundary effects involving its facilities or activities from which a release of radioactive material occurs or is likely to occur the Party shall notify other States which may be physically affected, directly or through the International Atomic Energy Agency (IAEA), and the IAEA itself, of the nature of the accident, its location, and the time of its occurrence.

The State Party is also required to provide other States and the IAEA promptly with specified information relevant to minimizing the radiological consequences in those States.

Parties are further required to respond to a request by an affected State for additional information or consultation.

In addition, each Party shall make known its competent authorities or point of contact responsible for issuing and receiving the notification and information referred to above.

States may voluntarily notify accidents related to military nuclear activities, with a view to minimizing the radiological consequences of the nuclear accident. All five nuclear-weapon States have declared their intention to make such notifications.

The information to be provided in case of a nuclear accident shall comprise the following data:
(a) the time, exact location where appropriate, and the nature of the accident;
(b) the facility or activity involved;
(c) the assumed or established cause and the foreseen development of the nuclear accident relevant to the transboundary release of the radioactive material;
(d) the general characteristics of the radioactive release, including as far as

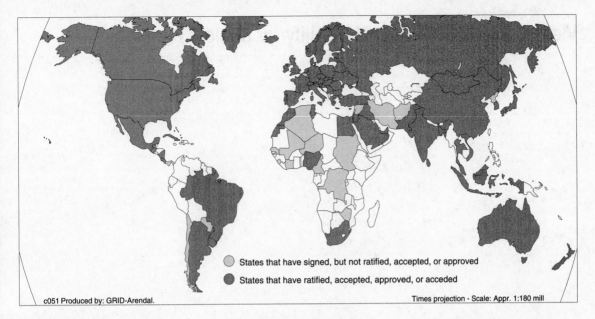

States that have signed, but not ratified, accepted, or approved

States that have ratified, accepted, approved, or acceded

c051 Produced by: GRID-Arendal.

Times projection - Scale: Appr. 1:180 mill

practicable and appropriate, the nature, probable physical and chemical form, quantity, composition, and effective height of the radioactive release;
(e) information on current and predicted meteorological and hydrological conditions necessary to forecasting the trans-boundary release of the radioactive materials;
(f) the results of environmental monitoring relevant to the transboundary release of the radioactive materials;
(g) the off-site protective measures taken or planned;
(h) the predicted behaviour over time of the radioactive release.

## Monitoring/implementation

### Review procedure
The information above shall be supplemented by further relevant information on the development of the emergency situation with the inclusion of its foreseeable and actual termination. Information may be used without restriction except when such information is provided in confidence by the notifying Party.

All information on implementation of the Convention is made available directly to Governments and the competent authorities designated. In addition, IAEA issues a wide range of public information materials relating to the Convention. There is no independent verification of data or information.

At national level, designated national authorities are responsible for issuing and receiving notifications and information.

### Observations or inspections
None by the Convention as such.

### Trade sanctions
None.

### Dispute-settlement mechanisms
In the event of a dispute between the Parties, or between a Party and the IAEA, concerning the interpretation and application of the Convention, the Parties shall consult with a view to settling the dispute by negotiation or by any other peaceful means.

However, if the dispute cannot be settled within one year from the request

for consultation, the dispute shall be submitted to arbitration or referred to the International Court of Justice for decision.

A Party may declare that it does not consider itself bound by either or both of these dispute settlement procedures when signing, ratifying, approving, or acceding to the Convention.

## Decision-making

### Political bodies
The only organ referred to in the Convention is the IAEA. No meetings of Parties have taken place so far.

### Scientific/technical bodies
Technical assistance is provided by the IAEA. No long-term scientific advisory functions or participation from NGOs and industry are foreseen.

## Publications

Up-to-date information is available through *IAEA Bulletin* (quarterly) and the IAEA's Annual Report.

# Vienna Convention on Civil Liability for Nuclear Damage

## Objectives

To establish minimum standards to provide financial protection against damage resulting from peaceful uses of nuclear energy.

## Scope

*Legal scope*
Open to all States members of the United Nations, or members of the UN specialized agencies, or the International Atomic Energy Agency (IAEA) (see IGOs). Not open to regional integration organizations.

*Geographic scope*
Global.

## Time and place of adoption

21 May 1963, Vienna.

## Entry into force

12 November 1977.

## Status of participation

24 Parties, by October 1994. 4 Signatories without ratification, acceptance, or approval.

## Affiliated protocols, annexes, and organizations

• *Optional Protocol Concerning the Compulsory Settlement of Disputes, Vienna, 1963* (see below). [Not yet in force.]
• *Joint Protocol Related to the Application of the Vienna Convention and the Paris Convention, Vienna, 1988.* Entered into force 27 April 1992. 16 Parties and 9 Signatories without ratification, acceptance, or approval, by October 1994. The Paris Convention on Third Party Liability in the Field of Nuclear Energy is regional in scope and administered by the Nuclear Energy Agency (NEA) of OECD (see IGOs).

The *International Atomic Energy Agency (IAEA)* (see IGOs) acts as depositary and is in charge of administering the Convention.

*Co-ordination with related instruments*
Since 1987, a review of all aspects of international law on liability for nuclear damage has been instituted by *The Standing Committee on Liability for Nuclear Damage*, within the framework of the IAEA. The first stage of this work led to the adoption of the Joint Protocol (see above). With respect to the revision of the Vienna Convention major issues under consideration concern the following: a revision of the limitations of liability of the Vienna Convention, as far as the minimum amount of

compensation, the period of time within which the compensation may be claimed, and the exclusion of preventive measures are concerned.

The Standing Committee has also evaluated possibilities for introducing additional compensation. Supplementary layers of compensation may either be incorporated into the Convention or become subject to a new draft instrument. Issues of State responsibility and liability are also under consideration.

## Secretariat

IAEA (see IGOs).

## Finance

*Budget*
No costs of administration.

*Special funds*
None.

## Rules and standards

The operator of a nuclear installation shall be liable for nuclear damage on provision of proof that such damage was caused by an incident within the installation, or involving nuclear material originating therefrom or being sent thereto.

The liability of the operator in such a case shall be absolute, but the courts may

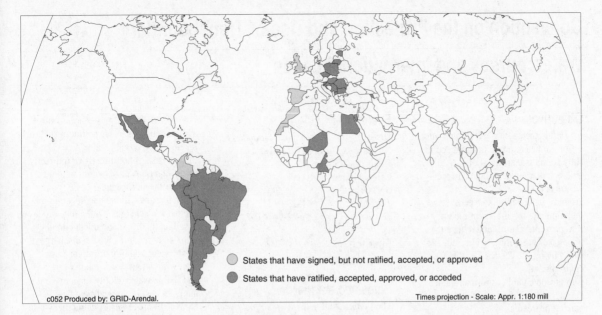

States that have signed, but not ratified, accepted, or approved

States that have ratified, accepted, approved, or acceded

c052 Produced by: GRID-Arendal.

Times projection - Scale: Appr. 1:180 mill

make a finding of contributory negligence on the part of the person suffering such damage; in any case the operator will not be liable if the nuclear incident was due directly to act of armed conflict, civil war, insurrection, or a grave natural disaster of an exceptional character.

The Convention has established limits of liability and limitation of action.

The operator is required to maintain insurance or financial security to cover liability.

Parties shall:
• ensure the payment of compensation in cases where they do not provide for insurance of the operator or beyond the yield of such insurance and up to the operator's liability;
• provide for necessary jurisdictional competences, recognize final judgements entered by foreign courts in accordance with the Convention.

They shall not invoke immunities in legal proceedings under the Convention.

The principal benefit for all countries participating in the Convention, is the right of their nationals to claim compensation in case of nuclear damage caused by installations situated in the territory of a Contracting Party. Currently, the minimum amount of compensation is subject to review and subsequent adoption; the benefit may be expected to increase substantially in the near future.

## Monitoring/implementation

### Review procedure
There is no mechanism for the promotion of implementation and follow-up on non-compliance. Parties do not regularly report about implementation and do not have to disclose or supply data.

### Dispute-settlement mechanisms
The Convention has no rules concerning the settlement of disputes. But the International Conference on Civil Liability for Nuclear Damage of 1963 adopted an Optional Protocol Concerning Compulsory Settlement of Disputes (see this section). The Protocol is subject to ratification. It comes into force upon the second ratification. Upto now one ratification has been deposited.

## Decision-making

### Political bodies
The Convention does not provide for institutional or administrative arrangements. No regular meetings or programme activities are envisaged. A *Standing Committee on Civil Liability for Nuclear Damage* was established within the framework of IAEA. This Committee met occasionally to discuss issues relevant to the Convention. The Committee was composed of 15 States. Limitations concerning participation were removed as the Committee was transformed into an open-ended negotiation forum and renamed a

*Standing Committee on Liability for Nuclear Damage.* Currently, about 60 delegations from both developing and industrialized countries as well as NGOs attend its sessions and the mandate of the Committee has been extended to include international liability matters. The Committee has a revision of the Convention under consideration.

### Scientific/technical bodies
There are no elaborated mechanisms for regular review of provisions or consideration of scientific and technical information. However, the Board of Governors of the IAEA (see IGOs) may take decisions on minor technical issues. The Board may also provide legal assistance if requested in case of countries without nuclear programmes. Participation does not imply any financial obligations.

## Publications
Up-to-date information is available through *IAEA Bulletin* (quarterly) and the IAEA's Annual Report.

# Convention on the Protection and Use of Transboundary Watercourses and International Lakes

## Objectives

• to strengthen national and international actions aimed at protection and ecologically sound management of transboundary waters, both surface waters and groundwaters, and related ecosystems, including the marine environment;
• to prevent, control, and reduce the releases of hazardous, acidifying, and eutrophying substances into the aquatic environment;
• to promote public information and public participation in relevant decision-making processes.

## Scope

*Legal scope*
Open to member countries of the United Nations Economic Commission for Europe (UN/ECE), the European Union (EU), and other European States having consultative status with the UN/ECE.

*Geographic scope*
Regional. UN/ECE region.

## Time and place of adoption

17 March 1992, Helsinki.

## Entry into force

Not yet in force. Enters into force ninety days after the deposit of 16 instruments of ratification, acceptance, approval, or accession.

## Status of participation

7 Parties, by 15 September 1994. 19 Signatories, including the European Union, without ratification, acceptance, or approval.

## Affiliated protocols, annexes, and organizations

The Convention contains also four *Annexes* which form an integral part of the Convention.

The *Executive Secretary of the UN/ECE* carries out the Secretariat functions.

## Secretariat

UN/ECE, Environment and Human Settlements Division (ENHS), Palais des Nations, CH-1211 Geneva 10, Switzerland
*Telephone*: +41-22-9171234
*Telefax*: +41-22-9070107

## Finance

Not applicable.

## Rules and standards

The Parties shall take all appropriate measures:
• to prevent, control, and reduce pollution of waters causing or likely to cause transboundary impact;
• to ensure that transboundary waters are used with the aim of ecologically sound and rational water management, conservation of water resources, and environmental protection;
• to ensure that transboundary waters are used in a reasonable and equitable way, taking into particular account their transboundary character, in the case of activities which cause or are likely to cause transboundary impact;
• to ensure conservation and, where necessary, restoration of ecosystems.

In taking these measures, the Parties shall be guided by the following principles:
• the *precautionary principle*, by virtue of which action to avoid the potential transboundary impact of the release of hazardous substances shall not be postponed on the ground that scientific research has not fully proved a causal link between those substances, on the one hand, and the potential transboundary impact, on the other hand;
• the *polluter-pays principle*, by virtue of which costs of pollution prevention, control, and reduction measures shall be borne by the polluter;
• water resources shall be managed so that the needs of the present generation are met without compromising the ability of future generations to meet their own needs.

Measures for the prevention, control, and reduction of water pollution shall be taken, where possible, at source. These measures shall not directly or indirectly result in a transfer of pollution to other parts of the environment.

The Parties will have to set emission limits for discharges from point sources based on the best available technology; issue authorizations for the discharge of waste water and monitor compliance therewith; adopt water-quality criteria and define water-quality objectives; apply at least biological treatment or equivalent processes to municipal waste water; develop contingency plans; apply environmental impact assessment and the ecosystem approach in water management; develop and implement appropriate measures and best environmental practices to reduce the input of nutrients and hazardous substances from diffuse sources, in particular from agriculture.

The Riparian Parties shall co-operate on the basis of equality and reciprocity, in particular through bilateral and multilateral agreements, in order to develop harmonized policies, programmes, and strategies covering the relevant catchment areas, or parts thereof, aimed at the prevention, control, and reduction of transboundary impact, and aimed at the protection of the environment of transboundary waters or the environment influenced by such waters, including the marine environment.

The Convention establishes the minimal requirements for the agreements or other arrangements between Parties bordering the same transboundary waters.

## Monitoring/implementation

*Review procedure*
The Parties shall report periodically on the implementation of this Convention.

The Meeting of the Parties (see below) shall keep the Convention under continuous review and, with this purpose in mind:
• review the policies for and methodo-

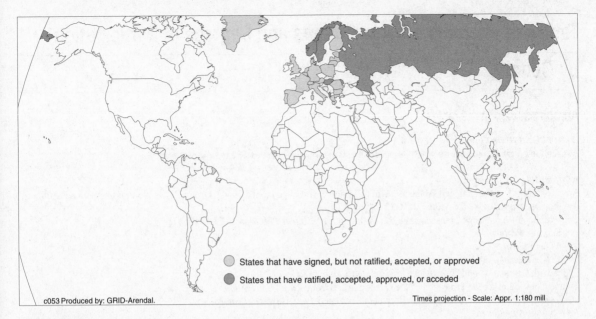

States that have signed, but not ratified, accepted, or approved

States that have ratified, accepted, approved, or acceded

c053 Produced by: GRID-Arendal.                    Times projection - Scale: Appr. 1:180 mill

logical approaches to the protection and use of transboundary waters of the Parties with a view to further improving the protection and use of transboundary waters;

• exchange information regarding experience gained in concluding and implementing bilateral and multilateral agreements or other arrangements regarding the protection and use of transboundary waters to which one or more of the Parties are party.

Under the auspices of the UN/ECE Committee on Environmental Policy, the Working Party on Water Problems at its annual sessions is reviewing action taken to implement the Convention pending its entry into force and taking steps to bring closer together their relevant policies and strategies. The Working Party also seeks to strengthen the capability of future Parties, particularly countries with economies in transition to a market economy, to comply with the obligations under the Convention.

*Environmental monitoring programmes*
Parties bordering the same transboundary water shall establish and implement joint programmes for monitoring the conditions of transboundary waters, including floods and ice drifts, as well as transboundary impact; agree upon pollution parameters and pollutants whose concentrations in transboundary waters shall be regularly monitored; carry out joint or co-ordinated assessments of the condition of trans-boundary

waters and the effectiveness of measures taken to prevent, control, and reduce transboundary impact; exchange reasonably available data on environmental conditions of transboundary waters, including monitoring data; inform each other about critical situations that may have transboundary impact; and make available to the public results of water and effluent sampling, together with the results of checking compliance with the water-quality objectives and the permit conditions.

The Convention obliges the Riparian Parties furthermore to harmonize rules for the setting-up and operation of monitoring programmes, measurement systems, devices, analytical techniques, data processing, and evaluation procedures.

*Dispute-settlement mechanisms*
If a dispute arises between two or more Parties as to the interpretation or application of the Convention, they shall seek a solution by negotiation or by any other method of dispute settlement acceptable to the parties to the dispute.

The Parties may submit the dispute to the International Court of Justice or to an arbitration procedure set out in Appendix IV.

## Decision-making

*Political bodies*
By the decision adopted in March 1992, the Senior Advisers to UN/ECE Govern-

ments on Environmental and Water Problems, now the Committee on Environmental Policy, entrusted the Working Party on Water Problems to undertake activities on such questions as may be deemed important pending the entry into force of the Convention.

Once the Convention has entered into force, the *Meeting of the Parties* shall be the decision-making body. The first meeting shall be convened not later than one year after the date of the entry into force of the Convention. Thereafter, meetings shall be held at least every three years.

At their meetings, the Parties shall keep under continuous review the implementation of the Convention.

*Scientific/technical bodies*
The Meeting of the Parties will seek, as appropriate, the services of relevant UN/ECE bodies as well as other competent international bodies and specific committees in all aspects pertinent to the achievement of the purposes of the Convention.

## Publications
• Water Series;
• *Environmental Conventions Elaborated under the Auspices of the UN/ECE*, 1992;
• *Bilateral and Multilateral Agreements and other Arrangements in Europe and North America on the Protection and Use of Transboundary Waters*, 1993.

# Tables of International Agreements and Degrees of Participation, by Country

## Acronyms used in the tables

### General Environmental Concerns
Convention on Environmental Impact Assessment in a Transboundary Context: ***Espoo Convention***

### Atmosphere
Annex 16, vol. II (Environmental Protection: Aircraft Engine Emissions) to the 1944 Chicago Convention on International Civil Aviation: ***Aircraft Engine Emissions (ICAO)***
Convention on Long-Range Transboundary Air Pollution: ***Transb. Air Pollution (LRTAP)***
 • ***Sulphur Protocol***
 • ***$NO_x$ Protocol***
 • ***VOC Protocol***
Framework Convention on Climate Change: ***Climate Change (FCCC)***
Vienna Convention for the Protection of the Ozone Layer: ***Ozone Layer Convention***
 • Montreal Protocol on Substances that Deplete the Ozone Layer: ***Montreal Protocol***
 • ***London Amendment***
 • ***Copenhagen Amendment***

### Hazardous Substances
Convention on the Ban of the Import into Africa and the Control of Transboundary Movements and Management of Hazardous Wastes within Africa: ***Bamako Convention***
Convention on Civil Liability for Damage Caused during Carriage of Dangerous Goods by Road, Rail, and Inland Navigation Vessels: ***CRTD***
Convention on the Control of Transboundary Movements of Hazardous Wastes and their Disposal: ***Basel Convention***
Convention on the Transboundary Effects of Industrial Accidents: ***Transb. Effects of Indust. Accidents***
European Agreement Concerning the International Carriage of Dangerous Goods by Road: ***Dangerous Goods by Road (ADR)***
FAO International Code of Conduct on the Distribution and Use of Pesticides: ***Distrib. and Use of Pesticides***

### Marine Environment
#### Global Conventions
Convention on the Prevention of Marine Pollution by Dumping of Wastes and Other Matter: ***London Convention 1972***
International Convention for the Prevention of Pollution from Ships, 1973, as modified by the Protocol of 1978 relating thereto: ***MARPOL 73/78***
International Convention on Civil Liability for Oil Pollution Damage: ***Civil Liab. for Oil Pollution (CLC)***
International Convention on the Establishment of an International Fund for Compensation for Oil Pollution Damage: ***Fund Convention***
International Convention on Oil Pollution Preparedness, Response, and Co-operation: ***OPRC***
International Convention Relating to Intervention on the High Seas in Cases of Oil Pollution Casualties: ***Intervention Convention***
United Nations Convention on the Law of the Sea: ***UNCLOS***

#### Regional Conventions
Convention for the Prevention of Marine Pollution by Dumping from Ships and Aircraft: ***Oslo Convention***
Convention for the Prevention of Marine Pollution from Land-based Sources: ***Paris Convention***
Convention for the Protection of the Marine Environment of the North East Atlantic: ***OSPAR Convention***
Convention on the Protection of the Marine Environment of the Baltic Sea Area: ***1974 Helsinki Convention***
Convention on the Protection of the Marine Environment of the Baltic Sea Area: ***1992 Helsinki Convention***
 ***Conventions within the UNEP Regional Seas Programme:***
 • Convention on the Protection of the ***Black Sea*** against Pollution
 • Convention for the Protection and Development of the Marine Environment of the Wider Caribbean Region: ***Wider Caribbean Region***
 • Convention for the Protection, Management, and Development of the Marine and Coastal Environment of the Eastern African Region: ***Eastern African Region***

- Kuwait Regional Convention for Co-operation on the Protection of the Marine Environment from Pollution: *Kuwait Region*
- Convention for the Protection of the Mediterranean Sea against Pollution: *Mediterranean Sea*
- Regional Convention for the Conservation of the Red Sea and Gulf of Aden Environment: *Red Sea and Gulf of Aden*
- Convention for the Protection of the Natural Resources and Environment of the South Pacific Region: *South Pacific Region*
- Convention for the Protection of the Marine Environment and Coastal Area of the South-East Pacific: *South-East Pacific*
- Convention for Co-operation in the Protection and Development of the Marine and Coastal Environment of the West and Central African Region: *West and Centr. African Region*

## Marine Living Resources
Convention on the Conservation of Antarctic Marine Living Resources: *Antarc. Marine Living Res. (CCAMLR)*
International Convention for the Conservation of Atlantic Tunas: *Atlantic Tunas (ICCAT)*
International Convention for the Regulation of Whaling: *Regulation of Whaling (ICRW)*

## Nature Conservation and Terrestrial Living Resources
*Antarctic Treaty*
Convention Concerning the Protection of the World Cultural and Natural Heritage: *World Heritage Convention*
Convention on Biological Diversity: *Biological Diversity (CBD)*
Convention on the Conservation of Migratory Species of Wild Animals: *Migr. Species of Wild Animals (CMS)*
Convention on International Trade in Endangered Species of Wild Fauna and Flora: *CITES*
Convention on Wetlands of International Importance especially as Waterfowl Habitat: *Ramsar Convention*
FAO International Undertaking on Plant Genetic Resources: *Plant Genetic Resources*
International Tropical Timber Agreement: *Tropical Timber Agreement (ITTA)*

## Nuclear Safety
Convention on Assistance in the Case of a Nuclear Accident or Radiological Emergency: *Assistance Convention*
Convention on Early Notification of a Nuclear Accident: *Notification Convention*
Vienna Convention on Civil Liability for Nuclear Damage: *Civil Liability for Nuclear Damage*

## Transboundary Freshwaters
Convention on the Protection and Use of Transboundary Watercourses and International Lakes: *Transb. Waterc. and Intern. Lakes*

# Keys

*General*
States that have signed, but not ratified, accepted, or approved

States that have ratified, accepted, approved, or acceded

*Antarctic Treaty*
Non-Consultative Parties to the Antarctic Treaty

Consultative Parties to the Antarctic Treaty

*Aircraft Engine Emissions (ICAO) and*
*Distrib. and Use of Pesticides*
Member States

*Plant Genetic Resources*
States that have adhered to the Undertaking

*Tropical Timber Agreement (ITTA)*
Member States

| | General Environmental Concerns | | | | | | Atmosphere | | | | | Hazardous Substances | | | | | | | Marine Environment — Global Conventions | | | | | | Regional Conventions | |
|---|---|---|---|---|---|---|---|---|---|---|---|---|---|---|---|---|---|---|---|---|---|---|---|---|---|---|
| | Espoo Convention | Aircraft Engine Emissions (ICAO) | Transb. Air Pollution (LRTAP) | Sulphur Protocol | NOx Protocol | VOC Protocol | Climate Change (FCCC) | Ozone Layer Convention | Montreal Protocol | London Amendment | Copenhagen Amendment | Bamako Convention | CRTD | Basel Convention | Transb. Effects of Indust. Accidents | Dangerous Goods by Road (ADR) | Distrib. and Use of Pesticides | London Convention 1972 | MARPOL 73/78 | Civil Liab. for Oil Pollution (CLC) | Fund Convention | OPRC | Intervention Convention | UNCLOS | Oslo Convention | Paris Convention |
| Afghanistan | | ○ | | | | | ○ | | | | | | | | | | | ○ | | | | ○ | | ○ | | |
| Albania | ● | ○ | | | | | ● | | | | | | | | | | | | | ● | | ○ | | | ● | ● |
| Algeria | | ○ | | | | | ● | ● | ● | ● | | | | | | | | | | | | | ● | ● | ● | ○ |
| Andorra | | | | | | | | | | | | | | | | | | | | | | | | | | |
| Angola | | ○ | | | | | ○ | | | | | | | | | | | | | | | ○ | | | | ● |
| Antigua & Barbuda | | ○ | | | | | ● | ● | ● | ● | ● | | | ● | | | | | ● | | | ○ | ● | ● | | ● |
| Argentina | | ○ | | | | | ● | ● | ● | ● | | | | ● | | | | | ● | | | ○ | ● | ● | ● | ● |
| Armenia | | ○ | | | | | ○ | | | | | | | | | | | | | | | | ○ | | | |
| Australia | | ○ | | | | | ● | ● | ● | ● | ● | | | ● | | | | | ● | | | ○ | | ● | ● | ● |
| Austria | ● | ○ | ● | ○ | ● | ○ | ● | ● | ● | ● | | | | ● | | | | | ● | ○ | | ● | | ○ | | |
| Azerbaijan | | ○ | | | | | ○ | | | | | | | | | | | | | | | | | | | |
| Bahamas | | ○ | | | | | ● | ● | ● | ● | ● | | | ● | | | | | ● | | | ○ | ● | ● | ● | ● |
| Bahrain | | ○ | | | | | ● | ● | ● | | | | | | | | | | ● | | | ○ | | | | ● |
| Bangladesh | | ○ | | | | | ● | ● | ● | | | | | | | | | | ● | | | | | | ● | ● |
| Barbados | | ○ | | | | | | | | | | | | | | | | | ○ | ● | ● | | ● | | | ● |
| Belarus | ○ | ○ | ● | | ● | | ○ | | | | | | | | | | | ● | | ● | ● | | | ○ | | |
| Belgium | ○ | ○ | ● | ○ | ○ | ○ | ● | ● | ● | ● | | | | ● | | ● | ● | ● | ● | ● | ● | ● | ● | ● | ● | ● |
| Belize | | ○ | | | | | ● | | | | | | | | | | | | | | | ○ | ● | | | |
| Benin | | ○ | | | | | ● | ● | ● | | | | | ○ | | | | | | | | ○ | ● | ● | ● | ● |
| Bhutan | | ○ | | | | | ○ | | | | | | | | | | | | | | | ○ | | ○ | | |
| Bolivia | | ○ | | | | | ● | | | | | | | | | | ○ | | | | | ○ | | ○ | | |
| Bosnia & Herzegovina | | ○ | ● | | | | | ● | ● | | | | | | | | | ● | | ● | | ○ | | ● | | |
| Botswana | | ○ | | | | | ● | ● | ● | | | | | | | | | | | | | ○ | | ● | | |
| Brazil | | ○ | | | | | ● | ● | ● | ● | | | | ● | | | | | ● | | | ○ | | ○ | ○ | ● |
| Brunei Darussalam | | | | | | | | ● | ● | | | | | | | | | | | | | | ● | ○ | | |
| Bulgaria | ○ | ○ | ● | ● | ● | ● | ● | ● | ● | | | | | | | | | ○ | | ● | | ○ | ● | | ● | ● |
| Burkina Faso | | ○ | | | | | ● | ● | ● | | ● | | | | | | ○ | | | | | ○ | | ○ | | |
| Burundi | | ○ | | | | | ● | | | | | | | ○ | | | | | | | | ○ | | ○ | | |
| Cambodia | | ○ | | | | | | | | | | | | | | | | | | | | ○ | | ○ | | |
| Cameroon (U. Rep. of) | | ○ | | | | | ● | ● | ● | ● | | | | | | | ○ | | | | | ○ | | ● | ● | ● |
| Canada | ○ | ○ | ● | ○ | ● | ○ | ● | ● | ● | ● | | | | ● | | | | | ● | ● | | ● | ● | ● | | ○ |

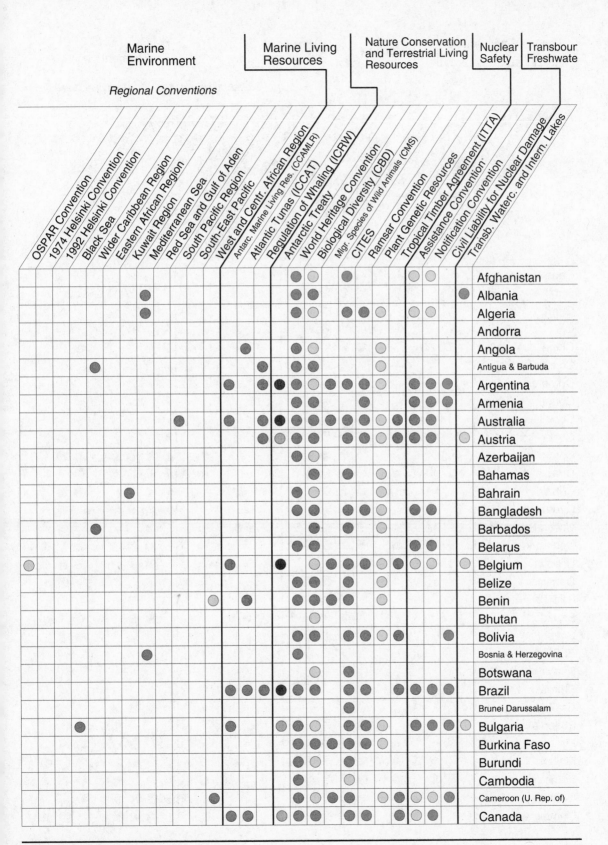

## General Environmental Concerns · Atmosphere · Hazardous Substances · Marine Environment

Marine Environment: Global Conventions / Regional Conventions

| Country | Espoo Convention | Aircraft Engine Emissions (ICAO) | Transb. Air Pollution (LRTAP) | Sulphur Protocol * | NOx Protocol * | VOC Protocol * | Climate Change (FCCC) | Ozone Layer Convention | Montreal Protocol * | London Amendment * | Copenhagen Amendment * | Bamako Convention | CRTD | Basel Convention | Transb. Effects of Indust. Accidents | Dangerous Goods by Road (ADR) | Distrib. and Use of Pesticides | London Convention 1972 | MARPOL 73/78 | Civil Liab. for Oil Pollution (CLC) | Fund Convention | OPRC | Intervention Convention | UNCLOS | Oslo Convention | Paris Convention |
|---|---|---|---|---|---|---|---|---|---|---|---|---|---|---|---|---|---|---|---|---|---|---|---|---|---|---|
| Cape Verde | | | | | | | ○ | | | | | ○ | | | | | | | | | | ○ | ● | | ● | |
| Central African Rep. | | | | | | | ○ | | ○ | ● | ● | | | | ○ | | | | | | | ○ | | | ○ | |
| Chad | | | | | | | ○ | | ● | ● | ● | | | | ○ | | | | | | | ○ | | | ○ | |
| Chile | | | | | | | ○ | | ● | ● | ● | ● | | ● | | | ● | | | ● | | ○ | ● | ● | | ○ |
| China | | | | | | | ○ | | ● | ● | ● | ● | | | | | ● | | | ● | ● | ○ | ● | ● | ● | ○ |
| Colombia | | | | | | | ○ | | ○ | ● | ● | | | | | | ○ | | | ● | | ○ | ● | ● | | ○ |
| Comoros | | | | | | | ○ | | ● | | | | | | | | | | | | | ○ | | | ● | |
| Congo | | | | | | | ○ | | ○ | | ○ | | | | | | | | | | | ○ | | | ○ | |
| Cook Islands | | | | | | | ○ | | ● | | | | | | | | | | | | | ○ | | | ○ | |
| Costa Rica | | | | | | | ○ | | ● | ● | ● | | | | | | | | | ● | | ○ | | | ● | |
| Côte d'Ivoire | | | | | | | ○ | | ● | ● | ● | | | ○ | | | | | | ● | ● | ○ | ● | ● | ● | ○ | ● |
| Croatia | | ○ | ● | ○ | | | | ○ | ● | ● | ● | | | ● | | ● | | | ● | | ○ | | ● | ● | ○ | |
| Cuba | | ○ | | | | | | ○ | ● | ● | | ● | | | | ● | | | ● | | ○ | | ● | ● | | |
| Cyprus | | ○ | ● | | | | | ○ | ● | ● | ● | | | | | ● | | | ● | ● | ● | ○ | ● | ● | ● | |
| Czech Republic | ○ | ○ | ● | ○ | ● | ● | | ● | ● | ● | | | | ● | | ● | | | | ● | ● | ○ | | | ○ | |
| Denmark | ○ | ○ | ● | ● | ● | ○ | ● | ● | ● | ● | ● | | | ● | ● | ● | ○ | ● | ● | ● | ● | ● | ● | ● | ● | ● |
| Djibouti | | | | | | | ○ | | ○ | | | | | ○ | | | | | | ● | ● | ○ | ● | | | |
| Dominica | | | | | | | | | ● | ● | ● | | | | | | | | | | | ○ | | | ● | |
| Dominican Republic | | | | | | | ○ | | ● | ● | ● | | | | | | | | ● | | ● | ○ | | | ● | ○ |
| Ecuador | | | | | | | ○ | | ● | ● | ● | ● | | ● | | | ● | | | ● | | ○ | | ● | ○ | ● |
| Egypt | | | | | | | ○ | | ○ | ● | ● | ● | | ● | ○ | | | ● | | | ● | ● | ○ | ● | ● | |
| El Salvador | | | | | | | ○ | | ○ | ● | ● | | | | | | | | | ● | | ○ | | | ○ | |
| Equatorial Guinea | | | | | | | ○ | | | ● | | | | | | | | | | | | ○ | | | ○ | |
| Eritrea | | | | | | | ○ | | | | | | | | | | | | | | | ○ | | | | |
| Estonia | | | | | | | ○ | | ● | | | | | | | | | ● | ○ | | | ○ | | ● | ● | ● |
| Ethiopia | | | | | | | ○ | | ● | | | | | | | | | | | | | ○ | | | ○ | |
| Fiji | | | | | | | ○ | | ● | ● | ● | | | | | | | | | ● | ● | | | ● | ● | |
| Finland | ○ | ○ | ● | ● | ○ | ● | ● | ● | ● | ● | ● | | | ● | | ● | | ● | ○ | ● | ● | ● | ● | ● | ● | ○ |
| France | ○ | ○ | ● | ● | ○ | ● | ○ | ● | ● | ● | ● | | | | | | ● | ● | ● | ● | ● | ● | ● | ● | ○ | ● |
| Gabon | | | | | | | ○ | | ○ | ● | ● | | | | | | | | | | | ○ | ● | ● | ○ | |
| Gambia | | | | | | | ○ | | ● | ● | ● | | | | | | | | ● | ● | ● | ○ | | ● | ● | |

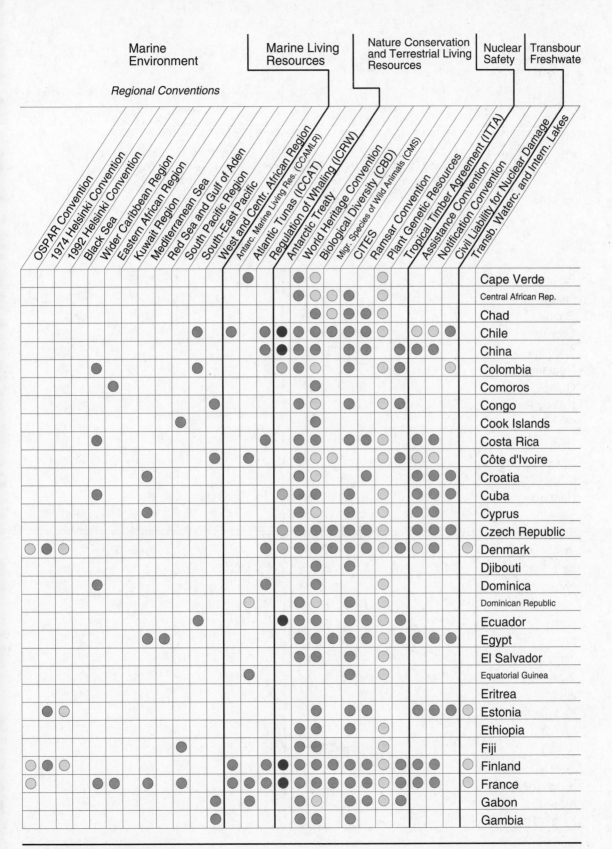

Convention participation table (countries Georgia–Kyrgyz Republic)

| Group | General Environmental Concerns | | | | | | | Atmosphere | | | | Hazardous Substances | | | | | | | Marine Environment — Global Conventions | | | | | | Marine Environment — Regional Conventions | |
|---|---|---|---|---|---|---|---|---|---|---|---|---|---|---|---|---|---|---|---|---|---|---|---|---|---|---|
| Country | Espoo Convention | Aircraft Engine Emissions (ICAO) | Transb. Air Pollution (LRTAP) | Sulphur Protocol * | NOx Protocol * | VOC Protocol * | Climate Change (FCCC) | Ozone Layer Convention | Montreal Protocol * | London Amendment * | Copenhagen Amendment * | Bamako Convention | CRTD | Basel Convention | Transb. Effects of Indust. Accidents | Dangerous Goods by Road (ADR) | Distrib. and Use of Pesticides | London Convention 1972 | MARPOL 73/78 | Civil Liab. for Oil Pollution (CLC) | Fund Convention | OPRC | Intervention Convention | UNCLOS | Oslo Convention | Paris Convention |
|---|---|---|---|---|---|---|---|---|---|---|---|---|---|---|---|---|---|---|---|---|---|---|---|---|---|---|
| Georgia | | | | | | | ○ | | | | | | ● | | | | | | | | | | | | ○ | |
| Germany | ○ | ● | ● | ● | ● | ● | ● | ● | ● | ● | ● | | ● | ● | | | | ○ | ○ | ● | ● | ● | ● | ● | ● | ● |
| Ghana | | | | | | | ○ | | | ○ | | ● | ● | ● | | | | | | | | ○ | ● | ● | ● | ● |
| Greece | ○ | ● | ● | ● | ● | ● | ● | | | | | ● | ● | ● | | | | ● | ● | ● | ● | ● | ● | ● | ○ | ○ |
| Grenada | | | | | | | ○ | | | | | ● | ● | ● | | | | | ○ | | | | | | ● | |
| Guatemala | | | | | | | ○ | | | | | ● | ● | ● | | | ○ | | ○ | ● | | ● | | ○ | ○ | |
| Guinea | | | | | | | ○ | | | | | ● | ● | ● | | ○ | | | ○ | | | ○ | | ● | | |
| Guinea-Bissau | | | | | | | ○ | | | | | ● | | | | ○ | | | ○ | | | | | ● | | |
| Guyana | | | | | | | ○ | | | | | ● | ● | ● | | | | | ○ | | | | | ● | | |
| Haiti | | | | | | | ○ | | | | | ○ | | | | | ○ | | ○ | ● | | | | ○ | | |
| Holy See (Vatican) | | ○ | | | | | | | | | | | | | | | | | | | | | | | | |
| Honduras | | | | | | | ○ | | | | ○ | | | | | | | | ○ | | | | | ● | | |
| Hungary | ○ | ○ | ● | | ○ | ○ | ● | ● | ● | ● | ● | | ● | ● | ● | ● | | | | | | ○ | | ○ | | |
| Iceland | ○ | ○ | ● | | | | ● | | | | | | | | | | | ○ | ● | ● | ● | ● | ● | ● | ● | ● |
| India | | | | | | | ○ | | | | | ● | ● | ● | | | | ● | | | | ○ | | ○ | | |
| Indonesia | | | | | | | ○ | | | | | ● | ● | ● | | | | ● | | | | ○ | | ● | | |
| Iran (Islamic Rep. of) | | | | | | | ○ | | | | ○ | ○ | ● | | | | | ● | | | | ○ | | ○ | | |
| Iraq | | | | | | | ○ | | | | | | | | | | | | | | | | | ● | | |
| Ireland | ○ | ○ | ● | | ○ | | ● | ● | ● | | | | ● | ● | | | ○ | | ● | | ● | ● | ○ | ● | ○ | ● |
| Israel | | | | | | | ○ | | | ○ | | ● | | | | ○ | | | ● | | ○ | | ○ | | | |
| Italy | ○ | ○ | ● | ○ | ● | ○ | ● | | | | | ● | ● | ● | | | ● | ○ | ● | | | ● | ● | ● | ● | ● |
| Jamaica | | | | | | | ○ | | | | | ● | ● | ● | | | | ● | ● | | | | | ● | ● | |
| Japan | | | | | | | ○ | | | | | ● | ● | ● | ● | | | ● | ● | ● | ● | | | ○ | ○ | |
| Jordan | | | | | | | ○ | | | | | ● | ● | ● | | | | ● | | | | ○ | | | | |
| Kazakhstan | | | | | | | ○ | | | | ○ | | | | | | | | | | ● | ● | ● | | | |
| Kenya | | | | | | | ○ | | | | | ● | ● | ● | | | | | ○ | ● | ● | ● | | ● | | |
| Kiribati | | | | | | | ○ | | | | | ○ | ● | ● | | | | ● | | | | | | | | |
| Korea (P. D. Rep. of) | | | | | | | ○ | | | | ○ | | | | | | | | ○ | ● | | | | ○ | | |
| Korea (Rep. of) | | | | | | | ○ | | | | | ● | ● | ● | ● | | | ● | | ● | ● | ● | | ○ | ○ | |
| Kuwait | | | | | | | ○ | | | | | | ● | ● | ● | ● | | ● | | ○ | ○ | | ● | ● | ● | ● |
| Kyrgyz Republic | | | | | | | ○ | | | | | | | | | | | ● | | | | | | | | |

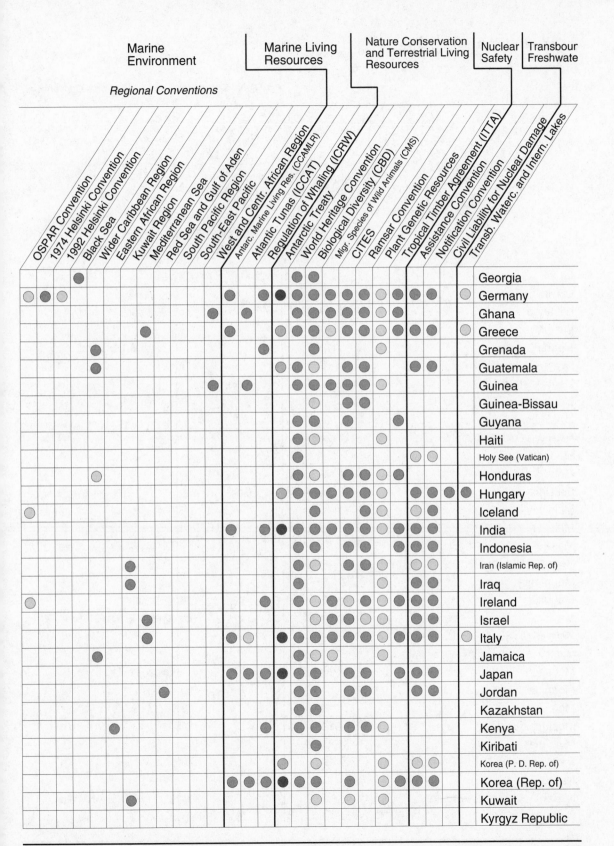

Marine Environment

Regional Conventions

Marine Living Resources

Nature Conservation and Terrestrial Living Resources

Nuclear Safety

Transbour Freshwate

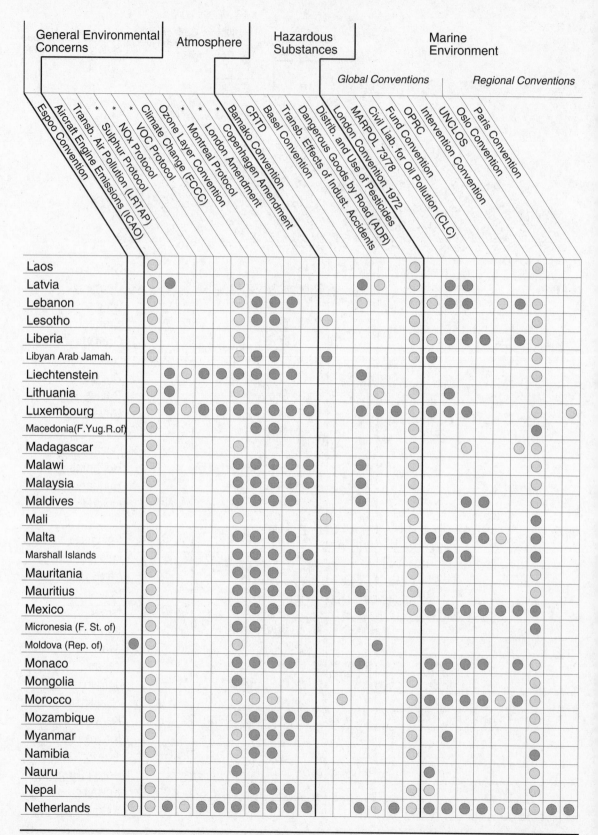

GREEN GLOBE YEARBOOK 1995

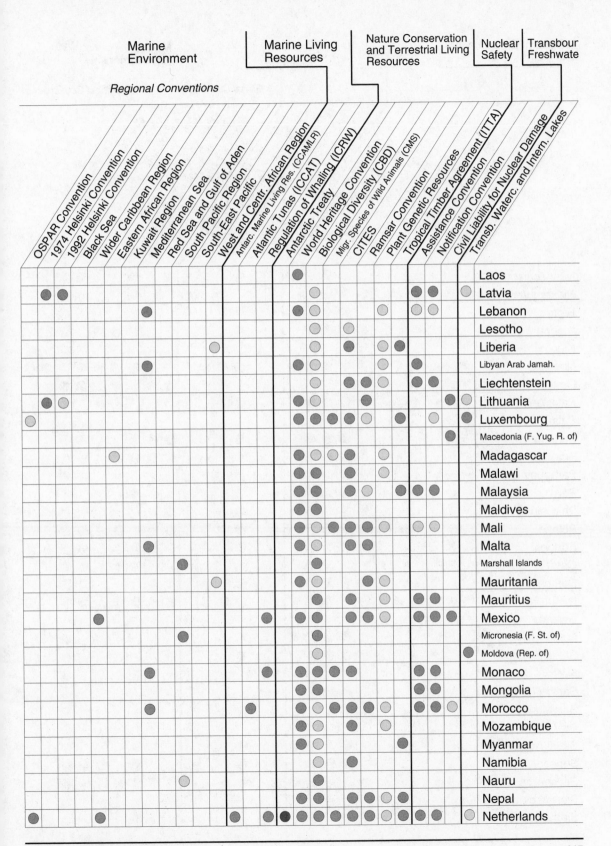

| | OSPAR Convention | 1974 Helsinki Convention | 1992 Helsinki Convention | Black Sea | Wider Caribbean Region | Eastern African Region | Kuwait Region | Mediterranean Sea | Red Sea and Gulf of Aden | South Pacific Region | South-East Pacific | West and Centr. African Region | Antarc. Marine Living Res. (CCAMLR) | Atlantic Tunas (ICCAT) | Regulation of Whaling (ICRW) | Antarctic Treaty | World Heritage Convention | Biological Diversity (CBD) | Migr. Species of Wild Animals (CMS) | CITES | Ramsar Convention | Plant Genetic Resources | Tropical Timber Agreement (ITTA) | Assistance Convention | Notification Convention | Civil Liability for Nuclear Damage | Transb. Waterc. and Intern. Lakes | |
|---|---|---|---|---|---|---|---|---|---|---|---|---|---|---|---|---|---|---|---|---|---|---|---|---|---|---|---|---|---|
| | | | | | | | | | | | | | | | ● | | | | | | | | | | | | | | Laos |
| | | ● | ● | | | | | | | | | | | | ○ | | | | | | | | | ● | ● | | ○ | Latvia |
| | | | | | | | ● | | | | | | | ● | ○ | | | | ○ | | | | ○ | ○ | | | | Lebanon |
| | | | | | | | | | | | | | | | ○ | ● | | | | | | | | | | | | Lesotho |
| | | | | | | | | | ○ | | | | | | ● | ● | | ● | ● | | | | | | | | | Liberia |
| | | | | | | | ● | | | | | | | ● | ○ | | | ○ | | | | ● | | | | | | Libyan Arab Jamah. |
| | | | | | | | | | | | | | | | ○ | ● | ● | ○ | | | ● | ● | | | | | | Liechtenstein |
| | ● | ○ | | | | | | | | | | | | ● | ● | | | | ○ | | | | | | ● | ● | ○ | Lithuania |
| ○ | | | | | | | | | | | | | | ● | ● | ● | ● | ● | ○ | | ● | | | ○ | | ● | Luxembourg |
| | | | | | | | | | | | | | | | | | | | | | | | | | | ● | Macedonia (F. Yug. R. of) |
| | | | | ○ | | | | | | | | | | ● | ○ | ● | ● | | ○ | | | | | | | | Madagascar |
| | | | | | | | | | | | | | | ● | ● | | ● | | ○ | | | | | | | | Malawi |
| | | | | | | | | | | | | | | ● | ● | | ● | ○ | | ● | ● | ● | | | | | Malaysia |
| | | | | | | | | | | | | | | ● | | | | | | | | | | | | | Maldives |
| | | | | | | | | | | | | | | ● | ● | ● | ● | ● | ○ | | | ○ | ○ | | | | Mali |
| | | | | | | | ● | | | | | | | ● | ○ | | ● | ● | | | | | | | | | Malta |
| | | | | | | | | | ● | | | | | ● | | | | | | | | | | | | | Marshall Islands |
| | | | | | | | | | | | ○ | | | ● | ● | | ● | ○ | | | | | | | | | Mauritania |
| | | | | | | | | | | | | | | ● | | | | | | ● | ● | | | | | | Mauritius |
| | | | ● | | | | | | | ● | | ● | ● | ● | | | ● | ● | ○ | | ● | ● | ● | | | | Mexico |
| | | | | | | | | | ○ | | | | | ● | | | | | | | | | | | | | Micronesia (F. St. of) |
| | | | | | | | | | | | | | | ○ | | | | | | | | | | | | ● | Moldova (Rep. of) |
| | | | | | | ● | | | | | ● | | ● | ● | ● | ● | | | | | | ● | ● | | | | Monaco |
| | | | | | | | | | | | | | ● | ● | | | | | | | | | ● | ● | | | Mongolia |
| | | | | | | | ● | | | | ● | | ● | ● | ● | ● | ● | ○ | ● | | | ● | ● | ○ | | | Morocco |
| | | | | | | | | | | | | | ● | ○ | | ● | | ● | | | | | | | | | Mozambique |
| | | | | | | | | | | | | | ● | ○ | | | | | ● | | | | | | | | Myanmar |
| | | | | | | | | | | | | | | ○ | | ● | | | | | | | | | | | Namibia |
| | | | | | | | | | ○ | | | | | ● | | | | | | | | | | | | | Nauru |
| | | | | | | | | | | | | | ● | ● | | ● | ● | ● | ○ | ● | | | | | | | Nepal |
| ● | | | ● | | | | | | | | | ● | | ● | ● | ● | ● | ● | ● | ● | ○ | ● | ● | ● | | ○ | Netherlands |

Matrix of participation in international environmental agreements.

Column groups and conventions (left to right):

**General Environmental Concerns / Atmosphere**
1. Espoo Convention
2. Aircraft Engine Emissions (ICAO) *
3. Transb. Air Pollution (LRTAP) *
4. Sulphur Protocol *
5. NOx Protocol *
6. VOC Protocol *
7. Climate Change (FCCC)
8. Ozone Layer Convention
9. Montreal Protocol *
10. London Amendment *
11. Copenhagen Amendment *

**Hazardous Substances**
12. Bamako Convention
13. CRTD
14. Basel Convention
15. Transb. Effects of Indust. Accidents
16. Dangerous Goods by Road (ADR)
17. Distrib. and Use of Pesticides

**Marine Environment — Global Conventions**
18. London Convention 1972
19. MARPOL 73/78
20. Civil Liab. for Oil Pollution (CLC)
21. Fund Convention
22. OPRC
23. Intervention Convention
24. UNCLOS

**Marine Environment — Regional Conventions**
25. Oslo Convention
26. Paris Convention

Key: ● = dark circle, ○ = light/shaded circle

| Country | 1 | 2 | 3 | 4 | 5 | 6 | 7 | 8 | 9 | 10 | 11 | 12 | 13 | 14 | 15 | 16 | 17 | 18 | 19 | 20 | 21 | 22 | 23 | 24 | 25 | 26 |
|---|---|---|---|---|---|---|---|---|---|---|---|---|---|---|---|---|---|---|---|---|---|---|---|---|---|---|
| New Zealand | | ○ | | | | | ● | ● | ● | ● | ● | | | | | | | ● | | | | ○ | | ● | ● | ● |
| Nicaragua | | ○ | | | | | ○ | ● | ● | | | | | | | | | | | | | ○ | | | ○ | |
| Niger | | ○ | | | | | ○ | ● | ● | | | | | | | | ○ | | | | | ○ | | | ○ | |
| Nigeria | | ○ | | | | | ● | ● | ● | | | | | | | | | ● | | ● | | ● | ● | ● | ● | |
| Niue | | | | | | | | | | | | | | | | | | | | | | | | | | |
| Norway | ● | ● | ● | ● | ● | ● | ● | ● | ● | ● | ● | | | | | | | ● | ● | ○ | ● | ● | ● | ● | ○ | ● |
| Oman | | ○ | | | | | ○ | | | | | | | | | | | | | | | ● | ● | ● | ● | ○ |
| Pakistan | | ○ | | | | | ● | ● | ● | ○ | | | | | | | | ● | | | | ○ | | | ● | ○ |
| Palau | | | | | | | | | | | | | | | | | | | | | | | | | | |
| Panama | | ○ | | | | | ○ | ● | ● | | | | | | | | | ● | | ● | ● | ○ | | ● | ● | ● |
| Papua New Guinea | | ○ | | | | | ● | ● | ● | | | | | | | | | ● | ● | ● | ● | ● | | ● | ● | ○ |
| Paraguay | | ○ | | | | | ● | ● | ● | | | | | | | | | | | | | ○ | | | ● | |
| Peru | | ○ | | | | | ● | ● | ● | | | | | | | | | ● | | | | ○ | | ● | ● | |
| Philippines | | ○ | | | | | ● | ● | ● | | | | | | | | | ● | | | | ○ | | ○ | ○ | |
| Poland | ○ | ● | ● | ○ | ○ | | ● | ● | ● | | | | | | | | | ● | ○ | ● | ● | ● | ● | ● | ● | ○ |
| Portugal | ○ | ● | ● | | | | ○ | ● | ● | | | | | | | | | ● | ● | ● | ● | ○ | | ● | ○ | ● ● |
| Qatar | | ○ | | | | | | | | | | | | | | | | | | | | ○ | | ● | ● | ○ |
| Romania | ○ | ● | ● | | | | ● | ● | ● | ● | | | | | | | | ● | | ○ | ○ | ● | | | ○ | ○ |
| Russian Federation | ○ | ● | ● | ○ | ○ | | ○ | ● | ● | ● | | | | | | | | ● | ● | ● | | ● | ● | | ● | ○ |
| Rwanda | | ○ | | | | | ○ | | | | | | | | ○ | | | | | | | ○ | | | ○ | |
| St Kitts & Nevis | | | | | | | ● | ● | ● | | ● | | | | | | | ● | | | | ○ | | | ● | |
| St Lucia | | ○ | | | | | ● | ● | ● | | | | | | | | | ● | | | | ○ | ● | | ● | |
| St Vinc. & Grenadines | | ○ | | | | | | | | | | | | | | | | | | | | ○ | ● | ● | ● | |
| Samoa (Western) | | | | | | | ○ | ● | ● | | | | | | | | | | | | | ○ | | | ○ | |
| San Marino | | ○ | ○ | | | | ● | | | | | | | | | | | | | | | | | | | |
| São Tomé & Principe | | ○ | | | | | ○ | | | | | | | | | | | | | | | ○ | | | ● | |
| Saudi Arabia | | ○ | | | | | | ● | ● | ● | ● | | | | | | | ● | | | | ○ | | ● | ● | ○ |
| Senegal | | ○ | | | | | ● | ● | ● | ● | | | | ● | | | | ● | | | | ○ | | | ● ● ● | ● |
| Seychelles | | ○ | | | | | ● | ● | ● | ● | ● | | | | | | | ● | | | | ○ | ● ● ● ● ● | ● | ● | |
| Sierra Leone | | ○ | | | | | ○ | | | | | | | | | | | | | | | ○ | ● | ● | ○ | |
| Singapore | | ○ | | | | | ○ | ● | ● | ● | | | | | | | | | | | | ○ | ● | ● | ○ | |

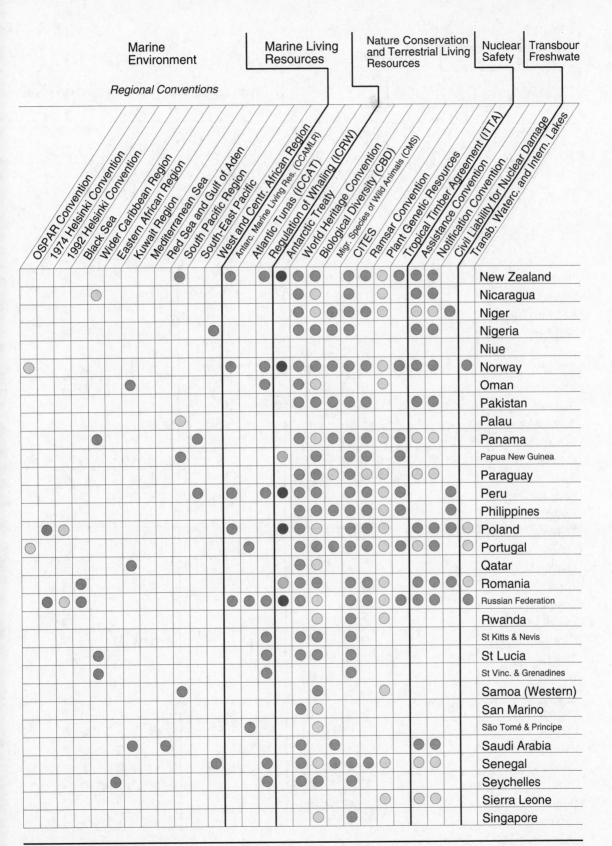

**GREEN GLOBE YEARBOOK 1995**

| Country | Espoo Convention | Aircraft Engine Emissions (ICAO) * | Transb. Air Pollution (LRTAP) | Sulphur Protocol * | NOx Protocol * | VOC Protocol * | Climate Change (FCCC) | Ozone Layer Convention | Montreal Protocol * | London Amendment * | Copenhagen Amendment * | Bamako Convention | CRTD | Basel Convention | Transb. Effects of Indust. Accidents | Dangerous Goods by Road (ADR) | Distrib. and Use of Pesticides | London Convention 1972 | MARPOL 73/78 | Civil Liab. for Oil Pollution (CLC) | Fund Convention | OPRC | Intervention Convention | UNCLOS | Oslo Convention | Paris Convention |
|---|---|---|---|---|---|---|---|---|---|---|---|---|---|---|---|---|---|---|---|---|---|---|---|---|---|---|
| Slovakia | ○ | ○ | ● | ● | ● | | | | | | | ● | ● | ● | ● | | | | ● | | ● | ● | ○ | | ○ | |
| Slovenia | | ○ | ● | ● | | | | | | | ○ | ● | ● | ● | | | | ● | | ● | ● | ○ | | ● | ● | ● |
| Solomon Islands | | ○ | | | | | | | | | | ○ | ● | ● | | | | | ● | ● | | | | | ○ | |
| Somalia | | ○ | | | | | | | | | | | | | | ○ | | | ○ | | | | | | ● | |
| South Africa | | ○ | | | | | | | ○ | ● | ● | | | | | ● | | ○ | ● | ● | ● | | | ● | ○ | |
| Spain | ● | ○ | ● | ● | ○ | ○ | ● | ● | ● | ● | ● | | | | | | | ● | ● | ○ | ● | ● | ● | ● | ● | ● |
| Sri Lanka | | ○ | | | | | | ● | ● | ● | | | | | | ● | | ○ | | | | ● | | ● | ● | |
| Sudan | | ○ | | | | | | ● | ● | ● | | ● | | | ○ | | | | | | | | | ● | | |
| Suriname | | ○ | | | | | | ○ | | | | | | | | ● | | | | | | | | | | |
| Swaziland | | ○ | | | | | | ○ | ● | | | | | | ○ | | | ● | | | | | | | | |
| Sweden | ● | ○ | ● | ● | ● | ● | ● | ● | ● | ● | ● | | | ● | ● | | ● | ● | ● | ● | ● | ● | ● | ○ | ● | ● |
| Switzerland | ○ | | ● | ● | ○ | ● | ● | ● | ● | | | | | ● | ● | | | | ● | ● | ● | ● | | ● | ● | ○ |
| Syrian Arab Rep. | | ○ | | | | | | ● | ● | | | | | | | | | ● | | | ○ | | ● | ● | | |
| Taiwan | | | | | | | | | | | | | | | | | | | | | | | | | | |
| Tajikistan | | ○ | | | | | | | | | | | | | | | | | | | | | | | | |
| Tanzania (U. Rep. of) | | ○ | | | | | | ○ | ● | ● | ● | | | ● | | ● | | ○ | | | | | | ● | | |
| Thailand | | ○ | | | | | | ○ | ● | ● | ● | | | ○ | | | | ○ | | | | | | ○ | | |
| Togo | | ○ | | | | | | ○ | ● | ● | ● | | | ○ | | ○ | | | ○ | ○ | ● | | | ● | | |
| Tonga | | ○ | | | | | | | | | | | | ○ | | | | | | | | | | | | |
| Trinidad & Tobago | | ○ | | | | | | ● | ● | ● | | | | ● | | | | | ○ | | | | | ● | | |
| Tunisia | | ○ | | | | | | ● | ● | ● | ● | | | ○ | | ● | | | ○ | | | ● | | ● | | |
| Turkey | | ○ | ● | | | | | | ● | ● | | | | | | | | ● | | | ○ | | ● | | | |
| Turkmenistan | | ○ | | | | | | | ● | ● | | | | | | | | | | | | | | | | |
| Tuvalu | | | | | | | | ● | ● | ● | | | | | | | | | | | | ● | ● | ● | ○ | |
| Uganda | | ○ | | | | | | ● | ● | ● | | | | | | | | ○ | | | | | | ● | | |
| Ukraine | ○ | ○ | ● | ○ | ● | ● | ● | ● | ● | | | | | | | | | ● | ● | | ● | | ● | ○ | | |
| United Arab Emirates | | ○ | | | | | | ● | ● | | | | | | | ● | | ○ | | ● | ● | ● | | ● | ○ | |
| United Kingdom | ○ | ○ | ● | ● | ● | ● | ● | ● | ● | ● | ● | | | ● | ○ | ● | ● | ● | ● | ● | ● | ● | ● | | ● | ● |
| USA | ○ | ○ | ● | | | | ● | ○ | ● | ● | ● | ● | | | | | ○ | ● | ● | ○ | | ● | ● | ● | | |
| Uruguay | | ○ | | | | | | ● | ● | ● | | | | ● | | | | ○ | | ○ | | ● | | ○ | ● | |
| Uzbekistan | | ○ | | | | | | ● | ● | ● | | | | | | | | | | | | | | | | |

Marine Environment · Marine Living Resources · Nature Conservation and Terrestrial Living Resources · Nuclear Safety · Transbour Freshwate

Regional Conventions

Legend: ● = party / ratified (filled); ○ = signatory / other status (open)

| Country | OSPAR | 1974 Helsinki | 1992 Helsinki | Black Sea | Wider Caribbean | Eastern African | Kuwait | Mediterranean | Red Sea & Gulf of Aden | South Pacific | South-East Pacific | West & Centr. African | CCAMLR | Atlantic Tunas (ICCAT) | Whaling (ICRW) | Antarctic Treaty | World Heritage | Biol. Diversity (CBD) | Migr. Species (CMS) | CITES | Ramsar | Plant Genetic Res. | Tropical Timber (ITTA) | Assistance | Notification | Civil Liability Nuclear | Transb. Waterc. & Lakes |
|---|---|---|---|---|---|---|---|---|---|---|---|---|---|---|---|---|---|---|---|---|---|---|---|---|---|---|---|
| Slovakia |  |  |  |  |  |  |  |  |  |  |  |  | ● | ● | ○ |  | ● | ● |  |  |  |  |  | ● | ● |  |  |
| Slovenia |  |  |  |  |  |  |  | ● |  |  |  |  |  |  | ● |  |  | ● |  |  |  |  |  | ● | ● | ● |  |
| Solomon Islands |  |  |  |  |  |  |  |  |  |  | ● |  |  |  | ● | ○ |  |  |  | ○ |  |  |  |  |  |  |  |
| Somalia |  |  |  |  |  | ● | ● |  |  |  |  |  |  |  |  | ● | ● |  |  |  |  |  |  |  |  |  |  |
| South Africa |  |  |  |  |  |  |  |  | ● | ● | ● | ● | ● | ● | ○ |  | ○ | ● |  | ○ | ● | ● |  |  |  |  |  |
| Spain | ● |  |  |  |  |  |  | ● |  |  |  |  | ● | ● | ● | ● | ● | ● | ● | ● | ● | ● |  | ● | ● | ○ | ○ |
| Sri Lanka |  |  |  |  |  |  |  |  |  |  |  |  |  |  | ● | ● | ● | ● | ● | ● |  |  |  | ● | ● |  |  |
| Sudan |  |  |  |  |  |  |  | ● |  |  |  |  |  |  | ● | ● | ● |  |  | ○ | ○ | ● |  |  |  |  |  |
| Suriname |  |  |  |  |  |  |  |  |  |  |  |  |  |  | ● |  |  | ● |  | ● | ● |  |  |  |  |  |  |
| Swaziland |  |  |  |  |  |  |  |  |  |  |  |  |  |  | ○ |  |  |  |  |  |  |  |  |  |  |  |  |
| Sweden | ● | ● | ● |  |  |  |  |  |  |  | ● |  | ● | ● | ● |  | ○ | ● | ● | ● | ● | ● |  | ● | ● |  | ● |
| Switzerland | ● |  |  |  |  |  |  |  |  |  |  |  |  | ● | ○ |  | ● | ○ | ● | ● | ● |  |  | ● | ● |  | ○ |
| Syrian Arab Rep. |  |  |  |  |  |  |  | ● |  |  |  |  |  |  | ● |  | ● |  |  | ○ |  |  |  | ○ | ○ |  |  |
| Taiwan |  |  |  |  |  |  |  |  |  |  |  |  |  |  |  |  |  |  |  |  |  |  |  |  |  |  |  |
| Tajikistan |  |  |  |  |  |  |  |  |  |  |  |  |  |  | ● |  |  | ○ |  |  |  |  |  |  |  |  |  |
| Tanzania (U. Rep. of) |  |  |  |  |  |  |  |  |  |  |  |  |  |  | ● | ○ |  | ● |  | ○ |  |  |  |  |  |  |  |
| Thailand |  |  |  |  |  |  |  |  |  |  |  |  |  |  | ● | ○ |  | ● |  | ● |  |  |  | ● | ● |  |  |
| Togo |  |  |  |  |  |  |  |  |  | ● |  |  |  |  | ○ | ○ | ● | ● |  | ● |  |  |  |  |  |  |  |
| Tonga |  |  |  |  |  |  |  |  |  |  |  |  |  |  |  |  |  |  |  | ○ |  |  |  |  |  |  |  |
| Trinidad & Tobago |  |  | ● |  |  |  |  |  |  |  |  |  |  |  | ○ |  | ● | ● | ● | ● |  |  | ● |  |  |  |  |
| Tunisia |  |  |  |  |  |  |  | ● |  |  |  |  |  |  | ● | ○ | ● | ● |  | ● |  |  |  | ● | ● |  |  |
| Turkey |  |  | ● |  |  |  |  | ● |  |  |  |  |  |  | ● | ○ | ● | ● |  | ● |  |  |  | ● | ● |  |  |
| Turkmenistan |  |  |  |  |  |  |  |  |  |  |  |  |  |  |  |  |  |  |  |  |  |  |  |  |  |  |  |
| Tuvalu |  |  |  |  |  |  |  |  |  | ○ |  |  |  |  | ○ |  |  |  |  |  |  |  |  |  |  |  |  |
| Uganda |  |  |  |  |  |  |  |  |  |  |  |  |  |  | ● | ● | ○ | ● |  | ● |  |  |  |  |  |  |  |
| Ukraine |  |  | ● |  |  |  |  |  |  |  |  | ● |  | ○ | ● | ○ |  |  |  |  |  |  |  | ● | ● |  |  |
| United Arab Emirates |  |  |  |  |  |  | ● |  |  |  |  |  |  |  |  | ○ |  | ● |  |  |  |  |  | ● | ● |  |  |
| United Kingdom | ○ |  |  | ● |  |  |  |  |  | ○ |  | ● | ● | ● | ● | ○ | ● | ● | ○ | ● | ● |  |  | ● | ● | ○ | ○ |
| USA |  |  | ● |  |  |  |  |  | ● |  |  |  | ● | ● | ● | ○ | ● |  | ● | ● |  |  | ● | ● | ● |  |  |
| Uruguay |  |  |  |  |  |  |  |  |  |  |  |  | ● | ● | ● | ● | ○ |  |  | ● |  |  |  | ● | ● |  |  |
| Uzbekistan |  |  |  |  |  |  |  |  |  |  |  |  |  |  | ● |  |  |  |  |  |  |  |  |  |  |  |  |

**General Environmental Concerns** | **Atmosphere** | **Hazardous Substances** | **Marine Environment** (*Global Conventions* / *Regional Conventions*)

| Country | Espoo Convention | Aircraft Engine Emissions (ICAO) | Transb. Air Pollution (LRTAP) | Sulphur Protocol * | NOx Protocol * | VOC Protocol * | Climate Change (FCCC) | Ozone Layer Convention | Montreal Protocol * | London Amendment | Copenhagen Amendment | Bamako Convention | CRTD | Basel Convention | Transb. Effects of Indust. Accidents | Dangerous Goods by Road (ADR) | Distrib. and Use of Pesticides | London Convention 1972 | MARPOL 73/78 | Civil Liab. for Oil Pollution (CLC) | Fund Convention | OPRC | Intervention Convention | UNCLOS | Oslo Convention | Paris Convention |
|---|---|---|---|---|---|---|---|---|---|---|---|---|---|---|---|---|---|---|---|---|---|---|---|---|---|---|
| Vanuatu | | | | | | | ○ | | | ● | | | | | | | | ○ | ● | ● | ● | ● | | ● | ○ | |
| Vatican (see Holy See) | | | | | | | | | | | | | | | | | | | | | | | | | | |
| Venezuela | | | | | | | ○ | ○ | ● | ● | ● | | | | | | | | | ○ | | ○ | ● | ● | ● | ○ |
| Viet Nam | | | | | | | ○ | ○ | ● | ● | ● | | | ● | | | | | | | | ○ | | ● | ● | |
| Yemen | | | | | | | ○ | | ○ | | | | | | | | | | | | | ○ | ● | ● | ● | |
| Yugoslavia | | | ● | | | | ○ | | ● | ● | | | | | | | | | | ● | | ○ | ● | ● | ● | |
| Zaïre | | | | | | | ○ | | ○ | | | | | | | ● | | | | ● | ● | ○ | | ● | | |
| Zambia | | | | | | | ○ | | ● | ● | ● | ● | | | | | | | | | | ○ | | ● | ● | |
| Zimbabwe | | | | | | | ○ | | ● | ● | ● | ● | | ● | ● | | | | | | | ○ | | ● | ● | |
| European Union | ○ | | ● | ○ | ● | ○ | ● | ● | ● | ● | | | | | | ● | ○ | ○ | | | | | | | ○ | ● |

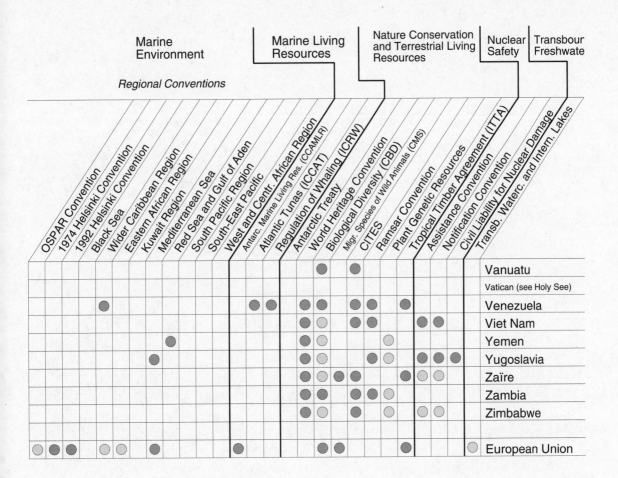

**Regional Conventions** — column groups: *Marine Environment* · *Marine Living Resources* · *Nature Conservation and Terrestrial Living Resources* · *Nuclear Safety* · *Transbour Freshwate*

Columns (left to right):
OSPAR Convention · 1974 Helsinki Convention · 1992 Helsinki Convention · Black Sea · Wider Caribbean Region · Eastern African Region · Kuwait Region · Mediterranean Sea · Red Sea and Gulf of Aden · South Pacific Region · South-East Pacific · West and Centr. African Region · Antarc. Marine Living Res. (CCAMLR) · Atlantic Tunas (ICCAT) · Regulation of Whaling (ICRW) · Antarctic Treaty · World Heritage Convention · Biological Diversity (CBD) · Migr. Species of Wild Animals (CMS) · CITES · Ramsar Convention · Plant Genetic Resources · Tropical Timber Agreement (ITTA) · Assistance Convention · Notification Convention · Civil Liability for Nuclear Damage · Transb. Waterc. and Intern. Lakes

| Country | Marine Environment | Marine Living Resources | Nature Conserv. & Terrestrial Living Resources | Nuclear Safety | Transb. Freshw. |
|---|---|---|---|---|---|
| Vanuatu | | | CBD ●, CITES ● | | |
| Vatican (see Holy See) | | | | | |
| Venezuela | Wider Caribbean ● | ICCAT ●, ICRW ● | World Heritage ●, CBD ●, CITES ●, ITTA ● | | |
| Viet Nam | | | World Heritage ●, CBD ○, CITES ● | Assistance ●, Notification ● | |
| Yemen | | | World Heritage ●, CBD ○, CITES ○ | | |
| Yugoslavia | Mediterranean Sea ● | | World Heritage ●, CBD ○, CMS ○ | Assistance ●, Notification ●, Civil Liability ● | |
| Zaïre | | | World Heritage ●, CBD ●, CMS ●, CITES ●, Plant Genetic Res. ○, ITTA ○ | | |
| Zambia | | | World Heritage ●, CBD ●, CMS ●, CITES ●, Ramsar ○ | | |
| Zimbabwe | | | World Heritage ●, CBD ○, CMS ●, CITES ○ | Assistance ○, Notification ○ | |
| European Union | OSPAR ○, 1974 Helsinki ●, 1992 Helsinki ●, Eastern African ○, Kuwait ○, Mediterranean Sea ● | CCAMLR ● | World Heritage ●, CBD ●, Ramsar ● | Assistance ○ | |

# Intergovernmental Organizations (IGOs)
*including United Nations specialized agencies*

# Commission on Sustainable Development (CSD)

## Objectives

- to monitor progress in the implementation of *Agenda 21* and activities related to the integration of environmental and developmental goals throughout the UN system;
- to consider information provided by governments regarding the activities they undertake to implement *Agenda 21*;
- to review the progress in the implementation of the commitments set forth in *Agenda 21*, including those related to the provision of financial resources and transfer of technology;
- to receive and analyse relevant input from competent non-governmental organizations, including the scientific and the private sector;
- to enhance the dialogue, within the framework of the UN, with non-governmental organizations, and the independent sector, as well as other entities outside the UN system.

## Organization

*Type*
Intergovernmental organ of the United Nations. Functional Commission of the UN Economic and Social Council (ECOSOC). Reports to the UN General Assembly through ECOSOC. Established as an institutional arrangement to the follow-up to the UN Conference on Environment and Development (UNCED) in Rio de Janeiro, June 1992.

*Membership*
The CSD is composed of representatives of 53 states, elected for a three-year period by ECOSOC. Other member States of the United Nations, non-member States, intergovernmental organizations (IGOs), including regional integration organizations, and accredited non-governmental organizations (NGOs) are participating in the work of the CSD as observers.

*Founded*
16 February 1993.

## Secretariat

Division on Sustainable Development, Department of Policy Co-ordination and Sustainable Development (DPCSD), Room DC-2270, United Nations, New York, NY 10017, USA
*Telephone*:     +1-212-9635949
*Telefax*:     +1-212-9634260
*E-mail*:     dpcsd@igc.apc.org

*Chairman*
Dr Klaus Töpfer.

*Director*
Ms Joke Waller-Hunter.

*Information Officer*
Ms Julie Thompson (UN Department for Public Information).

*Number of staff*
20 professionals and 15 support staff (Oct. 1994).

The DPCSD liaison office in Geneva: Department of Policy Co-ordination and Sustainable Development, 11, chemin des Anémones, PO Box 76, CH-1219 Châtelaine, Geneva, Switzerland
*Telephone*:     +41-22-9799111
*Telefax*:     +41-22-9799034
*E-mail*: secretariat.unfccc@unep.ch

## Activities

A *Multi-Year Thematic Programme of Work* is agreed with the following cross-sectoral clusters to be reviewed and monitored on a yearly basis:
- critical elements of sustainability (chs. 2–5 of *Agenda 21*);
- financial resources and mechanisms (ch. 33);
- education, science, transfer of environmentally sound technologies, cooperation and capacity-building (chs. 16 and 34–7);
- decision-making structures (chs. 8 and 38–40);
- roles of major groups (non-governmental sectors) (chs. 23–32).

The Programme also specifies the sectoral clusters that will receive special

attention between 1994 and 1996:
• 1994: Health, human settlements, and fresh water (chs. 6, 7, 18, and 21); and toxic chemicals and hazardous wastes (chs. 19, 20, and 22);
• 1995: Land, desertification, forests, and biodiversity (chs. 10–15);
• 1996: Atmosphere, oceans, and all kinds of seas (chs. 9 and 17).

The 1997 session will have an overall review and appraisal of *Agenda 21* in preparation for that year's special session of the UN General Assembly.

All cross-sectoral clusters will be under review annually, with particular emphasis on selected chapters within a cluster. The purpose in combining sectoral themes with cross-sectoral chapters is to enable a more integrated view of how the cross-sectoral elements interact and contribute to the sectoral issues in the *Agenda 21* implementation process.

According to a decision adopted at the Commission's first substantive meeting in June 1993, governments are encouraged to submit their national reports on *Agenda 21* implementation not less than six months before the Commission's session. It is up to individual governments to decide on the degree of detail and regularity of their reporting to the CSD. However, the information provided shall:
• be relevant to the *Agenda 21* clusters to be discussed that year;
• be concise (no more than fifty pages);
• be accompanied by an executive summary of no more than five pages.

Reports are also requested from organizations of the UN system, including international financial institutions and the GEF (see World Bank, UNDP, and UNEP in this section), as well as international, regional, and sub-regional intergovernmental organizations outside the UN system.

The secretariat shall prepare an annual overview report on progress made in the implementation of *Agenda 21*, with a focus on the cross-sectoral components of *Agenda 21* and critical elements of sustainability. In addition, it shall provide thematic reports, corresponding to the *Agenda 21* sectoral clusters, to be included on the agendas of forthcoming sessions of the Commission.

60 national reports and reports from regional organizations were submitted to the 1994 meeting of CSD.

In carrying out its programme of work, the CSD will take into account the results of major intergovernmental events and negotiating processes, with a view to integrating these activities in the review of the implementation of *Agenda 21*. The CSD will also take time-frames into account with regard to specific targets identified in *Agenda 21*.

## Decision-making bodies

The 53 members of the *Commission on Sustainable Development* are elected by the UN Economic and Social Council. The members serve for a three-year period and are encouraged to be represented at the ministerial level. Membership will rotate among governments of the UN, drawn on the following geographical basis: Africa (13), Asia (12), Latin America, and the Caribbean (10), and North America, Europe and other (18). The CSD has its sessions annually for two or three weeks.

The members of the CSD elect the Chair and four Vice-Chairs. These five members constitute the *Bureau* of the CSD.

The CSD has established inter-sessional *ad hoc* expert groups to assist the Commission on issues related to the financing of *Agenda 21* implementation (annual), and on sectoral issues for 1995.

*High-Level Advisory Board on Sustainable Development*
The UN secretary-general has also established a *High-Level Advisory Board on Sustainable Development*, comprised of twenty-one eminent persons knowledgeable about the environment and development, including relevant sciences. The Board will advise the secretary-general and the CSD on formulating policy proposals, elaborating innovative approaches, and identifying emerging issues to be brought to the attention of relevant intergovernmental bodies, particularly the CSD. It takes part in the annual CSD sessions.

The Board establishes *ad hoc* panels to focus on the various areas for the next two years. In spring 1994 the focus was on:
• linkages between economic, social, and political development;
• new approaches to finance and technology transfer;
• establishment of new partnerships between the UN and other bodies in the field of sustainable development.

At the session in October 1994, the panels focused on linkages between economic, social, and political development in the changing world; value-based education for sustainability, and concrete ways of forging alliances.

## Finance
CSD activities are financed mainly through the regular UN budget.

*Budget*
No information available.

## Publications
*CSD Update* (bi-monthly newsletter).

*Electronic conferences*
CSD documents on the CSD sessions, a menu item for the inter-sessional process, reporting guide-lines, the complete *Agenda 21*, and an electronic copy of the *CSD Update* newsletter are available on *CSD Gopher*. Further information is available from DPCSD.

# European Union (EU): Environment

## Objectives

According to Article 130(r) of the Single European Act, action by the European Union relating to the environment has the following objectives:
- to preserve, protect, and improve the quality of the environment;
- to contribute towards protecting human health;
- to ensure a prudent and rational utilization of natural resources.

Environmental protection requirements shall be a component of the Community's other policies and action by the Community shall be based on the principle that:
- preventive action should be taken;
- environmental damage should as a priority be rectified at source;
- polluter should pay.

According to Article 2 of the new Treaty on European Union, one of the basic aims is to promote a harmonious and balanced development of economic activities, sustainable and non-inflationary growth respecting the environment.

## Organization

*Type*
Intergovernmental organization (IGO). The institutions of the EU have a definite legal status and extensive powers of their own. The European Union, which incorporates the European Community (EC), comprise three juridically distinct entities: European Economic Community (EEC); Euratom; and European Coal and Steel Community (ECSC).

The EU consists of four main institutions which all play an important role in EU environmental policy:
- *Council of Ministers*;
- *European Commission*;
- *European Court of Justice*;
- *European Parliament*.

Due to the central role of the European Commission in preparing, proposing, and verifying environmental legislation,

in the following we shall focus on this organization.

*Membership*
Any European State can apply for membership. The terms of its admission will be agreed between the original member States and the applicant state. 12 member States (Belgium, Denmark, France, Germany, Greece, Italy, Ireland, Luxembourg, the Netherlands, Portugal, Spain, and the United Kingdom), by December 1994. Four states, Austria, Finland, Sweden, and Norway have applied for membership from 1 January 1995. Parliaments in the four candidate countries need to pass enabling legislation following a referendum. In Austria, Finland, and Sweden the result was in favour of membership. The referendum in Norway was on 28 November 1994.

*Founded*
The Treaty establishing the EEC was signed in Rome on 25 March 1957. (European Community was founded on 8 April 1965. European Union came into being on 1 November 1994).

## Secretariat

European Commission,
rue de la Loi 200,
B-1049 Brussels,
Belgium
*Telephone*:       +32-2-2991111
*Telefax*:        Information is available from the switchboard operator.

*President*
Mr Jacques Santer.

DG XI: Environment, Nuclear Safety & Civil Protection
Postal address and telephone: as above
Location: bld. du Triomphe 174

European Environment Agency (EEA),
6 Kongens Nytorv,
DK-1050 Copenhagen,
Denmark
*Telephone*:       +45-33-145075
*Telefax*:        +45-33-146599

*Commissioner for Environment*
Ms Ritt Bjerregaard.

*Information officer (DGXI)*
Mr Hans Jankowski.

*Number of staff*
18,576 at the Commission (1993). 412 at DGXI (1994).

## Activities

The major environmental activities consist of:
- *policy activities*, through developing EC Environmental Action Programmes (1973, 1977, 1983, 1987, and 1992). The fifth Programme lays out the EC's environmental goals to the year 2000. It identifies the most pressing environmental concerns, lists priorities, selects target sectors including industry, transport, agriculture, and tourism, broadens the range of instruments (political and financial) needed to achieve goals, and sets up three *ad hoc* dialogue groups—a consultative forum, an implementation network, and an environment policy review group—to promote a greater sense of responsibility among the principal actors targeted by the Programme, and to ensure effective and transparent application of measures. A Review of the Programme is set for 1995, which marks the midway point between the priming and full steam phases of the Programme. The Review will examine to what extent the Programme has been implemented, quantify the objectives set out for the year 2000, and in the light of this analyse critically the Programme's priorities;
- *legal activities*, through providing

environmental legislation in the form of Regulations, Directives, or Decisions. Approximately three hundred legal texts related to the environment currently exist;

• *research and technological development (RTD) activities*, through developing research and development programmes within the area of the environment. The *Science and Technology for Environment Protection (STEP)* Programme was adopted in June 1991. It replaces the previous STEP and the European Programme on Climatology and Natural Hazards). The STEP programme aims to develop the scientific knowledge and technical know-how which the Union needs in order to carry out its role concerning the environment. The programme ran until 31 December 1994. The *Fourth Framework Programme*, which is the Community's principal medium-term plan for research activities at Community level, has recently been adopted and runs for four years, from 1994 to 1998. There are four main activities, and the environment features in the first which deals with research, technological development, and demonstration programmes. The 'environment and climate programme' will establish networks of excellence and RTD in three areas:

• research into the natural environmental quality and global change;

• environmental technologies;

• space technology applied to earth observation and environmental research;

• *monitoring and implementation activities*. According to the Treaty of Rome, the Commission is responsible for ensuring that the EC environmental legislation is properly implemented and for reporting cases of infraction to the European Court of Justice.

The *CORINE Programme* (1985–90) had as its principal aim to gather, co-ordinate, and ensure the consistency of information on the state of the environment in the EU. The CORINE Programme was wound up in 1990, and the Commission proposed the setting up of an Agency, known as the *European Environment Agency (EEA)* the same year. In accordance with a decision by the European Council on 29 October 1993, the EEA is in the process of being put into operation. Its seat is in Copenhagen, Denmark. The EEA's overall task, as given by Council regulation 1210/30/EEC is to produce objective, reliable, and comparable information for those concerned with the implementation and further development of environment policy of the European Community, along the lines expressed in the Council resolution on the Fifth Environment Action Programme.

## Decision-making bodies

The *Council of Ministers* is the main decision-making body concerning environmental related legislation. According to the Single European Act, there are two main procedures:

(*a*) Decisions in accordance with Article 130 require unanimity and restrict the role of the European Parliament to non-binding consultation;

(*b*) Decisions in accordance with Article 100(*a*), require a qualified majority and increase the influence of the European Parliament, if a proposal relates to the establishment and functioning of the internal market.

In cases of majority voting, seventy-six votes are distributed among the member States in the Council, broadly reflecting the size of their populations.

## Finance

The budget is based on financial contributions of member States.

*Budget*
The total budget for the European Community was ECU67.9 billion in 1993, ECU72,4 billion in 1994, and is approximately ECU75.1 billion in 1995.

The budget of DGXI was approximately ECU100 million in 1993, approximately ECU110 million in 1994, and is approximately ECU50 million in 1995.

*Main contributors*
Main contributors in 1993 were Germany (28.5 per cent), France (18.0 per cent), Italy (15.5 per cent), and United Kingdom (12.0 per cent).

*Special funds*
The *Financial Instruments for the Environment (LIFE)* is established to assist the development and implementation of the EU's environmental policy. LIFE may also provide technical environmental assistance for non-EU countries bordering the Mediterranean and the Baltic, and for implementing international agreements relating to regional and global environmental problems. The finance required for the first operational phase, from 1992 until 1994, is an estimated ECU400 million. Of this, ECU140 million is made available for measures, demonstration schemes, awareness campaigns, incentives, and technical assistance.

## Publications

• *State of the Environment in the European Community*;
• *European Community Environmental Legislation*.

# Food and Agriculture Organization (FAO)

## Objectives
- to raise the levels of nutrition and standards of living of the populations of member countries;
- to secure improvements in the efficiency of production and distribution of all food and agricultural products;
- to improve the conditions of rural populations;
- to contribute towards an expanding world economy and towards ensuring freedom from hunger for humanity.

## Organization
*Type*
Intergovernmental organization (IGO). A specialized agency of the United Nations. Linked to UN Economic and Social Council (ECOSOC).

*Membership*
Membership is confined to Nations; Associate Membership to territories or groups of territories. The European Union is given membership as a regional integration organization. The total membership of FAO was 169 countries and the European Union, by 15 September 1994. Puerto Rico is an Associate Member.

*Founded*
16 October 1945.

## Secretariat
Food and Agricultural Organization (FAO),
Viale delle Terme di Caracalla,
I-00100 Rome, Italy
*Telephone*: +39-6-52251
*Telefax*: +39-6-52253152
*E-mail*: telex-room@fao.org

*Director General*
Dr Jacques Diouf.

*Director, Information Division*
Mr Richard Lydiker.

*Number of staff*
1,287 professionals and 1,975 support staff at headquarters in addition to 1,050 professionals and 1,637 support staff at field, regional, and country offices (Dec. 1993).

## Activities
In fulfilling its aims to combat poverty and malnutrition, FAO carries out four major functions; it collects, analyses, and disseminates information; advises governments on policies and programmes; provides technical assistance; and offers governments and experts a neutral forum in which to meet to discuss issues related to food and agriculture. The major areas of FAO activity are: crop production, livestock, natural resources, research and technology, rural development, nutrition, food and agricultural policy, fisheries, and forestry.

*Main conventions on environment under the auspices of FAO* (see Agreements)
- *International Convention for the Conservation of Atlantic Tunas (ICCAT), Rio de Janeiro, 1966*;
- *FAO International Code of Conduct on the Distribution and Use of Pesticides, Rome, 1985*;
- *FAO International Undertaking on Plant Genetic Resources, Rome, 1983*.

*Environmental activities*
The Organization has intensified its interdisciplinary work to ensure the integration of environmental considerations in all FAO activities; giving high priority to the prevention of environmental degradation and emphasizing sustainable development in agriculture, fisheries, and forestry.

FAO advises governments on policy-planning and environmental protection in a wide range of sectors, including the management of soil and water resources, farming systems, genetic resources, irrigation systems, integrated pest management, integrated plant nutrition, and watershed management.

## Decision-making bodies
The *Conference*, which meets every two years, is the major policy-making organ of FAO. All members are represented and each has one vote. The Conference is responsible for approving the FAO budget and Programme of Work, adopting procedural rules and financial regulations, admitting new members, formulating recommendations on food and agricultural questions, and reviewing the decisions of the *FAO Council* and subsidiary bodies. The FAO Council is composed of 49 members, elected by the Conference for three-year terms. The Council is the executive organ of the Conference and exercises powers delegated to it by the Conference. The FAO Council is assisted by eight major committees covering Agriculture, Commodity Problems, Constitutional and Legal Matters, Forestry, Fisheries, World Food Security, Finance, and FAO Programmes.

## Finance
Contributions from member countries for implementation of the Regular Programme of Work are based on per capita income. The Field Programme is financed by three major sources: government trust funds, the UNDP, and FAO's own Technical Co-operation Programme.

*Budget*
The budget for the biennium 1994–95 amounted to $US673.1 million.

*Special funds*
The *Technical Co-operation Programme (TCP)* allows the Organization to respond to special needs of member countries. TCP expenditure was $US35.9 million in 1991, $US36.1 million in 1992, and $US36.0 million in 1993, financed by member countries through the regular budget.

## Publications
- *FAO Plant Protection Bulletin* (quarterly);
- *Food Outlook* (monthly);
- *Rural Development* (annually);
- *Commodity Review and Outlook*;
- *FAO Annual Review*.

The library catalog at FAO's David Lubin Memorial Library is computerized and available on-line. It is using CDS/ISIS on Mainframe, and is affiliated with CGNET.

# Global Environment Facility (GEF)

## Objectives

To serve as a mechanism for international co-operation for the purpose of providing new and additional grant and concessional funding to meet the agreed global environmental benefits in the following focal areas:

- climate change;
- biological diversity;
- international waters; and
- ozone layer depletion.

Projects addressing land degradation, primarily desertification and deforestation, are also eligible.

The GEF shall ensure the cost-effectiveness of its activities in addressing the targeted global environmental issues, and shall fund programmes and projects which are country-driven and based on national priorities designed to support sustainable development.

## Organization

*Type*
Intergovernmental organization (IGO). The GEF is jointly managed by the World Bank, United Nations Development Programme (UNDP), and United Nations Environment Programme (UNEP) (see this section).

*Membership*
Any state member of the United Nations or any of its specialized agencies may be become a Participant in the GEF. Not open to regional integration organizations. 139 Participants, by 10 November 1994.

*Founded*
28 November 1991. The instrument establishing the new GEF entered into force on 1 July 1994.

## Secretariat

Global Environment Facility Secretariat,
The World Bank,
1818 H Street NW,
Washington, DC 20433,
USA
*Telephone*:     +1-202-4731053
*Telefax*:        +1-202-522-3240/3245
*E-mail*:  msubiza@worldbank.org
              or first initial last
              name@worldbank.org

*Chairman and Chief-Executive Officer*
Dr Mohamed T. El-Ashry.

*Head of Information*
Mr Nicholas van Praag.

*Number of staff*
15 professionals and 9 support staff (Nov. 1994).

## Activities

The Global Environment Facility (GEF) was initially set up in 1990 as a three-year pilot programme by the World Bank, UNDP, and UNEP. The aim was to provide grants and low-interest loans to developing countries to help them carry out programmes to relieve pressures on global ecosystems.

The restructured GEF is based on a set of principles agreed to by the Participants. The principles include the availability of the GEF to serve as the funding mechanism for agreed global environmental conventions. The GEF operates, on an interim basis, the financial mechanism for the implementation of the Framework Convention on Climate Change (see Agreements) and, on an interim basis, the institutional structure which carries out the operation of the financial mechanism for the implementation of the Convention on Biological Diversity (see Agreements). An operational strategy is in the process of being developed. It will include sub-strategies in the four areas covered by the GEF (see Objectives, above). The strategy will be completed in July 1995. In the meantime, the Facility is providing limited resources to a small number of urgent projects that are highly likely to fit into the operational strategy once it is agreed.

There is agreement that the GEF should work with the regional development banks, the UN agencies, and bilateral agencies to involve them in GEF technical assistance and investment projects. The implementing agencies are working with the regional development banks and UN agencies on the modalities for such co-operation.

## Decision-making bodies

The GEF has an *Assembly*, which consists of representatives of all Participants. The Assembly meets every three years. The Assembly reviews the general policies and in addition evaluates the operation of the Facility on the basis of reports submitted by the Council. The *Council* is the main governing body responsible for developing, adopting, and evaluating the operational policies and programmes for GEF-financed activities. It consists of 32 members with 16 members from developing countries (six each from Africa and Asia, with four seats for Latin America), 14 from developed countries and two from the countries of central and eastern Europe and the former Soviet Union. The Council meets twice a year, or as frequently as necessary.

When consensus is not possible, a double-majority voting system will be used, requiring 60 per cent Council members and 60 per cent donor support. It is intended that the system will protect the interests of both donor and recipient countries.

The GEF Secretariat will service and report to the Assembly and the Council and ensure that any project proposed for GEF funding is consistent with GEF policies, operational strategies, and work programme. It will be supported administratively by the World Bank, but will operate in a functionally independent and effective manner.

The Scientific and Technical Advisory Panel (STAP) is an advisory body. UNEP serves as the secretariat for STAP and operates as the liaison between the Facility and STAP.

## Finance

Funding comes in the form of grants from the donors, which include both developing and developed countries. Contributions from developed countries will be roughly in line with a formula based on their shares in the World Bank's International Development Association (see this section). 26 countries have announced pledges to the GEF, including eight developing countries.

*Budget*
Not available. The budget will be presented for approval to the GEF Council in January/February 1995.

*Special funds*
During the three years pilot phase the GEF provided financing for 117 environmental projects. Accumulated disbursement was $US730 million.

Total multilateral pledges and contributions to the Trust Fund is $US2 billion for 1994–97. GEF funding will be available for projects and other activities that address the objectives of GEF. The GEF has committed $US850 million to its first series of projects, which will be fully operational by the end of 1994.

*Main contributors*
The main contributors are the USA, Japan, Germany, and France. These countries provides 63 per cent of the Facility's funding for the 1994–97 period.

## Publications

In addition to annual reports and a working paper series:
• *Quarterly Bulletin*;
• *Quarterly Operational Report*.

*Electronic conferences*
GEF documents are available in the ECONET Conference under the name: gef.report

# International Atomic Energy Agency (IAEA)

## Objectives
- to encourage and assist research on and development and practical application of atomic energy for peaceful purposes throughout the world;
- to act as an intermediary in the supply of materials, services, equipment, and facilities;
- to foster the exchange of scientific and technical information;
- to encourage the exchange and training of scientists and experts;
- to establish standards and administer safeguards against the misuse of aid provided by or through the Agency;
- to carry out safeguards to verify compliance of non-nuclear weapon states party to Non-Proliferation Treaty (NPT), and other Treaties, that they use fissionable material for peaceful purposes only.

## Organization
*Type*
Intergovernmental organization (IGO). An independent IGO within the United Nations system.

*Membership*
Open to all States, whether UN member or not. 121 member States, by 1 November 1994. Not open to regional integration organizations.

*Founded*
29 July 1957.

## Secretariat
International Atomic Energy Agency (IAEA),
Vienna International Centre,
Wagramerstrasse 5,
PO Box 100,
A-1400 Vienna,
Austria
*Telephone*:     +43-1-23600
*Telefax*:     +43-1-234564
*E-mail*:     iaeo@iaea1.iaea.or.at

*Director General*
Dr Hans Blix.

*Director, Division of Public Information*
Mr David Kyd.

*Number of staff*
833 professionals and 1,355 support staff (Oct. 1994).

## Activities
There were over 825 nuclear installations and other locations under IAEA safeguards by end of 1993. This represents approximately 95 per cent of the world's nuclear facilities and materials outside the five nuclear-weapon states. IAEA safeguard inspections in these facilities to verify that the fissionable material is used for peaceful purposes only.

*Main conventions on environment under the auspices of IAEA*
- *Convention on Assistance in the Case of a Nuclear Accident or Radiological Emergency (Assistance Convention), Vienna, 1986* (see Agreements);
- *Convention on Early Notification of a Nuclear Accident (Notification Convention), Vienna, 1986* (see Agreements);
- *Vienna Convention on Civil Liability for Nuclear Damage, Vienna, 1963* (see Agreements);
- *Convention on the Physical Protection of Nuclear Material, Vienna, 1979.* 52 Parties, by 29 October 1994. 45 Signatories without ratification, acceptance, or approval;
- *Joint Protocol Relating to the Application of the Vienna Convention and the Paris Convention on Third Party Liability in the Field of Nuclear Energy, Vienna, 1988.* 16 Parties, by 29 October 1994. 22 Signatories without ratification, acceptance, or approval;

- *Convention on Nuclear Safety, Vienna, 1994.* [Not yet in force.] 1 Party, by 29 October 1994. 46 Signatories without ratification, acceptance, or approval.

*International conventions which request member States to conclude agreements with the IAEA*
- *Treaty on the Non-Proliferation of Nuclear Weapons (NPT), London, Moscow, Washington, DC, 1968.* 164 Parties, by 29 October 1994. No Signatories without ratification, acceptance, or approval;
- *Treaty for the Prohibition of Nuclear Weapons in Latin America (Tlateloco Treaty).* 24 Parties, by January 1994. 6 Signatories without ratification, acceptance, or approval;
- *South Pacific Nuclear Free Zone Treaty (Rarotonga Treaty), Rarotonga, 1985.* 11 Parties, by January 1994. 11 Signatories without ratification, acceptance, or approval.

*Environmental activities*
Many of the IAEA's programmes contribute directly or indirectly to the goals of sustainable development and protection of the environment as set out in *Agenda 21*, the outcome of the 1992 United Nations Conference on Environment and Development (UNCED). Of particular relevance in this context are the programmes on food and agriculture, isotope hydrology (work on both climate change and water resources), and waste management. The IAEA also takes an active role in inter-agency co-ordination of the implementation of *Agenda 21*.

An important example of the IAEA's activities in relation to monitoring of the environment in 1993, was the response to the concern expressed by the contracting parties to the Convention on the Prevention of Marine Pollution by Dumping of Wastes and Other Matter (London Convention 1972) (see Agreements) and by the international community over the dumping of radioactive wastes in the Arctic seas—a response reflected in the IAEA's involvement in the International Arctic Seas Assessment Project. Progress in this regard was made during the year, with the acquisition of basic source term information from the government of the Russian Federation and the establishment of a programme on environmental modelling. The IAEA Marine Environment Laboratory in Monaco (MEL) contributed to this assessment and participated in the 1993 Russian-Norwegian expedition to the Arctic dump sites to sample and subsequently analyse water, sediment, and biota.

IAEA has assisted States since 1956 in controlling the discharge or release of radioactive materials into the sea and in establishing internationally acceptable regulations to prevent pollution of the sea by radioactive materials in amounts which would adversely affect the human and marine environments. IAEA is the adviser to the London Convention 1972 on radiological matters.

At a meeting of the Contracting Parties to the London Convention 1972 in November 1993, a majority voted to prohibit totally the dumping of all types of radioactive wastes at sea. The IAEA was entrusted with the practical task of providing a definition of the levels of activity below which material may be considered as non-radioactive.

With the Marine Environment Laboratory (MEL) the IAEA runs the only marine environment laboratory in the United Nations system. The scientific objectives of the IAEA-MEL include more applied areas of marine radioactivity studies, e.g. radiological assessments, emergency response, marine modelling and database provision, isotopic tracers within the marine carbon cycle, and comparative radiological assessments between industries. In light of the increasing need to understand the carbon cycle, and the greenhouse effect, the

IAEA-MEL expanded its participation in oceanographic cruises in the Mediterranean Sea to measure the vertical flux and changes in the inventories of radionuclides and other elements, including carbon.

The IAEA-MEL continued to assist member States to obtain information on the transport and fate of marine pollutants. Of note in 1993 was the continuation of field work and laboratory analyses to assess the impact of oil related pollution in Kuwait and Saudi Arabia stemming from the 1991 Gulf war. IAEA-MEL staff carried out a third pollution survey and collected some fifty samples of sediment, biota, and sea water from the surface microlayer; analyses have just begun. Some of the polluted sediments samples have been 'fingerprinted' for oil by inductively coupled plasma mass spectrometry and cold neutron induced prompt gamma multielement analyses through a joint research project between IAEA-MEL and the Japan Atomic Energy Research Institute. Preliminary results suggest that oil-related metals such as nickel and vanadium are present in elevated concentrations in the most heavily affected areas.

*Agenda 21* of the 1992 UNCED identified the need to strengthen interagency co-operation. To this end, the IAEA signed a new Memorandum of Understanding with the Intergovernmental Oceanographic Commission (IOC) of UNESCO and UNEP (see this section) to ensure co-ordination of joint programmes centred at IAEA-MEL. 1993 saw the introduction of a new 'umbrella' project between UNEP and IAEA-MEL. Within this framework, IAEA-MEL provides comprehensive technical support to assess marine pollution. In 1993, staff conducted advisory and technical missions to 27 countries. Extended specialist training activities were provided in Albania, Cyprus, Egypt, Mexico, Nicaragua, Slovenia, and Tunisia. The instrument maintenance engineer installed new equipment (donated through UNEP and the World Bank) in Slovenia and Albania and conducted seven service visits to monitoring laboratories.

A significant part of the Agency's overall programme is the joint IAEA/ Food and Agriculture Organization

(FAO) (see this section) programme on nuclear techniques in food and agriculture, almost entirely devoted to increasing food production while reducing the environmental impact of fertilizer and pesticide use.

The IAEA's laboratory at Seibersdorf acts as a sample collection, data acquisition, and distribution centre in the World Maritime Organization's (WMO) (see this section) Background Air Pollution Monitoring Network (BAPMON).

The IAEA's Isotope Hydrology Programme is determined by the increasing demand in member States for the utilization of isotope methods, especially in water resources assessment in developing countries. Isotope methods have been recognized as being indispensable for solving problems such as characterization of palaeowater resources, evaluation of recharge and evaporative discharge under arid and semi-arid conditions, reconstruction of past climates, study of interrelationships between surface and groundwater, dating of groundwater, identification of pollution sources, and validation of contaminant transport models.

Under the IAEA's Radioactive Waste Management Advisory Programme (WAMAP), advisory services are available to member States needing advice on establishing national waste-management programmes and technical assistance on specific waste-management issues or problems.

The IAEA provides various services to member States in the field of safe operation of nuclear power plants and nuclear facilities to protect the environment from contamination.

*Environmental Monitoring Programmes*
The Isotopes-In-Precipitation Network was initiated by the IAEA in collaboration with the World Meteorological Organization (WMO) in 1958. In 1977, it was extended to fit within the framework of the United Nations Environment Programmes' (see this section) Global Environment Monitoring System (GEMS). The initial objective of the programme was to collect systematic data on isotope content of precipitation on a global scale. In 1988, 80 Network stations were in operation, while another 82 nationally implemented stations contributed data. Recently, the Project

objectives have changed in view of global climatic change. Data is valuable for global and/or regional scale atmospheric circulation models. Using such data should improve the understanding of what mechanisms control climatic conditions, thus making predictions of future climatic trends more reliable.

*Data and Information Management Programmes*
A database is affiliated to the Isotopes-In-Precipitation Network (see above).

## Decision-making bodies
The policy-making Organs of the IAEA are the *Board of Governors* and the *General Conference*. The General Conference is composed of representatives of all the IAEA member States. The Board of Governors, IAEA's executive body, is composed of representatives of 35 governments, of which 13 are designated by the Board itself for a period of one year and 22 are elected by the General Conference for a period of two years. The *Secretariat* is headed by a Director-General appointed by the Board with the approval of the General Conference.

## Finance
IAEA financial resources fall into two categories—the regular budget and the voluntary contributions. The regular budget provides for the normal administrative expenses of the IAEA (safeguard inspections, safety services, environmental activities, publications, research conferences, and information services). It is funded by contributions based on annual assessments of member States and by miscellaneous income. The Technical Assistance and Co-operation Fund consists of voluntary contributions used for financing the IAEA's technical

co-operation programme. It is funded by contributions from member States and the United Nations.

*Budget*
The regular budget was $US191 million in 1993, $US200 million in 1994, and is $US211 million in 1995.

*Main contributors*
Main contributors in 1994 were the USA (25.9%), Japan (11.7%), Russian Federation (10.3%), Germany (9.6%), and France (6.4%).

*Special funds*
The target for voluntary contributions for the IAEA Technical Assistance and Co-operation Fund (TACF), established in 1959, has been set at $US55.5 million for 1993, $US58.5 million for 1994, and $US61.5 million for 1995.

In line with world-wide trends in technical assistance, environmental issues were emphasized in IAEA's 1993 Technical Co-operation Programme. The IAEA was represented at several United Nations follow-up meetings to the UNCED, and IAEA proposals have been submitted to the Global Environment Facility (GEF) (see this section) and to Capacity 21 (launched by UNDP).

Total new resources available for technical co-operation in 1993 totalled $US52.9 million, the largest amount ever recorded. All sources of funding were higher than in the previous year, with the Technical Assistance and Co-operation Fund (TACF) rising by 31 per cent, extrabudgetary funding by 28 per cent, assistance in kind by 26 per cent, and funds from UNDP by 71 per cent. The major source of funds continued to be the TACF with 82.9 per cent, and the share of the $US55.5 million target met rose to 79.3 per cent, the highest percentage since 1989.

The adjusted programme, which includes assistance brought forward, totalled $US69,375,000. The overall implementation rate was 65.9 per cent, a significant improvement over the rate of 59.3 per cent in 1992. Total new obligations climbed to over $US45.7 million, an increase of more than $10 million over the previous year.

During 1993, there were 1,373 operational projects. This total comprised 860 projects continued from 1992, plus 412 new approved core projects for the start of the biennial cycle and 44 training courses, 11 Reserve Fund projects and three UNDP projects.

The area activity which received the largest share of disbursement in 1993 was food and agriculture, at 20.2 per cent. This was followed by safety-related activities, comprising radioactive waste management, radiation protection, and the safety of nuclear installations, which received 19.7 per cent. Physical and chemical sciences accounted for 18.1 per cent of the total. Other significant programmes included industry and earth sciences with 14.5 per cent and human health with 14.4 per cent.

## Publications and databases
IAEA publishes books, reports, proceedings, safety manuals, statistics, etc. Regular publications are:
• *IAEA Bulletin* (quarterly);
• *IAEA Newsbriefs* (bi-monthly);
• *IAEA Yearbook*;
• *International Nuclear Information System (INIS) Atomindex*;
• *Nuclear Fusion* (monthly);
• *Meetings on Atomic Energy* (quarterly).

Regular IAEA on-line databases are:
• *International Nuclear Information System (INIS)*;
• *Power Reactor Information System*

# International Council for the Exploration of the Sea (ICES)

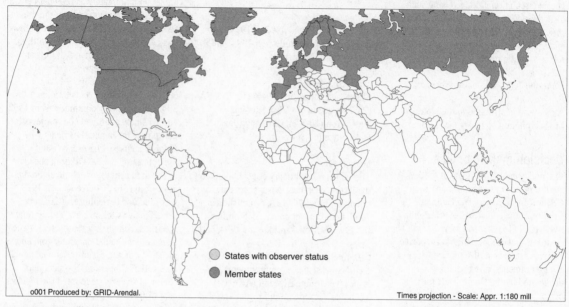

States with observer status

Member states

o001 Produced by: GRID-Arendal.

Times projection - Scale: Appr. 1:180 mill

## Objectives

• to promote and encourage research and investigations for the study of the marine environment and its living resources in the North Atlantic and adjacent seas;
• to publish or otherwise disseminate the results of this research, including the provision of scientific information and advice to national governments, regional fishery management, and pollution control commissions.

## Organization

*Type*
Intergovernmental organization (IGO).

*Membership*
Open to any state upon approval by three-quarters of its member states. Not open to regional integration organizations. 19 member states, by 6 October 1994. The European Commission and 28 intergovernmental organizations have observer status.

*Founded*
22 July 1902.

## Secretariat

International Council for the Exploration of the Sea (ICES), Palægade 2–4, DK-1261 Copenhagen K, Denmark

*Telephone*:     +45-33-154225
*Telefax*:     +45-33-934215
*E-mail*: ocean@server.ices.inst.dk
     ices.dk (Omnet)

*General Secretary*
Dr Christopher C. E. Hopkins.

*Number of staff*
10 professionals and 22 support staff (Oct. 1994).

## Activities

The work of the ICES concentrates on basic research co-ordinated by 12 standing committees. While the ICES itself is not a regulatory body, its Advisory Committee on Fishery Management (ACFM) and Advisory Committee on the Marine Environment (ACME) provide scientific information and advice, including recommendations for management measures, to several other international agreements and bodies in this field, and to its own member country governments. Further work is co-ordinated by standing area and subject committees including: Fish Capture, Hydrography, Statistics, Mariculture, Marine Environmental Quality, Biological Oceanography, Demersal Fish, Pelagic Fish, Baltic Fish, Shellfish, Anadromous and Catadromous Fish, and Marine Mammals. The work is conducted by approximately 90 working

groups and study groups.
The ICES co-ordinates international studies and co-operative monitoring of fisheries, oceanography, and marine pollution, including possible quantification of observed effects on living organisms. The Secretariat operates extensive data banks covering these fields.

## Decision-making bodies

The *ICES Council*, composed of two delegates appointed by each member Government, elects the *Bureau*. The Council holds statutory meetings, termed the Annual Science Conference.

## Finance

Contributions from the member country governments and from organizations.

*Budget*
The administrative budget for the biennium 1994–95 is DKr18.1 million.

## Publications

*ICES Annual Report*, *ICES Journal of Marine Science* (quarterly), *ICES/CIEM Information* (twice a year), *ICES Co-operative Research Reports* (approximately eight issues a year), and *ICES Techniques in Marine Environmental Sciences* (approximately four issues a year).

# International Fund for Agricultural Development (IFAD)

## Objectives
- to mobilize additional resources to be made available on concessional terms for agricultural development in member States;
- to focus attention on the needs of the poorest rural communities, in particular small farmers, the landless, fishermen, livestock herders, and impoverished rural women;
- to pay special attention to grass-roots development and innovative approaches which build on local participation and the preservation of the natural resource base;
- to provide financing primarily for projects and programmes specifically designed to introduce, expand, or improve food production systems and to strengthen related policies and institutions within the framework of national priorities and strategies, taking into consideration: the need to increase food production in the poorest food-deficient countries, the potential for increasing food production in other developing countries, and the importance of improving the nutritional level and living conditions of the poorest populations in developing countries.

## Organization
*Type*
Intergovernmental organization (IGO). International financing institution which is a specialized agency of the United Nations.

*Membership*
States. The Fund was established as a partnership of industrialized countries, oil producing and exporting countries, and other developing countries which joined together to raise funds and share in the governance arrangements. The Agreement Establishing IFAD organized membership into three categories in order to reflect this special character of the institution. That original Agreement is now being revised. Under the proposed Revised Agreement, while the historical partnership continues, membership will no longer be codified into rigid formal categories, but will reflect the need for flexibility. However, the membership continues to work through groupings of like-minded countries for decisions on policy and operational matters, for the purpose of consultation over financial affairs including fund raising, and for other reasons related to the governance of the inter-relationships that are a special feature of the joint character of IFAD. The formation of such groups will be negotiated and decided by the various member countries themselves.

Countries not original members of IFAD may join after approval of their membership by the Governing Council and accession to the IFAD agreement. Not open to regional integration organizations. Total of 157 member States, by October 1994.

*Founded:* 11 December 1977.

## Secretariat
International Fund for Agricultural Development (IFAD),
Via del Serafico, 107,
I-00142 Rome,
Italy
*Telephone:*     +39-6-54591
*Telefax:*     +39-6-5043463
*E-mail:* un.ifad@agora.stm.it

*President and Chairman of the Executive Board*
Mr Fawzi Hamad Al-Sultan.
(1993–96)

*Number of staff*
107 professionals and 154 general service staff (Dec. 1993). The Fund has no field, regional, or country offices.

## Activities

IFAD projects range from provision of farming inputs and services (seed, fertilizer, tools, and agricultural research and extension) to irrigation, storage facilities, access roads, and credit to poor farmers and workers who would have no other source of loans.

IFAD lends money, most of which is on highly concessional or low interest terms, and is concerned not only with raising agricultureal production but also with improving local prospects for employment, nutrition, and income distribution.

By the end of 1993, IFAD had supported 370 poverty alleviation projects in 102 developing countries, helping about 130–140 million rural people to increase their productivity and raise their income. The total investment cost of these projects is about $US14 billion, of which IFAD itself has provided about $US3.4 billion. The balance has come from other external donors, host governments, and the beneficiaries themselves.

*Environmental activities*
As the first international financial institution to respond to the socio-economic crisis in Sub-Saharan Africa, IFAD launched the Special Programme for sub-Saharan Africa (SPA) in January 1986, with a target for resource mobilization of $US300 million for the first phase (SPA I) of the programme. The resources contributed exceeded the Programme's original target and amounted to $US322.8 million.

The objectives of SPA I were to help restore the productive capacity of small farmers, promote traditional food crops grown mainly by smallholders, and initiate small-scale water control schemes as well as measures for environmental protection and policy assistance for governments. By the end of 1992 IFAD had fully exhausted all resources of SPA I in supporting 32 projects in 22 sub-Saharan African countries.

The second phase of the Programme (SPA II), which became effective in January 1993, preserves the focus of the first phase, while extending its conceptual frame and operational scope. Specifically it carries environmental and soil conservation objectives from on-farm to off-farm (particularly in the common property resource domain); and addresses overall coping strategies for households and communities through economic diversification. The list of countries eligible for assistance grew from 22 under SPA I to 27 under SPA II including Benin, Burundi, Central African Republic, Comoros, Equatorial Guinea, Madagascar, Malawi, Rwanda, and Sierra Leone. By 31 May 1993 the resources received by Phase 2 amounted to $US95 million.

The Fund started in 1990 to elaborate environmental principles and criteria into operational guide-lines for application in the project work. To this effect a preliminary development and testing phase of 'natural resources for rural poverty alleviation' consisting of pro-active environment assessment, natural reserve management studies, and environment related preassessment activities was initiated for the period 1992–93. The lessons emerging from this preliminary phase is guiding IFAD in developing environmentally sustainable rural poverty alleviation projects and results will be shared with the development community at large.

## Decision-making bodies

The highest directing body of IFAD is the *Governing Council*, where all the member States are represented by a Governor or an Alternate Governor. The Council meets annually and elects the President of the Fund by a two-third majority for a four-year term.

Current operations are supervised by an *Executive Board* composed of 18 members. The Board is elected by the Council for a three-year period. In addition to the conduct and general operation of IFAD, it approves loans and grants for projects and holds three regular sessions a year. Developing countries hold the majority of the votes and therefore have a major influence on the investment strategies of the Fund; while permitting the main donors to maintain close control on the use of resources in order to ensure cost effectiveness and higher output from IFAD operations.

The Secretariat is headed by the President of IFAD and is responsible for the management of the Fund. It has three main administrative departments:

• Economic Policy and Resource Strategy Department;
• Programme Management Department, with five Regional Divisions, as well as a Technical Advisory Division;
• Management and Personnel Services Department, including Office of the Secretary, Personnel Division, Management of Information Services, and an Administrative Services Unit.

Other units are: Offices of Evaluation and Studies, Internal Audit, Legal Services, and the Office of the Controller and Treasury.

## Finance

The Fund is financed by contributions from its member States. Its initial resources, in 1977, amounted to $US1,021 million. The First Replenishment (effective on 18 June 1982) amounted to $US1,102 million. The Second Replenishment (effective on 27 Nov. 1986) amounted to $US488 million. The Third Replenishment (effective on 24 Dec. 1990) amounted to $US567 million.

The Fund is currently discussing with donors a Fourth Replenishment. It is anticipated that this will become effective early in 1995 at a level higher than that of the Third Replenishment.

*Budget*
The administrative budget was $US53,822,000 in 1992, $US54.9 million in 1993, including a contingency of $US650,000, and $US50.9 million in 1994, including a contingency of $US350,000.

## Publications

• *Annual Reports*;
• *Reports of the Sessions of Governing Council* (annual);
• *IFAD Update Bulletin* (quarterly);
• IFAD Operations by country (IFAD in India, Indonesia, the Philippines, Uganda, Argentina, Chile, Venezuela, Tanzania, Zimbabwe, and Kenya);
• *The State of World Rural Poverty* (series);
• *Meeting the Challenge of Hunger and Poverty*;
• *Providing Food Security for All*.

# International Labour Organization (ILO)

## Objectives

To establish social justice as the foundation for universal and lasting peace, by unifying governments, employers, and workers in common action to promote human rights, generate employment, and improve living and working conditions.

## Organization

*Type*
Intergovernmental organization (IGO). A specialized agency within the United Nations system.

*Membership*
Open to members of the United Nations. Non-members of the United Nations must be approved by the General Conference by a two-thirds majority. Not open to regional integration organizations. 171 members, by 7 November 1994.

*Founded*
11 April 1919.

## Secretariat

International Labour Office,
4 route des Morillons,
CH-1211 Geneva,
Switzerland
*Telephone*: +41-22-7996111
*Telefax*: +41-22-7988685

*Director General*
Dr Michel Hansenne.

*Director of Public Information*
Mr Miguel Schapira.

*Number of staff*
687 professionals and 833 support staff (Nov. 1994).

## Activities

One of the oldest and most important functions of the ILO is the adoption, by the tripartite International Labour Conference, of conventions and recommendations which set international labour standards. The ILO has adopted 174 conventions and 181 recommendations, forming an international labour code as a guide-line for national law and practice in all spheres of labour activities. Through ratification by member States, conventions create binding obligations to put their provisions into effect. More than 5,700 ratifications have been registered. Recommendations provide guidance on policy, legislation, and practice.

International technical co-operation is carried out in the major fields of standards, employment, training, working conditions, labour administration and labour relations, enterprise development, and social security.

*Main conventions on environment under the auspices of ILO*
• *Convention No. 115 Concerning the Protection of Workers Against Ionizing Radiations, 1960;*
• *Convention No. 136 Concerning Protection Against Hazards of Poisoning Arising from Benzene, 1971;*
• *Convention No. 139 Concerning Prevention and Control of Occupational Hazards Caused by Carcinogenic Substances and Agents, 1974;*
• *Convention No. 148 Concerning the Protection of Workers Against Occupational Hazards in the Working Environment Due to Air Pollution, Noise, and Vibration, 1977;*
• *Convention No. 155 Concerning Occupational Safety and Health and the Working Environment, 1981;*
• *Convention No. 162 Concerning Safety in the Use of Asbestos, Geneva, 1986;*
• *Convention No. 170 on Safety in the Use of Chemicals at Work, 1990;*
• *Convention No. 174 Concerning the Prevention of Major Industrial Accidents, 1993.*

*Environmental activities*
In the area of the environment, the ILO's actions have been extended beyond the traditional emphasis on occupational safety and health and the working environment to include: strengthening the role of trade unions and employers' organizations in securing sustainable development; environment and development training; employment, poverty, and development issues; and environmental concerns related to women, and indigenous and tribal peoples.

## Decision-making bodies

The *International Labour Conference*, which meets annually, is composed of national delegations comprising two government delegates, one delegate representing employers and one representing workers. The *Governing Body*, composed of 56 members, supervises the work of the ILO. The *International Labour Office* acts as secretariat to the Organization.

## Finance

Apportioned among member governments according to a scale of contributions approved by the Conference.

*Budget*
The administrative budget was $US405.7 million for the biennium 1992–93 and is $US466.5 million for 1994–95.

## Publications

• *World of Work Magazine* (five times a year);
• *International Labour Review* (six times a year);
• *Yearbook of Labour Statistics*;
• *Conditions of Work Digest*;
• *World Labour Report*.

# International Maritime Organization (IMO)

## Objectives

• to provide machinery for co-operation among governments on technical matters affecting international merchant shipping, with special responsibility for safety at sea;
• to ensure that the highest possible standards of safety at sea and of efficient navigation are achieved;
• to prevent pollution of the sea caused by ships and other craft operating in the marine environment;
• to encourage removal of hindrances to international shipping services;
• to be responsible for convening international maritime conferences and drafting international maritime conventions.

## Organization

*Type*
Intergovernmental organization (IGO), specialized agency of the UN within the UN system, linked to ECOSOC.

*Membership*
Governments of 149 states, by 30 September 1994. Not open to regional integration organizations.

Consultative status with 36 intergovernmental organizations (Sept. 1994). 55 non-governmental organizations enjoy consultative status with IMO (Sept. 1994).

*Founded*
6 March 1948, Geneva.
The original name was Inter-Governmental Maritime Consultative Organization (IMCO). This was changed to International Maritime Organization (IMO) on 22 May 1982.

## Secretariat

International Maritime Organization (IMO),
4 Albert Embankment,
London SE1 7SR,
United Kingdom
*Telephone*:        +44-71-7357611
*Telefax*:        +44-71-5873210

*Secretary-General*
Mr William A. O'Neil (Canada).
(1 Jan. 1994–31 Dec. 1998)

*Head, Information Office*
Mr Roger Kohn.

*Number of staff*
115 professionals and 184 support staff (Oct. 1994).

## Activities

IMO has drawn up and promoted the adoption of 35 Conventions and Protocols, nearly all of which are now in force. Conventions and Protocols are binding legal instruments and, upon entry into force, their requirements must be implemented by all States Parties.

*Main conventions on environment under the auspices of IMO* (see Agreements)
• *Convention on the Prevention of Marine Pollution by Dumping of Wastes and Other Matter (London Convention 1972), London, 1972;*
• *International Convention for the Prevention of Pollution from Ships, 1973, as modified by the Protocol of 1978 relating thereto (MARPOL 73/78), London, 1973 and 1978;*
• *International Convention on Civil Liability for Oil Pollution Damage (CLC), Brussels, 1969, 1976, and 1984;*
• *International Convention on the Establishment of an International Fund for Compensation for Oil Pollution Damage (Fund Convention), Brussels, 1971;*
• *International Convention Relating to*

*Intervention on the High Seas in Cases of Oil Pollution Casualties (Intervention Convention), Brussels, 1969;*
• *International Convention on Oil Pollution Preparedness, Response, and Co-operation (OPRC), London, 1990.* Enters into force on 13 May 1995.

In addition IMO also adopts numerous non-treaty instruments such as codes of practice and recommendations which, although not mandatory, provide a basis for legislation in member States. This helps prevent unilateral, unco-ordinated, and possibly conflicting standards.

An important function of IMO is to facilitate technical co-operation within the scope of the Organization. For this purpose, IMO provides advice and assistance to developing countries in the technical, legal, and administrative fields. Its Technical Co-operation Programme assigns very high priority to maritime training at all levels. It provides opportunities for training in national and regional maritime training institutions and for specialized training for senior maritime personnel at the World Maritime University established by IMO in Malmö, Sweden. Branches of the World Maritime University have been established in countries throughout the world and these also provide training in specialized areas.

## Decision-making bodies

*Political bodies*
The *IMO Assembly* is the supreme governing body and meets biennially. It is open to all member States as well as representatives of the intergovernmental and non-governmental organizations in consultative status with IMO. One of the Assembly's most important tasks is to adopt the numerous resolutions and recommendations that have been prepared during the previous two years by subsidiary bodies.

It also elects the members of the *IMO*

*Council* for the next biennium. The Council is IMO's only elective body and consists of 32 member States who are chosen by a system designed to give appropriate representation to large shipowning and trading nations while also ensuring that smaller nations and all geographical areas of the world are represented.

The Council normally meets twice a year and acts as the governing body of IMO between sessions of the Assembly. It is also responsible for preparing for the Assembly's consideration the budget and work programme that it is to handle.

*Technical/Scientific bodies*
There are four main committees consisting of all member States:
• The *Maritime Safety Committee (MSC)*, the highest technical body for the Organization, was set up in 1973. It has 11 subcommittees dealing with different aspects of safety such as the carriage of dangerous goods, fire protection, training, etc. All members of IMO are entitled to take part, together with representatives of non-IMO states which are parties to treaties in respect of which the Committee exercises functions;
• The *Legal Committee* was set up after the *Torrey Canyon* disaster in 1967. Its functions are to consider any legal matters falling within the scope of IMO;
• The *Marine Environment Protection Committee (MEPC)*, set up in 1973, is responsible for co-ordinating and administering the activities of the organization concerning the prevention and control of pollution;

• *The Technical Co-operation Committee*, first set up in 1972, has the main functions of establishing directives and guide-lines for the execution of IMO's comprehensive programme of assistance to developing countries in maritime transport, of monitoring the programme's progressive development, and of reviewing its results. It acts to help governments implement IMO Conventions and other instruments through various forms of assistance;
• The *Facilitation Committee*, a subsidiary body of the IMO Council, has the main function of directing IMO efforts to reduce unnecessary formalities and obstructions to allied trade.

Most of the draft resolutions submitted to the Assembly for consideration have been prepared by the Maritime Safety Committee (MSC) and the Marine Environment Protection Committee (MEPC).

## Finance
Contributions to the IMO budget are based on a formula which is different from that used in other United Nations agencies. The amount paid by each member State depends primarily on the gross tonnage of its merchant fleet.

*Budget*
Total approved budget by appropriation for the biennium 1992–93 was £30,735,700, (£14,971,200 for 1992 and £15,764,500 for 1993) and the budget for the biennium 1994–95 amounts to £34,328,800 (£16,724,200 for 1994 and £17,604,600 for 1995). Assessments on member States amounted to £14,729,200 in 1992, £15,522,500 in 1993, and £16,482,200 in 1994.

The actual administrative costs at Headquarters were £14,747,725 in 1992 and £15,648,242 in 1993.

*Main contributors*
The top ten contributors for 1993 were Liberia, Panama, Japan, USA, Greece, Norway, Cyprus, Bahamas, Russian Federation, and China, and for 1994, Panama, Liberia, Japan, Greece, USA, Cyprus, Norway, Bahamas, Russian Federation, and China.

*Special funds*
Financial support for IMO projects is provided in various ways. IMO's Technical Co-operation Programme, with a total budget of $US13,370 million in 1994, is not funded from IMO's own resources, but mainly from United Nations Development Programme (UNDP) (see this section). The Programme was introduced over 25 years ago, with the main goal of bridging the gap between the developed and the developing maritime nations in matters concerning sea transport and related activities. Prominent among the aims of the Programme are improving safety at sea, reducing marine pollution, and mitigation of pollution effects. Various agencies like UNDP, United Nations Environment Programme (UNEP) (see this section), and governments make funds available on an *ad hoc* basis, contributing directly to environment/development-motivated projects within the framework provided by the Marine Environment Protection Committee.

## Publications
IMO publishes books, reports proceedings, conventions, pamphlets, codes, etc. A catalogue is available from the Secretariat.

*IMO News*, the magazine of IMO, is published quarterly.

# International Monetary Fund (IMF)

## Objectives

• to promote international monetary co-operation through a permanent institution which provides the machinery for consultation and collaboration on international monetary problems;
• to facilitate the expansion and balanced growth of international trade;
• to promote exchange stability and maintain orderly exchange agreements among Members and avoid competitive exchange depreciation.

## Organization

*Type*
Intergovernmental organization (IGO). An agreement of relationship concluded with the UN outlines a programme of mutual assistance between the UN and the Fund, as an independent international organization and a UN specialized agency. The IMF co-operates particularly with UNCTAD, GATT, and the World Bank (IBRD) (see this section).

*Membership*
Open to all countries. Not open to regional integration organizations. Ratification of the articles and acceptance of conditions laid down by the Fund are conditions of membership. Total of 179 members, by 1 October 1994. Membership resolutions for two other countries are pending.

*Founded*
27 December 1945.

## Secretariat

International Monetary Fund (IMF),
700 19th Street,
Washington, DC 20431,
USA
*Telephone*:     +1-202-6237000
*Telefax*:     +1-202-6234661

*Managing Director*
Mr Michel Camdessus.

*Director of External Relations*
Shailendra J. Anjaria.

*Number of staff*
1,532 professionals and 799 support staff (Oct. 1994).

## Activities

The Fund operates special facilities, including a Compensatory and Contingency Financing Facility, which makes additional resources available to compensate for unexpected temporary shortfalls in export earnings for commodities, and for certain contingencies, such as sudden increases in interest rates; a Structural Adjustment Facility, and, since 1987, an Enhanced Structural Adjustment Facility (ESAF), which provide concessional loans to low-income developing Members that qualify for assistance in order to support programmes to strengthen substantially and in a sustainable manner their balance-of-payments position and to foster growth, and, since April 1993, a systematic transformation facility to assist members facing balance of payments difficulties arising from severe disruptions in their trade and payments arrangements attributable to a shift to market-based trade.

*Environmental activities*
The Fund addresses environmental issues in a manner consistent with its specialized mandate to promote international monetary co-operation and stability. Fund staff seek to develop greater understanding of the interplay between economic policies, economic activity, and environmental change, drawing upon the expertise of other institutions with environmental competence and responsibilities. This work enables Fund staff to conduct better-informed discussions with national authorities who face macro-economic policy choices entailing major environmental implications.

## Decision-making bodies

The IMF operates through a Board of Governors, a Board of Executive Directors, an Interim Committee on the International Monetary System, and a Managing Director and staff. The *Board of Governors* consists of one Governor and one deputy appointed by each Member Country—typically the minister of finance or governor of a central bank. An annual meeting of the Board in conjunction with

that of the World Bank Group is held each autumn. All powers of the Fund are vested in the Board. The *Executive Board* is responsible for the daily business of the Fund. It consists of the Managing Director as Chair and 24 executive directors, who are appointed or elected by individual member countries or by groups of countries. Each Member has an assessed quota, which is subscribed and determines voting power. On 30 April 1994 the United States, as the largest contributor, had 18% of the voting power, while the smallest contributors held considerably less than 1% each. Access to use of the Fund's resources is also determined in relation to quota, taking account of the balance-of-payments needs of the Member and the strength of the policies it agrees to implement to restore balance-of-payments viability. France, Japan, Germany, the UK, and the United States have the largest quotas. The total of Members' quotas by 30 April 1994 was about $US211 billion.

## Finance

The general resources of the Fund have been supplemented by borrowing from Member Countries in strong payments positions. These borrowed resources are made available to member countries under a variety of facilities and policies.

*Use of Fund resources*
The total of stand-by and extended arrangements in effect by 30 September 1994 was about $US18.5 billion, of which about $US6.4 billion was undrawn. The total amount of Fund credit and loans outstanding under all its facilities by 30 September 1994, was about $US43.6 billion, of which about $US37.2 billion comprised general resources.

## Publications

• Annual Reports;
• *IMF Survey* (23 times a year);
• *Finance and Development* (quarterly);
• *World Economic Outlook* (twice a year);
• *World Economic and Financial Surveys* series;
• Staff Papers;
• Economic Reviews series.

# OECD, Environment Policy Committee (EPOC)

## Objectives

• to provide a forum for Member countries to share views on, and consider policy responses to, major environmental issues and threats;
• to encourage co-operation among Member countries in the pursuit of shared environmental objectives, including *inter alia*, co-ordinated consultation on policies, approaches, and major actions taken or proposed; data sharing; and joint research and analysis;
• to promote, in support of sustainable development, the integration of environmental and economic policies, technological innovation and diffusion, and protection of unique environmental values and natural ecosystems;
• to assess on a systematic basis the environmental performance of Member countries in relation to their national and international policies and commitments;
• to develop and promulgate environmental indicators, and standardized, comparable sets of data and statistics, as a basis for identifying environmental trends, progress, and deficiencies in individual Member countries and the OECD as a whole;
• to promote the sharing with non-Member countries of the environmental management expertise, information, and experience which reside in Member countries and the OECD;
• to ensure that the views and expertise of private-sector institutions are drawn

upon in the conduct of OECD's environmental work, utilizing the Business and Industry Advisory Committee to the OECD (BIAC) and the Trade Union Advisory Committee to the OECD (TUAC).

## Organization

*Type*
Intergovernmental organization (IGO).

*Membership*
Open to States and regional integration organizations. 25 member States and the Commission of the European Communities with full membership, by 31 October 1994. 5 states, UNEP (see IGOs), Council of Europe, and UN Economic Commission for Europe (UN/ECE) with observer status.

*Founded*
• OEEC: 1948, OECD: 1960.
• OECD Environment Committee: 1970, replaced by Environment Policy Committee (EPOC): 1992.

## Secretariat

OECD, Environment Policy Committee (EPOC),
2 Rue André Pascal,
F-75016 Paris,
France
*Telephone:*    +33-1-4524-8200/7039
*Telefax:*    +33-1-45247876

*Secretary General (OECD)*
To be designated.

*Director for the Environment*
Mr Bill Long.

*Executive Secretary, EPOC*
Ms Françoise Feypell.

*Number of staff*
80, including professional and support staff (Nov. 1994).

## Activities

OECD is developing a 'second generation' of environmental information for policy-makers and the public, including improved statistics and indicators on environmental conditions and trends.

It promotes a three-part strategy for integrating economic and environmental decision-making, improving environmental performance at home within the OECD region, and strengthening international co-operation.

It recommends an expanded and more consistent use of market mechanisms to achieve environmental quality objectives in OECD countries and a strengthening of international co-operation and monitoring in the use of these economic instruments.

It promotes co-operation in controlling chemicals on the commercial market

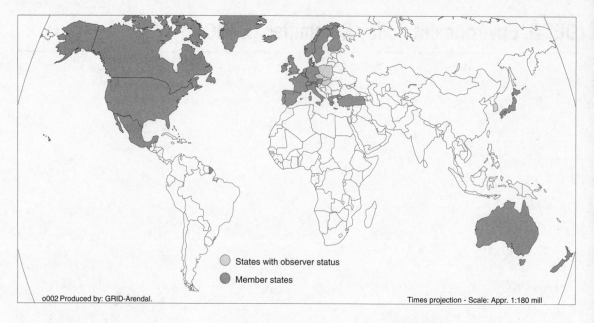

States with observer status

Member states

('Chemicals Programme').

*Polluter-pays principle* and *prevention is better than cure* are two main concepts in the achievement of the environmental programme.

The main pillars of the environmental programme are economics of sustainable development, energy and environment, environmental health and safety, and co-operation with non-OECD countries.

## Decision-making bodies

The supreme body of the OECD is its *Council*, composed of one representative from each Member country. The Council meets either at permanent representative level (about once a fortnight) under the chairmanship of the *Secretary-General*, or at ministerial level (usually once a year) under the chairmanship of a minister elected annually. Decisions and recommendations are adopted by mutual agreement of all members of the Council. The Council is assisted by an *Executive Committee* composed of 14 members of the Council designated annually by the latter. The major part of the OECD's work is, however, prepared and carried out by numerous specialized committees and working parties. The Environmental Policy Committee which is composed of high-level government officials, is serviced by the Environment Directorate. The Environment Directorate works closely with many other bodies, particularly those of the UN and the European Community—as well as other sectoral Directorates in OECD.

## Finance

The OECD is funded by contributions from its Member countries.

*Budget*
Confidential.

*Special funds*
Grants from the Member countries to promote specific projects.

## Publications

*State of the Environment* (every 3 years).
  Other relevant publications from OECD:
• *Directory of Non-governmental Environment and Development Organizations in OECD Member Countries*;
• *Main Economic Indicators* (monthly);
• *OECD Observer* (every 2 months);
• *OECD Economic Outlook* (twice a year).

# United Nations Children's Fund (UNICEF)

## Objectives

• to safeguard the rights of children to survival and protection in environments that are supportive of sound and healthy development;
• to promote the well-being of children throughout their formative years everywhere, particularly those in developing countries who are in the greatest need;
• to promote the implementation of the basic rights of children embodied in the Convention on the Rights of the Child, and to attain the goals set by the 1990 World Summit for Children, and the Rio Declaration and *Agenda 21* adopted by the 1992 United Nations Conference on Environment and Development (UNCED).

Major summit goals for the year 2000 are:
• A reduction of the infant and under-five child mortality rates by one third or to 50 per 1,000 live births respectively, whichever is less; a reduction of maternal mortality rates by half; a reduction of severe and moderate malnutrition among children under-five by half;
• Universal access to safe drinking-water and to sanitary means of excreta disposal;
• Universal access to basic education and completion of primary education by at least 80 per cent of primary-school-age children;

• A reduction of the adult illiteracy rate to at least half its 1990 level, with emphasis on female literacy;
• Improved protection for children in especially difficult circumstances.

Ten specific goals and three partial targets have been selected for accelerated achievement by the end of 1995.

## Organization

*Type*
Intergovernmental organization (IGO), an integral part of the United Nations system. Its work is reviewed annually by its Executive Board, UN Economic and Social Council (ECOSOC), and the UN General Assembly.

*Membership*
UNICEF has no formal membership, but countries, including non-members of the United Nations, participate in and contribute financially to its work. An Executive Board, consisting of 36 member states from all regions of the world, is elected by ECOSOC for a three-year term.

*Founded*
11 December 1946.

## Secretariat

United Nations Children's Fund (UNICEF),
UNICEF House,
3 United Nations Plaza,
New York, NY 10017,
USA
*Telephone*:      +1-212-3267000
*Telefax*:      +1-212-8887465
*Telex*:      760-7848
*E-mail*:      UNC007

*Executive Director*
Mr James P. Grant.

*Director of Division of Information*
Ms Mehr Khan.

*Number of staff*
1,398 international professionals, 975 national professionals, and 4,906 general service officers, serving in 235 locations world-wide (July 1994). 344 professionals and 453 general service staff at Headquarters. 1,098 professionals and 4,453 general service staff in field, regional, and country offices.

## Activities

Through its extensive field network in developing countries and within national development objectives, UNICEF carries out with governments, local communities, and other partners programmes in health, nutrition, education, water and sanitation, the environment, women in development, and other fields of importance to children.

UNICEF sets its priorities for children according to their vulnerability. Almost all its resources are therefore invested in the poorest developing countries, with the greatest share going to children in the high-risk early years, up to age five.

In emergency relief and rehabilitation, UNICEF works closely with United Nations Department of Humanitarian Affairs (DHA) and other UN agencies and many non-governmental organizations (NGOs). In 1993 it provided $US223 million worth of emergency assistance to 64 countries in Africa, Asia, Latin America, the Middle East, and central and eastern Europe, including Afghanistan, Angola, Ethiopia, Iraq, Kenya, Liberia, Mozambique, Somalia, the Sudan, and the former Yugoslavia. In 1994, UNICEF continued to help these countries and also responded to new emergency situations in Rwanda, a country which was given highest priority, and Burundi.

*Environmental activities*
UNICEF participated actively in UNCED and made successful efforts to include children's needs and interests in *Agenda 21* and is supporting countries to implement it. At the International Conference on Population and Development (ICPD) held in Cairo in September 1994, UNICEF underlined the linkage between poverty, population growth, and environmental deterioration and the need to resolve these problems to improve the situation of children.

UNICEF programmes have long supported community-based measures to improve the environment as part of the overall effort to promote the well-being of children and women. A broader approach is also being taken through advocacy and initiatives at national and international levels.

At the community level, there are several UNICEF-supported activities which help to improve the environment and alleviate the impact of environmental degradation and poverty. Factors that contribute to a healthy environment, such as clean water, adequate sanitation, health and hygiene education, are all part of programmes to combat diarrhoeal diseases in young children.

Household fuel problems and related issues of deforestation are addressed by promoting fuel-efficient and smoke-free stoves, solar stoves, small agroforestry projects, community wood lots, and alternative forms of energy in several countries.

Household food security poses an acute challenge in many developing countries, particularly in arid ones. In such cases, environment-friendly food production methods to ease pressure on scarce land resources are supported, including improved crop varieties, home gardening, nitrogen-fixing plants, small-scale irrigation, and appropriate technologies.

In the cities, UNICEF pays special attention to the needs of poor mothers and children through its urban basic services programmes in many countries. These involve maternal and child health services, water and sanitation, nutrition, and education.

Health, primary environmental care, and development education form a part of UNICEF-supported activities. Education about health and environmental issues is also a part of most ongoing UNICEF country programmes.

## Decision-making bodies

The *Executive Board* is the governing body of UNICEF, and at its annual meeting, establishes policies and approves programmes and expenditures.

The *Secretariat* is headed by an *Executive Director*, appointed by the United Nations Secretary-General in consultation with the Board. The Executive Director is responsible for the administration of UNICEF as well as for the appointment and direction of

UNICEF staff. Regional offices in Abidjan, Amman, Bangkok, Bogota, Kathmandu, and Nairobi provide and co-ordinate specialized support for the 82 country offices which are the key operational units for advocacy, advisory services, programming, and logistics.

Offices in New York, Geneva, Copenhagen, Tokyo, and Sydney service the Board, develop and direct policy, manage resources, and deal with donor governments, 36 National Committees for UNICEF, and non-governmental organizations (NGOs).

## Finance

UNICEF is unique among United Nations organizations in that it relies entirely upon voluntary contributions to finance its activities. Total income was $US938 million in 1992 and $US866 million in 1993. Slightly more than 30 per cent of the income in 1993 came from non-governmental sources. More than 100 governments, including those that benefit from UNICEF co-operation, provided nearly 75 per cent.

UNICEF supports programmes for children in 138 developing countries and territories. Total expenditure was $US932 million in 1992 and $US997 million in 1993.

*Budget*
Proposed administrative and programme support budget was $US391 million for 1992/93, $US445.6 million for 1993/94, and is $US431 million for 1994/95.

## Publications

- *First Call for Children* (quarterly);
- *The Progress of Nations* (annually);
- *The State of the World's Children* (annually);
- *UNICEF Facts and Figures* (annually);
- *UNICEF Annual Report*;
- *UNICEF at a Glance* (1994).

*Electronic conferences*
Telnet or Gopher to <hqfaus01.unicef.org> for the UNICEF Internet Gopher, or UNICEF under Gopher listing for UN organizations on the Internet.

# United Nations Development Programme (UNDP)

## Objectives
• to help the United Nations become a powerful and cohesive force for sustainable human development;
• to focus its own resources on a series of objectives central to sustainable human development: poverty elimination, environmental regeneration, job creation, and advancement of women;
• to strengthen international co-operation for sustainable human development and serve as a major substantive resource on how to achieve it.

## Organization
*Type*
Intergovernmental organization (IGO). An organ of the United Nations. Linked to the UN General Assembly through UN Economic and Social Council (ECOSOC).

*Membership*
Open to all members and observers of the United Nations, of its specialized agencies, and of the International Atomic Energy Agency (IAEA) (see this section). 195 member States, by 25 October 1994. In addition, many territories around the world are beneficiaries of UNDP assistance.

*Founded*
November 1965 through a merger of two predecessor programmes for United Nations technical co-operation.

## Secretariat
United Nations Development Programme (UNDP),
1 United Nations Plaza,
New York, NY 10017,
USA
*Telephone*: +1-212-9065000
*Telefax*: +1-212-9065364
*E-mail*: udp050

*Administrator*
Mr James Gustave Speth.

*Director, Division of Public Affairs*
Mr Peter Gall, Acting Director

*Number of staff*
Approximately 7,000 world-wide, over 85 per cent of whom serve in UNDP's programme country offices (Oct. 1994).

## Activities
Through a network of 132 offices world-wide, UNDP works with 174 governments to build developing-countries' capacities for sustainable human development. To execute the programmes and projects it supports, it draws upon developing-countries' national technical capacities, as well as the expertise of over 30 international and regional agencies and non-governmental organizations.

People are at the centre of all UNDP activities, which focus on six priority themes: poverty elimination and grass-roots development; environment and natural resources; management development; technical co-operation among developing countries; transfer and adaptation of technology; and women in development. Entrepreneurship is promoted as a means of creating jobs and reducing poverty. Requests for assistance in areas of good governance and human rights are increasing. Global and interregional programmes address world-wide problems, including food security and HIV/AIDS.

A UNDP *Human Development Report*, published yearly since 1990 and drafted by a team of independent consultants, assists the international community in developing new, practical, and pragmatic concepts, measures, and policy instruments for promoting more people-oriented development.

UNDP normally also plays the chief co-ordinating role for operational development activities undertaken by the whole United Nations system. This includes administering special-purpose funds such as the UN Sudano-Sahelian Office (UNSO); the UN Capital Development Fund (UNCDF); the United Nations Volunteers (UNV); and the UN Development Fund for Women (UNIFEM).

*Environmental activities*
Environment is one of the main themes for UNDP's 1992–96 programming cycle. Environmental objectives are therefore included in 87 per cent of the country programmes approved for this period and virtually all activities are screened for their environmental impact. Programmes to build capacities for sustainable development and natural resource management are supported in such sectors as food security, forestry, water and sanitation, energy, and urban development.

UNDP assisted developing-country governments and local NGOs and grassroots organizations in preparing for the 1992 United Nations Conference on Environment and Development (UNCED). As a follow-up to UNCED, it is (i) assisting the developing countries in integrating environmental concerns into development plans, and (ii) providing support in strengthening capacity for management of environment and sustainable development programmes as called for in *Agenda 21*, UNCED's blueprint for action. For this purpose UNDP launched *Capacity 21*, which became fully operational in June 1993. By 1 May 1994, Austria, Canada, Denmark, Finland, France, Germany, Italy, Japan, Norway, Sweden, and the USA had pledged a total of $US33 million and further support was expected. National Capacity 21 programmes had been initiated in 21 countries and preparatory activities were under way in several others.

UNDP promotes and supports environmental programmes in co-operation with a wide variety of partners in government, non-governmental organizations, community-based groups, UN organizations, and academic and research institutions. Global environmental programmes in which it participates include:
• The *Global Environment Facility (GEF)* (see this section), jointly managed by UNDP, the World Bank, and the United Nations Environment Programme (UNEP), which provides grants to help developing countries reduce global warming, protect international waters,

preserve biological diversity, and prevent further depletion of the ozone layer. Donor countries provided $US1.3 billion for the GEF's pilot phase, which began in 1991. Under the pilot phase UNDP developed a work programme valued at $US270 million, including 55 capacity-building projects and 19 pre-investment initiatives. UNDP also administers the GEF's $US10 million Small Grants Programme, which supports community-based NGO projects related to the GEF's global concerns. More than 125 small grants projects have been approved for funding, with many more in development or under review. UNDP will continue to be responsible for technical assistance, training, and pre-investment studies in the GEF's next stage, for which donors have agreed to $US2 billion in replenishment funding for a three-year period beginning July 1994;

• The *Multilateral Fund of the Montreal Protocol* (see Agreements). Currently UNDP is assisting 29 developing countries in the planning, preparation, and implementation of country programmes, projects, and sectoral activities to replace and phase out chlorofluorocarbons (CFCs), halons, and other ozone-depleting substances. Project funding of $US38.3 million was approved during the period 1991 to 1994, and it is expected that additional 1994 approvals could increase this amount to $US60 million. Nine Montreal Protocol country programmes have been approved and five technology transfer investment projects have been completed, phasing out 372 tonnes of CFCs;

• The *UN Sudano-Sahelian Office (UNSO)* is UNDP's focal point on drought and desertification. It has provided substantive support to the preparatory process for the Global Convention on Desertification (see Agreements), promoting regional and subregional consultations and giving technical support to the preparation of Africa's contribution to the Convention;

• UNDP's *Sustainable Development Networking Programme* makes relevant country-specific information on sustainable development readily available to a wide range of development partners, including decision-makers responsible for planning and implementing sustainable-development strategies and community-based organizations. It is currently

implemented in eight countries and is expected to begin in another 12 during 1994;

• *Environmental management guidelines* and a companion *training programme* developed by UNDP facilitate a consistent approach to the environmental aspects of all projects and programmes which receive support. By the end of 1993 a total of 80 workshops had been held, providing training for approximately 2,200 individuals, including representatives of governments, UN agencies, NGOs, the private sector, the media, and academia. Extension of this training to UNDP's some 50 other country offices is a priority;

• Forty-one new national UNDP *posts for sustainable development officers* were established in early 1994. The new national staff members will serve as advisors to UNDP Resident Representatives and other development professionals in their respective countries of service, advocate the integration of environmental considerations into UNDP-supported activities, and promote and support specific initiatives such as Capacity 21 and the GEF.

## Decision-making bodies

The UNDP is headed by an *Administrator*, who is responsible to a 36-nation *Executive Board*, representing all major regions and both donor and recipient countries. The Board, in turn, reports to the UN General Assembly through the Economic and Social Council (ECOSOC). In addition to setting policy guide-lines, the Board approves the volume of assistance allocated to each country, as well as all three-to-five-year country programmes.

## Finance

The UNDP is financed by yearly voluntary contributions from member States of the UN or its related agencies. Country contributions to UNDP totalled $US923.4 million in 1993 and $US928.2 million in 1994. Contributions to UNDP-Administered Funds (see below) and co-financing arrangements raised the total income to $US1.6 billion.

*Budget*
Expenditures were approximately $US1.4 billion in 1993 and approximately $US1.5 billion in 1994.

*Main contributors*
For 1994 the USA was the largest donor to UNDP ($US125.5 million, provisional), followed by Japan ($US100.1 million), Denmark ($US90.1 million), the Netherlands ($US87.8 million), Germany ($US82.1 million), Sweden ($US75.5 million), and Norway ($US69.5 million).

*Main recipients*
58 per cent of UNDP's total resources are allocated for the countries designated as 'least-developed' by UN General Assembly. 87 per cent of UNDP's country-programme funds go to countries with annual per capita GNPs of $US750 or less. For the 1992–96 period, allocations planned for the largest UNDP recipients are as follows: China ($US123.7 million), Bangladesh ($US114.2 million), India ($US109.3 million), Nigeria ($US84.0 million), Ethiopia ($US82.5 million), and Vietnam ($US70.4 million).

*Associated Funds*
The UNDP manages several associated funds, which received an estimated $US48 million in voluntary contributions in 1994. Among them are the United Nations Capital Development Fund (UNCDF), the United Nations Volunteers (UNV), and the United Nations Development Fund for Women (UNIFEM). UNDP also provides management support services for bilateral projects and programmes financed through multilateral financing institutions.

## Publications

• *Choices* (quarterly magazine covering development issues);
• *Update* (newsletter, every two weeks);
• *Annual Report*.

*Electronic conferences*
UNDP publications, documents, and speeches and statements by the Administrator are available on the Internet. The path is: *gopher.undp.org*

# United Nations Educational, Scientific, and Cultural Organization (UNESCO)

## Objectives

• to contribute to peace and security in the world by promoting collaboration among nations through education, science, culture, and communication in order to further universal respect for justice, for the rule of law, and for the human rights and fundamental freedoms which are affirmed for the peoples of the world, without distinction of race, sex, language, or religion by the Charter of the United Nations.

• in support of these objectives, UNESCO's principal functions are: to collaborate in the work of advancing mutual knowledge and understanding among people through all means of mass communications; to help provide basic education for all and the spread of culture; to maintain, increase, and diffuse knowledge; to encourage the teaching and understanding of science.

## Organization

*Type*
Intergovernmental organization (IGO). A specialized agency of the United Nations.

*Membership*
Member States of the United Nations. Non-members of the United Nations may be admitted as members by a two-thirds vote in the General Conference. Not open for regional integration organizations. 182 member States and three associate members, by 31 October 1994.

*Founded*
4 November 1946.

## Secretariat

United Nations Educational, Scientific, and Cultural Organization (UNESCO),
7 place de Fontenoy,
F-75352 Paris 07 SP,
France
*Telephone*:       +33-1-45681000
*Telefax*:       +33-1-45671690

*Director-General*
Dr Federico Mayor Zaragoza.

*Director, Office of Public Information*
Ms H.-M. Gosselin.

*Number of staff*
716 professionals and 1,372 support staff

at Headquarters (Oct. 1994). 297 professionals and 335 support staff in the field.

## Activities

UNESCO conducts expert studies, promotes the free flow of ideas by word and other forms of communication, encourages the exchange of persons and of information, and the conservation and protection of books, and collaborates with Member States in developing educational, scientific, and cultural programmes.

*Main conventions on environment under the auspices of UNESCO*
• *Convention Concerning the Protection of the World Cultural and Natural Heritage (World Heritage Convention), Paris, 1972* (see Agreements);
• *Convention on Wetlands of International Importance especially as Waterfowl Habitat (Ramsar Convention), Ramsar, 1971* (see Agreements).

*Environmental activities*
UNESCO's role in the field of environment is to: improve understanding of the natural and human environment and of complex environment and development issues; contribute to problem-solving by providing policy-relevant information to decision-makers; increase scientific and technical expertise; foster institutional development and change; provide the public with the knowledge and skills needed for sustainable development through both formal education programmes and public awareness activities; and promote international co-operation and exchange with emphasis on addressing the needs of developing countries.

UNESCO is actively involved in the implementation of *Agenda 21*, the Convention on Biological Diversity, and the Framework Convention on Climate Change (see Agreements). UNESCO's activities to follow up the UN Conference on Environment and Development (UNCED) cut across all its areas of competence, and include the following: Man and the Biosphere Programme (MAB); Intergovernmental Oceanographic Commission (IOC) and programmes on marine science related issues (MRI);

International Hydrological Programme, Earth Sciences and Natural Hazards Programmes, including the International Geological Correlation Programme (UNESCO-IUGS); Network of Microbial Resources Centres (MIRCENS); UNESCO-UNEP International Environmental Education Programme.

## Decision-making bodies

The *General Conference*, composed of representatives from Member States, meets biennially to decide the policy, programme, and budget of UNESCO. The *Executive Board*, consisting of 51 members elected by the General Conference for a single four-year term, meets twice a year and is responsible for the execution of the programme adopted by the Conference. The Secretariat carries out the programmes; it consists of a Director-General and staff.

## Finance

Each Member State contributes according to a percentage calculated on the basis of the scale of assessments adopted by the United Nations General Assembly.

*Budget*
The budget was $US444,704,000 for the biennium 1992–93 and is $US455,490,000 for the biennium 1994– 95 .

*Main contributors*
Extra-budgetary resources are used mostly to implement operational projects. A major part of these resources come from United Nations sources, particularly the United Nations Development Programme (UNDP) (see this section) and the United Nations Population Fund (UNFPA) (see this section). Operational activities are also financed by governments and institutions under funds-in-trust arrangements by the World Bank and regional development banks and funds, by governments, institutions, and individuals.

## Publications

• *UNESCO Courier* (monthly);
• *International Social Science Journal*;
• *Nature and Resources* (quarterly);
• *Prospects* (quarterly);
• *UNESCO Sources* (monthly);
• *UNESCOPRESS Weekly.*

# United Nations Environment Programme (UNEP)

## Objectives

- to promote international co-operation in all matters affecting the human environment;
- to ensure that environmental problems of wide international significance receive appropriate governmental consideration;
- to promote the acquisition, assessment, and exchange of environmental knowledge.

## Organization

*Type*
Intergovernmental organization (IGO). Subsidiary to the UN General Assembly and the Economic and Social Council (ECOSOC).

*Membership*
Member States of the United Nations. Non-member States, IGOs, and international non-governmental organizations (NGOs) with an interest in environment participate as observers. 184 member States, by 9 November 1994.

*Founded*
15 December 1972 by the UN General Assembly. Established as a result of the UN Conference on the Human Environment in Stockholm, June 1972.

## Secretariat

United Nations Environment Programme (UNEP),
PO Box 30552,
Nairobi,
Kenya

| | |
|---|---|
| *Telephone*: | +254-2-621234 |
| *Telefax*: | +254-2-2268-86/90 |
| *E-mail*: | ipa@unep |

*Executive Director*
Ms Elizabeth Dowdeswell.

*Head of Information and Public Affairs Branch*
Mr Tore J. Brevik.

*Number of staff*
222 professionals and 491 support staff at Headquarters (Oct. 1994). 132 professionals and 141 support staff at regional and other offices.

## Activities

The primary role of UNEP is to provide leadership and encourage partnership in caring for the environment by inspiring, informing, and enabling nations and peoples to improve their quality of life without compromising that of future generations. It works to win the co-operation and participation of governments, the international scientific and professional communities, and non-governmental organizations. The first UN agency to be based in a developing country (Nairobi, Kenya), UNEP also has regional or liaison offices in Bangkok, Cairo, Geneva, New York, Mexico City, Nairobi, Manama (Bahrain). Its programme is divided into three main sectors:

- *Environmental assessment*, comprising the Global Environment Monitoring System (GEMS), the Global Resource Information Database (GRID), the International Referral System for Sources of Environmental Information (INFOTERRA), the International Register of Potentially Toxic Chemicals (IRPTC), and Earthwatch, designed to provide early warnings of significant environmental risks and opportunities and to ensure that governments have access to information;
- *Environmental management*, covering terrestrial ecosystems, technology and the environment, industry and the environment, oceans and coastal areas, and desertification control;
- *Support measures*, covering environmental education and training, public information, development planning and co-operation, and environmental law and institutions.

In 1994 UNEP co-operated on 102 projects with other UN agencies and bodies, 194 international projects, and, with governments and other organiza-

tions, 196 projects and 11 PAC projects, making a total of 503 projects. The 12 priority areas are:
• protection of the atmosphere;
• environmental management of freshwater resources;
• environmental management of terrestrial ecosystems and their resources;
• environmental management of oceans and coastal areas;
• environmental health, settlements, and human welfare;
• environmental economies, accounting and management tools;
• environmental law, institutions and policies;
• toxic chemicals and waste management;
• industry, energy, and the environment;
• earthwatch: data, information assessment, and early warning;
• capacity-building for environmentally sound and sustainable development;
• support for and co-operation in environmental action (including global and regional co-operation).

The *Global Environment Facility (GEF)* (see this section) was created in 1991 as a pilot programme to help developing countries to contribute towards solving global environmental problems. In 1994 the operational phase began, initially for an additional three years. The GEF operates in four focal areas: the protection of biological diversity, the limitation of greenhouse gases, the protection of international waters, and the protection of the ozone layer. Responsibility for implementing the GEF is shared between United Nations Development Programme (UNDP) (see this section), World Bank (see this section), and UNEP. In order to fulfil its mandate in this collaboration UNEP established the Scientific and Technical Advisory Panel (STAP) comprising a group of 15 world renowned experts in the fields relevant to the GEF. UNEP facilitates the Panel's work by providing the secretariat for STAP. UNEP has ensured that the GEF has operated in line with existing global conventions and agreements and has contributed to ensuring a better focus on high-priority projects.

UNEP is also active in the areas of working environment, energy, technology, and human settlements.

*Main conventions on environment under the auspices of UNEP* (see Agreements)
• *Convention on International Trade in Endangered Species of Wild Fauna and Flora (CITES), Washington, DC, 1973*;
• *Convention on the Conservation of Migratory Species of Wild Animals (CMS), Bonn, 1979*;
• *Vienna Convention for the Protection of the Ozone Layer, Vienna, 1985*;
• *Montreal Protocol on Substances that Deplete the Ozone Layer, Montreal, 1987*;
• *Amendment to the Montreal Protocol on Substances that Deplete the Ozone Layer, London, 1990 (London Amendment)*;
• *Amendment to the Montreal Protocol on Substances that Deplete the Ozone Layer, Copenhagen, 1992 (Copenhagen Amendment)*;
• *Basel Convention on the Control of Transboundary Movements of Hazardous Wastes and their Disposal; Basel Convention, 1989*;
• *Convention on Biological Diversity, Rio de Janeiro, 1992*;
• Conventions within *UNEP Regional Seas Programme*.

## Decision-making bodies

UNEP has three main components: the *Governing Council*, composed of 58 member States elected for four years, which reports to the UN General Assembly through the Economic and Social Council (ECOSOC). The membership of the Governing Council is made up on the following geographical basis: Africa (16) Asia (13), Latin America and the Caribbean (10), Eastern Europe (6), Western Europe, North America, and other (13).

The *Secretariat*, headed by the *Executive Director*, supports the Governing Council, co-ordinates elements of the environment programme, and administers the *Environment Fund*.

In 1994–95, a new management style was introduced into the organization, based on the Results Model. Main elements of UNEP's strategy for delivering the 1994–95 programme are a focus on: achieving results; providing responsive service; regional delivery; and integration.

## Finance

UNEP is financed through the regular budget of the United Nations, the Environment Fund, Trust Funds, and counterpart contributions.

*Budget*
Total budget was $US97.900 million in 1991 and $US100.299 million in 1992. Total budget is $US120,086,000 for the biennium 1994–95 from the Environment Fund.

*Main contributors*
Main contributors in 1994 were the USA ($US21.0 million), Japan ($US9.0 million), United Kingdom ($US6.3 million), Germany ($US5.8 million), Finland ($US3.5 million), Switzerland ($US3.2 million), and Sweden ($US2.7 million).

*Special funds*
The Environment Fund is a voluntary fund used to finance the costs of environmental initiatives. Some programmes are totally financed by the Environment Fund which is based on voluntary contributions, others only from the UN Regular Budget, but most from more than one source, including the Trust Funds and Counterpart Contributions.

## Publications

• *Annual Report of the Executive Director*;
• *Our Planet* (six times a year);
• *Industry and Environment Bulletin* (quarterly);
• *Regional Bulletin for Africa* (quarterly);
• *Regional Bulletin for Europe* (quarterly);
• *Newsletter/Bulletins of Programme Activity Centres*;
• *Technical Reports Series*;
• *Environment and Trade Series* (18 publications).

# United Nations Industrial Development Organization (UNIDO)

## Objectives

The five development objectives of UNIDO are:
• industrial and technical growth and competitiveness;
• human resource development;
• equitable development through industrialization;
• environmentally sustainable industrial development;
• international co-operation in industrial investment and technology.

Working at three levels—policy, institutions, and enterprise—UNIDO acts as:
• focal point for industrial technology;
• honest broker for industrial co-operation;
• centre of excellence on industrial development issues;
• global source of industrial information.

UNIDO is specializing in promoting and accelerating industrialization in developing countries. It assists both governments and the public and private sectors through technical and investment promotion services, and with policy advice. Its services are available to developing countries and to countries in transition to a market economy wishing to strengthen their industrial base.

## Organization

*Type*
Intergovernmental organization (IGO). A specialized agency of the United Nations. Linked to ECOSOC on matters of inter-agency concern.

*Membership*
Open to members of the United Nations. 166 member States, by 31 October 1994.

*Founded*
1 January 1967. It gained status as a fully specialized agency on 17 December 1985.

## Secretariat

United Nations Industrial Development Organization (UNIDO),
Vienna International Centre,
Wagramerstrasse 5,
PO Box 300,
A-1400 Vienna, Austria

*Telephone*:      +43-1-21131
*Telefax*:      +43-1-237241
*E-mail*:      unido1 (Bitnet Earn)

*Director General*
Mr Mauricio de María y Campos. (1993–97)

*Chief, Public Information Section*
Mr Kemal Saiki.

*Number of staff*
402 professionals and 781 support staff at Headquarters (Jan. 1994).

## Activities

UNIDO programmes provide a range of specific services such as:
• policy advice, studies, and research;
• technological trends;
• national industrial reviews;
• investment services;
• technical support services and technology management;
• statistical services;
• industrial, technological, and business information processing and dissemination;
• public information.

Key programmes mobilize resources and enter into activities on the specific requirements of developing regions, least developed countries, and the role of women in industry.

*Environmental activities*
A cross-sectoral programme on environmentally sustainable industrial development (ESID) helps developing countries build policies, institutions, technical, and scientific capacity for pollution prevention, cleaner production, and efficient energy utilization. ESID will be characterized by (a) limitations on industrial emissions to protect the biosphere; (b) the efficient use of man-made and natural capital; and (c) equity in the social sphere as a basic principle in the transition to a sustainable society.

Growing focus has been placed on the danger of highly polluting industries moving from the industrialized to the developing countries.

## Decision-making bodies

The *General Conference*, comprising all member States, meets every two years, or as decided by the UN General Assembly. The Conference reviews UNIDO strategies and policy concepts on industrial development. The *Industrial Development Board*, consisting of 53 member States, meets annually. It reviews implementation of the approved work programme, the corresponding regular and operational budgets, and the implementation of General Conference decisions. The *Programme and Budget Committee*, comprising 27 member States, assists the board in preparing its work programmes and budget, and the draft scale assessment for regular budget expenditures.

## Finance

Sources include assessed contributions from member States, UN system funds, governments funds, development finance institutions and trust funds.

*Budget*
The budget was $US181 million for the biennium 1992–93 and is $US196 million for the biennium 1994–95.

*Special funds*
UNIDO administers the UN Industrial Development Fund (IDF), a voluntary fund established by a UN General Assembly resolution in 1976 and aimed at enhancing UNIDO's ability to meet the needs of developing countries promptly and flexibly, supplementing where necessary the assistance in the industrial sector provided by the UNDP (see this section) or other UN agencies. Total pledges were $US29.6 million for 1992 and $US37.0 million for 1993.

## Publications

• Annual Reports;
• *UNIDO Newsletter* (monthly);
• *Industry and Development* (annual);
• *Industrial Development Abstracts*;
• *Transfer of Technology Series*;
• *Energy and Environment Series*;
• *UNIDO Upadate* (quarterly).

# United Nations Population Fund (UNFPA)

## Objectives
• to build up, on an international basis, the knowledge and the capacity to respond to needs in population and family planning, and to promote co-ordination in planning and programming;
• to promote awareness of population problems in both industrialized and developing countries and of possible strategies to deal with them;
• to assist developing countries at their request in dealing with their population problems, in the forms and the means best suited to the individual country's needs;
• to play a leading role in the United Nations system in promoting population programmes, and to co-ordinate projects supported by the Fund.

## Organization
*Type*
Intergovernmental organization (IGO). Co-ordination with other UN agencies and organizations is maintained through the mechanism of the Administrative Committee on Co-ordination and through meetings of a 'Joint Consultative Group on Policy' composed of the following five funding agencies: UNDP, UNFPA, UNICEF, WFP, and IFAD (see this section).

*Membership*
Not applicable.

*Founded*
1969.

## Secretariat
United Nations Population Fund (UNFPA),
220 East 42nd Street,
New York, NY 10017,
USA
*Telephone*:          +1-212-2975011
*Telefax*:          +1-212-5576416
*E-mail*:          marshall@unfpa.org

*Executive Director*
Dr Nafis Sadik.

*Head of Information*
Mr Stirling Scruggs.

*Number of staff*
105 professionals and 135 support staff at Headquarters and 199 professionals and 398 support staff at field offices (Oct. 1994).

## Activities
UNFPA is involved in seven main areas, which, in order of priority, are:
family planning, communication and education, basic data collection, population dynamics, formulation and evaluation of population policies and programmes, multisector activities, and special programmes.

The Fund's Executive Director also served as the Secretary General of the International Conference on Population and Development (ICPD), held in Cairo in September 1994.

*Environmental activities*
UNFPA adopted policy guide-lines on 'Population and Environment' in 1989 to promote the integration of environmental concerns into population activities. In line with these guide-lines and *Agenda 21*, UNFPA supports a range of projects dealing with the impact on the environment and vice versa of population factors such as growth, distribution, age structure, and migration in particular. The Programme of Action of the International Conference on Population and Development (ICPD) in September 1994 in Cairo emphasized anew the close links between population issues, sustainable development, and environmental protection. As an integral part of the implementation of the Programme of Action, UNFPA will take new initiatives in many fields, including the field of population and environment.

## Decision-making bodies
The *Executive Board* of the United Nations Development Programme (UNDP) (see this section) and UNFPA act as the governing body, under the policy supervision of the UN Economic and Social Council (ECOSOC).

## Finance
The Fund's resources come in the form of voluntary contributions from governments and private donors, the majority of which pledge on a yearly basis.

*Budget*
Expenditure was $US193.6 million in 1992 and $US215.4 million in 1993. Total income from pledges and miscellaneous sources was $US238.2 million in 1992 and $US219.6 million in 1993. The administrative costs were $US45.1 million in 1993.

*Main contributors*
The largest donors in 1993 were Japan, The Netherlands, Germany, Norway, and Denmark. The total number of donors was 105 governments in 1992 and 101 governments in 1993.

## Publications
• *Populi*, the UNFPA magazine (10 issues a year);
• *Inventory of Population Projects in Developing Countries around the World* (annual);
• *State of World Population Report* (annual);
• *Population in the 21st Century: UNFPA and Agenda 21*;
• *Guide to Sources of International Population Assistance* (triennial).

# World Bank

## Objectives
- to help raise standards of living in developing countries by channelling financial resources to them from industrialized countries;
- to provide capital for productive purposes, particularly the development of productive facilities and resources in developing countries;
- to promote private foreign investment for productive purposes and, where necessary, supplement private investment by providing finance;
- to identify the more useful and urgent projects required to support economic and social development;
- to ensure that such projects are given appropriate priority by arranging or guaranteeing finance.

## Organization
The World Bank includes the International Bank for Reconstruction and Development (IBRD) and the International Development Association (IDA). IBRD was established on 27 December 1945 when representatives of 28 countries signed the Articles of Agreement which had been drawn up at the Bretton Woods Conference in July 1944. IDA was established on 24 September 1960 in Washington, DC. The name 'World Bank' is generally taken to mean the IBRD and IDA together.

*Type*
Intergovernmental organization (IGO). IBRD and IDA are both UN specialized agencies. Besides IBRD and IDA, the World Bank Group also includes the International Finance Corporation (IFC) and the Multilateral Investment Guarantee Agency (MIGA).

*Membership*
Membership is open to all members of the International Monetary Fund (IMF) (see this section). Not open to regional integration organizations. 178 member States, by 31 October 1994.

*Founded*
27 December 1945 (IBRD) and 24 September 1960 (IDA).

## Secretariat
The World Bank
1818 H Street NW
Washington, DC 20433
USA
*Telephone*:      +1-202-4771234
*Telefax*:      +1-202-4776391

*President*
Mr Lewis T. Preston.

*Director, Environment Department*
Mr Andrew Steer.

*Head of Information and Public Affairs*
Mr Mark Malloch Brown.

*Number of staff*
4,145 professionals and 2,193 support staff at Headquarters (June 1994). There are about 162 higher-level staff in the Environment Department and the four Regional Environment Divisions. Overall more than 300 environmental higher-level staff and long-term consultants work full-time on environmental matters in the Bank.

## Activities
The World Bank finances infrastructure facilities such as roads, railways, and power facilities as well as small-scale projects such as providing credits to microentrepreneurs and farmers. It has increased emphasis on investments which can directly affect the well-being of the masses of poor people, i.e. developing countries, by making them more productive and by including them as active participants in the development process.

*Environmental activities*
Policy and research work on the environment is conducted in all the Bank's sectors, but especially in energy, industry, urban infrastructure, and agriculture.

Incorporating environmental considerations into decision-making has been a prime focus of activity, and several activities are concerned with the effects of rapidly growing energy use on pollution.

Central to integrating environmental concerns into the Bank's activities is the 'Operational Directive on Environmental Assessment', approved in October 1989. The directive mandates an environmental assessment for all projects that may have a significant impact on the environment. In fiscal year 1992, the directive was revised to require that people affected by Bank-supported projects have access to the information contained in the assessment.

The Bank works closely with the United Nations Development Programme (UNDP) (see this section) and often serves as executing agency for UNDP projects.

The Bank co-operated with UNDP and United Nations Environment Programme (UNEP) in the three-year pilot programme, Global Environment Facility (GEF), which provided grants and low-interest loans to developing countries to help them carry out programmes to relieve pressures on global ecosystems. The pilot programme was adopted in 1991. The new restructured GEF was established by the same implementing agencies in 1994 (see this section).

World Bank lending for environmental projects in fiscal year 1994 totalled $US2.4 billion for 25 environmental projects to assist developing countries in three broad areas: pollution control and protection of the urban environment; natural resource management and protection of the rural environment; and institution building.

The Bank's environmental strategy has four basic objectives:
• to assist developing countries set priorities, build up institutions, and implement programmes for sound environmental stewardship;
• to ensure that potentially adverse environmental effects from World Bank-financed projects are addressed;
• to assist member States build up the links between poverty-reduction and environmental protection;
• to address global environmental challenges through participation in the Global Environment Facility (GEF).

## Decision-making bodies

All powers of the Bank are vested in a *Board of Governors*, which consists of one Governor appointed by each member State. The Governors have delegated most of their powers to the *Executive Directors* responsible for matters of policy and approval of all the loans made by the Bank. The Bank's operation is the responsibility of a *President*, selected by the Executive Directors and who is, *ex officio*, their *Chairman*.

*IDA* is a separate legal entity with its own financial resources. It has the same Board of Governors and the same Executive Directors representing countries that are members of both IBRD and IDA. The President of the Bank is *ex officio* President of IDA and the officers and staff of the Bank also serve IDA. Each member has an assessed quota which is subscribed and determines voting power in IDA and IBRD. By 30 June 1994 the USA, as the largest contributor, had 15.41% of the voting power in IDA. Japan (10.22%), Germany (6.81%), the UK (5.13%), and France (4.04%) have, together with the United States, the largest share of voting power. By June 1994, the voting power in IBRD of the five largest shareholders was as follows; USA (17.14%), Japan (6.47%), Germany (5.00%), the UK (4.79%), and France (4.79%).

## Finance

The IBRD, which accounts for about three-quarters of all World Bank lending, raises most of its money on the world's financial markets. It sells bonds and other debt securities to pension funds, insurance companies, corporations, other banks, and individuals around the world. In 1993, the IBRD borrowed $US8,900 million. Other sources of funds are shareholders' capital and retained earnings. IDA depends almost entirely on the wealthier member governments for its financial resources. Thirty-four countries committed $US18.0 billion for IDA operations from 1993 to 1995. IDA donors include not only industrial countries such as the United States, Japan, and Germany, but also developing countries such as Brazil, Hungary, Korea, and Turkey.

When combined with advance commitments against future repayments by IDA borrowers and the approved transfer of $US375 million equivalent from the IBRD's surplus account, IDA's commitment authority during the three-year period would total about SDR16 billion equivalent. This amount could be augmented further by transfer from the IBRD's net income once the commitments have been approved by the IBRD's board of governors.

*Budget*
Approved administrative budget for the World Bank was $US1,233,900 in 1993, $US1,388,700 in 1994, and is $US1,420,300 in 1995.

## Publications
• Numerous research studies, country reports, etc.;
• Annual Reports;
• Annual Report on the Environment;
• *World Development Report* (annually);
• *Environment Bulletin* (newsletter of the World Bank Environment Community);
• *World Debt Tables*;
• *Trends in Developing Countries*;
• *World Bank Atlas*.

# World Food Programme (WFP)

## Objectives

WFP provides food aid to developing countries both to promote economic and social development and to help meet emergency needs. To this end, WFP's assistance, targeted at the most vulnerable and neediest groups of people, is provided in support of a variety of government supported projects and emergency operations.

## Organization

*Type*
Intergovernmental organization (IGO).

*Membership*
No general members (see decision-making bodies, below).

*Founded*
24 November 1961.

## Secretariat

World Food Programme (WFP),
426 Via Cristoforo Colombo,
I-00145 Rome, Italy
*Telephone*:      +39-6-522821
*Telefax*:        +39-6-59602-348/111
*E-mail*:         diberto@wfp.org

*Executive Director*
Ms Catherine Bertini.

*Head of Information*
Mr Paul Mitchell.

*Number of staff*
178 professionals and 238 support staff at Headquarters (Jan. 1994). 480 professionals and 1,109 support staff are in the field.

## Activities

WFP-assisted development projects have traditionally fallen almost exclusively within two broad categories; (i) agricultural and rural development and (ii) human resource development. WFP's expenditures for projects aimed at assisting agricultural and rural development totalled $US217,380,000 in 1993. Expenditures for human resource development projects, mainly for mothers and pre-school and primary school children, in 1993 were valued at $US181,005,000. At the end of 1993, WFP was assisting 237 ongoing development projects with total commitments valued at $US2.8 billion. Projects to boost agricultural production accounted for $US141,684,000 of ongoing WFP-assisted development activities in 1993. Well over 50 per cent of WFP development assistance directly supports women's advancement.

During the past three decades, WFP has invested approximately $US13 billion involving more than 40 million tons of food to combat hunger, promote economic and social development, and provide relief assistance in emergencies throughout the world.

*Environmental activities*
WFP is one of the world's largest donors of resources for environmental activities, spending some $US1 million a day on projects for afforestation, soil conservation, and activities to promote environmentally sustainable agricultural production. By the end of 1992, WFP was assisting 148 projects with environmental components, with a total value of nearly $US1.1 billion, more than one third of all WFP development activities.

Increasingly, WFP is trying to combine environmental components in an integrated way, both at the micro level (on individual farms) and at the macro level (in entire drainage basins).

A checklist highlighting the types of projects supported by WFP that are particularly sensitive to environmental concerns has been devised for incorporation into WFP's project preparation guide-lines. The purpose of this approach is to: predict the most serious environmental impact of a project; help find ways to reduce possible negative impacts by designing projects in a way that preserves (and improves) the environment; organize project supervision in such a way as to reduce or eliminate possible risks.

## Decision-making bodies

WFP's Governing Body, the *Committee on Food Aid Policies and Programmes (CFA)*, is composed of 42 members, 21 elected by the FAO Council (see this section) and 21 by the UN Economic and Social Council (ECOSOC). Apart from exercising intergovernmental supervision of WFP, the CFA also serves as the international body designated to discuss global food aid issues and concerns, including bilateral food aid.

## Finance

The Programme is funded through voluntary contributions from donor countries and intergovernmental bodies such as the European Community (EC). Contributions are made in commodities, cash, and services.

*Budget*
WFP's annual expenditure amounted to $US1.7 billion in 1992 and $US1.8 billion in 1993. Total multilateral pledges and contributions to WFP for the biennium 1991–92 reached nearly $US3.0 billion, more than 70 per cent higher than the previous 1989–90 record.

*Main contributors*
Main contributors to the Programme are the USA, EC, Canada, the Netherlands, Sweden, Germany, Denmark, Finland, Japan, Australia, Norway, the United Kingdom, Switzerland, Italy, and France.

*Special funds*
WFP has special funds for dealing with emergency situations such as the IEFR (see above), which was operative in 1976 and the Intermediate Response Account (IRA) which was operative in 1991.

By 30 June 1993 these funds amounted to $US3.1 billion. Disbursement in 1992 was $US580 million and accumulated disbursement was $US2.75 billion.

## Publications

- *World Food Programme Food Aid Review*;
- *World Food Programme Journal*;
- *Food Aid and the Environment*;
- *Food Aid Works for the Environment*;
- *WFP in Africa*;
- *When Food is Hope*;
- *More Than Food Aid.*

# World Health Organization (WHO)

## Objectives

The WHO Global Strategy for Health and Environment is an organization-wide action plan for the programmes for the *Promotion of Environmental Health (PEH)* and *Promotion of Chemical Safety (PCS)*.

The objectives of the PEH are:
• to serve as the lead programme for implementing WHO's Global Strategy for Health and Environment;
• to devise and co-ordinate the organization's contribution to international programmes relating to major environmental factors.

The objectives of the PCS are:
• to accelerate the provision of internationally evaluated scientific information on chemicals;
• to promote the use of such information in national programmes;
• to enable member States to establish their own chemical safety measures and programmes;
• to help member States strengthen their capabilities in chemical emergency preparedness and response, and in chemical risk reduction;
• to seek improved international co-operation in the promotion of chemical safety.

## Organization

*Type*
Intergovernmental organization (IGO). A specialized agency of the United Nations, linked to the UN Economic and Social Council (ECOSOC).

*Membership*
All member States of the United Nations may become members of WHO by accepting its Constitution. Other countries may be admitted as members on approval of their application by a simple majority vote of the World Health Assembly. Territories not responsible for the conduct of their own international relations may become associate members. 189 member States and two associate members, by 31 October 1994.

*Founded*
7 April 1948.

## Secretariat

World Health Organization (WHO),
20 avenue Appia,
CH-1211 Geneva,
Switzerland
*Telephone*:      +41-22-7912111
*Telefax*:        +41-22-7910746
*E-mail*:  tawffik@who.ch (Internet)

*Director General*
Dr Hiroshi Nakajima.
(1993 98)

*Executive Director,*
*Health and Environment*
Dr W. Kreisel.

*Head of Information of WHO*
Mr M. S. Barton.

*Number of staff*
1,576 professionals and 3,066 support staff at WHO as a whole (Oct. 1994). 150 professionals (including Regional Offices) and 30 support staff (Headquarters only) at PEH and PCS.

## Activities

The Eighth General Programme of Work, covering the period 1990–95, was adopted in 1987. This programme promotes national, regional, and global strategies for the attainment of the main social target of the member states: Global Strategy for Health for All by the Year 2000.

*Environmental activities*
The WHO programmes for PEH and PCS will address priority issues concerning the physical and social environments. They will carry out WHO responsibilities for co-ordinating international work in

the areas of health and environment, and assist member States with the development and implementation of national health-and-environment programmes.

PEH comprises three sub-programmes, (i) urban environmental health, (ii) rural environmental health, and (iii) global and integrated environmental health.

PCS has four main areas of activities, (i) chemical risk assessment, (ii) chemical risk communication, (iii) chemical risk reduction, and (iv) strengthening of national capabilities in and capacities for management of chemicals. PCS also executes the International Programme on Chemical Safety (IPCS) in collaboration with the International Labour Organization (ILO) and United Nations Environment Programme (UNEP) (see this section). This activity has been implemented under the Programme for the Promotion of Chemical Safety since 1 March 1992.

The activities of PEH and PCS also include:
• support of the sustainable extension of water supplies and sanitation facilities, and monitoring of progress;
• support of member States in the development of national programmes for control of environmental health hazards including air quality, water quality, radiation monitoring, human exposure to pollutants, and environmental epidemiology;

• promotion of human health through measures to improve living conditions and mitigation of the adverse environmental and health impacts of socio-economic development actions.

## Decision-making bodies

The *World Health Assembly* is the policy-making body of WHO and meets in annual session. The *Executive Board*, which meets twice a year, acts as the executive organ of the Assembly. The Board is composed of 31 persons technically qualified in the field of health and each is designated by individual member States. They serve in a personal capacity, and not as government representatives. Six regional organizations have been established as integral parts of the Organization, each consisting of a regional committee and a regional office. Regional committees meet in annual sessions. The *Secretariat* consists of a Director General, six Regional Directors, and such technical and administrative staff as are required.

## Finance

The regular budget is provided basically by assessments of member States and associate members. PEH and PCS budget is provided by the regular budget of WHO, and funded from other UN agencies and support agencies.

*Budget*
The regular WHO administrative budget for the biennium 1994–95 is $US872,496,000 of which the share of PEH and PCS is $US45,811,600 (including regional offices).

*Associated funds*
In addition to regular funding through the UN system, WHO operates a Voluntary Fund for Health Promotion (VFHP), which has a funding level in the region of $US200 million. About one third of WHO's operating budget is now sustained through the contributions of donor governments, international agencies, foundations, and individuals to the VFHP, plus separate trust funds identified with specific donors.

## Publications
• *World Health* (12 times a year);
• *Environmental Health Newsletter* (quarterly);
• *Bulletin of the World Health Organization* (12 times a year).

*Electronic conferences*
Internet:        *gopher.who.ch*;
Telnet:          *telnet gopher.who.ch*

# World Meteorological Organization (WMO)

## Objectives

• to facilitate international co-operation in the establishment of networks of stations for the making of meterological observations as well as hydrological and other geophysical observations related to meteorology and to promote the establishment and maintenance of centres charged with the provision of meteorological and related services;
• to promote the establishment and maintenance of systems for rapid exchange of meteorological and related information;
• to promote standardization of meteorological and related observations and ensure the uniform publication of observations and statistics;
• to further the application of meteorology to aviation, shipping, water problems, agriculture, and other human activities;
• to promote activities in operational hydrology and further close co-operation between Meteorological and Hydrometeorological Services;
• to encourage research and training in meteorology, and, as appropriate, in related fields, and to assist in co-ordinating the international aspects of such research and training.

## Organization

*Type*
Intergovernmental organization (IGO). A specialized agency of the United Nations. Agreements and working arrangements with non-governmental organizations (NGOs).

*Membership*
States and territories, 172 member States and 5 Territories, by 28 October 1994.

*Founded*
23 March 1950.

## Secretariat

World Meterological Organization (WMO),
41, av. Giuseppe Motta,
PO Box 2300,
CH-1211 Geneva 2,
Switzerland
*Telephone*: +41-22-7308111
*Telefax*: +41-22-7342326
*Telex*: 414199 ommch

*Secretary-General*
Mr G. O. P. Obasi.

*Senior Information and Public Affairs Officer*
Ms E. Gorre-Dale.

*Number of staff*
128 professionals and 153 support staff at Headquarters (Oct. 1994). 14 professionals (including 5 national experts) and 32 support staff at field, regional, or country offices.

## Activities

WMO carries out its work through seven major scientific and technical programmes which have strong components in each region: the World Weather Watch Programme, World Climate Programme, Atmospheric Research and Environment Programme, Applications of Meteorology Programme, Hydrology and Water Resource Programme, Education and Training Programme, and Regional Programme. Technical assistance to members is provided through the Technical Co-operation Programme.

*Environmental activities*
The WMO works through its members to provide authoritative scientific measurements, as well as assessments and predictions of the state of the global atmosphere and of the Earth's freshwater resources.

The WMO promotes increasingly effective application of meteorological and hydrological information in seeking environmentally sound and sustainable development.

It calls attention to the need for global action to reduce pollution of the atmosphere, on the basis of scientific information now available.

It has several programmes and activities operated jointly with other IGOs and NGOs. These include the *Intergovernmental Panel on Climate Change (IPCC)* to provide assessments of available scientific information on climate change and the resulting environmental and socio-economic impacts, the *Global Climate Observing System (GCOS)* to provide observations for monitoring climate and detecting climate change, and to support climatological applications for national economic development and research for improved understanding and prediction of the climate system, and the *World Climate Research Programme (WCRP)*.

WMO is also actively involved in the intergovernmental Negotiating Committee of the Framework Convention on Climate Change (FCCC) (see Agreements), the Intergovernmental Negotiating Committee on Desertification (INCD), and some aspects of *Agenda 21* of the UN Conference on Environment and Development (UNCED).

The *Atmospheric Research and Environment Programme (AREP)* coordinates and fosters research on the structure and composition of the atmosphere and its related physical characteristics; the physics of weather processes; and weather forecasting. It consists of four major components: The Global Atmospheric Watch, the Programmes on Weather Prediction Research, Tropical Meteorology Research and Physics and Chemistry of Clouds, and Weather Modification Research.

A majority of natural disasters are weather- or climate-related, such as hurricane, tornado, storm surge, flood, and drought. WMO through its members and in co-operation with other UN agencies and international organizations is contributing to the disaster preparedness and mitigation by means of prediction and warnings.

## Decision-making bodies

Main bodies of WMO are the *World Meteorological Congress*, which meets every four years and in which all member States and Territories are represented. The *Executive Council*, composed of 36 directors of national Meteorological and Hydrometeorological Services, meets at least once a year to review the activities of the Organization and to implement the programmes approved by the Congress. The six Regional Associations (Africa, Asia, South America, North and Central America, South-West Pacific, and Europe) are composed of member governments, and work to co-ordinate meteorological and related activities within their respective regions. The eight Technical Commissions, composed of experts designated by members States, study matters within their specific areas of competence. The Secretariat, headed by a Secretary-General, serves as the administrative, documentation, and information centre of the Organization.

## Finance

Contributions of members according to a proportional scale adopted by percentage assessment of total contribution.

*Budget*
The approved budget for 1992–95 is SFr236.1 million.

*Special funds*
In addition to the extra-budgetary funds for activities in respect of technical co-operation projects, WMO is administering several trust-fund and special accounts financed by various member States and international organizations.

## Publications
- *WMO Bulletin*;
- Mandatory publications;
- Programme Supporting Publications;
- Special Environmental Reports.

# World Trade Organization (WTO)

## Objectives

The main objectives of World Trade Organization (WTO) are:
• to supervise and liberalize international trade;
• to supervise the settlements of commercial conflicts.

The WTO shall facilitate the implementation, administration and operation, and further the objectives of the General Agreement on Tariffs and Trade (GATT) 1994, the Multilateral Trade Agreements (which are binding on all members), and shall also provide the framework for the implementation, administration, and operation of the Plurilateral Trade Agreements (which are binding on the members that have accepted them, but which do not create either obligations or rights for members that have not accepted them).

The main objectives of GATT 1994 are:
• to enter into reciprocal and mutually advantageous arrangements directed to the substantial reduction of tariffs and other barriers to trade;
• to eliminate discriminatory treatment in international trade relations.

WTO members recognize that their relations in the field of trade and economic endeavour should be conducted with a view to contributing to the following objectives:

• to raise standards of living, ensuring full employment and a large and steadily growing volume of real income and effective demand;
• to expand the production of and trade in goods and services, while allowing for the optimal use of the world's resources in accordance with the objective of sustainable development, seeking both to protect and preserve the environment and to enhance the means for doing so in a manner consistent with the member's respective needs and concerns at different levels of economic development;
• to ensure that developing countries and especially the least-developed among them, secure a share in the growth in international trade commensurate with the needs of their economic development.

## Organization

### Type
Intergovernmental organization (IGO). An independent IGO within the UN system.

### Membership
Any state or separate customs territory possessing full autonomy in the conduct of external trade may apply for WTO membership. Membership entails accepting all the results of the Uruguay Round of Multilateral Trade Negotiations (1986–1994) without exception and the submission of national tariff schedules on goods and initial commitments on services. There were 125 participants in the Uruguay Round, including the European Union, by 15 April 1994. Contracting Parties to GATT 1947 which have submitted schedules on goods of services will automatically become members by accepting the WTO Agreement within two years of its entry into force.

*Founded*
1 January 1995.

## Secretariat
World Trade Organization,
Centre William Rappard,
Rue de Lausanne 154,
CH-1211 Geneva 21,
Switzerland
*Telephone*:      +41-22-7395111
*Telefax*:        +41-22-7314206
*Telex*:          412323 GATT CH

*General-Director*
To be decided in December 1994.

*Director of Information*
Mr David Woods.

*Number of staff*
400 at the GATT secretariat (Nov. 1994).

## Activities

*Environmental activities*
The terms of reference of the Committee on Trade and the Environment (see below) include:
• identification of the relationship between trade measures and environmental measures, in order to promote sustainable development;
• makeing appropriate recommendations on whether any modifications of the provisions of the multilateral trading system are required, compatible with the open, equitable, and non-discriminatory nature of the system, as regards in particular:
• the need for rules to enhance positive interaction between trade and environmental measures, for the promotion of sustainable development, with special consideration to the needs of developing countries, in particular those of the least developed among them;
• the avoidance of protectionist trade measures, and the adherence to effective multilateral disciplines to ensure responsiveness of the multilateral trading system to environmental objectives set forth in *Agenda 21* and the *Rio Declaration*;

• surveillance of trade measures used for environmental purposes, of trade-related aspects of environmental measures which have significant trade effects, and of effective implementation of the multilateral disciplines governing those measures.

## Decision-making bodies

The *Ministerial Conference*, comprising all members, is the main governing body of the WTO, and meets at least every 2 years. A *General Council*, composed of all members, oversees operation of the WTO between meetings of the Ministerial Conference, including acting as a dispute settlement body and administering the trade policy review mechanism.

The Council has established subsidiary bodies such as the *Council for Trade in Goods*, the *Council for Trade in Services*, and the *Trade-Related Aspects of Intellectual Property Rights (TRIPs) Council*, and the *Committee on Trade and the Environment*.

Decision-making is made by consensus. If a decision cannot be arrived at by consensus, the matter at issue shall be decided by voting. at meetings of the Ministerial Conference and the General Council. Each member of WTO has one vote.

## Finance

Each member contributes to the WTO its share in the expenses of the WTO in accordance with the financial regulations adopted by the General Council. Contributions by members reflect shares in international trade in goods, services, and intellectual property.

*Budget*
The administrative budget at the GATT Secretariat was SFr94.1 million in 1994.

*Main contributors*
The USA, Germany, Japan, France, United Kingdom, Italy, Canada, the Netherlands, Hong Kong, Belgium, the Republic of Korea, and Spain.

## Publications

• *GATT Focus* (monthly);
• *News of the Uruguay Round* (monthly);
• *Basic Instruments and Selected Documents* (annually);
• *GATT Activities* (annually).

## Non-Governmental Organizations (NGOs)

The NGOs are selected on the following criteria:
- multinational, with member organizations, national affiliated, or offices;
- a certain duration of activities, i.e. *ad hoc* organizations are not included. A few networks, which seem to have influence beyond a particular event, are included;
- a substantial part of the activities within environment and development. For organizations with a main focus on development, an environmental component is also required;
- reasonably independent of governments (an exception has been made for IUCN);
- foundations and research organizations are avoided.

The Editors

# Alliance of Northern People for Environment and Development (ANPED)

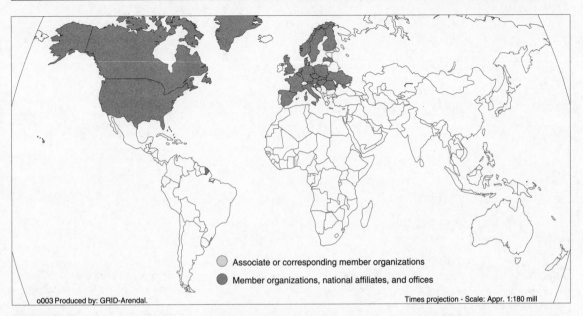

○ Associate or corresponding member organizations

● Member organizations, national affiliates, and offices

o003 Produced by: GRID-Arendal.                                       Times projection - Scale: Appr. 1:180 mill

## Objectives
• to facilitate continual co-operation among people's organizations within the ECE region for the purpose of promoting a holistic approach to environment and development, which necessarily includes the promotion of human rights, social and ecological justice, equity, cultural diversity, participating democracy, and peace;
• to co-ordinate common campaigns focused on environment and development, promoting equality in North–South and East–West relations, democratic and sustainable solutions to the global ecological and economic crisis, and the fulfilment of the responsibility of the peoples of the ECE region to join with the peoples of the South in a genuine partnership against global environmental degradation and human poverty.

## Organization
*Type*
Non-governmental organization (NGO).

*Membership*
Full membership in the Alliance is open to people's organizations within the region of the UN Economic Commission for Europe (UN/ECE). Associate

membership is offered to organizations in other regions or to organizations who do not wish to be full members. 80 full member organizations in 22 countries, by November 1994.

*Founded*
October 1991.

## Secretariat
Alliance of Northern People for Environment and Development (ANPED), c/o Women's Environmental Network, Aberdeen Studios, 22 Highbury Grove, London N5 2EA, United Kingdom
*Telephone*:        +44-71-3548823
*Telefax*:          +44-71-3540464
*E-mail*:           wenuk@gn.apc.org

*Secretary*
Ms Maite Bell.

*Number of staff*
1 professional and 1 support staff (Nov. 1994).

## Activities
The permanent working groups are the backbone of the activities, and there are working groups for: Women, UNCED follow-up, East–West relations, and changing consumption and production

patterns (CAP).
    The Alliance facilitates national and local action and promotes new relations within the NGO community.

## Decision-making bodies
The *Ordinary Meeting* of the alliance, taking place normally once a year, is composed of the member organizations, with one vote each, and associated organizations exercising no voting rights. The Ordinary Meeting decides upon the main principles and draws up policy-making guide-lines. The Alliance is directed by a *Co-ordinating Group* composed of nine to fifteen members, and the group is elected by the Ordinary Meeting for one year.

## Finance
Contributions from member organizations and individual supporters.

*Budget*
The administrative core budget was $US60,000 in 1994.

## Publications
• *Northern Lights* (quarterly newsletter);
• *Consumption and Production (CAP) Working Group*, newsletter (bimonthly).

# Centre for Our Common Future

## Objectives
• to promote and act as a focal point and catalyst in progress towards sustainable development as laid down in the report *Our Common Future* of the World Commission on Environment and Development (WCED);
• to encourage greater public and institutional involvement throughout the world in efforts to achieve sustainable development;
• to encourage and facilitate public participation in national and international decision-making processes and foster inter-sectoral dialogue on issues related to sustainable development.

## Organization
*Type*
Non-governmental organization (NGO). Consultative status with the Commission on Sustainable Development (CSD)(see IGOs) and several other UN agencies. The Centre is a non-profit foundation.

*Membership*
NGOs, intergovernmental organizations (IGOs), media, trade unions, industry organizations, and the scientific community. 265 organizations in 69 countries have associated with the Centre as Working Partners, by 3 October 1993.

*Founded*
1988.

## Secretariat
The Centre for Our Common Future,
33, route de Valavran,
CH-1293 Bellevue, Geneva,
Switzerland
*Telephone*:      +41-22-7744530
*Telefax*:          +41-22-7744536
*E-mail*:            commonfuture@gn.
                        apc.org

*Executive Director*
Mr Warren H. Lindner.

*Information Director*
Ms Ellen Permato.

*Number of staff*
10 professionals and 4 support staff (Oct. 1994).

## Activities
The Centre was active in the follow-up activities on the World Commission on Environment and Development. It assisted in laying down foundations for several 1990 regional conferences on follow-up on the Commission's report.

The Centre took an active interest and role in the preparations for the UN Conference on Environment and Development (UNCED) in Rio de Janeiro in 1992 and was a main contributor to the strengthening of the development aspects of the agenda for the conference and for the opening of the preparatory process to all key sectors of society.

The Centre organized a series of 'Eco '92 Public Forums' to provide an additional avenue of input for the public to the official UNCED preparatory process.

With the help and support of its network of Working Partner institutions, the Centre regularly collects information on sustainable-development initiatives taken by all sectors and disseminates it to individuals and organizations worldwide.

The Centre's database is a contact base for sustainable development and includes every sector of society, from grass-roots groups, religious organizations, research institutes, and environment and development activists to businesses, governments, and international organizations. Whether the institutions concerned deal with hands-on development projects or multilateral financial negotiations, they are part of the multi-faceted constituency that has a stake in sustainable development. The database is geographically balanced, with some 55 per cent of the records in the South and Eastern Europe, and 45 per cent in the North.

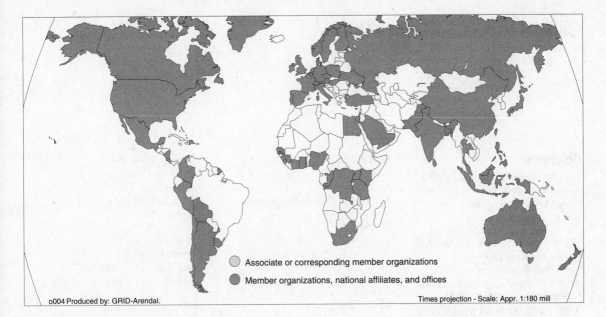

Associate or corresponding member organizations

Member organizations, national affiliates, and offices

o004 Produced by: GRID-Arendal.

Times projection - Scale: Appr. 1:180 mill

## Decision-making bodies

The *Board of Trustees* consists of five trustees and meets semi-annually.

## Finance

The Centre finances its activities by contributions from governments, UN agencies, and foundations; providing consultancies; message delivery/outreach services; sales of publications and other materials; individual contributions through the 'Friends of the Centre' programme.

*Budget*

The budget was SFr4.0 million in 1993, SFr4.0 million in 1994, and is SFr 4.5 million in 1995.

*Main contributors*

Main contributors in 1994 were the governments of Denmark, Finland, Germany, the Netherlands, Norway, Switzerland, and the City of Geneva, as well as the the International Development Research Centre, the Simons Foundation, UNEP, and the Centre's Friends and Working Partners.

## Publications

• *The Bulletin* (former Brundtland Bulletin), quarterly review of progress towards sustainable development;
• *Network*, monthly newsletter which monitors and reports on follow-up activities to the Earth Summit;
• *The Earth Summit's Agenda for Change*, a plain-language version of *Agenda 21* and the other Rio Agreements.

The Centre's database consists of 66,000 records (see above).

The Centre is committed to provide information on sustainable development to developing countries free of charge.

# Climate Action Network (CAN)

## Objectives

• to promote government and individual action to limit human-induced climate change to ecologically sustainable levels;
• to co-ordinate information exchange on international, regional, and national climate policies and issues;
• to formulate policy options and position papers on climate-related issues;
• to undertake further collaborative action to promote effective non-governmental organizations' (NGOs) involvement in efforts to avert the threat of global warming.

## Organization

*Type*
Non-governmental organization (NGO).

*Membership*
Non-governmental, citizen-based organizations with a special interest in climate-related issues. 8 regional offices covering 162 member organizations in 45 countries, by 12 October 1994.

*Founded*
March 1989.

## Secretariat

CAN has established the following regional focal points:

Climate Network Africa,
PO Box 76406,
Nairobi,
Kenya
*Telephone*:        +254-2-545241
*Telefax*:        +254-2-559-122
*E-mail*:  cna@elci.gn.apc.org

*CNA Co-ordinator*
Ms Grace Akumu.

Climate Action Network South Asia,
Bangladesh Centre for Advanced Studies,
620 Road 10a (New) Dhanmondi,
Dhaka,
Bangladesh
*Telephone*:        +880-2-815829
*Telefax*:        +880-2-863379
*E-mail*:  atiq.prdshta@cash.com

*CANSA Co-ordinator*
Mr Atiq Rahman.

Climate Action Network South East Asia,
Room 403 Cabrera Building II,
64 Timog Avenue,
Quezon City 1103,
The Philippines
*Telephone*:        +63-2-965362
*Telefax*:        +63-2-965362
*E-mail*:  cansea@phil.gn.apc.org

*CANSEA Co-ordinator*
Mr Lando Valasco.

Climate Action Network Central and Eastern Europe,
Radnicka cesta 22/1,
41000 Zagreb,
Croatia
*Telephone*:        +385-41-610951
*Telefax*:        +385-41-610951
*E-mail*:  za-zg@zamir-zg.ztn.zer.de

*CANCEE Co-ordinator*
Mr Toni Vidan.

Climate Network Europe,
44, rue du Taciturne,
B-1040 Brussels,
Belgium
*Telephone*:        +32-2-2310180
*Telefax*:        +32-2-2305713
*E-mail*:        canron@gn.apc.org

*CNE Co-ordinator*
Ms Lise Backer.

*Head of Information*
Ms Lynne Clark.

Climate Action Network UK,
Media Natura,
21 Tower Street,
London WC2H 9NS,
United Kingdom
*Telephone*:        +44-71-4972712
*Telefax*:        +44-71-2402291

*CAN UK Co-ordinator*
Ms Sally Cavanagh.

Climate Action Network Latin America,
Instituto de Ecologia Politica,
Casilla 16784 Correo 9,
Santiago,
Chile
*Telephone*:        +56-2-2746192
*Telefax*:        +56-2-2234522

*CANLA Co-ordinator*
Mr Eduardo Sanhuenza.

Climate Action Network US,
1350 New York Avenue, NW,
Suite 300,
Washington, DC 20005,
USA
*Telephone*:        +1-202-6249360
*Telefax*:        +1-202-7835917
*E-mail*:        uscan@igc.org

*CAN US Co-ordinator*
Ms Jennifer Morgan.

*Number of staff (all regional offices)*
8 professionals and 10 support staff (Oct. 1994).

## Activities

The activities are organized through the regional focal points:
• *Climate Network Africa (CNA)*, Kenya, is developing a working relationship with NGOs in all African regions to ensure a systematically wider coverage of the network;

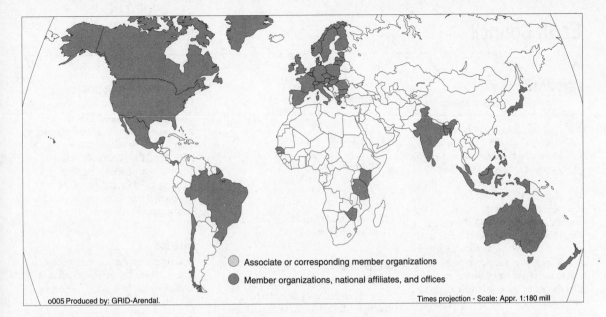

Associate or corresponding member organizations

Member organizations, national affiliates, and offices

o005 Produced by: GRID-Arendal.

Times projection - Scale: Appr. 1:180 mill

- *CAN South Asia (CANSA)*, Bangladesh, research activities include climate change and poverty; climate, environment, and population; and climate change and natural disasters;
- *CAN South East Asia (CANSEA)*, Philippines, has established Core Groups in the Philippines, Indonesia, and Malaysia and others are being sought in Thailand and other Indochinese countries;
- *Climate Action Network Central and Eastern Europe (CANCEE)*, newly established, has 19 NGOs affiliated;
- *CAN Latin America (CANLA)*, Chile, primarily consists of organizations from Brazil, Chile, Mexico, and Colombia;
- *Climate Network Europe (CNE)*, Belgium, was the first Climate Network node. It was created as an NGO service on climate change issues managed by the Stockholm Environment Institute (SEI). It has regularly co-ordinated activities between European NGOs and also acts as a resource centre for climate change information;
- *CAN UK* co-ordinates regular meetings of the Greenhouse Roundtable for information exchange and strategy building between 15 key NGOs in the United Kingdom, focusing on a range of issues such as transport, energy efficiency, water resources, development, and nature conservation;
- *CAN US* is the focal point of global warming research and advocacy by American NGOs. It has contributed to the scientific capacity of the NGOs within the UN climate convention negotiations and has benefited from interaction with Southern NGOs on the complexities of development issues in the South. CAN US is preparing to expand its domestic efforts at the state and local level by pursuing several legislative and administrative initiatives designed to reduce emissions of $CO_2$ and other greenhouse gases.

## Decision-making bodies

The regional co-ordinators meet twice a year. Common projects are discussed when appropriate.

## Finance

Core funding from foundations. Additional financing by membership dues and earnings from publications.

*Budget*
Not available.

*Main contributors*
Main contributors to Climate Network Europe in 1994 were the Stockholm Environment Institute, German Marshall Fund, Rockefeller Brothers Fund, and Alton Jones Foundation.

## Publications

- *ECO Climate Change Newsletter* (also available on electronic conference (see below);
- *CAN International NGO Directory*;
- *Everything You Ever Wanted to Know About Climate Change* (an annotated bibliography);
- *Joint Implementation from a European NGO Perspective*.

*Electronic conferences*
climate.forum

# Earth Council

## Objectives

• to serve as a global ombudsman for environment and development issues;
• to facilitate and support people's initiatives, particularly in implementation of the governmental and non-governmental results of the United Nations Conference on Environment and Development (UNCED);
• to help ensure that the experience, the concern, and the interests of people at the grass-roots are brought to bear at all levels of policy- and decision-making;
• to help ensure that public dialogue on environment and development issues is illuminated by the objective knowledge and opinions of scientists and experts;
• to monitor, compliment, and support the work and revision of the United Nations Commission on Sustainable Development (CSD) (see IGOs).

## Organization

*Type*
Non-governmental organization (NGO).

*Membership*
In addition to representatives of the sponsoring federations it consists of 21 distinguished citizens, scientists, and others serving in their personal capacities. National Councils on Sustainable Development or similar entities have been established world-wide during 1994. Information on the total number of entities were not confirmed, by November 1994.

*Founded*
September 1992.

## Secretariat

Earth Council Institute,
APDO 2323 - 1002,
San José,
Costa Rica
*Telephone:* +506-2233418
*Telefax:* +506-2552197
*E-mail:* ecouncil@igc.apc.org

*Chairman*
Mr Maurice Strong.

*Executive Director*
Ms Alicia Bárcena.

*Communications Officer*
Ms Aziyadé Poltier-Mutal.

*Number of staff*
15 professionals and 15 support staff at Headquarters (Nov. 1994).

## Activities

The Council's activities include:
• the organization of an ombudsman function which will facilitate equitable redress of environmental/development grievances and disputes;
• the provision of expanded access by grass-roots organizations and citizen groups to information, communication, and linkages which support their environmental/development activities and interests;
• the provision of information and materials in support of the development and implementation of the Rio Agreements by people, communities, and actors;
• the organization of public hearings, forums, and media events which focus public attention on environment and development issues and promote action in respect of them;
• the compilation and evaluation of indicators of environment and development performance;
• the provision of practical and financial support for people's projects and activities;
• the provision of practical support for communication and co-operation amongst people's organizations.
In all its programmes and activities the Earth Council will consult and co-operate closely with other organizations to avoid unnecessary duplication of effort and ensure the most effective use of limited resources and capacities.

## Decision-making bodies

An *Earth Council Organizing Committee* established the Council as a standing commission and took necessary action to bring it into full operation from March 1993. The 21 members of the Earth Council were officially nominated in November 1993 and they will be supported by the Earth Institute and the Earth Council Secretariat.

## Finance

Funding for the Earth Council comes from the Earth Council Foundation, a private non-profit-making foundation.

*Budget*
No information available.

*Main contributors*
Sponsoring institutions include the principal world federations of organizations dealing with development, environment, and science. They include the Stockholm Environment Institute (SEI); World Resources Institute (WRI); the International Development Research Center (IRDC); the Interamerican Institute on Co-operation for Agriculture (IICA); and small grants from the Netherlands and Switzerland representations in Costa Rica.
Additional support will be sought from foundations, corporations, and individuals in many countries.

## Publications

• Bulletins and reports;
• *Earth Council Information Letter* (six times a year).

*Electronic conferences*
Information on electronic communication systems and services is available from the Secretariat.

# Earthwatch

Associate or corresponding member organizations

Member organizations, national affiliates, and offices

o006 Produced by: GRID-Arendal.

Times projection - Scale: Appr. 1:180 mill

## Objectives
• to improve human understanding of the planet, the diversity of its inhabitants, and the processes that affect the quality of life on earth;
• to act as a bridge between science and the community by enabling members of the public to join scientists in the field and act as their assistants;
• to sustain the world's environment, to monitor global change, to conserve endangered species and habitats, to explore the vast heritage of the people, and to foster world health and international co-operation.

## Organization
*Type*
Non-governmental organization (NGO).

*Membership*
Individuals, organizations, corporations, and schools. About 75,000 individual members and 5 Earthwatch offices in five countries, by 7 November 1994.

*Founded*
1972.

## Secretariat
Earthwatch Europe,
Belsyre Court,
57 Woodstock Road,
Oxford OX2 6HU,
United Kingdom
*Telephone:* +44-865-311600
*Telefax:* +44-865-311383
*E-mail:* ewoxford@vax.oxford.ac.uk
(Internet)

*Director*
Mr Brian W. Walker.

*Deputy Director*
Mr Andrew Mitchell.

*Number of staff*
16 professionals (Nov. 1994).

## Activities
Earthwatch sponsors more than 165 projects in 50 countries. Projects are year-round and each volunteer pays a share of the cost to cover field-work, food, and lodging. The volunteers must be 16 years or older and no special skills are needed. Projects are 2–3 weeks in length.

Volunteer tasks can range from tracking endangered rhinos in Zimbabwe, excavating Mayan ruins in Mexico, surveying one of the last remaining fresh-water lakes in Kenya, to teaching dolphins sign language in Hawaii. Volunteers are an invaluable resource to scientists in collecting data pertaining to critical environmental issues.

Since 1972 over 35,000 volunteers (Earth Corps) have contributed over $US22.8 million to search for solutions to important environmental problems world-wide.

The Centre for Field Research receives over 400 proposals each year from scholars who need the help of volunteers. The Centre, with its academic advisory board, is responsible for peer review, screening, and selection of projects for Earthwatch support.

## Finance
Grants provided by foundations, corporations, and individual donors. More than three-quarters of its income is derived from subscribers and volunteers who share the cost and labour of the field research.

*Budget*
World-wide budget was $US7 million in 1993, $US10.3 million in 1994, and is $US10.3 million in 1995.

## Publications
• *Earthwatch* (six times a year);
• *President's Report* (annually).

# Environment Liaison Centre International (ELCI)

## Objectives

- to work towards socially, economically, and environmentally sustainable development by facilitating the voice and collective action of the grass-roots;
- to develop an equitable system of information processing and delivery that empowers people for community action;
- to promote voluntary community action as a necessary strategy for achieving sustainable development;
- to contribute towards recognition of cultural and ecological information that supports sustainable development while recognizing the intrinsic value of nature;
- to raise levels of technical expertise and management capacity for effective community action;
- to strengthen the participatory role of voluntary organizations by creating a democratic and responsible environment for enabling such participation;
- to promote the role and effectiveness of voluntary organizations in monitoring human actions that affect environmental quality and working for its improvement;
- to provide liaison between the UN system, the United Nations Environment Programme in particular, and environmental non-governmental organizations world-wide.

## Organization

*Type*
Non-governmental organization (NGO). ELCI is a networking instrument for NGOs. Consultative status with UN Environment Programme (UNEP) and UN Economic and Social Committee (ECOSOC).

*Membership*
Non-governmental organizations world-wide. Total of 840 full member organizations in 107 countries (105) or territories (2), by 19 October 1994.

*Founded*
1974.

## Secretariat

Environment Liaison Centre International (ELCI),
PO Box 72461,
Nairobi,
Kenya
*Telephone*:    +254-2-562-015/022/172
*Telefax*:      +254-2-562175
*E-mail*:       elci.gn.apc.org

*Co-Executive Directors*
Mr Rob Sinclair and Mr Ranil Senanayake.

*Head of Information*
Currently vacant, contact 'EDIE manager' (see Activities, no. 5, below).

*Number of staff*
11 professionals and 18 support staff (November 1993).

## Activities

From 1994, ELCI is to be organized around six strategic programme 'units'. These units will implement and manage specific programmes:
(1) *Issue-based Networks (IBN Unit)*. Through fostering these networks a group of members, working on a similar issue in different parts of the world, communicate with each other through mechanisms facilitated by ELCI. Issues being focused on the current period are: voluntary organizations' code of conduct and ethics; the convention of desertification; women in environment and development; cultural and ecological information; environment and economy; ecosystem-based networks; and 'roots of life'—models of sustainable development;

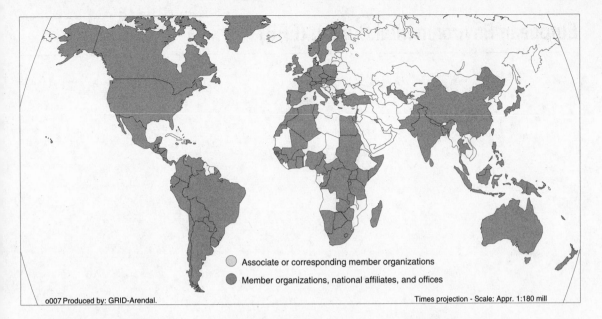

Associate or corresponding member organizations

Member organizations, national affiliates, and offices

o007 Produced by: GRID-Arendal.

Times projection - Scale: Appr. 1:180 mill

(2) *Constituency Development and Capacity-Building (CD/CB Unit)*. This unit is responsible for the provision of services to ELCI's members and constituency, including promotion and administration of membership, liaising with member organizations, and development and implementation of programmes aimed at supporting individual organizations, including a pilot *Eco-Volunteer* programme being implemented in collaboration with United Nations Volunteers (UNV) in eleven countries;

(3) *Research and Documentation Unit (RDU)*. RDU ensures that proper research and documentation functions are in place and gathers the information required to determine ELCI's appropriate response;

(4) *External Relations Unit (ERU)*. ERU is responsible for fostering strong working relationships with ELCI's peers in order to be more effective in supporting the work of grass-roots organizations. It works directly with intergovernmental and non-governmental organizations, donors, and the scientific and academic community;

(5) *Environment & Development Information Exchange (EDIE)*. EDIE is responsible for developing and maintaining systems for handling the inflow of information and directing it to action centres and for creating mechanisms for storage and retrieval of information.

(6) *Media and Publication Unit (MPU)*. MPU is responsible for overseeing the quality of all information that is disseminated to the constituency and general public by ELCI.

## Decision-making bodies

ELCI's main decision-making body is the *General Assembly* of members which meets annually to:
• review the state of global environment and development trends;
• determine policy directives;
• elect the Board of Directors which formulates policy.

The regionally balanced *Board of Directors*, which meets once a year, consists of 14 elected and up to 5 co-opted members. Each of the 5 continents is equally represented and women constitute around 50 per cent. The Board provides policy guide-lines which its elected *Executive Committee*, on which each continent is represented by one member, reviews twice a year.

The constitution regarding decision-making bodies will be restructured during 1994.

## Finance

The main sources of income are bilateral and multilateral donors, private foundations, members' fees, and sales of publications.

*Budget*
The administrative budget was $US1.1 million in 1992, $US1.4 million in 1993, and $US2.1 million in 1994.

*Main contributors*
Main contributors in 1994 were development agencies in the Netherlands, Norway, and Canada, as well as UNV/ United Nations Development Programme (UNDP) and United Nations Environment Programme (UNEP) (see IGOs).

## Publications

• *Ecoforum* (six times a year);
• *Global Action Guide: A Handbook for NGO Co-operation on Environment and Development*;
• *Directory of Francophone NGOs*;
• *Environment-Development News*;
• *WedLine;*
• *Circular Letters* (bi-monthly) on desertification and biological diversity;
• ELCI News/Nouvelles/Noticias (bi-monthly membership newsletter).

# European Environmental Bureau (EEB)

## Objectives
• to bring together environmental non-governmental organizations in the member States in order to strengthen their effect and impact on the environmental policy and projects of the European Union (EU);
• to promote an equitable and sustainable life-style;
• to promote the protection and conservation of the environment, the restoration and the better use of human resources;
• to use educational and other means to increase public awareness of these problems;
• to make all necessary information available to members and other organizations likely to assist in the realization of these aims;
• to promote and strengthen environmental policy at the global level. e.g. in the framework of the follow-up on the UN Conference of Environment and Development (UNCED).

## Organization
*Type*
Non-governmental organization (NGO). Consultative status with the Council of Europe, and relations with Commission of the European Union, European Parliament, Economic and Social Committee of the European Union, and OECD (see IGOs).

*Membership*
Non-governmental organizations, dealing with environmental conservation and protection, from EU and European Free Trade Association (EFTA) member States. Corresponding NGO members from non-EU member states. 83 full member organizations in 14 countries, by 4 November 1994. 34 associate, 24 affiliate, and 10 corresponding member organizations in 24 countries.

*Founded*
13 December 1974.

## Secretariat
European Environmental Bureau (EEB), 26 rue de la Victoire, B-1060 Brussels, Belgium
*Telephone*:       +32-2-5390037
*Telefax*:        +32-2-5390921

*Secretary-General*
Mr Raymond Van Ermen.

*Number of staff*
5 professionals and 2 support staff in Brussels (Oct. 1994).

## Activities
The activities of the EEB focus on the European Union's role in the field of environment, both within and beyond EU's borders.

The EEB monitors the European institutions' respect for the principles of the Single Act, according to which Commission proposals are to meet a high level of environmental protection, and environmental protection requirements are to be a component of the Union's other policies.

Main areas; environmental policy, education, nature protection, pollution control, land-use planning, transport, tourism, cultural heritage and education, energy, agriculture, and the environmental aspects of EU relations with developing countries.

It achieves its objectives through a mixture of lobbying, generalized and specific publications, in addition to 5 to 7 seminars/conferences, workshops, or round tables, which are open to the public..
Its regional office, the Mediterranean Information Office (MIO), which has become independent in order to have access to institutional funding, reinforces the capacities of Mediterranean NGOs through the sharing of experiences, dissemination of information, and setting-up of training programmes.

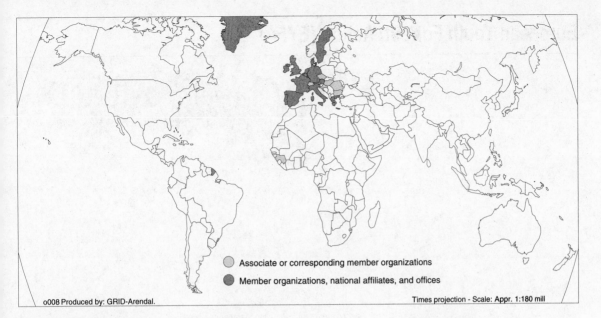

Associate or corresponding member organizations

Member organizations, national affiliates, and offices

o008 Produced by: GRID-Arendal.

Times projection - Scale: Appr. 1:180 mill

## Decision-making bodies

The *Annual General Meeting* (AGM), where each full member organization has one vote, elects the *Executive Board* for a two-year term. The Board consists, normally, of one member per EU member State. EEB draft position papers are prepared e.g. by EEB staff members, experts or expert groups, seldom by an 'outside' expert. They are always submitted for approval to the Board; depending on the issue and the time schedule they are first circulated for comments to EEB experts or all the members. Each member organization may attend the meetings. Full members of the working parties, with voting rights, are limited to one per country. In each of the EU member States national conferences of EEB members are organized several times a year.

## Finance

Members' dues, grants from official and private bodies, and contributions from the EU.

*Budget*
The budget was ECU1.5 million in 1993, ECU1.5 million in 1994, and is ECU1.7 million in 1995.

*Main contributors*
Belgium, Denmark, France, Germany, Greece, Luxembourg, the Netherlands, Sweden, the United Kingdom, and the European Commission.

## Publications

• Annual Reports;
• Conference Reports;
• *Metamorphosis* (newsletter in the nine EU languages);
• *Memorandum to the EU Presidency*;
• *The Mediterranean Information Office News Letter*;
• *In Brief* (newsletter for members only);
• *Your Rights under EU Environment Legislation*;
• *Towards a Sustainable Europe: The EU Policies and Central and Eastern European Countries*.

# European Youth For(est) Action (EYFA)

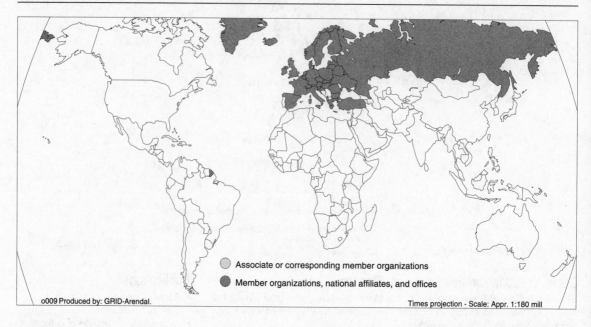

Associate or corresponding member organizations

Member organizations, national affiliates, and offices

o009 Produced by: GRID-Arendal.

Times projection - Scale: Appr. 1:180 mill

## Objectives

• to promote co-operation and co-ordination of youth environmentalists on an international level;
• to combine political non-violent activism with changes in life-style on the individual level;
• to fight nuclear energy and support new and renewable sources of energy;
• to develop sustainable life-styles.

## Organization

*Type*
Non-governmental organization (NGO). Platform of European environmental youth organizations.

*Membership*
More than 370 youth and environmental organizations in 35 countries in Europe, by October 1994.

*Founded*
1985.

## Secretariat

European Youth For(est) Action (EYFA),
International Office,
PO Box 94115,
1090 GC Amsterdam,
The Netherlands
*Telephone*:        +31-20-6657743

*Telefax*:        +31-20-6657743
*E-mail*:        eyfa@antenna.nl

*Director General*
Mr Loek Hilgersom.

*Number of staff*
Between 12 and 24 volunteers (Oct. 1994).

## Activities

EYFA organizes international bus and cycle tours to teach young people about environmental problems and to get them to act against polluters and for a better environmental policy. It is also engaged in several projects on the community level.

Information campaigns are arranged both on nuclear energy in the former Eastern Europe and on climate change.

In June 1992 EYFA co-ordinated the European youth activities around the United Nations Conference on Environment and Development (UNCED) meeting in Brazil in June 1992.

EYFA supports groups in Eastern Europe with communications (i.e. e-mail).

EYFA organizes in August every year the ecological summer university 'ECOTOPIA'. ECOTOPIA took place in Germany (1989), Hungary (1990), Estonia (1991), Bulgaria (1992), France (1993), and Romania in 1994. ECOTOPIA 1995 will be in Poland.

## Decision-making bodies

An *International Co-ordination Team*, which meets 4 times a year, consists of 7 members.

## Finance

Contributions from members, the Commission of the European Union, and European Youth Foundation, and other funds.

*Budget*
The budget was approximately Dutch FL500,000 in 1993, FL600,000 in 1994, and is FL500,000 in 1995.

## Publications

*The Verge* (six times a year).

# Friends of the Earth International (FoEI)

o010 Produced by: GRID-Arendal.

○ Associate or corresponding member organizations

● Member organizations, national affiliates, and offices

Times projection - Scale: Appr. 1:180 mill

## Objectives
• to promote conservation, restoration, and rational use of the environment and the Earth's natural resources through public education and campaigning at local, national, and international levels;
• to encourage international citizen action and improvement of social, economic, and cultural conditions influencing environmental degradation, stressing positive alternatives to destructive systems.

## Organization
*Type*
Non-governmental organization (NGO). Observer status at FAO, IMO, London Convention 1972, International Oil Pollution Compensation Fund, Barcelona Convention (see UNEP Regional Seas Programme, Agreements), International Whaling Commission (IWC) (see ICRW, Agreements), Ramsar Convention, International Tropical Timber Agreement (ITTA). Consultative status at UNESCO (see IGOs), UN Economic and Social Council (ECOSOC), and UN Economic Commission for Europe (UN/ ECE). Participates in the meetings of IAEA, Intergovernmental Panel on Climate Change (IPCC) (see Framework Convention on Climate Change, Agreements), Montreal Protocol on Substances

that Deplete the Ozone Layer, and others. Member of ELCI and IUCN (see this section).

*Membership*
National member groups and NGOs. Each national member group is an autonomous body with its own funding and strategy. National member groups in 50 countries and 1 territory, with nearly 1 million individual members, by 5 October 1994. 5 affiliated NGOs and 1 associate national member group.

*Founded*
1971.

## Secretariat
Friends of the Earth International (FoEI), PO Box 19199, 1000 GD Amsterdam, The Netherlands
*Telephone*: +31-20-6221369
*Telefax*: +31-20-6392181
*E-mail*: foeint@xs4all.nl

*Chairman*
Mr John Hontelez.

*Number of staff*
2 professionals and 2 support staff at the International Secretariat (Oct. 1994).

## Activities
Instrumental in creating networks of environmental, consumer, human-rights

organizations world-wide.

FoEI co-ordinates their activities at the international level through campaigns led by national members' groups. Main international co-ordinating areas; political lobbying, flow of information through the FoEI network, and citizen action with the following main areas; climate change, tropical rainforests, ozone pollution, and marine conservation.

## Decision-making bodies
An *Annual Meeting* of the national organizations elects the *FoEI Executive Committee*.

## Finance
Each national group is responsible for its own budget, and makes annual contributions to the FoEI Secretariat. Main sources are fees, donations, and subsidies.

*Budget*
The total budget of the International Secretariat was $US370,000 in 1993 and $US390,000 in 1994.

## Publications
• *FOE Link* (six times a year);
• *Activities Report* (annually).

# Greenpeace International

## Objectives

- to stop the chemicalization of the planet and the trade in toxic waste and dirty technology;
- to protect the Earth's biological diversity of species in the ocean and on land;
- to end the threat of nuclear weapons, nuclear weapons testing, nuclear power, and nuclear waste;
- to protect the Earth's atmosphere from ozone depletion and build-up of greenhouse gases and push for clean and alternative energy and refrigeration technologies.

## Organization

*Type*
Non-governmental organization (NGO), with offices world-wide. Consultative status with UN Economic and Social Committee (ECOSOC).

*Membership*
World-wide individual membership of over 3.5 million supporters in 143 countries, by 7 November 1994. Offices in 32 countries.

*Founded*
1971.

## Secretariat

Greenpeace International,
Keizersgracht 176,
1016 DW Amsterdam,
The Netherlands
*Telephone*:      +31-20-5236222
*Telefax*:        +31-20-5236200
*E-mail*: adam@greenpeace.org

*Executive Director*
Mr Steve D'Esposito.

*Head of Information Division*
Richard Titchen,
Greenpeace Communications,
5 Bakers Row,
London EC1R 3DB,
United Kingdom
*Telephone*:      +44-71-8330600
*Telefax*:        +44-71-8376606
*E-mail*: comms@greenpeace.org

*Number of staff*
About 1100 world-wide (Nov. 1994). Approximately 120 at the Amsterdam Secretariat.

## Activities

In 1995 Greenpeace will focus campaign resources in a number of areas. These will include special efforts to:
- ensure that a further step towards nuclear disarmament is taken by the conclusion of a Comprehensive Test Ban Treaty on the 50th anniversary of the bombings of Hiroshima and Nagasaki and that a new and more effective Non-Proliferation Treaty is established globally;
- protect the planet's climate and ozone layer by ensuring that industrialized-country governments agree at meetings in 1995 to radically cut emissions of polluting greenhouse and ozone-depleting gases;
- protect the marine environment from overfishing and pollution through adoption of new international regulations at intergovernmental meetings in the future;
- transform refrigeration, air conditioning, and other industries using ozone-depleting chemicals;
- monitor and ensure enforcement of global controls on the international waste trade;

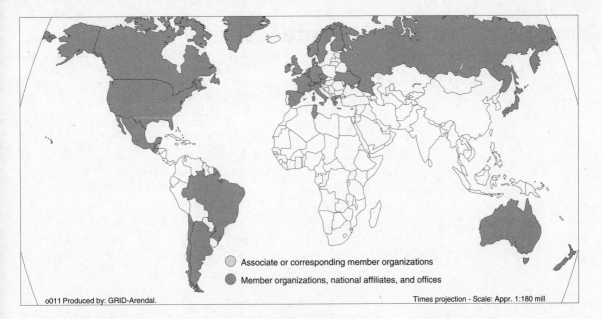

Associate or corresponding member organizations

Member organizations, national affiliates, and offices

o011 Produced by: GRID-Arendal.

Times projection - Scale: Appr. 1:180 mill

• stop clearcutting of temperate and tropical rainforests, and to promote economic alternatives;
• eliminate the use of hazardous chemicals, in particular chlorine, which is still used widely for paper bleaching, PVC, and other industrial applications in spite of mounting evidence of devastating impacts on human and animal health;
• stop commercial whaling;
• eliminate the use of drift-nets.

## Decision-making bodies

*Greenpeace Council*, consisting of one representative from each member country, defines objectives and strategies at the annual meeting. The Council elects seven members of the *Greenpeace International Board*, which appoints a chairperson and an administrative executive. The International Board is responsible for the supervision of the organization during the year. The national organizations have an autonomous position in their daily activities.

## Finance

Financed by voluntary contributions from the public and from the sale of merchandise.

*Budget*
The budget was $US40 million in 1992, $US39 million in 1993, and is $US30 million in 1995.

## Publications

*Annual Report* from the Amsterdam Secretariat. Various publications produced by national offices.

# International Chamber of Commerce (ICC)

## Objectives

The objectives of ICC are:
- to serve world business by promoting trade and investment and the market economy system;
- to represent business and defend the interests of the private sector in developed and developing countries, and in the economies in transition;
- to facilitate commercial transactions among nations through the provision of practical services and training for business people.

The ICC Commission on Environment represents world business in the United Nations and other international forums. It aims to ensure that environmental standards, UN conventions, and other internationally applicable regulations do not inhibit trade and investment, and are in conformity with the market economy system. The ICC Commission on Environment promotes the ICC's *Business Charter for Sustainable Development* and assists companies in implementing Charter principles.

The objectives of the World Industry Council for the Environment (WICE) are:
- to promote co-operation in technology between companies in developed and developing countries;
- to improve understanding of the global environment issues of greatest concern to business;
- to be a partner with governments and international organizations in influencing development of cost-effective environmental policies based on sound scientific conclusions;
- to be actively involved when environmental issues are dealt with in the UN and other intergovernmental agencies, particularly the UN Commission on Sustainable Development (CSD) and United Nations Environment Programme (UNEP) (see IGOs).

## Organization

*Type*
Non-governmental organization (NGO). WICE was established at the initiative of the ICC. The ICC has first-class consultative status with UN and its specialized agencies.

*Membership*
National Committees or groups in 61 countries, by November 1994. WICE's membership consisted of 87 companies in 23 countries, by November 1994.

*Founded*
ICC in June 1919, the Commission on Environment in 1978, and WICE on 26 February 1993.

## Secretariat

ICC,
38 Cours Albert 1er,
F-75008 Paris,
France
*Telephone*:        +33-1-49532828
*Telefax*:        +33-1-49532924

WICE,
40 Cours Albert 1er,
F-75008 Paris,
France
*Telephone*:        +33-1-49532891
*Telefax*:        +33-1-49532889

*ICC Secretary-General*
Mr Jean-Charles Rouher.

*Chairman of WICE*
Mr Rodney Chase.

*ICC, Head of Information*
Mr Lionel Walsh.

*WICE, Head of Information*
Ms Christine Elleboode.

*Number of staff*
ICC, Paris: 96 professionals; WICE: 7 professionals (Nov. 1994).

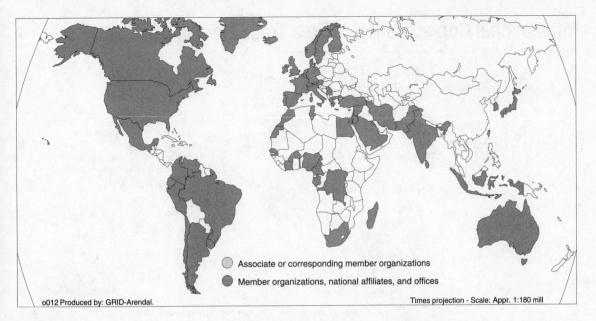

Associate or corresponding member organizations

Member organizations, national affiliates, and offices

o012 Produced by: GRID-Arendal.

Times projection - Scale: Appr. 1:180 mill

## Activities

The ICC Commission on Environment provided business input to sessions of the international negotiating committee on the UN Framework Convention on Climate Change (FCCC) (see Agreements), in preparation for first Conference of the Parties in Berlin in March/April 1995.

It participates in the technical committee of the International Standards Organization (ISO) responsible for negotiations on the development of standards related to environmental management systems.

The Commission has also developed a strategy in co-operation with the OECD Business and Industry Advisory Committee for the definition of hazardous and non-hazardous wastes.

The ICC adopted its *Business Charter for Sustainable Development* in 1990. The ICC uses its world-wide network to promote the Charter and encourage implementation of its 16 principles. WICE and the ICC assist companies by providing materials for in-house training along Charter lines.

ICC has twice organized World Industry Conferences on Environmental Management: WICEM I in 1984 jointly with UNEP and WICEM II in 1991.

## Decision-making bodies

The *ICC Council*, the supreme governing body, meets twice yearly. Members of the *Executive Board* are appointed by the Council on the recommendation of the President, who is elected by the Council, and holds office for two years.

The *WICE Board* meets once a year. It determines policy and launches specific projects. A 12-member *Steering Committee* meets four times a year to review strategic planning, policy developments, and the work programme.

## Finance

The ICC derives its income from services, publications, contributions from the National Committees and groups. WICE is funded from membership fees.

*Budget*
No information available.

## Publications

- *ICC Handbook*;
- *ICC Annual Report*;
- *From Ideas to Action: The Greening of Enterprise*;
- *ICC Business Charter for Sustainable Development*;
- *ICC Guide to Effective Environmental Auditing*;
- *ICC Code on Environmental Advertising*;
- *Environmental Reporting: A Manager's Guide*;
- *Design for Environment*.

# International Confederation of Free Trade Unions (ICFTU)

o013 Produced by: GRID-Arendal.

○ Associate or corresponding member organizations

● Member organizations, national affiliates, and offices

Times projection - Scale: Appr. 1:180 mill

## Objectives

• to maintain and develop a powerful and effective international organization at world-wide and regional levels, composed of free and democratic trade unions, independent of any external domination and pledged to the task of promoting the interests of working people throughout the world, and of enhancing the dignity of labour;
• to promote and defend human and trade-union rights world-wide;
• to promote fair and just economic development on the basis that this development can ultimately only be fair and socially just if it is at the same time sustainable.

## Organization

*Type*
Non-governmental organization (NGO). Consultative status with ECOSOC, UNESCO, ILO, and UNIDO (see IGOs).

*Membership*
Trade unions world-wide. 174 affiliated organizations in 114 countries and 8 territories representing 120 million working people, by October 1994.

*Founded*
December 1949.

## Secretariat

International Confederation of Free Trade Unions (ICFTU),
Blvd. Emile Jaqqmain 155,
B-1210 Brussels, Belgium
*Telephone:*      +32-2-2240211
*Telefax:*      +32-2-20-15815/30756

*General Secretary*
Mr Enzo Friso.

*Head, Press and Publications Departm.*
Mr Luc Demaret.

*Number of staff*
98 (Nov. 1994).

## Activities

The ICFTU made environment and development one of the main themes at its World Congress in 1992 and focuses particularly on the international aspects of sustainable development.

It stresses the importance of involving workers in the decision-making process as the only means of ensuring that the necessary changes are carried out fairly, efficiently, and with the minimum amount of social disruption commensurate with achieving the goal of sustainable development.

It further stresses the need for resources to be made available in and to developing countries in order to ensure

that they have the wherewithal to be able to undertake the sometimes costly activities that will be necessary to protect the environment.

## Decision-making bodies

The *Congress*, which meets every fourth year, elects the *Executive Board* and the *General Secretary*. The Executive Board meets at least once a year and elects the *President*, *Vice-Presidents*, and a *Steering Committee* of 17 members.

## Finance

Affiliation fees and voluntary contributions.

*Budget*
The total budget was $US13.0 million in 1994.

*Special funds*
General Fund: $US13.0 million (1994); and International Solidarity Fund: $US2.0 million (1994). Main contributors are affiliates of the ICFTU.

## Publications

• *Free Labour World* (12 times a year);
• *From Rio to the Workplace*;

*Electronic conferences*
poptel geo2:icftu.

# International Council of Voluntary Agencies (ICVA)

Associate or corresponding member organizations

Member organizations, national affiliates, and offices

o014 Produced by: GRID-Arendal.

Times projection - Scale: Appr. 1:180 mill

## Objectives

• to promote the development, growth, and improvement of voluntary agencies, and their activities throughout the world;
• to provide a forum where voluntary agencies may exchange views and information on all matters and questions of common interest;
• to serve as a means of informing peoples, governments, intergovernmental agencies, and non-governmental organizations throughout the world of the humanitarian problems to which the voluntary agencies address themselves.

## Organization

*Type*
International association of non-governmental organizations (NGO). Consultative status with UN Economic and Social Council (ECOSOC) and ILO (see IGOs).

*Membership*
Non-governmental organizations, non-profit organizations active in the fields of humanitarian assistance and sustainable development co-operation. Membership of 94 international, regional, and national organizations in 41 countries, by 10 October 1994.

*Founded*
6 March 1962.

## Secretariat

International Council of Voluntary Agencies (ICVA),
13 rue Gautier,
CH-1201 Geneva, Switzerland
*Postal address*
CP 216,
CH-1211 Geneva 21,
Switzerland
*Telephone*:       +41-22-7326600
*Telefax*:        +41-22-7389904
*E-mail*:  icva.geneva@cgnet.com

*Executive Director*
Mr Delmar Blasco.

*Number of staff*
8 professionals and 6 support staff (Oct. 1994).

## Activities

ICVA is not operational at the field level. ICVA implements programmes involving information exchange, analysis, and advocacy, on refugees, displaced persons, and migrants; on sustainable development (food security, debt, trade, consumption patterns, and popular participation); and on institutional development of NGOs.

## Decision-making bodies

*General Assembly*, which meets at least every three years, elects the *Executive Committee*. The Executive Committee, which meets twice a year, consists of 16 elected member agencies, 2 co-opted member agencies, and the chairs of 3 working groups.

## Finance

Member agencies pay membership fees (base, working group, sub-group, and assessed fees). Main sources are members' contributions, governments, development agencies, and foundations.

*Budget*
Budget for the biennium 1993–94 was SFr2,694,646.

*Main contributors*
Main contributors in 1994 were the Australian International Development Assistance Bureau, the Finnish International Development Agency, the Norwegian government, the Swedish International Development Authority, the Ford Foundation, the Albert Kundtadter Family Foundation, and the World Bank (see IGOs).

## Publications

• Mission reports;
• *ICVA Forum*.

# International Organization of Consumer Unions (IOCU)

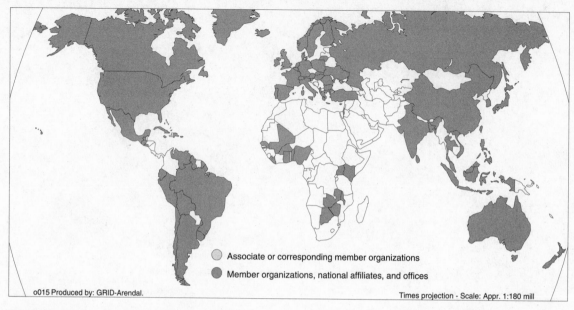

Associate or corresponding member organizations

Member organizations, national affiliates, and offices

o015 Produced by: GRID-Arendal.    Times projection - Scale: Appr. 1:180 mill

## Objectives

• to help build the organizations that make up the global consumer movement;
• to assist and promote genuine efforts throughout the world in consumer self-organization as well as governmental efforts to further the interests of the consumer;
• to give practical encouragement and aid to the development of consumer educational and protective programmes in the developing countries
• to influence the institutions which formulate global and regional policy affecting consumers.

## Organization

*Type*
Non-governmental organization (NGO). Consultative status with UN ECOSOC, UNESCO, FAO, WHO, UNICEF, and UNIDO (see IGOs).

*Membership*
Consumer associations, government-financed consumer councils, consumer bodies supported by family organizations, labour unions, and similar groups. IOCU had become a federation of 203 consumer organizations in 83 countries or territories, by September 1994. 121 corresponding member organizations in 53 countries, by March 1993.

*Founded*
1 April 1960.

## Secretariat

International Organization of Consumer Unions (IOCU), Head Office, 24 Highbury Crescent, London N5 1RX, United Kingdom
*Telephone*:        +44-71-2266663
*Telefax*:        +44-71-3540607

*Director-General*
Mr James Firebrace.

*Information officer*
Ms Carmelita McCarthy.

3 Regional Offices in Chile, Zimbabwe, and Malaysia, with Programme for Developed Economies (PRODEC) and Programme for Economies in Transition (PROECT) based in Head Office.

*Number of staff*
80 (March 1993).

## Activities

Three specific consumer rights and one consumer responsibility are directly related to sustainable development: the right to the satisfaction of basic needs; to safety; and to a healthy environment, as well as consumers' ecological responsibility to be sensitive to what their consumption of goods does to the environment.

Consumer Interpol (CI) is a global citizens' action network to check the international trade in hazardous products, technologies, and wastes.

IOCU organizes many conferences, seminars, and regional workshops.

## Decision-making bodies

*General Assembly*, the governing body, consists of one voting delegate from each associate organization. The *Council*, composed of 20 associate members elected by the *Assembly*, designates the eight-member *Executive Committee*.

## Finance

Membership dues, sale of publications, grants from governments, UN agencies, development organizations, development aid agencies, and donor institutions.

*Budget*
The total budget is approximately $US2.1 million in 1995.

## Publications

• Annual Reports;
• *World Consumer* (six times a year);
• *Consumer Current* (12 times a year);
• *Consumer Interpol Focus* (six times a year).

# International Planned Parenthood Federation (IPPF)

Associate or corresponding member organizations

Member organizations, national affiliates, and offices

o016 Produced by: GRID-Arendal.

Times projection - Scale: Appr. 1:180 mill

## Objectives
• to promote the formation of family planning programmes in all countries;
• to assist integration of family planning into development efforts;
• to further the training of physicians, nurses, health visitors, and social workers in the practical implementation of family planning services.

## Organization
*Type*
Non-governmental organization (NGO). Consultative status with UN ECOSOC, UNESCO, FAO, ILO, UNFPA, and WHO (see IGOs).

*Membership*
Member associations in 88 countries and 2 territories, by November 1994. Associate member organizations in 20 countries.

*Founded*
29 November 1952.

## Secretariat
IPPF,
Regent Park (Inner Circle),
London NW1 4NS,
United Kingdom
*Telephone*:      +44-71-4860741
*Telefax*:      +44-71-4877950

*Secretary General*
Dr Halfdan Mahler.

*Director of Public Affairs*
Ms Sunetra Puri.

*Number of staff*
127 at the Secretariat and 216 at field offices (Nov. 1994).

## Activities
The Federation, besides providing funding for some associations, offers technical support and training, and provides for the transfer of experience and expertise between its members.

Through its specialist panels and committees of international volunteers it is able to set standards and ensure levels of care which are recognized worldwide. It monitors the safety and acceptability of contraceptive methods, and provides contraceptive supplies on request. It has an important educational role and helps promote the cause of family planning at the international level.

IPPF co-operates with IUCN (see this section) and UNFPA (see IGOs), and together they publish the magazine 'People and the Planet'.

## Decision-making bodies
The *Members' Assembly* meets every three years and elects the *Central Council*, which meets every year. The *Executive Committee* meets twice a year. *IPPF International Medical Advisory Panel* and the *IPPF International Programme Advisory Panel* meet twice a year.

## Finance
Voluntary contributions both from governments (OECD countries and a number of developing countries), international organizations, and the private sector.

*Budget*
The total budget was $US81.1 million in 1993, and $US114.0 million in 1994. The administrative budget at the Secretariat was approximately $US47.0 million in 1994.

## Publications
• *People & the Planet*;
• *IPPF Medical Bulletin*;
• *Planned Parenthood Challenges*;
• Series of IPPF Medical publications;
• *Open File*, newsletter.

# International Solar Energy Society (ISES)

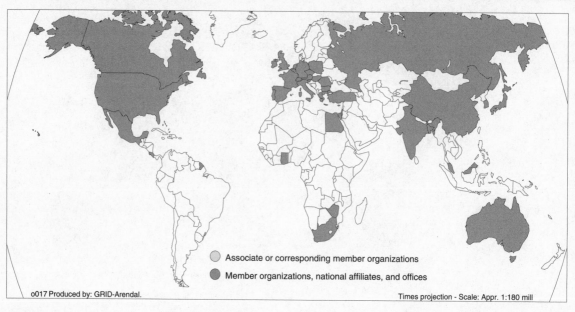

○ Associate or corresponding member organizations

● Member organizations, national affiliates, and offices

o017 Produced by: GRID-Arendal.

Times projection - Scale: Appr. 1:180 mill

## Objectives

• to provide a common meeting ground for all those concerned with the nature and utilization of solar energy;
• to foster science and technology relating to the applications of solar energy;
• to promote education and encourage research and development;
• to gather, compile, and disseminate information in these fields.

## Organization

*Type*
Non-governmental organization (NGO). Consultative status (category C) with UNESCO (see IGOs).

*Membership*
Organizations, corporations, individuals, scientists, engineers, and others with a special interest in solar energy. Members in more than 90 countries or territories. National and regional sections in 40 countries, by October 1994, representing 4,065 individual members.

*Founded*
24 December 1954.

## Secretariat

New location in 1995:
International Solar Energy Society (ISES),
Fraunhoffer Institute für Solare Energisystem,
Oltmannsstrasse 5,
D-19279 Freiburg,
Germany

*President*
Dr M. Nicklas.

*Secretary-Treasurer*
To be decided in January 1995.

*Number of staff*
1 professional and 3 support staff (Nov. 1994).

## Activities

Its interests embrace all aspects of solar energy, including characteristics, effects, and methods of use.

ISES organizes major International Congresses on solar energy at which numerous scientific and technical papers are presented and discussed. These congresses are held every two years in different countries.

ISES publishes the proceedings of each International Congress, usually in four volumes.

## Decision-making bodies

The Society is administered by a *Board of Directors*, elected by and representative of the world-wide membership. The Board meets annually, normally just prior to the *Annual General Meeting* of the Society's members. Day-to-day administration is provided by the *Secretary-Treasurer* and the *Administrative Secretary* in the Society's headquarters office.

## Finance

Membership dues, earnings from publications.

*Budget*
The total budget was $US220,000 in 1993, $US241,000 in 1994, and is $US461,480 in 1995.

## Publications

• *Solar Energy* (12 times a year);
• *Sunworld* (quarterly);
• *ISES News*.

# IUCN—The World Conservation Union

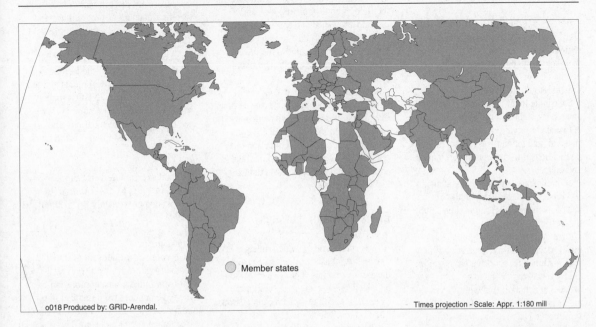

Member states

o018 Produced by: GRID-Arendal.

Times projection - Scale: Appr. 1:180 mill

## Objectives

The mission of IUCN is to influence, encourage, and assist societies throughout the world to conserve the integrity and diversity of nature. The objectives are:
• to secure the conservation of nature, and especially of biological diversity, as an essential foundation for the future;
• to ensure that where the Earth's natural resources are used this is done in a wise, equitable way;
• to guide the development of human communities towards ways of life that are both of good quality and in enduring harmony with other components of the biosphere.

## Organization

*Type*
Non-governmental organization (NGO). Consultative status with UN Economic and Social Council (ECOSOC) and several specialized agencies of the UN.

*Membership*
States (68), Government Agencies (100), National NGOs (550) and International NGOs (53). Total of 806 full members in 126 countries and territories, by May 1994. 35 non-voting affiliates.

*Founded*
5 October 1948.

## Secretariat

IUCN—The World Conservation Union, Rue Mauverney 28, CH-1196 Gland, Switzerland
*Telephone*:  +41-22-9990001
*Telefax*:  +41-22-9990002
*E-mail*:  iucnlib@gn.apc.org

*Director-General*
Mr David McDowell.

*Director of Communications and Corporate Relations*
Mr John Burke.

*Information Officer*
Ms Joanna Boddens Hosang.

IUCN Environmental Law Centre, Adenaueralle 214, D-53113 Bonn 53113, Germany
*Telephone*:  +49-228-2692231
*Telefax*:  +49-228-2692250

*Documentation Officer*
Ms Annie Lukacs.

In addition IUCN has regional offices in Asia, Central America, South America, Eastern Africa, Southern Africa, Western Africa, and numerous country offices, found mostly in developing countries.

*Number of staff*
540; of which 140 are based at headquarters and approximately 400 are outposted staff, including consultants (Oct 1993).

## Activities

IUCN carries out a single integrated Programme. Approved by the triennial General Assembly of members (see below) the Programme is co-ordinated by the central Secretariat (both in Headquarters and in the regional and country offices) and implemented with assistance from the network of volunteer experts in the IUCN Commissions, consultants, and a wide range of IUCN members and collaborating agencies. The Union's activities include to:
• harness the strengths of its members, Commissions, and other constituents to build global partnerships for conservation;
• catalyse action by the Union's members, Secretariat, and Commissions in order to achieve more effective conservation of nature and natural resources in

keeping with the principles set out in *Caring for the Earth*, the 1991 follow-up to the World Conservation Strategy (1980);

• provide a forum for government and NGO members to discuss global and regional conservation issues, including their scientific, educational, legal, economic, social, cultural, and political dimensions;

• contribute to an increased global awareness of the interrelationships between conservation, long-term survival, and human wellbeing, through publications, information dissemination, and education;

• communicate authoritative statements on conservation, drawing on the expertise of its members, Commissions, and Secretariat;

• develop national and regional strategies for sustainability, capacity building, and institutional support, a process often led by IUCN regional and country offices, in collaboration with governments and NGOs;

• influence national and international legal and administrative instruments to safeguard the environmental rights of future generations;

• participate actively in the preparation of international conventions relevant to the conservation of nature and natural resources and equitable and sustainable resource use.

The IUCN Commissions (see below) constitute a global network of more than 6,000 scientists and professionals.

The Environmental Law Centre (ELC) and the Commission on Environmental Law implement the legal aspects of the IUCN Programme. The main goals of the Environmental Law Programme are to promote the creation of sound international and national environmental legal instruments, to monitor developments in the field of environmental law, and provide assistance and service in this field, especially to developing countries. It has been instrumental in the development of several conservation conventions, and, in addition to practice-oriented legal analysis and studies, carries out specific projects in over 20 countries. Its Environmental Law Information System (ELIS) comprises a comprehensive collection of material on international and national environmental law with more than 115,000 citations.

## Decision-making bodies

*Political bodies*
A *General Assembly*, which meets every three years, consists of delegates from the member bodies. The General Assembly elects the *President*, the regional *Councillors* and the *Commission Chairs*. The *Council*, which meets at least annually, consists of the President, 4 Vice-Presidents, 24 regional Councillors, 5 co-opted Councillors, and 6 Chairs of Commissions.

*Scientific/technical bodies*
The six IUCN Commissions are:
• *Education and Communication*;
• *Environmental Law*;
• *Environmental Strategy and Planning*;
• *National Parks and Protected Areas*;
• *Species Survival*;
• *Ecology*.

## Finance
IUCN membership dues constitute a basic source of discretionary funds. Specific financing of programmes and projects is also provided by multilateral organizations (including UN agencies such as UNESCO and UNEP (see IGOs), and the Commission of the European Union), individual governments and aid agencies, international NGOs (such as World Wide Fund For Nature (WWF) (see this section)), foundations, the corporate sector, and individual donors.

*Budget*
The total expenditure was SFr55.2 million in 1992, SFr52.7 million in 1993, and approximately SFr57.0 million in 1994.

*Main sources*
IUCN received 72 per cent of its 1992 income from government sources, 13 per cent from foundations, corporations, and others, 10 per cent from membership, and 5 per cent from WWF. The largest government supporters were The Netherlands, Sweden, and Switzerland.

## Publications
IUCN regularly publishes reports and books on conservation issues. Key sources are:
• *The Red Data Books*;
• *United Nations List of National Parks and Protected Areas*;
• *IUCN Bulletin* (quarterly);
• *Caring for the Earth* (published with UNEP and WWF in 1991);
• *Interact*.

*Electronic conferences*
Greennet: iucn.news

# Sierra Club

Associate or corresponding member organizations

Member organizations, national affiliates, and offices

o019 Produced by: GRID-Arendal.                                    Times projection - Scale: Appr. 1:180 mill

## Objectives
• to protect wild places;
• to promote responsible use of the Earth's ecosystems and resources;
• to protect and restore the quality of the natural and human environment.

## Organization
*Type*
Non-governmental organization (NGO). Consultative status with UN Economic and Social Council (ECOSOC), working partner of Centre for our Common Future (see this section), and observer status with the International Whaling Commission (IWC) (see Agreements).

*Membership*
Individuals and groups, primarily in North America. 500,000 members in 27 countries and offices in 2 countries (75 in USA and 2 in Canada), by October 1994.

*Founded*
Sierra Club in 1892. The International Program, as the international arm of Sierra Club, in 1972.

## Secretariat
Sierra Club, International Program, 408 C Street, NE, Washington , DC 2000Z, USA

*Telephone:*       +1-202-5471141
*Telefax:*        +1-202-5476009
*E-mail:*  scdc1@igc.en.apc.org

*Executive Director*
Mr Carl Pope.

*International Program Director*
Mr Larry Williams.

*Number of staff*
200 professionals and 100 support staff (Oct. 1994).

## Activities
Sierra Club is currently working for legislation that guarantees clean air and water; to regulate the use and disposal of poisonous toxic chemicals; to set aside the most special places for parks and wilderness; for protection of tropical forests; and to ensure that environmental trade agreements do not override US environmental laws.

Sierra Club is politically active, endorses candidates for government office, and gives donations to 'environmentally proven' candidates.

## Decision-making bodies
The Sierra Club is guided by a *Board of Directors* with 15 members elected by the membership. It meets five times a year. Dozens of standing committees

assist the directors. Volunteer activity within the states is guided by 65 chapters, which in turn oversee work in over 400 localities. The Club is also assisted by two related organizations which are separately incorporated: the Sierra Club Legal Defense Fund and the Sierra Club Foundation (both of which have their own budgets and staff).

## Finance
Membership dues.

*Budget*
The total budget was $US41 million in 1993, $US44 million in 1994, and is $US42 million in 1995. The administrative budget at the Washington Secretariat was $US1.9 million in 1993, $US2.0 million in 1994, and is approximately $US2 million in 1995.

*Associated Funds*
Non-legislative work of the Club is funded by the *Sierra Club Foundation* with assets totalling $US15 million and grants totalling $US5 million. Main contributors are Sierra Club members.

## Publications
• *Sierra* (six times a year);
• *Planet* (monthly);
• *Earth Day Source Book*;
• *Earthcare Appeals* (quarterly);
• *International Activist* (quarterly).

# Society for International Development (SID)

## Objectives

• to promote international dialogue, understanding, and co-operation for social and economic development that furthers the well-being of all peoples and fosters the most equitable system of international relations;
• to advance the science, processes, and art of social and economic development through educational means.

## Organization

*Type*
Non-governmental organization (NGO). Consultative status with the Council of Europe, UN Economic and Social Council (ECOCOC), UNESCO, FAO, ILO, UNIDO, UNEP, UNFPA, and UNICEF (see IGOs).

*Membership*
Individual and corporate members, associated institutional and international sponsors. Over 10,000 individual members. Two-thirds of members were organized in 130 Chapters in 60 countries, by October 1994. Other categories of members in 132 countries.

*Founded*
19 October 1957.

## Secretariat

Society for International Development, Palazzo Civiltà del Lavoro, I-00144 Rome, EUR
Italy
*Telephone:*      +39-6-5925506
*Telefax:*      +39-6-5919836
*E-mail:*      s.i.d.@agora.stm.it

*President*
Ms Nafis Sadik.

*Secretary General*
Mr Roberto Savio.

*Number of staff*
8 professionals and 7 support staff (Oct. 1994).

## Activities

SID Programmes operate on a three-year cycle built around its triennial World Conference. These are major events which bring together participants from all parts of the world to review current issues in the field of international development and to highlight new lines of inquiry and response.

A significant portion of the Society's work is undertaken through the 130 SID Chapters which provide specific programmes geared to the interests of the communities and local members they serve.

The SID North–South Round Table serves as a sounding-board for new policy proposals, with attention focusing on international trends, problems, and interests of North and South. It has also served as a mobilizer of national and international support for such proposals as a private channel for exploring the possibilities for consensus by policy-makers, and as a public educator on global development issues through briefings and publications.

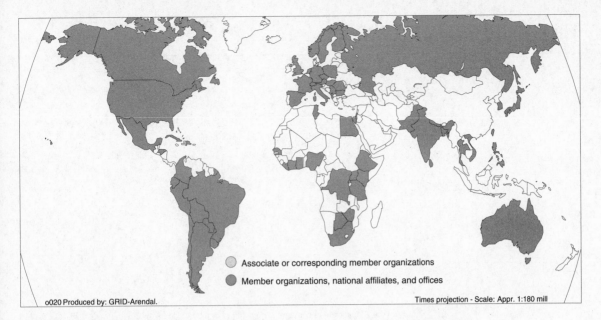

Associate or corresponding member organizations

Member organizations, national affiliates, and offices

o020 Produced by: GRID-Arendal.

Times projection - Scale: Appr. 1:180 mill

## Decision-making bodies

*General Assembly* (convenes every three years, at *World Conference*), composed of all members; *Governing Council* (meets annually) elected by membership for three-year terms. The Council consists of the three most recent *Presidents*, *Secretary General,* and a minimum of 28 and a maximum of 36 elected members from each of the major regions of the world. *Executive Committee,* consisting of six to nine members elected by the Council from among its membership and of *SID Secretary General* as an *ex officio* member.

   *Chapters*, organized at national and local levels, function autonomously under the broad guide-lines of the Society. *International Secretariat* has been established in Rome since 1975. Regional centres are present in the USA, South Asia, and Sub-Saharan Africa.

## Finance

Members' dues (income-rated). Contributions from private, public, international governmental and non-governmental organizations. Main sources are government sources, development banks, World Bank, UNFPA, UNICEF, and WFP (see IGOs).

*Budget*
The toal budget was $US1,076,920 in 1993, $US2,059,400 in 1994, and is $US1,747,500 in 1995. The administrative budget was $US334,907 in 1993, $US360,000 in 1994, and is $US375,000 in 1995.

*Main contributors*
Main contributors in 1994 were the governments of Canada, Sweden, the Netherlands, Italy, Norway, Germany, and Japan.

## Publications

• *Compass* (annual report);
• *Development* (quarterly journal);
• *Development Hotline* (bi-monthly news bulletin).

# Third World Network (TWN)

o021 Produced by: GRID-Arendal.

⬤ Associate or corresponding member organizations

⬤ Member organizations, national affiliates, and offices

Times projection - Scale: Appr. 1:180 mill

## Objectives
• to promote a greater articulation of the needs and rights of people of the Third World;
• to encourage a fair distribution of world resources and forms of development which fulfil people's needs and are ecologically and humanely harmonious;
• to exchange information and present Third World perspectives to the industrialized countries as well as within the Third World itself.

## Organization
*Type*
Non-governmental organization (NGO).

*Membership*
Non-governmental organizations and individuals. Consultative status with the UN Conference on Trade and Development (UNCTAD). 10 full member organizations in five countries. Offices in 5 countries, by 13 October 1994.

*Founded*
14 November 1984.

## Secretariat
Third World Network (TWN),
228 Macalister Road,
10400 Penang, Malaysia

*Telephone*: +60-4-2293-511/713
*Telefax*: +60-4-2298106
*E-mail*: twn@igc.apc.org

*Co-ordinator*
Mr S. M. Mohamed Idris.

*Information Officer*
Mr Martin Khor.

## Activities
The activities of TWN include:
• participation and involvement in global and regional processes such as the Commission on Sustainable Development (CSD) (see IGOs), the Biological Diversity Convention (see Agreements), the General Agreement on Tariffs and Trade (GATT), the World Bank (see IGOs), etc.;
• networking with NGOs on development and environment;
• research activities and production of research reports in the area of economics, environment, health, and other development issues;
• organizing seminars, conferences, and workshops.

## Decision-making bodies
The decision-making structure of TWN consists of an international steering committee, with affiliated and collaborating NGOs forming a separate part of the structure. The steering committee meets annually.

## Finance
Membership dues are the basic source of the funding.

*Budget*
No information available.

## Publications
In addition to booklets, books, and dossiers:
• *Third World Resurgence* (monthly), a magazine covering political, social, and environmental affairs;
• *Third World Economics* (fortnightly), specializing in international economic issues as they affect the Third World;
• *South–North Development Monitor (SUNS)*, a daily bulletin from Geneva;
• *Third World Network Features*, a service of 3–4 features a week sent to over 1,000 newspapers, magazines, and media writers world-wide.

*Electronic conferences*
• twn.info@conf.igc.apc.org;
• twn.features@conf.igc.apc.org;
• suns.feature@conf.igc.apc.org.

# Women's Environment and Development Organization (WEDO)

## Objectives

• to empower women world-wide to become activists, grass-roots leaders, and policy-makers in their respective countries;
• to move the 'Women's Action Agenda 21' into action;
• to strengthen citizens' efforts to address environment and development issues;
• to reshape institutions in order that women may rise to leadership positions and become active decision-makers from the community to national and international levels;
• to ensure gender balance on all parliamentary bodies, boards, commissions, and committees that deliberate on environment and development issues, and on all intergovernmental bodies including the United Nations.

## Organization

*Type*
Non-governmental organization (NGO). Consultative status with UN Economic and Social Council (ECOSOC).

*Membership*
Network of 16,000 individuals and groups in more than 100 countries.

*Founded*
1989.

## Secretariat

Women's Environment and Development Organization,
845 Third Avenue, 15th floor,
New York, NY 10022,
USA
*Telephone*:      +1-212-7597982
*Telefax*:        +1-212-7598647
*E-mail*:         wedo@igc.org

*Executive Director*
Ms Susan Davis.

*Number of staff*
9 professionals and 5 support staff (Oct. 1994).

## Activities

WEDO has put women's issues on the United Nations agenda through its organization of the women's caucus and created an international network of women activists and leaders concerned with environment, development, and social justice from the community to the global level.

In 1991, WEDO initiated 'Women's Action Agenda 21', a blueprint for incorporating women's concerns about the environment and sustainable development into local, national, and international decision-making. It was crafted by more than 1,500 women from 83 countries at the 8–12 November, 1991, 'World Women's Congress for a Healthy Planet' in Miami, Florida.

During the UN Conference on Environment and Development in Rio de Janeiro and its preparatory meetings, WEDO organized 'Women's Action Agenda' into the *Rio Declaration* and *Agenda 21*. The WEDO-sponsored 'Women's Tent', Planeta Femea, was the largest and most active at the grass-roots Global Forum in Rio, drawing thousands into its workshops, programmes, and panels every day.

WEDO continues to expand and strengthen its network through organizing women's caucus at UN conferences, encouraging women to organize locally, developing regional co-ordinators, and through projects such as the Community Report Card through which women evaluate the health of their communities on a range of issues, and Action for Cancer Prevention Campaign.

WEDO focuses on issues relating to the implementation of the 1994 UNFPA International Conference on Population and Development, the World Summit on Social Development, and the report of the CSD (see IGOs) on the effective implementation of *Agenda 21* in relation to women. WEDO plans to examine and

promote the role of NGOs in the UN in connection with the 50th Anniversary of the UN. In 1995 WEDO will organize special activities on International Women's Day at the World Summit on Social Development in Copenhagen.

WEDO is making the 1995 UN Fourth World Conference on Women in Beijing a major focus of activity. Its objectives are to ensure the maximum inclusion of women in official delegations to the meeting and the maximum access for women from NGOs and grass-roots groups to present relevant actions of the 'Women's Action Agenda 21', for inclusion in the final, updated 'Forward-Looking Strategies' document, which will be voted on by the full UN General Assembly. WEDO will organize a tent for networks on gender and environment issues and hold a second World Women's Congress for a Healthy Planet in Beijing.

## Decision-making bodies

The *Steering Committee* of WEDO consists of 10 co-chairs and meets twice a year. WEDO is advised by its *International Policy Action Committee* which consists of 53 members representing 30 countries.

## Finance

The main sources of income are donations from foundations, governments, and individuals.

*Budget*
The annual operating budget was $US570,000 in 1993, $US680,000 in 1994, and is $US1.0 million in 1995.

## Publications

*News and Views* (quarterly).

*Electronic conferences*
Internet:
• gopher@igc.apc.org;
• wedo@igc.apc.org

# World Federalist Movement (WFM)

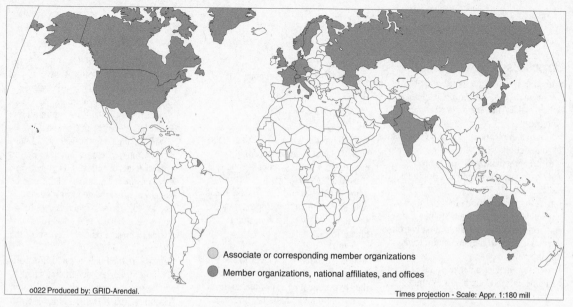

Associate or corresponding member organizations

Member organizations, national affiliates, and offices

o022 Produced by: GRID-Arendal.

Times projection - Scale: Appr. 1:180 mill

## Objectives

• to co-ordinate policies and activities of national organizations working for a World Federation having a defined sphere of jurisdiction, functioning through a legislature to make world law, a judiciary to interpret it, and an executive with adequate powers to enforce it upon individuals, associations, and states;
• to advocate measures to abolish war, by supporting efforts of the United Nations and its Specialized Agencies to preserve peace and protect life, and create and sustain environmental mechanisms and institutions.

## Organization

*Type*
Non-governmental organization (NGO). Consultative status with UN UN (ECOSOC) and UNESCO (see IGOs).

*Membership*
NGOs, parliamentary organizations, and individuals. 36 full member organizations in 21 countries, by November 1994.

*Founded*
1947.

## Secretariat

World Federalist Movement (WPM),
777 UN Plaza,
New York, NY 10017,
USA
*Telephone:*     +1-211-5991320
*Telefax:*     +1-212-5991332

*Number of staff*
2 professional and 2 support staff (Nov. 1994).

## Activities

During the WFM Congress in July 1991 the organization adopted an environmental policy resolution that recognizes that the remedies to global environmental problems require: real limitations of national sovereignty, transfer of technology and financial resources from wealthy to less wealthy nations, and restructuring and strengthening of the UN system. WFP will continue to lobby for this purpose.

WFM co-convenes the International NGO Task Group on Legal and Institutional Matters (INTGLIM).

Since UNCED, WFM has lobbied to ensure that the Commission on Sustainable Development (CSD) (see IGOs) has: just representation in membership; transparent and democratic procedures;

an extensive mandate with the ability to act; and effective NGO participation. INTGLIM has organized working groups on the CSD 'Cluster' issues, and makes information on the CSD process available to NGOs and individuals worldwide.

## Decision-making bodies

*WFM Congress* consists of representatives of all national and associate organizations. Congress elects members to the *Council* which also includes representatives of member organizations. Council elects officers to the *Executive Committee*, which consists of nine members, and also selects an *Advisory Board*.

## Finance

Membership dues, grants, foundations, and direct mail campaigns.

*Budget*
The budget was $US185,000 in 1994, and is $US180,000 in 1995.

## Publications

• *Transnational Perspective* (quarterly);
• *World Federalist News*.

# World Wide Fund For Nature (WWF)

Associate or corresponding member organizations

Member organizations, national affiliates, and offices

o023 Produced by: GRID-Arendal.

Times projection - Scale: Appr. 1:180 mill

## Objectives

To conserve nature and ecological processes by:
• preserving genetic, species, and ecosystem diversity;
• ensuring that the use of renewable resources is sustainable both now and in the longer term;
• promoting actions to reduce pollution and the wasteful exploitation and consumption of resources and energy.

## Organization

*Type*
Non-governmental organization (NGO). Works in conjunction with governments, other NGOs, scientists, business and industry, the world's major religions, and people at the local level.

*Membership*
More than 5.2 million regular supporters world-wide. Affiliate National Organizations in 22 countries and 1 territory, by 2 November 1994. 22 Programme Offices. Associate organizations in 4 countries.

*Founded*
11 September 1961. Formerly known as World Wildlife Fund, and continues to be known under its former name in Canada and the United States.

## Secretariat

WWF International,
Avenue du Mont-Blanc,
CH-1196 Gland, Switzerland
*Telephone*:       +41-22-3649111
*Telefax*:       +41-22-3645358
*E-mail*:       wwfpub@gn.apc.org

*Director General*
Dr Claude Martin.

*Head, Communications Department*
Mr Rob SanGeorge.

*Number of staff*
160 at Headquarters (Nov. 1994).

## Activities

Based on scientific evidence, WWF actively supports on-the-ground conservation programmes in Africa, Asia, Europe, and Latin America. Since 1961, the WWF network has invested over $US525 million in more than 11,000 projects in 130 countries.

Current WWF campaigns range from support of an international ban on ivory trade and promoting sustainable forestry practices to advocating a reduction in greenhouse-gas emissions and lobbying for more equitable trade between industrial and developing countries. It also sponsors educational and training programmes for park and wildlife managers, ecologists, and teachers; works with trade-and-industry associations to improve environmental practices; and significantly reinforces the effectiveness of wildlife-trade monitoring.

WWF, together with IUCN (see this section) and UNEP (see IGOs), launched 'Caring for the Earth: A Strategy for Sustainable Living', in October 1991 in more than 60 countries.

## Decision-making bodies

*Board of Trustees* (meets twice a year), *Executive Committee*, *Programme Committee* (meets twice a year), *Planning and Budget Committee* (four times a year), *Nominating Committee*, and *Business Committee*.

## Finance

Sources of income in 1993 were individuals and general donations (49%), legacies and bequests (8%), corporate subscriptions and donations (8%), governments and aid agencies (11%), trusts and foundations (4%), royalties (6%), other earned income (13%), and others (1%).

*Budget*
The overall income of WWF International including all national organizations was SFr50,233,000 in 1991/92 and SFr50,133,000 in 1992/93.

## Publications

• *Annual Review*;
• *WWF News* (four times a year).

# WorldWIDE Network

## Objectives

- to establish a world-wide network of women concerned about environmental management and sustainable development;
- to educate the public and its policy-makers about the vital linkages between women, natural resources, and sustainable development;
- to promote the inclusion of women and their environmental perceptions in the design and implementation of development policies and projects;
- to mobilize and support women, individually and in organizations, in environmental and natural resource activities.

## Organization

*Type*
Non-governmental organization (NGO). Consultative status with UN Environment Programme (UNEP) (see IGOs) and UN Economic and Social Council (ECOSOC).

*Membership*
Individuals and groups. The Network has more than 7,500 individual and group memberships and has established 16 WorldWIDE Forums (similar to chapters) in 14 countries, by early 1995.

*Founded*
1981.

## Secretariat

WorldWIDE Network,
1331 H Street,
NW, Suite 903,
Washington, DC 20005,
USA
*Telephone*:          +1-202-3471514
*Telefax*:             +1-202-3471524

*Executive Director*
Ms Elia García McComie.

*Director of Communications and Research*
Ms Susan Brackett.

*Administrative and Program Associate*
Ms Margaret S. Maringa.

*Number of staff*
3 professionals (Nov. 1994).

## Activities

The Network has established *Forums* (chapters) which are grass-roots organizations that nurture community participation and strengthen the role of women in natural and community resource management. Groups of colleagues, neighbours, or co-workers gather to explore common environmental problems and to identify appropriate local solutions. Each Forum determines its own goals and objectives, for which WorldWIDE provides assistance (information, training, materials, contacts, etc.)

when necessary. The solutions devised by the Forums often take the shape of technical training and education of women and girls, health education, improved water quality and sanitation facilities, community clean-ups, and the development of appropriate technology.

WorldWIDE Forums provide an institutional framework through which women can provide relevant information to policy-makers and the designers of development projects. Forums often lead to the development of income-generating activities, thus promoting economic self-sufficiency for participating communities. Finally, Forums lead to increased leadership and organizational skills among local women.

The *Global Assembly of Women and the Environment Project* was convened in 1991 and was implemented by WorldWIDE on behalf of UNEP (see IGOs). The Assembly demonstrated women's capacity as leaders in environmental management, the elements of leadership necessary for success, and the policies that can advance or retard women's efforts. WorldWIDE identified 218 successful environmental projects that had been initiated or managed by women—'success stories' in the areas of: energy, especially as it relates to climate change; environmentally friendly systems; products and technologies; waste; and water.

In June 1992, WorldWIDE presented a training workshop, 'Women's Voices on

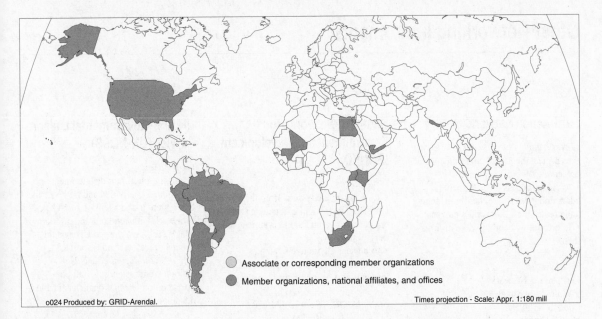

Associate or corresponding member organizations

Member organizations, national affiliates, and offices

o024 Produced by: GRID-Arendal.

Times projection - Scale: Appr. 1:180 mill

Community Action for Environmental Management' at the Global Forum of the UN Conference on Environment and Development (UNCED). WorldWIDE will facilitate a similar training workshop at the 1995 United Nations Fourth World Conference on Women in Beijing, to promote the inclusion of women, environment, and development issues in the Conference deliberations. Leading up to the UN Conference, WorldWIDE has held several training workshops at regional NGO Forums in Costa Rica, Argentina, and Austria in 1994. Similar workshops will be held in Jordan, Senegal, and California, USA in 1995. These workshops are arranged in collaboration with the WorldWIDE Forums and other NGOs on a variety of topics, including community organization and group facilitation techniques, leadership development, and environmentally sound agricultural practices.

Since 1987, WorldWIDE has published its annual *WorldWIDE Directory of Women in Environment*. Over the last few years the Directory has grown to include the names of 1,700 women from more than 115 countries or territories. The Directory is an important resource in facilitating the inclusion of women in environmental policy-making and project activities.

## Decision-making bodies

The *Board of Trustees* consists of twenty-five members of diverse disciplines and ethnic backgrounds. Each member serves on one or more internal committees in addition to attending the biennial Board meetings. The *International Advisory Council* is composed of women and men from all over the world, and serves as an advisory body for WorldWIDE projects and as contact points for WorldWIDE's international networkers and Forums.

## Finance

WorldWIDE activities have been financed by contributions from governments.

*Budget*
The total budget was $US135,542 in 1993 and the administrative core budget was $US60,300.

*Main contributors*
The governments of Canada, Norway, The Netherlands, and Sweden.

## Publications
• *WorldWIDE News*;
• *WorldWIDE Directory of Women in Environment* (annual).

# Other Networking Instruments

## EarthAction Network

*Objectives*
* to protect the global environment and preserve biological diversity;
* to ensure access to food, shelter, education, health care, family planning, and credit for all the world's citizens;
* to prevent war and promote disarmament.

*Secretariat*
EarthAction Network
9 White Lion Street,
London N1 9PD,
United Kingdom
*Telephone:*    +44-71-8659009
*Telefax:*    +44-71-2780345
*E-mail:*  earthaction@gn.apc.org

*Main publications*
* *EarthAction Alerts*;
* *EarthAction Editorial Advisories*;
* *EarthAction Parliamentary Alerts*.

## Green Belt Movement

*Objectives*
* to promote environmental conservation and sustainable development;
* to avert the desertification process throughout Africa by planting of trees;

*Secretariat*
Green Belt Movement,
c/o National Council of Women of Kenya,
Moi Avenue,
PO Box 67545,
Nairobi,
Kenya
*Telephone:*    +254-2-504264

## Southern Networks for Environment and Development (SONED)

*Objectives*
* to focus on the lessons from the UNCED process and articulate a southern perspective on the environment and development crisis;
* to present alternative strategies regarding institutional mechanisms and leadership to deal with these crises.

*Secretariat*
SONED Africa Region,
PO Box 12205,
Nairobi,
Kenya
*Telephone:*    +254-2-445893/4
*Telefax:*    +254-2-44-3241/5894
*E-mail:*  aacc.parti@econet.org

*Main publications*
* *The African Global Initiative on the New Environmental Economic Order*;
* *SONED on UNCED: A Southern Perspective on the Environment and Development Crisis*;
* *Africa Voices on UNCED '92 in Rio and Beyond*;
* *Green Africa People's Bank: An African Alternative to World Bank and IMF*.

## UN Non-Governmental Liaison Service (UN-NGLS)

*Objectives*
* to bring important development and environment activities and issues of the UN system to the attention of NGOs;
* to work with southern and northern NGOs seeking access to UN system events, processes, and resources;
* to promote increased UN/NGO dialogue, understanding, and co-operation on international sustainable development issues.

*Organization*
NGLS is an inter-agency project of the UN system established in 1975.

*Secretariat*
UN-NGLS,
Palais des Nations,
CH-1211 Geneva 10,
Switzerland
*Telephone:*    +41-22-7985850
*Telefax:*    +41-22-7887366

UN-NGLS
Room 6015,
866 UN Plaza,
New York, NY 10017,
USA
*Telephone:*    +1-212-9633125
*Telefax:*    +1-212-9638712
*E-mail:*    TCN (TCN4013)

*Main publications*
* *Go Between* (bi-monthly newsletter);
* *The NGLS Handbook: UN agencies programmes, and funds working for economic and social development*;
* *United Nations System: A Guide for NGOs*;
* *Voices from Africa* (series);
* *Women and World Development* (series);
* *Development Dossiers* (series).

# Tables of International Organizations and Degrees of Participation, by Country

## Intergovernmental Organizations (IGOs)*
International Council for the Exploration of the Sea (ICES)
OECD, Environment Policy Committee (EPOC)

### Keys

States with observer status

Member states

## Non-Governmental Organizations (NGOs)
Alliance of Northern People on Environment and Development (ANPED)
Centre for Our Common Future
Climate Action Network (CAN)
Earthwatch
Environmental Liaison Centre International (ELCI)
European Environmental Bureau (EEB)
European Youth For(est) Action (EYFA)
Friends of the Earth International (FoEI)
Greenpeace International
International Chamber of Commerce (ICC)
International Confederation of Free Trade Unions (ICFTU)
International Council of Voluntary Agencies (ICVA)
International Organization of Consumer Unions (IOCU)
International Planned Parenthood Federation (IPPF)
International Solar Energy Society (ISES)
IUCN—The World Conservation Union
Sierra Club
Society for International Development (SID)
Third World Network (TWN)
Women's Environment and Development Organization (WEDO)
World Federalist Movement (WFM)
World Wide Fund For Nature (WWF)
WorldWIDE Network

### Keys

*General*

Associate or corresponding member organizations

Member organizations, national affiliates, and offices

*IUCN—The World Conservation Union*

Members

*Note*: *Most of the IGOs are not included, as the degree of participation is almost universal. For the degree of participation regarding the European Union (EU) and the Commission on Sustainable Development (CSD), see entries in the IGO subsection.

| Country | ICES | EPOC | ANPED | CCF | CAN | EW | ELCI | EEB | EYFA | FoEI | GPI | ICC | ICFTU | ICVA | IOCU | IPPF | ISES | IUCN | SC | SID | TWN | WFM | WWF | WW |
|---|---|---|---|---|---|---|---|---|---|---|---|---|---|---|---|---|---|---|---|---|---|---|---|---|
| Afghanistan | | | | | | | | | | | | | | | | ● | | | | | | | | |
| Albania | | | | | | | | ● | | | | | | | ● | | | | | ● | | | | |
| Algeria | | | | | | | ● | | | | | | | | ● | | | ● | | | | | | |
| Andorra | | | | | | | | | | | | | | | | | | | | | | | | |
| Angola | | | | | | | | | | | | | | | | | | ● | | | | | | |
| Antigua & Barbuda | | | | | | | | | | | | | ● | | | | | | | | | | | |
| Argentina | | | | ● | | | ● | | | ● | ● | ● | ● | | ● | ● | | ● | | ● | | | ○ | ● |
| Armenia | | | | | | | | | | | | | | | | | | | | | | | | |
| Australia | | ● | | ● | ● | ● | ● | | | ● | ● | ● | ● | ● | ● | ● | ● | ● | | ● | | ● | ● | |
| Austria | | ● | ● | ● | ● | | ● | ● | ● | ● | ● | ● | ● | ● | ● | ● | | ● | | ● | | | ● | |
| Azerbaijan | | | | | | | | | | | | | | | | | | | | | | | | |
| Bahamas | | | | | | | | | | | | ● | | | | | | ● | | | | | | |
| Bahrain | | | | | | | | | | | | | | | | ● | | | | | | | | |
| Bangladesh | | | | ● | ● | | ● | | | ● | | ● | ● | | ● | ● | | | | ● | | ● | | |
| Barbados | | | | | ● | | | | | | | ● | | | | ● | | | | | | | | ● |
| Belarus | | | | | | | | | ● | | | | | | | | | | | | | | | |
| Belgium | ● | ● | ● | ● | | ● | ● | ● | ● | ● | ● | ● | ● | ● | ● | ● | | ● | | ● | | ● | ● | |
| Belize | | | | | | | ● | | | | | ● | | | | ○ | | ● | | | | | | |
| Benin | | | | | | | | | | ● | | ● | | | ● | ● | | | | | | | | |
| Bhutan | | | | | | | | | | | | | | | | | | | | | | | ● | |
| Bolivia | | | | ● | | | ● | | | | | ● | | | | | | ● | | ● | | | | |
| Bosnia & Herzegovina | | | | | | | | | | | | | | | | | | | | | | | | |
| Botswana | | | | | | | ● | | | | | ● | | | ● | ○ | | ● | | ● | | | | |
| Brazil | | | ● | | | | ● | | | ● | ● | ● | ● | | ● | | | ● | | ● | | | ● | ● |
| Brunei Darussalam | | | | | | | | | | | | | | | | | ● | | | | | | | |
| Bulgaria | | | | | ● | | ● | ○ | ● | ● | | ● | | | ● | ● | ● | ● | | ● | | | | |
| Burkina Faso | | | | | | | ● | | | ● | | ● | ● | | ● | ● | | | | | | | | |
| Burundi | | | | | | | ● | | | | | | | | | | | | | | | | | |
| Cambodia | | | | | | | | | | | | | | | | | | | | | | | | |
| Cameroon (U. Rep. of) | | | | | | | ● | | | | | ● | ● | | | ○ | | | | | | | ● | |
| Canada | ● | ● | ● | ● | ● | | ● | | | ● | ● | ● | ● | ● | ● | ● | ● | ● | ● | ● | | | ● | ● |
| Cape Verde | | | | | | | | | | | | | | | | ● | | | | | | | | |

Column key: ICES = Intern. Council for the Exploration of the Sea; EPOC = OECD, Environment Policy Committee; ANPED = Alliance of N. People on Env. and Developm.; CCF = Centre for Our Common Future; CAN = Climate Action Network; EW = Earthwatch; ELCI = Environm. Liaison Centre International; EEB = European Environmental Bureau; EYFA = European Youth For(est) Action; FoEI = Friends of the Earth International; GPI = Greenpeace International; ICC = Intern. Chamber of Commerce; ICFTU = Intern. Confederation of Free Trade Unions; ICVA = Intern. Council of Voluntary Agencies; IOCU = Intern. Organization of Consumer Unions; IPPF = Intern. Planned Parenthood Federation; ISES = Intern. Solar Energy Society; IUCN = IUCN--The World Conservation Union; SC = Sierra Club; SID = Society for International Development; TWN = Third World Network; WFM = World Federalist Movement; WWF = World Wide Fund for Nature; WW = WorldWIDE Network

| Country | ICES | EPOC | ANPED | Centre for Our Common Future | CAN | Earthwatch | ELCI | EEB | EYFA | FoEI | Greenpeace | ICC | ICFTU | ICVA | IOCU | IPPF | ISES | IUCN | Sierra Club | SID | TWN | WFM | WWF | WorldWIDE |
|---|---|---|---|---|---|---|---|---|---|---|---|---|---|---|---|---|---|---|---|---|---|---|---|---|
| Central African Rep. | | | | | | | ● | | | | | | | | | ○ | | | | | | | | |
| Chad | | | | | | | | | | | | | ● | | | | | | | | | | | |
| Chile | | | | ● | ● | | ● | | | ● | ● | ● | ● | | ● | ● | | ● | | ● | | | | |
| China | | | | ● | | | ● | | | | | | ● | ● | ○ | ● | ● | ● | | | | | | |
| Colombia | | | | ● | | | ● | | | | | ● | ● | | ● | ● | | ● | | | | | ● | |
| Comoros | | | | | | | | | | | | | | | | | | | | | | | | |
| Congo | | | | ● | | | ● | | | | | | | | | | | | | | | | | |
| Cook Islands | | | | | | | | | | | | | ● | | | | | | | | | | | |
| Costa Rica | | | | ● | | | ● | | | ● | | ● | ● | | | ● | ● | ● | | | | | ● | ● |
| Côte d'Ivoire | | | | ● | | | ● | | | | | ● | ● | | | ○ | | ● | | | | | ● | |
| Croatia | | ● | | ● | | | | ○ | ● | | | | | | | | | ● | | | | | | |
| Cuba | | | | | | | | | | | | | | | ● | ○ | | ● | | | | | | |
| Cyprus | | | | ● | | | | ○ | | ● | | ● | ● | | ● | ● | | ● | | | | | | |
| Czech Republic | | ○ | ● | ● | | | ● | ○ | ● | | | | ● | | | ● | | ● | | ● | | ● | | |
| Denmark | ● | ● | ● | ● | ● | | ● | ● | ● | ● | ● | ● | ● | | | | | ● | | | | ● | ● | |
| Djibouti | | | | | | | | | | | | | | | | | | | | | | | | |
| Dominica | | | | | | | | | | | | | ● | | | | | | | | | | | |
| Dominican Republic | | | | ● | | | ● | | | | | ● | ● | ● | ● | ● | | ● | | | | | | |
| Ecuador | | | | | | | ● | | | | | ● | ● | ● | ● | ● | | ● | | | | | ○ | |
| Egypt | | | | ● | | | ● | | | ● | | | | | | ● | ● | ● | | | | | | ● |
| El Salvador | | | | | | | ● | | | ● | | | ● | | ● | ● | | | | | | | | |
| Equatorial Guinea | | | | | | | | | | | | | | | | | | | | | | | | |
| Eritrea | | | | | | | | | | | | | | | | | | | | | | | | |
| Estonia | ● | | | | ● | | | ● | ● | | | ● | | | | | | ● | | | | | | |
| Ethiopia | | | | | | | | | | | | | | ● | | ● | | | | ● | | | | |
| Fiji | | | | | | | ● | | | ● | | | ● | ● | | | | | | | | | | |
| Finland | ● | ● | ● | ● | ● | | ● | ● | | ● | | ● | ● | | ● | ● | | ● | | ● | | | ● | |
| France | ● | ● | ● | ● | | | ● | ● | ● | ● | ● | ● | ● | ● | ● | ● | | ● | | | | ● | ● | |
| Gabon | | | | | | | | | | | | ● | ● | | | | | | | | | | ● | |
| Gambia | | | | ● | | | ● | | | | | | ● | ● | | | | | | | | | | ● |
| Georgia | | | | | | | | | | ● | | | | | | | | | | | | | | |
| Germany | ● | ● | ● | ● | | | ● | ● | ● | ● | ● | ● | ● | ● | ● | ● | ● | ● | | ● | | | ● | |

GREEN GLOBE YEARBOOK 1995

301

| Country | ICES | EPOC | ANPED | Centre for Our Common Future | CAN | Earthwatch | ELCI | EEB | EYFA | FoEI | Greenpeace | ICC | ICFTU | ICVA | IOCU | IPPF | ISES | IUCN | Sierra Club | SID | TWN | WFM | WWF | WorldWIDE |
|---|---|---|---|---|---|---|---|---|---|---|---|---|---|---|---|---|---|---|---|---|---|---|---|---|
| Ghana |  |  |  | ● |  |  | ● |  |  | ● |  | ● |  | ● | ● | ● |  | ● |  | ● |  |  |  |  |
| Greece |  | ● |  |  | ● |  | ● | ● | ● | ● | ● | ● |  | ● |  | ● |  |  |  |  |  |  | ● |  |
| Grenada |  |  |  |  |  |  |  | ● |  |  |  | ● |  |  |  |  |  |  |  |  |  |  |  |  |
| Guatemala |  |  |  |  |  |  | ● |  |  | ● |  | ● | ● | ● |  |  |  | ● |  |  |  |  |  |  |
| Guinea |  |  |  | ● |  |  | ● | ● |  |  |  |  |  |  |  | ● |  | ● |  |  |  |  |  |  |
| Guinea-Bissau |  |  |  |  |  |  | ● |  |  |  |  |  |  |  |  |  |  | ● |  |  |  |  |  |  |
| Guyana |  |  |  |  |  |  |  |  |  |  |  | ● |  |  | ● | ● |  |  |  |  |  |  |  |  |
| Haiti |  |  |  |  |  |  |  |  |  |  |  |  |  |  |  |  |  |  |  |  |  |  |  |  |
| Holy See (Vatican) |  |  |  |  |  |  |  |  |  |  |  | ● | ● |  |  |  |  |  |  |  |  |  |  |  |
| Honduras |  |  |  |  |  |  | ● |  |  |  |  | ● |  |  | ● |  |  | ● |  | ● |  |  |  |  |
| Hungary |  | ● | ● | ● | ● |  | ● | ● |  |  |  | ● |  |  | ● |  |  | ● |  | ● |  |  | ● |  |
| Iceland | ● | ● |  |  |  |  |  | ● |  |  |  | ● | ● |  |  |  |  | ● |  |  |  |  |  |  |
| India |  |  |  | ● | ● |  | ● |  |  | ● | ● | ● | ● | ● | ● | ● |  | ● |  |  | ● | ● | ● | ● |
| Indonesia |  |  |  | ● | ● |  | ● |  |  | ● |  | ● |  | ● | ● |  |  | ● |  |  |  |  | ● |  |
| Iran (Islamic Rep. of) |  |  |  |  |  |  |  |  |  |  | ● |  |  |  |  |  |  |  |  |  |  |  |  |  |
| Iraq |  |  |  |  |  |  |  |  |  |  |  |  |  |  |  | ● |  |  |  |  |  |  |  |  |
| Ireland | ● | ● |  | ● | ● |  | ● | ● | ● | ● | ● | ● | ● | ● | ● | ● |  | ● |  |  |  |  |  |  |
| Israel |  |  |  | ● | ● |  | ● |  |  |  |  | ● | ● |  | ● | ● |  | ● |  | ● |  |  |  |  |
| Italy |  | ● | ● | ● | ● |  | ● | ● | ● | ● | ● | ● | ● | ● | ● | ● | ● | ● |  | ● | ● |  | ● |  |
| Jamaica |  |  |  |  |  |  | ● |  |  |  |  | ● |  | ● | ● |  |  |  |  |  |  |  |  |  |
| Japan |  | ● |  | ● | ● | ● |  |  |  | ● | ● | ● | ● | ● | ● |  |  | ● |  | ● |  | ● | ● |  |
| Jordan |  |  |  |  |  |  |  |  |  |  |  | ● | ● |  |  |  |  |  |  |  |  |  |  |  |
| Kazakhstan |  |  |  |  |  |  |  |  |  |  |  |  |  |  |  |  |  |  |  |  |  |  |  |  |
| Kenya |  |  |  | ● | ● |  | ● |  |  |  |  | ● | ● |  | ● |  |  | ● |  | ● |  |  | ● | ● |
| Kiribati |  |  |  |  |  |  |  |  |  |  |  | ● |  |  |  |  |  |  |  |  |  |  |  |  |
| Korea (P. D. Rep. of) |  |  |  |  |  |  |  |  |  |  |  |  |  |  |  | ● |  | ● |  |  |  |  |  |  |
| Korea (Rep. of) |  | ● |  |  |  |  | ● |  |  |  |  | ● | ● |  | ● | ● | ● | ● |  | ● |  | ● |  |  |
| Kuwait |  |  |  |  |  |  | ● |  |  |  |  | ● |  |  |  |  |  | ● |  |  |  |  |  |  |
| Kyrgyz Republic |  |  |  |  |  |  |  |  |  |  |  |  |  |  |  |  |  |  |  |  |  |  |  |  |
| Laos |  |  |  |  |  |  |  |  |  |  |  |  |  |  |  |  |  | ● |  |  |  |  |  |  |
| Latvia | ● |  | ● | ● |  |  |  |  | ● | ● |  |  |  |  |  |  |  | ● |  |  |  |  | ● |  |
| Lebanon |  |  |  |  |  |  | ● |  |  |  |  | ● | ● | ● |  | ● |  | ● |  |  |  |  |  |  |

| Country | ICES | EPOC | ANPED | Centre for Our Common Future | CAN | Earthwatch | ELCI | EEB | EYFA | FoEI | Greenpeace Intern. | ICC | ICFTU | ICVA | IOCU | IPPF | ISES | IUCN | Sierra Club | SID | TWN | WFM | WWF | WorldWIDE Network |
|---|---|---|---|---|---|---|---|---|---|---|---|---|---|---|---|---|---|---|---|---|---|---|---|---|
| Lesotho | | | | | | | ● | | | | | | ● | | | ● | | ● | | | | | | |
| Liberia | | | | | | | | | | | | | ● | | ● | ● | | ● | | ● | | | | |
| Libyan Arab Jamah. | | | | | | | | | | | | | | | | | | | | | | | | |
| Liechtenstein | | | | | | | | ○ | ● | | | | | | | | | ● | | | | | | |
| Lithuania | | | | ● | | | | | ● | | | | | | | | | | | | | | | |
| Luxembourg | | ● | | ● | | | ● | ● | ● | ● | ● | ● | | | ● | ● | | ● | | | | | | |
| Macedonia (F.Yug.R.of) | | | | | | | | | | ● | | | | | | | | | | | | | | |
| Madagascar | | | | | | | ● | | | | | ● | ● | | | ● | | ● | | | | | ● | |
| Malawi | | | | | | | | | | | | | ● | | ● | | | ● | | | | | | |
| Malaysia | | | | ● | ● | | ● | | | ● | | | ● | | ● | ● | ● | ● | | | | ● | ● | |
| Maldives | | | | | | | | | | | | | | | | | | | | | | | | |
| Mali | | | | | | | ● | | | | | | ● | | ● | | | ● | | | | | | ● |
| Malta | | | | | | | ● | ○ | ● | ● | ● | | ● | | ● | | | ● | | | | | | |
| Marshall Islands | | | | | | | | | | | | | | | | | | | | | | | | |
| Mauritania | | | | | | | | | | | | | | | | ○ | | | | | | | | |
| Mauritius | | | | ● | | | ● | | | | | | ● | | ● | ● | | ● | | ● | | ● | | |
| Mexico | ● | | ● | ● | | | ● | | | | | ● | ● | ● | ● | ● | ● | ● | | ● | | | ● | |
| Micronesia (F. St. of) | | | | | | | | | | | | | | | | | | | | | | | | |
| Moldova (Rep. of) | | | | | | | | | | | | | | | | | | | | | | | | |
| Monaco | | | | | | | | | | | | | | | | | | ● | | | | | | |
| Mongolia | | | | | | | | | | | | | | | | | | ● | | | | | | |
| Morocco | | | | | | | ● | | | | | ● | ● | | | ● | | ● | | | | | | |
| Mozambique | | | | | | | | | | | | | | | | | | ● | | | | | | |
| Myanmar | | | | | | | | | | | | | | | | | | | | | | | | |
| Namibia | | | | | | | ● | | | | | | | | | | | ● | | | | | | |
| Nauru | | | | | | | | | | | | | | | | | | | | | | | | |
| Nepal | | | | | | | ● | | | | | | ● | | | ● | | ● | | ● | | | ● | ● |
| Netherlands | ● | ● | ● | ● | ● | | ● | ● | ● | ● | ● | ● | ● | ● | ● | ● | ● | ● | | ● | | ● | ● | |
| New Zealand | | ● | | ● | ● | | ● | | | ● | ● | | ● | | ● | | | ● | | | | | ● | |
| Nicaragua | | | | ● | | | ● | | | ● | | | ● | ● | | | | ● | | | | | | |
| Niger | | | | | | | | | | | | ● | | | | | | ● | | | | | | |
| Nigeria | | | | ● | | | ● | | | | | | ● | | ● | ● | | ● | | ● | | | ○ | |

| Country | ICES | EPOC | ANPED | Centre for Our Common Future | CAN | Earthwatch | ELCI | EEB | EYFA | FoEI | Greenpeace | ICC | ICFTU | ICVA | IOCU | IPPF | ISES | IUCN | Sierra Club | SID | TWN | WFM | WWF | WorldWIDE |
|---|---|---|---|---|---|---|---|---|---|---|---|---|---|---|---|---|---|---|---|---|---|---|---|---|
| Niue | | | | | | | | | | | | | | | | | | | | | | | | |
| Norway | ● | ● | ● | ● | ● | | ● | ● | ● | ● | ● | ● | ● | ● | ● | | | ● | | ● | | ● | ● | |
| Oman | | | | | | | | | | | | | | | | | | ● | | | | | | |
| Pakistan | | | | ● | | | ● | | | | | ● | ● | | | | | ● | | ● | | ● | ● | |
| Palau | | | | | | | | | | | | | | | | | | | | | | | | |
| Panama | | | | ● | | | ● | | | | | ● | ● | | ● | | | ● | | | | | | |
| Papua New Guinea | | | | | | | ● | | | ● | | ● | | | | | | ● | | | | | | |
| Paraguay | | | | | | | ● | | | ● | | | | | ● | | | | | ● | | | | |
| Peru | | | | ● | | | ● | | | | | ● | ● | | ● | ○ | | ● | | ● | | | | ● |
| Philippines | | | | ● | ● | | ● | | | ● | | ● | ● | | ● | | | ● | | ● | | | ● | |
| Poland | ● | ○ | ● | ● | ● | | ● | | | | | ● | ● | | ● | ● | ● | ● | | | | | | |
| Portugal | ● | ● | | ● | | | ● | ● | | | | ● | ● | | | | | ● | | | | | | |
| Qatar | | | | | | | | | | | | | | | | | | | | | | | | |
| Romania | | ● | | ● | | | | ○ | | | | ● | | | ○ | ● | | ● | | ● | | | | |
| Russian Federation | ● | | ● | | | | | ● | | ● | | | | | ○ | ● | | ● | | ● | ● | | | |
| Rwanda | | | ● | | | | ● | | | | | ● | | | | ○ | | ● | | ● | | | | |
| St Kitts & Nevis | | | | | | | | | | | | ● | | | | | | | | | | | | |
| St Lucia | | | | | | | | | | | | ● | | | | | | | | | | | | |
| St Vinc. & Grenadines | | | | ● | | | | | | | | ● | | | | | | | | | | | | |
| Samoa (Western) | | | | ● | | | ● | | | | | ● | | | ● | | | ● | | | | | | |
| San Marino | | | | | | | | | | | | ● | | | | | | | | | | | | |
| São Tomé & Principe | | | | | | | | | | | | | | | | | | | | | | | | |
| Saudi Arabia | | | | ● | | | | | | | | ● | | | | | | ● | | | | | | |
| Senegal | | | ● | ● | | | ● | | | | | ● | ● | ● | ● | | | | | ● | | | | |
| Seychelles | | | | | | | | | | | | ● | | | | | | ● | | | | | | |
| Sierra Leone | | | | ● | | | ● | | ● | | | | | | | | | | | | | | | |
| Singapore | | | | ● | | | | | | | | ● | ● | | ● | | | ● | | | | | | |
| Slovakia | | ○ | ● | | ● | | ● | ● | ● | | | ● | | | ● | | | | | | | | | |
| Slovenia | | | | | | | | ● | | | | | | | ● | | | ● | | ● | | | | |
| Solomon Islands | | | | | | | | | | | | | | | | | | | | | | | | |
| Somalia | | | | | | | ● | | | | | | | | | ○ | | | | | | | | |
| South Africa | | | ● | | | | ● | | | | | ● | | | | | | ● | ● | ● | | ● | ● | ● |

| Country | ICES | EPOC | ANPED | Centre for Our Common Future | CAN | Earthwatch | ELCI | EEB | EYFA | FoEI | Greenpeace | ICC | ICFTU | ICVA | IOCU | IPPF | ISES | IUCN | Sierra Club | SID | TWN | WFM | WWF | WorldWIDE |
|---|---|---|---|---|---|---|---|---|---|---|---|---|---|---|---|---|---|---|---|---|---|---|---|---|
| Spain | ● | ● | ● | ● | ● | ● | ● | ● | ● | ● | ● | ● | | | ● | ○ | ● | ● | | ● | | | ● | |
| Sri Lanka | | | | ● | ● | | ● | | | | | ● | ● | ● | ● | ● | | ● | | ● | | | | |
| Sudan | | | | | | | ● | | | | | | | ● | | ● | | ● | | | | | | |
| Suriname | | | | | | | | | | | | ● | | | | ○ | | | | | | | | |
| Swaziland | | | | | | | | | | | | ● | | | | | | ● | | | | | | |
| Sweden | ● | ● | ● | ● | ● | | ● | ● | ● | ● | ● | ● | ● | ● | ● | | ● | ● | | ● | | ● | ● | |
| Switzerland | | ● | | ● | ● | | ● | ○ | ● | | ● | ● | ● | ● | ● | ○ | ● | ● | | ● | ● | ● | ● | |
| Syrian Arab Rep. | | | | | | | | | | | | ● | | | | | | ● | | | | | | |
| Taiwan | | | | ● | | | ● | | | | | ● | | | ● | | | | | ● | | | | |
| Tajikistan | | | | | | | | | | | | | | | | | | | | | | | | |
| Tanzania (U. Rep. of) | | | | ● | ● | | ● | | | ● | | | | | | ● | | ● | | | | | ● | |
| Thailand | | | | ● | | | ● | | | | | | ● | | ● | ● | | ● | | | | | | |
| Togo | | | | ● | | | ● | | | ● | | ● | ● | | | | | ● | | | | | | |
| Tonga | | | | | | | | | | | | ● | | | | | | | | | | | | |
| Trinidad & Tobago | | | | | | | ● | | | | | | ● | | | | | | | | | | | |
| Tunisia | | | | | | | ● | | ● | ● | | | ● | | | ● | | ● | | ● | | | | |
| Turkey | | ● | | ● | | | ● | | ● | | | ● | ● | | ● | ● | ● | ● | | | | | | |
| Turkmenistan | | | | | | | | | | | | | | | | | | ● | | | | | | |
| Tuvalu | | | | | | | | | | | | | | | | | | | | | | | | |
| Uganda | | | | ● | | | ● | | | | | | ● | | ● | ● | | ● | | ● | | | | ● |
| Ukraine | | | ● | ● | | | | | ● | ● | ● | | | | | ● | | ● | | | | | | |
| United Arab Emirates | | | | | | | | | | | | | | | | | | ● | | | | | | |
| United Kingdom | ● | ● | ● | ● | ● | ● | ● | ● | ● | ● | ● | ● | ● | ● | ● | ● | ● | ● | | ● | ● | ● | ● | |
| USA | ● | ● | ● | ● | ● | ● | ● | | | ● | ● | ● | ● | ● | ● | ● | ● | ● | ● | ● | | | ● | ● |
| Uruguay | | | | ● | | | ● | | | ● | | ● | | | ● | ● | | ● | | | ● | | | |
| Uzbekistan | | | | | | | ● | | | | | | | | | | | | | | | | | |
| Vanuatu | | | | | | | | | | | | | | ● | | | | | | | | | | |
| Vatican (see Holy See) | | | | | | | | | | | | | | | | | | | | | | | | |
| Venezuela | | | | | | | ● | | | | | ● | ● | | ● | | | ● | | | | | ○ | |
| Viet Nam | | | | | | | | | | | | | | ● | ● | | | ● | | ● | | | ○ | |
| Yemen | | | | | | | | | | | | | | | | ● | | | | | | | | ● |
| Yugoslavia | | | | | | | | | | | | | ● | | | | | | | ● | | | | |

| Country | ICES | EPOC | ANPED | Centre for Our Common Future | CAN | Earthwatch | ELCI | EEB | EYFA | FoEI | Greenpeace | ICC | ICFTU | ICVA | IOCU | IPPF | ISES | IUCN | Sierra Club | SID | TWN | WFM | WWF | WorldWIDE |
|---|---|---|---|---|---|---|---|---|---|---|---|---|---|---|---|---|---|---|---|---|---|---|---|---|
| Zaïre | | | | ● | | | ● | | | | | ● | | | | ● | | ● | | ● | | | | |
| Zambia | | | | | | | ● | | | | | | ● | ● | ● | ● | | ● | | | | | ● | |
| Zimbabwe | | | | | ● | | ● | | | | | ● | | | ● | | ● | ● | | ● | | | | |
| European Union | ● | ● | | | | | | | | | | | | | | | | | | | | | | |
| | | | | | | | | | | | | | | | | | | | | | | | | |
| Anguilla | | | | | | | | | | | | | | | | | | | | | | | | |
| Aruba | | | | | | | | | | | | | | | | | | | | | | | | |
| Bermuda | | | | | | | | | | | | ● | | | | | | | | | | | | |
| Br. Virgin Islands | | | | | | | | | | | | | | | | | | | | | | | | |
| French Polynesia | | | | | | | | | | | | ● | | | | | | | | | | | | |
| Guadeloupe | | | | | | | | | | | | | | | | | | | | | | | | |
| Hong Kong | | | | | | | ● | | | | | ● | | ● | ● | | | | | | | | ● | |
| Macau | | | | | | | | | | | | | | | ● | | | | | | | | | |
| Montserrat | | | | | | | | | | | | ● | | | | | | | | | | | | |
| Neth. Antilles | | | | | | | | | | ● | | ● | | ● | | | | | | | | | | |
| New Caledonia | | | | | | | ● | | | | | ● | | | | | | | | | | | | |
| Puerto Rico | | | | | | | ● | | | | | ● | | ● | ● | | | | | | | | | |

# Index

*Entries in the reference section are denoted in italics*

environmental window, 89

environmentally-sound technologies, 17, 19, 23, 25-26, 47, 94-105

EPA, *see* Environmental Protection Agency

EPOC, *see* Organization for Economic Co-operation and Development, Environment Policy Committee

Espoo Convention, *see* Convention on Environmental Impact Assessment in a Transboundary Context

Europe, 21-22, 25-26, 35, 41-49, 54, 57, 59, 61-65, 71-73, 104
climate policy of, 41-49

*European Agreement Concerning the International Carriage of Dangerous Goods by Road (ADR), 134-135, 208-223*

European Auto Manufacturers (ACEA), 97

European Bank for Reconstruction and Development, 20, 26

European Chemical Manufacturers Association (CEFIC), 97

European Commission, *see* European Union (EU)

European Commission's Energy Directorate, *see* European Union (EU)

European Community, *see* European Union (EU)

European Confederation of Pulp, Paper, and Board Industries (CEPAC), 97

*European Environmental Bureau (EEB), 274-275, 299-306*

European Economic Community (EEC), *see* European Union (EU)

European ministerial conferences, 20

European Monitoring and Evaluation Programme (EMEP), 52, 60

European Parliament, *see* European Union (EU)

European Union (EU), 21, 41-49, 57, 62-65, 71-73, 104, *228-229*:
ALTENER, 44, 46
climate policy of, 41-49
Council Declarations, 43
Council of EC Energy and Environment Ministers of Member States, 43
Council of Ministers of, 43
environmental policy of, 41-49, 63
European Commission of, 43-48, 71
European Commission's Energy Directorate, 43
European Parliament, 44
global climate emissions from, 41-42
internal market, 48
JOULE, 44-45
Large Combustion Plant Directive, 47, 63
Maastricht Treaty, 44
Monitoring Decision, 43-47, 49
single European energy market, 65
Single European Market, 44
Specific Actions for Vigorous Energy Efficiency (SAVE), 44-46, 49
sulphur emissions of, 62
THERMIE, 44-45

*European Youth For(est) Action (EYFA), 276, 299-306*

Exxon Valdez, 53, 96, 98, 101

EYFA, *see* European Youth For(est) Action

FAO, *see* Food and Agriculture Organization

farmers rights, 72, 77

FASB, *see* Financial Advisory Standards Board

FCCC, *see* Framework Convention on Climate Change

Federchimica, 97

Ferber, Betty, 83-92

Ferretti, Janine, 83-92

financial assistance, 20-23, 26-27, 36, 56-58, 65-67, 69, 72, 74, 77-79, 87, 89-91, 101

Financial Advisory Standards Board (FASB), 102

Financial Times, 63

Finland, 23, 62-64:
environmental policy of, 63-64;
sulphur emissions of, 62

Fischer, Lynn M., 83-92

fishery, 22, 70, 80

FoEI, *see* Friends of the Earth International

food, 70, 77-79

food plants, 70, 78-79

Food and Agriculture Organization (FAO), 69, 71-73, 77, 79, *230*:
*Fund for Plant Genetic Resources*, 71-72, 77;
*Global System on Plant Genetic Resources*, 72, 77;
*International Code of Conduct on the Distribution and Use of Pesticides, 136-137, 208-223*;
International Undertaking on Plant Genetic Resources, 71-72, *192-194, 209-223*

foreign investment, 83, 85, 91, 93-105

forest, 20, 23, 25, 36, 58-60, 73, 80

forests convention, 36

forest management, 20

forestry, 58, 80

Framework Convention on Climate Change (FCCC), 19, 25, 29, 32-38, 41, 43-44, 51-53, 55-57, 97, 103, *117-119, 208-223*:
Intergovernmental Negotiating Committee (INC) of, 32-38, 52

France, 42, 44, 49, 60, 62-64:
climate policy of, 42;
environmental policy of, 60, 63-64;
global climate emissions from, 42, 44;
sulphur emissions of, 62

free-rider problem, 55-56, 74, 101

free-trade agreement, 66, 69, 72-74, 76, 83-91, 99

FRG, *see* Germany

*Friends of the Earth International (FoEI), 277, 299-306*

From Ideas to Action, *see* International Chamber of Commerce

Fund Convention, *see* Convention on the Establishment of an International Fund for Compensation for Oil

funds, *see* financial assistance

G-77, *see* Group of 77

Gallup, 93-94, 99

GAO, *see* United States of America, General Accounting Office

gas, 23, 26, 29, 64

GATT, *see* General Agreement on Tariffs and Trade

GCMs, *see* General Circulation Models

GEF, *see* Global Environment Facility

gene-banks, 70, 74-77, 79

gene transactions, 79

General Accounting Office, *see* United States of America

General Agreement on Tariffs and Trade (GATT) (*see also* World Trade Organization), 66, 69, 72-74, 76, 83, 85-86, 91, 99:
Trade-Related Aspects of Intellectual Property Rights (TRIPs), 72-73
Uruguay Round, 72, 76, 85, 99

General Circulation Models (GCMs), 31

genetic diversity, *see* genetic resources

genetic resources, 20, 60-80

genetically modified organisms, 75

Geneva, 31, 72

Georgia, 21

German Democratic Republic:
global climate emissions from, 44-46

Germany, East, *see* German Democratic Republic

Germany, Federal Republic of (FGR), 22-23, 35, 42, 44-46, 49, 59-60, 62-63, 71:
climate policy of, 42;
environmental policy of, 42, 59-60, 63;
Federal Supreme Court, 71;
global climate emissions from, 42, 44-46;
sulphur emissions of, 62

germplasm, 77

Gleckman, Harris, 93-106

Global Atmosphere Research Programme, 24

global climate, 20-49, 51-58, 63, 76, 78, 94

global climate emissions, 25-27, 29-38, 41-49, 51, 53, 55-58, 94

global climate negotiations, 29-40, 51-58

---

North American Agreement on Environmental Co-operation (NAAEC), 87-88, 90-91

North American Commission for Environmental Co-operation (NACEC), 87-91

North American Commission for Labor Co-operation, 88

North American Commission on Trade and the Environment, 87

North American Development Bank (NADBank), 87-90

North American Free Trade Agreement (NAFTA), 83-91

North Donets, 22

North Sea, 98

Norway, 23, 59, 61-64:
  Berntsen, Thorbjørn, environment minister of, 63;
  environmental policy of, 61, 63-64;
  sulphur emissions of, 62

Notification Convention, *see* Convention on Early Notification of a Nuclear Accident

NO$_x$ *see* nitrogen oxides

NO$_x$ Protocol, 60-61, 64, 66, *112-116, 208-223*

noxious substances, *see* hazardous substances

nuclear, 20-23, 31, 42

nuclear energy, 23, 42

*nuclear safety, 200-205, 209-223*

nuclear wastes, 22

nuclear weapons, 20

ocean pollution, *see* marine pollution

Occidental Petroleum, 98

Odén, Svante, 59

OECD, *see* Organisation for Economic Co-operation and Development

Official Development Assistance (ODA), *see* aid *or* development agencies

oil, 26, 29, 71

Oil Companies' European Organization for Environmental and Health Protection (CONCAWE), 96

oil crisis, 31

OPEC, *see* Organization of Petroleum Exporting Countries

OPRC, *see* Convention on Oil Pollution Preparedness, Response and Co-operation

Organization for Economic Co-operation and Development (OECD), 35, 41, 45, 48, 52-53, 56, 59-60, 66, 97, *243-244, 299-306*:
  *Environment Policy Committee (EPOC), 243-244, 299-306*

Organization of Petroleum Exporting Countries (OPEC), 56

Oslo Convention, *see* Convention for the Prevention of Marine Pollution by Dumping from Ships and Aircrafts

OSPAR Convention, *see* Convention for the Protection of the Marine Environment of the North East Atlantic

Ottawa, 60

overcropping, 84

overpopulation, *see* population growth

ozone depletion, 18, 21-24, 31, 52-54, 63, 78, 99, 102

ozone, ground-level, 65

ozone layer, 20, 23-24, 26, 52-55

Pardo, Arvid, Maltese ambassador to the UN, 70

Paris Convention, *see* Convention for the Prevention of Marine Pollution from Land-based Sources

patent law, 71-73, 77

patents, 70-74, 76-77, 94

patent system, 70-73, 76

Pechenganikel, 23

perestroika, 17-18, 27

pesticides, 78, 94, 98

pharmaceuticals, 69, 71-73, 98, 100

pharmaceutical sector, 71-73

PIC, *see* prior informed consent

plant breeders' rights, 70-72

plant genetic resources, 69-80

plant varieties, 72

pledge and review, 56

poaching, 25

Poland, 22-23, 60, 65:
  environmental policy of, 60;
  sulphur emissions of, 62, 65

polluter pays principle, 48, 103

pollution, *see* air- *or* marine pollution

pollution havens, 83

population, 30, 32

population growth, 32

Portugal, 42-45, 47, 62:
  climate policy of, 42;
  global climate emissions from, 43-45;
  sulphur emissions of, 62

power generation, *see* electricity

precautionary principle, 78, 105

prior informed consent, 74, 76-77, 79

property rights, 69-80, 96

Quebec, 88

Quayle, Dan, former vice-president of the United States, 75

radioactive, *see* nuclear

rainforests, *see* tropical forests

RAINS-ASIA, 67

RAINS Model, 62

Ramsar Convention, *see* Convention on Wetlands of International Importance, especially as Waterfowl Habitat

resource transfer, *see* financial assistance

recycling, 101-103

Red Dove Case, 71

*Regional Convention for the Conservation of the Red Sea and Gulf of Aden Environment, 168, 209-223*

Regional Seas Programme, *see* UN Environment Programme

renewable energy, 46, 56, 58

Review of US-Mexico Environmental Issues, 86

Rhine, 98

Rio de Janeiro, 33, 53, 56, 70, 74, 93-94, 96, 98, 102-104

River Dneper, 22

Rosendal, G. Kristin, 69-81

Rosy Periwinkle, 71

Russian Federation, 17-27, 33, 41, 61-62, 64:
  attitudes towards environment and development, 21;
  Danilov-Danilian, Viktor I., Minister of the Environment, 20
  environmental policy of, 17-27, 61, 64;
  environmental law of, 19;
  environmental security of, 19;
  global climate emissions from, 41;
  Law on Environmental Protection of, 19, 24;
  Ministry of the Environment and Natural Resources of, 18-19, 21, 23-24, 26;
  National Plan of Action for Realization of the UNCED Decisions, 19-20;
  non-governmental organization of, 26;
  State Committee on Environmental Protection of, 18;
  State Committee on Hydrometeorology, 25;
  sulphur emissions of, 62

San Antonio, 89

sanctions, 47, 54, 72, 74, 100

São Paulo, 97

Sandoz, 98

Saudi Arabia, 35

SAVE, *see* European Union, Specific Actions for Vigorous Energy Efficiency

Scandinavia, 23, 26, 41, 59-60, 63-64, 67

Schweizerische Gesellschaft für Chemische Industrie (SGCI), 97

Scotland, 63

seabed, 32

sea level, 30, 32, 35

Sebenius, J., 48

# Contents 1992–1995 volumes: Articles

This index is divided into a subject and an author index.

*International Controversy over Sustainable Forestry* (1993 volume)
Vandana Shiva, Professor and Director,
Research Foundation for Science and Ecology, Dehra Pur, India

*Protecting the Frozen South* (1992 volume)
Olav Schram Stokke, Research Fellow,
Fridtjof Nansen Institute, Lysaker, Norway

*Combating Desertification: Encouraging Local Action within a Global Framework* (1994 volume)
Camilla Toulmin, Research Fellow and Programme Director,
International Institute for Environment and Development (IIED), London, United Kingdom

## Nuclear Safety

*International Co-operation to Promote Nuclear Reactor Safety in the Former USSR and Eastern Europe* (1994 volume)
Michael Herttrich, Head,
Gesellschaft für Anlagen- und Reaktorsicherheit, Cologne, Germany, and
Rolf Janke and Peter Kelm, Research Fellows,
Gesellschaft für Anlagen- und Reaktorsicherheit, Berlin, Germany

## Intergovernmental Organizations (IGOs)

*The Global Challenges of Aids* (1992 volume)
Christer Jönsson, Professor,
Institute of Political Science, University of Lund, Sweden

*The Commission on Sustainable Development: Paper Tiger or Agency to Save the Earth?* (1994 volume)
Martin Khor, Director,
Third World Network, Penang, Malaysia

*Can GATT Survive the Environmental Challenge?* (1993 volume)
David Pearce, Professor and Director,
Centre for Social and Economic Research on the Global Environment (CSERGE), University College London, United Kingdom

*Has the World Bank Greened?* (1993 volume)
Amulya K. N. Reddy, Professor and President,
International Energy Initiative, Bangalore, India

## Non-Governmental Organizations (NGOs) and Civil Society

*The Inside Out, the Outside In, Pros and Cons of Foreign Influence on Brazilian Environmentalism* (1992 volume)
Ricardo Arnt, Journalist,
Folah de São Paulo, São Paulo, Brazil

*Indigenous People's Role in Achieving Sustainability* (1992 volume)
Russel Barsh, General Agent,
Mikmaq Grand Council, Seattle, Washington, USA

*International Attitudes Towards Environment and Development* (1994 volume)
Riley E. Dunlap, Professor and Project Director, George H. Gallup International Institute, Princeton, New Jersey, USA

*Non-governmental Organizations at UNCED: Another Successful Failure?* (1993 volume)
Elin Enge, Director and
Runar I. Malkenes, Information Officer,
Norwegian Campaign for Environment and Development, Oslo, Norway

*Building an Environmental Protection Framework for North America: The Role of the Non-Governmental Community* (1995 volume)
Betty Ferber, International Co-ordinator,
Group of 100, Lomas Barriloca, Mexico,
Lynn Fischer, Latin American Policy Specialist,
Natural Resources Defense Council (NRDC), Washington, USA, and
Janine Ferretti, Executive Director,
Pollution Probe Foundation, Toronto, Canada

*Democracy, Development, and Environmental Sustainability* (1992 volume)
Jeanette Hartmann, Social Scientist,
University of Dar-es-Salaam, Dar-es-Salaam, Tanzania

*Non-governmental Organizations: The Third Force in the Third World* (1993 volume)
Bill Hinchberger, Associate Editor and Correspondent,
Financial Times Bureau, São Paulo, Brazil

## Environment and Sustainable Development

*An Overview of Follow-up of Agenda 21 at the National Level* (1994 volume)
Alicia Bárcena, Executive Director,
Earth Council, San José, Costa Rica

*Promoting International Transfer of Environmentally Sound Technologies: The Case for National Incentive Schemes* (1994 volume)
Calestous Juma, Executive Director,
African Centre for Technology Studies (ACTS), Nairobi, Kenya

*Energy for Sustainable Development in the Third World* (1992 volume)
Amulya K. N. Reddy, Professor and President,
International Energy Initiative, Bangalore, India

## International Business and Industry

*Transnational Corporations' Strategic Responses to 'Sustainable Development'* (1995 volume)
Harris Gleckman, Consultant,
Benchmark Environmental Consulting, Portland, Maine, USA

*International Business and Sustainable Development* (1993 volume)
Alex Trisoglio, Manager,
Business and Industry Programmes, International Academy of the Environment, Geneva, Switzerland